Piety and Plurality

Piety and Plurality

Theological Education since 1960

GLENN T. MILLER

CASCADE *Books* • Eugene, Oregon

PIETY AND PLURALITY
Theological Education since 1960

Copyright © 2014 Glenn T. Miller. All rights reserved. Except for brief quotations in critical publications or reviews, no part of this book may be reproduced in any manner without prior written permission from the publisher. Write: Permissions. Wipf and Stock Publishers, 199 W. 8th Ave., Suite 3, Eugene, OR 97401.

Scriptures taken from the Holy Bible, New International Version®, NIV®. Copyright © 1973, 1978, 1984, 2011 by Biblica, Inc.™ Used by permission of Zondervan. All rights reserved worldwide. www.zondervan.com The "NIV" and "New International Version" are trademarks registered in the United States Patent and Trademark Office by Biblica, Inc.™

Cascade Books
An Imprint of Wipf and Stock Publishers
199 W. 8th Ave., Suite 3
Eugene, OR 97401

www.wipfandstock.com

ISBN 13: 978-1-62564-184-7

Cataloguing-in-Publication Data

Miller, Glenn T., 1942–

    Piety and plurality : theological education since 1960 / Glenn T. Miller

    xx + 386 p. ; 23 cm. Includes bibliographical references.

    ISBN 13: 978-1-62564-184-7

    1. Theology—Study and teaching—United States—History—20th century. 2. Theology—Study and Teaching—United States. 3. Protestant theological seminaries—United States—History—20th century. 4. Protestant theological seminaries—United States. 5. Catholic theological seminaries—United States—History. I. Title.

BV4030 M56 2014

Manufactured in the U.S.A.

For all those who have labored to educate an American Protestant ministry and, particularly, for my former colleagues at Bangor Theological Seminary, Southeastern Baptist Theological Seminary, St. Mary's Seminary and University, and Union Theological Seminary in the City of New York.

Contents

Preface | ix

Acknowledgments | xvii

List of Abbreviations | xviii

1. The Professional Model in the 1960s | 1
2. Finances, Professionalism, and New Directions | 32
3. The Rights Revolution and Theological Schools | 63
4. Catholic Theological Education | 140
5. Theology and Governance: Evangelicals, Missouri Synod Lutherans, and Southern Baptists in Crisis | 182
6. Basic Issues, the Theological Education Debate, and Globalization | 249
7. Under the Hood: A New Professional Model | 300
8. Visions: A Concluding Reflective Postscript | 347

Bibliography | 365

Index | 381

Preface

THIS VOLUME IS THE third volume of my study of the history of the goals and purposes of theological education. Like the two earlier volumes, *Piety and Intellect* and *Piety and Profession*, this volume focuses on the interaction between ideas about theological education and the institutions that were constructed in hopes of realizing those ideas. The first volume centered on the passion for theology that animated so many American Protestant Christians. How was the faith to be formulated, set forth rationally, and defended intellectually? Even the frontier and ethnic denominations, although their churches had their own self-understandings and theological formulations, accepted this formulation as the norm for their theological institutions. Not surprisingly, the founders of these institutions gathered treasures from abroad, particularly England and Germany, to buttress their own efforts. The second volume focused on the idea of the ministry as a modern profession. Driven in part by the rise of a new theology and theological method, the purposes of theological schools slowly but surely moved in the direction of professionalism. While the ideal graduate was still intellectually able, the overarching ideal was the competent professional who could interpret the faith and its applications to an increasingly urban and middle-class constituency. Even mighty Princeton, perhaps the best of the nineteenth-century houses of theology, was forced to follow this pattern after Gotham's Union Seminary set the pace in such areas as religious education, social ethics, and field education. Perhaps the greatest triumphs of this new educational order were the rise of clinical training and field education, both of which stood with one foot in the schools and the other in the midst of ministry. H. R. Niebuhr, Daniel Day Williams, and James Gustafson spoke for many who shared this vision when they published *The Advancement of Theological Education* in 1957. It was the high point of the new understanding of theological education, and only a few schools, notably confessional-oriented Westminster and Missouri Synod Concordia, stood outside the gates. All that seemed left was a mopping up operation in which this form of theological education raised the standards of existing schools and provided the foundations for new institutions. Schools might be conservative or liberal, but they shared a common goal and a similar understanding of what it meant to complete a theological school.

Looking back over the last fifty years, as I approached retirement, my original hope for this third volume was to find as dominant a theme for this period as I had for the other two periods. There were many reasons for this hope. The Roman Catholic

Church, which had followed its own trajectory since Trent, found itself apparently moving towards greater commonality with the various Protestant churches and, as I knew from my own experience at Baltimore's St. Mary's Seminary, had passed through an apparent theological renaissance. Some of the best theology of the period was Roman Catholic, and this theology was also studied in mainstream Protestant, Evangelical, and Orthodox schools. At the same time, the renamed American Association of Theological Schools expanded numerically and became a well-financed and very ably led organization, committed to both standardization (the accreditation process) and to the discussion of the issues involved in the day-by-day life of theological schools. My own Evangelical tradition, which had seemed locked into the narrow gauge of old fundamentalism, had shown that it still possessed both popular appeal and the ability to inspire the formation of new institutions. In many ways, the United States had replaced Germany as the center of new directions in theology and biblical studies.

Yet from the beginning, this was a fractured world, and the cracks became increasingly evident from the 1960s onward. The nation was in the midst of a rights revolution that demanded the liberation of minorities, including women, and in time, demanded their inclusion in theological schools. The smooth course of liberal and neo-orthodox theologies, that seemed set in the 1960s, gradually became rougher and finally almost impassable. Evangelicals, Catholics, and Southern Baptists found themselves locked in bitter battles as they struggled to make headway in a very complicated religious world. And despite the fact that many new schools were founded, just as educational costs were escalating, the funds began to dry up. In common with other educational institutions, the schools became increasing complex, raising the ante for schools again and again.

Equally seriously, deep changes occurred in American life. Americans were becoming notably less church oriented and deep demographic changes were eroding the position of the mainstream churches. Many wags repeated the adage that Catholics were the largest American religious demographic, and ex-Catholics the next largest. At the same time, Evangelical growth appears to have peaked in about 2003 and numerical decline to have begun at about the same time. At the same time, Evangelicals continued to found new schools, repeating an earlier mainstream pattern of too many schools serving too few students, with too few financial resources.

The full implications of the new computer technology for schools in general and seminaries more specifically have not been realized at the time of writing. In the midst of constant struggles for revenue, the economic appeal of distance education is clear. Schools, like students, are not limited by their location or their physical plants. Every institution is potentially national and even international in its scope and mission. Yet, whether this will prove as fruitful as its advocates hope remains unproven. The danger is that the tendency to see degrees as representing aggregates of credits, each one of which is in principle replaceable by another, may encourage students to shop for particular courses and only at the end to seek an institution to bundle them into a degree. If one purpose of theological education is the formation of identity, whether personal, Christian, or ecclesiastical, one wonders whether the computer interaction will provide the spark for that to occur.

Problems of scale and perspective also have complicated the task. The two previous studies had the advantage of covering relatively long periods of time. Being able to look back over a century or more enabled me both to form a perspective on events and to see the way that stories came to natural conclusions. Further, few of the people in those stories were known to me personally. Many, like Henry "Pitt" van Dusen, were leaving the stage just as I began to learn my part in the play; others were only figures that my teachers had mentioned, either in praise or in criticism, as part of my own studies. This volume, however, is largely about people and events that I experienced personally and that left their own impact on me. At times, that experience has enriched my understanding of events. I am sure that I understand more of the Catholic story from my brief time at St. Mary's than I would have otherwise. At other times, the turbulence and upset of the stories has left permanent marks on my soul that have healed at best slowly and in some cases not at all. I have struggled with those stories and my own place in them. I have sought to be objective. Yet, I know the best view of earth-moving equipment is not from under a steamroller, and I write about such events as the Union disruptions of the 1960s and the Southern Baptist controversy profoundly aware that these events shaped my life, my career, and my theology.

These are among the classic problems of a midlevel source in history. A middle-level source is one written by a contemporary but which references research and sources. It is not quite a primary source, a piece of evidence from an event; nor is it quite a secondary source, written by a third-party observer from research. Midlevel sources are never quite fish or fowl. They reflect personal, even idiosyncratic, experiences, and they reflect careful reading and rereading of primary materials. Unlike autobiography, middle-level studies do not primarily rely on memory, as the footnotes attest; but unlike more traditional history, they are influenced at every turn by the author's remembered experience of the events described in them. Hopefully, midlevel studies provide clues and approaches to the sources that make later secondary sources richer and more adequate. However, the reader is cautioned that this is not the final word, not even the penultimate word, on the events and ideas described within.

I tried, probably unsuccessfully, to avoid including two many references to individuals and personalities. In part this was an attempt to keep the focus on the aims and purposes of theological schools. In part it was because of my own fear that my judgment of people, particularly when it was based on my personal relationships with them, would color my interpretation too much. There is no subjectivity as invidious as interpersonal subjectivity with its friends, heroes, and villains. Yet there are other dangers. The fact that theological schools are small institutions—only the largest of them equally the size of a small liberal-arts college—means that there is a tendency to conflate the history of theological education with the history of the leadership of theological schools. Schools often seem to be the long institutional shadows of their leading personalities. To be sure, the development of the presidency is an important story, and references to foundation executives are also part of the story. But I did not want to make the impact of these leaders *the* story.

Is there one story that unites the last fifty years of theological education? Such a story may exist, but my own conclusion has been that no one story line made sense of both the data that I had and my own memories. What I found were a variety of stories that I have put together in a way that I hope is helpful. The primary filter that I have used is the idea of goals and purposes, which provides, I hope, at least a string on which the various stories can be located and some stories, alas, omitted.

One of those stories is the development of thought about how seminaries should be structured and financed. That story is told in the first two chapters and resumes in the seventh chapter. As of this writing, those stories form brackets around other material. The stories that form the brackets also contain discussions of other information that influenced seminaries as a whole, including a restatement of the professional ideal in terms of reflective religious leadership. There is clearly some overlap, especially, in the story of the evolution of administrations. I designed the brackets to say something. The story about the goals and purposes of seminary administrations ran on one level, while the other stories ran on other levels.

A second set of stories has to do with the gradual inclusion of racial, ethnic, and gender minorities. Given the complexity of ethnicity and gender in America—a complexity that grows almost daily—I have elected to concentrate on three such stories: the story of African Americans, the story of women, and the much more complex Hispanic (Latino/Latina) histories. These stories tend to follow a common pattern: a demand for inclusion, a demand that the particular insights of the group be included in theology and/or seen as having theological significance, and then the inclusion of the group into the larger patterns of the institution. Yet when one examines each story separately, the apparent commonalities tend to be less evident. All three groups contain people of many different social classes, educational levels, and religious denominations. In the case of women, they are actually the majority in all American denominations. Perhaps, most ironically, even the liberal churches, which have been most outspoken on these issues, basically kept pace with the larger society in their inclusion of these groups. In other words, the stories were no sooner constructed than they were deconstructed.

After several attempts to locate the story of Lesbian, Gay, Bisexual, and Transgendered persons at different places in the book, I finally moved it to the section on minorities. Although LGBT persons represent a different type of minority grouping, I did this because the LGBT leaders that I have known in theological education have often made their argument for inclusion on the grounds of civil rights.

When I began this study, my tendency was to treat the Roman Catholic story in terms of the expansion of the American, largely Protestant, model of theological education to yet another denomination, albeit, the largest one. Yet as I told the story, I became increasing convinced that the Catholic story was much more than this. To use fancy phraseology, the relationship between the Catholic story and the Protestant story came to be more morphological or formal than essential. To be sure, some of the formal equivalences were important: the expansion of many Catholic schools to include schools for ministry as well as institutions for training priests was perhaps most important of these similarities. Yet the Catholic character of these institutions, and particularities in the Catholic story, kept coming back to center stage. No Protestant equivalent of the Program of Priestly Formation or papal visitations exists. Perhaps my most important learning was that sacramental formation is not the same as piety or spirituality, even in traditions, like the Sulpician, that place a premium on the spiritual life of priests. I admit that my temptation was to retreat to making my story about Protestants, as I did in my earlier two volumes, but I decided that I needed to try to include the Catholic story (or, to be somewhat less prideful), parts of it, in this volume.

As someone who is both Evangelical and Baptist, I felt that the stories of the Evangelical and Southern Baptist battles of the 1980s had to be told. These were nasty battles that had continuing impact on a large number of schools and, perhaps most important, given the large size of some Evangelical and Southern Baptist schools, on a significant number of students and faculty members. Yet in ways that I may not have fully explained, I felt that those stories cut to the heart of what is particularly important in American theological education. At their center was the vexing and often confusing issue of the authority and centrality of the Bible, an issue that will simply not vanish, and the need for Protestants to come to terms with the difference between a deep and an abiding popular biblicism and what is actually taught about the Bible in theological schools. This issue simply refuses to go away, even in very progressive seminaries.

There were two great public discussions of theological education in the 1980s and 1990s: the discussion of what made theological education theological, and the discussion of globalization. The discussion of what made theological education theological was primarily conducted by mainstream Protestant theologians, although Evangelicals participated in it and learned from it. In many ways, this was the most sustained discussion about theological education conducted since the Reformation, and one of the few to penetrate to some of the more basic issues confronting the seminaries. In a sense, it was linked to the Evangelical controversies. Hidden beneath all the rhetoric and sophistication of the participants was a fundamental question: after biblical criticism and the subsequent erosion of biblical authority, what is theological education? At the same time, most of the debaters agreed that the classical professional model was no longer a satisfactory answer to this question, although they did not separate theological education from ecclesiastical or religious leadership. While the answer to the question had many nuances, the main thrust of their argument was towards an interpretation of theological education that leaned towards wisdom and avoided the (at least to them) dangers of either too much reliance on theory or practice.

The simultaneous discussion of globalization, although dominated by mainstream and Catholic theologians, was broader in its theological scope. While the discussion had many pragmatic elements, including the vexing question of the responsibility of the American churches for theological education of Christians in non-Western lands, it was primarily an attempt to come to terms, theoretically and practically, with the question of the relationship of Christianity and culture. On the one hand, the discussion wanted to find a way to affirm and strengthen the increasing sense of many in the world Christian community that their own cultures, including their religious past, had a significant role to play in theology and theological education. On the other hand, the discussion wanted to question the dependence of American theology and the American churches on their own culture, and enable them to hear the multitude of different voices abroad. In other words, the discussion had two foci that pulled it in very different directions. In effect, the participants had to explain why an American theology that drew on American motifs was not adequate even for Americans; at the same time, the participants had to encourage Christians abroad to draw on their own cultural traditions. This was a variation on the older question of Christianity and culture now restated as Christianity and cultures. Another troublesome question—exactly how did Christianity theologically relate to other religions—was also part of this complex array of issues. This was also a much older question. Liberal theologians from Schleiermacher onward had wrestled with it, as did the Second Vatican Council. Further, there were practical questions that had to be resolved (or at least honestly discussed) about such matters as scholarships, visiting faculty, travel courses, and immersions.

My final decision was to allow the plurality of these diverse stories to be the theme of the study as a whole. Plurality is itself a complex category. Unlike pluralism, plurality does not necessarily assume that any final resolution, including tolerance and goodwill, is the outcome of the stories that are told. Unlike the classic story of denominationalism in which Protestant beliefs that they had found the one true church gradually gave way to an ecumenism that allowed different traditions to interact with one another, plurality points to the depths of difference without necessarily arguing that any one future necessarily is the outcome of the whole. While I have noted the emergence of a new professional model, I am not sure that it has the same support or compelling social power of the earlier liberal vision of a professional understanding of ministry. In that sense, I do not necessarily believe or not believe that the various dialectics in the story to date will be resolved, although they may be. At one point Daniel Aleshire suggested, perhaps only partly in jest, that this volume be titled *Piety and Confusion*. Perhaps that title would be less pretentious and more accurate than *Piety and Plurality*!

I admit that *Piety and Plurality* also appeals to my own postmodern inclinations. Aside from the observation that the lack of a master narrative is itself a master narrative, it points to the observation that the world of theological schools is and is likely to remain—despite the best efforts of the ATS and the heartfelt hopes of many theological educators—irreducibly diverse. In that sense, this volume could have been, and perhaps should have been, titled *Chapters towards a History of Theological Education from 1960 to 2010*.

At the end of this study, I have tentatively offered some conclusions in which I try to formulate in very brief compass some of the visions that I see animating theological educators during the period. This is an attempt to bring the discussion of goals and purposes to a conclusion. But, from the beginning, the reader is warned that these concluding reflections are ideal types that do not necessarily represent any single thinker, institution, or even group. The actual stories are much less neat and tidy.

Another consideration in the writing of this volume was length. *Piety and Profession* was far too long for all but the most dedicated reader to complete, and I wanted this volume to be more accessible. Consequently, I cut many discussions down to a bare-bones description and omitted many items. At times the decision what to include was painful. I tried to use my overall understanding of my work as an intellectual historian interested in goals and purposes as my guide. In a more institutional history, the conclusions in many of the Auburn Studies of Theological Education would have been more important, but, as largely empirical studies, they did not contribute as much to the larger discussion and so did not get as much space. The book may still be too long, but I hope that what is here will be useful both to contemporaries and to later historians.

Finally, I would like to thank the Lilly Endowment for sponsoring my studies in theological education over the last four decades. Not only has the Endowment been generous in its funding, but Robert W. Lynn and Craig Dykstra have been important advisors and sources of information. Both have made major contributions to my understanding of the ecology of religion and education in America.

Acknowledgments

SPECIAL THANKS TO MALCOLM Warford, Robert W. Lynn, Christa Klein, Barbara G. Wheeler, Barbara Brown Zikmund, Fred Hofheinz, and Daniel A. Aleshire, who read the manuscript, all or in part, and made useful comments. They kept me from many a historical slip and helped to sharpen the study. The problems and errors in the text are, alas, my own responsibility.

Abbreviations

AA	Associate of Arts
AAR	American Academy of Religion
AATS	American Association of Theological Schools
AAUP	American Association of University Professors
AELC	Association of Evangelical Lutheran Churches
AETH	Asociación para la Educación Teológica Hispana
AIDS	Acquired Immunodeficiency Syndrome
ANTS	Andover-Newton Theological School
ATLA	American Theological Library Association
ATS	Association of Theological Schools
BA	Bachelor of Arts
BD	Bachelor of Divinity
BIOLA	Bible Institute of Los Angeles
CTU	Chicago Theological Union
DIAP	Development and Institutional Advancement Program
DMin	Doctor of Ministry
ELIM	Evangelical Lutherans in Mission
FTE	Full time Equivalent
GTU	Graduate Theological Union
ITC	Interdenominational Theological Center
LGBT	Lesbian, Gay, Bisexual, and Transgendered
MA	Master of Arts
MBA	Master of Business Administration
MDiv	Master of Divinity
MARC	Machine Readable Cataloging
NAE	National Association of Evangelicals
NIV	New International Version
NRSV	New Revised Standard Version of the Bible
OCLC	Ohio College Library Center
PADRES	Padres Asociados para Derechos Religiosos, Educativos, y Sociales
PhD	Doctor of Philosophy
RSV	Revised Standard Version of the Bible
SBC	Southern Baptist Convention

SBL	Society of Biblical Literature
TEDS	Trinity Evangelical Divinity School
ThEd	*Theological Education*
TEE	Theological Education by Extension
ThM	Master of Theology
WTU	Washington Theological Union
WOCATI	World Conference of Associations of Theological Institutions

1 The Professional Model in the 1960s

THE SIXTIES BEGAN ON a high note. Young President John F. Kennedy confidently proclaimed that the nation faced a new frontier that called for sacrifice and heroism. Kennedy was both product and symbol of what journalist Tom Brokaw labeled the greatest generation: those who matured during the Great Depression, fought the most extensive war in human history and returned to build the wealthiest and most technically advanced nation that the world had seen.[1] Like the young president himself, this generation moved into leadership at a young age and, partly because of medical advances, often remained in leadership for many years to come. The coming generation, the so-called baby boomers, found itself caught between its own aspirations—after all, their parents had succeeded at very early ages—and the reality that places in this new world would be difficult to find. The American youth culture began at the top and moved downward through the ranks. The parents of the baby boomers were, after all, a generation that married early and had its children early, often while enrolled in school. For a season, America was a land without grandparents, without those fonts of wisdom that impart stability and direction to a society. Ironically, the youth culture was not simply a phenomenon of alienated college students and young adults. The 1960s saw young people leading a society of even younger people.

Theological seminaries began this decade on a high note that matched the new president's exuberance. Although Protestant church membership had peaked several years earlier, the churches were well attended, with many congregations scheduling two Sunday morning services. Despite minor squabbling, the 1950s were a decade of good feelings. The Mainstream Protestant churches were growing closer together, and ecumenical dreams, soon to be fueled by the Pike–Blake proposals for church unity, occupied many of the church's leaders. The National Council of Churches (NCC), almost castled in its magnificent headquarters on Riverside Drive in New York City, seemed on the verge of even greater things. The Revised Standard Version of the Bible

---

1. Brokaw, *The Greatest Generation*.

was very well received, especially when compared with earlier revisions of the King James Bible. Quickly the RSV became the standard in college and seminary Bible classes; ordinary people also found it useful, and many congregations used the new translation in their worship services and educational programs. Evangelical churches, moving beyond the rigid sectarianism of the 1930s and 1940s, formed their own ecumenical agency, the National Association of Evangelicals (NAE), to forward their agenda. Conservatives had already succeeded in establishing a new flagship seminary, Fuller, in Pasadena, California, and they were actively developing their own network of seminaries. Many Bible schools were now degree-granting colleges with multiple academic programs.

Two hopeful signs seemed to announce an almost unlimited future. The first was the apparent triumph of the good feelings of the 1950s. To a remarkable extent, Protestant liberals and conservatives had cooperated in producing the religious revival. Billy Graham, religious celebrity and icon, had the broad support of many American Christians, with only critics on the far Left and far Right raising questions about his ministry. Other evangelists, including some sponsored by the NCC, were also influential. Canon Brian Green, if not as well known as Graham, was also a national figure.

The good feelings extended to the use of the media, as Graham himself experimented with radio, television, and film. Other media stars, including Bishop Fulton Sheen, a photogenic Catholic, had large followings that included Protestants of all convictions, Roman Catholics, and even some secularists. Public religious practice was encouraged; "the family that prays together, stays together" was a media catchphrase, blazed across billboards throughout the nation. The National Prayer Breakfast, founded in 1953 by members of Congress, enjoyed wide support.

Although few Christians, especially those in seminaries, noticed it, the churches had reached a high point in their influence on social questions. The postwar world interpreted international affairs as a struggle between conflicting ideologies about the nature of humankind, the role of personal freedom, and the best way forward. For most Americans, this meant a commitment to the expansion of freedom around the world, and Americans, often inspired by their large-scale missionary movement, were passionate advocates of decolonization. By 1960, the pink (British) and blue (French) areas on the world maps had shrunk and seemed destined to disappear. As classical imperialism receded, concern about the expansion of communist power increased. Anti-communism was a staple of American conservatism, and in the 1950s, more moderate and liberal voices took up the same cause. The struggle with the communists was a case of God versus godlessness, of freedom versus state slavery, of democracy versus dictatorship. The 1957 launch of a Russian satellite, nicknamed Sputnik, despite its lack of military significance, fired fears that America was behind in the space and missile race. Kennedy promised an all-out effort in this area, including placing people on the moon.

The primary sign of the power and influence of the churches was their participation in the first wave of the African American civil rights movement. Although Southern congregations often opposed the movement, ecumenical agencies, national denominations, and northern congregations were enthusiastic. Graham ordered his crusades in the South integrated. Demonstrations and marches often featured religious leaders, and many churchmen felt almost that they were reborn. The 1965 death of Episcopal seminarian Jonathan Daniels provided inspiration for many. Herbert Gezork, the president of Andover Newton, who had lived a life of social activism, noted:

> Nevertheless, having participated in a considerable number of such gatherings [ecumenical meetings] I must confess that I have never felt the true unity of the body of Christ as deeply as on that memorable day in Selma, Alabama, when we marched silently from Brown's chapel to Dallas County Court House, thousands of Whites and Negroes of many different denominations, led by a Greek Orthodox archbishop, a Baptist minister, a Methodist labor leader, and three Roman Catholic nuns.[2]

During the campaign for President Johnson's 1964 Civil Rights Act, letters to Congress from religious people were major factors in securing the passage of the controversial bill. This may have been the high point of the ecumenical churches' political influence.

The religious event of the decade was the Second Vatican Council.[3] Coming as it did shortly after the election of the first Catholic president, the Council appeared to be the beacon of a new ecumenical future. The Council stressed the role of the laity and called for a new, more pastoral and socially relevant understanding of ministry. These emphases fit a new mood among some American Catholics. Many Catholic priests and religious participated in the civil rights movement and actively supported programs for social change. The Church was the people of God on a mission. In addition, the Council mandated liturgical and structural reforms. Vatican II's influence extended to Protestants as well as Catholics. The identification of the Church as the people of God became almost universal, and many Protestants sought to allow the Spirit of the Council to inform their faith. The Mainstream churches began work on new orders of worship similar to those advocated by the Council. Not since the sixteenth century had the distance between Protestant and Catholic seemed so short or the possibilities for further narrowing of that distance so great.

The Vietnam War early polarized the nation, including various religious groups. College and university students early saw the struggle as an ethical issue and adopted the same techniques of nonviolent protest and resistance used in the civil rights movement. The issue consumed President Lyndon Johnson's term in office and overshadowed the substantial liberal achievements of his presidency. By 1968, the issue was

---

2. Gezork, "An End and a Beginning," 13–14.
3. See below, chapter 3.

divisive enough to lead to Johnson's decision not to run for a second term and to make a substantial contribution to Richard Nixon's 1968 defeat of Hubert Humphrey. College and seminary protests became more aggressive until the 1970 deaths at Kent State and Jackson State Universities, together with the draft lottery, signaled a period of resentful quiet on campuses.

Just as Vietnam moved to center stage, the civil rights movement became more radical. White Protestant and Catholic support for civil rights waned after the Watts Riots of 1965 and after the riots that followed the 1968 King assassination. The new militants had slogans such as Black Power and new demands such as for reparations from the churches. Many church people did not respond favorably to this reformulated program. Protestant church leaders who once believed that they were the conscience of the nation now saw themselves as a prophetic minority, standing against the tide, anxiously looking over their shoulders to see who, if anyone, followed them.

By 1968, the strong optimism of the early part of the decade was almost as distant as the Great War itself. The nation seemed embattled on every side with violent riots in the cities, an unpopular war abroad, and economic difficulties at home. The wave of progressive thought and legislation gave way to the cautious conservatism of Richard Nixon and an apparently chronic economic crisis. American religion was likewise undergoing significant alteration. The decade began with Harvey Cox's *Secular City*[4] and ended with the Jesus people. Although few saw the trend at the time, American Protestantism was shifting from Mainstream to Evangelical.

THE PROFESSIONAL MODEL

The life of America's seminaries reflected the exuberance of the decade and its despair. The schools began the decade buoyed by the H. Richard Niebuhr, Daniel Day Williams, and James Gustafson's report, significantly titled *The Advancement of Theological Education*.[5] While critical of the schools at some places, the Niebuhr-Williams-Gustafson study stressed the gains that the schools had made since the 1930s and indicated that more progress was on its way.[6]

The American Association of Theological Schools, recently strengthened by a Rockefeller grant, called Charles Taylor as its first executive secretary. Taylor was a wise choice. The former dean of Episcopal Theological Seminary in Cambridge, Massachusetts, the Oxford- and Harvard-educated biblical scholar was more than the administrator of an accrediting agency; Taylor was a cultivated representative for the schools and their mission. Significantly, Taylor's tenure at the Association ended in middecade, just as the darker side of the period began to exert increasing influence. His successor, Jesse Ziegler, was a Midwesterner and a minister in the Brethren

---

4. Cox, *The Secular City*.
5. Niebuhr et al., *The Advancement*.
6. For a detailed discussion of the Report, see Miller, *Piety and Profession*, 669–705.

church. Unlike Taylor, who spoke from the heritage of a long-established theological discipline, Ziegler had taught in the practical field. Significantly, Taylor led during a period of optimism, while Ziegler led during a period when people were increasingly aware of an impending crisis.

The common understanding of theological education in the 1960s was that the seminaries were graduate professional schools. Little agreement existed on the meaning of this shibboleth. For some, the language continued the triad of learned professions, ministry, theology, and law, inherited from the medieval period. Originally, a body of knowledge or literature defined all three professions. The person familiar with the liberal arts was best equipped to study this learned corpus. For others, graduate professional education was more a social category. A professional was anyone who had expert knowledge and the skill and insight to apply that knowledge to a concrete situation. In addition to medicine and law, perhaps the most prestigious professions, this understanding of professionalism included engineers, social workers, teachers, and business administrators: in short, anyone whose employment required specialized study or preparation. As economic life differentiated, the number of occupations requiring such training for entry or advancement grew. At the same time, the degree became required as a credential for beginning employment. For yet others, *professional* designated only that a person earned their living performing a task or tasks well. Many American ministers, perhaps 50 percent, had no special credentials for their work but were professionals in this sense.

The phrase *graduate professional education* stood as much for an ideal type as for a defined idea or clear definition. As for all ideal types, its multiple meanings in particular situations or incidences flowed together. Often the same speaker, sometimes in the same speech, mixed different definitions and usages. Yet just as various understandings emerge in discussions of other ideal types, so differing understandings emerge in discussions of graduate professional education, and all help illustrate the meaning of theological education. By training and inclination, Charles Taylor was an advocate of the view that the seminary graduate is the master of a body of knowledge. Not surprisingly, Taylor led the American Association of Theological Schools to study intensively the role of the biblical languages in their program of study.[7] The minister was a professional interpreter of the Bible who needed all the tools available. In contrast, his successor, Jesse Ziegler, an expert in Christian education, emphasized studies that enabled students to perform special tasks aimed more at working with people and organizations. Ziegler's signature program was Readiness for Ministry, a program of standardized tests that measured a person's preparation for the exercise of ecclesiastical leadership.

The phrase *graduate professional education* begged the question of where seminaries fit into the larger ecology of the nation's educational system. It was not an easy question to answer. The general movement of education for new professions, such as

---

7. Harrelson, "Introduction," 437–40, for an account of the study and its results.

social work and teaching, had been from independent freestanding schools to larger departments or schools under the auspices of a university. Educational programs for some professions, such as counseling, originated in the universities. Such programs were a response to innovative practitioners' development of professional standards for their work. While it was difficult in the post-World War II environment to speak of a definition of the university, universities were generally places that brought together teaching, research, and culture. Significantly, the universities had an almost complete monopoly of education for professors and administrators in higher education. While some seminaries offered research degrees, the shift towards the university as the place that credentialed seminary teachers was almost complete by 1960. The universities had other draws as well. Compared to the chronically economically challenged seminaries, the universities had an abundance of resources, including extensive libraries. The modern university benefitted greatly from the economics of scale, especially in fundraising, library, and administration. Intangibles also contributed to a university mystique. Universities shared in the prestige of science and technology; the schools were the harbingers of the modern, the new, and the creative.

Another reason for seminary fascination with the university was academic freedom. Although buffeted by the McCarthy era's virulent anti-communism, the universities had largely made good their claim to academic freedom. In America, academic freedom had two components: to teach whatever one's research supported and to express oneself freely as a public intellectual. Although teachers in theological schools related to universities had such freedoms, many doubted whether such freedoms were compatible with denominational seminaries

The professional ideal was part of the general fascination of seminary leaders with the university. Naturally, those divinity schools that were parts of universities were also the leaders in theological education. Conrad Cherry has rightly identified the university divinity schools as key players in the development of the graduate professional ideal among seminaries.[8] Like many generalizations in the history of American theological schools, the lines that separated university schools from others were not always clear. The principal schools in this designation were Yale Divinity School, Harvard Divinity School, the University of Chicago Divinity School, and Union Theological Seminary in the City of New York. The Methodists, in part because of financial reasons, had come to own the most important denominational family of similar schools: Boston, Duke, Emory, Southern Methodist (Perkins), Garrett-Evangelical, and Drew. In addition, the Methodists owned Claremont, part of the University of Southern California until 1958, and Wesley Seminary, formerly Westminster. Wesley moved to a location close to American University in Washington DC and established a working relationship with that school. The Methodist schools in the South benefitted both from the postwar economic growth of their region and from the steady growth of the so-called Sunbelt in the 1980s and 1990s. By the 1960s, these schools

---

8. Cherry, *Hurrying toward Zion*.

had acquired a national prominence that, if not equal to the older Ivy League schools, was not far behind.

In part, the preeminence of these university schools was financial. The university divinity schools had the money to innovate. Their prominence also came from their ecumenical character. The university schools were ecumenical in two important senses: first, these schools had students and teachers from different denominations; second, they saw themselves as public institutions. This public character of these impressed grant makers such as the Rockefeller administrators, who made the influential Sealantic grants of the 1950s,[9] and the Lilly Endowment's vice presidents for religion. Their public character also enabled them to concentrate on the education of the ministry apart from denominational restraints. Protestant confessions of faith defined the leadership of congregations in very specific ways. Church leaders were priests, elders, preachers, and ministers of Word and Sacrament. An ecumenical seminary could not hope to do more than honor this diversity. The divinity schools had to work around these differences. They did so in two ways.

First, the schools concentrated on those elements in religious leadership shared across Protestant lines by focusing on the mastery of common pastoral tasks, such as preaching or administration, which all ministers had to do. In addition, many practical areas, such as religious education and such newly minted forms of pastoral practice as counseling, had nondenominational origins. A professor could study these tasks, identify best practices, and point to areas of improvement. *Second*, the schools stressed the academic study of Christianity, usually with methods drawn from history or social science. Naturally, ethics, arguably the central discipline of the 1960s and inherently public, was part of the professional focus of the university-related schools.

The university divinity schools were also influential because they were good schools. These schools boasted excellent teachers and well-furnished libraries. At least up to the 1970s, historians could not write the history of biblical studies, church history, systematic theology and religious education apart from the contribution of their scholars. Intellectually, the university schools had flourished particularly in the 1950s when such scholars as Calhoun, Tillich, and the two Niebuhrs virtually defined American theology, and leading British theologians such as John Baillie enriched their ranks. The divinity schools provided the scholars that carried out the two great biblical projects the 1950s: the Revised Standard Version of the Bible and *The Interpreter's Bible*. After 1960, they faced stiff competition for academic talent from departments of religion. The most influential PhD programs were part of the same universities and used many of the same teachers. When schools as diverse as Perkins in Texas[10] and

---

9. See Miller, *Piety and Profession*.

10. For the impact of Yale on Perkins, see Robinson, ed., "Toward a Renewal of Perkins," 5–37. "We have come close to rebuilding the seminary on the model of Yale Divinity School of the fifties. Of course it would be wrong to take too much for granted. There is no reason for smugness about Perkins' academic achievement" (6). When I taught at SEBTS, Yale was the most cited exemplar of what made for an excellent theological education. Union (NY), where many of us did advanced degrees, was also

Southeastern Baptist in Wake Forest, North Carolina, looked to Union and Yale as exemplars of good theological education, their leaders had in mind both their academic quality and their methods of instruction.

The university divinity schools shared in the general academic freedom of their universities. This also made them models for other schools. Seminary leaders believed that the university schools proved that highest-quality theological education did not depend on subscription or enforcement of creeds or confessions of faith. In an important sense, the academic freedom associated with the American secular university was a homegrown product. In seeing academic freedom as the mark of good professional training, seminary leaders were not following the German model. German university theological faculties were confessionally organized, and German schools often required ordination as well as subscription for appointment. Hans Küng's later problems with ecclesiastical authority were not unique or uniquely Catholic. In contrast, the American ideal combined the academic and public speech. When the Death of God theologians, William Hamilton and Thomas Altizer, made their views known in 1964 and 1965, their works seriously tested this understanding of academic freedom. Hamilton and Altizer, unlike the other advocates of Christian atheism, held positions in theological schools: Hamilton taught at Colgate Rochester, and Altizer at Emory. Despite vigorous campaigns for their dismissals, both schools' administrations defended their right to publish and teach.

The 1960s saw a shift in the symbolic power of the university divinity schools. During the 1920s and 1930s, college religion courses, often listed as Bible courses, were common in denominational colleges that were often adjuncts to their churches' seminaries. In many ways, these schools were an important part of the Protestant ecology. Bible teachers steered young men to ministry and to the "proper" seminary, with some colleges and universities widely known as feeders for particular theological schools. After the Second World War religion departments in secular and state universities increased in numbers and influence. This was a major change. These new departments developed along much the same pathway as other components of the schools of arts and sciences, developing introductory courses (often part of the required liberal-arts or general-studies program), advanced courses, and finally master's and doctoral degrees. Although many religion departments, at least in their early days, resembled miniature theological schools (with courses in Bible, church history, and theology), this was only the first stage in their development. While Bible courses remained popular offerings, religion departments moved towards the study of world religions as well as to such fields as the sociology and psychology of religion. The religion departments quickly developed their own language for those courses that they had inherited from the past. New Testament, for example, became Christian Origins and American Church History became the History of American Religion. Perhaps significantly, such important schools as Yale and Duke separated their graduate

---

cited, although more often on scholarly matters rather than the academic program.

departments of religion from their divinity schools and restricted joint appointments to the most prominent scholars.

Many theological educators were slow to recognize the changing academic environment. As often happens, symbolic events were more important than actual happenings. Even in the heyday of high seminary enrollments, most seminaries were *de facto* open-admission institutions, open to anyone who had graduated from a recognized college. Yet, the logic of the professional model was that there should be a program, similar to college premed and prelaw courses, which prepared a student for the study of theology. However, the nature of such programs was unclear. The lists of preseminary courses recommended by the AATS were sketchy, but these recommendations stressed that a religion major was not the appropriate preparation for seminary study. To explore the relationship between college and seminary, the Lilly Endowment commissioned a major study of preseminary education,[11] conducted by Keith Bridston and Dwight W. Culver. The study concluded that the college provided the potential minister with a badly needed secular experience. Yet even in a world of somewhat sheltered late adolescent males, this argument was not convincing. Whether the traditional Protestant culture of Sunday schools, youth organizations, and campus ministries was a religious retreat from the world, most preseminary students had considerable exposure to the secular world in and apart from college.[12] Most seminary faculty might have agreed with John Bright's judgment:

> But, if my experience is any criterion, there is one point at which students tend to be distressingly similar: almost *all* of them exhibit a woeful ignorance of the fundamentals (in my case, a simple knowledge of Bible content). The typical student has come from a Christian home, has attended the church school from childhood, has come through the communicants' class, perhaps has been active in youth work and attended youth conferences. Quite likely, he has gone to a denominational college where Bible is required, and perhaps has even taken a major in religion. Yet he doesn't know the simplest facts of Biblical history and content.[13]

When challenged, seminary leaders, including Charles Taylor, claimed that the undergraduate standards in religion were below those in other departments. As true as this might have been in the 1940s, it was not the case in the 1960s.

The battle with the seminaries encouraged college and university religion teachers to see their work as an independent part of the academy. In 1964, they changed the name of their association, which had met for years at Union Seminary, New York, from the NABI (the National Association of Bible Instructors) to the American Academy

---

11. Bridston and Culver, *Pre-Seminary Education*.

12. Many of the best church-related colleges were formally moving away from denominational affiliation in the 1960s, a recognition of what had already occurred in their classrooms.

13. Bright, "The Academic Teacher," 41.

of Religion (AAR). The name change was important. The acronym NABI echoed the Hebrew word for *prophet*; *academy* referred to the world of college and university professors. The new organization abandoned their traditional meeting place, a symbol of their inferiority, for the hotels and convention centers characteristic of other professional societies. By the early 1970s, the AAR was the one professional meeting that young teachers in religion and theology, whatever their professional plans, had to attend. The leading publishers of religious books, including the denominational presses, made the AAR book exhibit the largest display of religious materials. Although criticized, often justly, by seminary leaders, the Welch Report,[14] published in 1971, made it clear that the university, not the seminary, was the natural home for the advanced study of religion. The only seminaries that escaped Welch's sharp pen were those who had clear university connections or alliances.

Walter Wagoner, at that time executive director of the Rockefeller Brothers Fund for Theological Education and later director of the Boston Theological Institute, was one of the few seminary leaders that saw the new religion departments as offering seminaries an opportunity. Like many other church leaders, Wagoner was deeply concerned with the quality of students attending seminaries and with the level of seminary instruction. In his article, "A Model for Theological Education," Wagoner listed five areas seminaries had to improve to more adequately serve the church:

1. There were too many and too-expensive schools.
2. The financial crisis had to be solved.
3. Better students had to be recruited.
4. Theological education had to be integrated more into general cultural studies.
5. Theological education had to be ecumenical.[15]

To achieve these goals, Wagoner proposed a variation on the German model that separated academic theology from explicitly professional preparation. The churches should use the departments of religion as the heart of their academic problem without worrying about the pastoral or confessional character of the teachers. The program would require four years and lead to a doctoral degree. Wagoner, who had encountered Catholic theological education after Vatican II, recognized that seminaries had a formative function and that denominations had their own ethos. To meet these needs, he believed that the churches should construct "houses of study" near the university to provide their candidates with worship and polity.

Wagoner's proposals were not as radical as they looked to his contemporaries. In 1971, Berkeley Divinity School affiliated with Yale Divinity School. Berkeley retained its mission to form Episcopal candidates, while allowing the divinity school and the university to establish and maintain academic standards. Earlier, the Disciples Divinity Houses at the University of Chicago and at Vanderbilt had established a similar

14. Welch, *Graduate Education in Religion*.
15. Wagoner, "A Model for Theological Education."

pattern. Ernest Colwell, the president of Claremont, formulated the most serious objection when he argued that "the ideal seminary is still the church's school. It should be independent of the university in ultimate responsibility. It should be ultimately responsible (preferably indirectly) to the church, to a church, to some churches (i.e., it should be either denominational or inter-denominational; but not non-denominational)."[16] Yet, as the quotation indicates, Colwell was not clear what this meant. The existing divinity schools, including the Methodist schools, were part of their universities, and the relationships between many seminaries and their sponsoring denominations was often nominal. Independent boards of trust, often self-perpetuating, owned most American theological schools. With few exceptions, the churches did not pay for the schools, appoint their officers, or determine their curriculum. In many cases, their influence was that of any major contributor. Moreover, that influence was declining. In 1960, AATS hired the accounting firm of Cresap, McCormick and Paget to study how much financial support the seminaries received from their sponsoring churches.[17] The results indicated that the churches gave very little, and that the seminaries depended on their endowments for the bulk of their operating expenses. Southern Baptists were almost alone in their willingness to support their schools financially.

CONSORTIA AND COOPERATION

The great prestige of the universities and their divinity schools inspired both imitation and some new directions. These seminaries not formally affiliated with universities sought to find ways to become part of the university orbit. The most common forms of such affiliation were consortia and clusters. Leon Pacata, later executive director of the Association of Theological Schools, observed:

> The 1960s was a time of the "great clusters." The Interdenominational Theological Center was incorporated in 1958; the Graduate Theological Union in 1962; the Toronto School of Theology in 1964 after many years of cooperative experience; Dubuque in 1967; the Rochester Center in 1968; the Chicago Cluster in 1972. During the same period, major consortia were established in Boston, Philadelphia, Minneapolis, Washington, D.C., together with many area and regional associations.[18]

The hope that the schools could consolidate around a university center formed the heart of many proposals, such as those made by the ATS Resources Commission, which sought to find ways to solve the financial and academic problems of Protestant theological education. Yet only a few succeeded in proportion to the hopes invested in them.

16. Colwell, "A Tertium Quid," 101.
17. Taylor, "Do Churches Support the Seminaries?"
18. Pacala, "ATS and the Corporate," 64.

The best known of these experiments was the Federated Faculty of the University of Chicago. The Divinity School of the University of Chicago, Disciples Divinity House, Meadville-Lombard, and Chicago Theological Seminary brought together their considerable resources in a cooperative venture that allowed their individual units to retain some measure of identity, while the whole gained the advantage of common planning and administration.[19] This should have been a marriage made in heaven. The schools shared a common commitment to liberal Protestantism, an interest in process theology, and a common commitment to the urban environment. They cooperated in raising the matching funds needed for participation in the Sealantic Grants. Yet, in 1960, the Federated Faculty dissolved into its component parts with all the bickering and faultfinding of a painful divorce. James Fraser noted:

> With the ending of the Chicago experiment in the early 1960s, it became an example of the potential issues awaiting future cooperative arrangements. Those in the 1960s who wanted cooperation always assured their audience that they were avoiding the Chicago mistakes. Those who opposed it had only to use the words 'Federated Faculty.'[20]

The problem was that it was not clear what mistakes the Federated Faculty actually made. It is too easy to resort to blaming individuals or to spend time analyzing the structural agreements for weaknesses. The deeper and more critical problem was definitional. While the University of Chicago wanted to continue to train pastors, its deepest loyalty was to the discussion between religion and the high culture of the university. Chicago Theological Seminary reversed these priorities. While Chicago Theological Seminary also wanted to address the high culture, the school's passion was the education of pastors and church workers. As long as resources were plentiful, the two priorities lived in relative harmony. Yet when the member schools had to make choices about scarce resources, the system fell apart.

Another successful attempt to build a university-related form of theological education was the establishment of the Interdenominational Theological Center in Atlanta. Atlanta was a center for African American education, and the city hosted a number of small black seminaries. The enrollment of these schools was low, their libraries meager, and their prestige almost nonexistent. To many they seemed beyond the capacity of even philanthropy to save. Yet, when Gammon, the largest of these schools, applied to the Sealantic Fund for aid, the Rockefeller charity responded with both a carrot and a stick—with a rejection and a suggestion. Technically, the foundation rejected the school's request, because Rockefeller restricted the Sealantic grants to schools related to a university. Yet, if Gammon could form a coalition with the other schools in the area and seek affiliation with Atlanta University, an African American graduate faculty, the Fund might make money available.

19. Carr, "The Federated Theological Faculty of the University of Chicago."
20. Fraser et al., *Cooperative Ventures in Theological Education*.

Ernest Cadman Colwell, former president of the University of Chicago; Merrill J. Holmes, president of Illinois Wesleyan University; F. D. Patterson, director of the Phelps Stokes Fund; Walter N. Roberts, president of the United Theological Seminary and AATS; and Henry P. Van Dusen, president of Union Theological Seminary, were appointed a committee to design the new seminary. Their proposal was that the Atlanta schools—Gammon, Morris Brown, Turner, and Phillips—close their existing facilities and move into new buildings on land donated by Atlanta University. Technically, the previously existing schools were the foundation of the new institution, and their boards appointed ten of the twenty members of the new governing board (the board elected the other ten). However, the heart of the proposal was that academic programs, libraries, and faculties merge into a single seminary under a single administration. The previously existing schools continued their work primarily as sponsors of residence halls for the students of their own denominations.

Interestingly, the three strongest African American theological schools, ITC, Howard, and Virginia Union were all university schools, affiliated with strong and growing African American universities. The civil rights movement marks an important divide in African American religious history. Before the civil rights movement, the African American ministry was the least educated of the major professions open to African Americans in a segregated society. People went easily from plowing to preaching. The civil rights movement marked the rise of a strong African American middle class. In turn, this new middle class had expectations for their ministers that often exceeded the capacity of their institutions. Many parallels existed between twentieth-century African Americans and nineteenth-century Methodists. As with the earlier Methodists, so with twentieth-century African Americans, rising social status led to educational innovation. Just as the Methodists had created the largest single family of university-related divinity schools in part out of their inability to afford seminaries, so African Americans founded university divinity schools, not seminaries, so that ministerial education might share expenses with the more profitable undergraduate and professional programs.

The Graduate Theological Union (GTU) was arguably the most successful consortium. The Union had two important links to the contemporary university ideal. The first, and perhaps as David Schuller of ATS suggested,[21] the most essential was the presence of the University of California with its massive research resources. In addition to an excellent library, California had strong departments in cognate disciplines and a strong presence in the Bay Area arts community. The other was the decision that the Union would confine its work to graduate studies. In addition to the churches and others who needed people with advanced theological training, this tied the school to the rising market for teachers of religion. Another easily overlooked advantage is that the schools, with one exception, were located in the same general area. Planning for the GTU began in 1958, shortly after the publication of the Niebuhr report,

---

21. Schuller, "Graduate Theological Union," 4.

and in 1962 four of the original schools, Berkeley Baptist, Church Divinity School of the Pacific, San Francisco Theological Seminary, and Pacific Lutheran Theological Seminary launched the venture. Pacific School of Religion, perhaps the strongest institution among the original planners, did not formally join until 1964 when Unitarian Starr King School for Ministry also joined. In 1964, the first Catholic school, St Albert's (Dominican School of Philosophy and Theology) joined, and two years later the Franciscans and the Jesuits followed. In 1968, the Union began to admit centers as components of its program—thus, eventually securing participation by Jewish, Buddhist, and Orthodox scholars.

In 1964, the GTU voted to establish a common library in a common location. The library was a major project that involved technical work consolidating collections, the design and financing of a new building, and, as always, much negotiation. Yet despite all the pain and expense involved in this project, the GTU library was a major achievement. As a specialized theological library, the GTU ranked with the more established theological libraries, such as Union Seminary's Burke Library, and legitimated the GTU as a university-level center for advanced research and study.

Why did the Graduate Theological Union succeed and the Federated Faculty fail? Part of the answer lies in the fact that the Union, for all its diversity, had a dominant academic purpose. The Union was a graduate department of theology and, as its scope expanded, of religious studies. The Graduate Theological Union confined itself to the more usual tasks of a graduate department. The standard of work for students and for faculty was, thus, part of the larger university world. In contrast, The Federated Faculty aspired to be a super-divinity school, educating pastors and professional church workers as well as serving as a center of theological research. Another reason was structural. While its member institutions created and governed the Union, the GTU had its own administration and identity. Its officers spoke for the Graduate Theological Union alone and not for its components. The Federated Faculty never attained that degree of integration.

The university ideal continued in the background of many proposals to reform the seminary. The university was, after all, part of the religious background of much of American Protestantism, and it was natural to see the seminary as a university faculty of theology separated from its natural home by the American system of church/state relations and ecclesiastical finances. The 1964 resolution of the Lutheran Church in America that theological education should be in a university environment reflected this tradition as did the location of its major new seminary in Chicago.[22] Two general trends in American religion made this yearning more heartfelt. After World War II, the rapid expansion of the state universities and the increasing proportion of college students who attended them made the seminaries' isolation more evident. These universities supplied seminaries with more and more of their student bodies. The other trend was the progressive secularization of traditionally church-related colleges. The

---

22. Horn, "The University Environment"; Skillrud, "The Fruits of Merger."

seminaries, which had long-term partnerships with these colleges, found themselves standing alone. Fueling at least part of the ecumenical movement was the hope that a reunited Protestantism might be able to claim or reclaim its traditional place in the academic order.

ESTABLISHING A UNIVERSITY STANDARD: THE TRANSFORMATION OF ACCREDITATION

Closely related to the seminary leaders' fascination with the university was the issue of academic accreditation. In most of the world, the state enforced educational standards, either by rigorous state examinations or by direct supervision. For various reasons, many related to the strategic place of the churches in the establishment of the American system of higher education, neither pattern developed in the United States. Instead, schools developed accrediting agencies that cooperatively set standards of educational quality. Although not all participants in an accrediting agency were equal, educators designed the system to produce a predictable level of education that institutions could use as the basis for the transfer of credits and for the acceptance of prior degrees for graduate study.

Generally, accrediting bodies make their standards and procedures more rigorous over time. While accreditation oriented in the need to establish the minimum criteria that made a school acceptable, once their members had attained that goal, the accrediting agencies worked towards the improvement of their member schools. Periodically, all accrediting agencies revised their standards to reflect the gains that their members had already made and to reflect a more contemporary understanding of education. In this way, accrediting agencies identified areas for improvement, exposed weaknesses, and set future directions. The 1958 revamping of the ATS library standards, for example, reflected the improvement of theological libraries since the Second World War. The level of library expense that was acceptable in the 1940s was no longer adequate in the 1960s, and the trend was for libraries to hire leaders with professional degrees to head their library staffs. The collections had also improved. The Sealantic Fund provided funds for the purchase of books, partly because the libraries had fallen behind during the depression and war years, and for increased purchases of contemporary materials.[23] In addition, the libraries had accepted responsibility for the microfilming of many works printed on high-acid paper that faced deterioration.

The 1960s saw a quantum leap in ATS accrediting procedures.[24] The older ATS procedure had been for schools to file schedules or forms reporting on the issues

---

23. Ziegler, "The AATS and Theological Education" has some details of the program. Dr. Raymond Morris was the primary director of the program.

24. The American Association of Theological Schools became the Association of Theological Schools in the 1970s. I have used Association of Theological Schools, abbreviated ATS, to refer to this group before and after the official name change.

covered in the standards. Although some schools had difficulties meeting the mark, the procedure was not rigorous or tightly controlled. In 1959, however, the Association decided that it needed to require a substantial self-study and campus visit[25] in addition to yearly reports. The ten-year self-study became a major event on seminary campuses, often involving the whole faculty as well as some students, and an occasion for important discussions of the school's future. Once the self-study method was established, the next step was to train the visitors and work to help secure a common understanding of the meaning of the standards. In 1966 the Association officially moved to the practice of reaffirming accreditation every ten years. The changes brought about by self-study were not accomplished overnight, but they did gradually improve the quality of seminary education and, especially, of seminary administration.

For a variety of resons, seminaries were not originally included in the regional accrediting system. The reason most often cited is that seminaries were single-purpose institutions, although different regions may have had additional reasons for their exclusion. Before the 1960s, this exclusion did not heavily affect most seminaries—after all, most seminary graduates went into some form of church-related employment; but in that decade, lack of larger accreditation became more problematic. Most professions had their own agencies to examine the schools that prepared practitioners, but since the vast majority of such schools were part of larger universities, they shared accreditation with other departments of their schools. Schools unaffiliated with universities did not. In the 1960s, many seminary graduates applied for admission to a variety of university graduate programs, and the universities often used internal standards for the recognition of credits and degrees that depended on regional accreditation. In those situations, those schools primarily evaluated the undergraduate transcript, often ignoring the more mature work done in the theological school. During the same decade significant numbers of ministers, Protestant and Catholic, left religious work and entered employment where employers did not understand or appreciate seminary education. If a seminary was not among the handful that enjoyed dual accreditation, then their graduates faced the problem of employers' internal standards that required degrees from regionally accredited institutions. Alums were naturally upset when someone questioned or denied their credentials. Lack of regional accreditation was a mark of institutional inferiority.[26]

Individual schools sought regional accreditation without involving ATS, and regional bodies accredited some schools, including Bangor Theological Seminary, before they became full members of the Association. Yet ATS executives recognized that they needed to take leadership. ATS took a major step forward when it affiliated with the National Commission on Accrediting. Part of the price of the affiliation was that

25. Ziegler, "The AATS and Theological Education," 69.

26. Ziegler, *ATS through Two Decades*. One of the problems in the 1970s and 1980s was the tendency of universities to transfer seminary credit only from those schools with regional accreditation. The model of *Credit Given*, a journal that reported on the exchange of credits, was almost absolute.

the National Commission required ATS to take over the task of establishing standards for degrees in religious education. This addition made the ATS the agency that accredited graduate professional degrees in religion. As seminaries offered more diverse degrees, this provided the charter for their incorporation into the ATS accreditation program. In turn, National Commission membership enabled the ATS to negotiate agreements with the various regional commissions to permit joint visits and self-studies. Such agreements limited the cost in time and treasure of accreditation and encouraged schools to take advantage of the opportunity. Although ATS continued as the sole accrediting agency for some schools, dual accreditation became normative.

In retrospect, National Commission recognition marked a subtle shift in the seminary ecology. The university divinity schools were one of the primary inspirations for the understanding of the seminary as graduate professional education. However, their influence was largely a matter of prestige. With the acquisition of National Commission status, this way of designating theological education became increasingly part of the legal structure of the schools. Graduate professional education was the formula that ATS used to differentiate its schools from Bible schools on the one hand and university religion departments on the other. The lines between these various institutions may have been murky in practice, but the formal process of accreditation made them more definite. Equally important, membership in first the National Commission and later the Council for Higher Education Accreditation meant that the ATS had to discuss changes in its understanding of theological education with both its members and with the broader educational community.

The selection of an executive director reinforced one of the traditional tasks of the Association: the promotion of knowledge and conversation about theological education. Unlike the various denominational forums, ATS was an open forum that included educators from widely differing theological backgrounds. When they came together, they discovered that other seminary leaders shared many of the same problems, hopes, and expectations. In 1965 the Association began the publication of a journal, *Theological Education*, designed to publish the results of its own studies as well as articles on current issues. The initial funding came from the Lilly Endowment, a leading financial sponsor of ATS initiatives.[27] The phrase *theological education* rapidly became the preferred term for what seminaries and divinity schools did collectively.

The popularity of the ecumenical movement contributed to the 1960s successes of the Association. During the 1960s, the National and World Councils were at the peak of their influence, and Vatican II suggested the expansion of the ecumenical movement to include all Christians. People became accustomed to Protestants, Catholics, and Orthodox acting together for common goals, and many people believed that organic unity between denominations was possible. Perhaps the Lutherans were the best example of this new optimism at work. In the 1960s, they consolidated the many small ethnic Lutheran churches, each with its own cultural and theological

---

27. Ziegler, "The ATS and Theological Education."

particularities, into three primary entities: The Lutheran Church–Missouri Synod, the Lutheran Church in America, and the American Lutheran Church. This was only a stopgap measure towards what they hoped would be further unification. In 1988, the Lutheran Church in America, the American Lutheran Church, and Association of Evangelical Lutheran Churches (moderate congregations earlier affiliated with the Missouri Synod) merged to form the Evangelical Lutheran Church in America.

ATS accreditation was, however, different from the major streams in American ecumenism. Unlike denominational movements that aimed at unity, ATS saw its diversity as part of its strength. ATS also differed from the federative movements, such as the NCC. Federative movements combined Faith and Order movements that rested on the hope of a common theological consensus, and Work and Life movements that saw the churches as having a common mission. In contrast, the Association provided its members with common services and recognized status.

THE LOGIC OF PROFESSIONALISM

Ideas often have their own historical logic. This was true of the ideal of graduate professional education. What made that ideal graduate was its connection to the larger university ideal and to the long tradition of Christian theological reflection. Yet, what made that ideal professional? This question was (and is) not easily answered. Throughout the 1960s, theological educators struggled with this question. Almost every seminary experimented with new curricula designed to accentuate the professional character of the seminary degree. To further the professional side of their program, schools added clinical programs, reformed their field-education programs, designed intern years, and developed programs in specialized ministries. Continuing education, a mark of most contemporary professions, also received attention.

At first glance, this emphasis on professionalism seems disconnected from other tendencies in seminary life. The 1960s saw blistering attacks on the ministry. Peter Berger, Harvey Cox, Martin E. Marty, and Gilson Winter eloquently pointed to the suburban captivity of the churches and to the ministry's lack of connection with the issues of contemporary life. More than a hint of sexism accompanied the emphasis on ministry as essentially serving women and children or in the mocking of the minister as a caring or healing professional. Almost every study of student opinion at the time reflected a similar understanding of parish ministry. The number of men who aspired to ordinary congregational service declined; the most prestigious schools, such as Union and Yale, reported the smallest percentage of parish-bound students. Enrollments did dip in the early 1960s until the pressures of the Vietnam War provided another answer to that question: the seminary was a good place to avoid the draft. Once the war ended, seminaries had to be much clearer about their rationale. George "Bill" Webber summed up the discussion with this judgment:

> For I am under the strong impression that for the last ten years the seminaries have been analyzing, dissecting, lambasting, and devastating the poor parish minister until he is likely to be bloody and bowed. Has any professional group ever been so threatened and criticized by its mentors as the clergy?[28]

Webber asked the right question, even if his proposals for theological education were avant garde.

One of the 1960s buzzwords, *relevance*, summarized the discussion. Like other overused catchphrases, *relevance* had more a suggestive than a precise or analytic meaning. On the one hand, it referred to the need for a theological approach to the questions of the day, particularly the civil rights movement, the Vietnam War, and the urban crisis. Despite church and National Council resolutions on those issues, the churches, especially on the congregational level, seemed isolated from what was happening around them. Even such orthodox thinkers as Southern Baptist George W. Bennett wondered where or even if the church could locate itself on the rapidly shifting urban frontier. Church pronouncements on social issues were increasingly less visible and effective. Church leaders did have public voices. Organizations such as Clergy and Laity Concerned about the War in Vietnam, founded in 1965, were vocal; yet, such voices were also marginal. In that sense, *relevance* pointed to the feeling that something more than moral suasion was needed to effect lasting change; something like direct political—or even revolutionary—action. *Relevance* was a council of despair for those searching for a professional understanding of congregational leadership. Ironically, Christian ethics, a stepchild in many seminaries, was itself undergoing its own process of professionalization as doctoral students increasingly elected it as their concentration, and seminaries—even small ones—included ethics courses in their required curriculum.

Theological change also affected the seminary's understanding of professionalism. The Barth–Brunner–Niebuhr theology of the 1950s rooted Christian life and ministry in a tradition that reached back to the Old Testament and forward into the future. The minister was part of a long procession of witnesses to the saving event of Jesus Christ. While the theologians of the fifties continued to take account of biblical criticism and of modern science, neo-orthodoxy provided an identity that could be a source of pride and of action. As the 1950s gave way to the 1960s, however, the consensus frayed and finally fell apart. The new era, perhaps best summarized as Bonhoeffer, Bultmann, and Tillich—although that trinity never had the power of the earlier triad—returned to fundamental theological questions: How can we speak of God in a technological and scientific age? How can the stories of the Old and New Testaments be existentially meaningful in an age that knows that they are mythical? How can we speak of the mighty acts of God in the face of a criticism that indicates that much of the biblical history, including the exodus, was legendary or just plain false? What did

---

28. Webber, "The Christian Minister," 15.

it mean for faith that modern people, especially in Europe and America, were less involved in religion and seemed to be moving beyond it? In particular, what was the public character of religion in a world that defined religion as a private matter? To paraphrase the classical question of Western philosophy, why was there something and not nothing? Why didn't the church close up shop or take up a mission that was more in line with humanity coming of age?

I have presented 1960s theology as a series of questions because the theologians of that decade had no answers to the issues that they had raised. The deep sense that modernity had shaken the foundations left some of the most promising theological developments stranded. Looking backward, Wilson Yates noted the rich growth of programs and discussion in theology and the arts in the early 1960s.[29] The foundation of these programs was Tillich's argument, based on German idealism, that the arts and religion discussed similar realities. For Tillich and his immediate successors, the point of contact was the human anxiety over finitude and the human need to create meaning. Although Tillich always insisted that theological symbols had to have some ontological basis, some grounding in being itself, many saw this as a wishing it were so. The promise of this movement was rarely realized. Only a few schools were able to incorporate theology and arts into their program, although many offered a course or two, and a journal *ARTS* provided a place for academic and practical discussion.

Another feature of the theology of the 1960s was the decade's self-absorption. Linguistic philosophy suggested that the most important inquiry was the nature of theological language itself. Traditional theology assumed, perhaps naively, that theological language was an attempt to describe the world, including the supernatural world, with a degree of accuracy. Most religious liberalism, while stripping away much of the superstructure of the traditional worldview, had continued to assume that religious language was about something "out there." The fatherhood of God and the brotherhood of humankind were, to be sure, minimal affirmations, but nonetheless they were affirmations. The language might involve a high degree of risk, a risk perhaps increased by the importance of what was at stake, but the language itself still pointed beyond itself. What made the risk real was that the leap of faith might be a leap into the void. The new analysis suggested that religious language was much more multivalent than had been supposed. Much of it might be language about the self or about a social or political group or only part of a larger language game.

Changing sexual mores also entered into this mixture. American attitudes and practices around sexuality had been changing since the 1920s, but the birth-control pill, easier divorce, and more explicit entertainment all pointed towards a sexual revolution. If nothing else, the change in sexual mores was yet another area where absolutes were no longer present, or at least no longer binding. Much seminary thinking about sexual matters, often summarized as situational or contextual ethics, was relatively modest, but it increased the sense of confusion. Almost all Mainstream seminaries

---

29. Yates, *The Arts in Theological Education*.

removed their elaborate rules around residence halls and student deportment. Symbolically, hosts at Mainstream schools served wine at faculty and, increasingly, student gatherings.

In this swirling confusion, which increased as the decade progressed, professionalism provided the seminary with what unity it possessed. Exactly what made seminary education professional education was less clear. Roger Hazelton, dean of Oberlin and later professor of theology at Andover Newton, proposed simply:

> Every professional minister is a theologian in spite of himself. He may not choose this role, and other roles may be forced upon him; but his own distinctive contribution to the church's ministry is necessarily a theological one. By virtue of his seminary education he is—or is thought to be—adept, as members of the laity are not, in communicating and interpreting the truth of faith.[30]

For others, the word *professional* simply meant that the purpose of the seminary was to produce people who could do a good job leading a church or (in the language of the times) could do a good job enabling a church to do its work. Others saw professionalism in terms of more abstract standards. Professional education provided people with the skills and insights that a particular profession required. A doctor, for example, had to diagnose illness in order to treat it, a social worker had to develop empathy in order to intervene in human tragedy, and teachers needed practice teaching to qualify for a first appointment. When a critic like Charles Feilding,[31] the Canadian author of "Education for Ministry," found theological schools "insufficiently professional," he had in mind primarily this later understanding of ministry. How did one go from what was taught in theological schools to the day-by-day work of the parish minister?

Part of what confused the question was the rose-tinted glasses through which theological educators viewed other professions and the dark lenses through which they viewed their own. Most professional work, in fact, consists of routine and not particularly challenging duties. The doctor sees multiple cases of grippe, sore throat, high blood pressure, and diabetes before he or she ever confronts an illness or a situation that requires sophisticated therapeutic knowledge or experience. Likewise, the practice of even the most dashing lawyer is often composed of wills, contracts, divorces, and the interpretation of government regulations. During the last fifty years, some professions have shifted much of this routine to lower-level professionals such as paralegals or nurse practitioners, but the general point remains valid. Professional life is a mixture of administration, routine, and—only occasionally—challenge. Paradoxically, much of professionals' daily work does not require the extensive training and experience that regulatory bodies mandate for entry into a given profession.

---

30. Hazelton, "Ministry as Servanthood," 521.

31. Feilding, "Education for Ministry." This was a major study of supervision, one of the principal marks of the professional model. The study was financed by the Lilly Endowment.

In one sense, ministers were freer to set their course than were members of other professional groups. The growth of government regulations had made other professions, including medicine, social work and teaching, progressively more embedded in administrative duties and general oversight. In comparison, most ministers did their work free of governmental regulation and with minimum supervision from judicatories and local congregational boards.

Much of the discussion of theological education as professional preparation focused on field education, including internships, and on clinical training. Theological educators intended both of these to mediate between the intellectual life of the study and the reality of congregational experience. Clinical Pastoral Education (CPE) had a long and successful history.[32] The basic idea of CPE was that the student would work in a center, most often a hospital, under close supervision. Clinical instructors used various techniques, such as the verbatim account of a conversation, group discussion of particular cases, and case studies to oversee the student's work with patients. Much of what the program developed was sensitivity to the emotional side of the encounter. This involved, particularly with young men who had lived largely in male environments, coming to terms with the ministerial candidates' own psychological needs and expectations, including their sexual identities. Karl Jung's psychology, which stressed the multiple dimensions of the inner life, was often used as part of this process. In many settings, particularly in hospitals, clinical training provided many seminarians with their first direct experiences of death and grief.

Clinical worked or, at least, theological educators believed that it worked. The courses were popular and well received. Significantly, counseling skills apparently improved, a significant achievement in a therapeutic age that interpreted the ministry as a helping profession. The question was whether theological educators could take the insights that they had gleaned from the clinical programs and use similar methods to teach more varied aspects of ministry.

One 1960s attempt to apply the lessons of clinical education was the popularity of the intern year. Just as clinical education borrowed language and techniques from medicine, so the idea of an intern year had medical analogues. The idea of an intern year also reverberated with some traditional emphases. Catholic Christianity, whether Roman or Anglican, had traditionally provided for a period as a deacon between the formal completion of training and ordination as a priest, and this year had some value as part of a young cleric's preparation for office. Among Reformation Protestants in America, Lutherans pioneered in the use of this educational technique, partially, because of the German precedent. In Germany, after students completed formal educational training and the first theological examinations, they entered a two-year period of intense professional study that included a year as an assistant pastor and practical studies. At the end of that period, the student took the second theological examination. A more direct inspiration for an intern year, especially among schools like the

---

32. For the development of clinical training, see Miller, *Piety and Profession*, chapter 25: 591–617.

University of Chicago and Andover Newton, was the medical model that had proven so successful in the clinical education movement. Just as the intern year forced the young doctor to deal with the full range of illness and treatment in a modern hospital, so (many believed) the intern year would force the young minister to deal with the full range of issues facing a modern minister.

These proposals rested on the quality of the supervisors. The major reason for the discontinuation of these programs was the difficulty that schools experienced in finding and retaining competent supervisors. Training and paying good pastoral supervisors posed a difficult and expensive task.[33] Moreover, the best supervisors often changed congregations as they advanced in their professional careers. In retrospect, the intern year may have rested on a misplaced metaphor. The medical intern year was done in a hospital in the midst of continual medical emergencies. The young doctor had to serve on different wards and had to respond instantly to the issues posed by those wards. The next step was an even more intensive residency. The local congregation was not analogous to a hospital. It was more like a doctor's office, characterized by routine illness and only rarely challenged by difficult cases.

Clinical training also inspired schools to undertake the reform of their field-education programs. As the 1960s inherited the program, field education was a combination of a source of revenue, an educational opportunity, and a chance for some pastoral experience. Students worked at a wide variety of tasks, including serving as the pastor of a small church, working in the local YMCA, running youth groups, and teaching church school. Often, strangely in line with a broader Catholic tradition, they also served as lectors during the Sunday worship service and took an occasional turn in the pulpit. The problems with the inherited system were legion. The student was rarely involved in the complex governance of the congregation and often was assigned the tasks that the senior pastor did not want to perform, and the need for financial support often decided who served in which placements. Ironically, fieldwork seemed to drive the seminary. Most schools had a four-day (or to be more accurate) a three-and-a-half-day schedule. Field education also took a disproportionate number of hours, twenty or more, from the student's week, leaving little time left over for serious study.

The most successful attempt to solve field education's problems was Russell Becker's In Parish program at Yale. Becker noted that one of the key elements in successful clinical programs was that the students functioned as a group. Group experience, in addition to its value as a pedagogic technique, allowed the students to face their supervisor in a much freer setting. Questions about the supervisor's practice, for example, could come from the group and not individuals. No one had to "find himself all alone in striking at the root of some pastor's pet enterprise."[34] Perhaps more

33. These two problems plagued every aspect of seminary education that relied on supervision, including field education.
34. Becker, "The Place of the Parish," 165.

important was the careful way that Becker trained his supervisors. They were required to meet together and to exchange insights:

> The major vehicle for supervision and training in supervision which we have provided is this: that the supervisor will meet with his cluster of students for at least an hour and a half every week throughout the school year and that *each meeting will be tape recorded in full.* These recordings are brought to the weekly meeting held by the supervisors with those of us at the school who take responsibility for leading the supervisory training sessions.[35]

In effect, Becker took the role of the supervising chaplain with the individual supervisors working directly with the small groups and the on-site experiences. Becker, thus, almost replicated the structure of contemporary clinical programs in a nonhospital setting.

The one problem that Becker did not solve, however, was the problem of supervision. This was the same problem that limited the yearlong internship programs. As Clinical Pastoral Education professionalized, clinical theological educators devised a method for training supervisors that took them through various stages in their preparation before they served as a supervising chaplain. When candidates became supervising chaplains, the system had prepared the candidates for that role. Equally important, the system rejected some less suited to the task or discouraged them from continuing. In contrast, Becker had to choose his supervisors from ministers in local positions of ecclesiastical leadership whose professional status was not dependent on either their own experience of supervision or their success as supervisors. Moreover, whereas the hospital setting could ensure with regularity, if not predictability, a supply of teaching moments, congregational ministry did not necessarily supply those moments with any predictability. Like a doctor's office, parish ministry involves routine—the regular administration of Word and Sacrament, the steady education of the young, the maintenance of organizations, and steady attention to financial matters. Teaching moments are few and far between and may (and often do) surprise the supervisor as much as they do the person receiving supervision.[36]

---

35. Becker, "In Parish Pastoral Studies 1960–1966," 409.

36. One of the central problems in all these schemes was, despite the tendency—partly marked among Baptists and Methodists—to make ordination a stage in professional development, the primary ministerial task was the administration of Word and Sacrament. Other ministerial tasks, even when those tasks took more of the minister's time, were secondary to this prime function or derived in some way from it. Churches in the Reformed tradition, historically more didactic than other branches of Protestantism, often combined Word and Sacrament with education and teaching. Since few students had a sacramental role or preaching role, aside from those involved in student pastorates, placements could not provide authentic experience of what ministry involved religiously. There is an infinite difference between guiding young people to adult faith through confirmation and marriage, and providing leadership for a youth group. In more Evangelical churches, admittedly, this distinction may not be as clear since the person charged with youth leadership is also charged with the task of leading their charges to saving faith.

The emphasis on specialized ministries and education specifically for these tasks also reflected the 1960s fascination with professionalism. In most professions, there was separation between those practitioners who dealt with a variety of clients and those who only consulted with people with special needs. This was particularly common among physicians where general practitioners and family doctors served as the front lines of medical treatment and diagnosis. Specialists treated individual diseases. Such doctors understood their own work as built on general medical education and practice. Where specialized practice differed was that specialists concentrated their practices on limited areas where they acquired experience not available to the generalists. Likewise, some attorneys became experts in tax law, employment law, trial law, or torts, and other areas. Social workers and educators showed similar patterns. In most professions, the line between specialized practice and general practice was, at least in part, the level of education required. The specialist received education in the general practice and then qualified through further study or experience in the specialty.

Ministry never completely fit this larger professional pattern of general/specialized practice. The chaplaincies came closest to this pattern. Military chaplains were a classic example of specialization. After a period of successful work as a congregational minister, usually three years in length, the military chaplain received specific training for work with the armed services. Once the chaplain had qualified, superior officers monitored the chaplain's work, subjected it to regular evaluation, and required periodic continued education. The military rewarded increasing proficiency with military rank and supervisory responsibility. Although less governmentally regulated, hospital chaplaincy followed a similar program: general practice was followed by specific training and evaluation; yet the requirement of prior general practice weakened over time. Missions also reflected a generalist/specialist pattern of education. Just as candidates for chaplaincy had to first gain pastoral experience before qualifying, so candidates for the mission field (at least male candidates) were required by sending agencies to have had experience in the ordinary ministry of Word and Sacrament before entering specialized training in languages and local cultures. The practice of granting missionaries periodic furloughs at home provided opportunities for continued education, either in theology or in social science, especially anthropology. Although less structured than the military or missionary specializations, hospital chaplaincy also represented a genuine ministerial specialty, building on general ministerial experience and providing special training and evaluation in work with patients, and in such areas as death and dying.

Theological educators in the sixties did not use the language of specialized ministries with any precision. For most faculty and students, specialized ministry was alternative ministry, a form of church or religious service that was an alternative to work in the congregation, not a development of it. Harold Fey, editor of the *Christian Century*, captured the widespread interest in finding religious employment not connected to the local church:

> For most seminary students today, the parish is no challenging frontier. In their view adventure, excitement and, more important, theological validity and sense of vocational fulfillment are to be found elsewhere: in the inner city, the mental institution, the social work center, the university. They have read some of the devastating sociological studies of the parish. They know all about the effects of bad locations of churches, of population shifts, and of competitive denominationalism.[37]

The term *mission*, carefully spelled without a final *s*, was often used to describe these alternatives. Theological educators dropped the *s* to distinguish their new sense of what God was doing in the world from the older program of foreign missions that many denominations were downsizing. American Christians had tied the traditional language of foreign and home missions to the expansion of Christianity as a religion at home and abroad. The missionary was, thus, a person who carried the faith to those without, a later-day apostle. To be sure, missionaries did other things, including founding hospitals, colleges, and schools, but the evangelistic thrust was never far from the surface. In contrast, *mission* resonated with the World Council's emphasis on the *missio dei*, God's larger project of bringing humanity to its full potential. Part of the advantage of the term was its open-ended character. The word *mission* was not necessarily tied to the religious expansion of the faith (although some believed that participation in God's cause would make the church more attractive), nor to the performance of traditional religious duties, such as preaching or administering the sacraments.

Christian charity was likewise not the focus of the new missioners. Home missionaries had conducted a variety of charities, ranging from food pantries to homeless shelters, throughout American history. These missions had deep and broad support among American Christians, whether Mainstream or Evangelical, and American Catholic charities were the best staffed and financed in the world. Yet, close observers of urban America believed, apparently correctly, that such measures were only a drop of cold water in a desert of human need and degradation. What the cities needed was social action that could alter the structure that created and sustained urban poverty. For a brief season, these hopes seemed realistic. After the conservative John Kennedy's assassination, his successor, Lyndon Johnson, launched the most extensive liberal program since the New Deal. Money was available for education, for children's programs, and for community organizations. Unlike New Deal programs, however, Johnson's programs required local participation and some measure of local control. This provided a window of opportunity for both liberals and radicals. The new social programs provided a base for direct Christian action. Urban training programs flourished in the mid-1960s and began to wane after the 1968 riots. Although some urban ministry

---

37 Fey, "Editorial: The Ideas of a Seminary," 518.

programs continued into the Nixon years, the changing political climate weakened their financial basis.

Although a few, like the MUST program in New York, headed by George "Bill" Webber, were housed in a seminary and used some of the seminary's resources, the urban training centers or programs, like clinical education programs, were largely independent of the seminary. At their height, there were at least fifteen such centers and programs at work and one, Intermet, in Washington DC, saw itself as offering an alternative to the traditional Master of Divinity degree. These centers attracted some of the most innovative leaders of 1960s theological education, including John Fletcher, the founder of Intermet; Tilden R. Edwards, who would later found the Shalem Institute; and Loren Mead, the founder of the Alban Institute.

The basic idea behind the urban training programs was that one could not existentially understand the problems of the inner city unless one experienced its problems directly. In the late 1940s, George "Bill" Webber established the East Harlem Protestant Parish with more or less traditional ideas of mission in mind. In the 1960s, he wrote:

> We began in East Harlem with the distinct impression that God needed us to get his work done. Christ had no other hands but ours. We went forth from the chapel at Union with the words of the great commandment urging us on, "Go ye into all the world and preach the gospel to every creature." We thought this meant we had to introduce Christ as though he were a stranger to the pagan, missionary world of East Harlem, as though we had to take him from Morningside Heights to a world from which, without us, he was absent. In the early days, with our self-righteousness, our confidence that now a radically new dimension had been added to East Harlem, we made all the social workers furious and alienated many of the devoted men and women who were engaged in the struggle for justice and brotherhood in the community.[38]

Webber also quickly learned that the best of what he knew—ranging from counseling techniques to Sunday school curriculum—required radical revision after he and his students immersed themselves in the culture that they sought to serve.

Webber's experience was not atypical. The image of the white explorer in the urban jungle, drawn from missionary lore, was no more real in Harlem than its prototype had been in Africa. What Webber and others found was a very complex world that one had to experience before one could understand. The student or prospective urban minister had to live on the field in order to understand what was happening. Above all, the minister had to encounter the various ways that members of the urban culture humanized their environment and made it serve the common good. Yet, urban educators did not have an uncritical belief in being there. The urban training centers sought to give their students tools, including sophisticated techniques from

---

38 Webber, "The Christian Minister," 19.

sociology and anthropology, to separate out what was significant from what was only factual. Further, urban educators used all the familiar tools of clinical education—intensely introspective group meetings, personal supervision, case studies, and reflective accounts—to accomplish their goals. Yet, they harnessed these techniques to a very different purpose: to change the world and not adjust to it. Students worked and studied with effective change agents. Perhaps most important, students did projects that enabled them to experiment with different approaches to the urban world. Teachers, students, and community members then evaluated those projects and helped the student formulate next steps. The pattern, at least ideally, was action-reflection-action. This was similar to what was happening in Latin America, mediated through such people as Princeton's M. Richard Shaull, who participated in both Latin America missions and the American urban scene.

The urban training programs vanished for much the same reason alternative ministries disappeared: finances. At the base of the Protestant financial system was the local congregation. Although urban training institutes received some money from individuals and particularly from foundations, those funds were largely to cover startup costs and initial expenses. When they ran out, the churches were the only source of funding left, and both they and their national bodies were increasingly strapped.

The subsequent careers of many urban educators should make us cautious about identifying the decline and closing of their institutional centers with the end of their influence on American theological education. George Webber was, after all, the only major seminary leader to rescue a dying theological school, New York Seminary, and give it a new vision and direction. Rather, many components of urban training continued. These included the so-called immersion experience as a tool for learning to minister in a new culture, the use of anthropological techniques (including the informant) to study a ministry site, and the belief in educational power of the project. Most urban training programs required students to devise, collectively or individually, a program that might effect change in a neighborhood and execute and evaluate that project. The project survived as part of many Doctor of Ministry programs. After all, the young people of one generation are the leaders of the next, and lessons learned in youth are the experience that guides age.

RIOTS AND UNREST

For many people, the student riots are almost symbols of the 1960s. Jesse Ziegler, the executive director of ATS, put the unrest on seminary campuses in the context of general student unrest:

> This is a task both of formation and of education. And we find ourselves caught today in a ferment the like of which the educational enterprise in North America has not known since its beginning. The campus on which we

meet today and the campuses of many other distinguished universities have been the scenes of major confrontations and demonstrations. We can't write these off as accidents; they level a profound judgment on the whole process of higher education. In effect, students are saying that they are getting answers to questions which they are not asking and are finding little manifest interest in the questions which are most vital in their lives.[39]

The students clearly believed that they were the vanguard of a radically new future in theological education that would replace the older church with a new, more prophetic religion. Even in schools where students did not seize offices or make explicit demands, there was widespread pressure for institutional and social change. Although growing unrest over the Vietnam War on almost all American campuses was the background of student unrest, racial issues were more often the spark that ignited the conflict. The Black Manifesto, with its demands for reparations from white organizations, sparked the unrest at Union Seminary, and the lesser known but equally upsetting events at Christian Theological Seminary in Indianapolis were a response to the racial crises at nearby Shortbridge High School.

The origins of student unrest varied. Many students had entered seminary to avoid the draft, an act that they understood as an act of protest against the Vietnam War. Demographic factors also contributed to the uneasiness. The seminary students of the 1960s were generally younger students, often entering seminary directly from college, who shared the youth culture with their only slightly younger peers.[40] Events that influenced college students as a whole, such as the tragic deaths at Kent State, were also events that rocked seminary communities. Further, the seminarians of the sixties were graduates of state or secular universities, unlike folks from earlier generations, who entered from denominational colleges. The events that affected public educational institutions also tended to affect them directly.

Ironically, student unrest was strongest in liberal institutions where the students and faculty often shared common social and political values. In part, this was because the schools had hired large numbers of instructors in the late 1950s and early 1960s who shared more of the worldview of the students than older colleagues did. Some older faculty members and administrators also shared those values. Union Seminary president John C. Bennett was a devoted advocate of racial justice. Moreover, Bennett had encouraged the formation of Clergy and Laity Concerned about the War in Vietnam and provided the group with meeting space and some secretarial support. Other members of his faculty were equally committed to social transformation.

---

39. Ziegler, "Conservation and Change in Theological Education," 104.

40. Seminarians of the 1960s were the youngest in the twentieth century. Early seminary students had often had to work for several years before entering seminary, and the generation after the War saw many students entering seminary after military service. By the 1960s, the older, postmilitary students were out of the pipeline, and a more prosperous America allowed many students to go directly from undergraduate to graduate education.

Bennett clearly did not want unrest on his beloved campus, but he was sympathetic to its causes and respected many of its leaders.

The unrest on liberal seminary campuses, I would suggest, came about through collaboration between some faculty and some students. While this was also true of much student unrest at universities where teach-ins often sparked more radical events, in retrospect, the close relationship between faculty and students may have defined the movement in theological schools. This observation also helps to explain the shifts in power and authority that occurred at many schools. Despite short-term increases in student participation in governance, the most substantial changes were those that strengthened faculty power over and against the administration, especially in such areas as faculty appointments and participation in presidential-selection procedures. The imperial presidency, so aptly modeled by Henry Pitney Van Dusen and John Mackay, declined at the more liberal schools. Many schools not directly affected by the unrest accepted the changed governance model. However, the remaining strong presidencies, including Princeton's James McCord and Southern Baptist Theological Seminary's Duke McCall, may have bent, but they did not break.

Attempts to include students in institutional decision making were not always successful. Such changes were very expensive in terms of the time needed to reach consensus or make decisions. Faculty committees had to update new student-members, but more important, seminary decision making, like decision making in other small institutions, became subject to pressure from the small numbers of those with time to participate. Although the complex committee structures of the 1960s and 1970s may have helped racial and other minorities, who earlier had little or no voice, this was not necessarily the case. A handful of students often were self-appointed representatives for the whole.

The 1960s were a decade of curricula experimentations. The changes in curriculum inspired by the unrest at decade's end increased student freedom to choose courses, instructors, and methods of instruction. These changes, some of which lasted, increased the costs of education. Instructors needed reduced class loads to prepare for more electives and individualized instruction. Less permanent was a widespread attempt to substitute written evaluations for grades. Many schools abandoned this comparatively quickly. Graduate schools, including graduate programs in seminaries, continued to expect grades as part of admission packets, but this was not the system's greatest flaw. Like participatory committees, evaluations took significant amounts of time and, despite the hope that students would receive detailed criticism, often contained more-or-less hackneyed generalities.[41] In many cases, the faculty adopted the

---

41. Miller, "Contemporary Threats to Theological Education," 139, offered this summary: "These new forms embody three characteristics: 1) There is less required work, with more freedom of choice and a wider range of elective offerings. 2) There is less formal class instruction, and more small group and individual study. 3) There is a closer relation to universities and to other seminary programs of instruction where possible, including Roman Catholic."

language of the older grading systems—words like *excellent* and *good*—to the new forms. No one was satisfied; the experiment died quickly.

How important was the unrest in determining a school's future? Perhaps not as important as either advocates or critics believed. Mainstream faculties already contained significant numbers of radical teachers, and while the new governance gave them more power and influence, the disturbances of the decade did not create them. In addition, many of these faculty members were young. The natural career curve would increase their influence as they rose in the ranks. Ironically, as the age of retirement rose, they served longer than previous academic generation. The sixties did cast a long shadow over Mainstream theological education. The shadow was not that cast by radical students; however, the shadow was cast by their teachers.

Some liberal schools did experience increased difficulties after the unrest ended. In many cases, these schools already had serious structural problems. Union in New York, the school most often associated with post-1960s decline, was never as healthy as outside observers supposed. When the Board elected John Bennett President, thoughtful observers were already raising questions about the institution's future. The *Christian Century* expressed its reservations in a single line: "His {Bennett's} ability to lead the school in meeting its increasing financial needs remains unknown solely because it has not yet been tested."[42] Structural problems continued to plague the school for the next fifty years. One can make similar observations about other seminaries believed permanently damaged by the unrest. At most, the student unrest, like other such natural events as earthquakes, exposed the structural weaknesses already present.

---

42. *Christian Century*, "Bennett Elected Union President," 7.

2 Finances, Professionalism, and New Directions

AFTER 1968, AMERICAN THEOLOGICAL education entered into a decade characterized by a deepening sense of financial crisis. In part, seminaries shared their sense of financial woe with much of the nation. The American economy seemingly experienced setback after setback. While inflation continued its steady rise, eroding the value of endowments and making potential donors more careful, little actual growth occurred in the economy. Military spending continued at a high level, and the liberal vision that Lyndon Johnson had so energetically embraced appeared less and less affordable. Economic shifts also occurred within the nation. The East and Midwest lost population and economic resources to the Sunbelt and the West. Since the nation's most noted seminaries were in the East, these schools faced increasing difficulties. At the same time, denominational contributions to theological education declined as Mainstream Protestantism began a decline in membership that would continue into the indefinite future. "Follow the money" is an important directive for this difficult period.

THE RESOURCES COMMISSION

The year 1968 was significant in the post–World War II development of theological education. Almost ten years after the Niebuhr-Williams-Gustafson project had spoken confidently of the advancement of theological education, the Resources Commission presented its four less glowing reports. The Resources Commission was part of the American Association of Theological Schools that was established, at least in part, in response to the Niebuhr-Williams-Gustafson study. The Resources Commission did not put forth any new understanding of theological education; the commission assumed that the graduate-professional understanding of theological schools was the natural order of things. Yet graduate professional education was expensive, and the schools often lacked the resources to implement their best insights. In many cases, schools stood at the edge of bankruptcy.[1]

---

1. McKay, "Resources Planning"; Jensen, "Protestant Theological Education"; Campbell et al.,

The Commission, appointed in 1966, represented some of the best minds in theological education at the time: Arthur R. McKay, chairman of the commission (McCormick Theological Seminary); John Dillenberger (Graduate Theological Union); Stanley B. Frost (McGill University); Paul M. Harrison (Pennsylvania State University); Lynn Leavenworth (American Baptist Convention); Edward F. Malone, MM (Maryknoll Seminary); Robert V. Moss Jr. (Lancaster Theological Seminary), and Henry P. Van Dusen (President Emeritus, Union Theological Seminary). The ATS leadership, headed by Jesse Ziegler and David S. Schuller, provided the staff work and research needed for the undertaking. Arthur Little and Company did the technical work of constructing financial models and providing sophisticated analysis. Arthur Little also provided the Commission with the services of Warren H. Deem, a skilled accountant who became an important figure in the professionalization of theological seminary administrations in the 1970s. Significantly, the Commission did not include either the new Evangelicals or the Southern Baptists, whose percentage of the total enrollment of AATS schools grew in the 1970s and 1980s.

The Commission quickly discovered that few seminaries had the resources to finance their programs as individual schools. The prospect of financing each school's improvement to an adequate level appeared difficult, if not impossible. The cost was just too great. Consequently, the Commission searched for another strategy. They noted a seeming paradox. While each school was comparatively poor, when considered collectively, the seminaries were comparatively prosperous. The trick was to rearrange the resources to make them more effective. The Commission's favored word for this new approach was *redeployment*. *Redeployment* was a military term used to describe the strategic movement of forces and material in order to attain specific goals, usually, to exert pressure at key points. The metaphor required clarity about two items: the extent of the resources available to be committed to the objective, and the objective itself. The objectives were what the schools needed to make seminary education truly professional and graduate:

> To achieve greater excellence in theological education;
>
> To further the advance of cooperative ecumenical endeavors in theological education; to enhance relevant denominational connections;
>
> To establish stronger ties between the enterprise of theological education and the teaching and research resources of major universities;
>
> To preserve meaningful cultural and regional differences found throughout the Association's membership and the life of the churches;
>
> To secure a fuller utilization of the economic resources required for theological education;
>
> To initiate a participative planning process which would further cooperative inter-institutional action in various areas of North America;
>
> To further cooperative developments by preparing a plan and materials which

---

"Theological Curriculum"; "Cooperative Structures."

would aid the planning effects of seminaries, denominational boards, and other interested parties.[2]

Each section of the report returned to these larger goals and objectives. One might summarize the thesis of the report, consequently, as, if you want your schools to attain their potential, attaining these objectives might enable you to do so. Warren Deem put this succinctly:

> For seminaries whose ambitions do not or cannot extend beyond "business as usual," it is probably safe to assume that recent experience with respect to cost and income will continue during the years ahead. If survival is the only goal, particularly survival in terms of today's program, it appears that most seminaries will be able to survive.[3]

In order to make this case, the Commission appointed a blue-ribbon task force to design a seminary curriculum for the 1970s. In many ways, this was an exercise in the creation of an ideal type. No one seriously thought that the seminaries might implement the Curriculum for the 1970s or even that they should do so.[4] The Commission recommended it only "as a particular kind of *illustration* . . . that . . . shows clearly and usefully the scale of resources" needed by theological schools in the coming decade.[5]

The Task Force's members painted the Curriculum for the Seventies on a broad canvas. Its report envisioned theological education as existing on three levels. The first was the college level where the student would become familiar with modern culture and master one modern and one ancient language. The second level was essentially classical theological study with special seminars to study the religious and theological dimensions of some aspect of contemporary culture. This level was to last for approximately two years, although the plan left open the possibility that it might take some students longer to achieve the competencies envisioned by the program. The academic load during this period was heavy, with long papers of forty to fifty pages and comprehensive examinations. Further, the students were to demonstrate that they could use the languages previously learned as an undergraduate in research! The third level was a series of centers that would concentrate on ministerial specialties and professional training, including pastoral ministry. This level would last eleven calendar months, half of which time would be in a field placement. Interestingly, those interested in theological teaching had their own specialized training that was supposed to follow the research doctorate. In concrete terms, this meant a faculty of around 92 members serving a student body of around 775 students.

---

2. McKay, "Resources Planning," 758.

3 Deem and Van de Mark, "1970s: Alternatives for Change," 43.

4. Few people referred to this document as the Curriculum for the 1970s, preferring the simpler, Curriculum for the Seventies. I have followed that practice.

5. McKay, "Resources Planning," 789.

The Curriculum for the 1970s suffered from too much detail at some points. Even now, the reader is easily lost in the specialized language, convoluted arguments, and pedantic style of the document. Where the reader wanted explanation, the Report failed to provide it; where the Report might have left some features to the reader's imagination, the Committee provided copious illustrations. The report's separation of theory and practice into levels 2 and 3, further, almost invited caricature. Yet, for all its flaws, the Curriculum of the 1970s made the Resources Commission's case. If the best that theological educators could devise required this level of resourcing or support, the present situation was woefully lacking.

The primary difficulty in the improvement of theological education, desired by the Resources Commission and most theological educators, was the problem of scale. Theological schools were small institutions that required comparatively large faculties and libraries. As a result, theological education was the most expensive form of professional education in America, apart from medical training. To complicate the problem further, seminaries lacked many sources of income open to other parts of the educational community, such as federal grants or wealthy graduates, and had to depend on the churches, directly and indirectly, for aid. The decline of the Mainstream denominations, already in evidence, pointed to increasing problems as did the demographics that indicated that fewer males in the twenty-one- to twenty-six-year age bracket were in the pipeline. As another commentator put it, "It is a disgrace if, in an affluent society, among the traditionally most generous people on the face of the earth, we find theological education scraping the bottom of the barrel for small change."[6]

The crisis depicted by the Resource's Commission was only the tip of the iceberg. One has only to consider faculty, the primary line item in the budget of most theological schools. During the 1950s and 1960s, the seminaries experimented with costly new programs. To implement these, the schools added and tenured new faculty members without regard to the long-term financial health of the institution. Increased competition from university departments of religion further complicated the picture. Theological schools, often without sufficient funds to compete in the larger educational marketplace, often paid for these new hires by granting faculty early tenure in exchange for lower salaries. Short of a formal declaration of fiscal exigency, the schools had little room to maneuver. Physical plant was another serious problem. The seminaries benefitted from the cheap energy available in the 1950s and 1960s; many of the new buildings that they constructed in those decades extravagantly consumed oil and electricity. Further, seminaries underutilized their buildings, leaving many buildings redundant and in some cases, unused. Unfortunately, these surplus buildings were virtually unsellable, except as part of the campus as a whole. In sharp language, "the Commission observes that the seminaries are paying a high price for what might be described as a sort of 'Babylonian captivity' to bricks and mortar."[7]

6. Nelson, "Trusteeship," 61.
7. McKay, "Resources Planning," 829.

The duplication of resources also impressed the Commission. The duplication of faculty was obvious. Each school replicated the same basic faculty, and, if there were more than one faculty member in a discipline, felt that it needed to hire specialists. Thus, for example, a two-person department of New Testament might include someone who specialized in Paul and someone who specialized in the Gospels. Thus, two seminaries had four underutilized faculty members. The rapid growth of specialization made it difficult for the seminaries to keep up with the development of the various disciplines. As field education replaced fieldwork, instructional costs went up yet again. Another major source of increased costs was the library. Aside from certain basic books, usually those on the reserve shelf, seminary librarians faced an avalanche of print, both books and journals, as the expanding American system of higher education placed increased pressure on faculties to publish. A patron, often a faculty member, might use a new book or journal once, if that, and yet the library had to catalog, record, shelve, and store that volume. These incidental costs were often as great as or greater than the initial outlay for the book or periodical. When one accounted for the cost of library duplication for several seminaries, the total, especially when measured over and against use, was excessive. In one area, served by three seminaries, "library expenses amount to approximately 11 percent of total operating costs." If the three could cooperate, the Commission estimated that savings could be "a reduction in annual operating costs of 3 percent at each of the three." Continuing its emphasis on quality, the Commission added, "furthermore, educators know one good library is worth many poor ones."[8]

In simple terms, the legacy of America's denominational past was that there were too many seminaries serving too few students, with too-small endowments. As Warren Deem noted, "small seminaries which are encountering increasing difficulties in financing current operations ought to give serious consideration to merger."[9] The Resources Commission did not reach this conclusion alone. When denominations merged, their study committees always recommended that the new church find ways of reducing the number of its seminaries. Some notable denominational consolidations did take place; for example, Garrett-Evangelical (Garrett and Evangelical), Lutheran Seminary in Chicago (Augustana Theological Seminary, Grand View Seminary, Chicago Lutheran Theological Seminary, and Suomi Theological Seminary), Luther Theological Seminary in Saint Paul (Luther Theological Seminary, Redwing, and United Church Seminary), and Colgate Rochester Crozer (Colgate Rochester and Crozer). However, the Resources Commission believed that few schools were able to negotiate such unions, especially if different confessional families owned or sponsored the seminaries. Even within confessional families or within the same denomination, some obvious mergers proved impossible, such as Gettysburg and Philadelphia, or United Seminary (Dayton) and the Methodist Seminary in Ohio. The only solution

8. Ibid., 807.
9. Deem and Van de Mark, "1970s: Alternatives for Change," 59.

was for theological educators to devise a way around denominational loyalty and institutional self-satisfaction.

The Resources Commission believed that clusters or consortia provided that way around the problems of institutional union. A cluster was a voluntary arrangement in which schools agreed to share certain resources, especially the high-cost items of faculty and libraries, in a particular region. In most cases, they believed that urban research universities, with their extensive libraries and resources in languages and social sciences, were the best anchors for such arrangements. To serve effectively as the core of a cluster, a participating university needed strong graduate schools and strong professional schools that the seminaries might use to strengthen their programs. The Resources Commission report, as published, listed eleven cities particularly suited to such clustering: Atlanta, Georgia; Austin, Texas; Denver, Colorado; Montreal, Quebec; Nashville, Tennessee; New Haven, Connecticut; Philadelphia, Pennsylvania; Rochester, New York; St. Louis, Missouri; Toronto, Ontario; and Vancouver, British Columbia.[10] The list was, of course, neither restrictive nor exhaustive. Other cities had the required university centers, and America was increasingly urban.

The word *cluster* was never carefully defined. In some ways, it suggested Thomas Jefferson's proposal that the various denominations establish their own schools around the University of Virginia and share its resources. Each school was to remain independent with its own officers and board and obedient to its own denominational rules and customs. Yet the schools were to form agreements that allowed them to share each other's faculties, libraries, and other resources. As least as the Commission envisioned these clusters, the various schools would engage in common planning to reduce duplication. Only one school might actually purchase a book or journal or hire a professor with expertise in a given area, such as Babylonian texts. The school would then share that book or instructor with the other participating schools and with their partnering university. As the schools experienced the financial benefits of cooperation, the savings would make available funds that the schools might use to innovate educationally, and, thus, better serve their publics as well as the public. In many ways, the plan was similar to the practice in Canada where even smaller enrollments encouraged divinity schools to locate near each other and near universities.

Warren Deem suggested a variation on the cluster concept. He believed that nearby seminaries should contract with each other for specific services or perhaps form a special corporation established to provide those services. In many ways, the Graduate Theological Union in Berkeley that Deem helped plan was an example of this type of cluster. The various schools established a separate entity, the Graduate Union, in order to create a strong graduate program in theology. Thus, Deem reasoned, several schools might establish a central academic administration for the purpose of planning and coordinating their academic programs or for such matters as

---

10. McKay, "Resources Planning." The list of possible sites caused much controversy, although the cities were intended primarily for illustration.

record keeping. Deem hoped that such service corporations might expand as time passed. He and others engaged in the establishment of the GTU hoped that the Union might provide its members with a taste of what cooperation might mean and inspire them to expand the sphere of their cooperative endeavors. However, such dreams were not to become reality.

CLUSTERS AND TECHNOLOGY: THE LIBRARY

Clusters never worked as well as the Resources Commission and the staff of the American Association of Theological Schools hoped that they might. This is not to say that there were not some successes.[11] Yet one area where they succeeded beyond even the optimistic hopes of the Resources Commission was the library. Librarians were an anomaly on seminary campuses. Increasingly drawn from the ranks of highly trained professionals, seminary librarians often possessed theological credentials and religious interests. Their influence, exerted through their own professional society, the American Theological Library Association, was great. Every time that the ATS revised its standards, the bar for libraries went up a notch or two. Yet the position of the librarian in the organization of the seminary was ambiguous. Most members of a seminary staff conducted their office under the guidance of the president or the president's delegate and pursued the goals and objectives of the administration. In contrast, the librarian was an independent professional hired by the seminary to perform an increasingly technical and precise task. Further, the librarians often had their own staffs, often assigned to specific tasks, such as cataloging, as well as a cadre of student workers. Next to the academic dean, librarians had the largest budget on campus. Most senior librarians believed that they should be members of the faculty, present at all faculty meetings, and granted faculty rank and privileges, including tenure and sabbatical leave.[12] Certainly librarians and library staff taught. Librarians conducted courses on theological research and bibliography, and they guided students in the preparation of papers and theses. Yet, the librarian, even when the institution granted that person faculty privileges, was not quite a faculty member. In many ways, the fact that most seminaries housed their library in a separate building symbolized the separation of the library and its leadership from the rest of the school.

Individual librarians were members of networks and peer groups that included professionals not engaged in theological education. After all, libraries were a feature of all academic institutions and of the towns and cities in which those institutions were located. Seminary librarians interacted with that larger library community, arranging borrowing privileges for faculty and students, extending hospitality to community residents with an interest in religion, and participating in statewide library networks. Further, members of this larger network of librarians often faced similar tasks and

---

11. For some of the effective examples of seminary cooperation, see chapter 1.
12. For example see Batsel, "Faculty Status."

challenges, including such technical matters as cataloging and managing staffs and budgets. Theological librarians were accustomed to cooperation with many different colleagues in varying types of institutions. Consequently, they found it easy to cooperate with other theological librarians.

One common problem that seminary librarians faced was the breakdown of their traditional cataloging systems. The problem was the increase in publication that accompanied the post-World War II education boom. In addition to the need for additional space and budget, librarians had to deal with catalog systems not designed with such growth in mind. For example, the Dewey system, invented in the late nineteenth century, lacked sufficient detail in its treatment of theological subjects to manage large seminary collections. Consequently, many seminary librarians had adopted the Union expansion of that system.[13] However, the Union system was also approaching its limits. Although the Library of Congress created its own system originally for its own use, many librarians adopted it, especially for research and university libraries. The Library of Congress also made available its own cataloging of every book that it received. At first, this was in the form of printed card-catalog entries; later, these were issued in electronic form as well. By the 1980s, the Library of Congress system was almost universal among seminaries, although some seminaries had part of their collection still under an older system.[14]

As early as 1968, librarians were viewing the new technology as part of a solution to their problems. Ronald Deering observed:

> We think of rapid access to bibliography, if not content information, printed out from computers and rapid print-out machines, of economical and compact micro-storage with instant selection and economical and rapid information retrieval. The hardware is already available to do a magnificent job of preparing bibliographies and of producing cumulative disposable book catalogs.[15]

A moment's reflection will reveal why this was a natural conclusion, even in the early days of the computer revolution. A library consists essentially of two parts: a collection of books and other resources, and a system of access to that collection. The system of access is essentially a database that includes fields that enable the user to locate materials under a variety of headings, such as author, title, subject, and date. The limit to the access system is the number of categories that a user can readily search. As anyone who has used a traditional card catalog will attest, time constraints often were as important a limit on access as the sophistication of the system. Electronic cataloging promised both to improve the system of access, making more categories available, and to increase the number of records that the user might search in a reasonable amount

---

13. This system was developed at Union Theological Seminary, originally to serve the Burke Library, one of the largest and best collections in the country.
14. Peterson, "Theological Libraries."
15. Deering, "Library Service," 218.

of time. The relatively easy linkage between a computer database and a printer or other output device made computer catalogs even more usable.

Clusters made the use of the new technology even more attractive. The task of providing a common catalog for the Boston Theological Institute or other large cooperative ventures by hand was daunting, but librarians could handle such tasks with comparative ease with the new computer technology. The translation of existing libraries' records into digital form was the most difficult task. However, once accomplished, a librarian or user might manipulate the records in a variety of ways.

The establishment of the Ohio College Library Center in 1967 was a major breakthrough in interlibrary cooperation. The purpose of the OCLC was:

> to increase availability of library resources for use in the educational and research programs of Ohio colleges and universities. The principal economic goal of the Center is to lower the rate of rise of per-student library costs, while increasing availability of library resources.[16]

In 1971, the year that United Seminary in Dayton, Ohio, joined the new organization, the digital cataloging of the state's libraries began at Ohio State. Part of what made the system work was the development of MARC (Machine Readable Cataloging), which allowed libraries to download entries directly into their own electronic catalogs. The easy availability online of WorldCat (World Catalogue), the world's largest electronic catalog of library resources, pushed seminary libraries into the digital age. In its earliest forms, OCLC services were only available at a library site; later, the expansion of the Internet made those services available from any computer.[17] At the same time, individual seminary library catalogs also became available online.

In a sense, the ideal of clustering and collaboration in libraries redefined libraries in terms of access rather than collection. In other words, a library was adequate when it provided its patrons with access to the materials that they needed in a timely manner whether it owned that material or not. Access, in a rapidly expanding world of printed materials and declining revenues, was more budget friendly than the individual library acquisition and cataloging of books and journals. Yet every improvement carried its own costs. Access meant a continually increasing budget for technology, both hardware and software, and fees for participation in WorldCat and other cooperative ventures. Further, students and faculty needed instruction in the effective use of the new means of access. In 1980, John Trotti put the issue in blunt terms: "who will pay for such access?"[18] His question was complicated by the fact that technological

---

16. O'Brien, "Challenges and Difficulties," 71.

17. I have chosen to highlight the development of OCLA because it became the standard national catalog in 2007 after it combined with RLG (Research Libraries Group) and RLIN (Research Libraries Information Network). This network was originally designed for use by research libraries and had such noted libraries as Yale, Harvard, and Stanford among its members. Aside from some university-related schools, few seminaries participated.

18. Trotti, "Dealing with Pain," 79.

advance continually updated the technologies that were making access possible. No sooner had a school paid for one technological improvement than a newer version appeared, and eventually the school had to adopt that innovation to keep up with other cooperating schools. If the new technologies were often less expensive—the cost of storage, for example, continually declined as did the cost of processing power—the reality of new expense seemed unending. Technology became a permanent budget line!

Seminary libraries also had to deal with a host of other new information technologies. Microfilm readers became standard in the 1960s, as did newer ways of accessing microform materials. Throughout the remainder of the twentieth century, libraries struggled to make microforms available and easy to use. Despite the advantages of the format—microforms were easy to store and comparatively inexpensive—they were never popular with library users. The 1970s also witnessed an explosion of new tape technologies. Although video- and audiotape technology existed from the early 1950s, the development of easy-to-use audio and video cassettes increased the content available for classroom use. Libraries had to provide access to these new materials. In many cases, they also had to manage the projectors and other technology that used them.

By the end of the 1970s, the future of theological libraries was technological. Librarians at the better seminaries had already joined interlibrary networks, such as OCLC, and interlibrary cooperation within clusters was the most effective part of those relationships. The daily van run between the various libraries of the Boston Theological Institute was a vivid symbol of the new order in library services. Although students might and some did use the new interconnection, the most evident beneficiaries were the researchers on the various faculties, who had more books and journals available than ever before. However, the libraries had not escaped the spiraling escalation of costs. Only very large libraries were able to use the new technology to save substantial amounts,[19] but, even before the Internet, technology had raised the standard for library service. If libraries did not achieve the dreamers' hope for coordinated collection policies, what they achieved was significant.[20]

EVANGELICALS AND THE ECONOMY OF SCALE

The essential problem that the Resources Commission located was the problem of scale. The seminaries were too small, faculty-student ratios too small, and facilities too large. The more conservative side of American Protestantism felt these problems more acutely than the liberal seminaries. The more liberal seminaries had significant endowments, many of which dated back to the Gilded Age or at least to the early 1920s. Although nothing decreases as rapidly as an endowment drawn down for current

---

19. Ohio State University claimed to have reduced its library salary line by seventeen positions in the first year of operation of the OCLC. No seminary library, even those at such bibliographic centers as Union (New York) operated at a scale that made such savings possible.

20. For the further effects of the technological revolution on libraries and librarians, see chapter 7.

expenses, endowments do provide a margin for difficult times. James McCord,[21] who became president of Princeton Seminary in 1959, was, if anyone was, the master of Mainstream seminary finance. McCord had no qualms about the seriousness of the situation before the seminaries in the 1970s. In a striking article, published in the *Christian Century* in 1971, he wrote:

> The answer to the crisis is simple: it is going to cost all of us something. By all of us, I mean seminaries, students, churches and parents. The seminaries must review their priorities in order to eliminate all but the truly important elements in their educational programs. For example, prestigious but money-losing publications constitute an area in which economy might be exercised. Administrative costs—academe's equivalent to corporate overhead—must be trimmed. In addition, proliferating doctoral programs must be curtailed.[22]

Like many administrators, McCord planned to shift much of the increasing costs to students, "who will be paying an increasing share of the total expenses."[23] McCord's strategy was more than raising tuition. A strong player in the game of Presbyterian politics, McCord fought for every penny available from the national denomination, artfully picturing Princeton's penury, but he knew that the funds available from this source was limited. His most successful initiative was his alliance with Sir John Templeton, a longtime trustee and board chair with extensive contacts on Wall Street. Partnered with the energetic financier, McCord managed to raise Princeton's modest endowment to more than 110 million dollars. His successor, Thomas Gillespie, would make Princeton the first seminary with a billion-dollar endowment.

McCord's large endowment allowed Princeton to become the largest Mainstream theological seminary and to offer a variety of programs. Although not as large as its more Evangelical competitors, Princeton became a theological university that was able to manage costs by operating on a large scale. The term *theological university* came from Robert Handy.[24] Basically, a theological university was an institution that provided education for a variety of Christian vocations. Early examples of the theological university were Hartford Seminary Foundation, which combined a school of theology, a school of education, and a school of missions, and Union Seminary in New York, which combined its theological program with a school of church music. Neither Union nor Hartford, however, realized their earlier potential after 1970. Finances and low enrollments forced Hartford to abandon its Bachelor of Divinity program and historic campus and to become a specialized institution, emphasizing continuing education, including a very successful Doctor of Ministry program, sociology of religion, and Islamic studies. Although Union's endowment was and remains one of the larger

---

21. McCord's influence on the development of the seminary presidency is discussed in chapter 7.
22. McCord, " Financing," 106.
23. Ibid.
24. Handy, "The Problem."

seminary funds, the school struggled with the very high cost of doing business in New York, declining enrollments, and its inability to raise the funds needed to sustain its earlier position as the nation's leading seminary. By contrast, Evangelicals and Southern Baptists constructed a string of theological universities that despite their small number, enrolled more than half of all American Protestant seminary students. Of the eleven largest seminaries, ten were consistently either Southern Baptists or Evangelical.

The Evangelical and Southern Baptist successes in constructing large seminaries in the 1970s and 1980s had many causes, including very strong leadership, clear statements of mission, and strong Christian identity. Evangelicals benefitted from the leadership of Billy Graham, Harold Ockenga, and Carl F. H. Henry, who provided the movement with national and international strategies. Southern Baptists also had outstanding national leadership, including the layman Porter Ruth, who strengthened the church's historic commitment to missions and education. Moreover, Evangelical and Southern Baptist schools had the benefit of a remarkable generation of seminary presidents. Few seminary leaders ranked with Fuller's David Hubbard or Trinity Evangelical Divinity School's Kenneth M. Kantzer, Southern Baptist Theological Seminary's Duke McCall, Southeastern Theological Seminary's Randall Lolley, or Southwestern Baptist Theological Seminary's Robert Naylor. Although not immune to the debates over governance that wracked many Mainstream seminaries, all of these presidents had firm control of their institutions and enjoyed the strong support of their boards.

Strong leadership was not the only cause of the rapid expansion of these institutions. In the case of both Southern Baptists and Evangelicals, the more mundane factors of underrepresented theological positions and underserved geographical areas aided their development. Significantly, as American Mainstream churches gradually moved away from foreign missions, these schools and their supporters retained close connections with the American missionary movement abroad. They were, consequently, in touch with the largest numerical expansion of Christianity since the early Roman Empire. They knew that the decline of Euro-American Christianity was not the only story in the twentieth century.

Regionalism is a defining factor in American religious history. Religion in the South and West, for example, differs from religion in the Northeast. Regional identity and location have had formative influence on theological education. Some areas, like the Northeast, early had a plethora of theological institutions; other areas, such as the western and mountain states, had fewer schools. Even within the Western region, there were subregional differences. In California, for instance, Northern California had too many schools for its Protestant population, while Southern California had too few. In the South, the poverty that followed the Civil War as well as a deeply entrenched tradition of lay religious leadership inhibited the growth of theological schools. Southern racial patterns, which restricted the public for theological schools largely to the white population, further restricted the growth of new institutions.

As their name suggested, Southern Baptists were essentially a regional church, concentrated in the eleven states of the Old Confederacy with strong representation in Texas, Oklahoma, and Arkansas. Before the Second World War and for some years after it, these states were at the bottom of the various national economic rankings: last in personal income; last in educational level; last in social services, hospitals, and libraries. The Southern United States and adjacent areas were America's Two-Thirds World—home of peonage, racial struggles, poor Whites, and poorer Blacks. The Second World War and the massive militarization of the nation during the Cold War led to a Southern renaissance, as the region's skillful congressional representatives snagged military base after military base. The rise of the Sunbelt in the 1970s and 1980s further created a new Southern prosperity. Whether the new prosperity begat urbanization or vice versa, the nationwide population shift from rural areas to the cities was particularly strong in the South. Although many Southern Baptist congregations remained rural, the denomination had significant numbers of large and very large churches with multiple staffs. Something similar to the expansion of churches into the suburbs of Northern cities occurred in the South in the 1960s and 1970s. The demand for pastors and other congregational professionals remained strong.

Before the Second World War, Southern Baptists established two large seminaries—Southern and Southwestern. Poor financial support dogged both institutions. Despite large enrollments, both verged on bankruptcy during the economic depressions of the 1920s and 1930s. Necessity, as is often the case, was the mother of invention. Building on suggestions about organization originally proposed by Shailer Matthew of Chicago, the denomination built its Cooperative Program in the 1920s to finance its missions and other programs that were, like its seminaries, facing financial ruin. The combination of the new program and aggressive fundraising paid off the denomination's debts and allowed it to face the postwar world with confidence and funding. Significantly, the seminaries became agencies of the Convention with funding from the common chest.

The new prosperity permitted the Southern Baptist seminary system to grow. New Orleans Baptist Theological Seminary, founded as the Baptist Bible Institute, became a full, graduate-level seminary, and the Convention established new schools in Kansas City, Wake Forest, North Carolina, and San Francisco. Southern Baptist schools, then, entered a period of rapid growth. By the 1980s, they enrolled almost one-half of all Protestant seminary candidates for the ministry.

All periods of growth are rocky, and various groups had different hopes and plans for the seminaries. Some, for example, still saw pre–World War II Southern with its emphasis on the gentleman scholar as the ideal, while others admired the more brash and entrepreneurial style of Southwestern. Many looked north for models. Many Southern Baptist scholars studied, at least during sabbaticals, at Union and Yale. The Union Summer School during the heyday of Niebuhr and Tillich was particularly popular. Despite these disagreements about the ideal form of seminary education, often strongest among faculty members, Southern Baptist seminaries had common characteristics that made them theological universities. Southern Baptist schools had five emphases: pastoral ministry, religious education and youth work, missions, music, and graduate study. In addition, following a pattern established in the nineteenth century, the schools maintained programs of undergraduate theological education.

The Southern Baptist seminaries were part of a network of institutions. They trained the pastors of the large city and suburban churches, educated most of the denomination's far-flung missionary force, provided instructors for denominational colleges, and educated most local church and denominational staff members. As Southern Baptist churches grew, inside and outside the South, they grew as well. Perhaps most important during this season of expansion, the denomination provided sufficient support for the schools not to charge tuition either for Baptists or for students from other denominations. When the seminaries combined this policy with vast networks of student churches (networks carefully maintained by the seminaries, of mostly rural churches served by seminary students), it meant that any person who wanted to attend could do so.

If the changing demographics of the South provided Southern Baptist institutions with an opportunity for growth, Evangelicals had a similar opportunity. The liberals and their moderate allies won the controversy in the 1920s, and if they never won over all the nation's congregations, they held power in the denominational hierarchies, the seminaries, and the ecumenical agencies. The growth of neo-orthodoxy further augmented this left-center coalition. Princeton, at one point the flagship of conservative Presbyterianism, became a center of neo-orthodox thinking under John Mackay, and the other Presbyterian seminaries followed suit. The liberal and moderate leadership fully expected that its opponents would vanish from the scene. People within the ruling Mainstream coalition, very mindful of their own internal differences, saw themselves as very theologically and socially diverse.

Despite the prophecies of their demise, conservative American Evangelicals were very much alive. Joel Carpenter has documented how Conservative Christians built a network of institutions in the 1930s and 1940s that had interlocking members and leaders.[25] The Billy Graham revivals of the 1950s indicated the power of these organizations as well as the general popularity of Conservative faith. The revivals also cemented the remarkable partnership of Billy Graham, Harold Ockenga, and Carl H. F. Henry. Together with other allies, including the English Anglican John Stott, these leaders created the so-called New Evangelical Movement. The New Evangelicals were instrumental in the creation of Fuller Seminary, in the merger and reestablishment of Gordon and Conwell, in the publication of *Christianity Today*, and in the establishment of the Lausanne movement.

The liberal and moderate churches won their greatest victory in the East and Upper Midwest. In the 1920s, this was the richest and most politically influential part of

---

25. Carpenter, *Revive Us Again*.

the United States. Much of the Midwest, the South, and Southern California remained conservative religiously, and these areas benefitted from the shift from the rust belt to the Sunbelt. Although it is only a rough analogy, the areas of the country that had supported abolition were essentially liberal and moderate, whereas the areas that supported slavery or which were less involved in the struggle were conservative.

Other American demographic and economic trends favored American Conservative Christians. The earlier fundamentalist movement had significant strength in the rural areas of the country, and the tendency was for population to move out of these areas and into more urban areas. The internal migrants found themselves forming new congregations—often self-consciously undenominational—that carried minimum theological baggage, often only an affirmation of the Bible's authority and inerrancy. Some of these congregations became very large. Occasionally called megachurches, these large congregations used their comparative lack of tradition to respond to new stimuli, including popular music and media. In some ways, these congregations resembled the immigrant congregations fifty years earlier. They provided both social and religious comfort as well as networks of people with similar hopes and fears. However, they also resembled an updated version of the large institutional and suburban churches that had sustained the Mainstream churches in their period of greatest growth. Many, for example, had gymnasiums, fully equipped educational rooms, and music programs with multiple choirs.

Pentecostal Christianity was also socially maturing. The Pentecostal movement had begun as an almost classic church of the dispossessed, but in a classic confirmation of Weber's famed hypothesis, Pentecostal Christians entered the middle class and became more like other Evangelical denominations. The Assemblies of God, for example, were among the original members of the influential NAE. Although Pentecostalism was more theologically Armenian than Calvinist, many ties existed between Pentecostalism and classical fundamentalism. Often Pentecostal Christians read books by fundamentalist authors, and they shared the fundamentalist belief in premillennial eschatology. Tongues and miracles were, after all, biblical signs of the coming of the end times.[26] In the 1960s, charismatic groups formed in Mainstream and Catholic churches. While charismatic Christians occasionally disrupted local congregations, they also enriched them with innovative church music and a general openness to spiritual experience.

The Jesus People of the 1970s highlighted another feature of American conservative religion: its attention to youth. At the same time as the Mainstream churches were downplaying their campus ministries, such Evangelical groups as Campus Crusade for Christ and InterVarsity expanded on the nation's campuses. While these organizations were present at Ivy League colleges, they were more numerous on state-university campuses. This was strategically important for Evangelical growth. The rapid expansion

---

26. For the relationship between early Pentecostalism and American Fundamentalism, I am indebted to Wacker, *Heaven Below*.

in higher education in the latter part of the twentieth century was predominately in the state universities. These Evangelical college organizations naturally served as feeders to Evangelical seminaries. They generated students who aspired to be leaders in various organizations in the Evangelical network, many of whom were candidates for increasingly popular Master of Arts programs, and also generated interest in other ministries, including the local church and foreign missions. When many Mainstream church colleges secularized in the 1960s and 1970s, Evangelical colleges remained Christian institutions with an Evangelical ethos. Further, the number of conservative Christian colleges increased as Bible schools became first degree-granting Bible colleges and then liberal-arts colleges. A handful, such as BIOLA (the Bible Institute of Los Angeles), became universities with relatively large divinity schools.

How important was theology in the growth of the larger Evangelical Seminaries? On the one hand, such secular factors as demographic shifts, effective leadership and organization, and the existence of strong networks of supporting institutions provide a sufficient explanation for their growth. In any economic market, the recipe for organizational growth is to bring together significant numbers of customers with those who provide commodities or services. On the other hand, in religion, belief matters. Evangelicalism is and was a compelling vision of the gospel and the Christian message. Moreover, it is a vision that combines both acceptance and criticism of the dominant secular culture, a way to be in and not of the world. Evangelical theology had a broad appeal, both to those joining churches, and to those desiring a professional career in ministry.

Fuller was a leader among the New Evangelical seminaries. Located in Southern California, the school had the support of its founder, Charles E. Fuller, a popular radio evangelist and missions advocate. After initial struggles, including a battle to secure ATS accreditation, Fuller began the systematic development of its program. With the very energetic support of board chairman C. Davis Weyerhaeuser, President Hubbard added schools of psychology and missions in 1965. The closely affiliated William Carey Library published early accounts of Theological Education by Extension and the Church Growth movement.[27] BIOLA's growth from a Bible college to a Christian university illustrates the size and scope of the conservative Christian market in Southern California.

In many ways, Trinity Evangelical Divinity School was also a new start. The very tiny Swedish, Norwegian, and Danish Free Churches owned the school. When the seminary moved from Chicago to Deerfield, Illinois, in the early 1960s, it resolved to change its identity. Calling Kenneth S. Kantzer, later editor of *Christianity Today*, as its dean, the school built a distinguished faculty of conservative scholars and began a period of rapid growth in enrollment. The choice of the phrase *Divinity School* in the name was deliberate. Kantzer, a Harvard graduate, wanted the school to operate at the

---

27. For Fuller, see Marsden, *Reforming Fundamentalism*.

highest intellectual and professional level, reaching standards similar to those attained by the university-related divinity schools.

Like Trinity, Gordon-Conwell underwent a transformation in the 1960s. The 1969 merger of Gordon with Conwell, a Pennsylvania seminary affiliated with Temple University, enabled the school to grow rapidly. Moving to South Hamilton, Massachusetts, the school had the considerable financial support of both J. Howard Pew (after his death in 1971, of the Pew Charitable Trust) and of Billy Graham. In 1976, Gordon-Conwell established its first extension campus in the heart of the Boston, continuing Gordon's historical emphasis on urban missions.

Other Evangelical seminaries also experienced growth on a similar scale. Dallas, the flagship dispensationalist school, grew rapidly as did Asbury, the leading conservative Wesleyan institution. Both schools, like Gordon, had histories that reached back to the early twentieth century, but both experienced their growth spurt in the 1960s and 1970s.[28] Both rebuilt their campuses, established new programs, and assumed leadership positions in important areas of American Evangelicalism. Like Fuller, Asbury became a major center for the study of Christian missions.

The Evangelical and Southern Baptist schools illustrate the truth of the Resources Commission basic insight: theological education was most efficient where there was sufficient size to reap the benefits of scale. What is interesting about these schools is their full-time equivalent (FTE) student bodies approached the size recommended by the Commission for a cluster of schools. There were other similarities between a cluster and these schools. With the exception of the Southern Baptist schools, these seminaries were independent of denominational control and served a variety of churches and independent Christian organizations. Whether they adopted an organizational model, with various schools (the model favored by Fuller and Southwestern), or a more unitary model, they were very complex institutions that offered education for a variety of Christian professional positions, ranging from pastoral ministry to counseling to missionary service. Further, the very size of these institutions served to limit faculty power. Their presidents were, consequently, able to innovate when the situation called for new approaches—especially in approaches to the delivery of theological education, first by extension and then by distance education.

Did size, as the Resources Commission implied, improve academic quality? Too many imponderables go into that question for a historian to offer an easy answer. Yet one may offer a cautious yes. Just as the size of Van Dusen's Union in the 1940s and 1950s contributed to that school's ability to hire a distinguished faculty, so the size of the Evangelical institutions permitted them to attract and keep highly qualified and competent teachers and scholars. Although the large university divinity schools continued to enjoy real advantages in the competition for scholars, the Evangelical schools were at least on a par with the average Protestant seminary. Evangelicals had come a long way intellectually from their marginal status in the 1930s and 1940s.

28. Hannah, *An Uncommon Union*; Kinghorn, *The Story of Asbury Seminary*.

Perhaps most important, scale enabled the Evangelical and Southern Baptist seminaries, which had not inherited large endowments, to use the resources they possessed effectively.

OLD DEGREES RENAMED AND NEW DEGREES BEGUN

The history of the Doctor of Ministry degree illustrates the combination of high aspirations and financial pressures during the 1960s and 1970s. For some years, theological educators in many of the better-financed schools had believed that the program should be a four-year program ending in a doctoral degree. Their reasoning was straightforward and was similar to the reasoning that produced the Curriculum for the 1970s. On the one hand, it was no longer possible to introduce students adequately to the academic study of Christianity in three years. The various disciplines had grown exponentially, and minimum professional competence demanded that the seminary programs had to keep up with these new developments. Further, there was the vexing question of field education and of internships. No room existed in the current curriculum for sufficient practical experience, especially if the students did their basic academic work well. The difficult question of prestige and status was also a factor. Seminary educators and pastors believed, whether it was the case or not, that the prestige of the ministry had declined in relation to that of other professions. The professional doctorate, earned after a more rigorous academic program, might go far to help with this difficulty. The eagerness with which ministers sought and used honorary doctorates seemed to confirm the depth of these concerns. The title Doctor did seem to give pastors an advantage in the complex ministerial job market.

Luther Weigel proposed a professional doctorate at the 1940 Association of Theological Schools meeting, thus launching twenty years of discussion and debate. Many smaller schools feared that they would not be able to meet the higher academic standards that a doctorate implied, and the more prestigious institutions did not want competition between their academic and their professional doctorates. By the 1960s, however, the advocates of the professional doctorate were ready to act without waiting for consensus. Both Claremont and the University of Chicago offered a professional doctorate as their basic degree. Vanderbilt and San Francisco experienced with variations: Vanderbilt offered the professional doctorate degree to a handful of its more able students, and San Francisco offered a professional doctorate at the end of a long program of continuing education.

In 1966 the Association of Theological Schools appointed a committee, headed by Seward Hiltner, to define the professional doctorate. The Hiltner proposal saw the professional doctorate as the primary theological degree. As envisioned by the committee, the professional doctorate was clearly parallel with the academic doctorate: there were language requirements, comprehensive examinations, and a dissertation. In many ways, it was a proposal for a doctorate in practical theology. The debate over the committee's proposals was one of the most bitter in the Association's history. Finally the Association appointed a new committee, chaired by Dean Krister Stendhal of Harvard, that included no members from the previous committee. The new report, which recommended the Master of Divinity degree as the first theological degree and a four-year professional doctorate, passed with a significant change. The prerequisite for the Doctor of Ministry was the Master of Divinity degree, not the Bachelor of Arts as the first committee had proposed. The new standards, adopted in 1972, allowed for both an in-sequence and an in-service Doctor of Ministry.[29]

When the new degree standards passed in 1972, most believed that the in-sequence form of the degree, mostly based in the larger and more equipped seminaries, would be the dominant form of the degree. This did not happen. The in-service Doctor of Ministry degree grew rapidly. In 1984, Jackson Carroll reported:

> One of the remarkable developments in theological education during the 1970s—one that has shown no sign of abating in the '80s—has been the rise in popularity of Doctor of Ministry programs. By 1984 more than 7,000 clergy had received the degree, and 6,345 persons were in enrolled in DMin programs during the 1985–1986 academic year. Some 90 schools that are members of the Association of Theological Schools now offer the degree.[30]

Why did this degree, so controversial only a decade earlier, become a regular feature of American seminary education? In an influential study of the Doctor of Ministry, Jackson Carroll and Barbara Wheeler noted that two factors influenced the growth of Doctor of Ministry programs: "The competitive position of certain schools versus others; and the growing demand for continuing education for ministers."[31] A third factor, not stressed by Carroll and Wheeler, was the internal financial structure of many seminaries. Each of these deserves consideration in turn.

The fact that much of the nation had too many seminaries for their population base meant that even a comparatively small competitive advantage was significant. In a small world, a few additional FTEs made a major difference. If school A attracted more MDiv students than school B because it had a DMin, then school B felt the pressure to add the degree to its program. Alumni were, further, crucial to seminary recruiting. The person with two degrees from an institution, after all, has closer ties to the school than the person with degrees from two institutions.

Carroll and Wheeler's second point was more significant. There was a widespread desire on the part of ministers for more knowledge and more highly developed skills. The formation of the Academy of Parish Clergy in 1968 provides evidence of this. Yet most programs of continuing education, despite all the efforts of their planners, failed to garner significant support. There were at least two reasons for this failure.

29. Carroll and Wheeler, "Doctor of Ministry. Program"
30. Carroll, "Why Is the DMin So Popular?" 106.
31. Carroll and Wheeler, "Doctor of Ministry Program."

The first was simply a lack of structure. One had to find ways to fit one's program into one's ministry, and the schedule of continuing-education events rarely fit neatly into the ebb and flow of church life. Further, the various continuing-education programs did not seem to go anywhere. If they were theoretical, the programs seemed to be only the same old same old; if practical, they seemed too concerned with nuts and bolts. The schools gave no recognition at the end of these programs. Most continuing education programs were also hard to explain to a church board or committee. Further, the family structure of many clergy had changed. Many, perhaps most, ministers in the 1970s were in marriages where both partners had full-time employment. Few continuing-education programs fit the changing style of clerical life. Consequently, while a busy pastor might resolve to do continuing education, it was hard to do so. In contrast, the in-service Doctor of Ministry program provided a structure and a final reward. While the program often required difficult adjustments of parish and family time, the candidate knew the schedule of the program and its demands in advance. Consequently, a participant was able to plan participation. Significantly, if a candidate had difficulty completing the Doctor of Ministry, the final project, the one element that had no set structure, was the hurdle. The degree was a very important incentive. Whether the degree—as many candidates hoped—improved chances for a larger parish assignment or not, the doctorate was a publicly recognized achievement. At a time when many ministers worried about prestige, the Doctor of Ministry increased their status in the local church.

The third reason for the success of the DMin lay in the tortured finances of the seminaries. In order to have a sufficiently diverse faculty to offer the Master of Divinity degree, schools had to hire more faculty than their enrollment warranted. There were always more faculty hours, at least as teaching slots, than there were students. There were two general solutions to this, both dating primarily to the 1980s. The first was the widespread decision to offer a Master of Theological Studies or where state law permitted, a Master of Arts. The new master's programs tended to require the same classes as the MDiv and to boast student-teacher ratios in such areas as biblical and theological studies. The other was the Doctor of Ministry that served a similar function for the practical fields and for some in more classical disciplines. Both allowed institutions to utilize existing faculty more effectively.

The importance of the Doctor of Ministry was consequently not that DMin programs provided sufficient income to cover their costs, but that the Doctor of Ministry allowed schools to use necessary faculty resources more efficiently than might otherwise have been the case. The same proved true with other resources. The DMin required little or no capital investment. Even where the seminars met at some distance from the main campus, schools located them in low-rental locations such as church basements. Despite initial fears that the new doctorates would require large additions to their libraries, this proved not to be the case. Theological libraries, as the Resources Commission had noted, were underutilized and the Doctor of Ministry programs made few demands for new purchases or concentrations. In short, the Doctor of Ministry programs allowed seminaries to make some use of the economics of scale, using existing resources to generate additional revenue.

Further, the Doctor of Ministry program was often the program that the ministers made. Since no clear academic definition of the degree existed, schools and candidates were free to shape the degree around clerical needs. Most programs provided generous blocks of time for ministers to discuss their own work and receive feedback from the other practicing ministers. Often these discussions and the fellowship that the more intensive form provided were the most important part of the program. In that sense, the DMin programs provided a noncompetitive space without the presence of denominational officials or nearby competitors. Practicing clergy used this safe space to work on their professional skills and competences. "Professionals teaching professionals" might serve as the motto for the degree's most valued component.

As the degree evolved over time, its most serious problem and the sticking point for many students was the project in ministry. Carroll and Wheeler noted that most schools failed to define the project component adequately. At some schools, the school required an experientially based project, while other schools permitted projects that were actually extended research projects, almost minidissertations.[32] Yet the lack of clarity was (and still is) more than formal. Urban-ministry teachers had used the term earlier to describe small initiatives designed to improve neighborhood conditions. The establishment of a place for teens to meet, for example, was a typical project.

The term *project* is common in business planning and management and in social science. In a project, the manager projects or plans something that should be accomplished, executes that plan, and evaluates the result. In the social-science model, the experimenter carefully monitors conditions before the experiment begins, projects the changes that the researcher hopes will occur as a result of the intervention, and establishes a set of evaluative criteria to see if the intervention explained the observed results. The ideal in either the business or the social sciences is, thus, for the basic evaluative criteria to be determined at the beginning and used at the end of the project. The best image for this method is a loop that compares the beginning point and the end point and determines the difference between them as part of an evaluative analysis. Further, both business and social-science models preferred quantification as a means of demonstrating the validity of the endeavor. Carroll and Wheeler gave a sharp description of the difficulties in this practice:

> One problem frequently cited is students' poor grasp of the empirical skills required to analyze ministry experiments. (No one argues that DMin students should learn sophisticated social research methods; but even a basic understanding of the structure of empirical reasoning is often absent from DMin students' work.)[33]

32. Carroll and Wheeler, "Doctor of Ministry Program."
33. Ibid.

The candidate was to show that he or she had effected measurable change in the way that a church structured itself or understood an educational or other program. The primary focus, consequently, was on the outward or empirical manifestation of faith. The more religiously fulfilling work of ministry—helping people to live a more holy and devout life, or developing sacramental depth, or opening hearts to the presence of the Spirit—were not quantifiable. They are vertical and not horizontal: a matter of depth, not breadth. Once the results were determined, the minister was to reflect theologically on the result.

The key religious term, *theological reflection*, remained undefined.[34] The reason that the language was so popular was that the classical disciplines had not defined it, and hence *theological reflection* could stand for any insight that came from the integration of the various disciplines. Edward Farley's later term, *habitus*, might be a good equivalent, except that a *habitus* is more a state of mind than the sustained theological analysis of a specific situation. This is not to say that ministers do not do theological reflection frequently during their ministry. Every sermon is a theological reflection that seeks to bring together a specific text and the church's traditions with the present situation of the congregation and world. Much the same is true of Bible study classes, catechism classes, counseling sessions, and other ministerial acts. Yet, either because faculties have difficulty with the down-and-dirty quality of much pastoral thinking about human life, or because pastors believe that more than this is required of an educational project, the element of theological reflection in the project was often among the least satisfactory parts of the process.

An unforeseen consequence of the popularity of the DMin degree was the decline of the Master of Theology or the Master of Sacred Theology. The Master of Theology (ThM) was a standard second theological degree, often used as preparation for doctoral studies. At some institutions, especially those with research doctorates, it continued to function in this way. However, many candidates for the degree had not taken it as part of preparation for further work. Those students had used it to get more education or to develop their own interests. Since the second theological degree, like the Doctor of Ministry, required only an additional year of study, many such students increasingly elected to do the Doctor of Ministry program instead of the older Master of Theology.

By 1980, the standard definition of the seminary had changed. Although the Master of Divinity degree remained the central degree, most seminaries also offered the Master of Theological Studies or Master of Arts[35] and the Doctor of Ministry. Many schools, especially the larger theological universities, often combined different

---

34. *Theological reflection* became a very important phrase in theological education after the various debates of the 1980s. See chapter 6, below. Again, part of its attractiveness was its lack of clear definition.

35. The nomenclature for this degree is not standardized, perhaps, because of varying state regulations around the granting of university degrees.

courses from different parts of the curriculum to form these new degrees (part of the economics of scale), and they were frequently offered at extension centers as well as the home campus.

The Association of Theological Schools adopted the nomenclature of the Master of Divinity at the same time it adopted the new Doctor of Ministry. The new title did not reflect substantial changes in the first theological degree program. At best, it highlighted the understanding of the seminary as a place for graduate professional education and made the seminary degree parallel to many other professional masters degrees, such as the Master of Business Administration, the Master of Social Work, and the Master of Education.

THE INFLUENCE OF WARREN H. DEEM[36]

During the 1970s, seminary administrations became increasingly complex. Externally, schools had to manage relations with other schools and increasingly had to relate to publics broader than their own judicatories, if any. This meant an increasing emphasis on public relations and specifically on fundraising. Increasing costs called for more careful monitoring of the school's financial position and increased attention to strategic and short- and long-range planning. Seminary staffs grew, and organizations required more coordination. The large theological universities came to resemble liberal-arts colleges in their administration. Each new crisis, whether rising fuel prices or deferred maintenance, called for sharpened managerial skills. The days of mom-and-pop operations were over. Of course, every added staffperson increased seminary costs, and the more highly trained that person, the greater the increase might be. Naturally, seminaries caught some young leaders just beginning and in need of a first position or other practical experience.

One of the most insistent voices calling for increasingly professionalized seminary administration was Warren H. Deem. Deem was a skilled business leader, a graduate of Princeton and the Harvard School of Business. He became involved in theological education late in his career through his work with the Graduate Theological Union and the Resources Commission. He was also a public member of the Executive Committee of the Association of Theological Schools. Deem was the first in a series of influential financial consultants to theological education that included Badgett Dillard and Tony Ruger. Deem wanted to apply modern business methods, especially planning and evaluation, to theological education. Deem was a person who deeply influenced those people who worked with him. Among those who heard him gladly were Jesse Ziegler, the executive director of the Association of Theological Schools, and Robert W. Lynn, who became vice president for religion at the Lilly Endowment

---

36. The story of efforts to improve seminary administrations and funding structures continues in chapters 7 and 8. This part of the story is put here because Deem was so influential in the various developments of the 1970s from the Resources Commission to the establishment of clusters.

in 1975. Through the people that he rallied to his cause, Deem's influence continued for many years both in ATS and in the Endowment's programs of grant making.

When Deem surveyed theological education from an accounting and business standpoint, the situation was grim. The schools' wasteful duplication, their hiring of untrained administrators, especially their presidents, and their failure to do business planning were signs of deep structural problems. In his more pessimistic moments, Deem wondered whether the schools (or to be more precise, many of them) could survive an economic crisis. An optimist, Deem believed that more could be done to make the schools successful than their current practices allowed. He was not one to be silent about his opinions. As a member of the ATS board, he constantly pushed the Association to lead the schools to establish new patterns of administration.

The professionalization of seminary staffs began with the larger schools. The university schools, of course, shared many staff functions with their universities, and these grew more or less in tandem with the staffs of their respective schools. The first to undergo this process were the business managers. In corporate terms, the evolution was from bookkeeper or accountant to chief financial officer (CFO). In part, this evolution took place because the skills needed to oversee the business activities of the average seminary were much more substantial than the office skills needed earlier.

With Ziegler's blessing, middle-level managers formed the Seminary Management Association to help managers with the performance of their task. In turn, the Seminary Management Association conducted three studies of seminary management and convinced the Association to establish a Commission on Institutional Management in 1974.[37] In addition, an informal committee composed of Dayton Huldgren, Barbara Wheeler, and Badgett Dillard advised Robert W. Lynn of the Lilly Endowment on the needs for further work in this area. With funding from the Lilly Endowment, the Commission on Institutional Management conducted workshops for those engaged in seminary management. Between 1975 and 1979, 137 schools or individuals received ATS Administrative Development Grants. Work with seminary administrators became part of ATS's continuing programming and came to include specialized work with development officers, student-enrollment specialists, academic deans, and workshops on academic and financial planning.

The most serious management problem was not with middle-level managers, many of whom held degrees in business. The most serious problem, Deem believed, were the seminary presidents, who came to their offices with little or no preparation for their work. The ATS held conferences for presidents in 1976, 1977, 1979 and 1981. Annual meetings also included presentations and seminars useful to seminary presidents. These programs did help, especially with institutional planning, but many, including Deem, felt the need for more presidential training. Significantly, the Association would name its most sustained effort at improving seminary presidencies the Warren Deem Institute.

37. Baumgaertner, "A Retrospective Study."

Deem also believed that seminary boards of trustees were crucial in determining the seminaries' future. This was particularly true in times of fiscal pressure:

> In many seminaries, the board of trustees is either inert or largely ineffective. As a consequence, the capacity of these seminaries to adapt and change is severely compromised. In one way or another, most of them will probably survive the severe financial problems they currently confront. But the central issue is not institutional survival; it is whether these seminaries will be able to sustain anything beyond the most marginal sort of relationship to the churches they were created to serve.[38]

The ideal trustee was a steward of an institution's fiduciary affairs, a wise participant in institution planning, and a source of funds. In the seminary world of the 1970s where every penny counted, each institutional decision confronted trustees with major policy issues.[39]

Deem's interest in basic industrywide research was closely related to his firm belief in the importance of institutional planning. His influence encouraged Robert W. Lynn and John Fletcher to develop a presentation, Theological Seminaries in the Future.[40] Although the research done for the project had its own inherent value, the primary focus of the Future project was a series of discussions with seminary trustees about what they needed to do to participate in institutional planning. The seminars followed a standard organization. First, the presenter or presenters discussed the overall situation of theological schools, the direction that Protestant churches were taking, and the most reasonable anticipations of future developments. Lynn and Fletcher often shaped this part of the presentation around the situation of particular schools. Second, the presenter led the group in a discussion of an institution's specific strategic position and helped board members formulate their own key questions. These seminars were the beginning of a series of major initiatives in trustee development that ran throughout the 1980s and 1990s.[41]

The bait for Lynn's sessions with trustees was the continuing financial crisis confronting most seminaries. Although the Lilly Endowment was never the only foundation making grants to theological schools, the Endowment was by far the most significant funder of new initiatives. Naturally, trustees were anxious to meet the person who might have their institution's future in his hands. Yet trustees and presidents benefited from these gatherings. Strategic planning, which often seemed part of the somewhat esoteric language of business schools, became part of the work of many presidents and boards and was incorporated into the ATS standards. Many 1970s

---

38. Deem, "Observations," 63. Also see Deem, "Evaluative Criteria."

39. Ibid. "Major policy issues" is my phrase.

40. The principal parts of this presentation were published Lynn and Fletcher, "Theological Seminaries in the Future."

41. See below, chapter 7.

seminary leaders, including Warren Deem, predicted that many seminaries would close. Why such dire predictions did not come true is unclear. Complex results rarely have one explanation. Yet the efforts at improving the administration, especially the emphasis on planning, contributed to this favorable outcome. Deem was essentially correct. The seminaries had to modernize their financial and planning work if they were to have a future. To their credit, many did so.

READINESS FOR MINISTRY

The most ambitious attempt to improve the efficiency of theological schools in the 1970s was the Readiness for Ministry program. Readiness was a program that originated in the increasingly theological and religious pluralism that followed the decline of neo-orthodoxy. In this new world, there was no consensus about what theological schools ought to do or what type of graduates they ought to produce. The university schools, important standard setters as late as the 1960s and 1970s (see above, chapter 1), lacked inner unity and direction. As theologian George Lindbeck noted in an influential study of the university-related schools:

> Instead of mediating, as professional schools characteristically do, between the university and specific spheres of organized activity in the wider society, the divinity schools are becoming more like departments in faculties of arts and science (or like miniature general education faculties).[42]

Lindbeck also noted that the university schools were now concentrating more on formal academic training. What the graduate of a good theological school ought to be was, consequently, not clearly defined in either theory or practice.

One approach to this question was to ask whether the schools had adequately prepared their graduates for their first ministerial assignment and to try to gauge their effectiveness in attaining this specific goal. The name Readiness for Ministry was shorthand for this objective. Readiness for Ministry did not attempt to measure what a student had learned or retained during their seminary career, or what skills a student may have developed. The focus was on whether a student was ready to begin ministry.

In developing Readiness for Ministry, David Schuller and his colleagues at ATS wanted to proceed as empirically as possible. The goal was to gather data from church officials, parishioners, seminary professors, and students about what was most desired in a beginning minister and to devise instruments that would measure those criteria.[43] The Readiness team envisioned a classic evaluation loop. The school was to administer tests at the beginning and the end of a students' career. By comparing before and after, the school and the student could ascertain what had been accomplished. The Readiness team designed the surveys to reflect differences in expectations among

---

42. Lindbeck, *University-Divinity Schools,* 13.
43. Schuller et al., *Readiness for Ministry.*

denominations. They wanted to avoid the assumption that one size fits all. Interestingly, Daniel Aleshire, who later became executive director of ATS, had his first sustained professional exposure to theological education as a researcher for this project.

Readiness for Ministry was the only the most recent in a series of tests for seminary students. Many schools used the Theological School Inventory, developed by the Education Testing Service in the late 1950s. This test sought to measure students' motivation for ministry.[44] Many schools also used a battery of psychological tests to help them counsel students vocationally and personally. What made Readiness unique was its emphasis on using criteria based on actual church experience.

The problems with Readiness did not have to do with its correlation with actual church life. Both the initial project and the 1987 revision called Profiles of Ministry had close correlations with actual experience, and the project was perhaps the most carefully evaluated in the history of theological education. Readiness for Ministry (Profiles of Ministry) has remained an important tool for institutional evaluation. Yet Readiness for Ministry never made the impact that its creators hoped that it would. Jesse Ziegler's dream that it might become the principal element in accreditation, in retrospect, seemed more than a step too far.

Why? We can suggest some reasons. First, the instrument, with its combination of case studies and interviews, took considerable time to administer and to interpret. At a time when seminaries were experiencing financial pressures and raising tuition and fees, even if the amount paid to the Association was comparatively small, it was more than many schools could pay. Further, most denominations had their own procedures for ordination that set forth their criteria for ecclesiastical service. These denominational criteria were under constant review. The Presbyterians, for example, added a test on the contents of the Bible to their usual tests and trials for ordination, and the Methodists extended their period of probationary membership. The more romantic atmosphere of American life in the 1970s and 1980s also worked against Readiness for Ministry. Both ministers and people tended to be more interested in spirituality, a vague category, than in criteria that were necessarily quantifiable. Another factor and one perhaps less obvious was that the Readiness reports, like the studies on which the Association relied, stressed more character-related criteria than they did theological criteria.

Readiness and its successor Profiles did not vanish. By 2000, there was an increasing emphasis on learning outcomes, both those of individual courses, and those of the schools as a whole. This pressure did not come from within the small world of theological education. The Department of Education, the largest single investor in American education, was pressuring the accrediting agencies to develop clearer criteria for educational outcomes so that consumers might make more intelligent choices before purchasing education. Such outcomes might also be useful for employers in their hiring procedures. This was where Profiles of Ministry (formerly Readiness

44. Cardwell, "The Theological School Inventory."

for Ministry) may yet come back into play as part of accreditation. Profiles remains the simplest and most consistently verified way to measure a prospective ministers' preparation for the first assignment. Given the high costs of measuring outcomes and doing the individual institutional research to support a seminary's educational claims, Profiles may turn out more cost-effective than the alternatives.

SPIRITUALITY

Many factors made the 1970s a period of intense interest in seminary spiritual life. Clearly, the most important was the Roman Catholic example. The most distinguishing aspect of Catholic theological education was the school's emphasis on priestly formation. The Catholic seminary sought to form its students into receptacles for the sacrament of ordination. The young priest was prepared as a vehicle for grace, a transit between God and humankind, who could mediate the divine presence through the sacramental order. While few Protestants understood all that was involved in this process and even fewer paid much attention to its theological underpinnings, they sensed that something was lacking in their own institutions. James I. McCord of Princeton reflected this new emphasis:

> It is not enough to import forms of piety from other traditions, but the seminaries are taking much more seriously now what the Catholics call "spiritual formation." . . . I believe the seminaries are taking this emphasis more seriously today than at any other time in my experience. Spiritual formation, piety, godliness, this goal is now a central objective, when only a short time ago this was taken for granted.[45]

Protestant educators had complained for years that students were not entering seminary sufficiently prepared. In retrospect, the Protestant system of Christian education—family prayer, Sunday schools, summer camps, youth and college organizations, and Sabbath observance—had eroded over time. The spiritual habits that sustained faith, even in the midst of its critical examination, were largely unformed. James T. Laney of Emory put the lament in these terms:

> After the battle over ecclesiastical control of the seminaries subsided, there was a generation of teachers whose inner lives evidenced the marks of piety. However sophisticated their language and thought, they were consciously a part of the people of God. There was a penumbra of piety, a recognizably religious quality to the lives of these memorable figures of the 1930s, 1940s, and 1950s.[46]

---

45. McCord, "The Understanding of Purpose," 64.
46. Laney, "The Identity Crisis in the Seminaries," 95.

More pungently, Frederick Ferré remembered the hours of prayer and personal biblical study that his father had invested, and lamented:

> For in 1967 and before I found such passages embarrassing and unprofessional. They threatened my sense of control over the argument: they derailed the careful train of thought; they sometimes left threads dangling that frustrated my demand for order, most of all, perhaps, they exposed the poverty of my own spiritual life and the thinness of my commitment to the church. He [his father, Nels] chose the seminary to be the forum for almost all his life's work; I choose the academy.[47]

Something had happened. In the late 1960s, Edward Farley wrote a perceptive little book, *A Requiem for a Lost Piety*.[48] Farley's thesis was that modernity had eroded the spiritual life of many of his contemporaries as well as himself. For Farley, this meant that the older liberal agenda had to expand to include the religious life as well as religious thought. One did not, however, have to accept his solution to appreciate his delineation of the problem.

In 1972, the American Association of Theological Schools published the results of a two-year emphasis on spiritual development.[49] The Task Force, however (the term *task force* was drawn from military practice), could do little more than lament existing conditions. In 1978, a grant from the Rockefeller Brothers Fund enabled the Association to establish a program for seminary teachers and administrators directed by Tilden Edwards and hosted at the Washington Theological Union.[50] However, the most successful attempts to deal with the issue came through the efforts of individual teachers. Yale Divinity School hired Catholic Henri J. M. Nouwen, a leading advocate for a deeper life combining a vital piety and Christian action. The student body enthusiastically received his courses, and his books sold very well on most Protestant campuses.

Perhaps the most successful response to the demand for more spirituality was at Southern Baptist Theological Seminary, where church historian E. Glenn Hinson and religious educator Findlay Edge developed a major emphasis on the spiritual life. On a more modest scale, William Clemmons developed an emphasis on spiritual direction as part of the program in religious education at Southeastern Baptist Theological Seminary. Other schools added courses in prayer and spiritual direction, usually as electives, taught by adjunct faculty.

Why didn't the drive for a renewed spirituality make more inroads among Mainstream Protestants and Evangelicals? Theological reasons existed, of course, that included the tendency for both Mainstream and Evangelical Protestants to define the

---

47. Ferré, "Toward Transformational Theology," 13.
48. Farley, *Requiem for a Lost Piety*.
49. "Voyage, Vision, Venture."
50. Edwards, "Integrating Contemplation and Action."

Christian life in active terms. The best Christian was the person who was engaged in the struggle, was working towards the kingdom, or was winning souls for Christ. Whether one defined church as mission or as missionary, the preference was for doing something in response to the gospel. Aside from the Quakers, few Protestants had a doctrine of contemplation or of the practice of the Presence of the Spirit. The popular spirituality that contributed to the interest in spiritual growth often lacked roots. One could practice meditation, for example, without any metaphysical assumptions about what may or may not have been at its roots, and the advocates of yoga—popular with many young Americans because of its supposed health benefits—thoroughly secularized the practice. Another clue lay in the very nature of American popular spirituality. Most Americans yearning for a spiritual life wanted to get in touch with their innermost being. This search for the true self was not necessarily rooted in the gospel, and it often yielded only the appearance of profundity. After all, the true self that one found might not be worth very much. In spirituality, as in computers, "garbage in" yielded "garbage out."

Perhaps more significant than these theological factors was the fact that Protestant seminary life was very busy and becoming even busier. Confronted with a full load of courses, field education, and often a family, the average student found life already crowded with obligations. The rising number of women, already close to 40 percent at the end of the 1970s, added other problems, as many women juggled caring for children, maintaining a home, and other obligations. In that world, students had to let something go, not because it was not valuable, but because they had to meet other obligations. After all, no one graded chapel, and attendance was not required. Protestant seminaries, like other professional schools and even most colleges and universities, were not organic communities. Faculty and often students were primarily on campus for their classes and office hours, and as time passed, even fewer students ate and slept on campus. Conversations between students and faculty members, consequently, were primarily about classes or on liberal campuses about social and political concerns. Even after Vatican II, strong community regulations, at times almost oppressive, sustained the sense of community in Catholic seminaries, and Protestant individualism rebelled, almost instinctively, against such restrictions on the individual. Protestant seminarians might have bewailed the lack of community, but they were unwilling to make the sacrifices that community entailed.

IMPORTANT QUESTIONS

The most significant developments of the 1970s were not institutional. Seminaries were moving from being all white, mainly male institutions to schools that included women and minorities among their student bodies and less frequently their faculties and administrations. At least part of the significance of the changes that took place in the 1960s and 1970s was that they helped institutions form the structures that would enable them to participate in rapid and fundamental social change. The heavy emphasis on theological education as graduate professional education, moreover, left seminaries with some unanswered questions: What is theological about theological education? Equally important, what was professional about it? Answering these questions would be the agenda for the remaining decades of the century and beyond.

3 The Rights Revolution and Theological Schools

THE MOST VISIBLE AND important development in American history from 1960 to 2011 was the Rights Revolution. In simple terms, the United States moved from a society in which Euro-Americans, especially males, held the bulk of political and economic power to a society in which African Americans, Latinas and Latinos, Asians, Women, and Gay and Lesbian (LGBT)[1] persons have a more visible stake in the nation and its future. The election of Barack Obama, although it did not mark the end of American racism, did indicate the distance that the nation had traveled. Few if any prophets would have predicted that the nation would elect an African American president fifty-three years after the passage of the 1964 Civil Rights Act. The figures in theological schools would seem to have reached a similar terminus. In 2009, Daniel Aleshire of the Association of Theological Schools reported that minorities, with the partial exception of Latino/Latina students,[2] had enrolled at roughly their percentage in the American population as a whole, and that the schools had made substantial progress in the hiring of racial and ethnic faculty and administrators. Interestingly, Asian students, one of the last groups to enter theological schools in large numbers, were somewhat overrepresented.[3]

Part of the difficulty in discussing the impact of the Rights Revolution is the diversity within each of these groups. All major American Protestant denominations as well as Roman Catholicism have African American members, and the largest

---

1. LGBT means Lesbian, Gay, Bisexual, and Transgendered, and is often used as shorthand for gender and/or sexual minorities.

2. Latina/Latino participation in theological education is difficult to compare with participation of African Americans or women, because the general level of religious observance among Latin Americans is significantly lower than among other groups. In the United States, ministry is financed by individual congregations. Where they are weak, the incentives to attend seminary is also weak. At the same time, Protestant Latina/Latinos are more like to be Pentecostal Christians. Pentecostal churches, whatever their racial or ethnic characteristics, are the last major denominational family to construct seminaries and have fewer members.

3. Aleshire, "Gifts Differing."

African American church traditions—Baptist, Methodist, and Pentecostal—have very different theological and educational traditions. An even greater diversity exists among women, who make up a majority of all Americans. Latino/Latina Americans are perhaps the most diverse. Although they share a common language, Latina/Latino Americans represent different national heritages and religious traditions. In many ways, they are similar to the various Eastern European immigrants in the last century. As had happened for Eastern Europeans, who often entered the United States with Russian or Austro-Hungarian passports, so for Latina/Latino immigrants, participation in a large, culturally dynamic empire shaped their cultures and their languages. Cloaks of imperialism and uniformity hid much diversity both in the Eastern European immigrant culture of the past century and in the Latin American culture of this century. All Latinos/Latinas are descended from residents of the former Spanish Empire—an empire with a somewhat common language and culture.

To place these various groups under one umbrella is a useful way of telling some similar stories. American law also provides a justification for this approach. In very concrete ways, government actions, ranging from the Civil Rights Act of 1964 to various affirmative action programs, have linked these groups by providing them with similar legal protections. The actions of the Association of Theological Schools also provides a precedent. In 1978 the Association of Theological Schools combined them under the Committee on Underrepresented Constituencies. This common treatment continued until 2008, a long time in ATS years, when the committee was renamed and split into two separate groups: the Committee on Race and Ethnicity and the Advisory Committee on Women in Leadership. Janice Edwards-Armstrong noted that the program of the Association went through five stages. These five stages roughly paralleled the experiences of the various groups as they entered into theological education. During the first phrase, which lasted from 1978 to 1990, the basic emphasis was on the recruitment of students, faculty, and administrators, and on curricula changes. The second phase from 1990 to 1999 emphasized the lived experience of underrepresented groups in theological education. This was a period in which ATS concentrated on holding consultations with representatives of the various groups and listening to their concerns. The third phase, from 2000 to 2004, was marked by a shift away from listening toward attending to the practices of schools in regard to their racial and ethnic constituencies. The fourth phrase, between 2005 and 2008, marked more of a concentration on Asian concerns; and the fifth and current stage, from 2008 to the present, is marked by an emphasis on teaching all students to minister in a multicultural and multiethnic world.[4]

Yet, having noted all of these commonalties, the stories remain different in very important ways. When they faced a common opponent, the various underrepresented

---

4. Edwards-Armstrong, "CORE: An Evolving Initiative." One might quibble with the decision to divide the period of 2000–2010 into three separate phases, but the overall usefulness of the paradigm makes it useful for the major 'underrepresented groups.

groups occasionally could act together, but they remained aware that each group had its own interests. Any alliance was, consequently, temporary. On a more fundamental level, their stories were different and distinctive. If theological educators have learned any lesson from the last fifty years, it is that difference matters. They should have known that from the beginning.

DEMOGRAPHICS AND DESTINY

As in the general story of the Rights Revolution, much of the change in theological education was incremental. Schools changed at much the same pace as did other areas of American life, illustrating again the close relationship between American religious institutions and American cultural and social structures. Naturally, there were differences in the speed in which different institutions made changes. Union Theological Seminary in New York took the lead, for example, in seeking a more diverse faculty and student body, and pioneered in providing theological education for gay and lesbian persons. Drew also changed relatively quickly. Other schools lagged behind the pacesetters, and some continue to do so. Regionalism, denominationalism, and theological orientation also affected individual institution's rate of change. Generally speaking, for example, Asian students moved more easily into Pacific Coast schools than they did into more Eastern institutions, while African American students were more concentrated in seminaries located in large Eastern and Midwestern cities. Sometimes these changes reflected other changes in theological education. The openness of an increasing number of seminaries to part-time, commuter students, beginning in the 1980s and continuing to the present, made it easier for underrepresented people to participate in theological education while continuing to meet other obligations. The same could be said of decisions, such as block scheduling and night classes—pioneered at the Boston Theological Institute as part of its effort at consortium building—that allowed students to fit coursework into very busy lives.

Several changes in American religious demographics influenced American seminaries, especially those related to the Protestant Mainstream. The baby-boomer generation did not continue to have children at their parents' rate, and institutions of higher education faced a demographics crunch. Fortunately for many colleges and universities, the steady increase in the percentage of young people entering college cushioned the blow. College became the new high school—the prerequisite to entry in the job market—and colleges and universities responded to their new status by increasing the number of professional and preprofessional programs available. As this general demographic shift was occurring, Mainstream Protestant churches entered a period of decline. These churches were an important part of the seminary ecology. The Reformation churches, for example, provided much of the intellectual leadership of American graduate theological education. Simultaneously, Evangelical churches grew, in part because of larger demographic shifts.[5] While seminary leaders had worried about declining enrollments in the 1960s, the end of the Vietnam War marked a dramatic decline in the number of young white male seminarians. Many students before the replacement of the military draft by the lottery attended seminaries to take advantage of the 4-D exemption from military conscription. Other observations may also provide possible explanations for the decline of white male students. The Protestant churches were increasingly female in membership and apparently more marginal to American public life. White males had other more profitable and prestigious options. The change itself was more important than an analysis of its causes. In simple terms, the decline in white male students meant that the schools had to find new students. Seminary finances were in a sorry state. Revenues were down, and expenses were up. The denominations, with the exception of the Southern Baptists, provided a smaller proportion of the needed revenues. Income from endowments declined. The expansion of schools' physical and human resources during the religious revival of the 1950s and 1960s raised the level of fixed expenditures. For good or ill, the seminaries were tuition driven. The seminaries could not solve their enrollment problems by lowering admission standards. With few exceptions, most seminaries were already open-admissions institutions, admitting all college graduates who applied. In short, the schools had places that they had to fill, and the only way to accomplish this was to find new sources of students. Not surprisingly, white women, the minority most able to pay, achieved parity in Mainstream and university divinity schools most quickly. Euro-American women had other advantages. In general, women already participated in the larger American culture, and many had attended good colleges and universities.[6] Women entered seminaries ready and able to do the work.

The logic of demographic stresses and income needs influenced almost all American seminaries. The Catholic vocations crisis, for example, created empty spaces at Catholic schools. Despite Rome's vigorous rejection of women's ordination, Catholic seminaries admitted an increasing number of Catholic women who were interested in a variety of church-related vocations. The new immigration from Latin America provided Catholic schools with another opportunity to enter a new market and increase their numbers. The role of women in the church was a major issue in the Southern

---

5. See above, chapter 2.

6. African American leaders were often conscious of the gap between African Americans and women, Charles Rooks noted at the 1981 session of the Society for the Study of Black Religion:

> A *third* way to look at what has happened to blacks in American theological education is to *review the situation of blacks in relation to women*—the response to feminism versus the response to racism. Both movements to correct historic injustices overlapped, but at least statistically women have fared better than blacks over the past decade. In 1972 there were 3,358 women enrolled in all degree programs or 10.2% of the total. In 1979 that enrollment had increased to 10,204 and 21.1% of the total enrollment. That's an increase of 6,846 persons. By contrast, the total black increase in the same years was 982 persons, from 1,061 to 2,043." Cited in John H. Cartwright, "The Cultural Context," 30.

Baptist controversy of the 1980s, and the battle ended with women all but excluded from the seminaries in the larger segment of that troubled denominational family. Yet before the fundamentalist takeover in the 1990s, Southern Baptists schools more or less followed the pattern of their Mainline and Evangelical counterparts in admitting growing numbers of women to all seminary programs.

A significant source of demographic change in the United States was the new immigration that followed the passage of Lyndon Johnson's 1964 Immigration Act. Although many of the newcomers were from non-Christian backgrounds, many were Christians who left their homeland seeking more religious and economic freedom. Both the Hispanic American and the Asian American communities grew significantly, because earlier immigrant communities had matured, and recent arrivals had their own needs. New immigrants fundamentally changed existing American minority communities. In some ways, this splintering effect was similar to what happened to Lutheranism in the nineteenth century when the Americanized Lutheran communities of the East had to deal with people from Denmark, Norway, and Sweden and with more confessional Lutherans from Germany. After 1990, African American churches had to confront strong congregations of persons who had come from African and Caribbean countries. Many of these new churches were either Pentecostal or related to one of the Mainstream denominations that had sent missionaries to the country of origin. Latin American communities had to deal with new immigrants from Mexico, Cuba, and Puerto Rico as well as new arrivals from the other Latin American countries. Many communities contained a mix of nationalities and a mix of generations as those born or educated in the United States had their own children and grandchildren.

AFRICAN AMERICAN THEOLOGICAL EDUCATION

The African American civil rights movement was the opening wedge in diversification of American theological education. Although other groups, particularly women, advanced more rapidly as a percentage of theological students, faculty, and administrators, African Americans were the paradigmatic minority group. The basic minority pattern was the one pioneered by African Americans: a period of protest was followed by a period of militancy. Affirmative action was the primary institutional demand of the militants, but it quickly gave way to a more fundamental concern with intellectual inclusion. In short, the more militant leaders discovered that they not only needed the right to participate in existing institutions, but they needed the right to use their own history and religious traditions as the foundation for academic work. Perhaps ironically, the concern for intellectual inclusion at first located black scholars on the margins of their institutions. The period on the margins did not last. As time passed, African American emphases became part of most scholars' theological thinking. Perhaps more significant, increasing numbers of African American faculty members moved from the ghetto of ethnic studies to the theological disciplines, such as New

Testament and church history, which were central to the theological curriculum. Following a similar pathway of protest, demands for enrollment and employment, and intellectual integration, women and Latinos/Latinas progressed at their own pace toward inclusion.

The civil rights movement was the most important event in postslavery African American history. After President Harry Truman ordered the desegregation of the American armed forces in 1948, the pressure for equal rights steadily gained strength in the United States. The drive had two separate foci: the courts and the streets. Lawyers, sponsored by the National Association for the Advancement of Colored People, brought a series of lawsuits challenging laws and practices that excluded African Americans. The court decision followed the logic of case law, declaring segregation unconstitutional in area after area of American life. These decisions were particularly important in education where the courts required formally all-white institutions to admit African Americans. Public support for these decisions grew steadily during the 1950s. The passage of the 1964 Civil Rights Act provided additional legal guarantees for African Americans, and laid the foundation for new court decisions that gradually expanded African American influence. At the same time, African Americans held a series of demonstrations, demanding the end of segregation. The 1955 Birmingham bus boycott, which began when Rosa Parks refused to surrender her seat on a municipal bus, brought Dr. Martin Luther King Jr. and the Southern Christian Leadership Conference to prominence. The next stage in the movement was the drive for voter registration. The 1965 march to Selma, Alabama, grew out of the efforts of African Americans to increase voter registration. After the original organizers invited Martin Luther King to lead the demonstration, a large number of clergy joined him. Pictures of ministers, priests, nuns, and rabbis marching side by side, often locking arms, spread across the American media. Seminarians and younger faculty members were very much in attendance. Selma was easily the most representative ecumenical event of the decade. The 1968 assassination of King marked major changes in the movement for black equality. Younger African Americans became more militant. The new radicalism, perhaps best symbolized by James Forman's presentation of the Black Manifesto, weakened the alliance between the African American movement and its ecumenical supporters. Some deserted the movement altogether, while others struggled to understand the movement's new direction.

Not surprisingly, the civil rights movement was also a watershed in the history of African American theological education. Despite the historical prominence of African American churches, few African American ministers were educated when the civil rights movement began. The reasons for this lack of education were complex. One was denominational. Among Euro-American Protestants, the primary advocates of theological education were those churches with a Reformation heritage—Episcopalians, Presbyterians, Lutherans, and Congregationalists. These churches had a deep tradition of an educated ministry and important European models for advanced schooling. However, Euro-American Baptists, Methodists, Disciples, and Pentecostals did not have as established traditions or rationales for the theological schooling of their pastors. These churches established their seminaries comparatively late and only gradually came to expect or require seminary education for their pastors. While the handful of African American pastors in the Reformation denominations were often highly educated, the vast majority of African American ministers were in denominations that lacked a firm tradition of an educated ministry. Like their white counterparts, these churches placed more emphasis on a minister's call than on a minister's preparation, and some members of these churches resisted theological education in principle. There were variations among the larger African American churches. The African Methodist Episcopal Church, with its strong roots in the North, had a social location among the African American upper middle class that encouraged a higher level of education. However, its standards required only high school and the completion of the Course of Study or college for ordination.

The social structure of African American communities also worked against a more educated clergy. African American communities had a chronic shortage of educated professionals, including teachers, doctors, lawyers, and businesspeople. When a young person acquired a high school or college education, these professions with their higher status and income often had first claim on those with aspirations for a better life. While African Americans participated in church life in large numbers, the ministry was not a prestigious profession in their communities. The civil rights movement partly changed this perception.

Perhaps most serious, there were few places for young African American ministers to acquire serious training. The American tradition of racial segregation and exclusion was strong in education. Most white colleges and seminaries, including those in the North, were not receptive to African Americans, and even the few that admitted African Americans often treated them as second-class students. Few had scholarship aid for African Americans or employed African American faculty members. Nor was the system of black colleges and seminaries strong. Segregated education was, as the Supreme Court noted, inherently unequal. In 1955 there were only two accredited African American theological seminaries, Gammon and Howard, and both struggled for students and funding.

Civil Rights and Theological Education

The civil rights movement and the Black Power movement that followed it redefined the African American church and provided it with models of leadership that promoted the development of a more educated ministry. The civil rights movement produced a remarkable degree of unity among African American Christians. This unity was not absolute. Significant numbers of African American churches and pastors stood apart from the struggle, however much their members may have sympathized with it, and these churches continued their historic stress on winning souls and personal morality. The largest African American denomination, the National Baptists, divided over the issue, and a new group, the National Progressive Baptists, claimed the allegiance of those committed to social action. Yet as time passed, African American Christians came to interpret their prior history as preparation for the movement and to see the demand for equality and justice as part of the essential core of their religious traditions. Further, the civil rights movement created a sense of unity among African American believers greater than the denominational and other differences between them. The next forty years of African American church experience would see common patterns of worship. Even in churches with long-standing traditions of decorum in worship, these changes included the use of both traditional and newer forms of gospel music and more spontaneous preaching and praise.

The civil rights movement generated a new model of pastoral effectiveness and success. The early leaders of the movement, such as Martin Luther King Jr., Ralph David Abernathy, Fred Shuttleworth, Gardner Taylor, and Joseph Lowry, were successful pastors who demonstrated that religion was not marginal to African American life. The leaders' use of the rhetoric and music rooted in the black church's own traditions pointed to religious and political vitality. An effective minister was one who stood at the center of his people's experience and used that position as a way of promoting the common good. The new African American minister was also an educated and sensitive leader. Although not all the civil rights leaders were educated, King, Abernathy, and Lowry were college-trained pastors, and King had earned both a seminary degree from Crozer and a doctoral degree in systematic theology from Boston University. Emmanuel L. McCall, longtime teacher at Louisville's Southern Baptist Theological Seminary, observed:

> It is attributable mostly to the new positive image radiated by the late Dr. Martin Luther King, Jr. King proved to young blacks that one could hold an earned Ph.D. and still communicate with the illiterate. He adequately demonstrated that one with training can be far more effective in ministry than one without.[7]

Pastoral education, despite resistance to it among some at the grass roots, did not separate one from one's tradition or people. Education could and did make one better able to lead a minority people in the midst of external hostility.

King's theological work was an important part of his example. Martin Luther King Jr. was the among the best-educated ministers of the early civil rights leaders, and his careful use of theological arguments and categories earned him respect outside the African American community as well as within it. In many ways, King was similar to Benjamin May, president of Morehouse, a person whom King greatly admired. May was a man at home in both the African American world and white academic culture, who spoke effectively to both. Like his mentor, King understood modern

---

7. McCall, "Theological Education," 418.

biblical criticism and had a sophisticated understanding of religious language. King's own theology derived not only from his African American heritage but also from sources as diverse as Boston Personalism and Paul Tillich. This intellectual framework, particularly Tillich, enabled King to reappropriate and redefine his African American heritage.[8] Essentially, King related his African American religious heritage to theology by correlating questions posed by the existential situation of his people to answers provided in African American Christian tradition. Whereas many white contemporaries used a similar philosophy to translate their traditional symbols into the language of existential philosophy, King translated those symbols into the language of freedom from oppression. Further, he recognized that the traditional language of African American religion functioned at a variety of levels. The same assertion might have a supernatural and a political reference. This fundamental method, something surprisingly akin to Paul van Buren's *Secular Meaning of the Gospel*, allowed King to draw freely from his tradition, including from its often-constricting biblicism, and use it evocatively as a call for action.[9] King's method also allowed him to use Gandhi and other advocates of nonviolence to strengthen his arguments. An important part of his intellectual baggage was his Baptist tradition that provided him with a prophetic understanding of ministry. Walter Rauschenbusch was as much a source of his theology as Paul Tillich.

Historians should not minimize the importance of King's theology. King's voice has been more studied than any other African American voice; scholars have pored over his writings and speeches, and new works on King appear regularly. Much later liberation theology drew on his writings, even when its authors doubted the wisdom of his tactic of nonviolence. King's blending of cultural traditions, theological insights, and calls for action has modeled a theology true to its African American roots while also sophisticated enough to appeal to other audiences. Some of his work, particularly his "I Have a Dream" speech, has become part of the American canon.

The sophistication of King's theology enabled him to speak across racial barriers. Euro-Americans and Europeans read King's theology and took it seriously. He was the one African American religious leader who everyone understood. Boston Personalism, one of the primary sources of his thought, originated in Methodism, and the position reflected many of the best insights of Evangelical Christianity. The person in all the complexities of historical location was the center of both epistemology and theology. King was a guest speaker at some of the South's leading theological schools,

---

8. King's dissertation was on Paul Tillich and Henry Nelson Wieman. One way to see the difference in the two primary influences on King's thought is to separate method from content. King consistently used Tillich's method to reinterpret African American religious experience. However, King, who was not an existentialist, often depended on personalism for the metaphysical foundations of his thought.

9. The literature on King is vast and growing. The following have contributed to my interpretation. Hill, *The Theology of Martin Luther King Jr. and Desmond Mpilo Tutu*; Dorrien, *The Making of American Liberal Theology*; Harding, *Martin Luther King*; Erskine, *King among the Theologians*; Miller, *Voice of Deliverance*; Cone, *Martin & Malcolm & America*.

including Southern Baptist Theological Seminary and Brite Divinity School, and did much to reinforce the decision of those schools to integrate their student bodies.

In short, King demonstrated that a theologically educated and sophisticated minister might live in two worlds: the minister could be an effective communicator to his or her own people and, at the same time, a thinker that the larger Euro-American world took seriously. In this, King was the role model that suggested that other African American ministers might also lead in both societies. King was not a white thinker in blackface; he was an African American thinker who spoke from his own heritage to white society in language that white society understood.

Further, King demonstrated to both black and white Americans that the African American churches were social organizations with religious and ethical significance. Before the civil rights movement, African American churches were almost invisible. Even the few scholars, such as W. E. B. Du Bois, who recognized the churches' influence in African American communities, saw the churches and their leaders as relics of the past. At best, these scholars believed that the churches were places where African Americans were in charge of their own lives, part of the shadow society of Black-dominated mutual-aid societies, Masonic lodges, and social clubs. A few scholars, to be sure, recognized the religious power of the spirituals, but few paid positive attention beyond their analysis of those songs. King's work made the African American churches visible within and without the African American community. This visibility had two consequences. First, younger African Americans could see their own religious institutions in a new light. The African American church was not a mere imitation of the white congregations. Second, the Euro-American churches and their leaders could see the African American church as something that they ignored at their peril. This new visibility changed the perception of African American theological education. If African American churches could inspire and lead a movement for social justice, then the question of the education of African American pastors became a high-priority matter for the African American churches, and equally important for the predominately white churches and seminaries.

African American Seminaries

Although the percentage of African American students in predominantly Euro-American seminaries increased steadily, the historically African American schools continued to educate a significant proportion of African American ministerial students and to provide important places for research into African American themes. In many ways, the post-King development of African American theological education is the account of the creation or maturation of schools explicitly related to African American churches. The beginning of the Interdenominational Theological Center (ITC) in

Atlanta, told earlier,[10] was an important part of this process. Rockefeller money had supported many African American educational institutions, and the willingness of Rockefeller money to contribute to this enterprise gave it immediate visibility as did its relationship with Atlanta University. Along with Howard in Washington DC, ITC was a university-related divinity school with the resources and prestige implied by that relationship. The president of ITC and the deans of Howard did not speak for all African American churches, but as representatives of elite African American institutions, they were in a strategic position to speak to those churches. Both schools were interested in the larger African Diaspora and in the survival of African culture. ITC took particular leadership in addressing the problems of local churches, including pastoral care, and church and denominational administration.

Both schools also maintained significant libraries of African American original materials. The Lawrence Neale Jones Library at Howard University Divinity School houses the African Heritage Collection. Originally founded in the 1960s to document the civil rights movement, the library is one of the largest collections of original material about African American religious history. ITC's Robert W. Woodruff Library also maintains extensive collections of African American archival material.

Other African American theological schools also matured. In 1971, The Association of Theological Schools fully accredited Virginia Union (Samuel DeWitt Proctor School of Theology), and the school's dean, Allix B. James served as the Association's first African American president. In the 1990s, the Association also accredited Shaw, Payne, and Hood. Interestingly, as time has passed, these schools have become multiracial and inclusive. Hood, located in eastern North Carolina, has become a major educator of white United Methodist pastors in the area as well as of its more traditional African Methodist Episcopal Zion student body.[11] In the same decade, American Baptist Theological Seminary of the West became a predominately African American institution, and Palmer (Eastern) in Philadelphia became a biracial institution.

Although many African American congregations resisted the ordination of women, their theological schools enrolled significant numbers of female students. The first African American woman to serve as the president of a seminary was Leah Gaskin Fitchue at Payne, the oldest seminary of the African Methodist Episcopal Church.

African American theological schools have played a particularly important role in the Association of Theological Schools. The Association's annual meetings and its various governing boards are predominately composed of presidents and deans, and through much of the last fifty years, despite the election of some African Americans to those positions in predominately white institutions, that has given the Association an overwhelmingly Euro-American cast. The presence of the African American seminaries has guaranteed African Americans an important seat at the table, and such leaders

---

10. See above, chapter 1.
11. Hutson, "Case Study."

as Allix B. James, James Costen, and John W. Kinney have played important public and behind-the-scenes roles in the determining the Association's policies.

African American schools had an expansive view of their mission and of the mission of the African American church. James Costen, president of ITC, said:

> Black theological education, in addition to its irreducible need to provide a sound classical theological framework for its community of learners, must also be centers lifting the fallen, inspiring the rejected, strengthening the weakened, educating the hopeless. These institutions must help people appreciate the sacred by moving them with skill and compassion through the secular to see God's will and love for them. How this is done is what I call the *Content of Black Theological Education*.[12]

Because the African American seminary was part of the black community, embedded in its life and practices, the needs of that community were not something that existed apart from the black seminary or its teachers. In this sense, black theological seminaries were like other seminaries with a distinctive mission or location. For example, the urban location defines New York Seminary and Union. Their students and faculty confront urban problems daily. Similarly, such schools as Bangor Theological Seminary and University of Dubuque Theological Seminary live and breathe in a small-church, rural atmosphere. Even when such schools follow an "industry standard curriculum," their programs reflect their location and mission. African American Seminaries did not have to research the problems of African American communities; they shared the life and experiences of those communities.

Another way to see these African American schools, including ITC to some extent, is to recognize that they are denominational institutions with special obligations to transmit a style of ministry and theology. The African American churches, if only judged by the strength of their membership and the number in attendance on Sunday morning, are statistically important components of American Protestantism. The National Baptists, for example, are the second-largest Baptist convention in the United States with almost ten million members. Among American churches, only the Roman Catholics, United Methodists, and Southern Baptists are larger. Similarly, the African Methodist Episcopal Church, the African Methodist Episcopal Church, Zion, and the Christian Methodist Episcopal Church are individually and collectively a significant proportion of American Wesleyans, larger than any of the Holiness denominations and second only to the United Methodist Church. Likewise, the Church of God in Christ (Pentecostal) ranks among the largest denominations in America with more than 5 million members. In short, the principal African American Churches are numerically part of the American mainstream, easily within the ten largest American denominations. If for no other reason than their relative strength, these churches need

---

12. Costen, "Black Theological Education," 4.

scholars who will pay appropriate attention to their particular history and individual theological traditions.[13]

The fact that African American churches are part of the statistical, if not the cultural, mainstream of American Protestantism in addition to their importance in their own communities, makes the question of the preparation of ministers for these churches an important one. Lincoln and Mamiya observed at the beginning of the 1990s that:

> If we were asked to make a single policy recommendation that we would consider critical for the future of black churches, it would be the need for more, better trained and better-educated black clergy. Although this need has been raised before by Woodson, Mays and Nicholson, and countless other denominational leaders, seminary presidents and professors, there is but meager evidence that it has been taken seriously by the Black Church as a whole.[14]

The simple fact of the matter is that, despite the success of African American megachurches and other congregations with less trained leadership, seminary-trained pastors do much of the most creative ministry in the African American community.[15] The most important argument for the inclusion of African Americans in theological education is that their churches are important outposts of the gospel in the United States.

One complication in discussing African American theological education is that African American Christianity is as varied as the African American community. Our language about race, inherited from racist traditions, tends to categorize people and institutions in the binary categories of white and black. Everyone falls on one side of the divide or the other. The binary division of American society obscures the important differences between African Americans, especially, the closely related categories of class and denomination. Among African Americans, members of the Reformation denominations, such as Presbyterians, Congregationalists (UCC), and Episcopalians, tend to be better educated and more economically secure than other African Americans. Not surprisingly, those who minister to these churches have an education and status similar to that of their congregations. The substantial African American membership in the United Methodist Church has also maintained consistently higher educational standards than most African American churches. Among the historically African American denominations, the African Methodist Episcopal Church often served the upper-middle-class African American community and, consequently, has higher educational standards than other African American churches. The National Baptists have served the urban middle class and many poorer rural congregations. In contrast, the Progressive National Baptists, formed when a number of pastors active

13. Edwards-Armstrong, "CORE: An Evolving Initiative."
14. Lincoln and Mamiya, *The Black Church*, 399.
15 Ibid.

in civil rights left the parent body in the 1960s, has served a more educated and activist public. The Church of God in Christ, the largest African American Pentecostal denomination, has primarily served the more dispossessed, although some of its members are rising socially. Not surprisingly, its ministers tend to come from that social demographic.

In short, the educational level of African American denominations follows basic class divisions. The more educated and socially prominent the denomination or the congregation, the higher its pastor's educational attainments are likely to be. Although race is a constant factor in African American history, it might be useful to compare the educational patterns of African American Baptist ministers with white Baptist pastors, particularly in the South. Although these white churches consistently have maintained higher educational expectations than their African American counterparts, their level of ministerial education was historically significantly lower than their Northern counterparts. Both Euro-American and African American Baptist ministerial education boomed after the Second World War, particularly following the 1960s.

Particularly in the South, African American denominations have divisions similar to those in the Euro-American churches. Many African Americans, for example, are strongly Evangelical in their theological outlook, sharing a strong doctrine of Scripture and an emphasis on the family with their Euro-American counterparts. Others, particularly those in predominantly Euro-American denominations, lean towards more liberal religious views. The more liberal churchmen, like their white counterparts, are often in dialog with African American humanists, a group often neglected in accounts of African American religion. This theological diversity means, for African American and Euro-American Protestants, that questions about theological education among African Americans do not have a single answer. Just as American theological education has always been diverse and has become more so over the last fifty years, so African American theological education is diverse. As among Euro-American Christians, the type of theological education ministers receive is often important to the churches that hire them. Very different people attended Union Theological Seminary in New York, the Interdenominational Theological Center in Atlanta, and Fuller Theological Seminary in Pasadena.

As the percentage of African Americans in predominantly Euro-American seminaries increased, the future importance of the predominantly African American seminaries became less clear. In 2010, these schools no longer had the same centrality as they had in the 1970s and 1980s; yet, historians need to be cautious. As we mentioned above, these schools serve important denominations and are the primary scholarly voices for those churches. My own sense is that these schools will not only continue to draw from their traditional constituencies, but that they will increase their enrollment of Euro-American students, students from the Caribbean basin, and African immigrants. Shared heritage will make them attractive to Caribbean students, whose background also includes enslavement, and the seminaries and their sponsoring churches interest in Africa will build bridges to immigrant and second-generation students from that continent. These schools, like other schools related to the Association of Theological Schools, are becoming commuter schools that draw their student body from nearby areas, making them available to Euro-American and Latina/Latino students as well. Further, these schools are in the most Protestant region of the country and, historically, the area with a highest percentage of ministers of all races without seminary training.

Dr. Charles Shelby Rooks and the Rockefeller Fund: Students and Teachers

American religious institutions were among the most segregated bodies in the United States. There was an irony in this. Many Euro-American leaders, Protestant and Catholic, actively participated in the civil rights movement and were willing to serve as advocates for equal rights in the churches and the seminaries. Yet goodwill does not necessarily move mountains. What the situation demanded in the 1960s was someone who could use the existing resources to recruit a substantial number of new African American students and teachers. The person who accomplished this was Charles Shelby Rooks. Rooks was a Union (New York) graduate, a Congregationalist, and a capable organizer and administrator. After graduation, he served as pastor of the influential Lincoln Memorial Congregational Temple in Washington DC and as an executive with the Rockefeller Brothers Fund. After his time as a foundation executive, Rooks was elected president of Chicago Theological Seminary. Rooks was the first African American to head a major Euro-American institution, and he ended his career as executive vice president of the United Church of Christ's Board of Homeland Ministries.

Rooks's career as a national leader began in 1959 after the NCC assembled a meeting of sixty-five white and African American leaders at Seabury House in Greenwich, Connecticut.[16] The meeting launched a decade of concerted interest in providing more educated leadership for African American churches. The meeting identified five crucial areas where someone needed to take action:

> (1) greatly increased black student registration in graduate theological schools; (2) sharp and sustained growth in the number of black faculty and staff in all theological schools; (3) significantly improved and strengthened black seminaries; (4) drastic change in the design and content of seminary curricula; and (5) the development of effective placement systems and strategies for black seminary graduates.[17]

These goals were interconnected. To increase enrollment in graduate theological schools, those schools would need to make the environment educationally and socially

---

16. Rooks, "Vision, Reality and Challenge." Rooks himself was not at the meeting.
17. Ibid., 39.

comfortable for African American students. Such an improvement involved the appointment of African American faculty, the design of new courses to help African American students live with their dual character as educated people and as African Americans, and perhaps most difficult, to devise new means of placing new graduates. This latter problem was most acute in the Baptist and Pentecostal denominations where clergy often received a call through a complex network of personal relationships in the community and where vocal opposition to an educated ministry existed. The other goal that theological educators needed to address was how to bring African American candidates up to graduate level so that they could enroll in seminaries and graduate programs in theology. The Conferences inspired the Rockefeller family, which had a long-standing interest in African American education.[18] Acting through the Sealantic Fund, the Rockefellers were the principal contributor to the Interdenominational Theological Center. Rockefeller philanthropic executives Yorke Allen and Walter Wagoner attended the Greenwich Conference and persuaded the family to begin two long-lived programs: the Protestant Fellowship Program and the Rockefeller Doctoral Program in Religion. Together the two programs aimed at meeting two of the Seabury goals: the recruitment of a significant number of African American students and the provision of well-trained African American faculty members. The most important decision that Allen and Wagoner made was to appoint Charles Shelby Rooks, whom Wagoner knew through his denomination, to direct these programs.

Rooks described his work with the Fund as *A Revolution in Zion*.[19] Rooks worked hard recruiting and financing young African American students and potential African American faculty members. His careful recruitment and the old-boys' network that it created helped to build the infrastructure that would make possible increased black participation.

Recruitment was a far more arduous task than contemporaries might assume. Rooks was determined that the two programs of the Fund would only finance young people with substantial promise, and that the programs would draw from all segments of the African American community. Part of the difficulty was geographic. Rooks traveled throughout the country, particularly the South, interviewing candidates and their teachers. He often had to stay in segregated housing or with friends, and he was not always greeted warmly when he visited campuses. As opportunities for African Americans expanded after the 1964 Civil Rights Act, a young, gifted African American had a more extensive choice of professions, including college and university teaching, as well as traditional opportunities in medicine and law.[20] Religion was neither as

---

18. Early Rockefeller contributions to African American education are detailed in Miller, *Piety and Profession*, chapter 16.

19. Rooks, *Revolution in Zion*.

20. The long tradition of segregation in these professions meant that independent African American professionals could establish their own practice within the confines of the African American community.

prestigious nor as well paid as the other possibilities. The fact that Rooks's position had the Rockefeller name and support from the nation's more influential seminaries admission officers opened doors, but ministry remained a hard sell. Rooks needed all of his considerable powers of persuasion to persuade college students to consider seminary and a career in religion.

If outcomes are the ultimate test of any foundation grant, the two Rockefeller funds were more than successful. The young men that Rooks recruited, both as seminary and graduate students, went on to have outstanding careers in church and academy. In turn, these graduates recruited other capable young African Americans to attend seminary and to undertake advanced study in religion. His work laid the foundation for the rapid growth of the number of African American students and faculty in the 1990s and 2000s.

Rooks also worked, particularly in his years at the Fund for Theological Education, as the unofficial and occasional official representative of African Americans to the Association of Theological Schools. Because of Rooks's influence, Jesse Ziegler, executive director of the Association of Theological Schools, made the inclusion of African Americans an important goal of the Association. Rooks also influenced Ziegler's most influential racial initiative the Black Religious Experience and Theological Education, held at the Howard University School of Religion, February 20–22, 1970.[21] The Conference contributed to a passionate search for African American faculty members, which meant that many, if not all, of those supported by the Rockefeller Brothers Fund might find jobs

The Rise of African American Theology and Theological Studies

By 1969, the racial atmosphere had changed. Unlike earlier generations, the newer African American leaders were less patient with slow, evolutionary change, and they demanded immediate responses to their complaints. The new movement had both cultural and political consequences. The most striking part of their program was their positive understanding of their own racial identity. For them, African American life had its own culture and its own positive values. An Afro haircut became a badge of pride, and many African Americans demanded that others call them black rather than Negro. Later, they called for *African American* to replace *black*. Like other ethnic terms in common use, such as *Irish American* or *German American*, the term referred to the continuation of cultural patterns in the New World as well as ethnic identity.[22]

21. Grigsby, "The Black Religious Experience."

22. The 1970s were a decade of ethnicity. Novak, *The Rise of the Unmeltable Ethnics* marked a period of intense ethnic conscious in American public life as politicians, especially Jimmy Carter and Ronald Reagan, appealed to ethnic blocks as part of their coalitions. This new movement had considerable influence on the American universities and, in particular, on the discipline of history. Histories of ethnic groups became very important, as did programs of ethnic studies. Interestingly, although religion departments had always included Judaism in world-religions courses and in courses

The new militancy had some negative effects on theological schools. The old alliance between white liberals and African American activists, for example, weakened and in some milieus, disappeared. Many schools with substantial African American student bodies noted that African American students increasingly organized their own campus organizations and pressure groups, and put increased pressure on seminary administrations for racial change. Affirmative action, both in hiring and admissions, were a common demand. Fear of destructive riots led many administrations to acquiesce to some of these demands.[23]

Yet the primary effect of the new militancy was cultural. African American scholars began creating both a distinctive African American theology and a number of theological disciplines, ranging from African American religious history to African American religious education, that offered alternative understandings of the Christian tradition. The event that marked this new theology was James Cone's 1969 publication of *Black Theology and Black Power*.[24] Cone's work was not the only quality theology being written by African Americans,[25] yet Cone's theology and terminology captured the moment. African American theologians were not content to be appendages to the history of Euro-American thought. They had their own voices and their own agenda. Cone's own position was a form of liberation theology:

> This view of the gospel has far-reaching consequences for theology and ethics. Simply put, it means that there can be no authentic investigation of Christianity which does not take seriously the liberation of the oppressed. Theology must become a theology of the helpless and weak, disclosing what is involved in the liberation of man.[26]

The witness of Scripture continually affirmed that God was on the side of the oppressed, and in America, that meant people of color. Hence, very aware that he was using symbolic language, Cone could affirm that God was "Black" and that those people seeking God needed to become "Black" as well. Like Martin Luther King Jr., Cone used a theology of correlation in which African American experience, especially

---

on Jewish themes, a new discipline, Jewish studies, became common on many campuses, particularly in the Northeast. Although Jewish studies included some material on Judaism, it was primarily interested in Judaism as a culture. Yiddish folktales were as important as rabbinic traditions.

23. Much of this agreement was, of course, subject to budgetary considerations. More was promised than delivered.

24. Cone, *Black Theology and Black Power*. See Cone and Wilmore, *Black Theology*, for a fuller examination of the context.

25. J. Deotis Roberts may have been the most able African American theologian. Dorrien saw his work has making a more significant contribution to the larger, more technical theological discussion. See Dorrien, The *Making of American Liberal Theology*, vol. 3, ch. 3: "Visions of Liberation." Dorrien also appreciates Cone's work.

26. Cone, "Black Power, Black Theology," 213. The fact that Cone was published in *Theological Education* at this early a stage in his own career demonstrates the impact of his work on the theological establishment.

the experience of oppression, addressed the questions to theologians, and, in turn, theologians formulated responses to those questions.

In some ways, Cone's position stood popular American Christianity on its head. American Christians had pictured Jesus consistently as White, often fair with blond or reddish hair, had spoken of the historical destiny of the Anglo-Saxon peoples, and had excluded African Americans even from the history of missions to Africa. Perhaps more serious, these distorted forms were often current in African American churches, poisoning ordinary people's understanding of themselves and of God. Yet Cone was not primarily concerned with these distortions. While others concentrated on these outward manifestations of racial bias, Cone's point was more radical: the gospel was that God was on the side of the oppressed, and that God's project was the ending of oppression. The gospel was political.

At the same time as black theology emerged, African American studies were becoming commonplace in American higher education. In 1969, for instance, Harvard University's library published *Afro-American Studies: A Guide to Resources of the Harvard University Library*,[27] and both Harvard and Yale published descriptions of their programs. Yet in 1973, the movement for increased black studies seemed less certain than it had earlier. Rooks reported in an article in the *Journal of the Interdenominational Theological Center*:

> For many reasons, black studies—albeit still a phenomenon—appears a phenomenon of a lesser order in 1973 than it promised in 1969. Very few institutions have student enrollments—black or white—which match their predictions and expectations. The appearance of parallel fields such as Chicano, American Indians, and Women's studies has led critics to claim that Black Studies was the first of a series of fads, none of them with serious staying power. Their competition has also contributed to stringent budget situations which have been cited as justification for reduced budget commitments to Black Studies in many institutions.[28]

In part, the problem was the multiplication of minorities. As each new group demanded to be included, fewer institutions had the resources to invest in classes and instructors for each separate group. However, the competition that Rooks noted only momentarily slowed the academic study of African American life. In many seminaries, African American theological studies had established themselves as academic disciplines.[29] The Society for the Study of Black Religion, which Rooks helped found, functioned as a scholarly society. Its yearly meetings and publications provided senior

---

27. The Harvard University Libraries, *Afro-American Studies*.

28. Rooks, "The First Dozen Years Are the Hardest," 101, citing the *Danforth Foundation News and Notes*.

29. The plural is deliberate, although the variety of studies at different schools varied. Many schools offered both African American History and black theology courses. More adventuresome schools offered others as well.

African American scholars with an avenue to make known new directions in their thinking, and allowed younger scholars to demonstrate their abilities and refine their arguments. Like all scholarly societies, the Society for the Study of Black Religion provided scholars might present their papers to a friendly audience.

Black theology (or, more accurately, black systematic theology) was perhaps the visible African American intellectual movement on many American seminary campuses. Even where it was not taught in separate courses, it was included in the very popular courses in liberation theology and feminist theology. The purpose of black theology was twofold. At one level, black theology located and critically appropriated elements in the African American tradition that affirmed black people's sense of identity and pride. Hence, many sought to translate Christian symbols from a Eurocentric to an Afrocentric world. God was "Black," and pictures of children in Sunday school literature were to show black faces. The other purpose of black theology was to find ways of articulating those elements in the tradition that promoted or encouraged African Americans to take the lead in their own liberation. Thus, theologians stressed such figures as Moses, very important in traditional African American thinking, and advocated worship and musical forms that pointed toward freedom. Like other liberation theologians, black theologians often drew upon contemporary Marxist thinking, but their commitment to understanding African and African American tradition also led them to consider other religious traditions, especially Islam.

For all its interest in African religious experience or perhaps because of it, African Americans theologians were able to highlight what had been distinctive in their own experience. J. Deotis Roberts wrote:

> Persons who have just arrived look like blacks, but they don't think the same way. What is lacking is the long history of oppression and the struggle for freedom in this society. They do not bear the psychological scars of the long struggle, what Dr. King referred to as "the long night of suffering."[30]

The experience of slavery followed by discrimination and exclusion, "the long night of suffering," marked African American theology as problem and as opportunity.[31] In that sense, serious study of black history was always more than just a study of the past. Warner R. Traynham noted in the *Harvard Divinity Review*:

> Black Studies in theological education is then first of all intended to give the black seminarian a place to stand, a real place that belongs to him, not the no-place afforded by the traditional theological enterprise. A process of reconstruction, of redemption in its truest sense, the buying back of a lost and deprecated past, the recovery of self is its goal.[32]

---

30. Roberts, "And We Are Not Saved," 366.

31. Cone, *The Cross and the Lynching Tree*, points to the way that black experience and early Christian experience illuminated one another.

32. Traynham, "Black Studies in Theological Education," 266.

In this sense, black studies were not unusual. In the wake of the ecumenical movement, many denominations required their candidates for ordination to take a denominational studies course, often called Polity and History, to forge needed group identity.

How influential was the black theology of liberation? Like all questions about historical influence, this inquiry is very difficult to answer. One must first ask influential with whom and in comparison with what standard. In 1990 Lincoln and Mimaya noted that less than two-thirds of black urban pastors knew anything about black theology,[33] but this may not tell us very much. Theological perspectives take a long time to filter down to local parish levels, even where the majority of pastors have seminary training, and the fact that almost of one-third of the pastors knew something about black theology might compare favorably to the percentage of pastors in Mainstream churches who knew anything about George Lindbeck, Edward Farley, or Langdon Gilkey. The influence of black theology, however, was on the pastors of large churches and, of course, within the academy. Teachers such as James Cone, located at Union, a major seminary for training theological instructors, taught many of those who would shape the African American presence in American theological education. Equally important, these scholars taught the pastors of the larger, more successful African American churches.

American theological schools, particularly the more liberal institutions, had struggled for academic freedom since the fundamentalist-modernist controversy of the 1920s. Like the death-of-God movement, black liberation theology, with its continual criticism of Euro-American theology, tested this commitment. Yet despite substantial contributions by scholars in traditionally African American institutions, those African American scholars in Mainstream schools did the bulk of the work. Social ethicist Peter J. Paris saw this as an irony:

> Ironically, most of these African American theologians were employed by the Euro-American institutions that they were criticizing, doing their research during sabbatical leave periods provided by the policies of these institutional adversaries and having their manuscripts published by publishing houses owned and controlled by white churches.[34]

From another point of view, no irony was present in these facts. The historically black seminaries, with the exception of Howard and Interdenominational Theological Center, had substantially smaller endowments and budgets than their Euro-American counterparts. Lack of resources meant less time for scholarship and reflection.

Yet this indirect influence was very important. African American churches were far less otherworldly in 2010 than they were in 1960, and almost all saw a vital connection between their work and the liberation of African American people. If the contribution of the black theology of liberation to this movement toward this

---

33. Lincoln and Mamiya, *The Black Church,* 187.
34. Paris, "Overcoming Alienation in Theological Education," 184.

transformation is not clear, we should remember that all theology reflects changes taking place deep in the structures of Christian life. If, when we get sufficient historical distance, we judge that black theology reflected rather than implemented change, its importance for theological education would not change. After all, that is the same judgment that scholars reached about Schleiermacher's romantic theology.

The African American theology of liberation's impact on the larger academy was considerable. Although American theologians read and studied the Latin American theologians of liberation, African American liberation theologies provided much of the language and model for other minority theologies. Without the work of African American theologians, for example, neither feminist nor Latina/Latino theology would have taken the course or had the success that these theologies did.

The black theology of liberation was part of a larger movement that we might call African American Christian studies. To be sure, much of the postwar study of the African American church followed an agenda set by the black theology movement. Scholars hoped to show that resistance to oppression, whether open or covert, was a mark of African American church history from the beginning.[35] While scholars had long appreciated the political dimension of some of the spirituals, they have recovered other aspects of the history of the connection between African American religion and work for black liberation and autonomy. African American theological scholars began discovering distinctive patterns of pastoral care and nurture that enabled people to build strong personalities. In turn, a deep sense of self-esteem enabled African American people to survive in very hostile environments.

Yet African American Christian studies were not only reflections on liberationist themes. In the 1960s, only a handful of monographs existed; by 2012, there were a number of standard reference works as well as monographs, dissertations, and substantial surveys. Slavery and slave religion have received fuller treatment, as has the period immediately after the Civil War. Important past leaders in the African American community, including Bishop Henry McNeal Turner, and some contemporary leaders, especially Martin Luther King Jr., have received careful attention. The post-Civil War period in African American religion has received a more sympathetic reading, and we have a picture of the changes in African American religion over the last half century that is often carefully nuanced to show the diversity and disagreements among African Americans.

African Americans have been interested in Africa and its religious practices since slavery times, and many of the most significant new directions in religious and theological studies have dealt with the influence of Africa on religion around the world. Scholars have explored such questions as the survival of African religious customs with research conducted in the United States, the Caribbean islands, Brazil, and Africa. Peter J. Paris's *The Spirituality of African Peoples* located many common themes that run throughout religion in both Africa and the African Diaspora. Interestingly,

---

35. See, for example, Wilmore, *Black Religion and Black Radicalism*.

while some advocates exaggerated the continuity between ancient Egyptian and Sub-Saharan African experiences, scholars became aware that Egypt in fact transmitted many African contributions to other ancient societies, including to Israel.

Perhaps most important, the study of the African American church moved beyond sociological studies into investigations that relied on humanistic interpretation.[36] As an academic discipline, the study of African American religion has matured. The Gardner Taylor lectures at Duke Divinity School, one of the earliest series in African American religious history, beginning in 1976, illustrate this growth. Initially, these lectures were primarily concerned with proving insight into the civil rights movement and the new black theology. As time has passed, their scope has expanded.[37] In many ways, these changes have reflected the development of the field into a classical liberal art that provides people with a variety of resources for exploring the meaning of the human condition. One can no longer think of American experience in any period without taking into account classical African American interpretations of that experience.

Scholars have noted the influence of African American Christianity on American Protestantism as a whole. Contemporary Evangelical praise music, for example, reflects the evolution of African American gospel, and most contemporary hymnals contain African American music, including "Take My Hand" and "Peace in the Valley," both by Tommy Dorsey, as well as traditional spirituals. More Evangelical congregations and Christian radio stations draw on a full range of contemporary African American musical expressions. The popularity of many charismatic religious practices, including raising the hands in prayer, is also an example of the influence of African Americans on the larger religious culture.

Teachers and Administrators

The 1970 conference noted three general goals for African Americans in theological education, apart from influence on the curriculum. These were the increase in African American enrollment in the MDiv program, an increase in the number of African American faculty, and an increase in the number of African American administrators. A historian might tell the story of these goals numerically, using the data published by the Association of Theological schools, perhaps presented in graph form. I have not adopted that form of presentation. Rather, I am more interested in locating what I might call a turning point in which the first generation after the civil rights movement begins to give way to a new generation that defined its understanding of theological education in different ways. To me, it seems that the decade of the 1990s marks such a

---

36. Lincoln and Mamiya, *The Black Church*, set a high standard for sociological study of the African American church. I would argue that this work also incorporates many of the more humanistic perspectives of recent scholarship.

37. The speakers at these lectures have included Gardner Taylor and Jeremiah Wright.

period. After and during the 1990s, African American students, faculty, and (to a lesser extent) African American administrators were no longer unusual in predominantly Euro American theological institutions. In simple terms, African Americans became a normal part of theological schools. They met the same entrance requirements as their Euro American counterparts, and schools hired African American scholars increasingly because of their expertise in the central or core disciplines. As Barbara Wheeler and others have noted, if the key to promotion in theological faculties is whether a person teaches in an area prized by an institution, then the important change was that African American scholars moved from the edges of seminaries' concerns to teaching courses at the center of their curricula.

What tipped the scale in that decade was twofold. Perhaps most important, although many African Americans continued to live in poverty, the combination of new opportunities, affirmative action, and raising numbers of high school and college graduates worked together to create a much larger and stronger black middle class. Not surprisingly, this middle class was often more churched than the African American community as a whole. While this new middle class continued to appreciate many marks of African American life, including music, they wanted more from their preachers. In fact, they were getting more. According to Jones and Mamiya, the majority of African American clergy at the time of their survey (1990) had college degrees, and in the more middle-class African American denominations, the college degree was normative. Once the congregations attained this point, the process was similar to that earlier experienced in such predominantly white denominations as the Methodists, Disciples of Christ, and American and Southern Baptists. This is almost a settled principle of seminary history: as the educational level of congregations rise, the education level of the ministry rises to the same or a greater level. African Americans may be passing through this process more rapidly than their white denominational counterparts since they have not had to found their own schools in order to participate.[38]

The numerical growth of African American students in predominantly Euro-American seminaries slowed experimentation with programs for folks who had not graduated from college. Among the most important of these were the Black Ministries Program at Hartford Seminary, New York Theological Seminary, and at Fuller Theological Seminary. They taught these programs at the undergraduate level with provisions for students to use their credits towards college degrees at other institutions.

---

38. The importance of the African American middle class for theological education is easy to overlook. Andrew Young has noted: "In all of this, a particularly heavy responsibility falls upon us as black Christians. For we, as black Christians, are among the affluent of the world, we are richer than anybody else on the face of this earth other than white Christians, and when you talk about the collective gross national product of a black America, you are talking about a gross national product of 147 billion dollars, annually, which is greater than the GNP of Canada, and greater than the GNP of all five Scandinavian nations combined. We are not poor, we who are black Christians" (Young, "Recent Directions in Black Theological Education," 108).

New York Seminary also experimented with a graduate program, initially offered in conjunction with New Brunswick Theological Seminary, shaped around the needs of African American pastors. One of the most interesting experiments in alternative forms of theological education was the Lilly Project at Colgate Rochester Divinity School in the late 1970s. The project combined presentations by the seminary's faculty with listening sessions with local African American pastors. One weakness of the experiment, at least in retrospect, was the conviction of the Euro-American faculty participants that European theology, particularly in the area of biblical studies, constituted a norm that African American pastors needed to appropriate. Unfortunately, the Euro-American faculty failed to realize that their own historical critical methodology was only one of the resources that they might have used for fruitful dialogue.[39]

The African American pattern of preparation for ministry not connected to postgraduate education moved out of the seminaries into the Bible schools. This was largely true, also, of Euro-American denominations. African American pastors entered Bible schools and Bible colleges in increasing numbers. This was particularly true of African American Pentecostals, who shared a Bible Institute tradition with their Euro-American counterparts.

Other consequences of the new African American middle class were equally important. Particularly among congregations in the free churches, dual affiliation with a Euro-American denomination became more commonplace. Both American and Southern Baptists experienced an increase in the number of dually affiliated churches as well as an increase in the number of predominantly African American churches. The United Church of Christ also had a significant number of new predominantly African American congregations. One attraction of dual affiliation was the greater range of denominational services available, including those provided by pension boards. Another effect was to encourage seminary enrollment and degree completion. The schools increasingly made this possible by offering part-time and other alternatively scheduled programs. Most seminaries, for example, adopted block scheduling and had a majority of their students enrolled part time. Many taught some courses as intensives.

In the 1990s, African American and Euro-American Evangelical Christians became aware that they shared much joint territory. One of the traditional emphases of African American churches was the need for strong families and strong family values, and Evangelical churches and seminaries shared this value. Moreover, the common interest in evangelism and missions often forged a bond. Gordon-Conwell was one of the leaders in reaching out to African Americans. Shortly after the two seminaries

---

39. The story of the Lilly Project is told in Wilmore et al., "Black Pastors/White Professors." In the introduction, Wilmore writes: "The judgment that the white teachers did not use all the resources available to them in white theological education is my own. To me, and this reflects my own evangelical bias, the rich biblical resources being produced at Evangelical seminaries might have formed a foundation for more useful educational dialogue than the more Germanic methods favored by the CRDS-Crozer faculty" (85).

united, the school gave its former Philadelphia campus to a school devoted to the education of African American leaders, and its first extension campus was in downtown Boston, convenient to Boston's large African American community.[40] Fuller Seminary also was a pioneer in developing programs for African American students. Further, Euro-American and African American Evangelicals began to look and feel more alike.[41] Many Evangelicals, influenced both by their own history and by exposure to Two-Thirds World liberation theologies thorough the Lausanne movement, became deeply socially concerned.[42] Both African American and Euro-American evangelicals adopted such forms of worship as praise bands, gospel and contemporary Christian music, and raised hands in worship. The preaching styles also came closer together. Unlike earlier periods of cross-fertilization, such as in the early days of the Pentecostal movement when the two races discovered that they could not work together, this period seems to be one in which the discovery of common elements is easier.

Theological schools actively sought African American faculty from 1970 onwards. In the difficult economic period of the 1970s and 1980s, searches were easier to declare than to fill. Many initial appointments were in part-time positions that despite promises that these might become full faculty hires, tended to remain part time. Some of the junior faculty recruited found themselves forced to do two jobs for one salary. As junior faculty members, they were part of the increasingly elaborate tenure processes that demanded more and more research, especially in the form of publications. African American teachers also had the job of serving as unofficial deans of African American students, advising African American students on their course of studies, encouraging them when the work became difficult, helping with placements, and often serving as recruiters. Together with learning the new profession of teaching, this was too much for any one individual. In the midst of these job-related stresses, African American professors, especially in predominately white institutions, faced the heavy burden of dual citizenship. Lawrence Jones observed:

---

40. Geyer, "Black Theological Education."

41. More than one thousand people attended Atlanta '88 a meeting of African American Evangelicals to plan for the evangelization of African Americans. The movement was related to the Lausanne Conference Movement. Like much American evangelicalism, Billy Graham had great influence. Graham had been among the first Euro-Americans to welcome African Americans to share the spotlight with him. Howard Jones began his work with Graham in 1957.

42. White US liberation theology tends to be allied more or less with various forms of liberal theology. While this is occasionally true of Two-Thirds World liberationists, it is more rare. Most Two-Third World liberationists often share the biblically based evangelicalism of the missionary movement, especially, of the missionary movement after the withdrawal of the Mainstream American churches in the 1960s. The various Lausanne documents, available online, reflect both a deep concern for the spread of the gospel and a commitment to a faith-based liberation movement. Interestingly, the Cape Town Commitment lists the fruits of the Spirit as "justice, compassion, humility, integrity, truthfulness, sexual chastity, generosity, kindness, self-denial, hospitality, peacemaking, non-retaliation, doing good, forgiveness, joy, contentment and love." It is no accident that justice comes first.

> As has been intimated above, perhaps the greatest risk to which the black scholar is subject in a predominantly white institution is that of becoming isolated in his new environment. To sustain the nurturance that comes to one from his ethnic community imposes the necessity of "shuttling" back and forth, of living in two worlds. He must establish and maintain an identity in the community where he works and where he may live, and he must cultivate his ties in and with the community to which he commutes.[43]

Many young African American scholars did not cross the tenure bar. As schools reached a critical mass of African American teachers and students, however, a more normal academic life became possible. By 1990, as with African American student enrollment, a more equitable future was in sight.

African Americans have made slower process in administrative positions. In part, this slowness was a residue of America's racist past, but it also may involve more long-range changes in academic life. Both the presidency and the deanship have passed through a process of professionalization that requires an increasingly long period of preparation. Although these positions have always required a senior leader, the various routes to the position have become more complex. If this observation is accurate, the number of African American deans and presidents should increase as those faculty appointed in the 1990s and 2000s reach professional maturity in the 2010s.

Viewed from the perspective of fifty years, African Americans, particularly those in the middle class and in predominately white denominations, have made significant gains. African American students and faculty are present on almost all campuses, and many African American churches are more open to seminary-trained pastors than before. Although not integrated into the seminary curriculum in many schools, African American studies have had a remarkable record of success. Scholars know more about the history of African American religion than before. If the seminaries have not completely resolved their problems with racial issues, they have made some progress.

WOMEN

At first glance, a discussion about the inclusion of women in a chapter that features racial and ethnic minorities seems out of place. After all, women were and are a majority of all Americans and almost all American demographic categories. Yet, women and minorities were linked in the Rights Revolution that began in the 1960s, and the various civil rights acts included the cause of women with others seeking inclusion in American society. The sixties were particularly important for women. The birth-control pill appeared in 1960; Betty Friedan's *The Feminine Mystique* in 1963, and the Civil Rights Act of 1964 prohibited discrimination because of sex along with discrimination because of race, ethnic origin, and religion. In line with other minorities,

---

43. Jones, "To Seize the Times," 334.

strong women leaders emerged to direct a very strong feminist movement that used many techniques pioneered by African Americans in the pursuit of their rights. The women's caucus joined black and other minority groups at ecclesiastical meetings, and ATS included women among underrepresented groups. Women seminary administrators and occasionally faculty met together to plan strategies to advance the cause of women in the two related professions of ministry and seminary instruction.

The apparent retreat of women from the workforce after World War II concealed long-term changes in the American economy that made the one-income family, except for short periods, outdated. The post-World War II prosperity that made it possible for many women to stay at home in the 1950s ended in the 1960s and 1970s. The period that followed saw real incomes decrease while the cost of everything from gas to food increased. The term *stagflation* best described the situation. Americans suffered the curse of inflation without the blessings of a booming economy that had accompanied inflation in the past. The hidden but real decline in male head-of-household wages also made female employment more necessary. The question was not so much, would women find such employment? but, would that employment be in traditional women's jobs, or in occupations traditionally held by men? Women, whether they wanted to or not, had to work outside the home in order for the family to maintain a middle-class lifestyle and especially to afford college for children. The mechanization of the home made this female employment outside the home almost inevitable. Increasingly after the Second World War, even modest homes had washing machines, clothes dryers, electric or gas ranges, vacuum cleaners, and, as time passed, also such innovative technologies as freezers, microwave ovens, and other labor-saving devices.

Changes in family life also encouraged occupational changes for women. Artificial birth control, widely practiced in the 1920s and 1930s, became more effective as manufacturers improved older technologies, based on mechanical blockage of the union of sperm and egg, and physicians developed newer medical approaches, such as the birth-control pill. Despite strong opposition by Rome, American Catholic families also adopted these practices. Whatever moralists and church leaders might say, the use of artificial means of birth control was the norm among Catholic middle-class and want-to-be middle-class families.

The expansion of education during the period encouraged women to enter new fields. Despite shifting demographics that seemed to predict an academic depression, colleges and universities entered new markets and entered a period of sustained growth. Women were the most obvious new market. Already blessed with a substantial high school graduation rate, they entered higher education in record numbers. The reasons for the growth were both obvious and not so obvious. The most obvious reason was that the college degree, often followed by professional certification, was the ticket to a better-paying and more satisfying job than those available in the so-called pink ghetto. Women sought education, in other words, for many of the same reasons that men did, and the abiding love of learning was not the primary item on that list.

At the same time, the sexual revolution and continuing economic problems made early marriage less attractive to both sexes, and high divorce rates made marriage at any age a less secure way to personal and economic security. Middle-class people, especially middle-class women, were seeking solutions to economic and social dilemmas, and education provided a possible way forward. Rising divorce rates also meant that even traditionally inclined women needed a second string for their bow. Heavy federal expenditures in education—including direct student aid, student loans, and work-study programs—were further incentives for women to take this road to professional advancement.

Admission to Seminary and to Ordination

Entry into seminary and into ministry followed these larger social trends. Women entered seminaries in significant numbers in the 1970s and 1980s, and by 1990, they came to be between one-third and one-half of seminary enrollments. Many Mainstream seminaries reported that the majority of their students were women, as did the influential university-related schools. Not surprisingly, the increase in female enrollment came at the same time that male enrollments declined after the Vietnam War. There were more places than applicants. John Fletcher believed that "the growing numbers of women in many of these schools obviously saved some {seminaries] from closure or merger."[44] Not surprisingly, seminary administrators were passionate advocates of women in ministry. Further, the seminaries had diversified their programs. Earlier, the schools had offered only the basic degree, the Bachelor of Divinity (after 1970, the Master of Divinity) and the Master of Religious Education. The latter degree had been almost a women's ghetto, enrolling the bulk of women students and providing one of the main opportunities for women to serve on faculties. To these, seminaries added a number of Master of Arts degrees, all of which required courses shared with the Master of Divinity curriculum. Even if a female student entered one of these Master of Arts programs, the seminaries encouraged her to transfer to the Master of Divinity and complete an additional year of study. The needs of seminaries and the needs of women came together. Another change benefitted both female and African American seminarians. Increasingly, schools admitted part-time and older candidates. These changes enabled women, especially those who had raised their young children, to enter seminary and to combine seminary either with family responsibilities or with other employment. The advent of distance education in the 2000–2010 decade would further expand these opportunities.

The popularity of professionalism in American culture further advanced the cause of women in both church and academy. Although the professional ideal originated in aristocratic cultures, its modern rendition held that entry into a position depended on

---

44. Fletcher, "Theological Seminaries in the Future," 76.

the knowledge appropriate to that occupation. If a person trained as an accountant, then they were qualified to work as an accountant. Professional training trumped other requirements for a position. Although the churches retained other criteria for ministry, the professional model dominated the Association of Theological Schools, especially during the period in which Jesse Ziegler was executive director, and set the stage for the seminaries' accommodation to larger cultural trends. The professional model also had considerable influence on the churches that hired seminary graduates. Since 1960, the denominations have moved steadily toward more professional placement procedures that stress abilities and achievements over recommendations and connections. As a consequence, the old-boys' networks that earlier played significant roles in clergy placement had their influence reduced, if not removed. Perhaps on the negative side, more bureaucratic structures reduced seminaries' influence on the placement process.

Official ecclesiastical restrictions on the ordination of women, at least among Mainstream Protestants, fell comparatively rapidly. Pamela Salazar reported that

> By 1970, ordination was a possibility in the American Lutheran Church, Lutheran Church in America, Southern Baptist Convention, United Church of Christ, American Baptist Convention, United Presbyterian Church, Christian Church (Disciples), Presbyterian Church U.S.A., United Methodist Church, Reform Judaism and Reconstructionist Judaism (its seminary was opened in 1968). Still excluded, among mainline denominations, were Episcopal, Roman Catholic, Orthodox, Conservative Jewish and Orthodox Jewish women.[45]

The issues in the remaining denominations varied. In the Episcopal Church, the issue was more a matter of churchmanship than biblical interpretation. Many Episcopalians understood their church, not in the terms of the Protestant Reformation, but as a historic Catholic church, united in faith and practice to the Roman and Eastern Orthodox churches. To break with the tradition of an all-male priesthood, consequently, was to step aside from this larger ecumenical consensus. In England, this consideration delayed women's ordination until 1996. The battle among American Episcopalians was colorful. A series of irregular ordinations and intense ecclesiastical debates revolved around the question of whether these ordinations were invalid or only irregular. The process finally resulted in the official approval of the ordination of women in 1976, although with an exemption for conscience that allowed individual bishops to refuse to perform the ritual. The Church repealed this exception, increasingly not used, in the 1990s with little fanfare.

Vatican II may have indirectly affected the Episcopal debates. In the wake of the Council, many observers believed that Rome would approve women's ordination in the near future, and some of the Roman church's most able women prepared themselves

---

45. Salazar, "Theological Education of Women," 74. This article has an excellent bibliography on the issue.

for ordination by enrolling in seminaries and divinity schools. However, those who hoped that the Roman Catholic Church might soon adopt women's ordination were bitterly disappointed. Paul VI maintained the need for all-male priesthood and made his position known both within and without the church. A more definitive no was on the horizon. The 1978 election of John Paul II marked a general Catholic movement in a more conservative direction. Influential Catholic theologians, especially those connected with liberation theology, were publicly criticized, as were the Jesuits. In 1994, John Paul II declared that the all-male priesthood was part of the church's constitution. He wrote:

> Although the teaching that priestly ordination is to be reserved to men alone has been preserved by the constant and universal Tradition of the Church and firmly taught by the Magisterium in its more recent documents, at the present time in some places it is nonetheless considered still open to debate, or the Church's judgment that women are not to be admitted to ordination is considered to have a merely disciplinary force.
>
> Wherefore, in order that all doubt may be removed regarding a matter of great importance, a matter which pertains to the Church's divine constitution itself, in virtue of my ministry of confirming the brethren (cf. Lk 22:32) I declare that the Church has no authority whatsoever to confer priestly ordination on women and that this judgment is to be definitively held by all the Church's faithful.[46]

His successor, Benedict XVI, reaffirmed this position, both as Prefect of the Congregation for the Doctrine of the Faith, and later as pope. Although Rome was not involved, St. Meinrad's dismissed M. Carmel McEnroy, RSM, for her participation in a public protest of the Church's official position. Such actions indicate the seriousness with which some American seminary leaders (including supporting bishops) took the papal position.[47] American Orthodox churches embraced a similar position.

An indirect result of the Catholic rejection of women's ordination was the significant number and importance of Catholic women theologians, including Rosemary Ruether and Mary Daly, who began and often stayed Roman Catholic. While one does not want to minimize the intellectual resources of their women—and these women were highly trained and acute thinkers—the passion of their position may have owed much to their constant awareness that their Church had largely rejected their work

---

46. John Paul II, *Apostolic Letter Ordinatio Sacerdotallis of John Paul II to the Bishops of the Catholic Church on Reserving Priestly Ordination to Men Alone*.

47. See *Academe*, "Report," for the results of the AAUP investigation of the case. There were many issues in the case. The Women's Ordination Conference, understandably among the most vocal participants in the investigation, undertook to secure signatures to an open letter addressed to the pope and the US Conference of Catholic bishops. The letter, asking for continuing discussion of the question of women's ordination, was published in the November 4, 1994, issue of the *National Catholic Reporter* and was signed by well over a thousand individuals and groups. One of the signers was Professor McEnroy. This act was cited in the letter dismissing her from her faculty position.

and, perhaps, equally important, their aspirations. One wonders if, given a different decision by Rome, they or their students might not have climaxed their careers with high ecclesiastical office.

The other major American religious bodies to reject women's ordination absolutely were the Southern Baptist Convention and the Lutheran Church–Missouri Synod. Unlike the Episcopal and Roman Catholic debate, the Southern Baptist debate revolved almost entirely around the Bible. Throughout the raucous debates of the 1980s, Conservatives and Moderates clashed frequently on the issue of women in ministry. Progressive Southern Baptist churches had ordained women since the 1960s, and the seminaries did not have formal gender restrictions on enrollment in their various degree programs.[48] Such Moderate leaders as Randall Lolley of Southeastern Baptist Theological Seminary and Roy Honeycutt of Southern Seminary led the battle for women in ministry.[49] With the Moderate defeat, Conservatives moved quickly to exclude women from leadership positions. The new president of Southern Baptist Theological Seminary, Albert Mohler, forced the resignation of Molly Marshall Green, a tenured professor of theology. Other SBC seminaries followed his lead. In 2000, the Convention modified the Baptist Faith and Message, its confession of faith, to affirm that only men can serve as pastors. Southern Baptist women seeking pastoral ordination, consequently, moved either to the Cooperative Baptist Fellowship or the Alliance of Baptists. Currently, more than 40 percent of the enrollment in seminaries related to the Cooperative Baptist Fellowship is female, a percentage similar to that in Mainstream schools. The Lutheran Church–Missouri Synod, which went through a passionate debate early in the 1970s, was not the scene of a major controversy explicitly over this issue.

With the exception of the African Methodist Episcopal Church, African American churches have not generally ordained or welcomed women in leadership positions. Pentecostal churches have also resisted the ordination of women. While these churches, often for reasons of polity, have not followed the Southern Baptist and Catholic pattern of adopting formal documents, the resistance to women in positions of pastoral leadership remains.

The question of why these groups have resisted women's ordination is complex. Aside from a pervasive biblicism, often exaggerated by outside observers, these groups had their own internal social dynamics. Both African Americans and Pentecostals

---

48. To be sure, women were encouraged to take the MRE degree, and what was often called the MRS and other seminary programs had a distinctly feminine focus. In many ways the seminaries, at least in the 1970s, were far ahead of general denominational opinion in the 1970s. This would radically change in the aftermath of the controversy in the 1980s (see below, chapter 5). The Cooperative Baptist fellowship and its seminaries have continued the more open policies of the older moderate party, and the percentage of women enrolled in schools related to it approaches the national average.

49. To be accurate, conservatives did not oppose women in ministry but women in positions of pastoral authority and in the diaconate. Everyone in the Convention, however, knew that "women in ministry" was a code phrase for the ordination of women to the pastoral office.

tended to draw their membership from less prosperous segments of American society, and the meaning of women's employment in those social strata was far different than it was in the middle- and upper-middle classes. The traditional family, with a working husband whose wife could afford to stay at home, was often a real aspiration for members of these groups. Womanist theologians, including such influential seminary teachers as Katie Cannon, Delores Carpenter, Jacquelyn Grant, Daisy Machado, and Elizabeth Conde-Frazier, have helped American theological educators to realize that not all women's experiences fit the larger Anglo-American pattern. Social location and race, as well as gender, count in understanding how churches and others conduct their business.

In the long run, the debates over ordination were less important than a psychological change that occurred among American women, especially middle-class, Euro-American women. They came to see that ordination and a career in the church was possible and desirable and that they had important allies in attaining this goal. Changes in seminary life, particularly a new openness to part-time and commuter students, also made significant contributions.

Yet the debates over ordination were significant. Do the Roman Catholic, Southern Baptist, Lutheran Church–Missouri Synod, and Evangelical cases represent a broader split among American Christians? Barbara Brown Zikmund noted that the decision to ordain women was part of a larger debate about the churches' approach to modern life. She wrote:

> In recent decades the ordination issue has become much more than a question of the status of women's leadership in the churches. It involves the basic ways Christians understand gender in church and society . . . The conflict is between those who want their denomination to display one sort of organizational identity in the modern world, and others who want their denomination to display another sort of organizational identity. Denominational rules about women's ordination give symbolic messages to the world, pointing to (or away from) the "broad liberal agenda associated with modernity and religious accommodation to the spirit of the age"[50]

Zikmund's argument also includes local congregations. The core factor distinguishing denominations endorsing women's ordination from those opposing it is their general response to modern cultural humanistic liberalism. Denominations that resist gender equality in ordination resist more than the single issue of women in pulpits and at altars.[51] A link exists between women's ordination and other political, cultural, and religious issues that divide Christians and churches. In this sense, the ordination of women is part of the larger so-called culture wars that divide American churches and

---

50. Zikmund, "The Protestant Women's Ordination Movement," 943.
51. Lehman, *Women's Path into Ministry*.

political parties. People opposed to women's ordination or uneasy about it often are pro-life on abortion and strong on other family-related issues.[52]

A common perspective on these issues has created an informal alliance among conservative Evangelicals and Roman Catholics that has influenced theological education as a whole. In 2008, for example, an alliance of Catholic and Evangelical schools defeated a revision of the ATS standards that required the inclusion of women in seminary leadership positions. While this alliance has not prevented ATS from being a bully pulpit for women's issues, the alliance has been strong enough to allow individual schools to define their own approach to gender issues.

Yet the denomination positions on women's ordination have not necessarily determined seminary policies or strategies. Among conservative Protestants, most seminaries serve an ecumenical public that includes people with many different denominational and confessional allegiances. If the women that they educate elect ordination, that decision was not the result of the seminary's official policy. The schools provide education for the profession of ministry; the churches provide authorization for ministry. A school may support women in ministry without necessarily affirming the ordination of women to the ministry of Word and Sacrament. Further, Evangelicals have historically employed large numbers of women in their vast missionary and parachurch subculture. Those organizations—which carefully do not call themselves churches—have needed increasingly sophisticated leaders and managers, and the Evangelical seminaries have educated women to take those positions. The megachurches, usually but not always nondenominational, are similar to other parts of the Evangelical subculture. Although the principal pastor of a megachurch is usually male, the ministry of those churches often involves a large professional staff, including people who specialize in youth work, in ministry to divorced people, in religious (pastoral) counseling, and in education. Women fill and have filled many of these positions. Evangelical seminaries offer a significant number of master's degrees for those seeking employment in these roles. Evangelical seminaries also train women for service as chaplains. Like Roman Catholic institutions, conservative Evangelical seminaries have hired women as seminary instructors.

The response of Catholic schools to women has been complex. Catholic schools have often administratively separated their programs of priestly formation from their other academic programs. This has enabled many to offer a standard three-year MDiv degree to their women students while reserving the canonically mandated four-year program for priestly ordination to males. Although most Catholic seminaries admit women to all master's programs, including the MDiv, the diversity of seminary programs provided a another way for these schools to reconcile their practices and their

---

52. The ordination of women was one of the issues that divided progressive and conservative Christians. Yet one should note that many conservative Christian theologians and churchmen affirmed women's ordination as an issue of social justice. While enrollment in specific seminaries might follow the larger debate over women's ordination, women were far more readily accepted in many seminaries than they were by more conservative denominations.

faith commitments. Catholic theological schools, further, have included women faculty, although generally not hiring women in the same proportion as men.

Evangelicals and Catholics share another characteristic. Like Evangelicals, the Roman Catholic Church has a vast array of organizations, ranging from hospitals and other charities to colleges and universities. When priests were plentiful, the Church often employed priests and women religious to administer these agencies. Yet many of these ministries were technically lay ministries, requiring neither ordination nor formal vows. As the number of priests and women religious declined, the Church opened many of these positions to laypeople. Women, not in orders, have served as teachers in Catholic schools; as chaplains in hospitals, colleges, and universities; and as charity administrators. The shortage of priests also created many new positions in local Catholic parishes. Catholic women performed many tasks traditionally done by priests, including serving as liturgists and parish administrators. Naturally, seminaries saw the theological education of such leaders as part of their mission.[53]

The Association of Theological Schools and Women

The Association of Theological Schools has advocated for women in ministry and for women in theological education. Beginning with Jesse Ziegler, the Association has expressed its official support for women and organized events, such as conferences, for those concerned with women in the leadership of theological institutions. During the 1970s, two issues of *Theological Education* were devoted to issues raised by the women's movement, and the journal has continued to publish important work on women's place in theological education. Meetings of women administrators, held in conjunction with the biennial meetings of the Association, have provided an occasion for women to network with each other, and the ATS leadership has identified and promoted women with the capacity to lead in theological education. Two studies of women in academic administration, both written by Barbara Brown Zikmund, have identified the problems that women administrators have faced.[54] Successive editions of the standards have urged schools to work towards greater representation of women in faculty and other positions. The Association itself has an affirmative action policy, and the leadership has carefully included women in its own leadership and on the very important visiting teams that evaluate schools for accreditation and reaccreditation.

The Association has also recognized and encouraged important women leaders. Barbara Brown Zikmund's career illustrates the importance of the ATS connection for a woman in theological education. A minister in the United Church of Christ and a graduate of Duke University, Zikmund was trained as an American religious historian.[55] She seemed destined to spend her career as a teacher in that discipline.

53. For the complexities of Catholic theological schools, see below, chapter 4.
54. Zikmund, "Walking the Narrow Path"; Zikmund, "Three Coins in the Fountain."
55. In addition to numerous articles, her writings include Zikmund et al., *Clergy Women*; Zikmund

However, while she was teaching at Chicago Theological Seminary, the Pacific School of Religion, the largest seminary related to her denomination, tapped her to serve as its academic dean. After leaving Pacific School of Religion, she became president of Hartford Seminary, where she guided that school in a difficult period of transition and financial hardship. Zikmund served as the first female president of the Association of Theological Schools and in a variety of other ATS positions. A person with a keen intellect and good administrative skills, Zikmund would have been prominent as a theological educator even without her ATS connection, but her role in the Association both provided other women with an important voice in theological education and gave her needed support in her career.

Another female leader who received strong support from the Association was Barbara Wheeler, who began her career at Union Theological Seminary in New York, moved to the Boston Theological Institute, and later became president of Auburn Seminary. Auburn, like Hartford, was a unique theological school that provided a variety of educational services for the Presbyterian churches of northern New York State, as well as continuing-education programs in conjunction with Union Theological Seminary, whose campus it shared. Wheeler first became involved in the larger work of the Association as an evaluator for the Lilly Endowment, where Robert W. Lynn was vice president for religion. Wheeler worked closely with Jackson Carroll on the first evaluation of the Doctor of Ministry degree, and she collaborated with David Kelsey on the evaluation of the Basic Issue program. In the process, she became one of the best-informed people about American theological education. Aided by a grant initiated by Craig Dykstra, Lynn's successor at Lilly, she led Auburn to establish the Center for the Study of Theological Education, which periodically reports on different aspects of theological education, such as on students, teachers, and finances. The Center is also one of the primary consultants in the field of theological education.

Just as that decade was important for African Americans in theological education, so the 1990s marked a watershed in the relationship of women to seminaries. By this point, women were a substantial minority or even a majority in many theological schools and were increasingly at home in seminary culture. This was also true in the Association of Theological Schools, an organization that largely reflects the views of seminary executives. In the Association, women leaders—such as the Canadian Dorcas Gordon and Virginia Theological Seminary's Martha Horne—rose more or less in parallel with their male counterparts in experience and institutional location.

Women were fortunate to have their revolution occur when it did. During the 1970s and 1980s, the Association of Theological Schools, although greatly enriched by the presence of Catholics and Evangelicals, was firmly under the control of progressive Protestants. Not only were the principal officers representatives of that point of view, but the more progressive seminaries still were recognized as the organization's

---

and Manschreck, *The American Religious Experiment*; Zikmund, *Hidden Histories in the United Church of Christ*; Zikmund, *The Living Theological Heritage of the United Church of Christ*.

intellectual leaders. Participation in the women's revolution came naturally to the organization's leadership, and they supported it by encouraging women as well as by including women in the standards.

The Reception of Women in Churches and Theological Education

What kind of reception did women get in theological education? Particularly in the 1970s, women reported considerable resistance to their being there, particularly in the form of demeaning remarks and exclusion from key discussions. There are some cases where arguably women appointed as junior faculty did not receive tenure due to gender-related discrimination. Often the failure of some women to attain tenure was related to the expectation of schools that female faculty would shepherd other women, including some high-maintenance students, through the program. Particularly in the early days, female faculty and administrators served as representatives of women, expected to make the case for their own gender as well as to demonstrate their own competence. Affirmative action was both a blessing and a curse. While affirmative programs may have helped some women get positions, in the minds of critics, the suspicion lingered that they had not been chosen because of their merits, but because of their gender.

Susan M. Shaw and Tisa Lewis provided a detailed study of the reception of women in their account of women graduate students at Southern Baptist Theological Seminary just before the Moderates lost control of that institution. The women that Shaw and Lewis interviewed deeply appreciated the support that President Honeycutt and the vast majority of the faculty provided them during that difficult period. Yet they also noted that even Camelot had its difficulties, including some cases of apparent sexual harassment and numerous problems adjusting to a pervasive male atmosphere. In many ways, their balance of appreciation and challenge may have been typical of women students before high female enrollments in the 1990s and 2000s changed the atmosphere of most Mainstream seminaries.[56]

Many women in the first generation of women clerical leaders reported also resistance to their service, particularly by fellow clergy. Interestingly, however, they trace many of their problems to doubts that had to do with their own inner need for a visible confirmation of their call, for evidence that they were doing things right. Such evidence was hard to find. The nature of pastoral work complicated their search for assurance. The type of professional verification that, for example, a woman lawyer might receive from winning a difficult case or negotiating a major contact, or that a

---

56. Shaw and Lewis, "'Once There Was a Camelot.'" The role of women in the denomination was one of the major issues in the SBC controversy, and women students at Southern and other Southern Baptist seminaries may have experienced more tensions than their counterparts at other seminaries, particularly those more related to Mainstream Protestant churches. Conservative students were very much part of the student body at SBC schools, and many deeply resented women students, who often served as graders and research assistants.

female physician might receive from making a complicated diagnosis, is rarely available. Congregations are not structured to give professional feedback, and much less to give assurance. Most churches are small institutions that operate according to their own internal traditions and structures. In practice, this means that the leaders of these organizations, the people who might reinforce a person's sense of accomplishment, are often unwilling or unable to do so. The primary qualification for service as a trustee, lay leader, or committee member is the willingness to serve, and many local leaders may be compensating for their own (perhaps comparative) inability to succeed. Consequently, many pastors experience more criticism than honest evaluation. Nor are other means of professional evaluation readily available. Few denominations provide close supervision of their pastors, and judicatory executives have to carefully balance their responsibilities to their clergy against their responsibility to the congregations under their care. Nor is self-evaluation readily available. The difficulty that many Doctor of Ministry students have with the required evaluation of their project illustrates this problem for clergy of both genders. The most difficult part of most Doctor of Ministry projects is the evaluation of the project undertaken for the degree. The best evidence of how well women in pastoral ministry did is that churches, even those on a call system, continued to accept women as pastoral leaders. Any widespread difficulty experienced by women leaders would have resulted in a radical reduction in the number of women called to those positions. Unfortunately, mere survival in ministry, the best test of ministerial effectiveness, does not provide the psychological support that one needs in the early days of ministry.

Did the Presence of Women Change Churches and Seminaries?

Feminist theologians believed that the presence of women in theological education would have a transforming effect on the seminaries and on the understanding of ministry. In this understanding, certain gender characteristics of women—a greater reliance on colleagueship and networking; emphasis on emotional and relational forms of teaching, knowing and leadership—would contribute to a more humane approach to theological education. Women would be, in short, the means for a major reform of theological education and ministry. However, attempts to establish this have not been wholly successful. While women have often seen a difference between their style of leadership and that of their male counterparts, their male counterparts have not been as sure that such differences exist. The same has been true of women in theological-school teaching and administration.

The answer to these conflicting perceptions may lie in the plastic character of gender. While sex is binary, gender identity and characteristics are fluid and only loosely connected with sexual differences. Psychologist Carl Jung saw every individual as manifesting male and female gender characteristics. In other words, normative maleness and femaleness are difficult to define, and most attempts at definition end up affirming or creating stereotypes that do not necessarily describe any particular individual. This difficulty is particularly acute in describing the gender identity of people who are professionally engaged in religious activities. Since the mid-nineteenth century, some Mainstream American Protestants have expressed concern that the male ministry was becoming too "feminine"[57] and have argued that the churches needed to embrace a more muscular Christianity. Further, the location of many Protestant congregations in suburbs and their close relationship with child rearing has accentuated the feminine side of ministry. At least since the 1960s, churches and church bureaucracies have emphasized such traits as empathy, capacity for relationships, and cooperative leadership—all culturally more feminine than masculine. The growing female majority, especially in the Protestant Mainstream, also pressures male ministers to express their feminine characteristics. In short, male ministers often have many female gender characteristics. At the same time, the women attracted to Protestant ministry may have traits more culturally associated with masculinity, such as a need to lead, interest in abstract thought, and the like. Women and men in theological education and ministry may share more of a gender identity, particularly in such areas as leadership styles, than binary gender distinctions imply.

The Wave of Feminist Theology and Feminist Theologies

The 1970s were a decade of intense feminist activity, inside and outside the churches, as the nation struggled with such issues as the guarantees of the 1964 Civil Rights Act and the Equal Rights Amendment. As in the earlier feminist movement, women took to the streets and to the polls in an effort to further their cause. Women used many techniques earlier successfully utilized in the African American Civil Rights struggle. Many denominations saw the founding of women's caucuses, as did many seminaries. These demanded the increased admission of women, more scholarships, the hiring of women faculty and administrators who could serve as role models, and curricula changes that included women's perspectives. Another demand was that seminaries provide childcare at little or no expense to the student. As the number of women on campuses increased, seminaries had to change their physical plant, including with the construction of new lavatories or with the designation of older ones as unisex facilities. The more liberal seminaries followed colleges in integrating women and men in their housing and dormitory facilities. Most schools adopted an inclusive-language policy. These policies ranged from those that required inclusive language only for women and men to policies that required inclusive language or gender-balanced language for God. As one might have expected, whether a given policy included God tended, at least among Protestants, to follow the growing conservative/modernist division. If a school was clearly on the modernist side, the policy was more likely to include

---

57. See Douglas, *The Feminization of American Culture*; and Kimmel, *Manhood in America*.

theological symbols than if it was either Evangelical or Moderate. Many schools included women in their affirmative-action plans, and some schools, such as Wesley and Drew, went for a number of years without adding any white male faculty. Women also challenged seminary publications to include pictures of women and men together in rough proportion to their percentage of the student body.

The effects of this pressure should not be underestimated. In the 1990s, Jackson Carroll, Barbara Wheeler, and Daniel Aleshire conducted an ethnographic study of two seminaries, the names of which were carefully kept anonymous, that was published as *Being There: Culture and Formation in Two Theological Schools*.[58] The purpose of the study was to examine the ways that seminaries socialized students, but in the process, *Being There* also provided an intimate glimpse into seminary life. One thing that was evident was the extent that feminist issues affected every part of the Mainstream seminary's life, in the classroom as well as extracurricularly; also evident was the bitterness with which students debated the issues. Generalizing from these results is, of course, difficult. Although the authors believed that the schools chosen were typical of their theological orientation, individual schools respond differently to a variety of factors: geography, denominational heritage, confessional traditions, and even date of origin.[59] Yet the picture may be more generally applicable. Like the moral crusades of the last century, seminary gender issues were battles in which the victors took few, if any, prisoners.

Christian feminist theology reflected the anger of the general feminist movement and the passions aroused on many campuses by women's demands.[60] One must be careful with language at this point. The words *feminist* and *feminism* had many meanings. In their broadest sense, they could mean little more than sympathy with many of the aims and goals of the larger women's movement. By this definition, feminists could include many theologically very conservative women and men, including David Hubbard of Fuller Seminary and Randall Lolley of Southeastern Baptist Theological Seminary. The term could also include many women in theological education, whose interest in the advancement of women was strong, but whose primary concern was with their own academic disciplines.[61] Almost all women in theological education were feminists in this broad sense. On other extreme, some critics of the word appear to have seen it as virtually synonymous with lesbianism.[62] As I am using the word, feminist theologians were those who adopted one or both of these propositions: first,

58. Carroll et al., *Being There*.

59. Personal experience is, of course, not necessarily historical evidence. However, the school where I taught at the time, Bangor Theological Seminary, had few of the internal tensions pictured in *Being There*, despite the fact that the school had significant faculty members who embraced liberationist and feminist theologies.

60. Both Judaism and Islam also produced feminist theologians who followed the scholarly canons of their own religious traditions.

61. See Cannon et al., *God's Fierce Whimsy*, 8.

62. Ibid., 12

that women's insights, drawn from their own and historical experience, had something vital to say to theology that was revolutionary; second, that women's style of teaching and/or leadership should transform both seminary and church. Although feminist theologians insisted on using a variety of nontraditional sources, including novels and other secular literature, diaries and theoretical discussions, they insisted that they were following academic guidelines while transforming them. Although a few feminist theologians were self-identified Evangelicals, such as Virginia Ramey Mollenkott,[63] most were liberal or progressive Christians.

The origins of Christian feminist theology in theological liberalism are important for understanding both its methods and its conclusions. Like all liberalisms, Christian feminist theology had deep roots in the Enlightenment and its ideals of personal self-fulfillment. The most just society, consequently, was the one where individuals might actualize themselves without undue restraint either from government or—more important—from history or biology. Like many heirs of the Enlightenment tradition, they often complimented this basic ethical stance with a passion for social justice for the poor, racial and ethnic minorities, and others disadvantaged by society. Many feminist theologians saw their work as worldwide in scope and were in communication with theologians in Two-Thirds-World countries. The Enlightenment not only provided ethical passion. Feminist theologians inherited the destructive and constructive biblical criticism of the previous two centuries with its important emphasis on the historicity of texts and their interpretation. Biblical criticism enabled them to acknowledge the heavily male-centered character of many biblical texts and to interpret that focus as related to the context in which the authors wrote. Like most theological liberals, feminists believed that the essential message of the Bible lay in the radical equalitarianism and demands for justice in Isaiah and the Synoptic Gospels.[64] Equally important, feminist theologians inherited the serious conversations about the nature of religious language that had been so important in the 1950s and 1960s. Like other liberal theologians, they believed that religious language was indirect in its references. Symbol and metaphor, narrative and myth, consequently pointed beyond themselves to the Source, but they did not describe God or ultimate reality. Any particular religious language was, consequently, replaceable or correctable. As Paul Tillich had argued, symbols could and did become broken and in need of replacement or repair. For feminists, such historical phrases as "God the Father" or the "kingdom of God" were broken because they had been used by generations of people to oppress women. Given the fractured traditional symbols, what symbols might women reasonably use to talk about God, humankind, and human destiny, that were liberating for themselves and others? For some feminist thinkers, particularly for Marjorie Hewitt Suchocki, Whitehead's process theology offered a way forward by offering a metaphysical framework that redefined transcendence and immanence. God worked

63. Mollenkott, *Sensuous Spirituality*.
64. Reinhold Niebuhr employed a similar hermeneutic in his preaching and writing.

in and through the natural order and not from above or beyond it. Other feminist theologians found the various theologies of liberation more comfortable dialogue partners.

Although it may not have been the most important issue raised by feminist theologians, inclusive language was the first that was visible publicly. In part, this was because Americans were gradually becoming used to language about people being used without gender references. For instance, the word *fisherman* was replaced by *fisher*, *postman* by *mail carrier*, *clergyman* by *clergy*, and so forth. Terms such as *men*, which had been used as collective expressions for the human race, were reformulated as *women and men*. The basic idea was to remove gender differentiation from language and thus remove an inherited bias towards the male sex. As noted above, many seminaries adopted inclusive-language policies. Theologically, however, the greatest victory was in biblical translation. In 1980, The National Council of Churches Division of Education and Ministry, the owner of the copyright on the Revised Standard Version, mandated that the revisers of that edition follow inclusive language wherever possible. The resultant translation, the New Revised Standard Version, appeared in 1989, and many Mainstream churches adopted it for use in worship and religious education. The New Revised Standard Version became the Bible of choice in many theological seminaries. Perhaps significantly, the more Evangelically oriented New International Version, (the full Bible was published in 1978 and revised in 1984) did not require its translators to follow inclusive language. However, when that version was itself revised in 2008, the revisers followed similar inclusive guidelines. A vigorous debate among Evangelicals followed the publication of this new edition, and this discussion forced the translators to agree to reconsider their methods. Current research into English usage, however, sustained most of the revisers' earlier decisions. The new NIV, printed in 2011, included these. Women biblical scholars were involved in both the NRSV and the 2008 and 2011 NIV revisions.

New biblical translations and versions influenced theological education. Some seminaries and their sponsoring churches still require a modicum of knowledge of the original languages for graduation and/or ordination. Yet even in those seminaries and churches, many (perhaps most) students depend on received translations for much of their biblical and theological study as well as their personal and practical biblical study. Standard theological texts, including those in biblical studies, often cite one or the other of the primary biblical translations. As pastors, graduates tend to use the translations that they used in seminary in their own preaching, teaching, and counseling. Changes in translations, consequently, subtly change the habits and practices of churches. Inclusive language received an important, almost ecclesiastical, imprimatur.

Although seminaries appointed more women faculty in the practical fields, feminist biblical scholars had more measurable effects on theological education as a whole. Harvard's Elisabeth Schüssler Fiorenza in New Testament and Union's Phyllis Trible in Old Testament were important pioneers. Trible, a graduate of Union Theological

Seminary in New York and an able rhetorical critic of the Old Testament, was particularly sensitive to the relationship between literary forms and the meaning of texts.[65] In her principal works she asks the question of how the presence of women affected biblical stories. Trible argued that many stories, including the story of the creation and fall, and the story of Ruth, have a new meaning when scholars reexamine the gender of the participants. The traditional meaning of these texts, she argued, does not stand up to a close reading. In the creation and fall story, for instance, Eve is clearly the strongest partner and the one whose actions move the story. Regarding Ruth, Trible shows that Ruth was not the humble and submissive daughter-in-law of tradition, but a strong woman capable of making her own choices. In a sense, these stories all point to a usable past for women in some parts of the Old Testament, even in parts that historically had an interpretation less favorable to women. Trible's concept of "texts of terror" was equally important. These texts, which include such stories as Hagar and Ishmael and the story of the sacrifice of Jephthah's daughter, highlight the negative view of women in the Old Testament. Her interpretation of the Hagar story is particularly moving. In most explications of the story, Hagar's story is quickly bypassed as is the story of Abraham's sale of Sarah to the Egyptians. A careful reading of the story, however, reveals the terror of Hagar's expulsion from Abraham's camp and her own inner strength in coping with this rejection. Hagar is the only woman in the Bible to receive a blessing from God. Although the story retains its terror, Hagar emerges as an important example of God's approval of independent female action. Part of Trible's theological message is that scholars should study the texts of terror with the same careful attention that they pay to other texts, even if they conclude that modern pastors must preach against the text. Other liberation theologians found that such stories as the story of Israel's conquest of Canaan require similar treatment.

Schüssler Fiorenza's reinterpretation of the New Testament and early Christian origins focused on the need for the application of a hermeneutics of suspicion to ancient Christian literature. A hermeneutics of suspicion seeks to recover the context behind the apparent meaning of words in the sources. Thus, one might recognize the influence of social class behind certain statements about women. Categorical statements, especially those presented without evidence, also often have a meaning that goes beyond and may contradict the evident meaning. Strong statements about the illegitimacy of female leadership, thus, may reflect the existence of significant numbers of female leaders. Condemnations are not issued in a vacuum. This type of suspicion, Schüssler Fiorenza assumed, was particularly appropriate in interpreting the references to women in the early church as male writers had a presumed interest in maintaining male supremacy. From this perspective, Schüssler Fiorenza saw

---

65. See Trible, *God and the Rhetoric of Sexuality;* Schüssler Fiorenza, *Aspects of Religious Propaganda*; Schüssler Fiorenza, *The Book of Revelation;* Schüssler Fiorenza, *Bread Not Stone*; Schüssler Fiorenza, *But She Said*; and Schüssler Fiorenza, *In Memory of Her*. Schüssler Fiorenza influenced many other aspects of feminist theology. Schüssler Fiorenza was one of the founders of the *Journal of Feminist Studies in Religion*, one of the most important journals in the field.

the first two hundred years of church history as the story of a small, sectarian group that was characterized by the tendency of such groups to charismatic leadership. The movement that Jesus founded was a reform movement within Judaism that drew its adherents from among all strata of society, particularly from among women, the poor, and the marginalized. In particular, Schüssler Fiorenza noted that women were often the first people to respond to the new movement, in both its Palestinian and its later phases, because many of Jesus's teachings related to their situation. In the canonical Scriptures, after all, the women are the first to proclaim the resurrection, and the earliest churches were often house churches with female patrons. The church continued to draw its membership and, of course, its leaders from these same groups. Crucial to Schüssler Fiorenza's argument was the belief that the appeal of early Christianity did not lie in its theology, which was, after all, only slowly developed, but in its social practices.

A key element of Schüssler Fiorenza's analysis was the special role of *Sophia* or wisdom in earliest Christianity. In her view, the earliest church saw Jesus as the messenger and voice of Sophia, while the missionary church saw him as Sophia himself. In her view, the Prologue to the Fourth Gospel replaced the earliest church's emphasis on Sophia with the more masculine Logos, thus hiding the original nature of the affirmation. Other feminist theologians found this interpretation compelling.

Did women scholars change the nature and direction of biblical and early Christian studies? No easy answer can be given. Both fields are vast and international. In 1988, Elizabeth Achtemeier noted:

> The task of evaluating the feminist approach to Bible and theology in brief scope is almost impossible for several reasons. First, there is no one feminist approach to Bible and theology, so that any evaluation must discuss not a single system of thought but a multitude of various views. Second, these views are constantly changing. There is an enormous difference between the feminist writings of the 1970's and of 1989, because feminist theology is experiential and pragmatic and has been developing in theory as it has worked its way out in practice. Third, the amount of literature is enormous.[66]

These observations are still valid in the 2000s. Yet, the contribution of such scholars as Trible and Schüssler Fiorenza was a significant part of the theological discussion of the last fifty years. While they and other women may suffer the usual scholarly fate of being buried in the small print of future footnotes, the arguments that they pioneered will be part of biblical and theological scholarship for the foreseeable future.

Much more controversial were feminist attempts to redefine Christian teaching or theology. In 1960, Valerie Sawing Goldstein argued in "The Human Situation: A Feminine View" that men's and women's experiences of faith was fundamentally different. Men, she noted, tended to see pride and self-assertion as the heart of sin;

---

66. Achtemeier, "Evaluating the Feminist Approach."

in contrast, women most often sinned through self-depreciation.[67] The essay opened up the question of how far women's experience should influence Christian teaching, particularly about God. Mary Daly posed a similar question in her very provocative works, *The Church and the Second Sex* and *Beyond God the Father*.[68] For Daly, the language, particularly the symbols that presented God, were hopelessly broken by their masculine references, reflecting the patriarchic world in which they originated. Theologians needed to replace these symbols (or at least supplement them) with new symbols that reflected contemporary women's experience. Since symbols for Daly, as for Tillich who deeply influenced her early work, were dynamic realities in their own right, changing the symbolic formulation of faith would itself contribute to the liberation of women. The symbolic world in which women lived was, thus, a key to their past enslavement and their future liberation.

Rosemary Radford Ruether was arguably the most comprehensive feminist theologian, writing on topics ranging from the history of Christian-Jewish relations, feminist contributions to ecology, medieval mysticism, and women in American religious history. What unites Ruether's diverse writings is her combination of historical study and ethical passion. In a retrospective of her work, she wrote:

> Since my training was in social and intellectual history of Christian thought, I have developed my theological work out of a historical methodology. I have gradually developed a methodology for approaching a number of social issues: racism, religious bigotry, especially anti-Semitism, sexism, class hierarchy, colonialism, militarism, and ecological damage. In the context of each of these social issues, I have traced the ideological patterns in Christian thought that have served to justify violence and oppression. These ideologies take the form of variants on a single root pattern. In each case the existing social hierarchy and system of power are justified and sacralized by defining them as the order of creation and the will of God.[69]

Feminism was an important part of this broader array of concerns. Feminist theology was both an object of inquiry in its own right as and a tool for the analysis of other issues. Ruether's was a broad-based theology of liberation written from a feminist perspective. The breadth of Ruether's concerns made her one of the most important contributors to feminist theology, because her work demonstrated that changes in the fundamental symbol system had implications for how all of theology and ethics were conceived.

Sallie McFague built on the linguistic emphasis in feminist theology through a vivid sense of metaphor. Using such categories as metaphor and model, she sought to remythologize the picture of God in terms of the images of God as mother, lover, and

---

67. Christ, "New Feminist Theology."
68. Daly, *The Church and the Second Sex*; Daly, *Beyond God the Father*.
69. Ruether, "Rosemary Radford Ruether," 2.

friend. The world, she proclaimed, was God's body, and what happened in the world happened in God. This naturally implied that God was both physical and spiritual, and that the interpretation of God was the interpretation of nature. Ecological awareness was, consequently, profoundly religious. Like Rosemary Radford Ruether, who was also deeply involved in the religious dimension of ecological issues, McFague believed that this way of talking about God, with its emphasis on mutuality, was a positive contribution to the liberation of people and of nature.[70]

Feminist theology experienced two crises in the 1980s and the 1990s. The first came with Mary Daly's decision to move beyond Christianity. The second was the Re Imagining controversy.

Marjorie Suchocki recognized the challenge that Daly had presented to Christian feminism:

> The challenge is of utmost seriousness, since it is Daly's work in *Beyond God the Father* which has inspired many women to find new ways of being as Christians who are also feminists. In *Gyn/Ecology*, however, the possibility of being both Christian and feminist is radically denied. Daly's reasons need to be heard and answered, not simply at the intellectual level, but at the existential level which is at the heart of the issue. For if the question to be raised is, "Can a woman be both feminist and Christian," then it is precisely we women who identify ourselves as both who are in question. We do not simply raise the question; we *are* the question.[71]

Carol Christ and Judith Plaskow noted that Daly's action split feminist theology into radical and reformist wings.[72] As with all such distinctions, scholars can debate the nuances of this distinction; typologies can be too narrow or vague, and in this case whose work was best discussed under one type of feminism or the other is not clear. Yet Daly forced feminist theologians to decide whether they were part of the Christian tradition or not.

The split among feminist theologians occurred during one of the classical periods of American metaphysical religion—that is to say, during the period under discussion here (from 1960 to 2000). In large numbers, Americans joined such movements as Wicca and other neopagan groups, and experimented with Native American and Asian religions. These new religious movements often had female leaders who wove their rituals and teachings from diverse historical and psychological sources. The rituals were particularly important to these expressions of women's spirituality, as they often reenacted women's experience in symbolic forms, with images of birth and gestation appearing frequently. Instead of wine, many women's rituals featured the use of milk or honey. Although different groups made differing truth claims, many

---

70. McFague, *Models of God*; McFague, *Life Abundant*.
71. Suchocki, "The Challenge of Mary Daly," 307.
72. McDougall, "Keeping Feminist Faith with Christian Traditions."

New Age advocates frankly admitted that the purpose of these religious movements was to elevate consciousness.[73] The new religions had many points in common with Mainstream feminist experience: the insistence that religion reflect women's experience, the belief that patriarchy lay at the root of many of society's problems, and the need for new ritual experience of faith.

Perhaps most important, the new religions and feminist movements shared a common apocalyptic myth in which the goodness of the world at the beginning of time is lost only to be recovered at the end of time. *Urzeit* will become *Endzeit*. In the feminist and in many New Age versions of this myth, the original matriarchic societies, reflected faithfully in their religions' goddesses and priestesses, were replaced by patriarchic societies, likewise reflected in their gods and priests. Even where goddess worship had survived the patriarchic revolution, gods and priests clearly ruled over goddesses and priestesses. The most important goddesses were, of course, the earth and the moon. Since ecological destruction was part of the end of the patriarchic period, the current crisis required humanity's return to the worship of the earth and of nature to avert disaster. The goddess was essential to life in these end times.

Carol P. Christ was the leading feminist theologian to embrace a goddess theology. Christ published several collections of women's writings, and was an unofficial historian and compiler of materials for American religious feminism. During a trip to Greece, she had a profound religious experience of the goddess, which integrated her world.[74] She devoted the rest of her career and her considerable intellectual talents to a scholarly exploration of the goddess tradition. Her keynote address at the Great Goddess Re-Emerging Conference at Santa Cruz in 1978, "Why Women Need the Goddess,"[75] was a key contribution to this type of radical feminist theology. Perhaps significantly, Christ did not take a position on whether the goddess was someone or some force out there, although she did not deny it, but she did stress the symbolic character of the affirmation. Her position was consequently not far from that of other theologians who used similar arguments about all attempts to describe God in language, including the language of ritual and myth. Interestingly enough, Starhawk, an influential pagan writer, took similar positions in her popular 1979 *Spiral Dance: A Rebirth of the Ancient Religion of the Great Goddess*. Both Starhawk and Christ stressed an ecstatic spirituality in which the individual became one with the symbol that reflected their deepest selves.

The second major shock to feminist theology was the 1993 Re-Imagining Conference, held in Minneapolis. The conference was a response to the World Council of Churches' designation of a decade of solidarity with women, and it was attended

---

73. The best study of American metaphysical religion is Albanese, *A Republic of Mind and Spirit*. See also Porterfield, *The Transformation of American Religion*.

74. The story is told, among other places, in Christ, "Reflections on the Initiation."

75. This article is reprinted in Christ and Plaskow, *Womanspirit Rising*, 273–87; and in Christ, *Laughter*. See also Christ, "Heretics and Outsiders."

by over two thousand people, with Presbyterians, Methodists, Lutherans, and United Church members providing the majority of the American representatives. The Presbyterian Church provided considerable funding for the planning of the event, and other Mainstream churches either sent official representatives or provided other support. The organizers planned for the meeting to be confidential, and they urged participants to speak freely and with passion. They did so. Many participants' statements about Christology, the doctrine of the atonement, and the ritual life of the church used slang and, occasionally, profanity.[76] Although many attending the meeting found the presentations useful and inspiring, writers for conservative religious journals, including the *Presbyterian Layman*, who received full accounts of the meeting, wrote searing critiques. Opponents charged that many participants were heretical or, at best, marginally within the Christian tradition. The reaction among Presbyterians was particularly strong. The denomination lost around two million dollars in donations, had to revise its annual budget, and devoted much of a General Assembly to the discussion of the conference and the church's participation in it. Six Princeton professors—Diogenes Allen, Charles Bartow, James Loder, Ulrich Mauser, Bruce McCormack and David Willis-Watkins—authored "An Open Letter to Presbyterians: Theological Issues Raised by the Re-Imagining Conference" that explicitly named the heresies that the authors believed participants had advocated.[77]

The controversy over the Re-Imagining Conference highlighted that many leaders had spoken about their own lesbianism, and some had defined their sexual preference as part of the opposition to male domination. Feminist writers had long noted the tendency to identify all feminists with lesbianism and to use that issue to separate women from their natural allies among women and men. In *God's Fierce Whimsy*, the Mudflower Collective noted:

> For now, we will simply say that heterosexism renders lesbians the focus of extravagant fear, anger, and projection. To the extent that feminism is assumed to be synonymous with lesbianism—a false equation—all feminists (single, married, mothers, grandmothers, lesbian, straight, bisexual) can expect to receive the harsh blows dealt systematically to "castrating bitches/man hating dykes" in a male dominated society.[78]

The frank embrace of lesbianism by some participants intensified some of the reaction to the conference. Homosexuality was the hot-button issue in almost all Mainstream

---

76. The profanity made the Conference appear more theologically radical than it actually was. For example, most liberal theologians, male and female, questioned the picture of God implied in the doctrine of the substitutionary atonement.

77. See Braaten, "What Price Unity?" Braaten was in sympathy with the critics, whom he saw as speaking an important word.

78. Cannon et al., *God's Fierce Whimsy*, 12. See also chapter 6, "Trashing the Terrible, Titillating Lesbian: Dialoging on Sexuality."

denominations in the 1990s, and the conference raised that issue and, in turn, the reaction to lesbianism made other issues appear more problematic.

Did the critics adequately understand what conference participants said? In some instances, they did not. Some of the participants restated arguments long debated in liberal theological circles in new language. This was particularly true of statements about the atonement. After all, most liberals had not known what to do either with the doctrine of the substitutionary atonement or with the popular religious language about the blood of Jesus. Traditionally, liberals appealed to the teachings of Christ as the heart of Jesus's work and mission. Delores Williams, the most outspoken on the issue, may have used badly chosen language, but her Union predecessor, William Adams Brown, maintained a similar position. In that sense, the conference and the commotion that followed it were part of the long, bitter debate between modernists and traditionalists, particularly in the Presbyterian Church. Nonetheless, the conference also marked the beginning of the end of exuberance in feminist theology. Afterwards, feminist theologians appear to have become more cautious, more precise in what they had to say.[79]

One of the central emphases of feminist theology was that women's experience was an important source for theology. Initially, the movement assumed that the binary nature of sexuality made that experience uniform. African American women theologians were among the first to challenge this assumption and the historical situation. Like other African Americans, these womanist thinkers, including Jacquelin Grant, Delores Williams, and Katie Geneva Cannon, argued that white feminists were bound to their own social location, a position echoed by Latina and Asian women theologians as well. To their credit, white feminist theologians accepted the critique and expanded their concerns, and the sources that they used, to include global women's concerns. Letty Russell's global DMin program illustrates the power of this alliance. In many ways, the most successful globalization of theological education was the expanding relationships between women theologians.

Did women and women theologians transform theological education? Theological seminaries are much different today than they were in 1960, and the presence of significant numbers of women as students, administrators, and theologians is part of that difference. Over the last half century, women provoked many of the most passionate debates over theology and over the nature of the churches. And, as in all passionate debates, especially debates predicated on rights, much productive conversation and argumentation may have been driven underground, increasing the polarization between liberals and conservatives. The women's movement also influenced seminary life indirectly. As seminaries became more open to part-time commuter students, for example, more women found it possible to attend seminaries. Despite the feminist

---

79. Nationally, feminism was entering a new stage that did not continue the angry rhetoric of the movement's early years. In some ways, Christian feminism was also entering a similar stage as women increasingly entered leadership positions in the church and in theological education.

rhetoric against bureaucracy, bureaucracy appears to have made possible increasing female participation and leadership.

As with the other underrepresented groups, the category of women hid many substantial differences as the Womanist and Latina theologians noted. The category of women cut across all other American social distinctions: class, income, geographical location, race, and sexual orientation. In religion, this also meant denominational differences. The religious experience of upper-classed white Presbyterian women was very different from that of poorer African American Pentecostals. These social differences were particularly important in determining which women had access to theological programs. Generally speaking, middle-classed women primarily faced psychological and theological barriers to graduate study. The question was whether they could make it in a man's world, not whether they could pay the price of the ticket. For some women, indeed, the inherited place of women may have made theological study easier. One could attend seminary after the hectic first years of childbearing had passed and before the high-expense years of college tuition forced employment. Substantial divorce settlements also enabled some middle-classed women to study in relative comfort. The barriers for poorer women were economic and social. They also faced gender definitions that made them the primary sustainers of family life. The absence of a middle-classed woman from family life required the other family members to make changes; the absence of poorer women threatened the ability of the family to survive.

HISPANIC LATINO/LATINA THEOLOGICAL EDUCATION

During the 1960s, César Chávez and the National Association of Farm Workers were at the center of a major civil rights movement that led to a boycott on grapes that finally won a contract with the grape growers of California. Together with the rising interest in Latin American theologies of liberation, this lead to the inclusion of Hispanics among what the Association of Theological Schools called underrepresented minorities. Over the next fifty years, both by natural increase and by immigration, the Latina/Latino population has become the largest minority group in the United States. Demographers are predicting that this group will become increasing prominent in the United States. Yet, despite these facts, theological schools have done less to provide seminary-trained leadership for this group than for other underrepresented groups.

The Problem of Definition

The Hispanic community is the most complex American minority, having its own internal diversity along religious, ethnic, racial, and class lines. In some ways, the larger context of the rights revolution helped to create the category of Hispanic or Latino/Latina peoples. As people struggled for their rights in a complicated American situation, they came to see themselves as having common interests that transcended their differences. In order to claim rights and privileges, including affirmative action programs or scholarships reserved for minority groups, a group must have an awareness of its particularity.

Much the same happened in theological education. Cuban American Methodist theologian Justo L. González was a key figure in making Latino/Latina Christians aware of their common interests, and in presenting their cause to theological educators. His 1988 study *The Theological Education of Hispanics* was an important contribution to this process of discovery.[80] González was in a key position to serve as an advocate. He was a graduate of Yale in historical theology and the author of a number of books, many of which seminaries used in classes on the history of theology and the history of Christianity. He also had broad contacts within the larger Latino/Latina community. These enabled him to contribute to the founding of *Apuntes*, a journal for Latino/Latina scholars, and to be instrumental in the founding of both the Hispanic Summer Program and the Hispanic Theological Initiative. González was also a major figure in the foundation of the Asociación para la Educación Teológica Hispana (AETH), begun in 1991, a broad alliance of people and institutions committed to the improvement of theological education among Hispanics. The AETH includes Bible schools, colleges, and seminaries among its institutional members. More than anyone else, González helped to form a common identity among Latino/Latina peoples interested in theological education.

Yet language is always a difficulty when discussing ethnic identity. Each ethnic group has its own favored self-identification that reflects its own history and its own sense of identity. Although I will use *Latino/Latina* and *Hispanic* interchangeably, I am aware that the preferred self-designation varies. Basically, four primary groups compose this underrepresented minority: Cubans, Puerto Ricans, Mexicans, and other people from Spanish America. These groups have their own history in the United States.

Cubans and Puerto Ricans

In the East, where the majority of Latin American immigrants and their descendants are rooted in the island cultures of Puerto Rico and Cuba, the preferred term is *Hispanic*, highlighting the language difference between the majority and this minority. The bonds between these two groups, however, are more than linguistic. They share a Caribbean island culture that also includes peoples who live on islands where the dominant language is French or English.

Cuba and the United States share a long and difficult history. Before the Civil War, American slaveholders contemplated the conquest of Cuba and its incorporation

---

80. González, *The Theological Education of Hispanics*.

into the United States as an additional slave territory. Slavery continued to exist in Cuba until 1886,[81] making the island a retreat for former Confederates. Americans from both regions invested heavily in Cuba before and after the Civil War, and close connections existed between the Cuban business community and their North American counterparts. These connections contributed to the Spanish-American War that made Cuba a virtual protectorate of the United States. After that war, American Protestant missionaries poured into the island, establishing churches, schools, and other institutions. As in other Latin American countries, Protestants were often middle-classed and professional. During the 1950s, Americans invested substantial amounts of money in Cuban tourism, including casinos and nightclubs.

Even before Castro there was immigration from Cuba, especially to nearby Florida, and the children of the elite frequently studied in American colleges and universities. When Fidel Castro, a Marxist-Leninist revolutionary, took over the island in 1959, he confiscated much of the property of Cuba's elite as well as American investments. Castro passed laws restricting religion in Cuba and closing religious institutions. The first wave of heavy emigration from Cuba after the takeover was largely made up of professionals and successful businesspeople. Often they had substantial business contacts in the United States before they left Cuba, and once in the States, they had powerful political allies. Many of these immigrants were Protestants. Their fellow religionists provided them with important contacts, especially in educational and philanthropic circles. The second wave of Cubans was by and large not from the elite. Castro used American openness to Cuban immigrants to rid his country of many poorer people, including formerly imprisoned criminals. Further, the first wave was often significantly whiter than the second wave of Cuban immigrants, reflecting the racial composition of the older Cuban ruling classes. First-wave Cuban immigrants quickly found places in American life, including church life, and amassed considerable financial and political power. Second-wave Cuban immigrants did not fare as well since they had fewer resources, fewer friends, and a different racial identity.

Puerto Rico's history had some similarities to that of Cuba. As in Cuba, so in Puerto Rico slavery lasted past the American Civil War, not being abolished until 1873. Also, as it had for Cuba, the Spanish-American War ended Puerto Rico's relationship to Spain. However, unlike its larger neighbor, Puerto Rico became an American possession. Puerto Ricans consequently entered the continental United States as citizens with full rights, including the right to vote, and eligibility for all federal and state social programs. As they had in Cuba, American missionaries entered Puerto Rico in significant numbers after the Spanish-American War. If many Cubans settled in Florida, many Puerto Ricans settled in New York and northern New Jersey, partially because of the good airline connections between that city and the island. Conditions in Puerto Rico encouraged many to move. Following the Second World War, rapid social and

---

81. Officially slavery ended in 1880, but slaves were not completely free until 1886. It was a gradual emancipation plan.

cultural changes destroyed both the traditional rural economy and the newer colonial economy. As in other rapidly changing rural environments, the choice for Puerto Ricans was not whether to move to a city but only to which city. New York and San Juan were attractive options. In many ways, twentieth-century Puerto Rican migrations were similar to those of earlier immigrants from Poland. The Poles were likewise colonials (Poland was divided between Germany, Russia, and Austria-Hungary) fleeing massive social changes.[82] Large-scale farming in rural Poland made traditional village life impossible for many. For the Poles, the choice was often between Warsaw or Berlin and Chicago, just as the Puerto Rican choice was between New York and San Juan. Also like the Poles, the migrants from Puerto Rico often had little capital other than their own labor.

Mexican Americans, the Southwest, and Subsequent Migrations

The story of Mexican Americans in the Southwest is longer and more complex. Long before Mexico ceded the territory to the United States after the Mexican-American War, the area was ethnically mixed. In addition to Native Americans still living in traditional or semitraditional ways, the region had a mixture of Spanish settlers and converted Native Americans, similar to the population of metropolitan Mexico, as well as Anglo-American settlers in Texas and California. To serve this population, the Mexican Catholic Church sent a number of priests and missionaries and created a nascent ecclesiastical system. Two streams of migrants entered this region after the Mexican–American War. One was composed of Euro-Americans and African Americans who were moving west; the other was composed of peasant farmers and others moving north from metropolitan Mexico. The two streams of migration had much in common. In both the United States and Mexico, the industrial and agricultural revolutions of the nineteenth century disrupted rural life and led to internal migrations.

A major period of immigration from East and South followed the American Civil War. The rapid expansion of the US railroad system made it easy for people to go west, particularly to California and Texas. Yet the railroads moved much more than people. First, the rails made possible the exploitation of the vast mineral wealth of the region. Second, especially after the invention of the refrigerator car, the railroads encouraged the development of large-scale agriculture and ranching. Both of these, particularly the latter, were labor intensive. Mexican migrants provided the unskilled labor force. The migrants constituted a new social class. Unlike many of the older Mexican settlers, some of whom owned vast estates, the new migrants were poor both

---

82. The comparison between Puerto Ricans and Poles also carries over into theological education. Although more Polish priests immigrated to the United States than did Puerto Rican priests, recruiting a second generation was difficult. In comparison, the Germans, who came supported by strong European missionary societies and often with substantial capital, very quickly became rivals of the Irish for the domination of American Catholic institutions.

before and after their resettlement. Further, unlike many of the Grandees,[83] they were Native Americans or mixed Spanish and Native American. This encouraged a system of segregation throughout the area. Although the signs read, No Mexicans, everyone knew that the "Mexicans" so excluded were those of visibly different race—the brown skinned—and not the descendants of wealthy Mexican settlers who called themselves Spanish.

César Chávez and the National Farm Workers Association (later Union) represented this first wave of Mexican immigrants. Significantly, traditional Catholic values shaped much of Chávez's thought and provided much of his appeal to migrants. Although Chávez had little formal education, his public speeches showed theological sophistication. Chávez took the best insights of traditional Catholic culture, particularly the Franciscan tradition, and combined these with demands for contemporary action. He often used fasts to popularize his message.

The second period of heavy migration was the post-World War II California boom. Again, this migration came predominantly from the Eastern and Southern United States, although there were significant numbers of Asians as well. The new defense and, later, technology companies, provided the economic incentive, and some California suburbs looked like the transplanted Midwest villages that they were. Another major component of the new migration was composed of people from the American South who settled predominantly in Southern California. Like the internal American migration to Chicago and Detroit, this movement was part of a larger swarming of Southerners to America's large cities. A significant proportion of these Southerners were African Americans, who quickly discovered that the California miracle did not include them; such cities as Los Angeles, long considered the Whitest city in America, developed large ghettos.

The new migration from the Mexican South differed from the earlier migrations. Whereas earlier immigrants had tended to follow the crops, the new immigrants often found themselves living in barrios or ghettos. In part, this ghettoization resulted from the increasing mechanization of farming, but it also reflected other trends in Western life that replaced human labor with machine labor. The problem was complicated by the presence of many immigrants who lacked the proper paperwork for permanent settlement in the United States, and who were consequently not eligible for many anti-poverty programs. In many ways, the new barrio immigrants represented a different challenge for churches and consequently for theological educators. Whereas the first wave of rural immigrants continued rural patterns of life, these newer immigrants faced painful adjustments both to a different culture and to urban conditions.

---

83. Grandees were Mexican landowners who stayed in the Southwest after the Mexican-American War. Most held very large landholdings and were part of the aristocracy. Almost all grandees were of pure Spanish descendent and considered themselves to be racially superior to the Native Americans and the Native American Spanish Mexican. Euro-Californians also considered them to be white and the signs prohibiting Mexicans did not apply to them.

The larger patterns of migration into the Southwest influenced the establishment of theological schools. The wave of settlers from the Midwest established a significant number of theological seminaries, many of which were located in and about Berkeley, that reflected the liberal culture of the Upper Midwest. Evangelical seminaries, such as Fuller and BIOLA, served the new migrants into Southern California. Texas, which shared many migration patterns with California, had large Baptist, Methodist, and Disciples of Christ seminaries, as well as smaller Episcopal and Presbyterian schools. Roman Catholics also had a variety of diocesan and order seminaries in the region. In many ways, these schools faced a challenge analogous to segregation in the states of the Old Confederacy. While few were officially segregated, these schools primarily served the immigrants from the East and South. They made little or no attempt to include the Mexican migrants and, in fact, discouraged their enrollment.

Other Latin Immigration

The changes in the 1964 immigration law also encouraged a variety of immigrants from Central and South America that did not share the history or the perspectives of the existing Cuban, Puerto Rican, and Mexican communities. The 1964 Act, for example, gave privileged status to people and their families where one member of a family had a skill or profession needed in the United States. Physicians and engineers were particularly favored under the act. The family provision may have provided a much broader gate than the authors of the act originally intended. Yet the one thing that appears clear is that the new immigration from Latin America, including Brazil, has been broader and more socially varied than the more traditional migrations from Cuba, Puerto Rico, and Mexico. The Hispanic community, like the Euro-American community, has become an ethnic community of many colors.[84]

Missions, Heritage, and Schools

The most abiding influence on Hispanics was the Spanish Empire. During the sixteenth and seventeenth centuries, the Spanish established an empire that included metropolitan Spain, most of Central and South America, the larger islands in the Caribbean Sea, and the Asian Philippine Islands. The vast extent of the empire created its own problems. Metropolitan Spain was not populous enough to settle such an extensive territory. The Spanish settlers actually formed a small but very important elite, throughout the Empire. This small minority faced the problem of incorporating the existing populations into their culture and establishing a common culture and common values. Religion was very much the handmaiden of this cultural imperialism, and the Catholic Church enforced and then reenforced linguistic and cultural norms.

---

84. Hernández and Davies, *Reconstructing the Sacred Tower*, 4–7.

The result was that the empire had a thin covering of Spanish culture and language that stretched over a variety of indigenous cultures. The final product was an apparent cultural unity that concealed much diversity. When the Spanish Empire dissolved because of revolutions and wars, diverse nations took its place. These nations also had their own ethnic diversity. Almost all had pockets inhabited by Native Americans who retained their own languages and cultures. In addition, slavery, especially in the Caribbean Islands and in the Portuguese colony of Brazil, added an African dimension to the region.

Catholicism in Latin America and the United States

Wherever the Spanish and Portuguese went, they established Catholicism. Secular clergy from the old country often served the colonists, while members of religious orders worked at converting and Christianizing the indigenous peoples. The clergy frequently held mass baptisms, similar to those in medieval Europe. Although these conversions were not in-depth—the church barred many recent converts from Communion—the hope was that subsequent instruction would complete the process. Although the Jesuits, Franciscans, and Dominicans worked hard at Christianization, they never had sufficient workers to educate the converts in the new faith. The religious orders also saw themselves as the protectors of the Native Americans against enslavement by Spanish colonists. Although the religious orders did not always succeed in protecting the indigenous population, the theologies and charismas of the religious orders provided a foundation for some later Latin American thinking. Gustavo Gutiérrez and Leonardo Boff, leading liberation theologians, were members of religious orders.

Spanish and Portuguese imperialism made Latin Americans, whatever their racial or ethnic background, heirs to a rich European tradition in theology, literature, and science. Spanish classics are also Latin American classics. In that sense, Latin America is part of Western culture and subject to the same cultural, political, and moral pressures as that larger culture. The Catholic Church was, of course, the primary medium of culture as well as religion. The Latin American educational tradition begins in the sixteenth century with the establishment of universities in Central and South America. While poverty often limited access to such advanced educational resources (both for clergy and for laypeople), universities have always been a feature of Latin American intellectual life. Much of the shock that Latin American immigrants to the United States feel—a pervasive sense of exile—comes from separation from this cultural heritage. In that sense, Hispanic theological education in the United States is about the transmission and appreciation of culture as well as the transmission and appreciation of faith or theology.

The colonial pattern of insufficient priests and religious has continued until today. Throughout its turbulent history, the Catholic Church in Latin America has relied on missionaries from abroad, especially from Europe, to carry out its ministry, a pattern repeated in the Southwest United States. Further, the role of the Church was often a central issue in the passionate political battles that pitted progressives (influenced by American and Enlightenment ideas) against traditionalists. As a result, most Latin American countries had a secular professional class that tended toward anticlericalism, and all Latin countries had periods when the progressives forcibly separated church and state. Marxism has also had a strong anticlerical influence. The struggles in Mexico, one of the primary homelands of American Hispanics, have had a particularly sharp anti-clerical edge. The Mexican constitution outlawed religious orders and foreign priests, secularized education, and seized much Catholic property. The law confined worship inside church buildings. A religious revolt, the revolt of the *Cristeros*, forced a relaxation of the anticlerical laws, although it was not until 1992 that the state allowed the Catholic Church to own property. Naturally, recruiting new priests and religious has continued to be difficult. Consequently, Latin America suffers from a chronic shortage of priests and other religious leaders

The shortage of priests means such Catholic practices as regular attendance at mass, confession, and catechesis are less common than in other Catholic countries. The Council of Trent had less impact on Latin American Catholicism than on European Catholicism as a whole, and often medieval religious practices continued longer in the region than elsewhere.[85] Consequently, much Latin American Catholic practice has focused on a vibrant popular Catholicism that exists largely apart from hierarchical control. Ordinary believers often invoke Mary and the saints for the healing of illnesses and other earthly needs, and other popular religious practices are in evidence. The most popular icons are those of the suffering Christ, often depicted, as in Spain, bloodied and beaten.

Significantly, Latin American Protestants also stress lay leadership and non-priestly (if not antipriestly) forms of ministry. For American missionaries in the nineteenth and early twentieth centuries, the Catholic Church was, not only religiously, but also politically, dangerous. Like other contemporary Protestants, the missionaries believed that the priests and hierarchy supported politically repressive governments and blocked social and political progress. Imported American Protestantism, thus, had its own anticlerical emphases. Further, although the missionaries tried to transfer American Protestant systems of church government, small congregations often were led by laypeople. Latin American Pentecostals, like their North American counterparts, stressed the immediate inspiration of the Holy Spirit as the criterion for ecclesiastic leadership. In both Latin America and the United States, the advocates

---

85. Protestant church histories have frequently neglected the reception of the degrees of the Council of Trent in favor of a view of papacy in which Rome speaks and all is accomplished. In fact, Trent took centuries to implement, and important pockets of medieval Catholic practices existed even in such Catholic and bureaucratic countries as France.

of Hispanic theological education have had first to establish that there is need for a ministry and then to establish institutions to educate people for that role.

The comparative unimportance of priests in Latin American Catholicism has made the task of incorporating Latin American minorities into North American Catholicism difficult. Generally speaking, previous waves of Catholic immigrants came to the United States accompanied by their own priests and with young men anxious to enter the clerical ranks. Members of religious orders were especially important in the establishment of ethnic ministries. Not only did some priests come with the financial and other support of missionary orders, but also both men and women religious actively recruited the next generation of Catholic leaders.

The missionary societies also helped shape immigrant religious practice. The societies affected almost every area of immigrant Catholic life: devotions, mass attendance, societies, parish schools, orphanages, hospitals, and poverty relief. In part because of their labors, ethnic Catholic communities in the United States often had a higher rate of religious practice than was customary in their homelands. Ethnic priests and religious served their coreligionists as organizers and community leaders, building a unique American Catholic culture. Latin American Catholics generally did not fit this pattern in either practice or piety. Justo González estimated that as many as 90 percent of Hispanic Catholics only attend church for rites of passage.[86] This posed new problems for the North American Catholic leadership. They had not only to recruit and educate new ministers to serve the immigrants; they also had to provide many of the basic structures of ecclesiastical life. Since there was little or no help from the homeland, they had to do so within existing American Catholic structures and practices. These structures were not necessarily Latino/Latina friendly. They had evolved to serve other ethnic groups and then to serve the new, more middle-classed Catholicism that followed the Second World War. New structures had to be developed.

Despite these problems, the North American Catholic experience with immigrant populations made a major contribution to the Church's attempts at creating a Hispanic priesthood. The Catholic Church has had a long and successful history of providing theological education for a number of immigrant groups. Despite the differences, many similarities between this immigration and earlier waves of new settlement existed. The battles over ethnic parishes in the last century left the Church open to the use of a variety of languages and religious practices. Further, important social parallels exist between the new immigrants and the old. For example, many earlier ethnic groups, including those who came to the United States after the Irish Famine, the Poles, and the Sicilians were poor and largely uneducated and were part of the worldwide migration from the countryside to the new metropolitan areas. They were peasants in two new homelands: in the new city and in the new nation. Of the two, the city was the one that most affected their lives. Early Catholic investments in the city, however, provided the new Hispanic immigrant communities with an important

---

86. González, *The Theological Education of Hispanics*.

foothold. Although it was often painful, parishes often transitioned from an old ethnic membership to a new Latino/Latina membership. If many of these church buildings had many signs of their earlier identities, including religious art rooted in the parish's earlier identity, the new Latin American immigrants did not have to bear the cost of constructing new buildings.

Likewise, the Catholic Church already possessed extensive facilities for training priests.[87] This provided a resource that the Church might adapt to the needs of Hispanic students. The Program of Priestly Formation[88] permitted and permits considerable variation in such areas as language and religious customs. The 1990 edition's emphases on traditional devotional practices permitted seminaries to adopt Hispanic devotional practices, particularly those related to Mary, as part of their program. These practices give the seminaries a comfortable feel. Although Catholic seminary leaders have long debated the use of languages other than English in instruction, some seminaries have accommodated to the needs of this new minority. Such seminaries as Saint Mary of the Lakes, near Chicago, and St. Vincent de Paul in Boynston Beach, Florida, have established bilingual programs, and other Catholic seminaries, particularly in the Southwest, have added courses on the Hispanic Church, and conduct part of their program in Spanish. Many Catholic seminaries actively recruit candidates from abroad for their programs. Seminaries with a missionary charisma or tradition, such as the Chicago Theological Union, provide extensive orientation to issues of Hispanic Catholicism, both in the United States and abroad.

Particularly important in creating Hispanic ministries are the actions of the American Catholic Church designed to make the Church more hospitable to Latino/Latina peoples. National Catholic interest in Hispanic ministry began with the establishment of an office for Spanish-speaking Americans under the National Catholic Welfare Council, the precursor to the National Conference of Catholic Bishops.[89] After Vatican II, this interest grew. Adapting church practices to a national Church's internal diversity seemed as mandated as the worldwide Church's adoption of its own rituals to local cultural situations.

The Medellín Conference of Latin American bishops, held in 1968, projected a new future of the churches of the region and—indirectly—also for the churches of the Hispanic Diaspora in the United States and Canada. We can suggest that the Medellín Conference had two important consequences for American theological education. First, Latin American Catholic theologians were part of a larger, churchwide theological discussion. Although their writings provoked strong negative responses from Pope Paul VI and especially from John Paul II and Cardinal Ratzinger, Medellín marked

87. See below, chapter 4.
88. See below, chapter 4.
89. The United States does not presently have a provincial organization. The United States Conference of Catholic Bishops provides much of the national leadership that one might expect to be conducted on a provincial level, including the approval of the Program of Priestly Formation.

Latin America's theological coming of age. Translators quickly translated theological texts, originally written in Spanish or Portuguese, into English, French, and German. Protestant and Catholic American seminaries, even very conservative schools, routinely assigned these works. Some knowledge of liberation theology became a mark of theological literacy. Second, the new theology served as a wake-up call to American bishops, who were increasingly interested in how to minister to the Hispanic minority in their own Church. Interestingly, the idea of base communities, very similar to the small groups, which have historically sustained many American Wesleyan congregations, became popular as an American home-missionary strategy as well as part of the outreach of Latin American churches.

PADRES (Padres Asociados para Derechos Religiosos, Educativos, y Sociales), an organization founded in 1969 largely by priests in the San Antonio area, became a national voice for Hispanic, particularly Mexican American, concerns in the Catholic Church. In many ways, PADRES was an organized pressure group that provided fellowship for its members and a means for expressing their concerns to the hierarchy. Many of the priests involved in PADRES, including Patrick Fernández Flores, who became Archbishop of San Antonio, Texas, understood the inner politics of the church and, consequently, could exerted considerable influence behind the scenes.

In an effort to promote a more active outreach to Latin Americans, the United States Conference of Catholic bishops have held four "*Encuentros.*" (1972, 1977, 1985, and 2000). *Encuentros* has no precise English translation. We might translate it as gathering, conference, or even as seminar, but no translation adequately captures the meaning of the term. Perhaps, the best is consultation since the *Encuentros* have adopted recommendations that later informed Catholic practice. The first three consultations aimed at the creation of a Spanish speaking ethnic church within the American Catholic Church. In so doing, the *Encuentros* repeated much of the common wisdom about the need for an increase in the number of Hispanic priests and bishops and for the need for seminaries to adopt policies and curricula that more open to Hispanic interests:

> We request that seminaries and houses of formation revise their programs and allow an atmosphere that is more favorable to various cultures and socioeconomic levels; more open to theologies that respond to Hispanic reality, and more flexible towards a pastoral training that will serve Hispanics.[90]

Despite the controversy over liberation theology, elements of this theological emphasis continued in these meetings and later meetings. The second and third *Encuentros* reflected liberationist perspectives, including requiring all those participating to be part of a base community. In line with other liberationist themes, the consultations placed considerable emphases on *pastoral de conjunto* or shared ministry. Even without these theological roots, the often priestless character of Latin American Catholicism made

---

90. Cited in González, *The Theological Education of Hispanics*, 46.

shared ministry necessary as did the Second Vatican Council's emphasis on the work of the laity.

Unlike earlier *Encuentros*, the fourth, held in 2000, had a different vision. Unlike earlier meetings, the Bishops did not confine the 2000 meeting to Hispanic Catholics. The 1999 invitation from the Bishops urged other Catholics to join Hispanics in the ministry to this community. The theme of IV *Encuentros* was, as the title of the parish guide put it, *Many Faces in God's House: A Catholic Vision for the Third Millennium*. Although this was a restatement of the ideal of *pastoral de conjunto*, articulated at the III *Encuentros*, the IV *Encuentros* expanded the original idea to include the diversity of both Hispanic and non-Hispanic Catholicism. The IV Encuentros signaled that the Church had moved from seeing Hispanics in terms of its older practices of Americanization to a stance that affirmed diversity as its ideal pastoral practice. In affirming the normative quality of Catholic diversity, the Fourth *Encuentros* affirmed that the various ethnic components in the church were partners, committed to complementary action. The United States Conference of Catholic Bishops went on to affirm that this diversity was essential to its mission and its character.

In 1987, the bishops issued their National Pastoral Plan for Hispanic Ministry. In 2002, reflecting the Fourth *Encuentro*, the bishops issued *Encuentro and Mission: A Renewed Pastoral Framework for Hispanic Ministry*. The Renewed Pastoral Framework moved from Remembering the Past with Gratitude to Living the Present with Enthusiasm to Looking Forward to the Future with Confidence. There was both a sense of accomplishment and an acknowledgement that the Church's work with Hispanics needed to be carefully rethought, especially, in the light of Catholic losses to other religious groups. Interestingly, the document affirmed three aspects of American Hispanics: the awareness of the Church's prophetic character, the belief in *pastoral de conjunto*, and the practice of consultation. While consultation might seem to be part of the *pastoral de conjunto*, the bishops had in mind a model more clearly based on Latin American liberation thinking:

> Since the I National *Encuentro* (1972), Hispanics have used a methodology of pastoral discernment that focuses on the needs and aspirations of the faithful, judges that reality in light of the Scriptures and Tradition, and moves into transforming action. This methodology, known as SEE—JUDGE—ACT—CELEBRATE—EVALUATE, has generated critical thinking and a strong commitment on the part of the leadership to the mission of the Church. This methodology has also led to strategies and pastoral actions that are relevant, timely, and effective. The components of celebration and evaluation have been very helpful in renewing and redirecting the efforts of Hispanic ministry over the years.[91]

---

91. *Encuentro and Mission*, item 5.

The primary shift in the document was toward the New Evangelization. Whereas the earlier plan had emphasized *missions*, a term that included both the gathering of souls and social witness and formation, the Renewed Framework stressed the importance of the awareness of God's presence:

> This process generates a *mística* (mystical theology) and a spirituality that lead to conversion, communion, and solidarity, touching every dimension of Christian life and transforming every human situation. As we have said in our national plan for evangelization, *Go and Make Disciples*, "The fruit of evangelization is changed lives and a changed world—holiness and justice, spirituality and peace."[92]

Hispanic priests were to share the religious, as well as the cultural, practices of their people. While this document cast the New Evangelization in Hispanic terms, other documents made similar demands on all students, regardless of ethnic background.

Has the Catholic Church in the United States found a model of theological education equal to its vision of Hispanic ministry? The steady increase in the number of Latino priests and bishops indicates some measure of success. Yet as *Encuentro and Mission* made clear, the church has continued to lose ground among people of Latin American descent. The continual rush of new immigration from Spanish-speaking countries may have hidden many changes in the Hispanic community from the Church and from historians. Every Hispanic community has newly arrived immigrants, the children of immigrants, and a third generation—a generation that has only lived in the new country. For the third generation, the imperative to maintain the language and culture of the old country becomes less pressing, and the consciousness of difference from other Americans is less highly developed. Hispanic ministry is very different, depending on the specific generation under discussion.

Those Hispanic Americans who entered the United States after 1980 came when the American Catholic Church was in disarray. The former network of parochial schools staffed by religious always on the lookout for vocations, of high schools and college seminaries, and Catholic youth organizations has weakened and in many areas of the country is almost nonexistent. The Catholic missionary orders, which staffed many American ethnic parishes and Catholic charities, are much fewer in numbers and resources. If the Catholic parishes (and some of the Protestant congregations) are the only stable institutions in many Latina/Latino communities, they are very different churches that those who greeted the Irish, French Canadians, Poles, Italians, Hungarians, Germans, and others earlier.[93] Fewer missionaries, fewer sisters, and far leaner resources are available than were provided to earlier generations. While the numerical declines among non-Hispanic Catholics have made the mission to Latino/Latina people more visible to the hierarchy, that same decline reduced the resources

---

92. Ibid.
93. See chapter 4, below.

available for effective theological education. One must also remember that factors weakening vocations among Catholics in general, such as the priest sexual scandals of the 1990s and 2000s, have also affected Hispanic communities.[94]

Protestantism: In Latin America and the United States

Protestantism initially entered Latin America in conjunction with American military and economic power. Protestants cheered the Spanish-American War and before the ink was dry on the treaties, the larger American Protestant churches had divided the new mission field among themselves. American missionaries entered Cuba and Puerto Rico, where they established churches and educational institutions. Although these schools usually had programs for those who had not graduated from college or university, the clear ideal was the American theological school. More equalitarian denominations, including the Baptists, were more open to a variety of educational approaches, although they also supported seminaries.

The Evangelical Seminary of Puerto Rico was among these missionary institutions. American missionaries from the largest Anglo-American denominations—Baptists, Disciples of Christ, Methodists, United Brethren, and Presbyterians—founded the school in 1919. In 1982, it received full accreditation from the Association of Theological Schools. Southern Baptists maintained the Seminario Teológico Bautista de Puerto Rico, which primarily served people on the Associate and Diploma levels. The Evangelical Seminary of Cuba, founded by the Methodists, Presbyterians, and Episcopalians in 1946, likewise had a measure of success. The Castro revolution dealt the school a serious blow: however, when Cuba loosened its restrictions on religion in the 1990s, the seminary began a slow, steady recovery. Other Protestant seminaries in Latin America were considerably smaller and less numerically successful. One of the sticking points between Latino/Latina pastors and American theological seminaries has been the inability of the seminaries to find a way to credit work done in these smaller schools.

American Presbyterian missionaries to Guatemala Ralph Winter and James Emery developed Theological Education by Extension (TEE) to expand the work of their small school by taking the instructors, not the students, to the villages. The model enabled the smaller seminaries to multiply their witness. TEE has spread throughout Latin America and Africa and has had considerable influence in Asia.

As Catholic seminaries have, Protestant seminaries with a strong missionary tradition have developed programs for Hispanic students, which provide both instructors and courses adapted to leaders in their denominations. Thus Eastern, Northern,

---

94. The difference between the Catholic Church at present and the Church in earlier periods needs to be repeated. While early immigrant communities were poor, the Church was developing rich resources with the aid of European coreligionists. The result was a Catholic Church in the United States that was more widely supported than the Church was in the European homelands.

and Andover Newton, among Baptist schools, have developed their own Hispanic programs and have appointed strong Latina/Latino faculty. Andover Newton, for example, elected Orlando Costas academic dean and appointed Robert Pazmino to its tenured faculty. Evangelical seminaries, such as Fuller, with strong ties to the Lausanne movement, have also reached out with various programs into the Latina/Latino community.

The Baptist Seminary of the Americas, founded by Southern Baptists as Mexican Baptist Bible Institute in San Antonio, provides an interesting glimpse into the development of missionary education sponsored by American denominations. It began as a typical Bible Institute with instruction only in Spanish, and for a number of years functioned without state or regional accreditation. However, in the 1990s, enrollment fell, and the school was on the verge of closing. Energetic leadership realized that the school had to change its basic model. While many students came from Spanish-only backgrounds, the churches that employed them were often bilingual communities. The new goal was for graduates to be bilingual. Consequently, the school adopted a program of intensive English-language instruction and sought state accreditation in 2003 for its degrees. The Baptist Seminary of the Americas currently offers a Bachelor of Arts degree, and many of its graduates enter Baptist theological seminaries.

Mainstream and Anglo-American Evangelical seminaries offer many opportunities for Latina/Latino students. Many of their graduates enter Hispanic ministries in predominantly Anglo denominations. However, the small number of Mainstream churches in the barrios—many of which Anglos abandoned when they fled to the suburbs—limits the opportunities to serve Spanish-only or second-generation communities. Consequently, a significant number serve churches or teach in seminaries that are predominately Anglo. Theological education, thus, can serve as a way out of Hispanic ministry as well as a way into it. For some, attendance at a Mainstream seminary is a means of social advance, enabling the minister to enter Mainstream American culture.[95]

Since the 1960s, Pentecostalism has flourished in Latin America, particularly, in the slums of the largest cities. Many Latin American Pentecostal denominations are stronger numerically than their North American counterparts are. For example, there are as many members of Assembly of God churches in Sao Paulo, Brazil, as in the United States.[96] In many ways, Pentecostalism was a religion of the people who, as in North America, often had an entrepreneurial spirit. Those called to leadership often have to establish new congregations or establish new ministries in order to have

---

95. This represents part of the problem with the discussion of Hispanic Americans. Is a Hispanic American who attends a Anglo-American seminary, who graduates, and who takes a position either in a predominantly Anglo church or seminary still a representative of that minority, or is that person a minister who has migrated out of their group? We should also note that many Hispanic laypeople move into predominantly Anglo Congregations when they prosper financially.

96. Wilkie, "Tremendous Growth in Latin American Churches."

a place to exercise their gifts. The lack of structure both promotes church growth and inhibits ministerial education.

To provide training for some of their leaders, Latin American Pentecostals have established Bible institutes and schools. Often a single teacher, usually an accomplished pastor, is both the faculty and administration of these informal institutions. Like the Pentecostal churches they serve, these schools reflect the entrepreneurial spirit of their founders and often concentrate their work on how to gather new churches. In Latin America, the post-1960 expansion of higher education spurred more advanced forms of theological education among all denominations.[97] In response to this demand, North American Pentecostals maintain centers for advanced study similar to the missionary seminaries of other United States–based denominations. The Latin American Assemblies of God seminary, for example, educates people from twenty countries.

Hispanic Pentecostal immigrants brought the Bible institute tradition with them.[98] In a sense, this is to bring a form of theological education full circle. These schools are similar to Anglo Bible schools and institutions, especially when those schools were first founded, and North American Pentecostal evangelists may have founded the first such schools. In the United States, the Bible institutes are nonaccredited and do not offer degrees. A Bible institute may exist one day and not exist the next. Although Bible institutes are located wherever substantial numbers of Pentecostals reside, it is difficult to get exact numbers. No governmental or accrediting agency recognizes these schools, and no denomination has an official list of recognized schools. As many as forty such institutions may exist in greater New York City, and other major cities have proportional numbers. Like other Evangelical churches, Pentecostal congregations are the product of a faith that encourages people to develop their abilities and their skills. The people who become pastors, largely self-selected, are often people with substantial leadership experience and a strong sense of self-worth and personal importance. In many ways, these institutes are limited in what they provide their graduates:

> Despite their success, we contend, these non-accredited institutions are insufficient for the adequate education of Hispanic ministers and professors. Furthermore, their graduates may not be accepted at accredited schools, and the data indicate that when they are accepted, there are significant challenges to their academic performance. Without accredited theological degrees, Hispanics will continue to be limited in church leadership.[99]

While these limitations are most evident when Hispanics move into Mainstream churches, the lack of skills also inhibits their ability to lead in their own communities.

97. This is similar to the situation in the United States.

98. It is difficult for an outside observer to determine whether the Hispanic immigrants established Bible colleges and schools because they knew them in their country of origin, or whether they discovered them when they came to the New World.

99. Hernández et al., "The Theological Education of U.S. Hispanics," 73.

Yet, the taste of education that Hispanic Pentecostals receive in Bible institutions and schools may whet their appetites for further training. George "Bill" Webber of New York Theological Seminary realized that his seminary might benefit from Hispanic interest in more standard American credentials. New York Seminary, consequently, developed a number of programs, often marked by partnerships with other degree-granting institutions, to enable students to earn first collegiate certifications (AA and BA degrees) and later professional degrees (Master of Divinity, Master of Professional Studies, Doctor of Ministry).

The concentration of Latino/Latina Christians in Pentecostal churches raises many questions for the interpreter of theological education. Anglo Pentecostals have only recently entered into graduate theological education in significant numbers, and many of them, like their Latino/Latina counterparts, move into Mainstream churches after graduation. Are Hispanic Pentecostal students less represented in theological education than their Anglo or African American Pentecostal counterparts are? Are there factors in Pentecostalism that make theological education less attractive or less avidly sought? Perhaps the right question is not, why are Latin Americans underrepresented in graduate theological education? Perhaps the question is, why are the poor and their denominations so underrepresented?

In short, Hispanic Christians are heirs of complex religious traditions that have inherited much from both European and American sources. Much of Hispanic theological education bears the marks of the larger Christian mission to the Americas and of the Protestant mission southward. The Bible institute, after all, was a characteristic invention of nineteenth-century Evangelicalism and closely tied to the missionary awakening of the 1890s and 1900s. Pentecostalism is nowhere more reflective of its American roots than in its use of this model of training, both at home and abroad. Moreover, the missionary movement has profoundly affected both Catholic and Protestant Latino/Latina theologians. Justo González was a Cuban Methodist who spoke often of the ways that his church bore the marks of its missionary history, and Orlando Costas served as a missionary to Latin America and worked in American congregations and agencies. Catholic liberation theology, arguably the most exciting theological development in Latin America, had strong roots in the Catholic missionary movement and among missionary priests. Such former Protestant missionaries as M. Richard Shaull and Alan Neely often carried it to the United States.

Hispanic Americans and American Life: Poverty, Race, and Theological Values.

What makes Hispanic Americans a distinctive ethnic group or at least a way of identifying several ethnic groups with common interests? Samuel Solivan offers the following set of generalizations:

> We are by and large of urban character, located in the major cities of the country; of low income; predominantly Roman Catholic in affiliation; young, high school graduates; theologically conservative; and politically liberal or independent. We are also people of color ... We are a mestizo people.[100]

Solivan's summary avoids the question of native language. In regard to language use, particularly in church, some evidence exists that Latina/Latino immigrants go through the same stages of linguistic adaptation as other immigrant groups:

> Older Hispanic *barrios* in cities like Los Angeles, San Antonio, Miami, New York, and Chicago, once dominated by first-generation Spanish-speaking *mexicanos, cubanos,* and *puertoriqueños* are now dominated by U.S.-born Mexicans, Cubans, and Puerto Ricans. Even more significantly, a growing number of Latinos are not only English dominant; they do not speak Spanish at all. Furthermore, they often feel little or no allegiance to their ancestral homelands or to the cultural and religious commitments their parents or grandparents brought with them from Mexico, Cuba, or Puerto Rico.[101]

Such findings suggest that theological education among Spanish-speakers will follow the same general pattern as it did with earlier European immigrants. At first, theological seminaries, serving a particular language group, such as German speakers or Danish speakers, would offer their classes in the language of the faith community that the prospective minister was to serve. As long as the first generation was the most important part of the prospective congregation, the goal was to produce ministers who could preach and pray in the language. However, early on in the history of these schools, they recognized the importance of bilingual pastors—not to speak to the outside world, but to speak to those in the second generation and almost all of the third. Finally, as ethnic identity weakened further, the schools often merged with schools of the same confessional tradition or became traditional seminaries.

Perhaps one reason that theological educators often overlook this larger pattern is the press of new immigration from Latin America after the Immigration Act of 1964. First-generation Hispanic churches are more visible than second-, third-, or later-generation churches. As a result, many people writing about the theological education of Latino/Latina candidates speak as if the primary problem were the provision of instruction in Spanish. Most existing programs for Latino/Latina students concentrate on instruction in Spanish, although most also require some competence in English. Some of these programs also stress cultural knowledge of the broader Spanish-speaking world and of the specific area from which students come, such as

---

100. Solivan, "Sources of a Hispanic/Latino American Theology," quoted in Conde-Frazier, *Hispanic Bible Institutes,* 6.

101. Rodríguez, "Hispanic Ministry," 433.

Cuba, Puerto Rico, and Mexico.[102] Language is not the only common denominator, however, and the others also influence theological education.

Poverty

Although not all Hispanic Americans are poor, the vast majority are, and their churches are islands of stability in the urban maelstrom. Over the last fifty years, the fact of poverty has defined almost every element of Latino/Latina theological education; especially scholarships, aid for doctoral candidates, the ability to complete degrees, and the need for particular attention to the problems of urban congregations. On a deeper level, Hispanic poverty has also sparked Hispanic theologians to articulate theologies that build cultural pride and enable Hispanic churches to proclaim the gospel more adequately in their own context. If the persistence of racism has defined African American theological education, poverty has played a similar role in Hispanic theological education.[103] Along with denominational affiliation, it remains the most visible reason that "Hispanics remain the most underrepresented racial/ethnic group in ATS schools, both in student enrollment and among faculty members."[104]

Hispanics share many circumstances with other poorer Americans. They are less likely to finish high school or complete college: they have fewer role models for effective leadership; and their institutions, especially their churches, must fulfill multiple social roles. The fact that almost all Hispanic students, even those with substantial financial aid, must work, often in full-time positions, limits academic achievement. Like Baptists and Methodists a century earlier, most Hispanic students serve churches while receiving schooling. The early efforts to build a Hispanic program at Fuller Seminary reflected this reality. When David Hubbard set up the Hispanic Advisory Committee at Fuller in 1974, the seminary planned to incorporate into the program folks who had not graduated from college:

> Using as an admissions model the existing theological studies program for black ministers, a program for Hispanic ministers was introduced with entrance requirements designed to enable Hispanic pastors without baccalaureate degrees to enroll as special students. The requirements were that the pastor be at least thirty-five years old, have at least five years' experience in the ministry, be able to study English, and have the endorsement of his own denomination and of the regional Hispanic ATS committee.[105]

---

102. See above, 112–17
103. Machado, "Ethnic Diversity."
104. Hernández et al., "The Theological Education of U.S. Hispanics," 73.
105. Gay, "Hispanic Ministries," 85.

Perhaps most important, this early program permitted the student to qualify for admission into a degree program, giving its students status within their community.[106] Fuller's program also featured case studies, not only for its more formal on-campus programs, but especially for gatherings of Hispanic pastors. Case-study instruction is particularly useful where people have substantial personal experience to bring to the examination of a case.

As in the case with other minorities and women, the most important way for Protestants into advanced theological study was the increasing variety of delivery systems, especially during the 1990s and 2000s. These new systems—block classes, evening classes, intensives, and various forms of distance (online) education—made it easier for students to enroll part time while maintaining the employment necessary for family life. For pastors serving churches, the variety of ways to take classes permitted them to balance complex schedules with classes. The willingness of seminaries to allow students to attend part time—even very part time (the so-called ten-year plan)—likewise, permitted juggling of schedules. As was the case with women and African American enrollees, the declining enrollment of white males meant that only the most prestigious schools were not virtually open-admission institutions. The Catholic insistence on residence for priestly candidates and the importance of programs of formation, however, has made these modifications less important for candidates for the priesthood, although candidates for nonordained ministries have taken advantage of them.

Scholarship programs were, of course, the most direct way to address the financial problem. As in the case of African Americans, the evidence is that there was substantial interest in all levels of theological education, but that many ministers and candidates for ministry found the costs daunting.[107] Finances were also crucial in determining Hispanic interest in Doctor of Ministry programs and Doctor of Theology and Doctor of Philosophy programs. The Fund for Theological Education, which had supported very influential programs for African American students, began its Hispanic Ministerial Fellow program to help met the need, and the Pew Charitable Trust provided the initial funding for the Hispanic Theological Initiative. The Hispanic Theological Initiative provided support for three out of five years of doctoral studies, including time for the writing of the dissertation.

The poverty of Latino/Latina people worked against the scholarship programs. Once a student had graduated from college, the opportunities for personal advancement, especially for higher salaries, increased geometrically. The inclusion of Hispanics in affirmative action further increased these opportunities. With only a small pool

---

106. Ibid.

107. The most exhaustive study of Hispanic theological education, The National Survey of Hispanic/Latino Theological Education, was conducted in the 1990s under the leadership of Edwin Hernández. The results were summarized in Hernández and Davies, *Reconstructing the Sacred Tower*. The survey revealed widespread interest in graduate theological study but much apprehension about funding.

of graduates ready for seminary, every potential candidate who elected another option further weakened the effort to recruit new Hispanic religious leaders. A similar drain affected the number of ministers for the barrios. As was often the case with white Pentecostals as well, seminary graduation opened up better-paying opportunities in the Mainstream church. The tendency was to move up denominationally and then to move out of the barrio.

Race

Hispanics faced two separate racial problems. Much of the Anglo world regarded them as people of color. Especially in the Southwest, Mexicans historically received much the same treatment as African Americans in the South. Both legal and informal segregation existed, and the Whites Only signs excluded both African Americans and Latina/Latino persons. This discrimination had harsh effects on those who experienced it. The 1964 Civil Rights Act targeted the eleven states of the Old Confederacy, but many Latina/o persons lived in the Southwest where enforcement of the law and its provisions was less rigorous. Informal patterns of segregation continued long after the legal prohibition of the practice. David Maldonado, who served as a seminary professor, dean, and president, recalled the problems that he had belonging to the theological community at Perkins:

> I was fortunate in that I had a full scholarship because I belonged to the Rio Grande Conference of the Methodist Church. I had the option of working on campus—not as a research or teaching assistant, nor as a dorm monitor, but as a yardman, as other Latinos had done in the past. I chose to not mow lawns and rake leaves, but rather, to tighten my belt and study.[108]

Despite his success as a theological educator, the Methodist University Senate found that race was a contributing factor in Maldonato's 2004 resignation as president of Iliff.[109] Outside of the Southwest, racism was more subtle, but still present. A pervasive distrust of Puerto Ricans, for example, was endemic in New York City and New Jersey.

Race is also a factor in the Hispanic community. Although the Spanish were not as reticent about interracial sexual relations as the English, their colonial societies were often a pyramid of racial and class differentiation. At the top, particularly in Puerto Rico and Cuba, were the Spanish born, who held power on the islands long after revolution had expelled them from the mainland Latin republics. Under them were the rich colonials, some of whom had lived in the New World for many generations, who had massive land holdings and considerable political power in their own right. Under them, various mixtures of two (Spanish and Native American) or three (Spanish, African, and Native American) races provided the bulk of agricultural and industrial workers.

---

108. Maldonado, "Latino/a Theological Education," 28.
109. Dart, "Iliff Seminary Warned," 14–15.

Substantial numbers of Native Americans, some of whom did not speak Spanish, also continued to exist. Since slavery ended later in Cuba, Puerto Rico, and Brazil than in the mainland republics or, for that matter, in the United States, those areas had large numbers of unassimilated Africans who had their own customs and religion. In the turbulent relationships between the United States and Latin America, those of pure Spanish descent often maintained close educational, economic, and cultural relationship with the United States. These enabled those of pure descent (or those whose skin appeared lighter) to assimilate easily into the larger Anglo-American culture. In addition, substantial Italian and German colonies existed in parts of Latin America, and recently Asians have also settled in Central and South American countries. The variety of racial self-identifications among Hispanics indicates the persistence of these distinctions.

Culture and Theology

Latin America has a long history of higher education and a highly developed literary tradition. Yet in many ways, Latin America remained an intellectual province of Spain, particularly, in such areas as theology. Vatican II occurred just as Latin American theologians were beginning to develop their own theological stance. Liberation theology both reflected local conditions and hoped to offer a way out of the poverty that gripped the region. Perhaps because Latin America is so vast and so diverse, the theology of liberation was not uniform. Some liberation theologians, following European practice at the time, actively dialoged with Marxists and others interested in social change; others drew significantly from such diverse sources as the North American Social Gospel, the New Testament, and the Catholic tradition of care for the poor. Institutionally, liberation theology responded to Latin America's chronic shortage of priests and other religious leaders by developing base communities, small religious groups devoted to prayer, biblical study, and social action.

Liberation theology spread rapidly. North American missionaries, both Protestant and Catholic, carried it with them when they returned home on furlough, usually to teach in a seminary or university, and the new theology was very popular among theologians attached to the World Council of Churches. The WCC based many of its pronouncements on it. For many theologians in the Two-Thirds World, some version of liberation theology became normative as African, Asian, and other liberation theologians developed their own variations. In the United States, both black and feminist theologians drew upon Latin American and other liberationists in developing their own positions. Orbis Books, the publishing arm of the Maryknoll missionary orders, became identified with these new theologies and published many liberationist theologians.

Liberation theology deeply influenced Latina/Latino theologians in the United States, both as a source for their own thought and as an example. Liberation theology was, after all, the first Latin American theology discussed by a variety of theologians around the world, and more than any other movement, it demonstrated the power and influence of Hispanic religious traditions. Ironically, liberation theology may have had more influence in the United States, Africa, and Asia than in Latin America itself. Although the rhetoric of preference for the poor persisted, Rome pressured Latin American bishops to adopt a more conservative theological and political course.

American Latino/Latina theologians have been slower to develop their own theological literature. Justo González has consistently argued that all American theologians need to have a deeper knowledge of Christianity in Latin America. He has also been a consistent advocate of the advanced theological education of American Hispanic students.

American Hispanic theologians are beginning to band together for mutual support and to review each others' work. In 1988, they formed the Academy of Hispanic Catholic Theologians to provide a place for mutual criticism and support. The Academy publishes the *Journal of Hispanic/Latino Theology*, which presents new research and thought directions. Clear outlines of the development of the Hispanic Church in the United States have appeared,[110] and church historians have begun to move beyond the older preoccupation with the emergence of modernity in Western Europe.[111] One can expect the next generation of texts in church history and American religious history to be quite different from those of a generation ago. As in the case of feminist theology so with liberation theology, the direction of theological study seems to have changed.

Beyond Poverty, Race, and Culture.

Hispanic Americans are the most complicated of the unrepresented groups in theological education. Considered as a whole, they are just beginning to enter Bible College and graduate theological education in significant numbers. Like most minority groups, they are a complex coalition. A large percentage are Roman Catholics who have inherited a particular strain of Catholic practice that does not encourage young men to enter the priesthood or young women to enter religious orders. Latin America has a chronic shortage of priests, and that shortage has continued to hinder Catholic work in North America. Among Protestants, most Latina/Latino believers are Pentecostals, a tradition that is just beginning to develop interest in Bible colleges and graduate theological schools. This tradition also resists theological education. The ideal Pentecostal pastor is a person whom the Spirit has called and equipped for the work of ministry. The case with African Americans is also the case with Hispanics: the group most open to traditional theological education are Hispanics who are members of Reformation traditions, Baptists, or Methodists. These churches, however, have few Spanish-speaking congregations, and many highly educated ministers are lost to the

---

110. Sandoval, *On the Move*.
111. See González, *The Changing Shape of Church History*.

Latina/Latino community as they move into predominantly Anglo congregations or seminaries.[112] How many of their coreligionists will follow them in this transformation is unknown.

THE LAST MINORITY

Throughout the last decades of the twentieth century, seminaries struggled with the intellectual and institutional consequences of an increasingly diverse America. African Americans, Latina/ Latino peoples, and women all demanded places in theological education as students, faculty members and researchers, and administrators. Although progress was slow, the twenty years between 1990 and 2010 saw significant progress in these areas as the percentage of underrepresented peoples moved slowly closer to their demographic percentage of the American population. Interestingly, Asian Americans, often demographic overachievers in other areas of American education, flourished in theological education as well.

The 1990s and 2000s saw the visibility of a new minority group, Lesbian, Gay, Bisexual, and Transgendered (LGBT) persons.[113] In one sense, this group was not new. Seminary administrators, faculty, and students had always known that a certain percentage of the seminary population was homosexual, and many of these people had graduated and entered ministry. Yet, homosexual persons were not visible as homosexual persons. They were "in the closet," hidden from view, and forced to remain invisible. The reason for this lay both in long-standing social custom and in specific Scripture passages that seemed to condemn all homosexual practices.

Just as they did around the civil rights issue and the women's issue, questions about homosexuality arose first in the larger culture. During the first wave of scientific study of sexuality, researchers and therapists had created the category of homosexuality to cover a wide variety of same-sex relations. Having created a category, therapists and others searched for a common explanation for the phenomenon. The basic idea was that if the researchers might identify the origin of the behavior, they could devise ways to treat the so-called disorder. These efforts were unsuccessful. Homosexual behavior and inclinations proved to be very difficult to treat, even when therapists applied extreme forms of behavior-modification therapy. To complicate the picture, homosexuality, unlike other behavioral patterns classified as disorders, did not seem to inhibit a person's daily functioning. In simple terms, researchers increasingly

---

112. Such social mobility among denominations is very common among Anglo-Americans. Many ex–Southern Baptists are Episcopalians, and at Andover Newton, many Baptists become UCC when they note that the salaries and benefits in that church are substantially greater. The reason given for these transformations are usually theological.

113. As with other groups, language is often a problem. In this chapter, we have tended to talk about gay and lesbian persons since these are the most visible in the church debates over ordination and marriage. Yet much of the discussion also includes bisexual and transgendered persons as well. Even if not explicitly named, they should be considered part of the discussion.

concluded that homosexuality was a variation, not an aberration, and, hence, not a legitimate area for therapeutic intervention.

Advanced research often takes much time to influence popular cultural perceptions. In this case, advanced thought and popular opinion came together quickly. Just as researchers were formulating a different understanding of homosexuality, American attitudes towards sexuality changed. Despite much controversy, popular opinion came to accept premarital sexual relations, easy and quick divorce, readily available birth control, and (much more controversial) abortion. In this world of popular discourse, many came to see homosexuality more as a preference or a choice, similar to other sexual choices and hence as a private matter between consenting adults. LGBT people began to come out of the closet.

The AIDS epidemic of the 1980s accelerated this development. At first, the primary response to AIDS was fear of the so-called homosexual disease, and some pastors and religious leaders played on this fear by labeling AIDS a punishment from God for a breach of the natural law. There were some religious precedents for this approach. Victorian Christians, faced by a major syphilis epidemic, had often interpreted venereal diseases as divine punishment. This approach had less popular support than expected. Once the initial fear wore down, people became increasingly sympathetic to those afflicted by a terrifying disease. The terrors of AIDS did not seem to meet the popular belief that the punishment should fit the crime. Increasingly, gay and lesbian people became more vocal about their rights. By the 1990s, they were demanding the protection of civil rights laws, that the government provide research funds for AIDS, and that the states adopt some form of legal recognition of gay and lesbian unions.

The debate over gay and lesbian persons and religion followed almost expected culture-wars lines. Despite the passion of the debate in the churches, the issue had little effect on Protestant seminaries. Those schools that strongly supported progressive causes quickly found room for LGBT students, student caucuses, and gay and lesbian faculty. Many progressive seminaries came to see themselves as spearheads for gay rights within the church and the society. Schools that are more Evangelical tended to continue the traditional view that homosexual behavior is sinful, although most had faculty members—particularly in counseling and pastoral psychology—who presented a variety of perspectives. Only a few schools seem deeply divided. In a 1993 debate over homosexual ordination in the Presbyterian Church USA, the publication of the Princeton Declaration and a widely circulated response by twenty-five other Princeton faculty members indicated that the school had a deep internal disagreement on the issue.[114] Robert A. J. Gagnon, in *The Bible and Homosexual Practice: Texts and Hermeneutics*, published in 2001, indicated that other Presbyterian thinkers maintained substantial antihomosexual arguments.[115] The majority of conservative

---

114. *Christian Century,* "Princeton Declaration Opposes Ordaining Gays"; *Christian Century,* "Princetonians against 'Princeton Declaration.'"

115. Gagnon, *The Bible and Homosexual Practice.*

thinkers appeared to agree with Stanley Grenz; these thinkers were "welcoming but not affirming."[116] In other words, they accept homosexual persons as persons, but they continue to believe that homosexual acts are wrong. Grenz's position was in line with the general Evangelical position that God loves the sinner, not the sin, and with the actual practice of many Evangelical congregations that did not make an effort to purge their membership.

Racial divisions were also occasionally visible. African American churches in general interpreted homosexual behavior as a sin that weakened their historic crusade to strengthen the black family. As the more progressive Mainstream seminaries identified with the LGBT-liberation movement, more African Americans enrolled in Evangelical seminaries. In the United Methodist Church, both racial and regional differences appeared in every effort to modify the *Book of Discipline* with African Americans and Southern Euro-Americans and generally allied against the more progressive Northern wing of the denomination. The United Methodist Church is also unusual in that churches established by United Methodist missionaries retain their close connection with the larger church. These overseas Methodists have also allied with Southern and African American Methodists to maintain the status quo.

The Catholic pattern here, as elsewhere, was very different from the Protestant pattern. In some ways, the homosexual issue would seem far from Catholic ministerial education. Catholic ethics had traditionally dealt with the interaction of will and action. Both homosexual and heterosexual priests vowed that they would not engage in sexual behavior of any sort, and this meant that both homosexual and heterosexual practices were equally violations of the oath. The question was whether the priest had the strength of will to maintain his resolve. Ironically, celibacy may have paradoxically enabled many gay men to deal with their sexuality. By entering the celibate world, they were removed from the world's tendency to separate gay and straight.

The continuing crisis over clergy sexual abuse that rocked the Church throughout the period from 1990 to 2012 formed the backdrop for much Catholic thought about homosexuals and seminaries in this period. Understandably, Catholics asked the question of what had gone wrong that allowed such a stain on the Church's honor. For some, including some in authority in Rome, homosexual priests provided an easy answer. Fewer gay priests, they reasoned, meant fewer priests engaged in abusive behavior. On this basis, the Church began to exclude homosexual candidates from the seminaries.[117] Catholic liberals and conservatives bitterly debated whether this had any effect on the larger problem. Aside from the ecclesiastical debate, Catholic moral theology continued to affirm that homosexuality was an "objective disorder" and that the Church was opposed to any form of gay marriage.

---

116. Grenz *Welcoming but Not Affirming.*

117. Catholic theology does not permit the wholesale removal of nonpracticing homosexuals from the ministry. Once a priest, always a priest.

Yet, the generalization holds true that the gay and lesbian issue, arguably the biggest hot-button social issue in the churches from 1990 to 2012, had less effect on the seminaries than on the churches. Although some seminaries prided themselves on their comprehensive character, most theological schools are small institutions that tend to uniformity of perspective. Colleagues are almost necessarily friends, and the power of friendship and the need for faculties to maintain a unified front are important social factors in the life of small schools. If the total body of seminaries tended to reflect the larger patterns in American religious life, each particular seminary tended to reflect the views of its immediate constituency, particularly its faculty. Those who pay the piper get to call the tune.

Yet, paradoxically, the gay and lesbian issue may show the power of the seminaries. Although no one seriously believes that the prophetic statements of seminary faculties—any more than the statements of the National or World Council of Churches—directly affect congregational life, seminaries do promote slow and steady change over time. In 1990, no one would have thought that the Presbyterian, Lutheran, Episcopal, and United Church judicatories would have approved LGBT ordination within twenty years; yet, they did so, despite the loss of many members and some whole congregations. Although this change has many origins, the slow and steady effect of much progressive seminary instruction over two decades was an important factor.

DIVERSITY

The Rights Revolution in theological education has not accomplished all of its goals. Traces of historical patterns of discrimination remain and perhaps will continue for some time to come. Yet, theological schools have made significant progress toward greater inclusivity. While no one would argue that the schools have moved more rapidly than the society as a whole on these issues, they have not lagged behind. Perhaps most significant, they adopted and have enforced the recommended policies, such as Affirmative Action, that supported these changes.

In retrospect, I am particularly impressed by the contribution of Jesse Ziegler and his much-maligned professional model to this process.[118] In the key decade of the 1970s, Ziegler led the American Association of Theological Schools to take advanced positions on race and on the role of women. While the Association and individual schools went far beyond the beginnings that Ziegler gently midwifed, he did set the

---

118. When I began my career in theological education, Dr. Ziegler's reputation was at its low point. Indeed, one reason for the original Auburn History of Theological Education project was to determine how and why the grand conceptions of the learned pastor had given way to the more mundane picture of the professional clergyperson. Yet as I have studied the record more intensively, I am more and more convinced that Ziegler rose to the occasion on a number of issues, not despite the professional model, but because he was so strongly motivated to see that it was implemented. In retrospect, it is striking that so many intellectual alternatives to the professional model based their arguments on ancient and medieval philosophical perspectives.

Association and theological schools on a firm course into the future. Interestingly enough, Ziegler also presided over the transformation of the Association from an organization that largely represented Mainstream liberal Protestantism into an organization that included Catholics and Evangelicals. By the time that this internal revolution was complete, liberal Protestants found themselves a minority, albeit one with many rights and privileges, in an organization that they had birthed.

The professional model was also an important factor in the growing diversity in and among theological schools. In a sense, this was because of the logic of a simple equation: if a person has the credentials to do a job adequately, then it is a violation of that person's rights to deprive them of the opportunity to do so. If all churches did not (and still do not) accept the logic of this argument, the argument still has logical force. In that sense, professional education provided much momentum for the inclusion of women, African Americans, and Hispanics in American church life.

4 Catholic Theological Education[1]

ONE OF THE MOST difficult problems in writing the current history of theological education is that a common language often separates Protestants and Catholics. The two religious movements shared a common history before the sixteenth century Reformation, and they carried much of the language of that early period into their subsequent history. However, the two traditions then reformulated that language to reflect the profound differences between the two approaches to Christian faith. Some of these differences were matters of scale. Even in the larger Protestant states of Europe, the Protestant churches were comparatively small, with limited bureaucracies. In contrast, the Catholic Church was a multinational organization that covered several continents and required a significantly larger bureaucracy to regulate its affairs. Other differences were less visible. Martin Luther and the other Reformers were the heirs of more than two hundred years of preaching by Catholic orders, mainly in the cities. The orders trained their members primarily in universities and taught them a comprehensive body of divinity that enabled their missioners to address an increasingly educated urban population. Although many Lutheran states adopted the educational reforms of the Renaissance, particularly the study of ancient languages, the basic focus of the education of a preacher remained the university program in biblical and systematic theology. Most Reformed countries adopted the same basic approach. Only England downplayed formal divinity in favor of a more classically oriented university program, although the mandated ordination examinations implied knowledge of the university course.

---

1. The literature on American Catholic education is vast and is only sampled in this chapter. For a guide, see Carey and Muller, "A Selected Bibliography," in Carey and Miller, *Theological Education*. The works by Katarina Schuth are particularly valuable. See especially, Schuth, *Seminaries*; and Schuth, *The Reason for the Hope*.

THE CATHOLIC HERITAGE IN THEOLOGICAL EDUCATION

Likewise, post-Tridentine Catholics continued the university tradition with some countries, particularly some German states, favoring the university as the primary center for Catholic theological education. Religious orders also maintained connections with the universities for the education of their membership, and the post-Tridentine orders, especially the Jesuits, played major roles in the creation of new Catholic universities around the world. However, the universities did not have the monopoly among Catholics that such schools had among Protestants. The reasons for this were both historical and theological. In part, also, it was a problem of scale. The countries that remained Catholic were often geographically extensive and uneven in the distribution of wealth. They could not afford (or thought that they could not afford) university education for all priests.

Many medieval priests, perhaps most, were not university trained. The university faculties of theology were largely dominated by the great religious orders: Franciscans, Dominicans, and Augustinians. The charisma of these orders was in education and preaching. They often provided the ministerial leadership for the cities where their learning and speaking were prized. In contrast, the average rural priest rarely preached and primarily administered the sacraments. Such priests learned their craft by working with older priests, spending time in a monastery, or living with the bishop's chapter. Some rural curates may have received less education than this. Some seemed to have received only rudimentary instruction in Latin and in the rubrics of the Mass. The Council of Trent did not try to redirect Catholic education away from the University; rather, it sought to regularize existing nonuniversity forms of ministerial preparation. Consequently, the Council required each bishop to establish a diocesan seminary, possibly housed in the Cathedral church, where candidates could become habituated to the Church's ritual and sacramental round and learn to pronounce Latin correctly. The traditions of the apostolic life movement shaped the Council's vision. The new seminary was to have many features of a monastery, and the ideal priest was a resident holy man. Even if the diocesan priest did not take all the vows of a professed religious, the priest was to live a similar life, marked by celibacy, renunciation, and distinctive dress. Theologically, the purpose of the Tridentine seminary was to form an *alter Christus*, another Christ, who embodied the religious and the sacramental ideal. Those who created this institution did not see themselves as beginning new directions in Church life.

The slow pace of the reception of the Tridentine reforms meant that the preparation of priests did not become regularized at the same time in all Catholic countries. In seventeenth-century France, the seminary was often a place of formation for those who had completed university training.[2] Both St. Vincent de Paul and Jean-Jacques

---

2. Trent fixed the minimum age for a person to receive priestly orders at twenty-five. Seminary could fill the years between study and ordination.

Olier, founders of influential societies of seminary teachers, worked to focus the purposes of the seminary by adding such features as the retreat before ordination and an emphasis on intense personal spirituality. Since one of the functions of the seminary was to produce obedient priests, the focus was on the mastery of the church's teachings, penitential practices, and canon law. The post-Napoleonic period would see further development of the ideals of Trent and of the seventeenth-century reformers as the Church responded to the criticisms of the Enlightenment. The goal of a "holy priest" serving in every parish became the norm, although even in an age of centralization, the ideal was not completely shared. Latin American churches, for example, often continued the folk priest traditions of the late medieval period.[3]

After the French Revolution and the reign of Napoleon, the Catholic Church intensified its defensive stance. The church became markedly more Tridentine. An important feature of this post-Revolutionary Catholic Church was an increasing centralization of ecclesiastical life in Rome, accompanied by an attempt at the standardization of Catholic faith and practice. As modern communications improved, this movement accelerated. Bishops were progressively expected to report to Rome on the work of their churches. The seminaries were a natural part of this larger movement. Up to the opening of Vatican II, new directives for seminary education periodically came from Rome, including an attempt to have all instruction in Latin.

Education is not only about learning; schools are nurseries of behaviors and practices that establish boundaries between human communities. Naturally, wherever competing bodies struggle with one another, educational institutions will stress these social markers more than they might in areas where one group or another has a virtual monopoly. The founders of American Catholic seminaries often came from two countries where Protestant and Catholic struggled: France and Ireland. These struggles led seminary educators (both abroad and in the United States) to stress celibacy, because it marked the symbolic boundary between the two groups. The difference between Protestant and Catholic was visually present in the contrast between the Catholic rectory and the Protestant manse. The manse was the home of a social and religious leader who lived, as other members of the ruling class lived, surrounded by wife, children and possessions. The rectory was the retreat of a holy man, one who had renounced the world, who lived alone or in community with other priests, and who possessed few worldly goods. The emphasis on the priest as the "other Christ," so important to the pre-Vatican II program of American seminaries, had social as well as theological origins.[4]

---

3. As church historians have moved away from an emphasis on the history of doctrine as the organizing principle for the history of Christianity, the diversity of Catholicism has become more apparent. In no areas, perhaps, of Christian life is this more evident than in the life and organization of local churches and local religious practices.

4. For the theological foundations, see Ciuba, "The Impact."

The political struggles in nineteenth-century Ireland and France further intensified the need for clear religious boundaries. In France, the aftermath of the revolution(s) pitted the church against secularists as well as Protestants. In Ireland, the struggle for national independence made the Catholic Church more central to Irish experience than it was earlier. In both, faithfulness to the Church and to Rome was the same as faithfulness to a political movement. Irish and French Catholic seminaries reflected this heightened awareness of Catholic social and political identity.

Irish and French Catholicism deeply influenced American seminary and church life. However, influence from abroad was not the only factor making for strong Catholic identity. Although the situation of Catholics in the United States differed, the need of Catholics and priests for a strong identity was similar to that abroad. American Catholics were a religious minority, although an increasingly important one, who faced social discrimination. Further, most Catholics were also members of ethnic minorities. Thus, an individual might be Irish Catholic, German Catholic, Italian Catholic, and so on. The Church's leaders wanted to fuse these very diverse elements into one church with common practices. The result was a Janus-like stance on the part of the Roman Church. Most bishops worked to strengthen Catholic identity in the midst of a Protestant majority. Ethnicity was an ally in this struggle. Since many ethnic groups tended to settle in relatively homogeneous urban areas, the church could use language and culture to reinforce Catholic identity.[5] This strategy worked very well. American working-class Catholics remained far more loyal to their religious traditions than western European Catholic workers, who often joined Socialist organizations.

Another strategy, related to ethnicity but different from it, was isolation. At the risk of overgeneralization, one can say that the Church sought to encourage Catholic life by building fences to protect its members from Protestant and secular influence. Education was the key to this strategy. At its height, the Catholic educational system reached from the parochial elementary schools through Catholic high schools to colleges and universities. The religious women and men who taught such schools stressed the importance of the marks of Catholic identity. Catholic youth organizations (such as the Catholic Youth Organization (CYO)) and catechetical classes (such as the Cofraternity of Christian Doctrine (CCD)) provided further educational protection. Yet, the same institutions that raised a fence around Catholic teaching also worked to break down that fence. Catholic schools taught a passionate American patriotism and enabled Catholics to rise socially and economically. Many Catholics later saw this as a period of ghetto Catholicism that limited the Church and its educational institutions as they tried to witness to the larger world of American culture.[6]

5. Dolan, *The American Catholic Experience*, deals with the impact of the varied ethnic pasts of American Catholics on the larger church. Like all standard histories of American Catholicism, he notes the predominant influence of the Irish on the hierarchy of the Church.

6. Perhaps most famously Ellis, "American Catholics and the Intellectual Life." The maturation of American Catholic higher education also highlighted this isolation. Although many people laughed at *Touchdown Jesus*, the mural on the Notre Dame library, opened in 1963, the library itself housed a

The American seminary participated in these larger movements. The goal was to produce obedient priests who would be effective symbols of Catholic unity. At the heart of the traditional program of priestly formation was the Catholic family that the Church urged to dedicate a child to the priesthood or to the religious life. Parents and education often set the child apart from an early age and marked him as a person destined for this vocation. Once the child was out of elementary school, formal educational formation began in the minor seminary (similar to a Catholic high school), which prepared prospective priests for the required eight-year program in philosophy and theology. While the minor seminaries were often good schools, their primary function was to shrink the pool of prospective priests. Many entered the minor seminaries; fewer went on to philosophy or theology. The student then went to the college seminary and, after another round of selection, to the major seminary or theologate. This chapter concentrates attention on the major seminaries.

Much of the program of both minor and major seminaries was in the habit or virtue of obedience. The seminaries minutely regulated the candidate's life, fixing times for rising, sleeping, studying, recreation, and classes. The seminary schedule provided little free time in the day.[7] The faculty periodically evaluated each student, and the major focus of their discussion was obedience to superiors and conformity to the seminary round. The schools also stressed the obedience of the faculty. Every year, the faculty publicly took the "oath against modernism" designed to limit instruction to the prevailing orthodoxy.[8] Although the changing direction of Catholic Scripture studies

---

world-class collection.

7. Poole, " Preparation" gives this as a typical pre-Vatican II seminary day:
AM
6:00 Morning prayers in common in the chapel
6:30 Mass
7:15 Breakfast
8:00 Class or study
11:30 Spiritual reading (twice a week, a spiritual talk by the spiritual director and one of the faculty)
12:00 Examination of conscience followed by lunch

PM.
1:00 Class/study
3:45 Recreation
5:30 Rosary, visit in chapel, examination of conscience
6:00 Supper
6:30 Recreation
7:30 Night prayers in common in the chapel, followed by study period.

8. The oath against modernism, imposed by Pius X in 1910, was to be taken by all Catholic seminary teachers and by all clergy. It was an implementation of the degrees against modernism, particularly *pascendi dominici gregis*, 1907. Catholic modernism was similar in many ways to Protestant liberalism, stressing nonpropositional understandings of revelation, and the growth and development of dogma. The emphases of these teachings were reaffirmed in *humani generis* by Pius XII in 1950. For an excellent discussion of the impact of modernism and its aftermath on the American Church, see Appleby, *"Church and Age Unite!"*

after 1943 produced some latitude, instruction was often by a recitation method that stressed memorization of the material in approved manuals. The manuals carefully summarized church teachings and dealt with easily refuted objections.[9] This method made the content of classes easy to control, and assured that instruction was in line with the Church's teaching. The educational goal of this instruction was to ensure that the prospective priest knew the Church's position on various theological and ethical issues and was able to transmit these teachings correctly to his people. The practical instruction also revolved around obedience and correctness. Despite the liturgical movement of the nineteenth and twentieth centuries, the seminaries emphasized proper administration and careful obedience to the rubrics. Many students suffered from scruples. In addition, Catholic seminaries devoted much curricular time to the confessional and the rules around absolution.

The word that best summarized this style of education was formation. The school shaped or formed a priestly person. The Church designed the seminary to prepare candidates for a role in a complex organization with clear lines of authority and clearly delineated tasks. Protestants often confuse formation with the development of personal piety. While pious practices, including meditation, Marian devotions, and regular prayer, were part of the process, the primary goal was not to shape personal habits. The purpose of the program was sacramental. The faculty prepared the student to receive the sacrament of ordination. Just as the Bread and Wine had to be prepared to receive the Body and Blood of Christ, so the seminary shaped the student to receive the grace of ordination that would transform him forever. The seminary formation program was consequently not professional education. The purpose of professional education is to shape persons who are the masters of their craft and, hence, able to make appropriate judgments about the proper way to perform its duties. The priest, at least the diocesan priest, was not to make independent judgments. In theory, priests were interchangeable; in fact, church authorities considered many things in promoting and assigning priests. A good Catholic attended the parish where he or she was canonically resident, received communion in that parish, and went to the next available confessor. The priest spoke with authority because the priest repeated what authority said. The system of promotion that moved priests slowly up the ladder from assistant in a large parish to pastor and beyond was hierarchical; promotion depended on earning and retaining the good graces of one's superiors. The pre-Vatican II process of formation involved almost constant supervision of students and their personal lives. In addition to the faculty's yearly evaluation of candidates and formal report to the student's bishop, the faculty might conduct special reviews of an individual or a group whenever an occasion or event suggested that a problem might exist. While

---

9. The manuals were an easy target in the period following Vatican II as was the pedagogy of memorization that often accompanied them. Yet they did have considerable philosophical and theological sophistication. Much like the Protestant scholasticism that was so central to the nineteenth-century Protestant seminary, they summarized very complex discussions and offered rational resolutions of dilemmas.

grades and academic performance were included in this process, the reviews were not primarily academic. The final authority in this process was the bishop or religious superior. Although the bishops usually supported the faculty and its recommendations, the bishop was not required to do so. The bishop might override a faculty's recommendation, particularly one primarily based on academic performance, and continue or ordain a candidate despite the faculty's reservations. These reviews were the external forum, and the regulations carefully separated them from the internal forum of a candidate's own conscience. Canon Law strictly prohibited confessors from disclosing anything shared with them under the seal, of course, but custom extended this protection to other, less formal, personal conversations. The system prohibited the confessor from participating in the faculty discussion or in the vote on his penitents.[10]

The sacred space of the pre-Vatican II seminary symbolized the goals and purposes of the seminaries. Urban dioceses such as New York and Chicago located their seminaries in rural areas somewhat distant from the cities that they served, and even the Jesuits, founders of a series of urban universities that included Georgetown, Boston College, and St. Louis, favored rural Woodstock as the location of their flagship school. In this, the seminaries often resembled the great monastic foundations of Europe, complete with areas set aside for meditation and reflection. One withdrew from the world in order to prepare to reenter it.[11]

The pre-Vatican II seminary picture also included the American College of the Roman Catholic Church of the United States. The school, like other national schools established in Rome, hoped to tie prospective priests (and especially prospective bishops) more closely to the Holy See. While the American College followed a similar

---

10. Ciuba, "The Impact," 66:

> 1. an environment isolated from society, very often in rural or park-like settings, 2. primary focus was upon the seminary as a "house of formation," 3. the general orientation of the theological education in the seminary was apologetic, defensive and lacking in creativity, originality and serious academic scholarship. 4. Faculty were responsible not only for theological instruction, but were also weighed down with heavy formational and pastoral responsibilities. 5. Student life featured a controlled environment, a strict daily schedule and a disciplined, orderly life intended to develop a man of virtue. 6. The central administration of the Seminary was usually vested in one person, the Rector, who was responsible only to the local Ordinary and to the Roman Congregations.

Also see White, *The Diocesan Seminary in the United States*. A similar description can be found in Kauffman, *Tradition and Transformation in Catholic Culture*.

11. The monastic ideal was also reflected at St. Meinrad's, a Benedictine monastery that also served as a house of formation and education for several Midwestern dioceses. Here the students lived the traditional monastic round as part of their formation. Many seminaries serving religious orders were, in effect, monasteries with an educational focus. Many of these would join theological unions.

program of priestly formation to that of American seminaries, it was not isolated from the city or from Rome's rich intellectual life.

The pre-Vatican II seminary was a complete system that had internal coherence. That was its glory and its fame. What is fascinating about the pre-Vatican II seminary is not that the Vatican or the bishops had to enforce orthodoxy occasionally, but that such intervention was comparatively rare. As long as students and faculty accepted the basic assumptions on which the Church based formative education, the seminary made theological and ecclesiastical sense. The purpose of the seminary was to form a holy man, set apart from the world, who bore the image of Christ. The system set the priest apart from the laity, and, equally important, the seminary helped to maintain the boundaries between Catholicism and its rivals. The problem was what would happen to the system of formation once people questioned its assumptions. How much, if anything, remained of the old system? What new directions were to shape the redefinition of priestly formation?

HINTS OF CHANGE

There were some significant hints of changes to come. These were not hints of reform, to be sure, but they were structures and precedents that people could use later to make other more significant changes.

The Third Plenary Council in 1884 adopted a six-year program for both minor and major seminaries, and perhaps more important, established a curriculum that included both biblical and historical studies.[12] It was a strong beginning. The American seminary had many curricular similarities to the European Catholic university. Like its American Protestant counterparts, the projected institutions were a blend of different European precedents with American experience. In common with many formal descriptions of seminary curricula Protestant and Catholic, the Third Plenary Council's theological encyclopedia had potential that would not (and could not) be realized until the Church made other changes. The Council also proposed the establishment of Catholic University, which opened in Washington DC in 1889. Its founders hoped that the new school would be a center of advanced theological study as well as general culture. While Catholic University did not initially fulfill the high hopes of its founders, the new school did establish an important institutional structure that aspired to the highest standards. Catholic University was one of the initial fourteen schools that formed the Association of American Universities in 1900. In 1934, moreover, Pius XI issued *deus scientiarum* requiring that seminary professors have a degree that included a dissertation as well as the approval of Rome.

In the 1950s, John Tracy Ellis had raised significant questions about the isolation of Catholic thought and life from the world and called for an end to the Catholic

12. This Council is discussed in all standard histories of American Catholicism. Carey, *Catholics in America: A History*, 54, observed that one-fourth of its decrees concerned education.

intellectual ghetto. Perhaps more important, Father Theodore Hesburgh had already begun the transformation of the University of Notre Dame into a world-class university. After the Council, Father Hesburgh took the lead in persuading Catholic educators to pledge academic freedom on their campuses and to seek accreditation at all levels. Despite all the jokes about "Touchdown Jesus," a large mural on the side of the library facing the football stadium, Hesburgh's new library was among the nation's best.[13] James Laubacher, a graduate of Louvain and the energetic rector of St. Mary's, Baltimore, in the 1950s, questioned the use of the various manuals and encouraged able young Sulpicians to seek advanced degrees, both abroad and at Johns Hopkins.

Perhaps the most important area of change in the pre-Vatican II seminary was in biblical studies. In 1943, the encyclical *Divino afflante spiritu*, issued by Pope Pius XII, opened the door for a more critical examination of Scripture. Young Catholic scholars were quick to take advantage of this permission, and such scholars as Raymond E. Brown, SS, a graduate of Johns Hopkins and St. Mary's, had made significant contributions to the discipline before the Second Vatican Council. The vitality of biblical studies was often in stark contrast to the much more restricted instruction in other subjects.

EXCURSUS: WOMEN AND THE PRE-VATICAN II SEMINARY

Both the seminary and the priesthood were masculine worlds. Faculties, spiritual directors, and students were exclusively male. The ideal was to separate the seminary from female presence and influence. This separation began in the minor seminary, which was a residential school, and became more structured as the candidate progressed. Religious women might serve more or less as household servants in some seminaries, just as many rectories were served by a nun or nuns, but they were ideally kept out of sight. Seminaries had markings on the floor that indicated where women might and, more important, might not go. Some seminaries were so suspicious of contact with the other sex that they established summer manors so that students would not be exposed to the corrupting influence of mothers and sisters during their vacations. In this environment, women were either feared or idealized, but in either case they were not real.

One consequence of gender separation was that seminaries had nothing to do with the education of the vitally important orders of women religious. As in many male orders, communities of women tended to train their own membership, but by the 1950s, Catholic sisters were actively entering colleges and universities for professional training in teaching and in nursing. In the 1950s, the University of Notre Dame and Catholic University made some beginnings in teaching women theology, partially because they often taught religion classes in parochial schools, but such education did

---

13. See note 4, above.

not enjoy the full support of the hierarchy. Women religious were also beginning to organize and to work for changes on their own behalf. Many sisters were aware that they knew much more about education than the parish priests charged with supervising their work and who, incidentally, were their direct employers. If the canonical pastor wanted to remove a religious order from his parish school, for whatever reason, he was free to do so. While many priests tried to handle this power responsibly, the structure occasioned many petty tyrannies. These injustices inspired many sisters' later demands for reform.

THE GREAT COUNCIL

The classical problem of interpreting a council distinguishes between a council's decrees and their reception. It took almost a century, for example, for France to receive the decrees of the Council of Trent. Other countries received the decrees at various times. The governments often controlled the editing of the documents, and local church authorities applied its teaching to their situation as they saw fit. Every official document, thus, has two meanings: the most accurate reading of the text as it was adopted and the meaning of the document as it was received in different locations. The text as it was written is not the same as the text as it was received.

The context for the American reception of Vatican II was the decade from 1955 to 1965, a crucial period for American Catholics. Aided by the GI Bill, significant numbers of Catholics attended colleges and universities after the Second World War. By the midfifties, those newly educated Catholics had left their ethnic enclaves and moved to the suburbs. Like their Protestant and Jewish neighbors, Catholics found themselves living in religiously pluralistic neighborhoods and working with non-Catholics on a variety of projects. Like other Americans, they looked to their churches for practical everyday wisdom on the living of their lives, and they welcomed their bishop, Fulton Sheen, to the ranks of television celebrities. The suburbanization of American Catholicism would have affected the history of Catholic theological education with or without Vatican II. Catholic birthrates were declining, making the traditional gift of a child to the Church more difficult. Particularly important, the economic and social futures of Catholic young people were much brighter. Being a priest or a sister was no longer as attractive economically or socially as it once had been. Demographic and social conditions sowed the seeds of the coming vocations' crisis, already present to some extent in France and Belgium, before the Council met. The combination of these larger trends with the rapid theological changes that followed Vatican II led to an almost perfect storm.

The reception of the decrees of Vatican II in the United States was further shaped by the character of the American Church at that time. To understand the impact of Vatican II on Catholic theological education, one must realize that the American Catholics who received the decrees, particularly younger Catholics, were in the midst of a period of optimism. The early 1960s were a golden age for America's Catholics. Catholic institutions thrived, mass attendance and contributions were up, and the religious orders and the secular priesthood turned away significant numbers of candidates. The prestige of the Church was high, as leading Catholic bishops took the lead in the struggle against communism. Moreover, Catholics were now soundly represented in the middle classes. The 1960 election of John F. Kennedy, the first Catholic to become President, further excited many Catholics. Kennedy was an all-American boy, a Harvard graduate, and the picture of self-confidence. His inauguration address, complete with language about a new frontier and sacrifice, called Americans to a new age. Catholics understood his brave language as a reflection of their shared faith. To many, the young president and the aging pope, John XXIII, seemed a pair of liberators. Robert Kennedy, a far more complex figure than his older brother, became part of this symbolic trinity. Further, the civil rights movement seemed to confirm the general atmosphere of hope. Young Catholics looked with pride at the seemingly endless parade of nuns and priests at Martin Luther King Jr.'s rallies, and they joined in the general exuberance of the early days of rock and roll and the youth culture. As they did for many Americans, the ideals of the Peace Corps excited them and testified to the depth of their and the nation's values. Just as Kennedy marked the coming of age for American Catholics politically, so Vatican II marked their coming of age religiously. They read the document as an expression of their hopeful view of the present world.

The Stopgap Pope

Pius XII's death in 1958 signaled a major change in Vatican direction. Pius had become pope in 1939, after a long period of service as Vatican secretary of state, and he served throughout the Second World War and during the early days of the Cold War that followed. Pius essentially continued the conservative traditions of the nineteenth-century papacy. As secretary of state, he negotiated treaties with the principal dictatorships of Europe that although designed to protect the Church, gave a measure of legitimacy to such rulers as Hitler, Mussolini, and Franco. Theologically, although he was more open to modern biblical study than his predecessors, such documents as *Humani generis* (1950) continued the theological traditions of the past. His 1950 decision to affirm the Assumption of Mary without a council was a high-water mark in a century-long development of Mariology and papal authority. Like his immediate predecessors, Pius XII continued to centralize the administration of the Church. Although later commentators criticized Pius for his actions during the war and for his failure to come to terms with the changed European situation, at the time of his death, Pius was one of the most admired men in the West. His picture often appeared in the windows of Catholic homes in the United States, and American leaders, including Harry Truman, considered his voice important in world affairs.

At the time of Pius's death, Europe was divided between East and West and seemed on the verge of another, perhaps nuclear, war. Many of the most Catholic areas of Europe—including Poland and Hungary—were communist states that actively persecuted the Catholic Church, and the Church was on defensive in Italy and France. In Asia, the Church faced serious persecution in Vietnam, and the Church in Africa seemed headed towards extended conflict with that continent's newly awakened nationalism. Pius XII's diplomatic skills had not been sufficient to ease the situation, and the Church was on the horns of a dilemma. In the binary political world of the Cold War, the Church could either make its peace with the liberal democracies of the West, including the United States, or face isolation. Peace with the communist East was impossible theologically and practically. No solution to these problems seemed at hand, and the Church faced a leadership crisis. Pius XII had not given Giovanni Montini (later Paul VI) the red hat when he promoted him to Milan, more or less excluding him from consideration as his successor, and no other figure stood out. Ironically, Pius's omission of Montini was almost providential. Whether intentional or not, this omission invited the consistory to experiment with an interim.

The interim was John XXIII (Angelo Giuseppe Roncalli). When the College of Cardinals elected him in 1958, John XXIII was an old man, and he died after a long battle with stomach cancer a scant four years later in 1963.[14] From the beginning, John XXIII's open personality and relations with ordinary people made him popular. After the ascetic and otherworldly Pius XII, John XXIII seemed a breath of fresh air, the people's pope, whose warm spirit could meet any challenge. In 1959, shortly after his election, John XXIII announced his intention to call a Council in 1959, and he officially summoned it in 1961. His motives for this action remain unclear. The First Vatican Council had not completed its work when Rome fell to Italian nationalists, and many items on its agenda remained unadjudicated. Perhaps part of John XXIII's hope was to complete these tasks, or perhaps he saw something new. Whatever the pope's motives, many assumed that the new pope's spirit would permeate the meeting. John XXIII's decision was popular with American Catholics before the council met.

The goals of the new council were vague. Clearly, John XXIII wanted to affirm ecumenism. He invited the Eastern Orthodox and the Protestant churches to send observers. Protestants responded to this invitation by sending some remarkable young theologians. Robert McAfee Brown, for example, was among those in attendance. Bishops from North and South America, Africa and Asia, further contributed to the breadth of the meeting. Vatican II was the most inclusive Council in Catholic history. Pope John XXIII also urged the council to adopt a pastoral tone rather than the canonical tone that had characterized earlier councils. Yet the curia dominated the

---

14. John XXIII was arguably the most beloved and influential pope of the twentieth century, and there has been an extensive literature written about his life and his work. Much of his genius was his ability to allow himself to be a symbol of the best of the Church's ministry. Like the meaning of any good symbol, John's meaning was not completely clear to contemporary or later observers.

preparation of the initial documents and determined the meeting's structure. What the curia proposed was the same old same old.

We cannot discuss the history of the Council in detail.[15] Perhaps the most important session was the first, when the bishops demanded that the Council take different paths than those prepared for it by the curia. The most obvious sign of this direction was that the bishops invited the "new theologians"—who had been suspect in the 1950s, and who were implicitly condemned in *Humani generis*, to be theological advisors to the Council. Although there had been theological advisors at Trent and Vatican I, this was a new role for modern Catholic theologians. For the first time since the almost endless disputes over the Avignon papacy, Catholic theologians were at the center of the Church's deliberations about its faith and its future. The next fifty years would see theologians, bishops, and popes struggle with the question of what this new role meant for the Church. Were theologians, so to speak, the soul of the magisterium, called to propel the Church toward its future, or were they primarily teachers of established Catholic doctrine? If the first, then theology was a creative attempt to recast traditional teachings. If the second, then the task of the theologian was to report what the magisterium had already decided. Shortly after the end of the council, some theologians assumed their new role as the avatars of the Church by urging hierarchy and people to reject on theological grounds the pope's teaching on birth control. Not surprisingly, the papacy pushed back. The conflict between the advocates of these two understandings of the work of the theologian was not resolved, and contributed to the complex cases of Hans Kung and Charles Curran. Before pope and council promulgated any documents, the Council had redefined the nature of theology and, hence, of theological education.

Almost all the documents produced by the Council influenced theological education. Unlike earlier councils, Vatican II did not produce a host of directives and modifications of canon law. Instead, the council focused on the pastoral work of the church around the world. To use language that was popular later, it was concerned with *praxis*, not with *theoria*.[16]

15. The literature on Vatican II is extensive. A quick search of the Hollis Library at Harvard yielded 1604 direct hits, and a search of the smaller library at Saint Joseph College, Portland, Maine, yielded 140 direct references. And neither search includes closely related volumes. I have found O'Malley *What Happened at Vatican II* to be particularly helpful in understanding the complex theological and political history of the Council. Also useful are Bulman and Parella, *From Trent to Vatican II*; Ratzinger, *Theological Highlights of Vatican II*; and Dulles, *Vatican II and the Extraordinary Synod*. I found Chinnici, "The Reception of Vatican II in the United States," invaluable for understanding the difference between the reception of a Council and the original intent, so far as it may be determined, of the authors of the various decrees. The documents of Vatican II are easily available online.

16. *Praxis* is a broader term than the English words *practice* or *practical*, which often carries pragmatic connotations. The Greek term carries more the implication of purposeful activity. In many ways, neoclassical philosopher Alasdair MacIntyre's use of *practice* in *After Virtue* (1983) might be a useful description. MacIntyre's understanding has the advantage of being closely related to the scholastic theology that informed both the conservatives and the new theologians at the Council. Karl Rahner, perhaps the most philosophical of the new theologians, described his position as "Transcendental

The first document the council officially approved was the *Constitution on the Sacred Liturgy*, which immediately impacted the perception of the Church. National churches were to translate the liturgy into the languages of their people. The decree assigned the task of translation and revision to national bishops, and their agents, usually scholars, translated the services into the vernacular. Liturgical scholars had long advocated the rearrangement of the sanctuary in the light of ancient Christian practice.[17] The new liturgies did this. The new rubrics replaced the medieval altar, mounted against the wall, with a table, with the priest facing the people. The new worship forms often renewed traditional elements in the services. Preaching was an excellent example. The service of the Word, often hurried through in pre-Vatican II services, became central, and the new order expected the priest to preach a homily based on the three readings in the lectionary. Vatican II climaxed a century of emphasis on frequent communion, and the new decree sped up the popular acceptance of that practice. Within a comparatively few years, reception of Communion by those attending became the norm. An unintended consequence of the new liturgical emphases was the rapid decline of confession among American Catholics.[18]

The designation of the Church as the people of God in *Lumen gentium* pointed to a style of ministry in which the priest, while still a sacerdotal person, served as the enabler of a people distinguished by a variety of gifts. The Decree on the Apostolate of the Laity (*Apostolican actuositatem*) reinforced this message by noting that many vital tasks in the modern church were primarily open only to laypeople involved in the world. The Council lifted up the theme of spiritual gifts, popular among Protestants during this same period, as a guiding principle.

Gaudium et spes, the Pastoral Constitution on the World, opened even more doors to changes in theological education. The Council pointedly addressed the document "not only to the sons of the Church and to all who invoke the name of Christ, but to the whole of humanity."[19] In struggling with human problems, the Council called

---

Thomism."

17. In the United States, this task fell to the US Conference of Catholic Bishops, which was reorganized in 1966 as a national voice for the Church in the United States. In many ways, this largely ad hoc arrangement was the consequence of the incomplete organization of the American Church after the Americanism controversy at the end of the nineteenth century.

18. Dolan et al., *Transforming Parish Ministry*, present a graphic picture of these changes. In my mind, the decline of the confessional was among the most important. Not only had confession taken much of the priest's time and energy, but seminaries had spent much time and energy preparing a priest to make the complex legal and moral judgments required for this sacrament.

19. The full quotation is, "Hence this Second Vatican Council, having probed more profoundly into the mystery of the Church, now addresses itself without hesitation, not only to the sons of the Church and to all who invoke the name of Christ, but to the whole of humanity. For the council yearns to explain to everyone how it conceives of the presence and activity of the Church in the world of today." Online: http://www.vatican.va/archive/hist_councils/ii_vatican_council/documents/vat-ii_cons_19651207_gaudium-et-spes_en.html/.

on the Church to ally itself with all people of goodwill who were seeking the improvement of the human condition:

> While faithfully adhering to the Gospel and fulfilling her mission to the world, the Church, whose duty it is to foster and elevate all that is found to be true, good and beautiful in the human community, strengthens peace among men for the glory of God.[20]

This broad humanism, reminiscent of Erasmus, required the Church to ally with those struggling for the betterment of human society. Hence, the Fathers carefully spoke about the importance of science and technology in the human enterprise and called for the Church to commit itself to the future envisioned for human beings by the technical revolution. The United Nations and other cooperative means to peace deserved full Christian support.

Gaudium et spes opened up almost unlimited spheres for human action. The place of the Church was to stand beside those working to correct human injustice and economic want. It summoned Catholics to go into the world and to work in the world for God's sake. This invitation was broad. Many priests and nuns heard it as a call to go into the world and fight poverty, and it suggested, perhaps not deliberately, that young people should consider such worldly service as a valid Christian alternative to religious life or priestly vocation. Others heard it as an invitation to formulate a theology that would firmly put the Church on the side of movements for liberation in the Two-Thirds World.

For theological educators in the United States, the Declaration on Religious Freedom (*Dignitatis humanae*) also had many implications. Although there are parts of the document that clearly point to religious situations very different from those in the United States, most Americans, Protestants and Catholics, read the document as a long-desired approval of the American form of church-state relations. By extension, the Declaration blessed other American institutions, quasi-governmental in character, including accrediting agencies. While like many complex events, the entry of Catholic seminaries into ATS had many causes, *Dignitatis* permitted and encouraged such participation.

Verbum dei showed how far Catholic biblical scholarship had advanced since the 1940s. The decree located God's revelation in the history of Israel and in Jesus Christ and saw the biblical text as the authoritative way that God transmitted this revelation to the Church. Although biblical studies had made important progress since 1943, this was the charter of a new seriousness in the Catholic relationship with Scripture. The Bible was the Church's treasure, and both clergy and laity were to be diligent in its study. Clergy were to study the Bible using the rules of interpretation and to preach its message to their congregations.[21] Scholars were to continue their explorations. These

---

20. Ibid.
21. Fogarty, "American Catholic Biblical Scholarship." Also see Fogarty, *American Catholic Biblical*

exhortations placed the Bible in the center of the Church's worship and pastoral care. As Catholic seminaries revised their curricula, this document justified devoting an increasing number of hours to scriptural studies often equal to or greater than the hours required by Protestant schools.

The Decree on the Training of Priests (*Optatam totius*) gathered up many themes from other documents. Perhaps most important, the decree reversed (at least partially) a century in which Rome made the basic decisions about theological education. Instead, each country was to put forth its own Program of Priestly Formation, revise it periodically, and adapt the program to the needs of their particular nation. Interestingly, the Decree saw the major seminary or theologate,[22] whether maintained by one diocese or several, as the heart of priestly formation. *Optatam totius* expressed the purpose of the seminary:

> They are therefore to be prepared for the ministry of the word: that they might understand ever more perfectly the revealed word of God; that, meditating on it they might possess it more firmly, and that they might express it in words and in example; for the ministry of worship and of sanctification: that through their prayers and their carrying out of the sacred liturgical celebrations they might perfect the work of salvation through the Eucharistic sacrifice and the sacraments; for the ministry of the parish: that they might know how to make Christ present to men, Him who did not "come to be served but to serve and to give His life as a ransom for many" (Mark 10:45; cf. John 13:12–17), and that, having become the servants of all, they might win over all the more (cf. 1 Cor. 9:19).[23]

In continuity with the older tradition, *Optatam* emphasized the spiritual formation of the seminary student. In addition to an appreciation of Catholic religious practice, the document stressed the importance of modern methods of education. The norms of Christian education were to be rigorously observed and complemented by the newer findings of sound psychology and pedagogy.

> Therefore, by a wisely planned training there is also to be developed in the students a due human maturity. This will be made especially evident in stability of mind, in an ability to make weighty decisions, and in a sound evaluation of men and events. The students should be accustomed to work properly at their own development.[24]

Scholarship.

22. Section 2 of the decree did deal with minor seminaries, although without as much focus and direction as section 3 on the major seminaries. It is doubtful whether any one at the Council envisioned the rapid decline of the college and high school seminaries that followed in the Council's wake. Online: http://www.vatican.va/archive/hist_councils/ii_vatican_council/documents/vat-ii_decree_19651028_optatam-totius_en.html/.

23. Ibid. The quote is from section 3, on major seminaries.

24. Ibid.

An emphasis on the pastoral arts, especially preaching, liturgics, and the care of souls was part of the work of the theologate. In these areas, the teachers were to stress the insights of psychology, sociology, and the pedagogy for their task. Interestingly, *Optatum* argued for "pastoral projects" to enable a student to learn to work effectively with others in realizing the goals of the Church.

The inclusion of instruction in the pastoral arts was not a cosmetic change for Catholic seminaries. The magnitude of this task should not be underestimated. The schools had to rearrange their curricula and faculties to include instruction in the pastoral arts. Unlike theology and biblical studies, where vibrant Catholic intellectual traditions already existed, these disciplines were new to Catholic theological education. Those interested in teaching these practical areas, consequently, often had to take their doctorates from such university divinity schools as Union and Yale. These fields often provided an entry for many laypeople, including women religious, into seminary teaching. They also broadened the Catholic theological discussion. Historically, Catholic theology dialoged primarily with philosophy, an arrangement that continued after Vatican II, but now Catholic theologians had to include the social sciences as well in the discussion. Particularly in the field of ethics, this was a fruitful combination, although one that generated controversy.

The key to understanding some documents is to ask, not what they said, but what they did not say. In the case of Vatican II, the call of the Council reserved the very important issue of priestly celibacy and the equally vexing question of birth control to the papacy. Whether these hopes were reasonable or not, many in and out of the Church, expected that the Church's positions on both issues would change. The existence of a special committee to examine birth control definitely fed the high expectations on that issue. Less reason existed to expect changes on celibacy, although everyone realized that this was a matter of discipline, not doctrine, and was only applicable to the Western rite. Eastern Rite churches in communion with Rome did not follow this practice, and many assumed that changed conditions made celibacy less vital. Both expectations were in vain.

Vatican II stressed the work of priests and the hierarchy, but it said little about religious orders or their work.[25] The principal exhortation contained in *Perfectae caritatis* was that these orders were to be true to their charisma, their original reason for being, and their distinctive ministries. Yet the male religious orders often provided many of the Church's most able scholars, and their members taught in and managed many of the Church's educational institutions. This left these orders to interpret the meaning of the Council's decrees for themselves. The orders were instructed, however,

---

25. The statement on the religious orders was *perfectae caritatis*. Online: http://www.vatican.va/archive/hist_councils/ii_vatican_council/documents/vat-ii_decree_19651028_perfectae-caritatis_en.html/. Although several other commentators have commented on the comparative thinness of the reflections on the religious life, the judgment in the text above is my own.

to bring their documents and practices into line with the teachings of the council; however, how this was to be done was not specified.

Historically, the women's orders provided the Church with an army of workers in fields including education, social work, and medicine. Their orders were already deeply involved in the Church's mission to the world. The most natural reading of *Perfectae caritatis* was the women's orders (with the exception of the contemplatives) were to reaffirm and expand their social and educational ministries. Many orders quickly took steps to follow this reading of their work, dropping their distinctive habits, and moving into new social situations. Further, the members of women's orders entered the new ministries in local parishes, such as directors of religious education and liturgical and music leadership.

In a sense, the failure of Vatican II to take the work of women religious more seriously was part of a centuries-old neglect of women's orders. The Council needed to note that women religious had become increasingly educated and self-conscious during the 1950s. Much more than the secular priesthood, they were prepared to implement the new directions that the Council had indicated. Yet, the Council's silence on women's issues had its own effects. Vatican II raised hopes that the Church might ordain women and, in the interim, use them in ministerial roles in local churches. The nature of the charismas stressed in the document seemed to demand no less.

THE COUNCIL IMPLEMENTED

Vatican II exploded the American seminary world, an indication that deep dissatisfaction may have existed before the Council met. In the rush for reform that followed, not all seminaries believed that they had to wait for the composition of the American *Program of Priestly Formation*. Many began changing their programs before the new directives appeared, and then had to interpret and modify their programs in the light of the official documents. Yet, the Program of Priestly Formation, first issued by the National Conference of Catholic Bishops in 1971, was the foundational document that defined the course of seminary reform. The document was frequently revised, with a second edition issued in 1976, and subsequent editions following in 1981, 1992, and 2005. The frequent revision of the *Program* was intentional. Unlike earlier Roman directives on seminary education, the *Program* was designed as a living document that the Church can and should update in the light of changing conditions. One illustration of this capacity of the document to respond to the changing nature of American Catholic life is the increasing emphasis from the third to the fifth edition on providing training for priests to serve congregations of the new immigration. The Program strongly urged the theologates to provide instruction and, particularly, worship in the language of the new immigrants.

Although most churches have statements about the goals and purposes of theological education, the *Program of Priestly Formation* is uniquely Catholic. On the one hand, the document is theological in its treatment of theological education. The *Program* begins with an understanding of the nature of priestly ministry and seeks to relate every issue discussed to that theological foundation. As the Catholic theology of priesthood changes, it follows that the *Program of Priestly Formation* changes. Hence, the fifth edition reflected the teachings of Pope John Paul II's *Pastores dabo vobis* (1992) and seeks to implement the theology contained in that document.

In addition to its theological foundations, The *Program of Priestly Formation* deals with a handful of organizational and academic matters, including the use of the Master of Divinity degree and the need for the seminaries to have a competent administration. The length of the major seminary program for priests, for example, is two years of philosophy and four years of theology.[26] In addition, the document deals with problems that theologates encountered in discharging their duties. For example, as the age of candidates has increased, the various editions have suggested adaptations of the inherited program. Yet the document is not primarily a set of standards or regulations for seminaries. Instead the document centers on the formation of priests for the ministry and deals with the various steps in that process. The focus is on how to form a man for a priestly vocation. At heart, as in the pre-Vatican II seminary, formation is preparation for reception of the sacrament of ordination.

The most important image in the *Program for Priestly Formation* is not school—the central image is community. The seminary is like the community that Jesus called into being when he summoned the disciples to spend time with him. During that period, the disciples learned the message of Christ, but they also learned to be with Christ, to take up Christ's mission, and to permit their intimate relationship with Christ to shape their personalities. The importance of community runs through all the dimensions of the formation of the priest. Academic formation, the training of the mind, was only part of the larger work of a seminary. The prospective priest was a person whose participation in communal life was to form his emotional, social, and professional life.

CATHOLIC SEMINARIES AND THE AMERICAN COMMUNITY OF THEOLOGICAL SCHOOLS

Almost as soon as the Second Vatican Council ended, American seminaries and houses of study interacted with the larger world of schools, particularly theological schools. During the period immediately following the council, Catholic seminaries, those for both religious and secular priests, joined the Association of Theological Schools. Within a decade, 52 out of 54 schools had joined. The association, then led by Protestant mainstream educators, saw Catholic priestly education largely in terms

---

26. Training in philosophy had historically taken place in the college seminaries. As these closed, the task fell increasingly to the theologates. Interestingly, some college courses in theology could be included in the two years of preparatory studies.

of their own view of Vatican II and their own emphasis on theological training. Few believed that Catholic participation in the association would substantially change the Association or its methods. Although some were aware that while the Association might have to make some compromises around academic freedom, most believed that these adjustments would be minor. Most perhaps saw the exchange as moving in the other direction; that is, they believed that the liberal Protestant model would further the reform of Catholic institutions. Jesse Ziegler, the executive director of ATS in the 1970s, was also genuinely committed to the ecumenical movement. Coming from the liberal wing of a relatively small American denomination, the Brethren, Ziegler saw society and the churches drawing together in an ever more common grasp of religious reality. The most important immediate effect on Catholic theological education was to reinforce the seminaries' identity as schools.

Did the Association of Theological Schools' leadership understand Catholic seminary education? Looking backwards over fifty years, my own opinion is that they did not. The Protestant tendency was to understand seminary education primarily as intellectual preparation for ministry and to see the various religious exercises practiced in Catholic seminaries as needed correctives to their own less pious educational practices. In simple terms, the leadership of ATS saw Catholicism as essentially a denominational form of Christianity and expected that the Catholic Church, like other American denominations, would gradually follow the same patterns of behavior as other American churches. But, whether the two parties understood each other or not, the welcome that the association extended to the Catholic schools was a confirmation that both sides saw Vatican II as opening new possibilities for cooperation and exchange.

Participation in ATS and accreditation contributed much to the development of the post-Vatican II seminary. Accreditation is primarily a judgment whether or not an institution meets a certain standard or rule. At each step towards accreditation, Catholic seminaries measured themselves against the association's rules. Since the dominant concept behind the ATS's self-understanding was graduate professional education, each such measurement suggests areas for further change and development. The process was slow and incremental. Consequently, Catholic theological schools came to acquire a dual character. On the one hand, they remained houses of formation, committed to shaping men for ordination; on the other hand, they became graduate professional schools preparing people for employment in the Church or churches. Some students attending the seminaries also wanted to prepare for careers in college or university teaching. The dual character of Catholic seminaries is the most characteristic feature of the post-Vatican II seminary. Naturally, few schools balanced these two emphases equally. In some schools, the formational model dominated; in others, the more graduate and professional understanding had more influence.

Nothing in history is completely unique. In many ways, the ATS-related Catholic seminary was close to the German model. In a German Catholic university, candidates for the priesthood attend classes taught by the theology faculty. However, at the same time, they reside in houses of study where they follow a strict program of priestly formation. I do not think that there was a direct link between the German and the American model, but there are important similarities. Yet, post-Vatican II seminaries are different in that they often combine what are almost separate organizations in a single institution. Interestingly, as the students have aged, the schools have often added the required two years of philosophy to their programs.

One symbol of the new seminary was the awarding of degrees to seminary graduates. The traditional Catholic system of minor seminary, college seminary, and major seminary had not marked its students' advance by awarding degrees. Rather, the system moved students steadily toward priesthood through a sequence of faculty evaluations accompanied by a steady progression through the various minor and major orders of ministry, ending with priestly ordination. After Catholic schools were accredited, a series of diplomas and degrees that other institutions recognized supplemented this traditional order. Minor seminary graduates received a high school diploma; college seminary graduates, a Bachelor of Arts; theologate graduates, an Master of Arts, a Master of Divinity, or Master of Theology. Although the *Program* did mandate the Master of Divinity as the required degree for ordination, the Catholic *Priestly Formation* never completely fit the ATS or regional accrediting standards for that degree. For example, the ATS approved MDiv program was a three-year degree, based on previous college graduation. Most Catholic seminaries awarded the degree on this basis. Yet the *Program of Priestly Formation* continued to require a four-year formation program (with at least two years of philosophy as preparation). Catholic seminaries often rewarded the additional year with a Master of Sacred Theology or Master of Arts. A few enterprising schools used it as an intern year.

As the number of seminary degrees multiplied in the 1970s and 1980s, many seminary degrees did not lead to ordained ministry. A person could, for example, earn a Master of Arts degree, and use it as a qualification for admission to a PhD program or for a position as a lay administrator of a Catholic program or parish. The multiplicity of degrees encouraged Catholic schools to admit people to their degree programs who were not part of their program of formation. The Catholic MDiv was essentially a graduate professional degree, similar to the degrees issued by Protestant institutions, requiring three years of study. Protestant students enrolled in Catholic seminaries could use it to meet their ordination requirements. Yet, Catholic schools also awarded the Master of Divinity degree as a purely professional degree for laypeople who did not want or who could not be ordained (married men or women). The lay degree was sharply distinguished from the priestly program. The degree was a year shorter than the mandated four-year program of priestly formation and did not require the two years of philosophy; and, most important, the MDiv program was defined in purely academic and professional terms. Lay Master of Divinity candidates did not participate in the programs of priestly formation, nor did the seminaries provide a program of spiritual formation more suited to their lay status.[27]

Acceptance into the Association of Theological Schools exposed Catholic seminary leaders to a community of educators who were rapidly expanding their own administrations and working on issues of funding and governance. This was a new world for most Catholic seminary leaders. Canonically and actually, a bishop or bishops owned diocesan seminaries. Those seminaries operated by religious orders were under the firm control of the religious superior. In one sense, this structure, mandated by canon law, did not change, but the various seminaries responded to it by adding different offices or by redefining old ones. The rector became *de facto* the chief executive officer, who exerted much of his control of the school through the various officers, including the dean and spiritual director, who were appointed by and responsible to him. Each revision of the *Program of Priestly Formation* revisited the nature of these offices and made changes in their general description. Yet, as in the case of the degrees, the result was a deep split in the schools. The administration consisted of the mandated officers as well as those necessitated by the school's work as a graduate professional institution. As in Protestant schools, academic deans, chief financial officers, or development offices of the school had to incorporate their functions under existing rubrics.

Compared with administration, changes in governance were more difficult to achieve. The basic change was the addition of boards of trustees, although these boards had differing names and functions. Part of the rationale for boards was the acute need of the schools, like their Protestant counterparts, to find new means of fundraising, but the new boards were more than conduits for funds. Gradually, they took on many of the functions of other American seminary boards, approving budgets and mission statements, and providing the rector and/or the ordinary with advice on polity. The importance of the Lilly Endowment in helping with this transition cannot be overstated. Using a combination of well-directed grants and wise advice, Fred Hofheinz, the Lilly officer who worked with Catholic schools in the late 1970s and 1980s, provided opportunities for the leaders of schools to exchange ideas with each other. The Keystone Conferences, which brought together experts on governance, rectors, and board members, were important contributors to this development and served as a model for Board education in Protestant theological schools. For all the change, most diocesan seminaries, whether serving one diocese or many, remained firmly under thecontrol of their ordinaries. The power of boards and faculties depended on the bishop's goodwill. However, this observation should not obscure the importance of this seemingly minor change in seminary governance. The advent of trustees may have been the most important, although less obvious, change brought about by accreditation.[28]

27. In the documents, formation is always preparation for the sacramental grace of ordination. While spiritual formation is a part of this, spiritual and priestly formation should never be equated.

28. Wister, "The Effects of Institutional Change," 88, shows the impact of boards on the governance

RELIGIOUS-ORDER SEMINARIES

Neither Vatican II nor the subsequent *Programs of Priestly Formation* dealt in any depth with the special educational needs of members of religious orders. Vatican II issued a strong call for the orders to return to their original charismas and ministries, without too much specificity as what that might mean. Somewhat like Protestant Evangelicals, who established large numbers of parachurch organizations to carry out specific missions, Catholics had formed religious orders in response to concrete social situations, often involving the poor or foreign missions. To return to their origins meant to return to those original ministries that, in the light of *Gaudium et spes*, meant active concern for those who were poor or those outside of the Church

Before Vatican II, almost all the religious-order seminaries were small, many were in rural locations, and with the exception of some Jesuit theologates, they lacked the academic facilities needed to carry out their renewed understanding of their mission. How could the religious-order seminaries reorder themselves to recover their original charisma? How could they replace the existing schools, often monastic or semimonastic, with renewed or newly created institutions?

One solution was through alliances with Protestant seminaries. The ATS Resources Commission (see below) had called for schools to find ways of cooperating with each other. Consortia in Chicago, Boston, and Washington DC included Catholic seminaries in their agreements. This cooperation included sharing library resources and allowing cross registration as well as some shared faculty activities. Yet these cooperative ventures did not require any sharing of power with non-Catholic institutions. The Graduate Theological Union (GTU), founded in 1962, was different. The GTU permitted individual schools to retain their own faculties and student programs, while allowing students to enroll in graduate theological degrees, particularly the MA and the PhD, conducted by the Union itself. The Jesuits joined the Union in 1966 and the Franciscans and Dominicans quickly followed. The GTU schools were something new in Catholic history. While the original seminaries retained control of the formation programs, the students had the academic resources of a major center of theological and religious research as well as the advantage of companionship with already-ordained brothers seeking additional graduate degrees. As in the case of other Catholic seminaries, this marked a separation of the academic and professional program from the formation programs. The difference at the GTU was that the university community was not Catholic: it was Protestant, Unitarian, Jewish, Buddhist, and secular. From the standpoint of governance, the GTU was an important experiment. While the individual seminaries retained control of their own faculties and students, the overall control of significant theological programs was in non-Catholic hands.

---

of schools. A later series of Keystone Conferences was primarily concerned with teaching. See Klimoski et al., *Educating Leaders for Ministry*.

Jesuit Woodstock, the oldest Jesuit theologate in America and arguably the order's flagship institution, tried another form of cooperation. The Jesuits located the school in rural Maryland in 1869, and the school had a national reputation, with Avery Dulles and John Courtney Murray serving on the faculty. The model that intrigued the Jesuits was the Columbia cooperative model, similar to a proposal made by Thomas Jefferson for the University of Virginia. Seminaries located near Columbia were encouraged to integrate their programs with those of the University. Students from Jewish Theological Seminary and Union (New York) attended classes at Columbia, and Columbia and Union had a joint PhD degree. Cooperation among the Morningside Heights institutions seemed the way of the future. Consequently, Woodstock moved to New York in 1969, but the experiment did not last long. The order reduced the number of its theologates in 1972, and Woodstock became a research center, affiliated with Georgetown University.

Another path forward was the establishment of theological unions, bringing together several orders in one school. The Chicago Theological Union (CTU) was established in 1968,[29] and the Washington Theological Coalition (later Union) in 1969. These schools brought together teachers and students from a wide variety of religious orders that created a new institution, jointly owned, to serve their needs. Shortly after their founding, both institutions became important centers of Catholic thought, and Vincent Cushing, the president of the WTU from 1975 to 1999, was president of the Association of Theological Schools from 1982–1984. Cushing was one of the major contributors to the Keystone Conferences, organized by Fred Hofheinz of Lilly, to help Catholic schools with the twin problems of governance and finances.

The two union seminaries, CTU and WTU, were pioneers. They admitted women religious and laypeople shortly after their foundings, and they experimented with different academic programs and degrees. The union schools also pioneered in the practical fields, including field education. Both early added lay teachers and invited laymen and women to serve on their boards. The diocesan seminaries made similar changes, although not at the same rate or with the same impact on the governance of the schools.

Why were these schools such centers of innovation? I admit that as an outsider to Catholic life, I was first tempted to seek the roots of their creativity in the charisma of the various orders involved in their creation, and in those orders' histories in America. However, a remark in the report of the most recent Roman visitation provided me with a clue. The visitors noted that these seminaries preferred to speak of ministry rather than priesthood, and speculated that this was because they had instructors committed to women's ordination. While the latter speculation might or might not be true, the observation was acute. What is obvious about the two unions is that they are schools of theology and ministry. Although both unions have some corporate programs of formation, formation remains in the hands of the religious

29. See the excellent study, Bechtold, *Catholic Theological Union at Chicago.*

orders that sponsor the schools. This enables the common structure to function more as an ecumenical Protestant seminary might, gathering a variety of students and faculty, to accomplish multiple goals and purposes. Formation remains very important to the various orders, but it is not as central to the structure of the unions. In other words, the separation between the formational and the academic that we noted in all accredited schools acquired a different structure in these innovative institutions.

Unlike diocesan seminaries, the union seminaries lacked a direct link to the hierarchy. They are not owned by the bishop or by any single religious order. To survive, they have to raise students, funds, and supporters. While endowments and ecclesiastical support are blessings, they are not the origin of innovation. Just as finances necessitated that Evangelical seminaries innovate in such areas as managing multiple locations and using technology, so finances have encouraged the unions to try new things and new programs.

Poverty is rarely a blessing. Like their Protestant counterparts, the union seminaries have faced increasing costs. As the number of lay teachers has increased, for example, they have also had to face the problem of funding salaries on par with those at other ATS schools. Higher costs mean increasing dependence on tuition and enrollment. As a result, both schools had to face the financial implications of the crisis in the number of vocations. The sponsoring orders have declined in the number of novices, and the number of women religious, both novices and absolute numbers, has also dropped precipitously. As the vocations crisis has continued, the schools have had to replace the revenue from priestly candidates and women religious with revenue from other students, many of whom are part time. Each priestly candidate and woman religious who does not enter the seminary means that the school has to recruit two or more lay students to replace them. To date, CTU, located in a very heavily Catholic area, has been able to keep up the pace, but WTU has not. Washington DC does not have as concentrated a Catholic population as Chicago, and the school faces stiff competition from other Catholic schools for lay and Protestant students, including the Ecumenical Institute of St. Mary's Seminary and University, founded in 1968. Consequently, Washington Theological Union ceased its academic programs in 2013 and will seek other ways of continuing its mission.

Pre-Vatican II theologates did not publish catalogs, and their publication was one of the most visible signs of the academic renewal that was taking place. Yet the most basic changes were not in the morphology of the programs. The familiar courses in Bible, Church history, and theology remained in the curriculum, but instructors refashioned these courses in a radically new way. The older manuals quickly disappeared, and the more American mixture of lectures, library research papers, discussions, examinations, and seminars took their place. Students were much more involved in their own learning, and the courses often stressed the importance of critical thinking and the examination of sources. Since many issues were left open ended, questioning was encouraged, and further study and reflection also encouraged. Seminaries added electives to their programs, and students did not take their courses in as rigid an order. As the Second Vatican Council had directed, biblical studies, the most ecumenical of Catholic theological studies, moved to the center of the curriculum, often having the largest number of credit hours. The libraries, which before the council had been often reserved for the use of the priest instructors, became important parts of the educational programs.

The most dramatic development was in professional studies. Pre-Vatican II seminaries stressed the correct administration of the sacraments and pastoral responses to confessions. Yet these same schools paid little attention to liturgics, preaching, religious education, counseling, ethics or spiritual direction. After Vatican II, these courses, together with field education, took up more than a quarter of the program. In part, this was in response to the pastoral direction taken by the Council itself, and to the picture of priesthood in *Presbyterorum ordinis*. These documents defined priesthood in terms of building up the community and educating Christians about their faith. Even in parish administration, the priest was to share insights and governance with the laity, and together with his fellow priests was to share the larger ministry of the bishop. At the same time, American Catholic expectations of their priests were changing in response to both the Council and to American conditions. The old custom of saying rosary during Mass or engaging in other devotions declined. Catholics expected their liturgies to be well prepared with a biblical message.

The new practical courses replaced the time and effort that pre-Vatican II seminaries had spent on confession and penance. The most visible sign of the new Catholicism was not Sunday mornings; it was the continually shrinking lines on Saturday afternoons.[30] There were many reasons for this decline. Many married Catholics did not go to confession, because they did not want to discuss their birth-control decisions with their priest. More fundamentally, confession as a practice seems to have worn out. In addition to relatively minor sexual peccadilloes, most confessions were relatively minor moral or ritual offenses. Where serious moral or psychological problems existed, the practice did not provide equally serious remedial measures. Like other Americans in the 1970s and 1980s, Catholic laity yearned for spirituality and spiritual direction, but the judicial ritual of confession and penance did not meet their needs.

The decline of confession was part of the larger post-Vatican II redefinition of the priesthood. The practice of confession and penance was essentially juridical. The layperson laid his or her sins before the priest, who made an authoritative judgment and imposed the proper penance. The good confessor was an authority whose pronouncement was the word of the Church. In contrast, the new professional courses, and the understanding of ministry that they implied, required priests to exercise discernment. In simple terms, the priest no longer had only to know what the Church taught; the new priest had to make those teachings meaningful to both individuals

---

30. Dolan et al., *Transforming Parish Ministry*.

and communities. This interpretative task required the priest to do more than repeat the teachings of the Church; the priest had to interpret those teachings in their context. Developing the priest's ability to do theological reflection was as important as teaching the priest the content of doctrine. This was, also, parallel to developments in Protestant theological education.[31]

The new professional program of the seminaries blurred the distinction between priests and laity. Although the priest was clearly the administrator of the sacraments, the other tasks of parish ministry did not require ordination. Laypeople, including women religious, entered into congregational leadership as liturgists, educators, parish administrators, and counselors. Many served as hospital chaplains. Spiritual direction was another new ministry. Unlike a confessor, who rendered a judicial decision, a spiritual director was concerned with the practice of the presence of God. Women religious were particularly attracted to this ministry, and they established retreat centers that served laity interested in developing their own spiritual lives. Some seminaries called women spiritual directors to direct their formation programs, until the Vatican ruled that seminary spiritual directors could only be priests. All programs of priestly formation involved spiritual direction, but not all programs of spiritual direction involved priestly formation. The distinction was important, if not always clear.

These new ministries were similar to tasks performed previously by priests, but they were not the same as those more traditional priestly roles. I find it useful to think of them as new forms of ministry created by the Second Vatican Council. Here again the line between these two interpretations is narrow and may be overdrawn. Clearly, the expansion of lay ministries was one way for the Church to compensate for the declining number of priests. In the pre-Vatican II Church, priests served in almost all ecclesiastical offices, including administrative offices, and the declining number of priests meant that someone else had to perform the tasks that priests could no longer accomplish. Further, the redefinition of the priesthood by the Council added many difficult and time-consuming tasks to the work of the local pastor and his assistants. Preaching, for example, took much time, and participatory administration added meetings, phone calls, and preparations to the workload. Pastors clearly needed help. Yet one must avoid too simple an interpretation of what occurred. The new ministers were not old priests writ small; they did tasks that no one had done before. The new ministries were fundamentally a response to the emphasis on the pastoral character of the Church affirmed in all the Vatican II documents. Even had the number of priests increased, many laypeople, including women religious, would have felt called to perform the new ministries as their own vocation. Something new was present in the work of the lay liturgist, the pastoral director, and the other offices in the new parish that was not merely helping the pastor with his work.

---

31. See below, chapters 6 and 7.

THE NEW WORK OF CATHOLIC THEOLOGIANS

As in American Protestantism, much Catholic theology moved outside of the seminary orb. The expansion of college theology classes began in the 1950s, and those who taught in that area formed the College Theological Society in 1953. This beginning mushroomed after Vatican II when a massive expansion of the teaching of theology in Catholic colleges and universities occurred, both on the undergraduate and the graduate levels. In many ways, this expansion was parallel to the growth of religion departments on secular campuses, and Catholic theology departments frequently taught courses that secular institutions designate as religion. At the same time, many Catholics entered historically Protestant divinity schools and graduate programs in religion. Many Catholic teachers carried the understanding of religion as an academic discipline into their work as teachers and scholars. The combination of what many American institutions consider separate fields complicates attempts to understand the particular relationship between the Church's magisterium and its related schools.

The post-1960s American Catholic university was, moreover, a far different place than its pre-Vatican II predecessor. In 1967, Catholic-university presidents at the Land of Lakes Conference had declared that they would abide by the contemporary standards for academic freedom in universities and not seek confessional exceptions. A year later, the publication of Pope Paul's encyclical *Humanae vitae* touched off a major protest by twenty-one theologians at the Catholic University of America. Eventually, the protesters left, voluntarily or involuntarily. In 1971, perhaps equally important in an age of rising costs, the US Supreme Court in *Tilden v Richardson*, made academic freedom a condition for religious colleges to receive federal aid. Regional accreditation reinforced this requirement. From that point, it became very difficult to remove a tenured professor from an American Catholic institution.[32]

What then was a Catholic university? The traditional definition of a Catholic college or university was a school owned by the Church and, more typically, a religious order. As with many Protestant colleges, ownership became increasingly blurred. Catholic boards became increasingly mixed bodies, containing laity, public members, and often non-Catholics. Unlike seminary boards, these boards owned the schools

---

32. For the effects of professionalization on the teaching of Catholic theology, see Curran, "Academic Freedom," 112. What might be described as the professionalization of Catholic higher education in general also took place with regard to the teaching of theology and religion on Catholic college campuses. Theology courses were traditionally required in Catholic institutions, but before 1960 they were frequently taught by people who did not have doctoral degrees. It was often thought that the mere fact of religious profession or priestly ordination was a sufficient training for teaching theology. The first national meeting of the Society of Catholic College Teachers of Sacred Doctrine (later called the College Theology Society) was held in 1955. One of the primary concerns of this group was the poor quality of undergraduate theology courses and the need for a greater professionalization. Accrediting agencies had been critical of Catholic theology courses. The founders of this new society recognized the legitimacy of these criticisms and wanted to raise the standards of such theology and religious programs to reach the standards for other faculties and courses in Catholic colleges and universities.

and approved the school's policies. Faculty, including those who taught theology, religion, and philosophy, were under the board's policies that were enforceable at law.

In theory, Catholic colleges and universities taught the Catholic faith to Catholic students. Yet in practice, what this meant was not clear. While some cases of conflict between Rome and American theological teachers did involve seminary teachers, the most newsworthy cases, such as those of Charles Curran, and in the 2010s Elizabeth Johnston and Margaret Farley, involved people teaching in universities. The case of Charles Curran revolved around the employment of a Catholic teacher in a Catholic university subject to hierarchical ownership and control. At the behest of the Vatican, Catholic University removed Curran, and he subsequently lost his court case challenging the decision.

The recent dispute over Elizabeth Johnson, a professor at Fordham University and past president of the College Theological Society, involved similar issues. The American bishops condemned Johnson, but they were not able to have her removed from Jesuit Fordham, nor did the Jesuits request her dismissal. The case of Margaret Farley is more complex. Her case has much in common with that of Elizabeth Johnson but with one important difference. Although a member of a religious order, Farley was a tenured professor in the Yale University Divinity School, and the Church had no way to dismiss her. Yet the Church went through many of the same procedures as though she were so employed. The Congregation for the Doctrine of the Faith, reviewed her book, *Just Love*, and asked for clarifications. Not satisfied with her responses, the Congregation officially warned the faithful not to read the book and declared that it was not to be used as a guide by priests or others.

These cases had many layers. One of the most important was Catholic identity. All three insisted that they were Catholic theologians who taught theology and ethics from a Catholic perspective. How could this be the case if the Church did not recognize their work as within the Catholic consensus? Who speaks for the Church? In enlisting the services of the so-called new theologians, the Church had implied that theology had an exploratory as well as an explanatory function. In other words, that the task of theology was not only to teach and explain what the magisterium decided, but to examine theological issues from a fresh perspective. In a sense, the model was similar to that of historical and biblical issues, where the nature of research demands that no issue have a final resolution.

An early attempt to resolve this dilemma was the 1983 revision of canon law. Paragraph 812 required all teachers of theology in Catholic universities to have the "mandate [*mandatum*] of the competent ecclesiastical authority."[33] In other words, a Catholic theologian was a person recognized by the Church as such. The provision

---

33. Orsy, "The Mandate," 476. The new rule read, "Qui in studiorum institutis quibuslibet disciplinas tradunt theologicas, auctoritatis ecclesiasticae competentis mandatum habeant oportet." (Those who in any kind of institute of higher studies teach theological disciplines must have the mandate of the competent ecclesiastical authority. [Orsy's translation])

did not recognize the unique character of American Catholic institutions. In Europe, treaties or concordats, defined the relationship between Catholic faculties, the Vatican, and the state. Ordinarily, these agreements required faculty to obtain and retain ecclesiastical approval for their teaching. In the Hans Küng case, when ecclesiastical approval was withdrawn, the university had to transfer him to another faculty (he had tenure under civil law), and he was prohibited from participation in the examination of students in the Catholic faculty. In America, the question of a mandate (*mandatum*) went to the boards of trustees. When they did not modify their faculty handbooks to require this formal approval, it became a matter of the teacher's conscience whether he or she chose to seek such a mandate or not.

Pope John Paul II attempted a definition of the Catholic university in his 1990 apostolic constitution *Ex corde ecclesiae*.[34] In this, John Paul went back to an older understanding of the relationship of the university to the Church and to Western culture.

> Born from the heart of the Church, a Catholic University is located in that course of tradition which may be traced back to the very origin of the University as an institution. It has always been recognized as an incomparable centre of creativity and dissemination of knowledge for the good of humanity. By vocation, the *Universitas magistrorum et scholarium* is dedicated to research, to teaching and to the education of students who freely associate with their teachers in a common love of knowledge. With every other University it shares that *gaudium de veritate,* so precious to St. Augustine, which is that joy of searching for, discovering and communicating truth in every field of knowledge. A Catholic University's privileged task is "to unite existentially by intellectual effort two orders of reality that too frequently tend to be placed in opposition as though they were antithetical: the search for truth, and the certainty of already knowing the fount of truth."[35]

In many ways, this understanding reflected much in Catholic tradition. Cardinal John Henry Newman made a similar point in his *The Idea of the University.* Part of the question was the status of this ancient ideal in a world in which truth is primarily understood as a report on the latest research and not as a conclusion valid for all ages and peoples.

Another difficulty, as noted above, was that the phrase *theological studies* did not have a precise meaning. Catholic universities included many different disciplines under theology, much like the discipline of religious studies does in other institutions, and instructors taught many subjects with theological import in other departments. Notre Dame, for example, hired such Evangelicals as George Marsden and Mark Noll to teach in the school's history division. The day had passed when whatever looked like a duck had to be studied in the department of biology. Particularly in larger schools,

---

34. John Paul II, *Apostolic Constitution: On Catholic Universities.*
35. Ibid.

the lines between broad fields, such as theology, and other areas of the curriculum, such as history, art, or philosophy, were not sharply drawn.

The relationship that existed between college and university theology departments and seminaries remained, as in the case of Protestantism, unclear. Seminaries, including the diocesan schools, depended on the graduate universities for the scholarly certification of their faculties, and, as in Protestantism, some seminary teachers saw themselves as essentially members of a graduate theological faculty. In many ways, the internal diversity of the post-Vatican II seminary made it easy for teachers to define themselves in disciplinary terms. If the work of formation was, as Rome insisted, in the hands of priests, what was the role of the layperson who taught in those institutions? Were they not professionals whose primary role was that of a teacher of a recognized academic discipline? If so, the ultimate standard was that of the larger educational world, which defined what it meant to a professional scholar and teacher.

The relation between seminaries and universities posed another, less visible problem. If some of those teaching in university departments of theology and in university divinity schools were not acceptable to the Church theologically, how could they teach those who would later direct the formation of priestly candidates? Wasn't the well poisoned at the source? Granted that few students are mirror images of their teachers, the problem did not admit of a simple solution. Protestant schools face a similar dilemma. How can the Church (or churches) use secular scholarship, including secular studies of its own sources, to train its priests (or ministers)? The Church faced a similar issue in the medieval period when its theologians confronted the philosophy of Aristotle. Perhaps a new Thomas is what is needed today.

COMPLICATIONS[36]

After Vatican II, Catholic seminary education in the United States virtually recreated itself. Almost no facet of preparation for priesthood or for preparation for ministry was unchanged: curriculum, pedagogy, ethos, sacramental and spiritual life, faculty, and governance. Change on such a massive level carried out so quickly would have been difficult in the best of times, but these were not the best of times. Vatican II marked the beginning of a half century of painful adjustments for the Catholic community in America. By the 1980s, some people, perhaps especially the young, were looking backward at the pre-Vatican II Church with nostalgia and yearning. The sense

---

36. I have chosen the term *complications* to include a variety of challenges to the new seminary. For those who struggled with many of these issues, they were crises, and the language of crisis does run through the literature from 1980 to 2010. I am not ignoring that as part of the story. One effect of the massive changes that Catholic theological education underwent is a sense of disorientation and confusion. Yet, and this is definitely a perspective from without, the course of post-Vatican II Catholic theological education seems relatively smooth. Once the revolution had past, curricular and educational change proceeded on more or less a steady course. Such features of recent theological education as an emphasis on reflection entered into the Catholic story in due course.

that something had gone awry was everywhere. Progressive Catholics felt that the hierarchy had betrayed the Second Vatican Council, and that the Church was drifting back toward its authoritarian past. The failure of the Church to ordain women priests was one reason for this dissatisfaction, but it was not the only reason. If many liberals were so-called cafeteria Catholics, as their conservative critics claimed, they were also cafeteria dissenters, finding many diverse points of disagreement. Conservative Catholics were also disillusioned. Although only a few wanted to return to the pre-Vatican II Latin liturgy, many wanted the return of traditional devotional practices and, above all, the renewal of Church authority. These Catholics were not alone. Many American mainstream Protestants wanted a return to the old-time religion, and the nation as a whole turned to the right with the election of Ronald Reagan.

The first shock to the Catholic system was the significant number of priests and women religious who left their ministries. In hindsight, what led to the exodus is not completely clear. Many former priests argued that it was the failure of the Church to end celibacy, and this must have entered into their decisions. The issue had been reserved to the pope by the documents constituting the Second Vatican Council, and Paul VI issued his letter on celibacy in 1971. Yet one must be careful to put this into context. The essential problem was deeper. While Vatican II had not ended celibacy, the Council's actions removed much of its theological justification.[37]

Not only had the meaning of priesthood been called into fundamental question, but the principal theological supports for celibacy had in consequence been radically undermined. The social supports for celibacy were simultaneously evaporating, as younger Catholics embraced essentially secular standards with regard to sexual morality. Celibacy quickly emerged as the principal issue in terms of which clerical discontent was articulated. Compulsory clerical celibacy was and is a legitimate issue in its own right. But it quickly became a convenient and inevitably distorting symbol of more complicated priestly difficulties. Debates over celibacy proved an excellent way to sidestep engagement with troubling questions about belief, though these questions were arguably at the heart of the crisis in clerical identity.[38] If priests and women religious were to engage actively in the world in the name of faith, they needed to be part of the world, participating in its structures.

Uneasiness about celibacy permeated the system. Ironically, education for celibacy was more featured in Catholic seminary education after Vatican II than before. Each successive edition of the *Program of Priestly Formation* placed an increased emphasis on preparing men for this practice. If the old seminary had sought to teach celibacy by isolating the prospective priest from temptation, the new seminary made it a focus of its program. However, the problem was theological, not practical or educational. Priests no longer saw themselves as residential holy men, and newer definitions of

---

37. Tentler, "'God's Representative.'"
38. Ibid., 348.

priests as servants did not seemingly require celibacy any more than they required the cassock and biretta.

Yet celibacy alone does not explain either the heavy exodus or the lack of new recruits. Young priests had a multitude of secular opportunities. The disintegration of the Catholic ethnic communities stripped the priesthood of much of its prestige. Vatican II's idealism about service in the world also had its effects. The traditional round of sacraments and devotional activities was part of the great drama of salvation, the presence of the supernatural in the midst of the natural, but this theology was eroding. In the light of the world's needs, it was hard to make a case for a life of relative self-denial. Many no longer found the old case convincing, and no one made a new case for parochial ministry.

The case of women religious is easier to explain. The convent had offered the primary way for young Catholic women to enter into a career. The women's movement meant that this was no longer the case. New possibilities opened almost daily. Further, the theological justifications for religious vocations weakened after Vatican II. Families no longer saw the prayers and devotions of a daughter in the nunnery as part of their eternal security. If the primary motive for religious work was this worldly, not otherworldly, why should one not seek a secular outlet for one's professional energies? The issue of women's ordination also played a role. As it became clearer that Rome would not ordain women as priests, fewer elected the religious life. Perhaps the deeper problem was the centuries of neglect on the part of the hierarchy. While women religious had lived and worked closely with lay Catholics, who by and large respect their unique gifts, the Church's leadership had often not respected or rewarded their contributions.

For both men and women, the most important reason for the decline in vocations was slow, steady deterioration of the Catholic religious ecology or environment. Pre-Vatican II Catholicism provided young Catholics with a variety of institutions that built their religious and Catholic identity. This religious ecology was the primary recruiter of religious leaders. The weakening of the Catholic school system, where the instructors routinely urged children and teenagers to vocations, was the loss of a major pipeline. The falling numbers of women religious was both cause and effect of the vocations crisis. In the pre-Vatican II Church, nuns were the primary teachers in Catholic schools and in catechism. One of their tasks was to locate prospective priests and sisters and convince them of the importance of the religious life. As the number of nuns declined, fewer teachers encouraged new vocations. In turn, the lack of new vocations meant fewer teachers. Another major shift in the Catholic ecology was the decline and disappearance of high school and college seminaries in many areas. In short, theologates lost the pipelines that provided them with students prepared academically and accustomed to personal discipline. The system that had generated more candidates than needed was in shambles.

Another contributing cause was the gradual drift away from social idealism towards social values that stressed status and wealth. The election of John Paul II was part of a larger movement towards more conservative social positions. The 1979 election of Margaret Thatcher in Great Britain and the 1980 election of Ronald Reagan in the United States marked a turn away from interest in progressive causes. If the fall of the Soviet Union at the end of the decade was not the celebrated "End of History," it did reinforce other social trends in America and Europe that stressed individualism, self-determination, and capitalist values. The advocacy of rights remained popular; the push for social action and social consciousness was less so. This new conservatism was far from the traditional Catholic doctrine of social solidarity. The individual was king. In less than twenty years, the most profound insights of the Great Council seemed dated.

The vocations crisis was the most serious complication for the new seminaries. The schools had demonstrated a remarkable capacity for change. In less than twenty years, they changed curricula, the gender and clerical nature of their faculties, the composition of their student bodies, and their form of governance. They had also adopted new academic and professional standards. Few institutions have changed so much, so quickly. Yet the best of programs without students cannot sustain an educational institution. Catholic seminaries were underutilized, underappreciated, and underfinanced. Declining enrollment and lack of support had their effects on administrators and teachers. In 1970, the seminaries were the avatars of God's new Church, still blessed with abundant enrollments, and filled with intellectual and religious excitement. In 1990, these same seminaries often had a handful of students rattling around in buildings far too spacious for their needs.

The second major trend that complicated the post-Vatican II seminary was the general turn to religious conservatism in the 1980s and 1990s.[39] John Paul II was a very popular pope whose travels made him familiar to most Catholics. In many ways, he was the product of his experiences. Before he became pope, he had struggled against the communist government of Poland that was determined to weaken the Church, if not to destroy it altogether. The experience convinced him that the Church needed to assert itself and its own positions. John Paul II's theology was far from a simple return to the pre-Vatican II Church; he wanted the Church to establish clear boundaries between itself and the world. Aided by Cardinal Ratzinger, John Paul II skillfully used the powers of his office, including his pulpit, to correct what he felt were some mistaken directions.

Both John Paul II and Cardinal Ratzinger saw theological education as the key to a renewal of Catholicism. They understood the seminary very much in formational terms, and they wanted to reaffirm its character as the place where the Church prepared men for the sacrament of ordination. Perhaps the best description of their goal

---

39. This also affected Protestants. See chapter 5, below.

was to prepare priests for the New Evangelization, an ambitious attempt to present the gospel anew to those who had lost faith or ceased religious practice.

One unintended consequence of the post-Vatican II seminary reforms was the loss of flexibility. The seminary had changed quickly, because authority demanded that it change. The new post-Vatican II seminaries were far more complicated institutions than their predecessors. Like their Protestant counterparts, Catholic theologate instructors adapted the various privileges of American higher education to their own situation. Instructors had professional rank, tenure, and stated terms of employment. As among Protestants, so for Catholics this meant that a career in seminary teaching was more likely to last a lifetime than it had been earlier. Those instructors appointed in the late 1960s and 1970s continued to teach until the 1990s and, in many cases, the 2000s. The shadow of the idealism of the 1960s was consequently long. Moreover, many Catholic professors were educated in historically Protestant university divinity schools. Unlike denominational seminaries, the divinity schools were not responsible to any particular Church and tended to define the church in terms of its mission, particularly its social mission, not in terms of its historic faith commitments. This professionalization of the seminary made radical change difficult. Although it is speculative, the new boards of trustees may have also made radical course changes more difficult. Ironically, the students may have been more influenced by cultural changes than their faculty members. Many schools reported conflicts between the faculties shaped by the Second Vatican Council and their more conservative students.

VISITATIONS

The tensions in the seminaries as well as questions about seminary teaching led to a demand that Rome conduct official visitations of the schools. The Church conducted two such visitations: in 1985 and in 2002. Two events separated the two visitations: the sex scandals of the 1990s and 2000s and the publication of *Pastores dabo vobis*. *Pastores* was a summary document that brought together John Paul II's and Cardinal Ratzinger's teachings on the preparation of priests.

John Marshall, bishop of Burlington, Vermont, directed the first visitation in 1985, under the leadership of William Cardinal Baum, archbishop of Washington and newly appointed head of the Congregation of Catholic Education. The basis of the visitation was the third edition (1981) of the *Program of Priestly Formation*. In many ways, the Visitation followed a path similar to an accreditation visit. Each school prepared a self-study based on the *Program of Priestly Formation*, which was the basis of a four-day visit that interviewed administrators, faculty, staff members, and students. On that basis, the visitors sent each individual school an evaluation, and Cardinal Baum prepared a general report. The evaluation, while generally positive, noted some areas where seminaries needed improvement. Cardinal Baum wrote:

> Our most serious recommendations have been about the need to develop a clearer concept of the ordained priesthood, to promote the specialized nature of priestly formation in accordance with Vatican Council II's affirmation of seminaries, to deepen the academic formation so that it becomes more properly and adequately theological . . . and to ensure that the seminarians develop a good grasp of the specific contribution that the priest has to make to each pastoral situation.[40]

More pointedly, Cardinal Baum noted that some seminaries tended to confuse preparation for priestly ordination with education for ministry in general:

> The emergence and popularity in recent years of the language of "ministry" has enabled many people to understand their roles in the Church, but it has also led in some instances to the blurring of the concept of priesthood in a generally undifferentiated notion of ministry.[41]

To guard against this problem, Cardinal Baum recommended that the seminaries appoint more priests to their faculty. Baum also noted problems with governance and called for strengthening the role of rectors and diocesan bishops.

Although the Church did not publish all results of the visitation, the public reports were positive. The visitors concluded that the seminaries were doing good work and noted that the schools had implemented Vatican II in constructive ways. Although some conservatives thought that the visitation might have whitewashed the schools, the visitors carefully stayed within official (public) standards. Yet it was clear that the Vatican was firmly but surely pushing the seminaries towards its own theological program. That program became clearer before the second visitation in 2002.

PASTORES DABO VOBIS

In 1990, the International Synod, an international advisory assembly of bishops meeting in Rome, considered the preparation of priests. Along with other documents, they considered Baum's report on the American churches as support for their recommendations to Pope John Paul II. In 1992, the pope issued arguably the most important document on theological education since Vatican II. The document influenced the fourth edition of the *Program of Priestly Formation* (1993) and was the primary source for the fifth edition.

Pastores begin by noting that the Church faces a crisis in vocations that demands that the church pay special attention to the recruitment, formation, and retention of priests. At a time when the need was for a "New Evangelization," the Church must raise up new apostles to carry out its work. In a passage that recalls the Council, John Paul II said:

40. Quoted in Wister, "The Effects of Institutional Change," 127.
41. Ibid.

> Despite many contradictions, society is increasingly witnessing a powerful thirst for justice and peace; a more lively sense that humanity must care for creation and respect nature; a more open search for truth; a greater effort to safeguard human dignity; a growing commitment in many sectors of the world population to a more specific international solidarity and a new ordering of the world in freedom and justice. Parallel to the continued development of the potential offered by science and technology and the exchange of information and interaction of cultures, there is a new call for ethics, that is, a quest for meaning—and therefore for an objective standard of values which will delineate the possibilities and limits of progress.[42]

The way to address such a society is through a priest who fully participates in the holiness of Christ and who, indeed, Christ forms to take up this work. The seminary, consequently, is:

> more than a place, a material space, should be a spiritual place, a way of life, an atmosphere that fosters and ensures a process of formation, so that the person who is called to the priesthood by God may become, with the sacrament of orders, a living image of Jesus Christ, head and shepherd of the Church.[43]

The seminary is not a school apart from the Church. Rather, the seminary is the continuation of the earliest community around Jesus:

> In its deepest identity the seminary is called to be, in its own way, a continuation in the Church of the apostolic community gathered about Jesus, listening to his word, proceeding toward the Easter experience, awaiting the gift of the Spirit for the mission. Such an identity constitutes the normative ideal which stimulates the seminary in the many diverse forms and varied aspects which it assumes historically as a human institution, to find a concrete realization, faithful to the Gospel values from which it takes its inspiration and able to respond to the situations and needs of the times.[44]

Seminaries are the Church formational, and as God constitutes the Church local and the Church universal, God constitutes the Church formational through the Word of God and the presence of Christ in the sacraments.

Pastores sees the formation of the priest as involving four different, but interrelated, processes: human formation, spiritual formation, academic formation, and professional formation. Previous documents mentioned these four aspects of seminary life, including the American *Program of Priestly Formation*, but this document stated them more clearly. In particular, *Pastores* emphases the human foundation of the formation of a faithful priest:

---

42. John Paul II, *Pastores Dabo Vobis*.
43. Ibid.
44. Ibid.

> Future priests should therefore cultivate a series of human qualities, not only out of proper and due growth and realization of self, but also with a view to the ministry. These qualities are needed for them to be balanced people, strong and free, capable of bearing the weight of pastoral responsibilities. They need to be educated to love the truth, to be loyal, to respect every person, to have a sense of justice, to be true to their word, to be genuinely compassionate, to be men of integrity and, especially, to be balanced in judgment and behavior. (124) A simple and demanding program for this human formation can be found in the words of the apostle Paul to the Philippians: "Whatever is true, whatever is honorable, whatever is just, whatever is pure, whatever is lovely, whatever is gracious, if there is any excellence, if there is anything worthy of praise, think about these things." (Phil. 4:8).[45]

Before one can become a priest, one must become fully human, a person at home in the world, and a person marked by personal integrity.

For John Paul II, the model for the interaction of these four types of formation is the Thomistic understanding of the virtues in which the supernatural virtues complete the human virtues and perfect them. Just as the other sacraments bring the natural virtues to their fulfillment in faith, hope, and love, so ordination completes the human and supernatural virtues and joins the person to Christ:

> Human formation, when it is carried out in the context of an anthropology which is open to the full truth regarding the human person, leads to and finds its completion in spiritual formation. Every human being, as God's creature who has been redeemed by Christ's blood, is called to be reborn "of water and the Spirit" (Jn. 3:5) and to become a "son in the Son." In this wonderful plan of God is to be found the basis of the essentially religious dimension of the human person, which moreover can be grasped and recognized by reason itself: The human individual is open to transcendence, to the absolute; he has a heart which is restless until it rests in the Lord.[46]

Pastores separation of the four aspects of priestly formation distinguished different modes of priestly formation, but it did not separate or compartmentalize them. I find a sacramental model useful here. Just as Jesus Christ is the One Sacrament that is presented in the seven sacraments, the sacraments work together to bring the person of faith to completion or wholeness. So the four aspects of formation represent the formation of the individual into completeness or wholeness. Each aspect is distinguishable but not separable from the others. Thus, the study of theology has a spiritual dimension just as the professional studies have a theological dimension. *Lectio divina*, meditative reading of the Bible, and scholarly studies come together in the preparation of the priest. In a similar way, John Paul II speaks of the relationship of priestly

---

45. Ibid.
46. Ibid.

formation to philosophy and the social sciences. These sciences enable the priest to extend the contemporary character of Christ into the present.

The pope's pronouncement on priestly formation came just as the sex scandals in the Catholic Church began to become public knowledge. Almost every level of Catholic life felt the shock of the scandals, and seminaries were no exception. Almost certainly they complicated the long-standing vocations crisis and made it more difficult to recruit students. Yet some good news for seminaries came out of the scandals.

The John Jay study of priest sexual abuse indicated that the vast majority of the abusers in America received their seminary training before the Vatican II reforms had taken effect. The seminaries had clearly improved their psychological evaluations of students and their other evaluative techniques. American seminaries were doing a much better job of forming men for priestly vocations than had been supposed.[47]

The scandals focused sharp attention on the question of seminaries and homosexual students. While the Catholic Church had long regarded homosexual acts as sin, the Church had not necessarily so regarded homosexual tendencies. The Church expected people to overcome them much in the same way that an individual overcame other temptations. In regard to the seminaries and priesthood, many felt that was no reason why a person could not be homosexual in orientation and celibate as easily (or with similar difficulties) as a heterosexual and celibate. Both broke their vows when they engaged in sexual acts with partners of either gender, and both equally had to confess impure thoughts. How many homosexual priests were there in fact? Vincent Cushing, the influential president of the Washington Theological Union, ventured the guess that it might be five times the number in the general population, but he had no firm evidence to surround his claim.[48] Yet the scandals led many to demand the Church clarify its position on homosexuals in the priesthood. The rule that emerged was that seminaries were not to admit men who engaged in homosexual acts or who had homosexual urges during the last two years. What was new was the examination of homosexual urges. Vocation directors only required heterosexual men to maintain a period of physical chastity before admission.

This was not a radically new policy. During the yearly evaluations of students, past faculties paid careful attention in the external forum to any signs of homosexual inclination or activity. Yet as the views of the psychological community changed along with general public sentiment, so did seminary practice. Rome returned the theologates to older ways of examining students' personal lives.

---

47. John Jay College Research Team, "The Causes and Context of Sexual Abuse of Minors by Catholic Priests in the United States, 1950–2010."

48. Cushing, "Some Reflections."

THE SECOND VISITATION

Pastores dabo Vobis and the sex scandals formed the basis of the second Vatican visitation of the seminaries, which the pope ordered in 2002. Edwin F. O'Brien, then archbishop for military services and an experienced seminary leader, directed the visitation. As had the first visitation, this process involved self-study, interviews, and reports to the ordinary and/or superiors. At the insistence of the American bishops, the Church appointed lay visitors to each team, although their formal power was limited. The report stated that many of the difficulties noted in the previous visitation were no longer present. The most serious problem was that many schools, in their efforts to educate both lay leaders and priests, tended to downplay the distinction between the common priesthood and the hierarchical priesthood:

> Problems can also arise when the seminary aims at offering a theological education to all—seminarians and laity—for, unless proper safeguards are put in place, the seminary can lose much of its finality, which is to offer a specifically priestly formation to men chosen by the church to embark on the way to Holy Orders.[49]

The report called for an increasing separation between lay and priestly students, including classes and libraries. Ironically, the fact that the priestly formation program and the various lay programs shared resources made many seminaries economically viable. Significantly, the report noted that the resolute action by seminary rectors had largely resolved the questions about homosexuality and homosexual practice.

Pastores Dabo Vobis deeply influenced the fifth edition of the *Program of Priestly Formation*, published in 2005–2006. The compilers cited the exhortation on almost every page, and structured the document around the fourfold formation of that document. The human formation of the priest is equal to the spiritual, academic, and pastoral formation in importance. The emphasis is on the students' integration of these aspects of their formation into a personal readiness for ordination and service. The document makes clear that formation is a priestly task. All seminary officers concerned with formation should be priests, although seminaries might hire lay faculty to teach academic subjects.

At one point, the fifth edition reflects a change in practice that had been gaining popularity, at least with students, since the 1980s. The *Program* stressed traditional Catholic devotional practices as part of the formation program:

> Devotion to the Blessed Sacrament must be encouraged. Scheduled hours of Eucharistic exposition are particularly desirable to provide for special opportunities for the adoration of the Blessed Sacrament in the seminary. It is also desirable that seminarians develop a habit of personal visits to the Blessed Sacrament in the tabernacle.

49. Online: http://www.ewtn.com/library/CURIA/ccefinalreport.HTM/.

> ... Devotion to the Blessed Virgin Mary, the Mother of God, and to the saints must be encouraged. Opportunities for devotional prayer should be made available and encouraged. The rosary, "a compendium of the Gospel," is especially recommended as a means of contemplating Christ "in the school of Mary."[50]

The document also called on American seminaries to offer the devotional practices of the various immigrant communities served by the Church. Many of these communities, especially various Latin American communities, had widely practiced devotions to Mary and the saints. The devotional ethos gave the theologates more of a Catholic feel.

Does the fifth edition of the *Program of Priestly Formation* represent a retreat from some of the insights of Vatican II? One must be careful to distinguish between actions and policies that Church and seminary leaders adopted to implement the Council, and the teachings of the Council itself. Clearly, the fifth edition signaled the return of many pre-Vatican II devotional practices to the seminary. Yet those practices had not been condemned by the Council, nor does evidence exist that the bishops at the Council intended for these practices to lapse. On many points, especially the earthly work of the priesthood, the *Program of Priestly Formation* actually elaborated the Council's insights. Although the *Program* retained two years of philosophy, for example, the emphasis on human formation required a pastoral awareness of the social sciences and of psychology.

REFLECTIONS

The transformation of Catholic seminaries that followed the Second Vatican Council was one of the quickest and most complete changes in the history of American theological education. Within less than a decade, schools adopted new curricula and new forms of governance, and came to include students who were not candidates for the priesthood. Those seminaries related to religious orders made these adjustments more quickly than diocesan schools, but the diocesan schools followed a similar pathway. Change on this massive a scale is difficult for any institution or set of institutions. In retrospect, the most remarkable fact about this season of change is not that controversies and disagreements remained, but that these were so minor.

The current American Catholic theological school is a remarkable combination. The Catholic belief in priestly formation, one of the bedrocks in the Catholic tradition, requires a school that is a community that can shape the individual candidate. Whatever else a present-day priest may be, the priest must possess the charisma of celebrating the sacraments and, thus, mediating the presence and work of Christ to the present world. On this foundation, the present-day Catholic seminary has engrafted

---

50. United States Council of Catholic Bishops, *Program of Priestly Formation*.

different elements. Clearly, one set of elements comes from the European and American university tradition. Vatican II's mandate that priests must be able to engage the present world requires thorough intellectual training. The Catholic seminary is thus linked to both Catholic universities and to private universities with divinity schools and/or graduate programs in religion. Like the better Protestant seminaries, the schools often function as mini-universities granting a variety of master's degrees. The influence of the universities was not unknown in the pre-Vatican II seminary, especially in those orders, such as the Jesuits, who had a long and vibrant university tradition; but Vatican II replaced the traditional manuals and recitation methods with a much more thoroughly university standard. A student studying New Testament at a Catholic seminary would learn much the same material as a student undertaking the same study in a university context. The most dramatic shift was in the importance of the pastoral fields. Whereas before pastoral studies tended to emphasize the confessional and the performance of ritual acts, the new practical disciplines saw the priests as actively engaged at every level with the life of the parish.

In a sense, many post-Vatican II seminaries became theological universities that served different students with very different career possibilities. Although Catholic seminaries tended to mix lay and cleric candidates in the same classrooms, especially in the more university-oriented disciplines, the two or more student bodies did not always blend with each other. This was even more so in the professionally oriented classes. Perhaps most obvious, the priestly formation program remained visibly separate from the rest of the program. Was the priest to be formed sacramentally in a New Testament course taught by a laywoman or layman, or was this class primarily intellectual formation?

As I read the history, the most amazing thing about the last fifty years is the amount of freedom that the Vatican and hierarchy has given the theological schools and university departments of religion. At least in theological education, the centralization and top-down control of the Vatican I Church has been in abeyance. The development of midlevel bodies of governance, especially trustee boards and shared governance procedures, has created something new in Catholic life. Most of this change took place behind the scenes as the result of the very patient work of people like Fred Hofheinz of Lilly, Katarina Schuth, and Jesse Ziegler. In this area, Jesse Ziegler, who worked so carefully to incorporate Catholic schools into the Association of Theological Schools, was among the most important actors. More than anyone else, he saw the Catholic schools in the light of their future and not the light of their past.

5 Theology and Governance
Evangelicals, Missouri Synod Lutherans, and Southern Baptists in Crisis

BY THE LATE 1970s, the realignment in American religion was already far advanced and with it, a realignment in American theological education. Evangelicals, who had seemed a minority in the early 1960s, had become the largest single Protestant grouping, while the Mainstream Protestant churches had declined in numbers and influence. As improbable as it might have seemed to many Mainstream seminary leaders, religious Conservatives now had the largest seminaries and enrolled approximately half of the nation's Protestant seminarians. Nor was the Conservative renaissance confined to graduate theological education. Many Bible schools had become Bible colleges, and some, such as BIOLA, were becoming Christian universities, offering education for a variety of religious professions.[1] Moreover, the secularization of many Mainstream colleges left the large majority of the nation's Christian liberal-arts colleges under Conservative control. The most vital Christian student movements, InterVarsity and Campus Crusade, were Conservative in orientation, providing Conservative seminaries with an extensive feeder network. Further, religious Conservatives had more apparent political power than ever before. In 1976, a year that *Time* magazine dubbed the "Year of the Evangelical," the United States elected Jimmy Carter, a soft-spoken Southern Sunday school teacher, president. In 1980, Ronald Reagan, who followed him, if he was not a regular church attendee, spoke the language of Zion. Whether it was "springtime in America" or not, American religious Conservatives had not been as prominent or as successful since the heady days of the missionary revival of the 1910s.[2]

Yet, all was not well in Zion. Evangelical seminaries were entering a decade of intense conflict that threatened their newly won academic standing and the academic

---

1. For an excellent study of the development of Biblical colleges and schools, see Patterson, *Shining Lights*.

2. See Miller, *Piety and Profession*, 619–47.

freedom of their leading scholars. The formal issue in this dispute was biblical inerrancy, but like other theological disputes in Christian history, this battle was not only about doctrine and perhaps not even particularly about doctrine. From the 1808 foundation of Andover, theological schools had struggled with the related issues of control and accountability. Over more than a century, two broad patterns of governance had emerged. In both paradigms, the keystone of governance is the board of trustees, virtually required by state laws governing educational institutions. For convenience, I will call one model the public paradigm. In this configuration, the institution ultimately invests authority in a board of trustees that although self-perpetuating, represents the public that supports the school and controls the school's purse strings. The other model, the ecclesiastical model, assigns the real responsibility for the direction of the school to a church that elects the board directly. The inerrancy controversy will play itself out in different ways in these two venues. Fuller Theological Seminary and other publicly governed schools (under model 1) will largely escape the full effects of the blast, although many of their supporters may have supported the inerrantist side. In those schools, the board and its president served as a buffer between the institution, particularly the faculty, and the institution's critics. In contrast, the inerrancy controversy reshaped the ecclesiastical governed seminaries (under model 2)—the Southern Baptists and the Missouri Synod—and replaced their leadership with a new cohort of administrators and teachers. Although not immune from controversy, Christian Reformed Calvin College and Seminary was largely undisturbed.

PROBLEMS OF DEFINITION

Any discussion of American Protestant conservatism runs into the problem of language. Both the words *conservative* and *Evangelical* describe eddies in a very fluid religious landscape, in which individuals, institutions, denominations, and congregations are only loosely related to specific theological and ethical positions. At best, these terms attempt to locate particular segments of the American religious spectrum. The same observation is valid for the terms *liberal* and *Mainstream*. On both sides of the spectrum, groups may exhibit significant diversity on particular questions, and lived faith often combines elements that might seem incompatible with each other. Yet as imperfect as the language might be, the words had considerable power. Since many of the controversies of the 1970s and 1980s were about who was or was not an Evangelical or a Missouri Synod Lutheran or a Southern Baptist, we need to start with some very preliminary definitions.

The terms *conservative* and *Evangelical* overlap with each other. Protestant religious conservatives are all those who hold the convictions and structures of the past, especially the theology in the classic confessions, to still have meaning and relevance for the present. Evangelicals are those Conservatives who emphasize Scripture, the substitutionary atonement, and an experience of conversion. All Evangelicals are

Conservatives, but not all Conservatives are Evangelicals. Some Conservative groups, such as the various orthodox Presbyterian denominations and the Dutch Reformed, do not emphasize conversion, although they may align themselves with Evangelicals on other issues. American Evangelicals, who see themselves as the heirs of the revival tradition, are open to using technology to spread their message. As we shall see, the issue of who was and who was not an Evangelical was an important question in the 1980s and 1990s and one largely settled, not so much by a theological definition, as by a historical one.

One perspective on American Evangelicalism is that Evangelicalism is a community constituted by certain alliances that allow each group to maintain its own identity. Even before the 1942 founding of the National Association of Evangelicals (NAE), American Evangelicalism was a loose federation of denominations, voluntary societies, and concerned individuals. The Billy Graham crusades expanded the scope of this sphere of cooperation. Carl F. Henry wrote:

> During the 1960s I somewhat romanced the possibility that a vast Evangelical alliance might arise in the United States to coordinate effectively a national impact in evangelism, education, publication and sociopolitical action. Such an alliance is not the same thing as a new denomination. Quite apart from the question of its desirability, the remote possibility of such a national Evangelical alliance was both shaped and lost, it seems to me, by evangelist Billy Graham. Penetrating the so-called mainline denominations with an Evangelical rallying point, the Graham crusades reached far beyond the orbit of the National Association of Evangelicals. As the tide of enthusiasm for pluralistic ecumenism began to ebb, the prospect emerged for a mighty Evangelical movement that transcended secondary denominational distinctions; it held in promise a transdenominational link involving Southern Baptists, the National Association of Evangelicals, Missouri Synod Lutherans, perhaps some associates of the American Council of Churches, and large numbers of disaffected Evangelicals in ecumenically affiliated churches whom the NAE seemed unable to attract. *Christianity Today* became during my editorship (1956-68) an intellectual fulcrum for these overlapping Evangelical concerns.[3]

As in any alliance, especially one not defined by institutional arrangements, the various participants do not equally share their common commitments. Some are more in line with key convictions and others less so. In this sense, we can interpret Evangelicalism as a circle with some groups and individuals near its center and others more on its periphery.

The New Evangelicals, a loose federation of Conservatives headed by Carl F. Henry and Harold Ockenga, and the supporters of the various Graham enterprises formed the center of the Evangelical movement. Also in the center were the various parachurch organizations. Voluntary religious societies were part of the very fabric of

---

3. Henry, "American Evangelicals in a Turning Time," 1060.

nineteenth-century American religious life, and Conservative Christians continued the tradition throughout the twentieth century. Organizations existed for youth work, for missionary outreach, for social service, for radio and later television ministry, and for world relief. Theologically, most of these traveled light with only a requirement that all employees accept the Bible as the sole infallible guide to faith and practice.

Furthest from the center were the religious Conservatives with strong ethnic roots, such as the Missouri Synod and the Christian Reformed. Southern Baptists, who functioned in many ways as an ethnic church, were in a similar position, although the Convention had significant minorities that saw themselves either as Evangelical or Mainstream. Interestingly, ethnic identity declined in all three groups as their children moved around the nation, particularly as they migrated to more urban areas. The confessional emphasis of all three groups also marked them off from the larger Evangelical movement. If push came to shove, Missouri Synod Lutherans were Lutherans first, Evangelicals second; Christian Reformed were Reformed first, Evangelicals second. Southern Baptists, who shared both a heritage with other Conservatives from the 1920s and, more important, deep roots in the revival tradition, were always Baptists first.

Much of the rest of American Evangelicalism found itself somewhere between the ethnic Conservatives and the center. This included those heirs of fundamentalism that stood somewhat apart from the Evangelical center. Most Evangelicals at the center were former fundamentalists, but not all fundamentalists were Evangelicals. They shared a common theology with the New Evangelicals but did not always share the same institutional commitments. Historically, the fundamentalists and their New Evangelical successors were the public intellectuals on the Protestant right, active in building Bible schools and colleges, and publishing much of the Conservative religious literature. At the heart of fundamentalism were three emphases: the Princeton Theology (especially its doctrine of inspiration), premillennial dispensationalism, and Keswickian holiness. Most fundamentalists were Reformed in theological orientation, although niceties about such matters as the divine decrees was not required. Organizationally, fundamentalism was a somewhat unstable amalgamation of Baptists (both convention and independent), Presbyterians (inside and outside the larger Presbyterian churches), and some Conservative Episcopalians, Lutherans, and Congregationalists. Fundamentalists drifted in and out of relationship with others of equally conservative views, often depending on their view of the necessity of separating from those who had any contact with Modernism or on their support for a particular religious cause. Varying conservative Wesleyan groups were also part of the larger circle. These included the Holiness and Pentecostal churches, now becoming much more visible on the American scene, and many supporters and employees of the parachurch bodies. The Jesus People and many charismatics or neo-Pentecostals also fit into this broad category. Numerically, these Wesleyan groups may have contained the majority of Evangelicals. During the 1980s and 1990s, Wesleyan theology produced many of the innovations in Evangelicalism. Gospel and praise music, two marks of Evangelical worship, grew out of Holiness and Pentecostal churches, as did the popular Evangelical practice of raising hands during singing or praying. Just as Wesleyan Evangelicals were open to popular music, they were early adopters of technological innovation, ranging from overhead projectors to the latest computer programs. Many of the most successful radio and TV evangelists came from a Wesleyan or charismatic background. Although Wesleyan Evangelicals were deeply committed to religious experience and activism, most were biblicists who consulted the Bible on each issue. Further, dispensationalism was common among Wesleyan preachers and people. Among Pentecostals, one argument for the resumption of the gifts of healing, prophecy, and tongues was that they were signs of the impending rapture.

Wesleyan conservatism was not, however, at the intellectual center of American Evangelicalism. Few strong seminaries were committed to Wesleyan or Pentecostal theology. The last fifty years have seen significant changes in this situation. Some were schools that matured as their denominations have become stronger. The most notable of these is interdenominational Asbury Seminary. Since the 1960s, Asbury has experienced sustained growth in enrollment, faculty, and facilities. It is now the largest Wesleyan seminary in the United States. In many ways, Asbury is the Wesleyan equivalent of Fuller or Trinity Evangelical Divinity School. Nazarene Theological Seminary in Kansas City, founded in 1944, has also experienced steady growth in this period. Pentecostals also entered into theological education, founding the Assemblies of God Seminary in 1972. The Church of God (Cleveland, Tennessee) opened its seminary, Pentecostal Theological Seminary, in 1975. Equally significant, the Methodist university divinity schools, most notably those in the South, have made a commitment to serving the whole Wesleyan family of churches and to the development of Wesleyan studies. These universities are important centers for the education of teachers in the new Wesleyan and Pentecostal seminaries. As these institutions and the larger Wesleyan network grow and develop, one can expect Wesleyan intellectual perspectives to move closer to the Evangelical intellectual center.

If these observations are correct, then the reason for the public character of the majority of Evangelical schools was part of the nature of Evangelicalism itself. Like Mainstream Protestantism, Evangelicalism is a loose alliance of very different churches, organizations, groups, and individuals. In most cases, the small size of the various components forces these groups to work together, formally or informally, to maintain theological schools of sufficient size to meet modern educational expectations. While this is true of most seminaries, Conservatives lost most of their stake in earlier seminaries after the 1920s controversy, and they had to start over with new institutions. They lacked endowments and historical patterns of support. Moreover, the cost of beginning new educational institutions increased as time passed. It took more to do less. The more rapidly costs increase, the more variety must be included in the supporting alliance. Indeed, one of the tasks of a seminary president, no matter what the character of a school, is to form and sustain a community of like-minded people that can cooperate financially in the support of the school. If the presidents of the more confessional Conservative seminaries had to find such support primarily in the ebb and flow of denominational politics, the presidents of the more publicly oriented seminaries had to make and maintain their own alliances. In addition, as Richard Mouw observed in 1978, the small pool of potential givers means that each school has to defend itself against other, similar schools that want some of its supporters for itself:

> American Evangelicalism is not an organized movement but a *de facto* coalition. Funds are not distributed by committees; they are solicited by urgent pleas. In this kind of competitive situation it is often convenient to assure one's constituency that one's cause is truly "the Lord's work" by suggesting that competing institutions and organizations are weakening in their commitment to the Evangelical faith. Thus when Clarke Pinnock observed that the inerrancy defenders are trying to "control and limit membership in the orthodox party," he was substantially correct.[4]

The controversies in the 1980s and 1990s ultimately tested the strength of these alliances. Strong conservative presidents, including David Hubbard of Fuller and Robert Cooley of Gordon-Conwell, were master coalition builders and maestros of the board podium. They were able to withstand considerable pressure from their publics and financial supporters. Less able presidents were less able to do so.

THE INERRANCY CRISIS AND THE PUBLIC EVANGELICAL SEMINARIES

Protestants have a history of battling that went back to the Reformation, and the free air of America permitted and perhaps even encouraged religious controversy. Both conservative and Mainstream churches inherited this passion for conflict and theological precision. Religious disagreements serve many purposes. In addition to the definition or defense of truth, controversies establish boundaries. In any free market—and religion is America's most free market—successful groups and individuals maintain clear borders that define themselves and their products. Every religious debate is, thus, not only an exchange of ideas about religious faith, but at the same time an attempt to gather new allies, to win new adherents, to increase contributions, or to retain existing supporters. Truly irenic individuals are rare, and one of the most striking aspects of Evangelical theological controversies is that Billy Graham, the great symbol of the Evangelical alliance and one of the principal architects of its seminary system, managed to retain his position more or less above the battle. Yet, even Graham could not completely escape the pressure to take a stand on inerrancy and use his influence to aid one side or the other.

---

4. Mouw, "Evangelicals in Search of Maturity," 45.

The battles over the Bible began at Fuller Seminary. In the 1960s, Fuller Seminary, the recently established and very successful Evangelical flagship seminary, moved steadily away first from a belief in premillennial dispensationalism and then from formal adherence to biblical inerrancy.[5] Well before the effects of this change became matters of public dispute, the effects of Fuller's decisions were felt throughout Evangelical circles. Kenneth Kantzer, a Harvard graduate and a master motivator, took the small seminary of the Evangelical Covenant Church and transformed it into Trinity Evangelical Divinity School (TEDS). Kantzer, like the New Evangelicals who had founded Fuller, was deeply committed to the university ideal and to thorough scholarship and research. Kantzer's choice of a name for the refounded school was significant. Trinity was to be a divinity school, tied to the highest academic standards, and requiring the best from its students and faculty. It was a remade Fuller, appealing to much the same clientele. Within a few years, it rivaled Fuller for the leadership and support of American Evangelicalism.

The disturbances at Fuller also influenced events in the East. Although Harold Ockenga never denounced his old school, where he had been president, he turned his attention to developing Gordon, one of the old-line Conservative institutions. Gordon's history stretched back to the great missionary revival and the training school movement. Ockenga used his friendships with Billy Graham and with Howard Pew, an oil millionaire, to broker the union of Gordon and Conwell, a Philadelphia-area school affiliated with Temple University. To pay for this school, which, like TEDS, was a refounding of an older institution, Ockenga relied on an agreement with Pew to help finance the venture. The deal with Pew, however, was like many alliances between unequal partners. The partner with the money had the power. To be sure, Ockenga got his Fuller of the East, and Pew made a major contribution to its new campus. Yet Pew's gifts came with financial strings attached. Pew opposed the school establishing an endowment and made an agreement to contribute sufficient funds every year to make an endowment unnecessary. Pew planned to transform this gift into a permanent financial gift after five years, if the school proved its ability to generate strong Conservative ministers. Unfortunately, the arrangement had an expiration date, and Pew died before he made the commitment permanent. Anxious negotiations between the school and the Pew Charitable Trusts eventually netted the school five million dollars. Robert Cooley, Gordon-Conwell's president from 1981 to 1997, faced the difficult

---

5. The original Fuller statement reads, "The books which form the canon of the Old and New Testaments as originally given are plenarily inspired and free from all error in the whole and in the part. These books constitute the written Word of God, the only infallible rule of faith and practice." In contrast, the revised version read, "All the books of the Old and New Testaments are the written word of God, the only infallible rule of faith and practice." For the text of the older Fuller Statement, see "Statement of Faith of Fuller Seminary," *Fuller Bulletin* 6/5 (Oct.–Dec. 1956) 1, 7. The more recent statement is online: http://www.fuller.edu/about-fuller/mission-and-history/statement-of-faith.aspx/. For an excellent discussion of the meaning of the original statement, see Marsden, *Reforming Fundamentalism*, 113–15.

task of finding ways to finance what was always an ambitious undertaking. With the strong help of Billy Graham, his board chair, he proved equal to the task.

Harold Lindsell fired the first public shots in the new controversy. Lindsell, trained as a historian, was a graduate of Wheaton, a former member and dean of the Fuller faculty, and Henry's successor as editor of *Christianity Today*. Unlike Henry and Ockenga, Lindsell was not part of the broader theological conversation and was less aware or at least less careful about theological nuances. His 1976 *Battle for the Bible*[6] was an exposé of Fuller that alleged that the flagship school of American conservatism was unsound on the Bible. Lindsell's diatribe included sideswipes at Southern Baptist Theological Seminary and Concordia. He continued his attack in the 1979 *Bible in the Balance*. Francis Schaeffer, an energetic Christian apologist and youth worker, strongly supported Lindsell. Schaeffer, whose writings influenced many young Evangelicals to take up academic life, believed that secular humanism penetrated all areas of American cultural life, particularly colleges and universities. Schaeffer saw biblical criticism as part of the same deadly infection. Like Lindsell, Schaeffer believed that Christian educational institutions were on a slippery slope.

Lindsell's attack had three foci. *First*, Lindsell charged that some scholars in Evangelical schools had moved to a noninerrantist position on the Bible. While one might argue about the definition of *inerrancy*, on the face of it, Lindsell may have been right, at least about the use of historical criticism in Evangelical seminaries.[7] Both the Word Biblical Commentary and the Broadman Commentary series showed that the authors were thoroughly familiar with modern critical techniques, and such Evangelical scholars as TEDS's Grant Osborne openly advocated redaction criticism, as did Westmont's Robert Gundry. *Second*, Lindsell argued that the use of these techniques necessarily led seminaries and churches away from the traditional basics of Christian faith. Ironically, most liberal theologians agreed with this statement. For such thinkers as Edward Farley of Vanderbilt, the fall of the House of Authority meant the revision or even the reformation of most Christian doctrine. For Lindsell, as for many liberals, only a few short steps separated a person or a school from advocating biblical criticism to denying the doctrine of the Trinity or the divinity of Christ. *Third*, Lindsell raised an ethical question. Essentially, Lindsell charged that Evangelical teachers had lied or had mental reservations when they signed the confessions of faith at their respective institutions.[8] This was far more serious than the accusation that they had used biblical criticism. If true, perjury had compromised the personal and Christian

---

6. Lindsell, *The Battle for the Bible*.

7. In general, Evangelical biblical scholars have insisted that confessional statements extend only to doctrinal issues and do not include questions of scholarly method (*Theological Education*, "ATS Luce Consultation on Theological Scholarship"). Lindsell, however, may have been closer to the intent of the authors of those statements than subsequent Evangelical opinion. Method and its application are not easily separated.

8. Payne, "Ethical Issues." The issue of ethics is present in all of the discussions of inerrancy and subscription.

integrity of the leaders of the schools and their faculties. Neither donors nor potential students could trust the institutions. Yet the ethical issue was a bridge too far. People who might have agreed with Lindsell about the danger of biblical criticism or even about restricting the freedom of those who taught it were less likely to agree that the faculty who they knew and trusted were liars and cheats.

Lindsell's charges also awakened painful memories. Most Conservatives remembered that subscription was an issue in the painful separation of Princeton and Westminster, and that the looser form of subscription practiced at 1940s Princeton opened the gate to neo-orthodoxy. The issue of subscription was hoary with age in American theological education. At least as far back as Moses Stuart and Andover, churches and Christian movements attempted to use confessional statements to regulate theological teaching. These confessional statements ranged from the very elaborate, such as the Augsburg or the Westminster Confessions, to the very simple, such as Southern Baptist Theological Seminary's Abstract of Principles. Liberal theological schools abandoned subscription when they adopted the new theology, especially the newer biblical studies, and those Mainstream seminaries that continued it did so as a way of identifying with their theological tradition.

In the experience of these Mainstream churches and schools, strict subscription never provided the guidance that churches believed that it might. Further, they believed that strict subscription led almost inevitably to conflicts that weakened a school's institutional fabric. However, the more Conservative schools continued it, most using statements inherited from the past, and some schools required a yearly public assent to the official confessional document. Only a handful, including Fuller, attempted to update their confessions to correspond to their practice. Interestingly, few seminary confessions mentioned biblical inerrancy. Most Conservative seminaries preferred statements about biblical infallibility, occasionally modifying that affirmation to refer to faith and practice. Southern Baptist Theological Seminary avoided both inerrancy and infallibility: "The Scriptures of the Old and New Testament were given by inspiration of God, and are the only sufficient, certain and authoritative rule of all saving knowledge, faith and obedience."

Many Conservative scholars agreed with Lindsell's basic argument that any questioning of inerrancy called biblical authority into question. They formed the International Council for Biblical Inerrancy to protect this teaching. The Council had a mixed membership from the beginning. Some advocated a strict or closed understanding of biblical inerrancy that essentially said that the plain meaning of the Bible, as given in the original autographs, was inerrant. Others favored a more open understanding that allowed for considerable nuance. The council's 1978 Chicago Statement on Biblical Inerrancy was a compromise. The document itself carefully balanced affirmations and denials. Most important for many biblical scholars, the document insisted that the reader had to take into account such matters as literary genre, historical usage, and linguistic forms when interpreting Scripture. In other words, the meaning of the Bible was not self-evident when one read a biblical text. Only careful study might reveal what the Bible actually said. Thus contemporary readers had to judge ancient historians, not by our standards of contemporary historical writing, but by the standards of their own time and place. The numbers in Exodus, thus, were inerrant, not by our current statistical methods, but by the standards of ancient historians. Most Evangelical scholars reconciled themselves to the Chicago Statement, often by insisting that many critical issues were not matters of fact, hence, of error or truth, but matters of interpretation (hermeneutics). As interpreted, inerrancy was a much broader category than many people might have imagined, and to some, the Chicago Statement buried its plain meaning under a thousand qualifications.

In most cases, the combination of the Chicago Statement and the strong support of a school's board provided individual scholars with the protection that they needed. Nonetheless, some careers were disrupted. Perhaps the most serious immediate causality of the controversy was scholar J. Ramsey Michaels, a twenty-five-year veteran at Gordon-Conwell. Michaels had used biblical criticism in his 1981 study of Jesus, *Servant and Son*, and had concluded that only Jesus saw the dove at his baptism. The decisive action in the Michaels's case was not by the board but by the Gordon-Conwell faculty. The faculty report that recommended Michaels's dismissal found that he "*appears* to aver that something asserted in Scripture as historical *may* not in fact have occurred *as represented* in the Gospel record."[9] However, the faculty agreed that Michaels said nothing in the book that he had not taught consistently throughout his tenure at the school. Michaels's teaching and writing appeared more heretical after the battles over inerrancy than they had before, but one wonders whether the board would have dismissed Michaels, apart from the faculty action.

The debate over biblical inerrancy did result in a major division of the house of Evangelical scholarship. The Institute for Biblical Research, formed in 1973, originally hoped to establish an American equivalent of Tyndale House, Cambridge. Tyndale House had provided a home base for English conservative biblical scholars and graduate students while they were working at Cambridge. Perhaps most important, Tyndale House was a think tank for English Evangelicals where they exchanged ideas and resources. Although founders of the Institute for Biblical Research did not realize their original dream (American education was too diffuse for such a center), the Institute for Biblical Research became the professional society for Evangelical biblical scholars, meeting on Saturday mornings in conjunction with the Society of Biblical Literature. In many ways, the Institute functioned as a subguild within the larger American biblical community, setting standards for Evangelical biblical scholarship and publishing its own journal. The Institute also provides a scholarly society free from the doctrinal controversies that often dominate the Evangelical Theological Society. Although not strictly parallel to scholarly societies formed to support Black, women, and Latino/Latina theologians, it functioned much the same way for Evangelicals.

9. Quoted in Noll, "Evangelicals and the Study of the Bible," 16.

While other specialized Evangelical scholarly societies existed, including the Conference on Faith and History[10] and the Society of Christian Philosophers, the Institute for Biblical Research was the one that most clearly demonstrated the divided opinion of American Evangelical scholars. One sign of the maturation of a movement is that it generates places for its critics to ply their trade in relative peace from the rest of the movement. In that sense, the institute also indicates the maturation of American Evangelical scholarship.

If the initial furor of the inerrancy debate died down, the debate itself dragged on and still continues. In 2008, Westminster forced its brilliant Old Testament teacher Peter Enns to resign. The problem was his 2005 book *Inspiration and Incarnation: Evangelicals and the Problem of the Old Testament*. In that book, Enns tackled some of the most difficult questions for a Conservative view of the Scriptures. These questions included the similarity between the Old Testament and other ancient writings, and the nature of the Old Testament quotations in the New Testament. As one approach to these and other difficulties, Enns proposed what he called an incarnational approach to the Scriptures that frankly acknowledged the human elements in their composition. For Westminster's Board of Trustees, this was a step too far. They requested Enns's resignation.[11] In 2010, the board of Reformed Theological Seminary forced Bruce Waltke to resign his position due to his advocacy of theistic evolution and his statements critical of Evangelicals who ignored the evidence for that position. Waltke's position was not unusual, even at Reformed, but he had to find other employment nonetheless. Both schools had boards that were closer to the denominational boards of the Missouri Synod or the Southern Baptists, although both also represented a broader Evangelical public.

The inerrancy debate cast a long shadow over Evangelical theological education. While "publish and perish" did not replace "publish or perish" as liberals expected, Conservative scholars were more cautious in their work. Perhaps the most important effect was not visible. For a movement based on the Bible, one would expect biblical scholars to lead theologically. Yet the most important public Evangelical voices are not the Bible interpreters but the historians, the theologians, and the philosophers. Moreover, most of them did not teach in Evangelical theological institutions. They taught in colleges and universities where it was more difficult to censure their opinions.

Other Conservative Theological Battles

Another reason that the biblical argument moderated in the 1990s was that Conservatives had two new theological opponents within: the open theists and the postconservatives. Although some scholars had explored these ideas earlier, the 1994 publication of *The Openness of God: A Biblical Challenge to Traditional Theism* by Clark Pinnock,

10. Pierard, "Evangelicals Seek Their Roots."
11. Pulliam, "Westminster Theological Suspension."

Richard Rice, John Sanders, William Hasker, and David Bassinger marked the beginning of another round in the battles in the Evangelical Theological Society and among Evangelicals generally. Although there are a variety of perspectives included in open theism, the basic argument is that neither Scripture nor reason supports the traditional picture of God as unchangeable, and that theologians need to revise the doctrine of God to make that teaching more biblical. This line of reasoning did not surprise those outside Evangelicalism. Harnack and other historians of doctrine had shown that classical theism was the result of the amalgamation of Greco-Roman philosophical thought and biblical concepts, and modern process philosophy and theology had attempted a restatement of the doctrine of God based on modern science's picture of a dynamic and changing universe.

What made open theism a threat to the Evangelical establishment, particularly its more Calvinistic members, was that the new theists argued their position from the biblical text itself. Particularly in the Old Testament, God is very much a participant in the course of human events and apparently shares in the contingency of those events. God makes promises that are conditional upon the performance of certain acts. If Israel obeys, then there one future will occur; if Israel disobeys, another future will follow. Jonah gives Nineveh the choice of repenting or not repenting, and when Nineveh repents, God turns aside from the threatened punishment. The advocates of the new theology could and did multiply examples of similar events and sayings in the biblical story. Perhaps the most important part of their argument, however, was the adequacy of the position to two key Evangelical practices: conversion and prayer. According to the new theists, prayer influenced God, and God acted in response to prayer; prayer, thus, could change the future. In the words of one of Pinnock's books, God was a most moved mover. Moreover, conversion implied a change in one's status before God and not merely the confirmation of a prior action on God's part. The sinner was once lost and now was found. The human choice was real and eternally important.

Open theism was strongly debated in the Evangelical Theological Society. Interestingly enough, the society conducted what amounted to a trial of John Sanders and Clark Pinnock, complete with hearings, and a formal vote. The ETS voted to retain both as members, although Sanders was subsequently dismissed from Huntington University, where he had taught religion. The open theism debate was only the beginning of an increasing doctrinal diversity among American conservatives. Evangelical theologians took up such issues as inclusive theology (salvation apart from profession of faith in Christ) and the whole realm of issues associated with postmodernism. Stanley Grenz, who taught at Regent College, was the leading advocate of this new approach to theology. In a postmodern world, the modern desire to see truth as a series of propositions is set aside, necessitating a new understanding of theological language. Theology is not so much a series of true or false statements about God as a historical report on the human experience of God at certain times and in certain places. While this dispute is continuing, significantly many Evangelical institutions, especially those with a publicly responsible board, have found ways to include advocates of the position on their faculties.

This brief account of the theological controversies of the last thirty years has not done justice to the nuances of any particular position. Good theology involves point and counterpoint, and theological discussions rarely move in a linear direction. Yet, the controversies marked a shift in Evangelical theological education that was largely supported by the trustees of Evangelical institutions. In simple terms, the conservative side of the equation came to look like a mirror image of the Mainstream theological world, with opinions and methods spread along an ever-widening spectrum. While the difference between scholars and theologians on the extreme left and right of the discussion remained visible, as one moved towards the center, the distinctions became less clear. Social and cultural forces also served to obscure disagreements. Evangelical Christians were and are passionate supporters of the missionary movement, and the Lausanne movement has had a central place in much of Two-Thirds World Christianity. Liberationist perspectives, popular abroad, have flowed naturally into American Evangelicalism from this source. On the American scene, although the political left has been a minority among American Evangelicals, Evangelicalism has also supported its own prophetic wing. African American Evangelicals and Evangelical feminist theologians have contributed to this increasing diversity as well. The theological diversity of American Evangelicalism resembles its organizational diversity.

Was Harold Lindsell right that the changes in Fuller heralded radical changes in Evangelical theological education, the first steps on a slippery slope? In retrospect, he was right, but perhaps for the wrong reasons. American Evangelical theological education developed along lines set by the American academy and by the give-and-take of academic discourse. As Evangelical scholars participated more in these larger discussions, they became more and more in tune with their contemporaries on major issues. There were also important changes in the training of Evangelical theological teachers. As the schools became more academically powerful, they tended to send their best graduates to the more established graduate programs and to hire their new instructors from the same sources. Although the tendency for young Evangelicals to do their doctorates in nontheological fields continued, this tendency was not as marked as in the first New Evangelical generation. Today more young Evangelicals attend the same leading university graduate schools as their Mainstream counterparts. In other words, young Evangelicals spend their most formative intellectual years in a pluralistic intellectual atmosphere where others judged their work by the standards accepted in that milieu.

Does this mean that all differences between conservative and liberal are erased? *Being There*, an ethnographic comparison of an Evangelical and a liberal seminary conducted by Jackson W. Carroll, Barbara G. Wheeler, Daniel O. Aleshire, and Penny Long Marler, indicated that there were substantial differences in ethos between the two institutions they studied. In part, the difference was political. The Evangelical seminary and its students were committed to opposing abortion, for example, and the Mainstream seminary to theological and personal inclusiveness. Yet the similarities were striking as well. Classrooms grew more and more similar as the distance in ethos widened.

What or Who Is an Evangelical? Historians Attempt a Definition

From its beginning, the question of what and who is an Evangelical has been a difficult one to answer, and it has become more difficult to answer as Evangelical seminaries have matured. Many of the founders of the New Evangelicalism, particularly Harold John Ockenga, Carl. F. Henry, and Billy Graham, began their careers as fundamentalists. Like other leaders of minority movements, including African Americans, these leaders needed a self-designation that avoided cultural stereotypes. The popular understanding of the word *fundamentalism*, although first used as a comprehensive term for a broad alliance of American Christians, was rural backwardness, extreme right-wing politics, and anti-intellectualism. In part, the American popular media created this caricature. The coverage of the 1925 Scopes Trial pictured the conservatives as resolutely anti-intellectual and backward, and the subsequent play and film, *Inherit the Wind*, reinforced the stereotype. The stereotype then passed into common parlance: those truths that everyone knows, but no one verifies. The picture was not without merit. Carl McIntire and John R. Rice incarnated and revealed the worst features of fundamentalism. If fundamentalism was to have a future, the movement needed a less loaded self-designation. The word *Evangelical* seemed perfect. During the Reformation, many reformers preferred it to *Protestant*, a term derived from the political conflicts of the German Reichstag. During the nineteenth century, those Protestants who supported revivals, missions, and Christian activism called themselves Evangelicals and often cooperated in common ventures. The nineteenth-century Evangelicals were the Protestant Mainstream; the New Evangelicals were their legitimate heirs. It was the liberals who had departed from the American way.

The founding of the National Association of Evangelicals, the rise of Billy Graham crusades, and the establishment of Fuller Theological Seminary were part of an effort to restore Protestant conservatism. The New Evangelicals wanted to move religious conservatism from the margins of American life to its center, and the ministry of Billy Graham, one of the most successful religious leaders in United States history, provided the impetus for this movement towards the center. Graham was an irenic conservative committed to working with people across theological and racial lines and, despite his notable relationship with Richard Nixon, was largely above politics. Like such past evangelists as Dwight L. Moody and Charles Finney, Graham saw education as an important part of his legacy. Graham was a major investor in the Billy Graham Center for the Study of American Evangelicals at his alma mater, Wheaton College; a member of the Board of Trustees at Gordon-Conwell Theological Seminary;

and a friend and coworker of Harold Ockenga. Carl F. Henry was the most serious theologian of this group as well as a popular author. Like many others in the 1940s and 1950s, Henry perceived that Western civilization was in the midst of a deep crisis, and he saw historic Christianity as the only way to halt the crisis. In order to remake the society, however, conservatism had to establish its own intellectual credentials and stand toe to toe with the other forces competing for leadership. Henry's work ranged from his contribution to the establishment of Fuller Seminary and *Christianity Today*, where he was the first editor, to his role in the establishment of the Lausanne movement, a very successful counterpart to the World Council of Churches. Perhaps most important, Henry provided intellectual leadership. Like many conservative scholars, he read or at least was familiar with most of the contemporary works in theology and was able to discuss them intelligently. Harold Ockenga was the third member of this group. Ockenga was the behind-the-scenes organizer, the person who could recruit others for his various causes.

One of the goals of the New Evangelicals was to claim a heritage as broad as their aspirations. History provided an avenue for a claim. Leaders of the new discipline of American church history, including William Warren Sweet, Robert T. Handy, and Winthrop Hudson, stressed the influence of the great revivals on the nation's development in the nineteenth century. From Edwards to Moody, the revivalists established schools and missions, at home and abroad, and carried the gospel to first the rural and then the urban frontier. Almost as one untimely born, Billy Graham embodied this tradition. Graham was a compelling figure: articulate, clean cut, soft spoken, personally honest, and physically attractive. His preaching, like that of his great predecessors, often included personal stories, and his services always included generous amounts of the gospel music of previous generations. Although he was personally very conservative (he called himself a fundamentalist in his early years), Graham's ministry emphasized comprehension. Like such earlier evangelists as Dwight L. Moody, he invited all, even religious liberals, who shared his concern for evangelism to join him. Graham's mild political liberalism, particularly on issues of race and poverty, fit into this program nicely. Although much of the funding for the new conservatism came from people like Howard Pew, an aggressive free-market advocate, Billy Graham's progressive conservatism—similar to that advocated in Henry's important book, *The Uneasy Conscience of American Fundamentalism* (1948)—was firmly in the American center. Graham's position was not far from that of Dwight Eisenhower. This was not the conservatism of the Old Religious Right. One early definition of what Evangelicals were was that they were people like Billy Graham.

Like Graham, the New Evangelicals were coalition builders. From the founding of the National Association of Evangelicals and the launching of Graham's great religious crusades, they sought to build alliances on the right similar to those that sustained the Mainstream. All of the great early Evangelical enterprises—the NAE, the Graham crusades, Key '73, Lausanne, Fuller Seminary, Asbury Seminary, Gordon-Conwell

Seminary, and TEDS—were interdenominational, and few of the New Evangelicals saw themselves in denominational terms. In many ways, the parachurch organizations—themselves interdenominational bodies that depended on a variety of people for financial support—were their real homes. In a similar way, American religious progressives often saw themselves as ecumenical rather than denominational.

Whom did the New Evangelicals want to enlist? In broad terms, they sought like-minded folk. These comprised many of the smaller religious denominations, including the Holiness and Pentecostal churches, and those ethnic churches, such as the Dutch Reformed, who had maintained an orthodox religious tradition. They hoped that the Southern Baptists might join them, as many individual Southern Baptists did, but the denomination remained aloof. Theologically, they wanted to bring together all those who felt themselves to be religiously more conservative than the Mainstream leadership of the older American denominations, and this included the dissenters within the Mainstream churches, far more of whom existed than many supposed, especially among Presbyterians and Baptists. In many ways, one might say that they sought support in the somewhat unorganized followers of the parachurch organizations. Parachurch members seemed only to share common membership on a mailing list and the willingness to contribute to a particular ministry. From the beginning, New Evangelicalism was interested in radio ministry and later TV ministry. Charles Fuller, the founder of Fuller Theological Seminary, had ministered through the radio, and Billy Graham was a master of media. When megachurches began to appear in the 1970s and 1980s, the leaders of these largely independent churches were another cadre that the New Evangelicals hoped to attract.

Were Evangelicals more than the friends of Billy Graham? From the beginning of the New Evangelical movement, the question of identity was a primary issue. Who exactly was or was not an Evangelical, and how did one know? By the time of Lindsell's *Battle for the Bible*, the question was becoming acute. The original founders of New Evangelicalism were aging, and there was a need for a second and third generation to take their place. Lindsell's book and its reluctant support by other New Evangelical leaders, many of whom disliked its tone, made the issue painfully obvious. Aside from their rejection of the term *fundamentalist*, what made the movement distinct?

Like the earlier Bible colleges, Evangelical seminaries provided an institutional answer to the question. Each school's alumni often functioned almost as an informal denomination, providing a network of contacts and friendships that helped to sustain the schools and their fundraising efforts. In this sense, the schools meant more to their graduates and their constituencies than Mainstream schools did to theirs. The schools lovingly maintained these networks, both for their own sake and for the sake of the movement. Many schools, such as Dallas Theological Seminary, were almost minidenominations in the services that they provided to their graduates. Yet while this enabled individual schools to maintain their identities, it did not provide a means of uniting the schools.

The movement, particularly as it affected theological education, needed a stronger intellectual foundation. As we mentioned earlier, Evangelical biblical scholarship had made and continued to make significant strides. Logically speaking, the biblical scholars should have been the primary intellectual architects of a new Evangelical identity, as they often were in the Southern Baptist Convention. Yet, the continuing battles over the Bible limited their capacity to shape the movement. Instead, the primary task of Evangelical definition fell to a group that I will call the New Evangelical church historians. This group included Joel Carpenter, Donald Dayton, Edith Blumhofer, Mark Noll, Nathan Hatch, Grant Wacker, and George Marsden as well as a number of less well-known scholars. Significantly, although all of them were very influential Evangelical scholars, they were not often employed by Evangelical theological schools. Of the principal voices, only Harry Stout and Grant Wacker spent significant parts of their teaching careers in university divinity schools, and only Donald Dayton taught in a self-identified Evangelical seminary. The others elected to teach in colleges and universities. Significantly, only George Marsden (MDiv), Donald Dayton (MDiv) and Mark Noll (MA) held degrees from a theological seminary, although Harry Stout attended Princeton Theological Seminary for a season.

The Evangelical historians were part of the larger trend for scholars outside theological institutions to do the most significant religious scholarship. The freedom of the college and university context permitted anyone who established their academic credentials freedom to set their own research agenda and to speak frankly on a variety of issues. This general rule also applied to schools like Wheaton College, where those in the history department had more freedom than those who taught religion courses. In addition, a professional location in a college, a university, or a university divinity school conveyed prestige on the larger stage and opened the doors of prestigious publishers and scholarly societies. Although Evangelical seminaries were flourishing, many of Evangelicalism's brightest minds found their primary professional identity elsewhere.

Although Mark Noll had interests in the transatlantic character of Evangelicalism, perhaps the most significant aspect of the new Evangelical historians was that they were specialists in American history. American history and American studies in general is a wide-open field, with Americanists investigating the varieties of United States social experience. Religion fit nicely into the discipline and its increasing concern with popular American life.

Equally important, there was a tradition of the theological interpretation of American church history. In the 1950s and 1960s, William Warren Sweet, Winthrop Hudson, and Robert T. Handy painted sweeping pictures of the nation's religious development that climaxed in the apparent triumph of ecumenical Christianity. If, as Sydney Ahlstrom pointed out, this consensus view of history omitted many churches, it had the advantage of demonstrating the unity behind the booming confusion of the American religious market.

What the Evangelical historians did was to change the lens through which they read America's religious past. While the 1960s mood did not permit them as imperial a view as the ecumenical historians enjoyed, it did encourage significant reinterpretation. Just as the ecumenical historians had argued that American Protestant history moved in a liberal direction, so the new Evangelical historians maintained that the common tradition moved in a more Evangelical direction. The revivals, the place of the Bible in American life and culture, the voluntary societies, American fundamentalism, and the various Holiness and Pentecostal movements provided the core to the story. Perhaps most important, these historians rehabilitated the reputation of the original fundamentalist movement and demonstrated that conservatives represented important streams in American religious life.

This metanarrative rested on substantial research into original sources. In this sense, the construction of the Billy Graham Center for the Study of American Evangelicalism at Wheaton College was an important contribution to the new history.[12] Billy Graham eventually donated over thirty million dollars to the enterprise.[13] The Center, initially headed by Mark Noll, combined a library and a museum and brought together an impressive array of sources and scholars.[14] The 1980 conference that opened the Center, Evangelical Christianity and Modern America, was among the most comprehensive scholarly meetings held to that date on the Wheaton campus. The conference brought together an impressive array of Evangelical and non-Evangelical religious scholars. The Lilly Endowment, although historically committed to Mainstream American Christianity, partially funded the opening conference.

The links between the Lilly Endowment and the Evangelical historians were deep and personal. Timothy Smith at Johns Hopkins University introduced Robert W. Lynn, the vice president for religion at the Lilly Endowment, to an array of younger Evangelical scholars, including George Marsden, Mark Noll, Joel Carpenter, Nathan Hatch, Harry Stout, and Grant Wacker. Lynn was deeply impressed with their work as historians and with the way that their personal faith informed their scholarly work. He was instrumental in securing a Lilly grant for two million dollars to establish the Institute for the Study of American Evangelicals, initially directed by Joel Carpenter. Other Lilly grants followed. The connection between Lynn and Carpenter led to Lynn's introducing Carpenter to the leadership at the Pew Foundation and his eventual position of leadership there.[15] In turn, Carpenter's grants provided much of the support for Evangelical work in philosophy of religion.

One result of the new Evangelical history was the increasing recognition that conservative Wesleyan and Holiness perspectives were a crucial part of the Evangelical coalition. Both the early New Evangelicals and their fundamentalist precursors were

12. Pierard, "Evangelicals Seek Their Roots"; Noll, "What Has Wheaton to Do with Jerusalem?"
13. According to the study guide at the Graham Center.
14. Noll, "What Has Wheaton to Do with Jerusalem?"
15. Hamilton and Yngvason, "Patrons of the Evangelical Mind."

Calvinists, and they assumed that the Holiness and Pentecostal churches they invited into their fellowship would continue to pay Calvinism at least intellectual deference. After all, fundamentalism had provided the bulk of popular and scholarly conservative literature during the long dry spell of the 1940s and 1950s. However, John Hopkins historian Timothy Smith had long argued that the Holiness movements had an important role in the shaping of American faith, and Northern Seminary's Donald Dayton continued his crusade to have the crucial role of Holiness thinking included in the history of American religion. Holiness and Pentecostal traditions were particularly important during the inerrancy crisis. Both Holiness and Pentecostal traditions stressed the role of religious experience and ethical practice over theological niceties. In particular, appreciation of Holiness and Pentecostal perspectives were important for Evangelical leadership in world Christianity. Many of the new Christians in Africa and Latin America were Pentecostals, whose representatives were crucial at the series of meetings associated with the Lausanne conference and its successors. If Henry and Ockenga contributed to the transformation of fundamentalism into Evangelicalism, Smith and Dayton contributed to the transformation of Evangelicalism into a more theologically comprehensive movement.

The new history presented a vibrant rereading of America's religious history. Charles Finney, for example, with his passion for holiness and his willingness to see the power of the Spirit, made major contributions to the conservative as well as the liberal side of American religion, and American popular biblicism, perhaps the most potent single force in American religious history, is never far from the surface of American religious practices. Seen from this perspective, Billy Graham and the rapid expansion of Evangelical Christianity in postwar America makes good sense. Graham represented a renewal of long-standing American cultural patterns. Given this history, it is not a surprise that Evangelicals have continued the traditional American Protestant emphasis on the family and on the state as the protector of family values.

Like all good history, the new Evangelical history had a critical edge. In his 1994 *The Scandal of the Evangelical Mind*, Mark Noll exposed the anti-intellectualism that lay at the heart of much of Evangelical life. Noll knew that the achievements of contemporary Evangelical scholars, including Bible scholars, historians, and philosophers, had given Evangelicalism a very different cast than it had in the past. This was not Carl F. Henry's world with Carl F. Henry's problems. Yet creation science and the continuing bitter battles over inerrancy endangered this progress. Further, Noll realized that Evangelicals did not exert the influence on the nation's intellectual life that their numbers might seem to warrant. In a religious nation where half of those attending church on a given Sunday were Evangelicals, this lack of influence was a call to Evangelical self-reflection.[16] However, Evangelicalism's problems were not primarily external; the challenges to Evangelical intellectual life were within its history. Although Noll agreed with those, such as Hofstadter, who saw a broad anti-intellectualism as part

---

16. Noll, *The Scandal of the Evangelical Mind*, 10.

of American life, he was more interested in specific trends in Evangelical history that gave the Evangelical resistance to the life of the mind its own particular cast. In fact, Evangelicals invested a considerable amount of energy in intellectual arguments, but the most serious point was that Evangelicals have often invested their mental energies in the wrong things.

One major force misshaping the Evangelical mind, Noll argued, was "fundamentalism." As Noll interpreted the fundamentalists, particularly after the largely symbolic year of 1925,[17] they were so preoccupied with biblical criticism and evolution that they were unable to appreciate the good in the emerging scientific and historical worlds of thought. In turn, they found it easy to fall into such travesties as creationism, with its assertion that the creation of the world was comparatively recent. Further, seemingly endless variations on the dispensational theme (perhaps most evident in the *Late Great Planet Earth*, a 1970s best seller, or the more contemporary Left Behind book series) also used up considerable Evangelical energy. The corrective needed, Noll believed, was an awareness of the historicity of the interpreter. The literal interpretation of the Bible was not as literal as some thought. Noll's book ended on a positive note. Since Evangelicalism stressed both the Scriptures and the message of the cross of Christ, the movement had a future.

The other significant attempt to define Evangelicalism was through a renewed Christian philosophy. Both Noll and Marsden noted that Scottish Common Sense Realism had influenced American Evangelicals. Common Sense philosophy placed a premium on sense perception and on the ability of ordinary people to weigh carefully the data or facts before them and to arrive at truth. This philosophy was particularly attractive because it had clear democratic implications and deeply influenced early American intellectual life. In addition to its popular manifestations, this philosophy shaped much early nineteenth-century theology, especially the theology of Princeton Seminary. The Bible provided the facts for both the theologian and the believer. When either had all of the biblical facts, they could draw the obvious and necessary conclusions. Like all science, theological teachings combined facts into theory. A consistent theology should have resulted from the application of this method that any believer could verify. Yet, one must be cautious about carrying this line of analysis too far. Much of Princeton theology as well as much popular Christian theology rested on the Aristotelianism of Protestant and Catholic scholasticism. Few theologians confined their thought to the facts of Scripture.

Christian Reformed thinkers in the 1980s and 1990s shaped an alternative philosophical basis for orthodox theology. Princeton Seminary's faculty and later Westminster's had a long-standing dialog with the Christian Reformed churches' theologians, in both their European and American branches, and was aware of shifting Reformed perspectives abroad. Cornelius Van Til was one who moved easily between both camps. Van Til's emphasis on propositional truth, however, was not the only way that

---

17. The year of both the Scopes Trial and the death of William Jennings Bryan.

Evangelicals might understand the Dutch tradition. The Dutch theological tradition had several intellectual strands. Adopting part of the Kantian revolution, such thinkers as Abraham Kuyper and his successors turned their attention to the analysis of worldviews. What this philosophy assumed that was the learner or subject brought a view of the world or a preunderstanding to every act of thought or cognition. In 1987, Richard Mouw saw this approach as the way forward:

> Seminary philosophical teaching and scholarship, as I see it, should focus much more than has been the case in the past on that area of discussion that Arthur Holmes refers to as "world-viewish philosophy." Holmes introduces this notion toward the beginning of his book, *Contours of a World View*, in the course of discussing the contributions that both theology and philosophy could make to the shaping of an explicitly Christian world view. He distinguishes "theologians' theology" from "world-viewish theology," and then goes on to draw a parallel distinction with reference to philosophy.[18]

What this approach permitted was for a thinker to bring a Christian perspective to any area of discourse and allow that perspective to share his or her apprehension of the data. One might understand other perspectives by analyzing the worldviews that informed them. This meant that worldview analysis was both subjective and sufficiently public to permit learned discourse.

Worldview type philosophies had implications across the spectrum of theological disciplines. The most visible theological voices in the 1990s and 2000s were those who sought to make theology speak in the voice of a particular gender, racial group, or economic class. In a similar way, Evangelicalism represents a consistent biblical worldview, and this worldview might constitute its contribution to the larger discussion of any topic. Equally important, worldview philosophy also opened critical possibilities. Open theists routinely noted that classical theism was not simply the result of the intellectual appropriation of Greek and Roman theology but also the product of viewing the Bible through the prism of an ancient, non-Christian worldview.

As influential as worldview approaches to Christian philosophy were, the Society of Christian Philosophy, established in 1978, represented a variety of philosophical and denominational perspectives. Although many Evangelical philosophers attained national stature, including Alvin Plantinga, Nicholas Wolterstorff, William Alston, and Robert Adams, the movement had institutional as well as intellectual effects. If nothing else, it proved that committed believers could make arguments that other philosophers had to take seriously, even if they did not share the conclusions. Whatever else might be true of Christian beliefs broadly considered, they were not without substantial intellectual warrant. Interestingly, BIOLA, which was in the process of becoming a Christian university, was a center for Christian philosophy and sent many of its most qualified students to leading graduate schools.

18. Mouw, "Evangelicalism and Philosophy," 328.

Philosophy and history, significantly, were two areas where Catholics and Evangelicals began to find common ground. The University of Notre Dame was the center of this wider academic dialog. The university provided support for the Center for Philosophy of Religion, headed for some years by Alvin Plantinga. The center provided a place for both research and discussion.[19] Notre Dame also included prominent Evangelical scholars in his faculty. At different times, its faculty has included Nathan Hatch, Mark Noll, Alvin Plantinga, and George Marsden. Notre Dame also served as a model for an American Christian university. Among other institutions, historically Baptist Baylor University in Waco, Texas, found Notre Dame to be an attractive model, particularly under the presidency of Robert B. Sloan.

Evangelicals and Catholics Together

After 1990, Evangelicals and Catholics were the new odd couple. Certainly not all Catholics and not all Evangelicals joined the new alliance. Liberal Catholics felt much more at home with Mainstream Protestants, particularly the socially active, and many Evangelicals continued to see Rome as a dangerous and relentless enemy. Yet significant number of intellectuals on both sides found themselves impressed with the assets that the other brought to the table and hopeful about future cooperation.[20]

After Vatican II, Catholic theologians began to look at the topic of justification afresh. In part, this was because of the Second Vatican Council's emphasis on ecumenism, but it also reflected deeper currents in Catholic theological thought. At the same time, Protestants, especially Lutherans, reexamined their own theological traditions. When they did so, they saw many places where the two traditions agreed on the intent of the two doctrines even where they disagreed on the best way to word those doctrines. More than thirty years of discussion led to the 1999 Catholic and Lutheran Joint Declaration on the Doctrine of Justification, with its emphasis on the importance of grace rather than on the more traditional categories of faith and works. This statement was among the most important ecumenical documents of the century.

The 1990s also marked the beginning of a series of conversions from Protestantism to Catholicism. Francis Beckwith of Baylor, one of the most prominent Evangelicals and at one time president of the Evangelical Theological Society, and ethicist and gadfly Richard Neuhaus, were highly visible converts. The list of those moving included Reinhold Huetter (Duke University), Mickey Maddox (Southern Methodist University), R. R. Reno (Creighton University), and Robert Wilkens (University of Virginia). As earlier converts had discovered, these converts found that Protestantism failed to protect sufficiently the basic truth of the gospel. They felt that it was far better with Rome to believe too much than with most Protestant churches to confess too little. Most Evangelical institutions continued their Catholic converts on the

19. This was funded by Pew in its early days. Joel Carpenter was the grant officer.
20. Shea, *The Lion and the Lamb*.

faculties, largely because of the overlap between conservative Protestant and Catholic beliefs, but Wheaton College dismissed philosophy professor Joshua Hochschild after his conversion.[21] Hochschild moved to Mount St. Mary's, a Catholic school. Despite Hochschild's dismissal, he continued to believe that private religious schools should set theological limits on who taught at their institutions. Hochschild maintained that his theology remained within Wheaton's confessional boundaries.[22]

Another important consideration for Evangelicals considering Rome was worship style. Robert Webber, who spent much of his teaching career at Wheaton College, noted the hunger of many Evangelicals for a style of worship that united past and present. Beginning with his 1985 book *Evangelicals on the Canterbury Trail*, Webber published extensively on the Evangelical need for roots in the ancient church and its worship practices. His works had wide influence, inside and outside Evangelical circles, particularly on the Emerging Church movement.

What moved Catholics and Evangelicals closer together, however, was more than theology or respect for past worship practices. The most important issues were ethical, and particularly the issue of abortion. The 1973 Supreme Court decision *Roe v. Wade* caught Evangelicals napping. In part, this was because Evangelicals had many other political issues on their plates. In the early 1970s, for example, Evangelicals actively supported family and public sexual morality, opposed sex education in the public schools, and resisted regulation of their religious schools and academies. Home schooling was a comparatively recent addition to this agenda. Given Evangelicals' preoccupation with these issues, abortion seemed a Roman Catholic issue, and the early anti-abortion voices were almost exclusively Catholic. As disappointment with President Carter grew, especially around family-related issues, Evangelicals became more politically involved on a variety of fronts. Contact with Catholics and their concerns led to greater attention to the abortion issue.

Francis Schaeffer, the popular apologist and author who earlier popularized the crusade against so-called secular humanism, joined C. Everett Koop in producing *Whatever Happened to the Human Race?*, a popular film that labeled America "a culture of death."[23] Schaeffer, who spent much of his career in Europe, was aware that the churches failed to address such issues as compulsory sterilization or euthanasia during the early Hitler years. Schaeffer believed that this early pattern of ethical avoidance led, albeit by a circuitous route, to the death camps. Consequently, Schaeffer argued that resistance to abortion was the first step in preserving American culture. James Dobson, whose popular radio show *Focus on the Family* began in 1977, was

---

21. This dismissal was unusual enough to be reported in the *New York Times*, on page 1, on January 7, 2006.

22. Post-Vatican II Catholic theology has stressed the continuity between Scripture and tradition while assigning Scripture a normative place. Given this interpretation of the Catholic position, it is difficult to see where Rome and Wheaton disagree on the formal issue.

23. Schaeffer and Koop, *Whatever Happened to the Human Race?*

another important shaper of Evangelical opinion. Dobson identified abortion as a crucial family issue, linking it to the traditional Evangelical emphasis on the family and family life. Dobson also added a psychological argument: abortion left women with a burden of guilt and shame that might take a lifetime to overcome. By the time that Jerry Falwell organized the Moral Majority in 1979—an organization that hoped to unite conservative Protestants, Roman Catholics, and conservative Jews—anti-abortion was fast becoming a mark of American Evangelicalism.[24]

One important Catholic contribution to Evangelical thought was the breadth of the Catholic right-to-life position. This was particularly true for those on the Evangelical Left. Coming out of the 1960s, some Evangelicals saw their faith as implying a more radical social witness. Jim Wallis and *Sojourners* magazine were the most visible advocates of Evangelical social action, but Wallis was not alone. Such prominent Evangelical teachers as Tony Campolo as well as Evangelical liberation theologians in Latin America and Africa kept social issues in the forefront of Evangelical concern, and some seminaries, such as Philadelphia's Eastern—currently Palmer Theological Seminary—were important centers for this version of the Protestant Social Gospel. By defining the right to life as an operative principle for all types of ethical concern, including opposition to war, capital punishment, and poverty, the Catholic bishops broadened the range of argument. This encouraged Evangelical Social Gospel advocates to cooperate with their more conservative brethren in advocating pro-life positions.

In 1994, Evangelical and Catholic scholars and representatives produced "Evangelicals & Catholics Together," a statement of common concerns and commitments. The statement on abortion was plain:

> The pattern of convergence and cooperation between Evangelicals and Catholics is, in large part, a result of common effort to protect human life, especially the lives of the most vulnerable among us . . . we hold that all human beings are endowed by their Creator with the right to life, liberty, and the pursuit of happiness. The statement that the unborn child is a human life that—barring natural misfortune or lethal intervention—will become what everyone recognizes as a human baby is not a religious assertion. It is a statement of simple biological fact. That the unborn child has a right to protection, including the protection of law, is a moral statement supported by moral reason and biblical truth.[25]

Catholics and Evangelicals Together continued to meet and to produce theologically and ethically sensitive materials, despite the deaths of its principal architects, Richard Neuhaus, Charles Colson, and Cardinal Avery Dulles. While differences remained

---

24. One faculty member commented that opposing abortion "has become the social badge of honor [for Evangelicals]. It defines you culturally and institutionally as an Evangelical . . . [much as] inerrancy has done" (Carroll and Marler, "Culture Wars?," 6).

25. Colson, "Evangelicals & Catholics Together."

between the participants—not to mention among the broader Evangelical and Catholic communities—the group achieved much.[26]

Evangelicals and Catholics cooperated in the Association of Theological Schools. Together, they represented a majority of the schools in the association, and they had common interests in such areas as academic freedom and women in theological education. They tended to see their common issues as involving the right of a school to maintain confessional integrity. Although publicly governed Evangelical schools and more confessional bodies (particularly of Southern Baptists and Missouri Synod Lutherans) experience these issues differently, ATS and accreditation were one place where they stood with other conservatives.

LUTHERAN CHURCH-MISSOURI SYNOD

In the 1970s and 1980s, controversies over theological education wracked two of America's largest and most prosperous denominations: the Lutheran Church–Missouri Synod and the Southern Baptist Convention (SBC). Because of these battles, three of the nation's premier seminaries—Concordia in St. Louis, Southern Baptist Theological Seminary, and Southeastern Baptist Theological Seminary—lost the bulk of their faculties and administrations. Further, both the Lutheran Church–Missouri Synod and the SBC experienced schisms that led to the formation of new seminaries and the establishment of stricter theological controls on the older ones. In many ways, these two controversies heralded a theological revolution.

As we mentioned earlier, the two crises had one striking fact in common: the seminaries were well integrated into the larger church structure. The Missouri system was the simplest. The church elected an eleven-member board of control, with five members elected at one biennial convention, and six at the next. The president of the Synod played a major role in the selection of board members. The governance of Southern Baptist seminaries was more complex. The president of the denomination had the right to nominate the members of the Convention nominating committee, which, in turn, proposed names for the various boards of all Convention agencies. Traditionally, the president consulted with the leaders of the various state Baptist conventions, but there was no constitutional requirement to do so. Variations in the size of the various boards—Southern Baptist Seminary in Louisville had the largest—determined the length of time it took to change control on the various boards. Behind these formal governance procedures, both denominations had extensive old-boys' networks that supported their members and provided the denominations with stability. Significantly, the Southern Baptists constructed their governance structure—the Cooperative Program—during the 1920s in the shadow of the fundamentalist-modernist controversy and the adoption of the Baptist Faith and Message. Many people

---

26. For an account of subsequent meetings and their statements, see Harper, "Regensburg Redux."

linked the two actions. In accepting the financial security offered by the Cooperative Program, the seminaries accepted denominational ownership and control. At that time, Southern Baptist Theological Seminary in Louisville surrendered its earlier right to a self-perpetuating board, although it retained (unlike the other seminaries) its board's right to elect its own successors. Although Southern (and later Southeastern) followed the Abstract of Principles, the other seminaries, like other Baptist agencies, accepted the Baptist Faith and Message as their standard.

The Lutheran and Southern Baptist pattern of a close relationship between seminaries and their sponsoring denominations paid rich dividends. Neither the Southern Baptists nor the Missouri Synod suffered from the tendency of American Protestant churches to establish too many schools for their membership. Equally important, the arrangement made the task of financing the schools easier. The seminaries were part of a uniform program of church finance that recognized that theological education was an essential part of the church's mission. In this sense, the schools were very much part of their denomination's identity. The only other seminary system with this measure of integration was the Roman Catholic diocesan seminary under the direct governance of its ordinary.

Both Southern Baptists and Missouri Synod Lutherans had strong traditions of theological identity. The Synod proudly traced its history to a handful of Saxon immigrants who had left Germany in order to preserve their identity as a confessional church. While others were meekly submitting to apostate church governments, the women and men of Missouri had stood for Lutheran truth. The study of the great orthodox Lutheran theologians was part of the stock-in-trade of Missouri's theological faculties. In contrast, a combination of Landmarkism and Civil War ideology shaped Southern Baptist identity. Landmarkism, although never the official theology of the denomination, was commonplace among Southern Baptist pastors and churches. Landmark Baptists believed that God had always preserved a faithful remnant of believers and that these believers had transmitted the truth from generation to generation. In many ways, landmarkism was a variation on the traditional Catholic idea of heresy as an alternative succession to the ordered succession of bishops. The other major shaper of SBC identity was the Civil War. During the theological battles leading up to the conflict, Southern theologians had maintained that the plain and obvious reading of the Bible supported the lawfulness of slavery. Theologically, the War was, consequently, traceable to Northern apostasy. Yet, despite Dixie's defeat, the South had remained firm in its adherence to biblical truth. In short, both churches had long and comparatively recent histories of standing and battling on the Lord's side. Those identities did not promote compromise.

Another common element was a similar theological history. From the end of the Second World War to the mid-1960s, neo-orthodoxy was the reigning Protestant theology. To conservatives, emerging from theological isolation, neo-orthodoxy seemed a promised land. The new theology quickly became normative among Presbyterians, gradually replacing the older confessional theologies still in place at such schools as Princeton and McCormick, and making major inroads at liberal Union. The lure of the new theology for conservatives was obvious: it offered a way to be both biblical and intellectual at the same time. One could continue to emphasize the Word of God; indeed, one could sound like one was repeating the traditional affirmations while accepting the newer biblical criticism. In both the Missouri Synod and the SBC, although individual faculty members had clearer ideas of the meaning of theological change, many teachers did not realize how far they had traveled from traditional orthodoxy. Rather than criticizing and reformulating a tradition, they were translating the faith once delivered to the saints into a new, more modern form.

Yet, by 1965 or earlier in some schools, neo-orthodoxy was dying. The older liberal agenda, never completely out of the theological discussion, reemerged. In particular, such issues as the meaning of historical criticism, new investigations of the meaning of science, and a close identification of mission with social and ecclesiastical change took center stage. Scholars reopened the historical Jesus debate, one of the most passionate arguments of the earlier liberal period, and the quest for the historical Jesus entered its second, third, and subsequent forms. Instead of Billy Graham, *Time* and other opinion makers (reflectors) reported on the Death of God. The transition from neo-orthodoxy to the new liberalism was generally smooth. The critics did not need to argue that neo-orthodoxy was a slippery slope. That was evident in every newspaper report on current theology.

Although the conservative opponents in the SBC and the Missouri Synod were not necessarily current theologically, they were in the midst of a theological world that increasingly stressed the importance of choice or will in the formation of Christian teaching. First African American and then feminist and Latina/Latino, theologians argued that their cultural heritage had the same right to a place in theology as the more dominant culture. In so doing, they often used deconstruction and the hermeneutics of suspicion. The new cultural relativism removed many theological certainties, especially, around the interpretation of the Bible. Historical criticism had seemed to many earlier theologians to have almost invincible warrants; scholars now saw the same method as socially and culturally rooted. In particular, scientific history seemed outdated, dissolved or dissolvable into class, gender, and other political perspectives. If so, any specific group might determine its own hermeneutical location and advocate its own specific worldview, particularly if that worldview had its own coherence and its own warrants. If relativism was good for the goose, it was good for the gander.[27]

Other parallels contributed to the similarity of the course of events. Perhaps the most important was that both the Missouri Synod and the SBC were adjusting to a major change in social location. Following the Second World War, both young Missourians and young Southern Baptists poured into the nation's urban areas. As with

---

27. The importance of this world of intellectual voluntarism cannot be underestimated. Historical relativism undercut all claims to truth, including its own.

other migrants from rural areas, urbanization and suburbanization was often a shock to their systems. Some even more deeply identified with their churches, which were oases of their rural culture; others embraced the new urban world with wide-open arms. Many wanted to preserve the best of their heritage, and such strangers in a strange land were, naturally, conservative. In this sense, socially this wave of conservatism was similar to the conservative wave in the 1920s and 1930s when northern Protestants experienced a similar migration to the cities, and many big-city churches, despite the urban cast of Protestant liberalism, elected to become fundamentalist and to preserve, insofar as they could, the customs of rural culture.

The Case of Concordia: The Missouri Synod Controversy[28]

The Lutheran Church–Missouri Synod prospered in the postwar period, and its period of growth continued into the 1960s and beyond. This was nowhere more evident than in its leading seminary, Concordia in St. Louis. Concordia was the largest Lutheran seminary in the world, larger than any German university theological faculty, and among the best-equipped schools in the nation. Its faculty included graduates from major American graduate schools; and some of Missouri's leading lights, such as Martin E. Marty of the University of Chicago, and Jaroslav Pelikan of Yale, were major American theologians in their own right. At a time when many schools were beginning to feel the financial pinch that accompanied denominational decline, Concordia flourished.

To be sure, there had been growing pains throughout the 1950s and early 1960s. As the seminary grew in power and influence, many ordinary church members worried about whether it was losing its grip theologically. This did not seem to be a major problem for either Concordia's administration or its staff. The Missouri Synod seemed to be passing through the same stages as other denominations. Such noted historians as Lefferts Loescher in his study of Presbyterianism, *The Broadening Church*, and H. Richard Niebuhr in his *Social Sources of Denominationalism* traced a pattern in which religious organizations became American denominations. Although Missouri's self-understanding remained more European, many in and out of the Synod believed that it was becoming a denomination in a nation of denominations.

Further, Lutheranism as a whole provided a textbook example of denominationalization. Negotiations and mergers reduced the large number of small ethnic

---

28. The literature on the Missouri controversy is extensive. Much of it was written by people who participated in the struggle, and it has the advantages and disadvantages of personal memory. Among the works that I consulted in writing this synopsis were Todd, *Authority Vested*; Montgomery, *Crisis in Lutheran Theology*; Tietjen, *Memoirs in Exile*; Burkee, *Power, Politics, and the Missouri Synod*; Board of Control, "Exodus from Concordia"; Marquart, *Anatomy of an Explosion*; and Zimmerman, *A Seminary in Crisis*. In addition, the controversy and its aftermath were extensively reported in both *Christianity Today* and the *Christian Century*. In general, the narrative reflects a consensus of these sources. I did not feel a need to footnote, for example, the chronology.

Lutheran churches to three separate denominations, and most Lutherans believed that the time was coming when these would unite in a single church. Concordia strongly supported this development toward unity. The seminary strongly affirmed existing cooperative agreements with the American Lutheran Church and hoped to see them expanded to include the Lutheran Church in America.

The seminary's openness to ecumenism had long included openness to Catholicism, both as expressed in the church fathers and the classical creeds, and the contemporary Roman Catholic Church. Arthur C. Piepkorn,[29] professor of systematic theology, was a passionate advocate of ecumenical causes. Piepkorn, a graduate of the University of Chicago, served as a military chaplain in the Second World War. He was a leader in the Lutheran-Catholic Dialogue and had many Catholic friends, including the Bible scholar Raymond Brown. One of his principal works, which appeared in multiple volumes after his death, was *Profiles in Belief*, a study of the theological beliefs of American and Canadian churches. Piepkorn died in the midst of the controversy, after having been pointedly "honorably retired" by the seminary's board of control. In 1965, he had published an article, "What Does Inerrancy Mean?," that traced the history of the doctrine and listed the problems with the usual interpretation of the teaching.[30] In many ways, this article spelled out many of the issues in the coming controversy.

In its desire to promote Christian, especially Lutheran, unity, the seminary stood with Oliver Raymond Harms, Missouri Synod president from 1962 to 1969. Two of Harms's principal achievements were agreements with the American Lutheran Church and the Missions Affirmations, which invited service and cooperation with missionaries of other denominations in the mission field. The later document, passed by the Synod in 1965, was a wake-up call for many of the denomination's more conservative ministers, and the Missions Affirmations remained a focal point for discontent during the controversy. Reaction to the Missions Affirmation was the principal issue that encouraged Missouri's conservatives to vote as a block in the 1967. Although they did not win at that meeting, the conservatives discovered that they were stronger than they had supposed. With careful organization, they might control the denomination. To do this, they needed to form alliances with both the far right of the denomination and with the denomination's center.

The central figure in this alliance building was Jacob O. A. Preus, the president of Concordia in Fort Wayne, Indiana. Preus, ironically elected to his seminary position by a synod committee that included Harms, reached out to the far right. In particular, he allied himself with Herman Otten. Otten was the conservative party's attack dog. Denied ordination after he denounced the faculty at Concordia for heresy, Otten pastored a small Lutheran church and published the *Lutheran News*, later the *Christian*

---

29. He was featured in a *Time* article in 1938: "Piepkorn vs. Merriment." He had adopted somewhat strict rules for weddings in the congregation he was serving.

30. Piepkorn, "What Does Inerrancy Mean?"

News. Otten's specialty was investigative journalism. His publications claimed that it looked beyond the surface to find the real story that authority had covered up. To support his interpretations, Otten marshaled an impressive list of sources: faculty lectures and conversations, student notes, and off-the-record interviews. Otten saw himself as plainspoken and forthright, but many in and out of Missouri saw him as abrasive, ill informed, and demagogic. Preus's alliance with Otten was risky. Otten might alienate as many as he attracted, but Preus believed that it was a strategic gamble worth taking.

How important was Otten to the eventual victory of the conservative coalition? Appraising the influence of particular books or authors is always historically difficult, and those who felt his sting, including church historian Martin E. Marty, may have overestimated his influence. One thing appears clear. Otten did not expose Missouri's leftward drift. The Synod was a moderately sized, relatively homogeneous body that trained its leadership in two principal institutions. Many Missouri laypeople were also products of the system, having attended parochial schools controlled and often staffed by graduates of synodically controlled teachers' colleges in River Forest, Illinois, and Seward, Nebraska. What faculty taught in seminary classes, thus, filtered down through the certification process to parochial teachers and continuing education sessions for pastors and teachers held at annual conferences. There was nothing new in Otten's revelations. Yet his way of presenting his material contributed to the atmosphere of distrust. By relying on unofficial sources, especially student notes and classroom handouts, Otten created the illusion that a network of spies was ferreting out the truth. This suggested that what happened in Concordia's classrooms was different from what the faculty maintained publicly. Somehow the faculty and administration were part of a conspiracy to hide the truth. In the context of the widespread belief in conspiracies following the Kennedy assassination and later Watergate, such charges had more credibility than they warranted.

Otten's disclosures put the seminary's administration and faculty on the defensive. Even when further investigation revealed that Otten had taken statements out of context or that the faculty presented controversial material as part of current scholarly debate, the faculty looked like it was hiding its real opinions under highly technical language. Although conservatives among Presbyterians and Baptists had used a similar technique in the 1920s, professing to expose their opponents' real opinions, the technique had backfired. The liberal faculty members published as radical or even more radical material than their critics alleged that they taught. The most damaging material was readily available at any local bookstore. Further, such early liberal leaders as A. C. McGiffert and Shailer Mathews shouted their most controversial positions from the housetops, or at least from the pages of the New York and Chicago newspapers. In short, one did not need John R. Rice or other critics to expose what liberals taught. Liberal opinions were a matter of public record. The Concordia faculty might have learned from this precedent.

The 1967 New York meeting demonstrated that the conservatives had more power than they suspected, and the United Planning Council, led by Jacob Preus, Karl Barth, Waldo Werning, and Edwin Webber, began regularly meeting to plan for the next meeting. Realizing that their right flank was secure, they devised a strategy, part of which was to ally themselves and the more centrist, but very conservative, members of the synod, especially in the Midwest where the membership of the Synod was concentrated. In the Presbyterian struggles of the 1920s, the more liberal party had allied with this central party, often reinforcing its decision by threatening to leave the denomination. Missouri's conservatives would not make the same mistake. The conservatives had decided that they would run the risk of schism and that it would not have disastrous consequences for the denomination. *Affirm*, a more moderate version of the *Christian News*, was a central part of this campaign. In 1969, Preus defeated Harms by 55 percent to 45 percent, one of the few times in American religious history that a sitting denominational leader was defeated in an open vote. At this time, Preus made it clear that one goal of his presidency was to remove recently elected Concordia president, John Tietjen, from office. Preus wasted no time appointing new members to the seminary's board of control, and appointing a fact-finding committee. The committee proceeded to interview all members of the faculty, and, sometimes by a narrow vote, to find them all within the seminary's confessional requirements.

Despite this apparent faculty win, the battle did not end. Preus won the presidency again in 1971 and secured a strong majority on the seminary's board of control. The Synod ordered the board of control to report to Preus on the charges against the faculty.[31] In September 1972, Preus published his Report to the Synod containing the results of his investigation. People nicknamed the report the Blue Book because the report interleaved Preus's interpretation of faculty positions, printed on blue paper, with transcripts of faculty interviews. The report was nothing less than an indictment of the seminary faculty and President John Tietjen. Every pastor in the Synod received a copy. Conservative Daniel Preus, reflecting on the Blue Book, noted:

> A cursory reading of *The Blue Book*, which was 160 8½ by 11 single spaced pages, will reveal that the overwhelming focus of attention was upon the doctrine of Scripture. *The Blue Book* was a bombshell not just for those whose views it condemned but for the entire complacent crowd of Missouri Synod members who had refused to believe that there were any problems at the St. Louis seminary. The issue at the heart of the entire controversy was to what extent Scripture could be considered and accepted as the Word of God. And it all centered around the historical-critical method and whether or not it could be properly used by Lutheran theologians.[32]

---

31. Resolution 2-28 of the 1971 Milwaukee convention.
32. Preus, "The Lutheran Church–Missouri Synod."

The only remaining question was whether biblical inerrancy was, in fact, part of the confessional documents, or whether they had a more limited view of biblical authority. This same issue, of course, was at the heart of the Southern Baptist debate and the debate over Fuller Seminary. In one sense, the question was more a quibble than a distinction. Theology and narrative are so interwoven in the Bible that it is difficult, if not impossible, to separate the doctrinal and ethical parts of Scripture from the stories that inspired them. Further, biblical inerrancy was a consequence of the intense polemical theological controversies that birthed Lutheran (and Reformed) scholasticism. Martin E. Marty, at the height of the controversy, wrote:

> He [Preus] knows that on his chosen issue the synodical forefathers, however different the context and background of their world, *did* speak the language of inerrancy, and that it still has attractions for many. The fathers derived this concept from 17th century scholasticism; as exiles from a lax European state church and strangers in bewildering 19th century American environments, they became more defensive. Early in the 20th century the concept and the word itself were even worked into some synodical resolutions and doctrinal statements.[33]

Tietjen replied with his own *Fact Finding or Fault Finding?*, which was likewise widely distributed. It is more difficult to appraise the influence of this work. Preus's Blue Book had defined the issues and set the terms of the future synodical debates and decisions, and Tietjen's response was too little, too late. It also failed to state openly that the faculty did not accept the traditional Lutheran understanding of the Bible.

The Blue Book and Tietjen's response are remarkable documents. Seldom has so much dialogue been recorded without including a conversation![34] The books made it clear that the seminary and the synod president lived in two different worlds and had two different approaches to the issues. The one thing that the Blue Book made clear was that there was no way to settle the issues except through the exercise of raw political power. The next meeting of the synod would be, for good or ill, a vote on the majority of the faculty members at Concordia.

---

33. Marty, "Showdown in the Missouri Synod," 942.
34. Ibid., 943.

> Report of the Synodical President has been mailed free of charge to 18,000 leaders of the Lutheran Church-Missouri Synod . . . The book's blue pages represent the position of the Synod's embattled president, J. A. O. Preus. With the help of a hand-picked fact-finding committee, he is currently on the attack against the faculty of St. Louis' Concordia Seminary. The contrasting white pages offer excerpts from the faculty members' writings, and transcripts of their interviews with the committee. The two-color format would not have been necessary: every line of the text shows that the antagonists live in different worlds.

Although the Blue Book found six major areas of concern,[35] in retrospect, the problem was the neo-orthodoxy of the faculty.[36] Much of neo-orthodoxy theology rested on a duality. On the one hand, neo-orthodoxy appealed to and reinterpreted the best of inherited Christian doctrine. On the other hand, the same theology argued that modern modes of thought, especially biblical criticism, did not substantially modify that message. For Lutheranism, part of neo-orthodoxy was the Luther renaissance. Beginning in the 1920s, Lutheran theologians and historians reinterpreted Luther's career, particularly his early years, in terms of Luther's existential decision for Christ, stressing the Reformer's sense that he stood alone and defenseless. Particularly among younger scholars, this interpretation corrected, at least partially, the older readings of Luther. Although much of the basic European research that constituted the Luther renaissance was done in the 1920s and 1930s, the new Luther became almost a cult figure in American seminaries in the 1950s and 1960s. Implicit in the Luther renaissance was the belief that while the issues might be different for us, present-day believers could do in their day what Luther did in his. Most German theologians of the period—including Karl Barth, Martin Niemöller, and Werner Elert—were influenced by this movement. In the United States, one response to the new Luther studies was the publication of a new edition of Luther's works.

For Missouri's moderates, the word *confessing* captured the essence of their position. The word *confessing* had a special place in the neo-orthodox canon. In contrast to the term *confessional*—a well-recognized term in German ecclesiastical politics—the term *confessing* had the advantage of bypassing many of the disputed issues between the traditional parties in European church politics, especially those separating Lutheran and Reformed.[37] For some, *confessing* suggested the importance of proclamation over teaching (*kerygma* over *didache*) and stressed an existential response to the gospel. Many Lutheran theologians looked to the work of Werner Elert, a popular

---

35. According to Tietjen, these were:

   1. A false doctrine of the nature of Holy Scriptures coupled with methods of interpretation which effectually erode the authority of the Scriptures.
   2. A substantial undermining of the confessional doctrine of original sin by *de facto* denial of the historical events on which it was based.
   3. A permissiveness towards certain false doctrines
   4. A tendency to deny that the law is a normative guide for Christian behavior
   5. A conditional acceptance of the Lutheran confessions.
   6. A strong claim that the Seminary faculty need not teach in accord with the Synod's doctrinal stance as expressed in the Synod's official doctrinal statements and resolutions. (Tietjen, *Memoirs in Exile*, 109; quoted exactly except that numbers have replaced the letters in the original list)

36. The word *neo-orthodoxy* is (and was) shorthand for a variety of theological perspectives that ranged from a chastened liberalism to a position close to confessional orthodoxy. This ambiguity confused the discussion both in the Southern Baptist Convention and in the Missouri Synod.

37. This was its use in the Confessing Church movement in Nazi Germany, which brought together leading Reformed and Lutheran pastors.

German interpreter of Lutheranism, who urged a more existential approach to the confessions of the church.

The term also had more heroic connotations. *Confessing* was a term taken from the German Church Struggle. Most German believers, whether they were comfortable with the Nazi interference with church government or not, stayed within their churches and remained faithful communicants. A handful, led by Karl Barth, formed a party to oppose Nazi-supported slates for church offices and to support those churches that continued church administrations from the pre-Hitler period. In 1934 this group offered the Barmen Declaration as a statement of its theological position. Like all such documents, Barmen was a compromise; in this case, the document attempted to avoid both the traditional Reformed understanding of government as a means to righteousness and the Lutheran doctrine of the two kingdoms. The self-conscious decision to call it a declaration rather than a confession reflected this delicate balance. As critics at the time and later noted, Barmen did not explicitly condemn Nazi anti-Judaism.

The heroic young Luther of the Luther renaissance was an important influence on the Confessing Church. The carrying of a red card, the sign of membership in the movement, was a Luther-like act. The Barmen Declaration and the Confessing Church were popular among American churchmen and, especially, among American theologians. Dietrich Bonhoeffer, the best-known martyr of the Nazi era, was a cult hero in some seminaries, and part of the four *B*'s—Barth, Bultmann, Brunner, and Bonhoeffer—that composed the neo-orthodox academic canon.

The appeal to the Confessing Church was somewhat disingenuous. The German issues were the right of the state to dictate church teaching on the Old Testament and to regulate the appointment or removal of ministers to ecclesiastical positions. The essential claim was that the Church had the right, under God, to determine its own teachings and its own officers. Ironically, the German debate often revolved around the continuing authority of the Old Testament. The German Christians wanted to interpret the Old Testament as only one divine preparation for the gospel, whereas the Confessing Church insisted that it was unique. Although Karl Barth might have agreed theologically with the Concordia faculty, the Confessing Church would not necessarily have followed his lead. Many Confessing Christians were biblical and confessional conservatives uneasy with their alliance with Reformed and liberal churchmen. Apart from the Nazi crisis, they might have sided with Preus and the conservatives.

Leaving aside the vexing issue of whether the faculty appropriately appealed to German experience, the implications of the term *confessing* as a self-designation were staggering. If the faculty were the confessing church, then their opponents—if we extend the metaphor—were at best oppressors of the true faith and themselves deniers of Scripture. Given the prominent place of the Old Testament in this as in other conservative/liberal battles, this shifted attention away from the question of the authority of the Old Testament—one of the real questions in the German Christian/Confessing Church battle—to the character of the combatants. Conservatives—and more important the politically vital center—did not see themselves or their allies in such stark terms.

The popularity of the confessing metaphor may have also managed to obscure other issues in the debate. The key issue in Preus's assault on Concordia was historical criticism, and this term figured prominently in all the documents, both as attack and as defense. Yet the term was never defined or critically examined. This would also be true of the Southern Baptist controversy. In retrospect, the two sides continually spoke by each other. For conservatives, the battle was not over criticism, but over the results of criticism. They used historical materials in their interpretations as much, if not more, than the Moderates did. For the faculty, the question was how to approach the text, and the results of that approach were beside the point. For conservatives, research ended in a conclusion; for the Moderates, it ended in further discussion.

Tietjen himself recognized later that attempts to claim that Concordia was only doing what the Missouri Synod had always done, only in more modern dress, were by the point. In his memoirs, Tietjen wrote:

> But I did not appreciate what I thought was less than candor in the seminary's repeated claims that nothing had really changed in CS [Concordia Seminary] teaching. I resented the efforts to demonstrate that what was happening at CS was really the 'old' Missouri Synod after all. I thought that it would have been not only more honest but also more hopeful for CS to capitalize on the changes that were going on by showing how those changes were enabling CS and the LCMS [Lutheran Church–Missouri Synod] to be more faithful to the Synod's confessional position.[38]

Left unanswered, even years later, was the question of what that more-faithful might have been. One assumes that at least part of that was the unification of Lutheranism around a modern reinterpretation of the confessional documents, particularly the Augsburg Confession. This is indeed what happened in the eventual merger of the larger Lutheran churches, a merger brokered in large part by Tietjen and supported by those who left the Synod in sympathy with the Concordia faculty.

The decision to defend a method, rather than the conclusions actually reached as a result of the application of that method, also forced the faculty into some strange uses of language. Perhaps the strangest was the phrase "the Lutheran way of doing historical criticism." Aside from the fact that much modern biblical study originated in Germany among Lutherans, I am a loss to understand what this might mean. The renaissance in Luther studies, which stressed the early writings of Luther, had tended to see Luther's approach to the Bible as existential, almost Kierkegaardian. This Luther was perhaps best illustrated in the *Preface to the New Testament* of 1522. Yet the critical edge of Luther's biblical study was not history. For him, as for John Calvin, the historicity of the Bible was largely intact. His essential question was the distance

---

38. Tietjen, *Memoirs in Exile*, 22.

between a biblical book and the teaching about Christ. By the time of the great debate over the Supper, Luther's own hermeneutic had shifted radically to a position very similar to that of later Lutheran orthodoxy.

Whether it is possible or not, the goal of historical study is to form a publicly accessible and verifiable picture of the past. Historians rarely, if ever, attain this goal. In any historical investigation, the evidence is never complete. Moreover, all historians interject, consciously or unconsciously, their own perspectives and prejudices into the discussion. Histories are as marked by social class, gender, and other ideological distortions, as are the sources that historians study. Nonetheless, the purpose of publication and discussion is to move closer and closer to the best understanding of the past available.

The Concordia faculty elected to make its case on theological grounds rather than on the grounds of academic freedom. In retrospect, the decision may have made more strategic sense than first appears. Although theological advocates of academic freedom have won approval from such secular organizations as the American Association of University Professors, they have rarely won more than punic victories in the Association of Theological Schools. Although he Association of Theological Schools was right when the visiting team appointed to investigate Concordia noted undue influence by the Synod on the teaching at the institution, the penalties imposed—two successive probations in 1972 and 1974—were less than a serious hand slap.[39] Many reasons may be offered for the comparative inaction of the agency: it was largely an organization of administrators, who tended to side with authority; the association was adding new schools, mostly Catholic and Evangelical, that were worried about whether accreditation might interfere with the right of churches to enforce their rules; and this case lacked meaningful precedents. However, the most serious barrier to effective action was the association's standards and expectations. ATS always accepted the right of any school to define its own theological standards and to enforce those standards by rules and procedures that guaranteed due process. In effect, faculty members accepted those rules—and the means of adjudicating them—when they accepted appointment to such institutions. Yet, despite the clarity of the association's standards, what they mean in practice is less clear. In modern Protestant history, theology varies from generation to generation. Yesterday's heresy easily becomes tomorrow's orthodoxy. As a result, confessional documents are continually reinterpreted and reapplied. Thus, a gap exists between the adherents of past interpretations and those have adopted new interpretations. Those who argue that "this is what it says" and those who argue that "this is what it means" are almost inevitably at odds with one another. Each side has sound reasons for the actions that it takes. In short, the meaning of a confessional statement is political, not procedural, and finally comes down to who controls the decision-making body.

---

39. Ziegler, *ATS through Two Decades*, 151

Even more than other confessional controversies, Concordia's struggles illustrated the tension in confessional schools. Ironically, Preus was highly skilled as a historical critic and exegete. He was an expert on historic Lutheran orthodoxy who was well qualified, as he and others recognized, to pass judgment on the meaning of the theological standards enumerated in Missouri's standards. Tietjen and his colleagues, many of whom had attended some of the finest graduate schools in the country, were thoroughly immersed in the problems of contemporary thought. The people who educated them and their ecumenical partners urged them to address the question of what those documents meant in the contemporary world. Concordia's *via media* between strict confessionalism and liberalism was suspect on all sides.

In both the Missouri Synod and the Southern Baptist controversies, the more liberal side preferred to call itself Moderate. At the time, Richard Neuhaus noted that the choice of language was unfortunate. "'Moderate' sounded namby-pamby to Missouri Lutherans. It would sound as if a Missouri Lutheran didn't know for sure what he believed, taught, and confessed, or as if he believed, taught, and confessed those truths only half way."[40] Unfortunately, the word *moderate* had other implications as well. Americans have historically been inclined to see change as good. The language of reform, which had historically aided the old liberals in the 1920s, was, by default, surrendered to the conservatives who had a clear, definite program for the future.

Whatever the merits of the two positions, however, the publication of the Blue Book marked a major turn in the controversy. Despite the fact that the faculty was officially cleared by the board of control in January 1973, the tide had turned decisively in Preus's direction. The issue came to a head with the decision of the board of control not to renew the contract of Arlis J. Ehlen, a rising faculty star and Harvard graduate, and to deny him, thereby, academic tenure. In some ways, the battle was a scrimmage for the coming meeting of the Synod. There was no doubt that Ehlen used the historical approach to the Old Testament, and likewise no doubt that the board of control found this unacceptable. Ironically, the board of control finally voted to pay Ehlen's salary for one additional year, provided that he had no faculty rank or teaching duties. He would subsequently appeal this decision to the American Association of University Professors, which eventually agreed with him, long after the decision had any relevance.

All the Conservatives had to do was to hold on to their supporters, while the Moderates had to win adherents or to convince the center that a conservative victory would be more destructive of the denomination than a compromise. In the 1920s, liberals had forced a compromise by threatening to leave the Presbyterian Church; Preus and his followers, however, were willing to run the risk of a liberal withdrawal. New Orleans was a spectacular victory for the conservatives. The synod put the board of control firmly into conservative hands and censured the faculty for teaching false

---

40. Quoted in Adams, *Preus of Missouri: And the Great Lutheran Civil War*, iv.

doctrine. Perhaps the clearest sign of conservative power was a resolution directing the board of control to deal with Tietjen's leadership.

In August 1973, the board of control suspended Tietjen for the first time, and then it vacated its action, allowing negotiations leading to a possible compromise. Was the situation as fluid as some hoped? Later events seemed to follow with the precision of a choreographed dance, but this may be only an illusion created by later events. The Moderates established the ELIM (Evangelical Lutherans in Mission), a precursor to a break-away denomination, and the conservatives appear to have offered a compromise that removed only Tietjen and a handful of faculty. Behind the scenes, emotions were building. The students at Concordia, led by such effective spokespersons as James Wind and George Miller, began to line up behind their faculty. In addition to their meetings on campus, students visited churches throughout the nation to explain what was happening. Did the students contribute to the genesis of Seminex—the Seminary in Exile? The students' determination to continue their education under their current teachers was an important component of future events, and it may have strengthened faculty resolve. At a minimum, the faculty knew that they would not be alone, if they took decisive action. At a maximum, the students pushed the faculty steadily towards more radical action. When the board suspended Tietjen for a second time, the students declared a moratorium on attending classes. The faculty joined them in declaring their solidarity with the deposed president. After a dramatic ceremony, complete with the pealing of bells—the traditional German prelude to a funeral—the faculty and students walked out and established Siminex with temporary headquarters at Saint Louis University and Eden Seminary.

The anticlimactic process of starting anew followed the dramatic walkout. Faculty had to vacate their offices and in many cases, their seminary houses or apartments. Students also had to find new residences. All had to accustom themselves to life in very different environments. Saint Louis University was and is a Jesuit University with a strong Catholic ethos, while Eden, the seminary that trained both Reinhold and H. Richard Niebuhr, was a liberal school related to the United Church of Christ. Once settled, the little details of separation began to accumulate. At least until the formation of the Association of Evangelical Lutheran Churches (AELC), the issue of the who and how of certifying graduates of the new school for ordination and placement was almost impossible to settle. Preus and the other conservative leaders used the issue as part of their campaign to purify the denomination, and removed District Presidents who persisted in including Seminex graduates in the process. The formation of the AELC did not end Seminex's—after 1977 Christ Seminary's—difficulties with placement. The new denomination did not have enough pulpits to accommodate the number of graduates.

Despite the loss of forty-five faculty members and most of its student body, Concordia recovered quickly. Within a few years, the older school had passed Seminex in enrollment and had recruited an adequate faculty. The Association of Theological

Schools, which had imposed very light sanctions, removed them, and Concordia was again the Synod's most prestigious institution. In contrast, despite the initial enthusiasm, Christ Seminary–Seminex found itself short of funds, students, and placements. The school searched for partners, and in 1983 dispersed its faculty and students to other Lutheran schools, especially the Lutheran School of Theology, Chicago. In 1987, the school officially closed its books. The protest was over. The new denomination, the Association of Evangelical Lutheran Churches, merged with the two larger Lutheran bodies as part of a new Evangelical Lutheran Church in America.

If nothing else, Christ Seminary–Seminex provided faculty with an opportunity to continue their careers until the larger Lutheran community could devise a more long-lasting solution. The damage that the controversy inflicted on faculty, administrators, students, and churches was deep and abiding. Careers were redirected, opportunities missed, and psychological trauma experienced. Lost potential, unwritten books, disrupted theological development do not always leave the historical evidence that careful researchers might desire, but they were part of the residue of this battle. To provide a place where such wounds might begin to heal was no small achievement. Further, one should not minimize the role of Christ Seminary–Seminex in promoting Lutheran unity. The Lutheran Church in America and the American Lutheran Church were, of course, well on the way to merger when the Missouri crisis began, and they probably would have continued on that path with or without the small number of congregations from the AELC. Yet the substantial talents of John Tietjen, the president of Christ Seminary, and the theological strength of the exiled faculty made substantial contributions to Lutheran reunion. The new denomination and new seminary did not reverse Missouri's conservative tide, but they did point to an alternative future.

The Missouri battle was over quickly. Once the conservatives had power, it was only a matter of three years before their control was complete. In retrospect, one wonders whether the issue might have turned out otherwise had the Synod taken more time to debate the issue. Many elements of the controversy, particularly the undercurrent of conspiracy and plot, were more believable in the days of Watergate than they might have been earlier. Further, the speed did not permit Concordia's spokespeople to develop a more contemporary defense. The seminary's leadership was defending the theology of the 1950s in a rapidly changing theological environment. In contrast, however much the conservatives might have resisted comparison with Evangelicalism, the conservatives were riding on the crest of a popular movement that was gaining in American Protestantism.

The Missouri controversy did influence other events. Anxious conservatives in the SBC realized that it was possible for a conservative movement in a denomination to topple the leadership of a major seminary and to reverse that seminary's direction. This had never happened before—the liberals consistently won in the 1920s and 1930s—but that was then, this was now.

SOUTHERN BAPTIST CONTROVERSY[41]

In many ways, the Southern Baptist controversy resembled the passionate battle among Missouri Synod Lutherans. In both, the conservative majority was an uneasy league between some conservative intellectuals and a larger, more populist, body of supporters. To maintain that alliance, the conservatives had to use a variety of appeals, including highly partisan newspapers, that often reported without nuance and without charity. Like the Moderates in the Missouri case, the Moderates here were also an uneasy and unstable alliance of seminary professors, denominational officials, and

---

41. In many ways, writing about controversies among Roman Catholics and Missouri Synod Lutherans was comparatively easy. I did not, as they say, have a horse in those races. The Southern Baptist Convention battle was otherwise. I had left the SBC after the Elliott controversy to attend Andover Newton, and when I returned to teach at Southeastern Baptist, the battle was just beginning. The struggle raged for most of my time there. It was one of the most painful periods of my life, and my memories of it are anything but pleasant.

Perhaps because I was, at least, a partial outsider, I had a different perspective on the battle than either my Moderate colleagues or their Fundamentalist opponents. I was convinced that American Christianity in general was in the midst of a crisis that would eventually shake it to its foundations, and that the American churches needed to prepare for declining memberships, increasing tensions with secular society, and a world that was at best indifferent to faith and at worse hostile. Never inclined to optimism about the world, I saw the period as more like the slow and steady erosion of the Roman Empire than the self-confident world of the nineteenth century. If there was hope, I felt that it was in a rebirth of Catholic Christianity or a new Reformed Christianity with an emphasis on creeds, confessions, sacraments, and ecclesiastical discipline. I still feel that way. Highly individualized Christianity will only survive under these post-Christian conditions as a fad. In that sense, I was ill at ease with either the Moderate emphasis on the "soul liberty" of the individual or with the Conservative emphasis on a text that had intrinsic authority apart from the worshiping community.

I did three major studies of Jonathan Edwards during my theological career. The first was a somewhat hasty study done in undergraduate school in a course on colonial American history, the second was a somewhat more focused study for Earl Thompson at Andover Newton, and the third was my dissertation under Robert Handy at Union. Edwards believed that true religion was necessarily a matter of the heart—a new sense—but he also believed that not all religious experiences were valid. Only when experience was tested and verified could be accepted as evidence of saving grace. Scripture without the new sense was only notional; experience without Scripture and, above all, without love, became fanatical.

I was and still am not completely sure that so-called academic freedom is a necessary value for theological seminaries. This does not mean that I do not believe in it for universities. Research must proceed without any preestablished norms other than perhaps the commitment to inquiry itself. Yet the purpose of theological education is not to find truth wherever it may be found, but to study that which strengthens the Christian community in its striving to give God glory and praise. Theological schools exist to increase the love of God and neighbor. In that sense, seminaries serve a higher law than universities, even if seminaries appear "enslaved" to the secular world.

I consider Evangelical Christianity to be marked by four C's: an emphasis on conversion, cross, canon, and community. These four emphases were and are still the central points of my own understanding of faith that I use to organize my thoughts, my ministry, and my work in theological education. Ironically, both my Moderate companions and my Conservative friends shared these same emphases. By any stretch of the imagination, they were all Evangelicals and not Liberals. Anyone who studied in liberal schools, as I did, was aware of the points of agreement. In an ideal world, these points of contact would and should have permitted free exchanges of views, but that was not to be. In this controversy, the middle was roundly condemned by those to the left and to the right.

successful pastors. They were the elite of the denomination, and they presented their views in careful articles in such journals as the *Review and Expositor*, *Faith and Mission*, and the *Theological Educator*. The editors of the influential state Baptist papers also tended to express Moderate views.

In the 1960s and 1970s, those that would compose the Moderate party were at the top of their game. The postwar SBC was among the great success stories in American religion. Not only had the denomination managed a major transition in its core population as Southerners, like Northerners a generation earlier, poured from the countryside into the newly booming Southern metropolitan areas, but Southern Baptists also became a national denomination, spanning the continent—north and south, east and west. Abroad, Southern Baptist missions were the best-equipped and best financially supported of the old-line denominations. Critics might laugh at the denomination's "Bold Mission Thrust," but it was the nation's most successful denominational program.

The Southern Baptist seminaries had also developed. At the beginning of the World War, the denomination was served by two poorly financed schools: Southern and Southwestern, and by the New Orleans Bible Institute. By 1960, the seminary system had expanded to six large seminaries: Southern, Southwestern, New Orleans, Golden Gate, Southeastern, and Midwestern. Over the next two decades, these schools grew numerically and qualitatively. By the time of the controversy, the seminaries had strong administrative staffs and able presidents, including Roy Honeycutt, Randall Lolley, and Russell Dilday.

These schools were not only the showpieces of a successful denomination. After the World War, they had enlisted increasingly distinguished faculty with impressive intellectual credentials. Southern Seminary, for example, could boast of Dale Moody and Eric Rust, and Southwestern had a distinguished line of church historians, including Robert Baker, William Estep, and Leon McBeth. Southern's Dale Moody, Southwestern's John Newport, and Southeastern's James Tull had worked with Paul Tillich at Union. Oxford doctorates were common.

As in the Missouri Synod, so in the SBC the dominant theology at the six seminaries was a conservative version of neo-orthodoxy. Neo-orthodoxy enabled Southern Baptist theologians to draw heavily on the Bible, while being attentive to the new criticism and the cultural emphases around them. The heavy reliance on neo-orthodox categories was one source of the seminary faculties' favorite self-designation as Moderates. Southern Baptist faculty members believed the neo-orthodox were the great middle party between the errors of the liberalism on the one hand and the intolerance of fundamentalism on the other. Ironically, by the time of the controversy, many American Mainstream Protestant theologians had abandoned this position for various more liberal or conservative alternatives. In a world with increasingly liberal and liberationist theologians on one side and Evangelical theologians on the other, SBC seminary faculties were out of step with both branches of American Protestantism.

The seminaries were also in a culture undergoing significant political and cultural change. A new Republican South, in part the result of Southern reaction to national issues, gradually replaced the older Democratic establishment, beginning with the presidential races, and moving gradually to include the senate, house, governorships, and state legislatures. At the same time, the Republicans added socially and culturally conservative emphases to their traditional economic conservatism. These emphases, including a strong emphasis on the family, were in line with deep regional values. During the 1920s, for example, white Southerners had strongly supported prohibition, because they believed that alcohol weakened families. During the 1960s and 1970s, further, many white Southerners, deeply dissatisfied with public education, had built and supported private religious schools. The fear that these schools were under attack from the government, or seemed so, hastened the transformation.

Most Southern pastors, including W. A. Criswell at Dallas and Jerry Falwell, did not initially recognize the religious centrality of the new Religious Right issues, especially abortion, and only gradually realized their importance. However, the people that would spearhead the conservative movement, especially Paige Patterson and Richard Land, recognized the importance of these issues from the beginning, as did such TV preachers as Charles Stanley and Adrian Rogers. Identifying the time frame in which changes in popular apprehension take place is difficult, but my sense is that Southern attitudes on abortion shifted significantly between 1973, when the Supreme Court handed down *Roe v. Wade*, and 1979, when Jerry Falwell and others formed the Moral Majority. If I am right on this, the change in attitudes about abortion and by extension other New Right political issues preceded the major conservative push in the SBC. Thus, SBC conservatives did not create the New Religious Right among Southern Baptists as much as the already popular New Religious Right ensured their success.

The Crisis Begins

Although one of the commonplaces of Southern Baptist history is that the denomination escaped the fundamentalist crisis, this is strictly not true. To be sure, the denomination did not have a significant liberal party, although such educational leaders as William Louis Poteat, president of Wake Forest University, were significant progressive voices. The issue of whether Baptist seminary and college faculty might teach evolution was a constant item on the agenda of both the SBC and the state Baptist conventions. Conservative strength, largely mobilized by the evolution debate, led the denomination to adopt its first confession of faith, the Baptist Faith and Message—a revision of the New Hampshire Baptist Confession—with its strong affirmation of biblical authority. Both E. Y. Mullins, president of Southern, and Lee Scarborough, president of Southwestern, publicly stated their opposition to evolution.

These debates formed the context in which Southern Baptists, cursed by a poverty inherited from the Civil War period, devised the Cooperative Program to fund their enterprises. Under the Cooperative Program, the denomination assumed both the major funding of the seminaries and the right to name their boards of trustees. A similar model brought many of the colleges under the control and sponsorship of their state conventions. This was perhaps the most important revolution in the way that Southern Baptists did education, and its success made it difficult for Southern Baptists to consider other alternatives. The polity also made the Conservative revolution possible.

The new plan vested considerable power in the national and state Baptist conventions. To use language popular in the SBC, the schools were Convention agencies, carrying out the will of the body. They were part of the larger denominational structure. E. Y. Mullins and Lee Scarborough, the two seminary presidents who helped devise the new structure, knew the danger of popular control. Both presidents recognized that the emotionalism of a particular meeting of the SBC messengers might result in intemperate actions that could weaken the schools.[42] Membership in the Convention varied radically from year to year. Since local churches elected messengers, usually from among those who could afford to go, the location of a meeting determined much of its composition. A meeting in Richmond or Atlanta had a very different composition from a meeting in Dallas. The meetings, especially considering the numerical size of the convention, were comparatively small. Two constants gave the convention some stability. First, both the cost of attending the convention and the urban location of its meeting favored representation from the larger and more prosperous Southern Baptist churches. As a rule, these tended to have seminary graduates, often with doctorates from Southern or Southwestern, as pastors. Even J. Frank Norris, the highly controversial fundamentalist pastor of the First Baptist Church of Fort Worth and for years a disturbing presence at convention meetings, was a graduate of Baylor and of Southern Baptist Theological Seminary.[43] Second, the Convention's bureaucrats were overrepresented. Their agencies paid their expenses, and their congregations elected them as messengers. Thus, denominational executives were voting messengers at all sessions of the convention, no matter where it met, and the experts on its rules and procedures. The executives controlled much of the formal agenda through their reports, and they operated in the hallways, pleading their cause and making alliances. Second, the convention president, again usually chosen from among the denomination's elite, had the power to appoint the committee that nominated the members of the boards, including the six seminaries' trustees. These protections were not only

---

42. *Messenger* is a technical term in Southern Baptist polity. In theory, messengers are bringing the opinions of the members of their local churches to the national body and are independent representatives.

43. Interestingly, William Bell Riley, his closest Northern Baptist counterpart, also attended Southern Baptist Theological Seminary.

geographical and customary. The Cooperative Program included significant constitutional protections for the schools. The seminaries were shielded—as were the various other denominational boards—by a system that allowed the convention to appoint only a limited number of trustees or board members at any given meeting or series of meetings. This check and balance allowed controversies to cool down before they affected the seminaries.

Did Southern Baptist governance rest on a grand compromise?[44] Not really, the convention was a theoretical democracy ruled by a very real and very powerful oligarchy. In practical terms, the system worked to keep both extremes out of power. More liberal elements, especially in North Carolina and Virginia, might have their innings when the convention met in the Southeast, and more fundamentalist elements might have their innings when the convention met in the Southwest. Geographical mobility, finances, and bureaucracy worked to keep those in power, in power. No matter how successful, oligarchies separate the powerful from the less powerful and encourage a politics of resentment.

Further, the 1960s were not good for oligarchies. Although historians have noted the many fractures in postwar American life, the various social movements of the 1960s and 1970s transformed those fractures into fissures. From either side of the divides that opened up, people viewed each other and, equally important, each other's leaders with suspicion. Many of those issues, including race, gender, immigration, sexual mores, and sexual orientation, continued to the end of the twentieth century and beyond. In what looks like an acting out of Hegel, every new left leads to a new right, every major liberalizing movement to a new conservatism. The two sides battle until one or the other has an apparent victory, and the process beings again. In a religious free market—and whatever else the United States might be, it is the world's largest free market in religion—there is an option to this continual warfare. A person can simply leave and go to another religious organization or to none. Competition can, thus, mute controversy as well as generate it.

Given the prominence of the racial issue in the South, one might have expected it to be the wedge that divided the SBC. While race did disrupt many local Southern Baptist churches, the denomination rode out that storm nicely. The issue that exposed the deep divisions was the Bible. Southern Baptists prided themselves on being a biblical people, on having no creed but the Bible, on standing fast on biblical grounds. When they attended church, often twice on Sundays and every Wednesday night, Bible study occupied the central place in their worship. Anthropologists often examine wedding customs as guides to the values of a people or tribe. They might note that most Southern Baptist brides carried a small white Bible, often carefully placed under their flowers, during the service. The bride threw her flowers to the bridesmaids, but she kept the Bible as the foundation of her new Christian home.

---

44. See Leonard, *God's Last and Only Hope*, for another point of view.

The Bible was often a gift from the Women's Missionary Union and represented incorporation into the "women's church" that was a significant power in most Southern Baptist congregations.

Theologian James W. McClendon described Baptist biblicism in terms of a formula: this is that and then is now.[45] The slogan identifies the present moment in terms of the biblical past. Old and New Testament stories are not merely historical; they are guides to contemporary life and experience. What is happening now is the same thing as what happened then. In other words, the biblical text is the hermeneutic that the believer uses to understand his or her own experience. In terms of biblical references, this is a biblical doctrine based more on Psalm 119:105[46] than on 2 Timothy 3:15–18.[47] An appreciation of this underlying hermeneutic is important for understanding why so much of the controversy revolved around biblical stories rather than around biblical doctrine or biblical ethics. Since the hermeneutic rested on the identification of this passage and this experience, then if one questioned the story, many Southern Baptists felt that one also questioned the experience, including the experience of salvation.

The first round of the controversy involved biblical scholar Ralph Elliott, who taught at the newly established Midwestern Baptist Theological Seminary.[48] In 1961, Broadman Press—the SBC Sunday School's publishing arm—published Elliot's *The Meaning of Genesis: A Theological Interpretation*. Measured by then-contemporary scholarship, *The Meaning of Genesis* was not a radical book. If anything, it leaned more toward the neo-orthodox consensus represented in the *Interpreter's Bible* than toward the more radical criticism common in Europe or at the leading American seminaries. In commissioning the work, Broadman apparently had in mind the publication of a middle-level type book; that is, one designed for pastors and serious readers, not necessarily for other scholars. *The Meaning of Genesis* was consensus scholarship, represented ideas held in common by teachers in Baptist seminaries and colleges.

Part of the furor over the *Meaning of Genesis* was an issue little noted outside of Conservative circles. Genesis referred to Melchizedek, as the Prince of Peace (Salem), the priest of God Most High. Melchizedek brought bread to Abraham and blessed him. In the New Testament book of Hebrews, Melchizedek is the type of the high priestly Christ who offers salvation through his ministry. In contrast, Elliott argued that the historical Melchizedek was probably the Canaanite priest of a local god, if he existed at all. Among Old Testament scholars, Elliott's interpretation was not unusual or shocking. However, to many Southern Baptist ministers, Elliott appeared to negate an important christological affirmation.

---

45. Westmoreland-White, "Reading Scripture in the Baptist Vision."

46. "Your word is a lamp for my feet, a light on my path" (NIV).

47. "All Scripture is God-breathed and is useful for teaching, rebuking, correcting and training in righteousness, so that the servant of God[a] may be thoroughly equipped for every good work" (NIV).

48. For the centrality of the Elliott case, see Howe, "From Houston to Dallas."

The Meaning of Genesis stirred up a hornets' nest. Herschel H. Hobbs, pastor of the First Baptist Church of Oklahoma City, was president of the Southern Baptist Convention in 1962 and 1963. Hobbs was a graduate of Southern Baptist Theological Seminary in Louisville with a master's and a doctoral degree in New Testament, and a popular writer on Baptist theology. He used his power as president to ensure that Midwestern Seminary received more Conservative trustees. Hobbs also presided over a convention-mandated revision of the Baptist Faith and Message, adopted in 1963. Although no seminary professors served on the committee that revised the statement, the final draft included the important provision that the center of the Scriptures was Jesus Christ.

The governance of the SBC permitted the Midwestern Board of Trustees to examine Elliott twice. The difference between the two hearings illustrates the power of a Conservative SBC president to influence the course of events at a seminary. The first time, the board exonerated him; the second time, the board split 15–15. The issue then went to a committee that negotiated with Elliott. Finally, Elliott and the committee agreed on 9 out of 10 points in a compromise document. The tenth was, however, the sticking point. Elliott had to agree not to republish his book. Unless the full board asked him to do so, Elliott refused this requirement. The board removed Elliott for insubordination.

The Elliott case was not resolved to anyone's satisfaction. Faculty in SBC seminaries and some state Baptist colleges felt that the Elliott case endangered their own academic freedom. Conservatives believed that the churches had spoken clearly through both convention action and the reaffirmation of the Baptist Faith and Message. Yet, the new faculty members chosen to replace Elliott and Heber Peacock, who resigned in sympathy, were equally committed to the same approach to Genesis, and reached many of the same conclusions. The decision appalled the handful of liberals in the denomination. They believed that the board should have protected Elliott's academic freedom. The liberals were surprised that the number of seminary faculty resigning in solidarity was so small. If Elliott had, in fact, said in public what everyone said in the privacy of their classrooms, then the other faculty who had reached similar conclusions should have stood up and recorded their agreement with their fellow scholar. Heber Peacock spoke for them when he said, as reported in the *Christian Century*,

> I no longer believe that we can have a school here. Appeasement and sacrifice ... cannot create a situation in which the truth can be spoken. Other men will be sacrificed as soon as they speak publicly what they teach in their classes, for most of us believe and teach as Ralph Elliott did. Since I must refuse to proclaim my theological and biblical understanding only in private and since I must refuse to bring my public teaching into conformity with the views of the literalists, I cannot remain.[49]

---

49. Peacock, "Seminary Loses Another Teacher," 326.

Later, Elliott expressed his own disappointment with the result.[50] As he saw it, his colleagues were willing to engage in a form of double-speak, saying one thing and meaning another, in dealing with their classes and with the church. If Elliott exaggerated his charges somewhat, they did highlight the seminaries' loss of legitimacy. Many young Southern Baptists fled north to Colgate Rochester, Andover Newton, Princeton, Union, and Yale.

Ironically, another Southern Baptist seminary, Southeastern, was more affected by doctrinal controversy than Midwestern. At Southeastern, however, the problem was (alleged) "Bultmannism" among the New Testament faculty. This internal controversy eventually led to the resignation of a number of teachers, including the very able scholars Harold Oliver and R. C. Briggs. Religious educator Denton Coker followed, and church historian Pope Duncan also left.[51] Unlike the Midwestern controversy, the Southeastern battle was within the faculty itself, with professors charging other teachers with departing from the seminary's Abstract of Principles. In one sense, this was how the system was supposed to work—with the faculties and administration working together to secure a broad orthodoxy. Yet it also demonstrated, to those inside and outside the convention how fragile Southern Baptist academic freedom actually was.

The next round was the controversy over the Broadman Commentary series.[52] The Broadman Commentary series was among the high points in Southern Baptist intellectual history. The Sunday School Board, the owners of Broadman Press, commissioned a commentary series that would cover the whole Bible and demonstrate the strength of Southern Baptist scholarship. The board hoped that the series would mark the emergence of Broadman as a serious, albeit Conservative, press, and a worthy denominational counterpart to the Lutheran and Presbyterian publishers that then led in theological publishing. Eventually, the board hoped that its catalog would include serious works in theology, church history, and other theological disciplines as well as the lay literature and excellent Baptist history materials that it traditionally produced. The Old Testament editors for the series were Roy Honeycutt, soon-to-be president of Southern Seminary, and John I. Durham of Southeastern. The New Testament editors were John William MacGorman of Southwestern and Frank Stagg of Southern.

The editors decided to head off controversy by asking distinguished English Baptist scholar, G. Henton Davies, to author the first volume, Genesis to Exodus. Davies seemed a safe choice. The Welsh scholar was Principal of Regents Park College, the Baptist House of Studies at Oxford, and widely recognized in England and in America as a conservative biblical scholar. At Regent, Davies supervised John I. Durham's doctoral work, and he served as the unofficial sponsor of many of the Southern Baptist students who enrolled in advanced study at that English university. Davies's commentary appeared in 1969. In that same year W. A. Criswell, the patriarch of Southern

---

50. Elliott. *The "Genesis Controversy."*
51. See Cook, "'Our Message Be the Gospel Plain.'"
52. Howe, "From Houston to Dallas," has a good discussion of the Broadman controversy.

Baptist Conservatives and 1969–1970 president of the convention, published *Why I Preach the Bible as Literally True*. Criswell had a doctorate in biblical studies from Southern Seminary in Louisville and was a convinced premillennial dispensationalist.

The conjunction of the publication of the two volumes was symbolic. The 1970 convention was one of the most bitter in Southern Baptist history. Messengers shouted down speakers who sought to defend the new commentary, including Conservative Hershel Hobbs, one of the main shapers of the 1963 revision of the Baptist Faith and Message. In addition to the usual battles over the first chapters of Genesis, the issue revolved around Davies's straightforward statement that he did not believe the account of Abraham's sacrifice of Isaac. In addition to the usual critical observations, Davies noted that this was a theological issue for him: God would simply not order anyone to commit such a heinous act. This removed the issue from the usual exchanges over biblical criticism. Christian theologians had often appealed to the Abraham story as a type of the cross of Christ. If God could not order Isaac's death, how could God will the cross of Christ for the salvation of souls? In other words, the inherited teaching on the atonement, often debated between Protestant conservatives and liberals, was part of this controversy.

The result of the dispute was not surprising. The conservatives won the battle, and they ordered the volume withdrawn and instructed Broadman to secure another writer to redraft the volume with an eye to more conservative perspectives. The author chosen was Clyde T. Francisco, the author of a popular *Introduction to the Old Testament* and professor at Southern. Francisco had all the right connections. He was a graduate of the University of Richmond, deeply influenced by Solon B. Cousins, an early Southern Baptist liberal, and he graduated from Southern before neo-orthodoxy was popular. Interestingly enough, Francisco was Elliott's major professor at Southern, and many Southern Baptists believed that the *Meaning of Genesis* reflected his opinions. Although Francisco's book did not satisfy either side, it managed to stay in print, a major achievement for any Southern Baptist volume on Genesis.

The Elliott and Genesis controversies convinced Conservatives that they had a problem. They won the battles on the convention floor and elected strong Conservatives as presidents of the convention. Yet nothing apparently changed. Like many dissenters in American religious history, they turned to the establishment of alternative theological institutions, establishing the Criswell Biblical Institute, later Criswell College, (1971); Mid America Baptist Theological Seminary (1971); and Palm Beach Atlantic University (1968). They also strengthened Luther Rice University and Seminary (1962).[53] The convention leadership showed little inclination to nurse these schools to academic maturity, and they remained outside official Southern Baptist

---

53. For the founding of these schools, see May, "Southern Baptist Perspectives." May correctly notes that Beeson Divinity School had a different origin. Beeson was founded because a leading conservative philanthropist, who had also provided considerable funds for Asbury Seminary, was willing to endow a school. His contribution to the endowment was larger than the then-endowments of Southern or Southwestern Seminaries. The school still prospers.

structures, although supported largely by individual Southern Baptist churches. Significantly, many leaders of the Conservative party in the controversy had ties to these counterseminaries, including Patterson, who was president of Criswell, or received their doctoral degrees from one of them.[54]

What is significant about this decision not to recognize counterseminaries, strongly supported by the existing seminary leadership, was that it closed off one of the traditional Baptist ways of handling disagreements: the establishment of parallel institutions. Northern Baptists (later American Baptists), with a much weaker central authority, had almost paired conservative and liberal schools in the 1920s: Crozer (liberal), Eastern (conservative); Newton, later Andover Newton (liberal), Gordon (conservative); the University of Chicago Divinity School (liberal) Northern Baptist Seminary (conservative); and often ordained graduates of the various Bible colleges, including Moody Bible Institute.[55] Although these divisions weakened funding for all the seminaries, they did give each major party places for the free exchange of its views. Ironically, when Southern Baptist Conservatives took over the established seminaries, the Moderates and the more liberal elements responded by establishing their own string of counterseminaries, beginning with the Baptist Theological Seminary at Richmond in 1989.[56]

Holy War and Heresy

Conservative resentment toward the Southern Baptist leadership simmered during the remainder of the 1970s. The basic alliance between Paige Patterson and Paul Pressler seems to have begun when the two met in New Orleans in 1967 to discuss how the Conservative majority might exert its power in the convention. Patterson was an unlikely crusader. At the time that he met Paul Pressler, Patterson was a graduate student in theology at New Orleans Baptist Seminary where he studied under David Muller, a student of Karl Barth, and Clark Pinnock, then the enfant terrible of the Southern Baptist right. Pinnock was a recent convert to theological conservatism after spending his childhood in a very liberal Canadian Baptist congregation. At this time, Pinnock maintained that Southern Baptists were a people in danger of slipping almost unconsciously into the liberalism that had all but destroyed the churches in Canada and Great Britain. He appealed to alienated young people in the 1960s, because his position was profoundly countercultural and antiestablishment at the same time it was deeply biblical. Young Conservatives who journeyed to Switzerland found a less

---

54. Howe, "From Houston to Dallas," discusses the various ties that united the Conservative party and the Counter Seminaries.

55. See Miller, *Piety and Profession*, chapter 18, for a discussion of the different ways that the two Baptist conventions handled the problem of diversity in theological education.

56. Those of us who had received all or part of our training under American Baptist auspices never understood the passionate nature of the rejection of the alternative-seminaries model as a way of maintaining theological peace.

scholarly but very similar mix in Francis Schaeffer. Patterson's 1970s experience at Criswell Bible Institute further fed Patterson's conservative activism. Although W. A. Criswell, a former convention president, founded the thoroughly orthodox school, the SBC leadership kept it and its leader at the edge of Southern Baptist life. By his going there, friend and foe marked Patterson as someone outside the walls. Yet, the same leadership welcomed more liberal Southern and Southeastern. Given Patterson's family connections, his graduation from a mainstream SBC seminary, and his natural ability, fate destined him to become a card-carrying member of the SBC establishment. Experience and inclination made him otherwise.[57] When the convention leadership did not welcome him, he decided that change was necessary.

Paul Pressler was the older member of the partnership. Pressler was the offspring of a wealthy Texas family, was educated at Exeter and at Princeton, and served on the Texas Court of Appeals. Although often credited with being the one that saw the flaw in the SBC constitution (i.e., if one could control the presidency for ten years or five successive two-year presidencies one could control the boards of the various agencies), this was common knowledge in the convention. Pressler's contribution was more political. Schooled in the traditional Texas Democratic Party, Pressler realized that the Conservative party needed not only to mobilize the Conservatives at the base of the SBC; the Conservatives also needed keep them mobilized. In part, Pressler planned to accomplish this through such conservative journals as the fire-breathing *Southern Baptist Advocate* and the *Southern Baptist Journal*. However, Pressler knew that populism and agitation only worked for a season; political power came from organization and continual attention to one's supporters. Like the skilled Texas operator he was, Pressler never lost track of this basic law of political life.

Pressler also recognized the value of enlisting successful pastors, men whose success in the pulpit made them important role models for other ministers. The conservative decision to feature such men as Charles Stanley and Adrian Rogers in the pastors' conferences that preceded the convention was an essential part of the plan. Not only did the appearance of such prominent speakers, often candidates for the denomination's presidency, ensure large conservative crowds, but they illustrated also the link between successful ministry and Conservative theology. Many of these pastors had six-figure salaries at a time when most convention ministers made less than thirty thousand dollars a year. Megachurch pastors also demonstrated that acceptance by the denominational hierarchy was not the only road to professional advancement.

Yet when viewed across the spectrum of American denominational life, the most important part of the Pressler-Patterson plan was one that they had in common with African American and feminist groups in the mainline denominations: identify yourself as a persecuted minority and demand that the majority acknowledge your rights.

---

57. I admit that historians should be very careful in trying to find the origins of behavior in personal reactions to events. This interpretation of Patterson's actions makes sense to me of his actions. It is easy to forget that he was to the "manor born" in the complex old-boy networks of the old SBC.

This was not as difficult as it may have seemed to outsiders. The Moderates, particularly in the seminaries, often put Conservative students down and made fun of fundamentalists. As the tension rose, the Moderate rhetoric accelerated as Conservative pressure grew. Conservatives easily found example after example of Moderates treating their position with less than full respect or in some cases with derision. Was the Conservative picture accurate? Not completely, but it did not have to be 100-percent accurate. A few documented cases were sufficient to confirm the common wisdom. Further, the seminary faculty had an important place in the old boys' network that often determined convention hiring. "Fundamentalists"—no matter how bright—did not receive the unofficial imprimatur required for appointment.

The Conservatives also followed the central rule of 1970s and 1980s minority politics: find a single issue and organize around it. This issue need not be the only issue at stake, but the leaders had to keep this issue front and center. The Conservative issue at hand was biblical inerrancy. The issue enabled Conservatives to demonize their opposition. After all, what Baptist theologian would say bluntly that the Bible was incorrect in what it said?

Like other Americans, the Conservatives inherited the mournful American tradition of the jeremiad, a style of preaching that has been traced back to the Puritans. The basic formula was simple: in the past, we were faithful and God blessed us. In the present we have drifted from our past faithfulness, and God has withdrawn God's blessing. For the new Jeremiahs, the turning away from the Bible was the first step toward the moral and physical decline of America. Inerrancy was, thus, useful as a way to discuss such issues as abortion, the decline of the family, and moral decay. The fact that almost all American denominations had active Conservative pressure groups, the members of which argued for inerrancy, also made the issue appear less parochial. The Conservatives could maintain that inerrancy was the central theological issue in the 1980s.

Was the Pressler-Patterson party a cover for the New Religious Right? The Moderates certainly thought so. Yet, one has to discuss this question with care. Since the 1960s, all American denominations, including the Catholic Church, have increasingly involved themselves as advocates for various secular causes. Many SBC Conservative leaders, including Paul Pressler, had connections with the American right, especially, the New Religious Right. Yet, the Moderates were also politically motivated. Contemporary Mainstream seminary faculties often advocated either a liberal version of the Social Gospel or its more radical offspring, liberation theology; and Southern Baptist faculty often fit the Mainstream paradigm. John Rawls's theory of public life may have masked the religious motives behind many liberal crusades. Rawls argued that advocates should confine their religious opinions to the private sphere. Those speaking in the public sphere should stress more universal concerns, such as justice or fairness, in making their points. In theory, political conversations about justice were, thus, secular. Yet, the very fact that most liberationist theologians forged a visible link between religious tradition and secular advocacy makes this assumption problematic. The question of whose justice was never far from the surface. The culture war, noted by Hunter, was a religious civil war.

For these reasons, we should interpret both Moderates and Conservatives in the SBC in terms of their profound connections to the larger public sphere. If the Conservatives had less difficulty acknowledging their relationship to the Religious Right than liberals to the Left, they were not for that reason more political than their Moderate counterparts were. In both cases, political opinions had deep religious roots that inspired struggle both within the church and within society. Of course, there were variations in each camp. Richard Land, who became chair of the Christian Life Commission, was always politically vocal, as was liberation theologian Alan Neely, one of the founders of the Alliance of Baptists. To be sure, some Conservatives and Moderates were less involved in the causes that influenced their respective parties with a handful politically neutral on both sides.

To use a historical analogy, the various Southern Baptist parties were similar to pre-Civil War Evangelicals. The Evangelicals were an important part of both the abolitionists and the pro-slavery parties, and both sides spoke from profoundly religious motives. Between the two extremes were a number of Evangelicals who might have leaned one way or the other. Just as the pre-Civil War crisis forced the wavering to choose sides, so the SBC crisis pressured the broad middle to stand up and be counted.

One characteristic of late twentieth-century theology in general was the passionate interest of American theologians in the German Church Struggle. It was almost an axiom of religion that the German churches had failed to criticize Hitler, much less to use their political power to stop him from attaining power. Whether or not this reading of the German situation had historical merit, it was all the more powerful for being unexamined. Francis Schaeffer, whose experiences in Europe made him acutely aware of the sexual and biological issues involved in genocide, helped make the Confessing Church a model for contemporary Conservative social action.[58] In embracing abortion, Schaeffer argued, America had embraced a "culture of death." Many found his analysis convincing.

The Moderates' inability to recognize the importance of the abortion issue made an important contribution to their defeat.[59] Historical amnesia was a large part of their problem. Southern Baptists had historically advocated laws protecting family

58. One of my electives at Southeastern was a course on the German Church Struggle. Students always hated the fact that they had to study German politics in order to understand why certain people acted as they did. They were also shocked to learn how many people in the Church Struggle had less than democratic points of view.

59. One of the first acts of the new Board of Trustees at Southern in 1990 was to adopt a resolution calling on all employees of then seminary to "cease and desist" from all activity that implied that abortion was justified, except in cases where the life of the mother was at stake. The same meeting singled out Paul Simmons for special censure because of his arguments on behalf of the right to an abortion. If he did not cease these activities, the Board served notice that he would be fired. (Leonard, "Roy Lee Honeycutt").

life, and they had joined with other churches in passionately battling against gambling and alcohol. The struggle against abortion had many features in common with these earlier battles. The advocates of gambling and alcohol, for example, had claimed that they were defending the individual's right to choose, while the churches and their supporters argued that the restriction, even the prohibition of these vices, protected the common good. In effect, the Conservatives made abortion part of a larger constellation of issues—family values—already popular among Southern Baptists.

Roe v. Wade moved the abortion issue close to the center of historic Baptist thought. Before *Roe v. Wade*, many—perhaps most—Baptists in the South favored therapeutic abortions, a fact reflected in the near unanimity with which the convention adopted pro-abortion resolutions in the 1970s. However, the controversy over *Roe v. Wade* moved abortion, for both Left and Right, from the realm of therapy to the realm of personal maternal choice. The question became one of civil and personal rights as opposed to the family and the common good. This phrasing of the question, perhaps best symbolized by abortion clinics advertising the price of their services, made it difficult for the Moderates to claim the sanction of tradition. Abortions conducted under the guidance of a physician were one issue; abortions conducted "on demand" to satisfy a potential mother's private interests were another. The Moderates' attempt to use church-state language to describe this aspect of the controversy flew in the face of the traditional Baptist position on the family.

For the first five years of the controversy, the Moderates did not fully enter the debate.[60] They assumed that the Conservatives would eventually defeat themselves as they had in the past. After a few years of emotional conventions, the body would return to a more normal condition. After all, the Moderates controlled the denominational machinery, and they had the advantage of the support of many traditionally strong churches. In 1984, the Moderates realized that they had to act. By that year, the Conservatives had won four successive presidencies, and they expected to reelect

---

60. This does not mean that no Moderate published any material on the questions under discussion. Southern Seminary's Eric Rust wrote:

> Because it is concerned with historical happening, the biblical material must be open to the historical method of investigation. Ever since the Enlightenment, the historical method has been applied to human religious consciousness in general and to the biblical religion in particular. It has become a part of the accepted approach to biblical studies in this Seminary as well as in any like reputable institution. I should be the last to condemn the method of historical criticism, for our general historical awareness and our understanding of the historical nature of the divine disclosure make it imperative that we should adopt such an approach. Historical criticism has helped to clarify the life-situations of the prophetic oracles and to understand the historical milieu to which they were addressed. It is of value, for example, to know that Isaiah and Deutero-Isaiah were two distinct prophets, belonging to different times and associated with very different movements of Hebrew history. We can thus grasp more clearly the significance of the divine disclosure through them.

Rust, "Theological Emphases of the Past Three Decades," 265.

President Charles Stanley in Dallas. If the Moderates were to stop the Conservative movement, they had to act quickly. Surprisingly, the strongest call to action was that of Roy Honeycutt, the president of Southern Baptist Seminary and an able biblical scholar, who preached a sermon in the seminary chapel popularly known as the Holy War sermon.

Honeycutt's sermon surprised both friends and enemies. A year earlier Honeycutt had taken the extraordinary step of firing theologian Dale Moody. Moody, a Conservative neo-orthodox theologian who had studied with Tillich, was among the most biblical of the denomination's theologians. He peppered his speech with biblical citations, often from the Greek or Hebrew, and his then-recently published dogmatics, *The Word of Truth* (1981), cited Scripture on almost every page. Arguably, *The Word of Truth* was the most explicitly biblical Baptist theology to appear since Augustus Strong's *Systematic Theology*, a favorite among many Conservative Baptists; and many thought that it would replace Strong on Conservative bookshelves. The only comparable work published by a Baptist was Millard Erickson's *Christian Theology*.

The immediate cause of Moody's dismissal was his well-known and thoroughly public dissent from the seminary's official confessional statement, the Abstract of Principles. The Abstract affirmed the traditional Baptist belief in eternal security ("once saved, always saved"); Moody did not. His signature on the document included a note in which he dissented from this doctrine, and he consistently argued that apostasy was a rare possibility, but a dread possibility nonetheless, that Christians needed to fear. Faced with wide spread Conservative criticism of Southern's faculty for affirming one thing when they signed the statement when they, in fact, believed something else, Honeycutt fired Moody, despite his academic tenure. The act caught Southern's faculty and graduates off guard. If Moody was heretical, who was orthodox? If Honeycutt thought that his sacrifice of Moody might satisfy the Conservatives, he was wrong. They were after heresy rather than heretics. The assault from the Right grew even louder. The sacrifice of one of the seminary's leading lights accomplished nothing.[61]

Honeycutt preached his famed "Holy War" sermon on August 28, 1984. The address was a classic example of Baptist hermeneutics. Honeycutt skillfully interwove biblical themes with current events, moving from the time of the prophets to the present. The full title of the sermon revealed its purpose: "To Your Tents O Israel! A Biblical Call to Duty, Unity and Honor." To Honeycutt, what was at stake was much more than a theology or an institution. For him, the issues were

> the priesthood of the believer, the primacy and authority of Scripture, competence of the individual, soul freedom of conscience, pluralism in worship and

---

61. For another view of Honeycutt's action, see McSwain, "Roy Lee Honeycutt as Theological Educator." McSwain believed that Honeycutt was genuinely defending a theological tradition in the Moody Case. However, my own experience as an SBC professor suggests otherwise. The Abstract was always presented as a guide (in accord with and not contrary to) and as a document subject to interpretation.

witness, liberation through Christ as the Lord of Life, leadership of the Holy Spirit in our Convention decision making, a world view of the Gospel through cooperative missions, and excellence marked by integrity in all aspects of our election to be on mission with God in the world.[62]

Honeycutt also fell into the trap of returning the theological insults almost blow by blow. He thundered:

> persons in our generation seeking unity by autocratic and dictatorial control, should remember that individuals cannot be coerced into community. History is replete with horror stories of political bosses and dictatorial tyrants. Then, as now, that style of leadership can only exist in the context of dishonesty, manipulation, and depersonalization.[63]

Perhaps Honeycutt's' weakest argument was his defense of pluralism as the mark of the SBC. As he saw their history, Southern Baptists had modeled diversity throughout. He believed that Southern Baptists had always cooperated despite their differing theologies, local practices, and customs. It was an exciting vision, but it was also a major rewrite of Southern Baptist history.

That same year, Southwestern Seminary president Russell Dilday preached his sermon "Higher Ground," which stressed the importance of freedom in the Convention. In the summer of 1985, however, Dilday argued that premillennial dispensationalism, a position identified with W. A. Criswell, was a "Southern Baptist heresy." How dispensational other SBC Conservatives were was unclear, but the received wisdom was that fundamentalism was a synthesis of dispensationalism and Princeton theology. Dilday's message, unfortunately, indicated that he, at least, did not accept the idea of a large enough SBC tent to include all conservatives! This played directly into his opponents' hands.[64]

---

62. Honeycutt, "To Your Tents O Israel!," 125.
63. Ibid., 128.
64. Pressler, "An Interview with Paul Pressler," 23:

> Russell Dilday is the one who raised the millennial issue when he declared that, in a talk on July 5, 1984, using the campus facilities at Southwestern Seminary, that dispensational pre-millennialism was a Southern Baptist heresy. Now, this to me is absolutely shocking, because Conservatives have been talking about what Scripture is and that, under the priesthood of the believer, we are free to interpret Scripture. Now we have a man who is the head of one of our seminaries, who is branding a large number of Southern Baptists heretics because they do not believe in the eschatological interpretation to which he holds. Now this is shocking, it's disturbing, it cuts to the very basis of what Southern Baptists should believe. I believe that we can have pluralism about the eschatological position. Evidently, Dr. Dilday does not, because he says that those who hold to a dispensational pre-millennialism, that is a heresy, therefore those who hold to it are heretics. Now that brands a large number of ones in the Southern Baptist Convention as heretic.

The Moderates' rhetoric of 1985 made denominational loyalty the central plank of their position. Around this they clustered a number of other issues, including the role of women and academic freedom. The choice of Winfred Moore to carry the Moderates' standard at the 1985 Dallas convention reinforced this central concern. Moore was a biblical conservative, at least as conservative on biblical questions as Patterson or Criswell, but he was also a strong advocate of the Convention's leadership. Moore's opponent was the sitting president, Charles F. Stanley, pastor of the First Baptist Church in Atlanta. In many ways, he was the ideal opponent for the Moderates.[65] A popular TV preacher whose sermons often stressed an upbeat piety, he conducted most of his ministry outside the normal SBC bounds. Further, although he supported many new Religious Right causes, his theology had many liberal overtones. Listening to Stanley, as when listening to Harry Emerson Fosdick or to Norman Vincent Peale, one heard as much a call to a healthy attitude on life as a summons to a life of repentance. Further, Stanley's First Baptist Church of Atlanta was not a strong supporter of the Cooperative Program. Nonetheless, Stanley won a very close race at the largest Southern Baptist Convention to that date.

In many ways, the Dallas convention was the high point of the Moderates' cause. Although the Moderates came close to winning at San Antonio, the Conservatives were clearly in control. The clearest sign of their dominant position was the 1985 appointment of the Peace Committee, charged with determining how to reestablish good relations between the two factions. Although some prominent members of the Moderate party served, including Cecil Sherman and Winfred Moore, they left the committee after a short period. The real focus of the committee was an investigation of the seminaries. In simple terms, the Conservative members of the committee wanted to establish that their charges against the seminaries were in fact true. Many Moderates questioned whether they should take part in the Peace committee or reply to its questions. Roy Honeycutt took the wise step of considering the Peace Committee's concerns to be formal charges, thus ensuring Southern's faculty due process, while Randall Lolley, at Southeastern, elected to treat them less formally.

In 1986, the Peace Committee met with the six seminary presidents and during an all-night prayer meeting persuaded the presidents to accept the Glorieta Statement, named after the conference center near Santa Fe, New Mexico, where it was adopted. The statement had two parts. The theological part committed the seminaries to a belief that the Bible "not errant in any area of reality," a statement that pleased neither Moderates nor Conservatives.[66] The second part committed the seminaries to a policy

---

65. Although Stanley often claims to believe in biblical inerrancy, his sermons and books often show a mixing of Christianity and popular psychology that is more characteristic of liberal theology and such thinkers as Norman Vincent Peale. Rather than offering the usual fundamentalist attacks on sin, Stanley is much more likely to speak about "hurting people" and their need for love and acceptance than about hell and damnation. He was an early supporter of the Moral Majority.

66. The full statement on Scripture read, "We believe that the Bible is fully inspired; it is 'God-breathed' (II Tim. 3:16), utterly unique. No other book or collection of books can justify that

of parity in hiring; that is, to hiring a sufficient number of Conservatives to secure a balance between Conservative and Moderate members. This later statement was, in fact, a major revision of the governance of the schools.[67] Like other ATS schools, Southern Baptist schools practiced "shared governance." By mandating new appointments, a collaborative process became a largely administrative one. Further, it meant that the faculties would have, in effect, two doctrinal statements. The first was either the Abstract of Principles or the Baptist Faith and Message, and the other was their trustees' interpretation of inerrancy. This put the Conservatives on the spot. Although many inerrantist scholars accepted the very carefully drawn Chicago Statement, the average Southern Baptist understood the term *inerrancy* to mean "God said it, I believe it." Later on, inerrantist faculty members, appointed under the policy, would shock SBC Conservatives by insisting that belief in inerrancy did not mean that the Bible prohibited women pastors or deacons![68]

One less widely observed effect of the Glorieta Statement was that it weakened the strong relationships between the faculties and their presidents. Up until Glorieta, the seminary faculties had confidence in the way that the presidents were handling the controversy. Among other things, this meant that the faculties had tended to allow the administration to speak for them and to follow their lead. After the Glorieta Statement, this strong bond broke. Many faculty members believed that the controversy was over and that the Moderates had lost.[69]

The controversy in fact rapidly ended shortly thereafter. In 1987, the conservatives won control of the Southeastern Theological Seminary Board and resolved that the school would strictly follow the Peace Committee dictates on hiring. As a result, the president, Randall Lolley and the dean, Morris Ashcraft, resigned their offices, carefully giving the board sufficient notice to secure their replacements. Common wisdom in the Convention was that Southeastern's faculty was the most liberal in the Convention, although this was probably not true; but under the leadership of Richard Hester, Professor of Pastoral Care, the faculty resolved to defend its rights.[70] The cho-

---

claim. The sixty-six books of the Bible are not errant in any area of reality. We hold to their infallible power and binding authority." Cited in Wittman, "Freedom and Irresponsibility."

67. Culpepper, "Reflections on Baptist Theological Education."

> In October of 1986, the six SBC seminary presidents gathered at Glorieta and issued the Glorieta Statement, which stated that "the sixty-six books of the Bible are not errant in any area of reality." Many of the faculty at Southern and at Southeastern felt that the presidents had capitulated to the convention leadership, and in retrospect it is clear that the adoption of the Glorieta Statement marked the beginning of the end of the controversy.

68. At the time, I thought that this compromise could not stand. Even if all sides had accepted it in goodwill, which they did not, it was too instable to survive the multiple pressures of academic life. Professors, if nothing else, change their minds and their theologies as their studies lead them. Today's inerrantist is tomorrow's liberationist or neo-Catholic.

69. Leonard, "Roy Lee Honeycutt."

70. This action was not always understood by those outside the denomination. Dennis Campbell

sen method was through the organization of a chapter of the American Association of University Professors.[71] The AAUP was, of course, a noted defender of academic freedom, and its chapters often functioned as *de facto* faculty unions. The choice of the AAUP as a means of protest was deliberate. As Southeastern's faculty saw the battle, it was a question of academic freedom, including the right to participate in the hiring of new faculty. Alan Neely, Professor of Missions and one of the later founders of the Alliance of Baptists (originally the Southern Baptist Alliance), was also very active in this group.

The Southeastern trustees elected Lewis Drummond as Lolley's successor. Why the trustees turned to Drummond remains a mystery. Drummond was a successful evangelist, a close friend of Billy Graham, with worldwide connections in the larger Baptist community. Drummond's academic passion was the history of evangelism, and he published studies of such evangelists as Charles Finney, Bertha Smith (a noted SBC missionary to China), and Billy Graham. His magnum opus was a study of

---

said at a meeting held shortly after Lewis A. Drummond's installation: Campbell then ventured out on a limb by engaging the issue of academic freedom. This, he indicated, hit close to home:

> Here in North Carolina I've been somewhat troubled that the faculty and some of the students at Southeastern Baptist Theological Seminary in Wake Forest have used the issue of academic freedom to get at their problems regarding authority. I do not want to be misunderstood here: I believe in academic freedom. A faculty must have the freedom to represent extraordinary opinions. But for most institutions nowadays—and for most universities—that is not the primary problem. The other side of the question seems more important in our time What about the responsibility of faculty members to an institution? What about institutional discipline?"
>
> Last Tuesday I represented Duke at the inauguration of a new president in Wake Forest. By no means do I celebrate what has happened there. The framing of the question is what I am asking about. The question is this: In a theological seminary or in a theological tradition—say, the Southern Baptist tradition—where is the place for internal critique? It has to be remembered that such a critique is undertaken in the content of a faith community, a community of memory. That understanding of the issue of academic freedom might be more fruitful and less problematic in the long run.

Stallsworth, "The Story of An Encounter" in Richard John Neuhaus, *Theological Education and Moral Education*.

71. Hester, "AAUP Censures Southeastern Seminary."

> Southeastern's faculty solidarity in this situation has been advanced by the establishment of a campus AAUP chapter, organized in April 1987. Between April and October of that year the chapter enlisted all full-time faculty, retained legal counsel, secured a media consultant and began raising funds. The chapter developed the following consensus: (1) members would not give assent to any confessional statement presented by the trustees—signing the seminary's Articles of Faith was sufficient; (2) the members would consent to an investigation of their teaching only on the basis of due process spelled out in the school's documents; (3) the school's policy manuals set forth the highest standards of higher education, and the faculty would strive to uphold those policies even when the administration violated them; and (4) for consistency's sake, members would express the chapter's position through one person, the chapter president.

Charles Haddon Spurgeon, the great English preacher and evangelist who had stood for conservative doctrine during the "Downgrade" controversy. Not surprisingly, after he left Southeastern, Drummond authored a book with his wife, Betty, *Women of Awakenings* that traced women's contribution to the revival tradition.[72]

Drummond lacked administrative talent. Despite his real skills in the pulpit and as a revivalist, he had little knowledge of how one could or should run a present-day theological institution, especially one in crisis. In many ways it seemed, at least to me, that Drummond was following a life script drawn from the lives of Finney and Spurgeon.[73] Both had climaxed their revival ministries by serving as presidents of theological institutions. Those examples of piety and intellect did not aid Drummond in dealing with a deeply conflicted institution. The school went into a tailspin as enrollment declined and prominent faculty began to leave. Alan Neely and Morris Ashcraft both worked hard to bring the first counterseminary, the Baptist Seminary at Richmond, into being.[74] Significantly, the first president of that school was Thomas Graves, formerly Southeastern's professor of philosophy of religion, and its first dean was G. Thomas Halbrooks, formerly a professor of church history at Southeastern. Although the situation somewhat stabilized with the appointment of L. Russ Bush, a philosopher of religion previously at Southwestern Seminary, as dean, Drummond was unable to summon the loyalty of a significant number of faculty, including the new so-called inerrantist hires that he recruited. Faculty and others easily turned Drummond's administrative slips into public scandals, as when his overspending on his office and the president's home became a prominent story in the Raleigh newspaper. As the problems mounted, the board maneuvered his resignation and replaced him with Paige Patterson, the engineer of the Conservative victory. Many remaining Moderate faculty departed, as did many of the more recent inerrantist appointments.

---

72. I felt at the time that for all his problems, Lewis Drummond was Southeastern Seminary's best hope. He was a person of outstanding piety and personal conviction. His inerrancy was not of the dogmatic sort; at one point, he asked me about the doctrine, and I told him that I had difficulties with reading the first chapters of Genesis as history. He then asked me if I could affirm them as inerrant myth? My own sense of his position was that he loosely agreed with the Chicago Statement, but not to the more rigorous views of inerrancy that characterized the Board at that time.

73. During the semester that I served as acting dean, Drummond and I had the opportunity to have many long and involved conversations. Both of us were interested in the history of American Evangelicalism and the history of American education.

74. Ashcraft had worked towards a counterseminary from the first establishment of the Alliance of Baptists.

> Ashcraft's involvement with the Richmond enterprise began with his participation in the early life of the Alliance of Baptists. From its beginning in 1987, the Alliance focused on the need to provide alternatives in theological education. In fact, one of the central tenants of the Alliance Covenant proclaims a commitment to "'theological education in congregations, colleges and seminaries characterized by reverence for biblical authority and respect for open inquiry and responsible scholarship. (Graves, "The Influence of Morris Ashcraft," 185–92).

The troubles at Southeastern led directly to the founding of the first counterseminary in 1991. Yet the school was not Southeastern in exile; it was more oriented toward the preservation of the Southern Baptist Theological Seminary tradition. As conditions at that seminary became more strained, Richmond enlisted many of Southern's most eminent professors, including E. Glenn Hinson. The new school was supported by the Virginia State Baptist Convention, the Southern Baptist Alliance, and, after it was formed, the Cooperative Baptist Fellowship. Perhaps the close relationship between many of the Moderate counterseminaries and Southern is best illustrated by the fact that the *Review and Expositor*, the scholarly journal of Southern Baptist Seminary, passed into the hands of a coalition of the Moderate alternative schools.[75]

The Conservative wave swept over Southern Baptist Theological Seminary as well. Roy Honeycutt was the only seminary president who had a chance to save his institution. Southern's original charter provided for a self-renewing board of trustees, and its current charter required the board to elect the new members nominated by the Convention. The right to elect is also the right to decline to elect. Many, including the former president, Duke McCall, believed that Southern's board should reclaim its right of nomination and preserve the school's Moderate character. However, to have done so might have cost the school its Convention funding. Perhaps more significantly, Honeycutt, like the other seminary presidents, had talked himself into a corner. In his public statements about the controversy, Honeycutt had insisted that Southern's primary loyalty was not to a theology but to the Convention's Cooperative Program. To leave the Convention would expose him and his school to the charge of hypocrisy. Interestingly enough, in 1984, the same year that Roy Honeycutt preached his so-called Holy War sermon at Southern, Moderate Dan Vestal called for a meeting of conservative Moderates in Atlanta that eventually led to the establishment of the Cooperative Baptist Fellowship, a more conservative alternative to the liberal Alliance of Baptists. The Cooperative Baptist Fellowship might have had the strength, especially if Honeycutt had joined, to sustain the school during a period of transition.

It was not to be. Whether Honeycutt's concerns were primarily pragmatic or ideological, he did not ask the board to declare its independence. The Conservatives acquired a majority on that board in 1990, and Honeycutt set out to negotiate an agreement, largely based on the Glorieta Statement, that would allow existing faculty to remain at the seminary. The agreement was simple enough: Southern would appoint only inerrantist faculty until the faculty achieved numerical parity. As part of this agreement, Honeycutt persuaded his faculty to take part in the faculty selection process, nominating their future colleagues, as long as they were Conservatives. Perhaps as a sign of good faith, Honeycutt selected David Dockery, editor of the New American Commentary and a former Southern Seminary New Testament teacher, as

---

75. Allen, "The Review & Expositor." Like other seminary journals published by seminaries established in the nineteenth century, the *Review and Expositor* was "owned" by a corporation separate from the seminary's Board of Trustees.

dean of the School of Theology and later academic vice president. As his later experience as president of Union University in Tennessee demonstrated, Dockery was an able administrator. He also knew many of the younger Evangelical scholars personally and recruited some of the brightest, including Timothy Weber. For a few years, the compromise appeared to work, sparing Southern the house cleaning that had occurred at Southeastern. Barry Hankins described Dockery's hiring policy: "Under Honeycutt, Dockery had been assembling a faculty of what might be called Mainstream, *Christianity Today*, Evangelicals."[76] There were, to be sure, tensions between the new faculty and the older faculty that included some derogatory remarks and social isolation. This also happened at Southeastern. However, as time passed, the two sides gradually found that they had much common ground. Southern appeared on the way to stability.

After Roy Honeycutt's resignation in 1993, new crises completed the Conservative takeover of Southern. Like his Southeastern counterpart, Randall Lolley, Honeycutt deeply believed in women in ministry, and his compromise with the Conservatives had included tenure for Molly Marshall Green, a systematic theologian and a strong advocate for women's rights in the churches. Over the years, Conservatives expressed a variety of concerns about Marshall's teachings, including her supposed universalism, but the granting of tenure legally ensured her future. The new president, Albert Mohler, might have allowed sleeping dogs to lie. However, Mohler made Marshall's removal a priority of his administration, and he forced her resignation in 1994.[77] The next defining issue came over a dispute between Mohler and Diana Garland, dean of the Carver School of Social Work, the only seminary-related school of social work in the country. There was a vacancy in the school, and she recommended David Sherwood of Gordon College for the position. Sherwood, who supported women in ministry, passed the faculty committee easily, and the faculty sent his name to Mohler

---

76. Hankins, *Uneasy In Babylon*, 81.

77. The reasons for the forced resignation are difficult to discover. On the one hand, outside observers believed that it was part of the general Conservative campaign against women in ordained ministry. Molly Marshall was both a symbol and an advocate of that position. On the other hand, Mohler insisted that the issues were doctrinal; see *Christian Century*, "Tenured SBC Woman Forced to Resign." Mohler denied that Marshall's gender had anything to do with the effort to oust her but acknowledged that "feminist theology, as distinct from the issue of the service of women in the church, is and has been one of proper concern related to Southern Baptist theological education." He went on to say that "without apology, Southern Seminary will not be open to a revision of basic Christian doctrine or of the text and character of Christian scripture in order to meet the demands of what is now considered the Mainstream of feminist theology." There are good reasons to credit Mohler's argument. Almost all feminist theology rested on an analogical understanding of religious language that was ultimately nonpropositional in its understanding of religious truth. Mohler, an admirer of Carl Henry, firmly believed that revelation conveyed propositional truth, and that theological statements, based on Scripture, shared those truth claims. By this standard, Marshall was outside of the Conservative understanding of the Abstract. Whether her colleagues agreed with her or not (and many did), her colleagues believed that she was within the acceptable boundaries of the Abstract as she and they had understood it at the time of subscription. If the issue had been handled according to the Southern Faculty Handbook, Marshall would have been cleared.

for his confirmation. To everyone's surprise, Mohler rejected Sherwood, although he did not make his reasons public at that time. Garland faced an almost impossible situation. She knew the reasons for Sherwood's rejection, but the president had instructed her to keep them confidential. Nonetheless, she went public with them, and Mohler either asked for her resignation and received what he believed was agreement or, as Garland was convinced, Mohler fired her outright.

The Garland dismissal marked the end of the Honeycutt experiment. The School of Social Work, ironically one place where Mohler's commitment to anti-abortion might have influenced the larger society, eventually closed. On Black Wednesday, the faculty confronted Mohler on the Garland decision and his grounds for it. The new Evangelical professors began their steady exodus from Southern, led by Timothy Weber and David Dockery. The difference between Southern conservatism and Northern Evangelicalism was nowhere as evident. As Weber said:

> The great middle space occupied by most Evangelical seminaries today allows for flex on this issue of women in ministry. Trinity Evangelical, Gordon Conwell, Bethel and Denver all have faculties that have agreed to disagree . . . But the current criteria push Southern Seminary toward the far right. We are not even in the Mainstream of Evangelical seminaries anymore.[78]

The remaining new Evangelical faculty members gradually left. Six went to Union University, where David Dockery became president.

The firing of Diana Garland was thus one of the decisive events in Southern Baptist seminary history. Almost alone among American theological institutions, the six Southern Baptist seminaries restricted the place of women on their faculties and in their student bodies. Not even the Roman Catholic Church has as many restrictions on women in their theological schools, although it likewise restricts ordination to males. The Convention itself went on record as approving the doctrine of complementary gender roles in marriage, and opposing the selection of women as senior pastors. To make this rejection even more formal, the Convention added this understanding to the Baptist Faith and Message and thus made it binding on all Convention agencies and employees. Perhaps the great irony is that Dorothy Patterson, one of the most able women theologians in Southern Baptist circles and the wife of the Conservative leader, was a major voice in the wording of this revision.

The Mohler revolution at Southern involved more than the women's issue, as important as that issue was to all participants. Part of what was happening was a purge of the Moderates and their supporters. When Paul Debusman dared to correct SBC president Tom Eliff's claim that earlier administrations would not have invited Eliff to speak in chapel, Mohler dismissed Debusman, despite his thirty-five years of faithful service in the seminary library.[79] The record indicates that Honeycutt had routinely

---

78. Quoted in Hankins, *Uneasy in Babylon*, 84.
79. The dismissal of Debusman was unexpected and still has not been adequately explained. For

invited Conservative SBC presidents to address the school, and that they accepted his invitation. Whatever sins Honeycutt may have committed, he was not politically naïve.

Mohler was a convinced Calvinist who believed that the Calvinist tradition among Baptists was an important thread in the churches' history and a major resource for the churches' renewal.[80] At least historically, Mohler had a point. Most of the founders of SBC colleges and seminaries were Calvinists, and Calvinist theologians have often led in the history of American theological education. Calvinism's combination of reason and biblical faith is a potent tradition that inspires people to found schools, colleges, and seminaries. Timothy George of Beeson Divinity School, perhaps the most capable Conservative scholar, likewise tends towards Calvinism, as does R. Philip Roberts at Midwestern.[81] At the more grassroots level, Founders' Ministries, established in 1982, provided a forum for serious discussion of Calvinist themes by professors and local ministers. Yet, historically, the acids of frontier revivalism eroded the Calvinist foundations of Baptist theology, and whether the Convention will sustain a strongly Calvinist presence among its six seminaries remains to be seen. Mohler may yet find himself and his school as isolated theologically as the more liberal party was at Southern earlier. If so, Moody might triumph after death in a way denied him in life.

Conservatives had one last step to complete their domination of the seminaries: Southwestern Baptist Theological Seminary. Although Southwestern was widely believed to the most conservative of the seminaries, the school was much more complex than it appeared to those outside. Texas Baptists, the group most served by Southwestern, often combined biblical conservatism with a Midwestern Social Gospel. Further, Texas itself was almost a country in its own right with great cultural and economic differences between its various regions. Despite their differences, Texas Baptists took pride in their seminary, whose president, Russell Dilday, symbolized the strength of the state's churches. Although theologically conservative,[82] Dilday was a convinced denominational loyalist. However, Dilday's denunciation of premillennial dispensa-

---

an account of the action, see *Christian Century*, "Breaking Ranks." In point of fact, all SBC seminaries invited the presidents of the Convention to speak, despite their political affiliation or theological affirmations. Mohler must have known this policy since he was the student assistant to President Honeycutt.

80. Ironically, Mohler's Calvinism comes closest to my own understanding of theology, although I, like many Baptist Calvinist theologians, oppose Mohler on the issue of women's ordination. Whether Calvinism can be other than a minority voice in SBC is a different issue than whether Calvinism is theologically viable. The frontier revivals still have as much influence on Baptist life, particularly in Texas and Oklahoma, as any theological position, no matter how biblically based.

81. Weaver and Finn, "Youth for Calvin."

82. Dilday wrote the doctrinal study for 1983, *The Doctrine of Biblical Authority*. Although he did not use the word *inerrancy*, his understanding of the Bible was closer to that of the Conservatives than to many of the Moderate authors of the Boardman Commentary. Like the other presidents, he was apparently more personally Conservative than the majority of his faculty. Dilday's doctoral degree was in the philosophy of religion.

tionalism and his prominent leadership among other SBC presidents were rocks of offense to the Conservative party. The board unceremoniously fired Dilday on March 9, 1994, and had him escorted physically from the campus. Association of THeological Schools executive director James L. Waits complained:

> We view with utmost seriousness the dismissal of Russell Dilday from the presidency of Southwestern Baptist Theological Seminary. Such precipitous action on the part of any board of trustees is a clear violation of accepted governance practices and places in jeopardy the vitality and basic integrity of the institution. I urge the trustees immediately to reconsider their action.[83]

Such laments were of no avail. The trustees had the legal power to dismiss Dilday; he served at their pleasure.[84] Despite a very favorable evaluation of Dilday's work as president, the trustees were not pleased. The law did not require them to give reasons, and they offered none.

In many ways, the firing of Dilday climaxed a series of battles between Moderates and Conservatives in Texas, most of which the Moderates won. In 1990, Baylor University, the great symbol of Texas Baptist achievements and aspirations, had won from the state government the right to name its own trustees and had launched a major campaign to become a major Christian university. In many ways, the model for this development was Catholic Notre Dame. In 1990, Baylor had registered the name George W. Truett Theological Seminary with the Texas Board of Regents, and the school methodically moved towards the establishment of a full divinity school. The new school opened in 1994. The establishment of Truett is only one of many conservative setbacks in Texas. Not only did Moderates found other divinity schools in the state, but they retained control of the influential Texas State Baptist Convention. As in Virginia, where the Moderates controlled the state organization, Conservatives had to organize their own counterconvention.[85]

The Triumph of Pluralism and Regionalism

New seminaries in Texas and Virginia were only part of the rapid expansion of Baptist seminaries in the South, a numerical growth that continues today. For those who appreciate ironies, the conservatives, who earlier had established counterseminaries, were now in control of the six historically Southern Baptist schools. Although these schools had a temporary enrollment decline after the conservative victory, they have recovered their numbers and are presently among the nation's largest theological

---

83 *Christian Century*, "SBC Seminary President Fired," 308

84. Southwestern's trustees were, like the Trustees of other SBC agencies, selected from the different state conventions. Had the Board represented only Texas Baptists, Dilday would have remained as president.

85. For a good summary of this activity, see Clark, "Twilight Breaking."

schools. With the exodus of the Evangelical scholars from Southern and Southeastern, these schools came to reflect a similar parochialism to that which characterized earlier Southern Baptist theological education under Moderate control. Neither the Conservatives or the Moderates, for example, had significant clout in the Association of Theological Schools.

The Moderates, who earlier rallied their supporters around the cry of denominational loyalty, have become the founders of new seminaries. At one point, this chapter contained short accounts of the founding of these schools, but the material came to be too long and repetitive. With the very important exception of Baptist Seminary at Richmond, Moderate Southern Baptists tended to establish seminaries, often called divinity schools, in conjunction with colleges controlled by Moderate trustees. This was an old Baptist pattern. The Baptist theology of ministry has never seen the minister as a person set aside from the other members of the congregation, and many outstanding Baptist schools, including Southern, Southwestern, Eastern, Gordon-Conwell, and Northern, began with some relationship to a college. James Boyce, the founder of Southern Baptist Seminary, had seen the education of both college graduates and high school graduates in the same institution as a necessary part of his plan. Interestingly, the Conservative counterseminaries also elected to integrate graduate and undergraduate work, at least in some areas.

The new seminaries are more regional than the older Convention-related schools. In part, this is because their founders piggybacked them onto existing Baptist colleges, historically related to state Baptist conventions. Yet this was not the only reason. The schools came into being at a time when theological schools were increasingly commuter schools (serving nonresidential students). Heavy investment of limited capital in residences was, consequently, a poor use of those funds. This may have permitted the founding of more schools, since the Moderates could invest their limited resources in more institutions. The savings from nonresidential operation also enabled them to make a comparatively larger investment in faculty and scholarships.

The central problem facing the new Moderate seminaries was and is financial. Neither the Alliance of Baptists nor the new Cooperative Baptist Fellowship has developed a denominational structure or a means of corporate financing. In part, this was a reaction to the disappointment over the defeat of the Moderate party in the struggle. Forced to develop its own independent funding system, each new seminary would be able to resist any attempt to take them over. The problem was, of course, maintaining momentum and building endowments. The earliest faculty at the new schools were beloved former teachers whose ouster from their teaching positions cried out for justice; the problem came as these leaders and their students passed from the scene. Do Baptists in the South need so many different, small, and expensive schools? Only time will tell whether they can or will finance them.

A Concluding Unscientific and Unhistorical Observation

Gregory Wills, one of the new faculty members at Southern Baptist Theological Seminary, wrote one of the most important histories after the controversy, *Southern Baptist Theological Seminary, 1859–2009*.[86] The book is a fine volume, well written and well researched, and a contribution to the history of American theological education. Like all historians, Wills wrote his volume from a specific perspective: the belief that the Conservatives were essentially right in their charge that the seminary had abandoned the doctrinal foundations on which it was established. Significantly, he identifies the key figure in this story as E. Y. Mullins, the 1920s figure that Moderate historians also identify as the key in the development of modern Southern Baptist theological education. Was Mullins, who had much influence in the formation of the Baptist Faith and Message and Cooperative Program, somehow responsible for what happened later?

To a reader of Wills's book looking backward, his insight may have been accurate. Mullins did not end a golden age of Baptist Calvinism at the seminary, to be sure, but his book *Axioms of Religion*, a brief but very well-crafted exposition of Baptist principles and a Baptist classic, was a pivotal volume in the development of the Moderate Baptist cause. As Mullins examined the Baptist tradition that he had inherited, he interpreted that tradition in terms of American individualism. The heart of Baptist life was what Mullins styled "soul liberty," the belief that the individual, guided by his or her study of Scripture, was the supreme authority in religious matters. While never standing alone, "soul liberty" provided Mullins with the organizational principles for his development of other Baptist distinctives, including the separation of church and state.

Such individualism was, of course, one element in the Baptist story, particularly on the frontier, and many modern Baptists have felt comfortable with it. Yet—and this *yet* is an important reservation—it was far from the whole story. From the Anabaptists through the Puritans to many of the evangelists, many Baptists, including Roger Williams, Isaac Backus, Walter Rauschenbusch, and Martin Luther King Jr., sounded another note: God's call to the churches was to construct a "beloved community" united by God's Word into a powerful force for righteousness. Local church discipline, vigorously applied up to the Civil War, reflected this deep devotion to a Christian common good as churches excluded members for sins against the divine and secular order. As Rauschenbusch famously remarked, we have a social gospel, we need a theology adequate to it.

In the world long after the nineteenth century, especially as the so-called culture wars heated up in the 1970s and 1980s, rugged individualism did not appear to be a substantial religious value. No matter what side of the various controversies one came down on, the object of all sides was to find laws that might shape the development of the larger culture. The purpose of affirmative action, for example, was to help create a

---

86. Wills, *Southern Baptist Theological Seminary*.

multiracial culture, and Black, feminist, Latino/Latina, and Two-Thirds World theologians believed that they were the harbingers of a new cultural formulation that would right ancient social wrongs. Likewise, Conservatives saw themselves as the supporters of traditional and godly social values. Abortion was not merely an individual evil, but part of a larger culture of death that devalued the lives of everyone. The New Right very much wanted to make America again a "city upon a hill." Both New Left and New Right were willing to use law to accomplish their cultural aspirations, and law requires the use of the state's power to coerce and punish those who refuse to conform.

Moderate Southern Baptists had no language to help them through this thicket. They never recognized, for example, that demands for social change and reform were as Baptist as appeals to individual conscience. Hence, they had no choice but to fit such explosive issues as abortion under the rubric of church-state separation or individual rights. World War II analogies are overdrawn in American Protestantism in general—everyone wants to play Confessing Church versus Nazis—but the Moderates were in much the same position as the classical German liberals caught between an aggressive social Right and Left. The center could not hold then or in the SBC controversy.

Another place that the Mullins tradition weakened the Moderates was in the Moderate defense of academic freedom. Moderates tended to speak as if academic freedom made the individual professor a lord in his or her own classroom. Yet, academic freedom is a far from simple concept, and one that rests on social assumptions as much if not more than on individual rights. Ultimately, the state and the society abandon the immediate supervision of expert academic and scientific opinion, because the academic and scientific community will correct the mistakes made by its individual members. In this sense, academic freedom is a social trust in a process of shifting positions and arguments that will eventually separate the wheat from the chaff. American society has learned, after long trial and error, that the risks of allowing free inquiry are less than the risk of missing the truth. The history of history—historiography—shows this process in action. Each generation views the work of its academic parents with jaundiced eyes and the discussion moves steadily onward.

The question of academic freedom in theological education is the question of whether, given the fragmentation of religion in modern societies, a community of accountability analogous to that in other academic disciplines exists nor not. Unlike the community of chemists or historians, the community of theologians is a Babel of competing and dissonant voices. As we shall see, one of the key questions in the 1980s was the question of exactly what theological schools taught that set them apart from other institutions concerned with the study of religion.

6 Basic Issues, the Theological Education Debate, and Globalization

THE EVANGELICALS EMERGED FROM the 1980s and 1990s bruised but still growing and still establishing and strengthening new schools and strengthening older ones. If anything, the Evangelicals demonstrated their capacity to span the Conservative side of American Protestantism with institutions that served different parts of a large, comparatively thriving community. However, the Mainstream churches, the 1980s and 1990s were in a cultural twilight. The Mainstream denominations continued to have considerable social prestige and to dominate traditional ecumenical organizations. In this sense, they often appeared stronger and more influential than they actually were. This was certainly true in theological education. The period from 1980 to 1995 was the last period in which the larger world of theological education reflected the inherited dominance of the Mainstream's educational institutions, especially, in the Association of Theological Schools. In part, the lack of dominance was a matter of numbers. The Conservative schools, especially if combined with the Roman Catholic ones, educated a majority of American seminarians. Further, the university divinity schools, which had been close to the heart of Mainstream theological education, were changing. Although Yale continued to train pastors for elite churches, the classic university divinity schools, Harvard, Chicago, and the Graduate Theological Union, moved progressively towards a more religious-studies orientation. Union, once the epitome of Mainstream theological education, devoted itself to a modified and radicalized Social Gospel. Interestingly, the Methodist divinity schools in the South, where the Methodists shared cultural hegemony with Baptists and Presbyterians, continued more of the traditional divinity-school pattern. One of the most original contributions to theological education, the Congregational Studies Movement, began at Emory. The Mainstream denominational seminaries were not as fortunate. The decline of their supporting denominations forced them to broaden their definitions of their missions as well as consciously or unconsciously to lower academic standards. The schools faced older student bodies that attended increasingly part time, and a growing number of degree programs. The schools were also losing their denominational character.

Increasingly complex bureaucratic requirements for ordination, especially among American Baptists and Methodists, meant that a progressively smaller proportion of seminary teachers were ordained ministers in their denominations. This reinforced, especially among historians and biblical scholars, the tendency to define themselves primarily as scholars. As a result, Mainstream seminaries increasingly looked alike. In a real sense, theological schools ceased to reflect the rich, almost luxuriant, diversity of America's denominational heritage.

Although the influence of generational change on larger historical patterns is controversial, the 1980s and 1990s saw a major shift in theological faculties. The late 1940s and 1950s period of growth in Mainstream theological education was also a period of faculty expansion. Since the schools faced severe restrictions on employment during the Great Depression and World War II years, the schools hired people to fill these neglected positions. At the same time, the increasing complexity of theology and ministry led to new positions in practical theology as well as the need to have diverse specialties represented in the so-called classical disciplines. To make matters more complicated, the growth of religious studies departments created more demand for new faculty. Consequently, these professors had a smooth career pattern and often received tenure and power at an early age. At the other end of their careers, government regulations ending mandatory retirement extended their careers. As a result, this cohort spent a long time at the apex of American theological education. Yet for all their professional and institutional success, this was not a happy generation. People expected much from those trained in the 1940s and 1950s, and at different times they anointed various members of this generation as the next Niebuhr or the next Tillich. Robert McAfee Brown, James M. Gustafson, Gordon Kaufman, and Langdon Gilkey all wore this mantle, but none fulfilled the dreams that others had for them. The expectations were greater than any individual or any generation might have reasonably fulfilled. The generation did not fail the promise that people had imposed on it; rather, the tasks were greater than any generation, not to mention any particular individual, might have performed.

The theological consensus that sustained American neo-orthodoxy dissolved in the 1950s and 1960s. In part, this was because many unresolved theological problems moved to center stage. These included serious intellectual questions about the doctrine of God, questions posed by a new intellectual and social humanism and, above all, questions about the lack of a hermeneutic that yielded any coherent picture of the meaning of the biblical text. Gary Dorrien noted the changed character of the liberal tradition:

> In previous generations the mainstay of liberal theology was its liberal Evangelical tradition. Liberal theology reached beyond its academic base only when it preached the gospel. That is, it spoke with convincing spiritual power

to large audiences only when it featured a gospel-centered language of incarnational faith, personal theism, and personal and social salvation. By the 1960s, however, the Evangelical liberal tradition was expiring, even as King gave a historic witness to it. The mainstay of the new liberalism, for better and worse, was a metaphysical vision of process divine creativity, relativity, wholeness, human flourishing, ecological sustainability, and divine good.[1]

The problems were not merely intellectual; they were also institutional. The social basis of Mainstream ministry was eroding. Congregations were becoming smaller and beginning to age; the "pastoral director" of the Niebuhr-Williams-Gustafson report was no longer common. Mainstream ministry was increasingly single-pastor and smaller-church oriented, and the demographics suggested that in the future, many seminary-trained ministers might serve part time. The 1950s and 1960s Mainstream seminaries had educated leaders for high-steeple churches. Part-time ministers who, even in the more educated denominations, often lacked college or seminary training served the smaller churches. Unlike earlier times, this pattern was reversing. Seminary graduates were now moving down, rather than up, the ladder of clerical success. Fear of falling off the ladder, as much as desire for advancement, fueled much of the growth of the Doctor of Ministry programs. The popular language about ministry as a profession, almost a mantra in Jesse Ziegler's ATS, no longer rang true to those working in the Mainstream. Education for professional ministry was a compelling vision in the 1960s and 1970s that suggested parity with other forms of education for community leadership. By the 1980s, that language lacked conviction. Were clergy part of the social and cultural elite or were they something else? Moreover, if not part of the elite, how did they have a public voice?

The third crisis was less evident but nonetheless real. American Mainstream Christianity had put much of its faith in the worldwide ecumenical movement. In the 1950s and the 1960s, the excitement about the new expressions of worldwide Christianity—especially, the WCC—appeared a possible replacement for the more traditional American enthusiasm for foreign missions. Mainstream denominations, in fact, began to withdraw from work abroad about 1967. In that same year, although the European and American churches kept control of a few major offices in the WCC, the new churches of Africa and Asia were increasingly in control of the WCC agenda and programs. Although it is a slight exaggeration, ecumenical and liberation theology became almost synonymous. Although liberation theologies did influence Evangelicalism as well, especially through the Lausanne movement, Evangelicalism retained both a vibrant missionary presence and a more traditional missionary theology. In a world increasingly aware of the worldwide dimensions of all issues, liberalism appeared increasingly parochial and self-centered. Just as women's voices and ethnic- and racial-minority voices demanded a hearing in Mainstream churches, so

---

1. Dorrien, *The Making of American Liberal Theology*, 8.

the various liberation theologies from abroad were demanding a hearing. Although the largest American minorities were African American and Latina/Latino, growing African, Korean, and Asian minority groups raised global issues close to home. Mainstream theologians, especially those in the liberal tradition, were also aware that the question of the relationship between Christianity and other world religions was still on the agenda, especially now that those world religions also had significant presences on American soil. Moreover, some world religions, especially Buddhism and Islam, had significant convert memberships.

Three primarily Mainstream discussions, largely brokered by ATS and the Lilly Endowment, revolved around these questions: 1. the basic issues program of the ATS, 2. the discussion among systematic theologians of what made theological education theological, and 3. the discussion of globalization in (or perhaps better, of) theological education. A fourth related discussion, that of Christian practices and theological education, also supported strongly by the Lilly Endowment, offered another approach to many of the same questions.

THE DISCUSSION OF BASIC ISSUES

Jesse Ziegler's period as executive director of the Association of Theological Schools ended with a sense of widespread dissatisfaction. Part of this dissatisfaction was with specific Association programs, particularly Readiness in Ministry. Part was general uneasiness about where theological education fit in the larger scholarly world. Even more important than these, however, was dissatisfaction with the reigning professional understanding of theological education. As critics saw it, the professional model with its emphasis on the social status of the minister and the performance of specific tasks was antiquated. Equally important, it posed both pedagogic and theological problems. Pedagogically, the problem was the almost insurmountable problem of the relationship of the theological disciplines, often represented as theory and practice. Theologically, professionalism did not seem adequate for those who saw the minister as part of the vanguard of social change. Prophets and professionals seemed a categorical confusion. Many also sensed that theological schools, even if not as nearly bankrupt as the Resources Commission had indicated, were in serious financial trouble. The new director of ATS, Leon Pacala, formerly president of Colgate Rochester Divinity School, began his term of office by appointing a Transition Committee to set priorities for his coming administration. The committee set six such priorities:

> (1) Review and Update accrediting standards and processes; (2) support the scholarship and research of theological faculties; (3) identify, research, and deliberate basic issues confronting theological education; (4) enable executive leadership of theological schools to acquire current administrative and managerial study and training; (5) advance the capacity of theological schools to benefit in their financial development efforts from state of the art practices

and professional nurture of development officers; and (6) identify the state, needs, and issues confronting theological libraries and resources needed for the twenty-first century.[2]

It was an ambitious program.[3] We will discuss many of the more practical parts of the program, especially the education of presidents and trustees, in a subsequent chapter. In this chapter, we will concentrate on the intellectual components of this agenda. In simple terms, Pacala wanted American theological educators to ask fundamental intellectual questions about what they did and who they were.

Pacala's program demanded a reexamination of the foundations of theological education. In the past, the schools had passed through two major periods of fundamental thought about theological education: the confessional period in which denominational standards provided the framework for institutional standards, and the liberal period in which professionalism and scholarship had provided that framework. Pacala believed that the time was ripe for a third such examination. A modest and somewhat scholarly leader, Pacala did not know the answer to the larger questions before theological educators. Like a biblical scholar seeking to correct the received text, he only knew that the questions needed to be asked.

Leon Pacala had an important ally in Robert W. Lynn, vice president for religion of the Lilly Endowment. Lynn, a former professor of religious education at New York's Union Seminary, had a deep interest in the history and future of American Christian institutions. Lynn was important as a researcher in his own right and did important work in the history of American Christian education, including histories of both the Sunday Schools and the seminaries. Yet, Lynn's most important contribution to theological education was his capacity to midwife the broader discussion of theological education. Lynn had a unique style of leadership. His preferred mode of operation was conversation and dialog, and he was always willing to allow others to take credit for ideas that either he generated or substantially shaped. This style was particularly important in the small world of theological education. Like congregations and other small institutions, seminaries offer a place where people with strong egos can and do waste their own and others' energy jostling for position and prestige. Disputes often are out of proportion to the importance, real or imagined, of the question at hand. Lynn navigated this world with ease. He took a suggestion here, an idea there, or a topic interjected in a conversation, and he involved others in the development of that insight. Robert Lynn initiated much of the discussion in the 1980s and early 1990s, including my own historical studies, and he saw that the projects funded by the Endowment were carefully planned and evaluated.

The Basic Issues program and such related studies as those of Edward Farley, Joseph Hough and John Cobb, and David Kelsey were ideally suited to Lynn's style of

---

2. Pacala, *The Role of ATS in Theological Education*, 19.
3. See Carroll, "Project Transition."

leadership. The concept of issues is important. Unlike a program, such as the need for more effective work in development, the product of the discussion of an issue is not a set of best practices or a cadre of trained leaders. Almost by definition, an issue yields the exposure of the multiple paths forward. In assessing the work of Convocation 1984, a group of 120 theological educators called together to identify the basic issues before theological schools, David Kelsey wrote:

> As Leon Pacala pointed out, some well-focused questions deal largely with "problems." They are characteristically put in a "how" form e.g., "How do we increase the pool of able applicants to our schools?" In principle they admit of practical solutions. Once solved, such problems disappear. By contrast, other well-focused questions raise "issues." Issues regarding theological education do not admit of "solution." They arise at the point of conflict between different perspectives on the nature and purposes of theological education. Issues are characteristically put in a "should" form: e.g., "Should there be a different theological curriculum for each different minority group in the student body?"[4]

In *Vision and Discernment,* Charles Wood's exposition of theological study, Wood defined the purpose of theological education as enabling a person to adequate form cognitive patterns that enabled them to see Christian realties from a broad (vision) and a particular perspective (discernment). The study of a basic issue was to provide theological educators with just such perspectives on their own work.

From the beginning, ATS planned the Basic Issues Program around serious faculty and administrative participation. In that sense, the Basic Issues Program itself expressed a pedagogy as well as an understanding of theological education. At the heart of the program were a series of meetings, called to discuss commissioned papers, with carefully selected participants. The hope was to generate significant conversations about the issue under discussion. The advantage of this format was that most theological administrators and all faculty participants were already familiar with it from their professional meetings. The format, perhaps equally important, permitted continued discussion at meals and in other less formal situations. Moreover, the hope was that participants might continue these conversations after they returned to their home campuses. In 1982 and 1983, the association held regional meetings to set the agenda of the program. A national meeting of 120 scholars, held in 1984, determined the issues that future meetings would discuss, and although ATS did not implement all its suggestions, it did set the goals and direction of the program as a whole. In addition, those who presented the papers attended annual sessions where they received additional criticism and reported any further reflection on their earlier study.

The combination of freedom and participation in the Basic Issues Program might have resulted in a loss of focus or, perhaps more serious, in a series of idiosyncratic

---

4. Kelsey, "Reflections on Convocation '84," 115.

studies. To guard against such problems, ATS assigned the program to the Issues Research Advisory Council. Composed of leading scholars, the Advisory Council functioned in many ways as a source of peer review, providing a scholarly imprimatur for the work. Equally important, Robert Lynn recommended and ATS accepted the services of David Kelsey and Barbara Wheeler as the formal evaluators of the program. In addition to providing formal evaluation, essential to any effective foundation program, Wheeler and Kelsey attended the key meetings of the Advisory Council as well as the larger sessions. In many subtle ways, mainly informal, they kept the program on track.

One important achievement of the Basic Issue Program was that it generated an extensive literature on theological education. In 1989, Clark Gilpin of the University of Chicago published a representative bibliography of the materials generated, directly and indirectly, by the emphasis on basic issues.[5] The article, which contains very little discussion, took up six large pages in *Theological Education* and listed more than seventy items. Gilpin carefully noted that his list was only a selection of the studies that the program had inspired.[6] The authors included Mainstream Protestants, Evangelicals, Roman Catholics; theologians, historians, practical theologians, and seminary administrators; men, a handful of women, and a few representatives of racial minorities. The Basic Issues literature continued to appear into the 1990s and beyond as works in progress and more important, as discussions not yet concluded found printed form. Lists of printed works do not necessarily indicate the importance of the research undertaken, but bibliographies do provide a rough indicator of interest in the topic. No other movement in American theological education, not even the early founding of theological schools, generated so much and such rich literature about theological education and institutions.[7] If one mark of a profession or an academic discipline is the possession of a technical literature of its own, the Basic Issues initiative was an important step in the professionalization of theological education.

Four Reflections

Four of the works published in response to this initiative offered a different, not necessarily new, approach to the question of what made theological education theological: Edward Farley, *Theologia*; Charles Wood, *Vision and Discernment*; David Tracy, *Understanding God Truly*; and John Cobb and Joseph C. Hough, *Christian Identity and Theological Education*. These works shared certain characteristics. First, all accepted

---

5. Gilpin, "Basic Issues."

6. Gilpin did not consider important works, not connected to the Basic Issues initiative, that began to appear in this decade. Katharina Schuth's works, for example, began to appear in this decade and established her as one of the leading commentators on Catholic theological education.

7. One might compare Gilpin's list with any decade in Day, *Protestant Theological Education in America: A Bibliography*.

the belief that biblical authority no longer defined theological education. In this sense, they based their augments on what Farley called the fall of the house of authority and were, in some sense, responses to the situation created by that situation. At the same time that they accepted and even, particularly in Farley's case, celebrated that changed situation, they had doubts and more than doubts about how critical studies, whether of Scripture or of church history, fit into theological education. In part, these questions had to do with the socialization of the historical disciplines in academic guilds and specialties, although the authors admitted that these problems also were part of pastoral studies and systematic theology. Interestingly, Christian ethics was in the process of becoming an academic discipline at this time—with its own peer-reviewed journal, discussions of methods, and recognized centers for training. However, the reservations of these authors were not a protest against a distant social structure. The authors were children of the academy. University divinity schools employed three authors, and Claremont, similar to a university school, employed the other two. The authors shared the widespread dissatisfaction with the separation of theory and practice. In engineering, the role of physics was clear. The good engineer used the laws of physics to establish tolerances, to define materials, and to measure forces. Nothing like this intimate relationship existed between the theological theoretical and the practical disciplines. Viewed from another perspective, the issue of theory and practice was often a restatement of a basic modern theological dilemma: the relationship between the historical and the normative. The philosopher Lessing called this the "big ugly ditch" that separated the modern world from its religious past, and whether self-consciously treated as the problem of history or not, it was the problem that underlay all the difficulties. The difficulty of relating theory and practice suggested that the reigning professional understanding of theological education needed to be replaced or radically modified. Another issue involved in all of the studies was the question of how theological study related, if it did, to the new religion departments. Since the religion departments were, by and large, committed to a descriptive understanding of the world's faiths, this was another variation on the relationship between faith and history.

The four studies shared important links to the works of the nineteenth-century theologian Friedrich Schleiermacher.[8] Schleiermacher, often called the father of liberal Protestantism, was a key figure in the development of modern theological education. He was one of the founders of the University of Berlin. After the fall of Prussia and its great university at Halle to Napoleon, the Prussian king resolved to create a new university as part of his plan of national regeneration. Much of the new university, of course, was not new at all. Such features as legally guaranteed academic freedom, the focus on research, the doctoral degree, and the need to prepare students for the dreaded German state examinations were already in place at Halle and Göttingen, and the new University of Berlin followed these existing models.

---

8. Strege, "Chasing Schleiermacher's Ghost."

Schleiermacher and others founded their new university in the midst of a major cultural revolution. The eighteenth-century vision of education was largely rational and scientific. Insofar as the Enlightenment continued the classical tradition, the Latin classics provided the foundation for its work. Early nineteenth-century thinkers, however, participated in a revival of interest in Greek philosophy and life. When these thinkers, often called the Romantics, thought about education, they did so in terms of *Bildung*, usually translated as cultured, a rough German equivalent to the ancient Greek ideal of *paideia*. Hegel, the great romantic philosopher, saw the task of his generation as the synthesis of the scientific, the ethical, and the artistic. This academic idealism defined the cultured leader as someone who would put his or her scientific knowledge at the service of the state.[9] The professional, whether a bureaucrat, army officer, university teacher, or pastor, was to serve the common good. In this sense, Schleiermacher's advocacy of the professional ideal both affirmed and criticized the Enlightenment ideal of science and the priority of research. As important as those might be, they had to contribute to the student's *Bildung*, if the student were to be a competent professional. In that sense, the education provided by the state served a higher purpose than mere knowledge. Thus, ministry, law, and medicine, the three medieval disciplines based on the mastery of distinctive canons of knowledge, had a common mission: to provide leaders who embodied the German cultural ideal, including the capacity for research and scientific study. Medicine did not fit as easily into this professional paradigm as the other professions, although Germans even today expect their physicians to be cultured individuals.

Schleiermacher's classic *A Brief Outline of the Study of Theology* was originally a privately published textbook for his own lectures on theological encyclopedia. The book was not a description of any existing theological curricula or a justification of what he or his colleagues taught at the university. I would suggest that we should read the *Brief Outline* as a "thought experiment" designed to suggest an approach to the study of theology that would enable Schleiermacher's students to prepare for the first and second theological examinations. In *Vision and Discernment*, Charles Wood attempts a similar thought experiment that outlined an ideal structure for theological thinking, although he realized that its value did not depend on anyone implementing it. From a different perspective, Kelsey's analysis points in a similar way. Since Kelsey argues that each theological school preserves its own uniqueness, his discussion is more a grammar or language for knowing God truly than a program of studies. Yet, Kelsey's basic point is similar to the advice that Schleiermacher gave his entering students in theology: begin with the goal of theology in mind.

---

9. Americans do not generally share the German appreciation of the state as the embodiment of the common good. For Americans and for much British thought, the state is primarily the enforcer of laws and regulations, especially, in times of emergency. When Schleiermacher and other German thinkers saw the ministry as the servant of the state, they saw the church as one of the instruments of the common good, a positive—perhaps even *the* positive—embodiment of the common good.

I cannot offer an exhaustive analysis of Schleiermacher's proposal at this point, but I do need to make a few observations. First, we should not read the *Brief Outline* apart from Schleiermacher's magnum opus, *The Christian Faith*. *The Christian Faith* moves along the pathway indicated in the *Brief Outline*. The study begins with the nature of religion, compares Christianity to other monotheistic faiths, and then centers its exposition on Reformation Christianity. What is characteristic of the Reformation churches is the alternation of sin and grace within the experience of the believer. Second, Schleiermacher's own practice as the preacher in the largest church in Berlin also followed this outline. His sermons did not invite his hearers to an intellectual experience. Schleiermacher designed his sermons to awaken in his hearers the full range of Christian emotions, including awe at the infinite God of nature, and, in particular, the personal awareness of sin and grace. This "romantic" style of preaching was, of course, not limited to Germany or to Schleiermacher. Boston transcendentalists and frontier revivalists both hoped to awaken experiences within the hearts or consciousness of the believer. The American Charles Hodge, whose understanding of religion was substantially different from either Schleiermacher's or the revivalists', was not impressed with Schleiermacher's or Charles Finney's preaching. Hodge believed that Schleiermacher and Finney were two sides of the same coin.

The value of regarding the 1980s discussions as similar thought experiments makes their contribution to theological education more evident. While Farley occasionally spoke of his work as having implications for a reform of theological education, these were not reformist documents. Their goal was to change people's perspective, inside and outside theological education, on what they and their institutions were doing. To use an overworked phrase from the period, the goal of these reflections on theological education was a *paradigm shift*. The proposed change was from studying theology to doing theology or "theological praxis." While such a shift might, as Charles Wood suggested, lead to some new theological courses, it did not necessarily do so. Schools might keep the same basic texts and courses, but approach those courses and their outcomes in a different way. Such a change may have been more common in courses in systematic and practical theology where many instructors moved toward the student's theological reflection about the material and away from the mastery of set body of material. However, instructors in more historical fields also left behind or modified the older goal that the students demonstrate mastery of the field or its principal texts.[10] This trend towards reflection was particularly evident in faculty deliberations on the overall goal of the degree programs. Many faculties expressed the hope, both formally and informally, that their graduates might think theologically about

---

10. This movement, of course, had many different sources, including a new emphasis on pedagogy that became current in the 1990s. It influenced biblical studies and church history (the two theological areas with the most clearly established disciplinary character) less than the other fields. Both of these fields were, of course, deeply influenced by changes in hermeneutics, and in particular by the new emphasis on cultural standpoints, such as race, gender, and class.

their own work and that their theological thinking would influence their subsequent daily ministerial practice.

In many ways, Edward Farley's *Theologia: the Fragmentation of Theological Education* was both the first and the key document. Like the importance of other seminal texts, its importance lay not only in its central ideas but also in the fact that later commentators felt called upon to comment on these ideas or to take issue with particular observations. Farley structured his argument as a classic jeremiad; that is, the argument rested on the idea that the best insights of a classical age had eroded and that the present needed to recover those insights in fresh and innovative ways. The classical world that we lost was a form of theological education that Farley styled *theologia*. *Theologia* was a theological habit of mind that integrated the work of the mind with the daily experience of the person. The classic expression of this *habitus* was life in the Benedictine monastery. This tradition was substantially modified in the Middle Ages when the application of Aristotelian methods to theology led to the creation of theology as a "science or discipline."[11] Despite this change, "the meaning of theology did not displace what was the more primary sense of the term in the same period, theology as a practical *habitus* of knowledge whose end is salvation."[12] The great change came in the eighteenth and nineteenth centuries when the various theological areas of theological study divided into separate academic disciplines such as Old and New Testament. Although Farley associated this primarily with the research emphasis of such schools as Berlin, the specialization of the theological disciplines was the slow and steady result of a half century of institutional development. The more a researcher needed to know to study and teach a particular discipline, the more rapidly it became a separate department. Naturally, Old Testament, with its heavy reliance on Hebrew studies, was the first to develop in this way, while New Testament and church history, which rested on the Latin and Greek common to classically educated people, came later. In the nineteenth century, particularly in America, schools became interested in the "practical know how" related to church work.[13] These changes shattered the unity of the theological enterprise and forced people to ask how the various courses related to each other and how one could conceive of how these disciplines related to ministerial practice.

The most usual way of doing this was to define the theological school and its curriculum as a place for the professional preparation of ministers, the clerical paradigm. This definition, in term, raised the question of theory and practice with the so-called classical disciplines comprising theory and the arts of ministry comprising practice. Farley put this argument directly:

---

11. Farley, *Theologia*, 38.
12. Ibid., 40.
13. Ibid., 40.

> The major elements structuring the North American approach to theological education are the continued dominance of the fourfold pattern, the absence of a material unity of studies, a functionalist version of the clerical paradigm as that unity, and a theory practice mindset.[14]

The keyword in Farley's analysis is "functionalist." Farley did not envision divinity schools or seminaries that did not train pastors and other religious leaders. The difficulty that he saw was that the various practical disciplines, preaching, religious education, and evangelism, originated in a sociological analysis of the ministry, not in a theological analysis.[15] Hence, when scholars studied these disciplines, they often left behind their theological content and allowed sociological or other social-scientific perspectives to dominate.[16] Moreover, these functions tended to define the career path of a ministry. A "good pastor" was one whose performance of these tasks was good or outstanding, not one who conformed to the theological demands of the gospel.

> The education of a leadership for a redemptive community cannot be defined by reference to the public tasks and acts by which the community endures (a formal approach), but rather by the requirements set by the nature of that community as redemptive.[17]

In turn, this clerical paradigm ended in paradox: "Accordingly, the more the external tasks themselves are focused on as the one and only telos of theological education, the less the minister is qualified to carry them out."[18] All of Farley's carefully worded specificities, such as "the one and only telos," need emphasis. He is dealing strictly with the world of theory, of a thought experiment, and not with what teachers actually do or not do in particular classrooms.

Further complicating this problem was the fact that several theological fields, particularly church history and biblical studies, also existed as independent scholarly disciplines in the universities, and many (if not all) of their practitioners were trained in the canons of university scholarship and drew their standards for teaching and scholarship from that source.[19] In a sense, this was also true of the practical fields, par-

14. Ibid., 127.

15. Ibid., 127.

16. One disadvantage of writing about history that has one has lived through is one's personal experience may be otherwise. Perhaps because I attended a denominational seminary (Andover Newton), my own experience of practical theology courses was often intensely theological, especially the work in religious education and in preaching. This was also my experience of the practical teachers at Union where I did my doctoral studies. In many ways, Robert Lynn and C. Ellis Nelson modeled theological existence for all of us as did Paul Hoon and the preaching faculty.

17. Farley, *Theologia*, 127.

18. Ibid., 128.

19. Part of the problem is that most religious-studies programs are heavily dependent on historical method or on social science as their entry into the university and its standards. Farley's proposals also include finding another way to teach university religious studies that will include theological understanding. Thus, in addition to a Christian studies program that highlights theological understanding,

ticularly, their functionalist emphases. When university schools and later seminaries sought to educate students from many different bodies, each claiming to be the church in some way, those disciplines had to find a common way of approaching Christian leadership. What it meant to lead a redemptive community meant something far different for an Anglican than for a Baptist or Disciples congregation. Yet certain tasks do seem common to ministry: preaching, education, and so forth. By concentrating on the tasks, the functions, the schools hoped to avoid the scandal of particularity. Systematic theology developed from a similar need to speak across theological diversity. More confessional churches insisted on courses on Christian teaching (dogmatics) taught according to their own confessions of faith. Seminaries that enrolled a variety of students from different ecclesiastical backgrounds had to take a broader approach.[20] In effect, ecumenical schools replaced dogmatics with something akin to the philosophy of the Christian religion.

Farley's solution was to bring back *theologia* as "a personal and existential wisdom or understanding" as the goal of theological education.[21] *Theologia*, understood in this sense, is the theological equivalent of the Greek concept of *paideia*.[22] The identification is apt. The goal of ancient Greek education was to develop a leader whose sensitivity to the *polis* and its needs enabled her/him to help the *polis* attain its human potential; likewise, the goal of *theologia* was to develop a leader whose sensitivity to the church and its needs enabled the church to attain God's rule and reign.

Farley argues that *theologia* exists (or should exist) on three levels. There is the *theologia* of the believer that is foundational for all understandings of *theologia*. The *theologia* of the believer is the movement from personal insight into a situation to an examination of the redemptive possibilities present in a situation. "This mode of understanding is theological reflection."[23] The second level is that of leadership, both lay and clerical, that is more directed or intentional than the reflection of the ordinary believer. The leader wants to evoke the believer's understanding and action. "Diaconal understanding is descriptive but awkward."[24] The third level of theological understanding is "inquiry and scholarship" that seeks to find the truth. This, Farley insists,

---

a Jewish or Buddhist studies course should also highlight *theologia* of those faiths. In many ways, Farley's demands on the university were similar to the demands of other cognitive minorities—especially women and African Americans—that courses serve to build racial or gender self-consciousness. This is one of the most serious problems with Farley's proposals. In theory, the courses in the university are all available to anyone who wishes to inquire about a subject and who is willing to accept the discipline of the university in so doing.

20. Part of the paradox is that at the same time that Farley was writing *Theologia*, various American denominations were adding specific requirements for education in the theology of their own denomination to their ordination requirements. Among the churches making such a move were the Methodist Church and the United Church of Christ, neither of which was particularly confessional.

21. Ibid., 153.
22. Ibid., 155.
23. Ibid., 157.
24. Ibid., 158.

is "theological knowledge."[25] However, one need not separate these three modes from each other. The leader is, after all, also a believer as the theological scholar is also a leader. Since these modes relate to each other as levels, rather than separate things, the individual may move up or down the ladder depending on their own situation.

Farley was committed, intellectually and professionally, to the broadening of the work of theological schools. In many ways, this was the mantra of the 1980s as theological schools developed a number of MA and lay leadership education programs as well as a number of extension centers. By moving theological education away from the technical task of preparing a specific type of religious professional, Farley hoped to open up theological schooling to a wider public and to involve more people in the enterprise. What was economically necessarily, Farley suggested, was also intellectually or theologically necessary. Like Andover Newton's president, George Peck, he wanted the laity theologically equipped, not as little ministers, but as fully equipped leaders in the church.

Farley's book appeared at the right time to provoke agreement and disagreement. Although Farley very carefully united the argument in *Theologia*, individual readers found parts of the discussion that rang true to their own diagnosis of the needs of theological schools. Many cited *paideia*, for example, as the goal of education, and almost all educators of professionals, not just ministers, were interested in how to develop leadership. As important as technical work was in many areas—the word processor was just becoming a necessary scholarly tool—people were aware of the limitations of technical reason. Farley's use of Greek images was also part of the general atmosphere. People talked about *theoria* and *praxis*, *techné* and *sophia*. David Tracy, one of the most evocative theologians of the period, peppered his writings with references to the classics and indeed saw the idea of the classic as a root of "foundational" theology.

Farley was a theologian's theologian, and his writings were often difficult for the nonspecialist to understand. Although disagreeing with Farley at a number of significant points, including offering a more positive view of disciplinary studies, John Cobb and Joseph Hough were much more readily accessible than Farley. In their *Christian Identity and Theological Education*,[26] they began their inquiry by noting that institutions had always linked theological education to professional preparation and that Christian churches will always need professional leaders.

Like medical studies and legal studies, there were various aspects of theological studies, especially the historical disciplines, that had a distinct methodology and that yielded verifiable positive knowledge. But also like law and medicine, theology as a whole was unified by its concern for matters affecting the practice of a major profession. In other words, the unity of theological studies lay in the fact that all parts of

---

25. Ibid.
26. Hough and Cobb, *Christian Identity*.

its subject matter were determined by their relevance to the needs of the church for leadership.[27]

The fact that the church needs leadership, trained leadership, does not mean that we can best understand ministry in terms of theory and practice. Instead, the book argues that two types or aspects of leadership are necessary: the practical Christian thinker and the reflective practitioner. The practical Christian thinker reflects on the stories of the church—its fundamental identity—in the midst of the present situation. What is most important in this thinking is the Christian identity of the practical Christian thinker, her or his roots, in those things that are basic to Christian life. This grasp permits the practical Christian thinker to cast light on the situation in which believers find themselves. The other side of this is the reflective practitioner. Using current models of professional practice, they argue that the professionalism that theological schools should teach is that of the "reflective practitioner." A reflective practitioner is a person who continually monitors or evaluates their own professional work, their *praxis*, and makes needed corrections as they become more experienced. Ideally, the practitioner moves from what are thought of as best practices to even better practices. Over time, this pattern of professional life will enable a particular profession to develop new techniques and to respond to a constantly changing environment.[28]

Cobb and Hough's emphasis on professional leadership did not imply what Farley styled the clerical paradigm. Cobb and Hough saw the church as continually engaged with the world, and the task of leadership, as they saw it, was not primarily concerned with institutional maintenance. They believed that the effective Christian leader was a person who midwifes the gospel and makes it applicable to public life. The key to such successful practice was a clear sense of Christian identity and of the church's mission. In a passage that reflected much of modern theology since Schleiermacher, they wrote: "For the Christian it will always be finally an event—the event of Jesus' life, death and resurrection. This event will always have its meaning in large part as mediating the story of Jesus' people, the Jews."[29] The Christ event, however, was always broader than its necessary particularity. Just as Christian theology had absorbed the ancient Greek philosophers, so it had a place for the "great sages and spiritual giants of China and India."[30]

The global nature of Christianity was not only intellectual or spiritual. It was natural and multinational. Christian identity had to include "the growing interconnectedness of all aspects of the biosphere and human involvement in it." We are part of the natural order. Further, Christians had to deal with "the threat of nuclear holocaust, and the rising demands for justice, often expressed in revolutionary movements."[31]

---

27. Ibid., 2.
28. Hough and Cobb, *Christian Identity*, chapter 4.
29. Ibid., 31.
30. Ibid., 31.
31. Ibid., 43ff.

Our situation, its dangers, hopes, and potentials, are all global in their reach. While leadership took place in local situations, a leader's vision was not confined to the local.

Indeed, Christians cannot solve local problems without understanding their broader context. There are two reasons for this. "First, the local problems are the manifestations of systems that extend far beyond the locality . . . Second, to treat local problems in their local context is to fail to approach them as Christians. As Christians, our concern is with the indivisible salvation of the whole world."[32] In other words, the local was not isolated, either politically or theologically. Perhaps one way to describe this is to see the order of theological reflection as moving from the local outward until it was as universal as the gospel itself.

Perhaps because of Hough's long experience as an administrator, the book makes some concrete recommendations about curriculum. Perhaps the most interestingly, neither theology nor ethics should consider themselves as disciplines; rather, they were methods or modes of thought that the neophyte can only learn through practice. One learns theological thinking by thinking theologically, just as one learns any practical activity by participating in that activity. Although not as critical of the disciplinary character of much instruction in Bible and church history, in part because of "the subject matter . . . [of these courses] and the deepening, broadening and clarifying of Christian identity," they believed that these disciplines played too large a role in actual instruction.[33]

Cobb and Hough felt that they needed to address every issue in the 1980s seminary, at least briefly, and their lists included chapel, denominational studies, and spirituality or, as they preferred, devotion. Much of the argument, at least in retrospect, broke down as Cobb and Hough moved towards the solution of specific problems

The emphasis on theological education as reflective participation in leadership has the advantage of highlighting theological education as part of a larger process. Craig Dykstra, Robert Lynn's successor as vice president for religion at Lilly, based much of his work at the Endowment on a similar insight. Ministry develops from early leadership experiences through professional preparation through sustained and reflective practice. Hence the order of ministry moves from a person's early formation in the church, through the seminary, to a career in which professional practice leads to increasing proficiency. Dykstra used the concept of practice, as developed by such thinkers as Alasdair MacIntyre, as a theoretic framework for his work, but his ideas had important affinities with Cobb and Hough's concept of "Christian Identity."

Charles Wood published *Discernment and Vision* in the same year that Farley's *Theologia* appeared. Wood taught at Perkins, one of the Methodist schools just emerging into prominence, and Schubert Ogden, a fellow member of the faculty, influenced

---

32. Ibid., 102.

33. Ibid., 93. One wonders if these courses, at least in part, may not have had the character of a cold bath, awakening students to the possibility of future growth. Historical-critical approaches suggest that the common wisdom is not necessarily so.

him[34] Ogden passionately argued that the task of theology was not primarily interpretative or hermeneutical—as important as those tasks might be—but that theology was always a critical inquiry into the validity and truth of the gospel. Consequently, although Wood's work shared much with the other literature about theological education—including a sharp critique of the fourfold curriculum—Wood began his study from a slightly different angle of vision. For Wood, "Christian Theology is a critical inquiry into the validity of the Christian witness."[35]

"Critical inquiry" is a complex idea that required much explanation and very careful argument. Wood does not mean that it is the task of theology simply to pass negative judgments on Christian witness (one of the more common understandings of criticism) or to stand apart from Christian witness as its judge or arbitrator. At the same time, Wood is confident that critical inquiry, while it recognizes the value of such traditions as *theologia*, is not simply reflection on what is given in the Christian witness.[36] Wood argues, persuasively, that *theologia* often left the church unable to cope with such major external challenges as the rise of historical studies and modern science. If we have learned anything from modernity's struggle with faith, it is that the Christian witness must, like all aspects of life, answer for its own content and claims. However, historically conditioned the Enlightenment might have been and no matter how limited its claims to truth, modernity is not something reversible. In an eloquent passage, Wood writes:

> To bear witness is to represent something as the truth: to assert it, to commend it, to endorse it as worthy of acceptance. Whether or not this is all explicit in given instance, it is at least implicit in every genuine act of Christian witness (as distinguished from, say, a descriptive account of what Christians believe). It belongs to the nature of Christianity that such a claim to truth is present. The critical theological question which corresponds to this feature of its object is, naturally enough: Is this witness really true?[37]

Yet theological judgments are more than an evaluation of truth claims. Theology, Wood insists, is second-level discourse that reflects or thinks about something else, in

---

34. I believe that Ogden's influence can be found in many places in the development of the argument. One specific place where it is discussed is page 63, footnote 12, where Wood mentions Ogden's classic essay, "What Is Theology?" In writing this chapter, I wrestled with whether this seminal essay should have introduced the chapter. Dorrien's judgment on Ogden (and on James Gustafson) was accurate and acute: Exacting, scholarly, a bit dour, and known for acerbic judgments, Ogden and Gustafson were thoroughgoing master teachers who won disciples through their analytical rigor and distinctive positions. Both were radical monotheists, although they argued for theocentricism on different grounds (Dorrien, *The Making of American Liberal Theology*, 3:289).

35. Ibid., 21.

36. Wood, *Vision and Discernment*, 31–33, offers an extensive critique of Farley's attempted revival of *Theologia*.

37. Ibid., 41.

particular, Christian witness. Theologians need to examine every area of church life in the light of the internal logic of Christian faith and its claims.

Like Schleiermacher, Wood proposes a structure for theology and theological studies. In addition, like his liberal predecessor, Wood admits that these disciplines might well be "ghosts" that never existed and never will.[38]

"Theological inquiry, as understood in this book, does not depend absolutely upon the existence of corresponding disciplinary arrangements. It can be conducted, with more or less success, within a great variety of arrangements, each of which may facilitate the inquiry in some respects or distort it in others."[39] Theological inquiry, consequently, can be conducted under the disciplinary rubric of biblical studies or church history. Equally important, not all disciplinary work in systematic theology or philosophy of religion qualifies as theological inquiry.

Wood's position has some ambiguity. On the one hand, he is deeply appreciative of the modern achievements of scholarship. On the other hand, he realizes that the means that achieved those gains contained serious flaws, including the separation of theoretic and practical interest (in all areas of scholarly inquiry) and the tendency for institutions to confine scholarly freedom to academic matters, excluding such areas of life as the political.[40] Echoing Karl Barth's well-known exhortation to biblical scholars that they were not critical enough, Wood calls for theology to expand and deepen its critical reach.

The key metaphors in Wood's argument are vision and discernment. Vision is a "grasp of things in their wholeness and relatedness, a seeing of connections"; discernment is the capacity to understand particular situations.[41] Wood admits that these may seem opposing approaches to the world, but he feels that they are necessary to one other. Only if and when a viewer perceives a situation in terms of a larger picture can that viewer discern the situation's meaning. The interrelationship between them is somewhat similar to the role of facts and interpretation in history. Every historian, no matter how concerned with factual accuracy, fits facts into a larger framework. Without this interplay, facts would not make sense, and the historian would not know how this piece of information related to other data. Perhaps most important, Wood's use of *vision* and *discernment* allows him to move between theological education and Christian community. Since theological inquiry is a practice, students learn it by doing. Having learned it, however, inquiry becomes itself a *habitus* that develops critical perspective on the student's subsequent Christian life. In many ways, Wood's argument resembles the classic defense of the liberal arts. By reflecting and studying the breadth of human experience, a person becomes able to function effectively in the world. Business school graduates become managers; liberal-arts majors become lead-

38. Ibid., 57.
39. Ibid., 58.
40. Ibid., 62–63.
41. Ibid., 69.

ers. *Vision and Discernment* projects a similar educational outcome, at least ideally, for those who major in the Christian arts.

In retrospect, Wood's work was never as central to the larger discussion as the work of Farley, Cobb and Hough, or, later, David Kelsey. Why is not evident. *Vision and Discernment* is clear and well argued, and makes immediate contact with much that was actually done in theological schools, particularly in schools in the liberal tradition. In many ways, although it was part of the chorus complaining about the theological curriculum, *Vision and Discernment* pointed to the type of leadership that university divinity schools at their best often produced: critical, discerning, and intentional study of the Christian tradition. In that sense, *Vision and Discernment* contained an explicit apology for the university-related schools that Wood might have made more explicit.

Theologian David Kelsey was part of the theological discussion of theological education from the beginning, both as coevaluator of the Basic Issues Program of ATS, and is a frequent contributor of articles on the project. In the early 1990s, he contributed two important volumes of his own to the discussion: *To Understand God Truly: What Is Theological about a Theological School* and *Between Athens and Berlin: The Theological Education Debate*.[42] In the latter of these, Kelsey offered his own interpretation of the larger discussion and an expansion of his categories of Athens and Berlin. For him, Athens presented the long tradition of formative thinking, dating back to the ancient ideal of *paideia*, the understanding of education as the intellectual formation of the citizen. John Henry Newman in the last century was a more modern figure who held this belief in the formative quality of study. In contrast, Berlin stood for the modern scholarly approach to inquiry and, in particular, to the ideal of the professional. For Kelsey, subsequent approaches to education, including theological education, could be located somewhere on these two roads. Like all typologies, this typology had more than a few difficulties, including the fact that each type suffered the slow death of an excessive number of qualifications,[43] but the typology did highlight the very important place of Werner Jaeger's *Paideia* on the discussion.

Kelsey's survey of the other contributors to the conversation was generally careful and fair. However, Kelsey sometimes brings into the discussion an educational idealism in tension with his more empirical approach. In his treatment of Cobb and Hough, Kelsey notes that they often overlook the value, not of the results of modern scientific study, but of the methods by which modern study obtained those results:

> Rather, the difficulty is that they fail to appreciate how education into the practice of disciplined critical thinking is crucial to church leaders' capacities to offer both vision and implementation in a fashion that involves genuinely perceptive assessment of the present situation and truly insightful grasp of

---

42. Kelsey, *To Understand God Truly*; Kelsey, *Between Athens and Berlin*.

43. See the excellent review: Welch, "Between Athens and Berlin." Welch also noted Kelsey somewhat shortchanged the Enlightenment in his analysis.

> Christian identity. Knowledgeability about the results of such studies of the world historical situation and about the results of biblical and historical studies, but not about their methods, would not be sufficient for that type of leadership.[44]

Yet one wonders whether it is possible, even at Yale, for a student to do more than sample the variety of valid methods used in different scholarly enterprises. The theological curriculum is too diverse, too complicated, to permit more than a sampling of the results of any serious study.

The most serious problem in Kelsey's typology was his analysis of the Berlin model. He tended to see Berlin as a combination of scientific study and professionalism. While aspects of this interpretation are useful, particularly when we ask what Americans took from the German model, it lost very important elements of the German understanding. We mentioned earlier the German belief that the way to secure the common good was through the state. The German official, whether in education, law, medicine, or ministry, was an agent of the common good and not what Americans term a mere bureaucrat. Further, German educational life and theory interwove the ideals of *Bildung* (*paideia* and *Kultur*) with the ideals of science and technology. Germans expected their exemplars of *wissenschaft* to exemplify culture and refinement as well. Einstein, with his love of music, and Tillich, with his love of art, are two examples well known in America, of the classical German professional ideal. Present-day German education, like its French and American counterparts, has more room for technical and scientific specialization at an earlier age. Yet theological students even today enter the university only after a thorough exposure to culture in the gymnasium. In more Victorian language, one had to become a "gentleman" before one became a "professional." Seen against this background, the most important aspect of the classical Berlin model—the combination of *Kultur* and occupation—was not included in Kelsey's typology. Had he included them, his argument might have noted that the loss of the requirement of the Bachelor of Arts as an essential prerequisite to theological study meant that the current American appropriation of the Berlin model was defective. The purpose of the Bachelor of Arts was to produce a cultured person prepared to take social leadership; without the liberal arts, the Master of Divinity lacked deep roots in the common good.

Kelsey's more important contribution to the discussion, however, was *To Understand God Truly: What's Theological About A Theological School*. Although Kelsey wrote from a definite theological viewpoint, the major theme of his discussion of theological education is pluralism and diversity. His concern is with what is the theological character of those schools that are self-consciously concerned with "the Christian thing." The term, borrowed from G. K. Chesterton, is simply a "placeholder" for all

---

44. Kelsey, *To Understand God Truly*, 171.

communities of "practice and belief who call *themselves* Christian."[45] Despite overlaps and similarities, these bodies are irreducibly different from each other:

> there is no one "core" or "basic" or "essential" material theme or doctrine, not any one pattern of them, that is the Christian thing. The generally accepted conclusion of historical studies is that there never has been. There is not even a past, perhaps originating, 'essential" or "core" construal of the Christian thing from which Christians have departed in different ways to which they might return.[46]

At a minimum, the result is a diversity of maps—Kelsey likes the metaphor of roads—by which different groups approach Christianity. This diversity, naturally, continues in the schools maintained by or for these groups.

Each presents its own way or ways of knowing God. Kelsey notes some of these approaches: contemplation, discursive reason, and speculation, the affections, and action. Kelsey wrote:

> It is because theological schools are *theological* that they are irreducibly plural ways in which the idea of "understanding God" is itself theologically understood, combined with the irreducibly diverse ways in which the subject matter (the Christian thing), whose study is believed to bring us to a better understanding of God, is construed.[47]

Individual schools reflect this diversity in their self-understanding and distinctive practices. This pluralism exists not only among different schools; one can often detect it within particular institutions.

Kelsey argues the schools reflect other diversities. Although theological schools are generally small-scale organizations, they range from very large to very small, and their variations in scale contribute to the diversity of organizational forms and procedures. For Kelsey, these differences are not incidental. How a school governs itself, how students and faculty interact with each other, how the administration raises funds, each of these influences the way in which the school models "knowing God." In this sense, every aspect of a theological school has a theological component whether or not the institution is engaged in a conscious process of theological reasoning. In other words, theological significance is not limited to verbal or even intellectual matters but is present in various areas of a school's life and practices.[48]

Kelsey is a careful wordsmith, and he avoids using such words as *unique* in his descriptions. For pluralism to be a constant fact in theological education it is only

---

45. Ibid., 32.
46. Ibid., 33.
47. Ibid., 49.
48. Kelsey began his career with an exposition of Tillich's theology and with an appreciation of that theology's ability to enter into discussion with the work around it. See Kelsey, *The Fabric of Tillich's Theology*.

necessary that it be irreducible; that is, that the differences between different schools and approaches are such that they cannot be explained away. This means that much of the language of the discussion of theological education, such as words like *curriculum* or even *scholarly*, always needs nuance. There is no "thing" that corresponds to theological curriculum, for example, and no "thing" that corresponds to scholarly discourse. Diversity and freedom are, thus, necessary correlates. "God" calls each school to find its own order. If each school exists, as Kelsey's typology suggests, at a particular intersection of the Berlin and Athens roads, then these two highways define something more like the classical New England patchwork of small towns that help us pinpoint locations.

Kelsey sees three issues involved in further reflection about theological education:

> a) How shall the theological course of study be unified? b) How shall the theological source of study be made adequate to the pluralism of ways in which the Christian thing is actually construed; that is, interpreted and lived in concrete reality. c) How can theological education be understood concretely, that how can it be described concretely, that is so that what makes it "theological" is made clear without denying or ignoring its concreteness and the ways in which that concreteness makes it deeply pluralistic in actual practice.[49]

Kelsey's "thought experiment" was to turn to the most pluralistic manifestation of American religion: the local congregation. His proposal was:

> I will argue that the Christian thing is present in concrete reality in and as various Christian congregations or worshipping communities in all their radical pluralism . . . A Christian theological school is a community of persons trying to understand God truly by focusing study of various subject matters through the lens of questions about the place and role of those subject matters in diverse Christian worshipping communities in all their radical pluralism.

Kelsey's suggestion was in line with a then-current emphasis in theological education. The 1980s and 1990s saw a revival of interest in congregations and their value. Beginning with James Hopewell's *Congregations: Stories and Structures*[50] and continuing through James P. Wind's and James Welborn Lewis's two-volume *American Congregations*[51] to Nancy Tatom Ammerman's and Arthur Emery Farnsley's *Congregation & Community*,[52] serious work on the congregational substructure of American religious life was commonplace. Two editions of a practical guide for studying American congregations also appeared.[53] Hartford Seminary, where both

49. Ibid., 105.
50. Hopewell, *Congregation*.
51. Wind and Lewis, *American Congregations*.
52. Ammerman et al., *Congregation & Community*.
53. Ammerman et al., *Studying Congregations*; Ammerman et al., *Handbook for Congregational Studies*.

Carl Dudley and Nancy Ammerman worked, held a popular series of workshops for pastors, congregational leaders, and theological educators. Many Doctor of Ministry programs included elements from congregational studies, and many schools included some work in congregational studies as an elective part of their MDiv curriculum. Many, including Robert W. Lynn and Barbara Wheeler, maintained that this was the most important contemporary development in the study of American religion.

Part of what made congregational studies exciting was the promise of a new and more imaginative way of understanding American religion. In many ways, James Hopewell understood the promise of the congregational-studies movement for theological education. A graduate of Episcopal Theological School and Columbia University (the joint program with Union), Hopewell served as a missionary educator in Africa and as director of the Theological Education Fund Committee of the WCC. He taught at Hartford Seminary Foundation before moving to Emory University. Interestingly enough, Hopewell was active in establishing a new congregation in Cummings, Georgia, which he also served as first vicar. His work with congregations had three important elements: his own training in comparative religion and ethnography, his awareness of place and context, and his capacity to summon his own mythic and poetic sensibility. Hopewell's combination of sensitivity to context and theological acuity set the bar high. Every congregation approached in that way demonstrated some aspect of the meaning of Christianity as people actually lived it in the world. Correctly and carefully read, such an apprehension of a congregation was invaluable to the person charged with the weekly preaching of the Word and the pastoral care of souls. If one might educate a minister to make these judgments, then the seminary might have made a quantum leap in its work.[54]

In my opinion, Kelsey's proposal did not capture this excitement or promise. Part of the problem was that Kelsey's proposal died the death of overqualification. Yet, there was a more serious problem. Kelsey may not have understood some of the promise of congregational studies or the fact that, almost by definition, the fact that every congregation was Christian in its own way, meant that no congregation was Christian in every way. In a passage that sounds almost like the 1960s, Kelsey wrote:

> Behind these reasoned objections and giving them their power lies a deep offense, Christian congregations are occasions for offense. One need hardly be a theological education in a seminary about theological schools to feel that. The morally earnest, the spiritually perceptive, the intellectually sophisticated, not to mention the ascetically sensitive, are often scandalized by the actualities of Christian congregational life. And justifiably so. The phrase "the scandal of particularity" has usually been associated with Christian claims about Jesus of Nazareth . . . But the phrase applied with even more cause to traditional Christian claims that congregations are somehow part of the "people of God," the "body of Christ," the "Bride of Christ," that they are communities on which

---

54. See Hopewell, "A Congregational Paradigm."

the Holy Spirit is particularly poured out. It is naturally and appropriate to be scandalized that such claims should be made of just these all-too-well-known groups, faithless to their self-descriptions, thoroughly assimilated to the value system of the larger culture in which they live, complacent and at ease, often trivial and banal, subtly using the rhetoric of the faith to sanction their privileges and to obscure society's injustices.[55]

Kelsey may have intended this assertion to highlight his theme that the only way to the general is through the particular; but, unfortunately, it set the tone for much of the subsequent development of Kelsey's proposal. If the situation is as Kelsey describes it, then the task of theological school and of local church leadership is essentially theological criticism of congregations or perhaps proposing some other way to actualize faith. The genius of the congregational-studies movement was its exhortation that we needed to listen to congregations first in order to discern their structure, their theological understanding, and their possibilities. Only after listening carefully could one move to a theological or sociological critique. In contrast, Kelsey argues that a "theological school's study would be *against* and *for* Christian congregations, and only for that reason also in a way *about* them."[56]

The idea of the congregation as the focus of theological education, Kelsey felt, should not obscure the different practices that were characteristic of each. "The central practice of Christian congregations are ordered to the end of worshipping God; the central practice of a theological school are ordered to the goal of understanding God truly."[57] The distinction was, of course, finely drawn. For Kelsey, schools remain public places of inquiry. In principle, consequently, it must be possible for a person to engage in theological study without making any religious commitment to the object of studies; that is, it must be possible for a person to understand God truly without worshipping God.[58]

Like Wood and Farley, although with a different emphasis, Kelsey believed that theological education prepares ministers best when it does so indirectly. If theological

---

55. Kelsey, *To Understand God Truly*, 133. In reading Kelsey, I wondered whether he had ever been in the congregations that I have attended or served. In even the worst of them, the Word of God was preached and the sacraments administered, and people struggled with the problems, including the sin, in their own lives. There was also a capacity for change and for self-criticism that I have rarely seen in theological schools. Kelsey was not unusual among theological educators, particularly in the classical disciplines, in having negative views of empirical church life, and some had fled from the churches to what they believed were the safer grounds of the seminary. As I have watched the Mainstream churches decline over much of my career, I have often wondered how much the negative view of actual church life held by so many in theological education was not a major part of their decline. Interesting enough is that such negative attitudes were much rarer among colleagues and friends when I served in the Southern Baptist context than in more Mainstream Protestantism, perhaps because many of us in Southern Baptist seminary life also served as interim or even congregational pastors.

56. Ibid., 207.

57. Ibid., 197.

58. This is explicitly stated in ibid., 198.

schools define their goal as producing church leadership, they will fail to attain that goal. To acquire this sensitivity, Kelsey proposes that the course of studies concentrate on three questions about Christian congregations: "What is the Christian thing in that congregation? Is it faithful to its own identity? Is it true?"[59] This would tie the particular course offered to the central purpose of the school while allowing a full appreciation of all of the pluralisms present among faculty and students. In effect, if the range of participants in the study, congregations, students, and faculty, were sufficient, the class would come to a picture of the whole that recognized all the differences between them.

From a later standpoint, Kelsey's emphasis on the radical pluralism of American religion, especially American Protestantism, reflected the declining place of the university divinity schools. The architects of the university divinity schools hoped that sound scholarship, open investigation of differences of opinion, and the idea of professional practice might make it possible for people from a variety of backgrounds to study in one institution with a single faculty.[60] As other seminaries broadened their student bodies and faculties, they came to share this same ideal. Even in the twenty-first century, university divinity schools continue to do this well. Kelsey has not offered a convincing alternative to this tradition, despite all of its intellectual problems. In many ways, his proposal brings us back to Lessing's big ugly ditch: how can the truths of history (particularity) become the eternal truths of reason? Kelsey has, in effect, hidden the problem behind the pluralism of the contemporary church, but this is only to highlight the issue.

Feminist educators made two contributions to the discussion: Katie Cannon and The Mudflower Collective, *God's Fierce Whimsy: Christian Feminism and Theological Education* (1985); and Rebecca Chopp, *Saving Work: Feminist Practices of Theological Education* (1995). Unfortunately, these books were often at the edge of the larger discussion.[61] *God's Fierce Whimsy*, a collection of essays, did not develop a particular perspective on theological education, although the essays did stress the role of experience, of story, and of personal reflection. In contrast, Rebecca Chopp's *Saving Work* was a more sustained theological argument. In many ways, Chopp stood outside the questions of theory and practice and curriculum construction that shaped the larger discussion. Beginning with a more experiential view of theology, she argues that theological education should follow practices that promote personal growth and wholeness. The pedagogy and the content of theological education had to be integrated with each other. Good theological education involves every type of human intellect and creativity.[62] Good theological practice, consequently, necessarily participates in the

---

59. Ibid., 212.

60. See Miller, *Piety and Profession*.

61. Cannon et al., *God's Fierce Whimsy*; Chopp, *Saving Work*.

62. Chopp was a graduate of the University of Chicago and often combined elements of feminism and process thought.

divine creativity and self-disclosure. In that sense, theological education liberates the student, the teacher, and, by extension, the church. In effect, theological education consists of providing students with a place where they can share their experiences, using symbols and images drawn from a variety of religious sources. As in the creation of all forms of art, the categories of right and wrong, of proper and improper, do not apply.

A New Practical Theology

Closely related to the debate over what made theological education theological was a reappraisal of the nature of practical theology. Led by Chicago's Don Browning, practical theologians stepped beyond the limitations of a functionalist interpretation of their discipline. Practical theologians faced pressures from different directions.[63] Many theological schools had an informal hierarchy that, whether conscious or not, tended to see practical theology as lacking intellectual rigor.[64] In part, this was because of the phenomenological character of social sciences. Following a pattern that reached back to Aristotle and Plato, the intellectual life was one that dealt with abstractions and with final or ultimate causes. The practical fields had also lost ground within theological education. In simple terms, these disciplines moved from the center to the edges of theological education, especially in the university-related schools. In 1930, the professors in the practical fields had led in the construction of the characteristic liberal theological curricula; that was clearly no longer the case. As the 1960s and 1970s passed, the last remnants of this early position were lost. Perhaps the most striking thing, for example, about the discussion of what is theological about theological education is that the primary participants ignored the serious discussions of Christian identity and its formation by such practical theologians as C. Ellis Nelson. Moreover, despite the rising abstract interest in the congregation, the anticongregational bias of the 1960s lived on in theological thinking. Even such realistic thinkers as Cobb and Hough spoke too glibly of the middle-class captivity of the local churches as a hindrance to effective Christian or theological practice.[65] People found it too easy to

---

63. For the immediate relationship to the Cobb and Hough volume, see Browning et al., *The Education of the Practical Theologian*. The larger debate can be followed in Browning, *Practical Theology*; Mudge and Poling, *Formation and Reflection*; Poling and Miller, *Foundations*; and Browning, *A Fundamental Practical Theology*.

64. Interestingly enough is that Gary Dorrien only mentions Browning once in his history of liberal theology since the 1950s, and that is as a student of Bernard Loomer. Browning's serious contributions to liberal thought about church and society and theological issues is never considered. Yet his contributions as a teacher and as a scholar rivaled those of his teacher and other Chicago faculty members.

65. My own personal memories have colored my reading of this situation. For middle-class people deeply concerned with their own professional status and promotions to be constantly condemning other middle-class people often without all the higher education of faculty members seemed pretentious or even an example of false consciousness. Somehow one was to do contextual theology in every

think that what strengthened the local body somehow helped the enemy. Another complicating factor was the shifting role of the church in society. During a period of rapid religious change, the changes in the ministry demanded that instructors in the practical fields continually update their basic paradigms and address a rapidly changing ministerial profession. Practical theologies wore out quickly as yesterday's wisdom became today's folly.

The discussion of what made practical theology theological had many ins and outs. Leroy T. Howe of Perkins offered a useful summary of the discussion:

> Most practical theologians writing today work with a definition of the field in something like the following terms: practical theology is critical reflection on the ministry of the church, with emphasis upon assessing the faithfulness and effectiveness of that ministry as a witness to Christ in the present. On this definition, it is fruitful to construe pastoral theology as a "sub-field" of practical theology, as critical reflection on the work of the ordained ministers of the church, which presupposes the calling of all followers of Christ to ministry.[66]

James Fowler offered a similar redefinition. Practical theology is

> theological reflection and construction arising out of and giving guidance to a community of faith in the praxis of its mission. Practical theology is critical and constructive reflection on the praxis of the Christian community's life and work in its various dimensions.[67]

Such redefinitions pointed to a close relationship between ethics and practical theology. Historically, much American ethical theory, especially in social ethics, had evolved from the Social Gospel argument that what the churches needed was an applied Christianity. The pastoral ministry was one way, as Howe noted, that Christianity became incarnate in the life of church and community. Browning demonstrated the intellectual acuity of the new understanding in such theoretical studies as *A Fundamental Practical Theology: Descriptive and Strategic Proposals*, but these were often hard for all but trained theologians to grasp. More important was Browning's own practical demonstration of what the new practical theology might yield in his work on faith and law and, particularly, in his contributions to the discussion of Christian marriage.

Significantly, the new practical theologians did not surrender their interest in social science. The gains from the scientific study of religion, especially psychology

---

context except the one in which one lived, worked, and worshiped. The failure to take the context of American Protestantism with real seriousness weakened the churches as they faced an increasingly secular society.

66. Howe, "A Future for Pastoral Theology," 7.
67. Quoted in Fowler, "Practical Theology," 49.

and sociology, were too great to be ignored.[68] Interestingly, the publicly ascertained facts played significant roles in their disciplined reflections.

By the 1990s, a new practical theology had clearly emerged. One of the major contributions to this subsequent development was Craig Dykstra and Dorothy Bass's insistence on practice as a primary category for understanding faith.[69] Like the idea of *paideia*, the idea of practice had its roots in ancient Greek educational theory. Alasdair MacIntyre and other virtue ethicists interpreted Aristotle's ethics as practice. For MacIntyre, a practice was a repeated behavior that the practitioner or doer continually enriched by rational reflection. In *After Virtue,* he gave the example of playing chess. A good chess player both studies the games of past masters and analyses his or her current performance as it develops. The best symbol of MacInytre's view of chess is the record of games kept by each player in a club or tournament. The classical idea of virtue provides another example. One becomes a brave person each time one acts bravely in a dangerous situation. Each act of bravery leads the person to reflect on that action and to deepen attachment to that virtue. We become virtuous by doing virtuous deeds. Practices are, consequently, habits, but they are rational habits developed by a person struggling with actual situations. Interpreted from this perspective, ministry is rooted in character and self-reflection that follows an arc from early childhood faith through professional maturity. The seeds of the minister's practice are thus sowed, nurtured, and matured.

The relatively new Doctor of Ministry programs, despite their unpopularity with many faculty members in classical disciplines, provide an important testing ground for both the idea of the practical theologian as reflective practitioner and the new practical theology. Although many Doctor of Ministry programs featured the traditional specializations in ministry, such as pastoral care or preaching, others used the idea of the reflective practitioner to help define the DMin project, one of the perpetual problems in the program. Projects were to demonstrate theological thinking or theological reflection in both their design and in their evaluation. The demand for evaluation as part of the project design, further, pushed many DMin students to consider statistical means of validation.

Did the theological-education debate influence Mainstream theological education as a whole? The question admits of more than one answer. As in the case of Schleiermacher's *Brief Outline*, no school accepted all of the proposals, either as a

---

68. Perhaps the most serious problem of the Farley–Kelsey–Wood discussions was their comparative neglect of social science as a source for theological reflection. Interestingly, Catholic thinkers, who had known firsthand the consequences of ignoring this type of inquiry, were much more open to modern psychology and sociology.

69. See Bass and Dykstra, *For Life Abundant*. Particularly important is the essay by Cahalan and Nieman, "Mapping the Field of Practical Theology," 62–85. The essay is best read as a summary piece, containing insights gathered over more than two decades. Cahalan was among the strongest advocates of theological reflection as part of ministerial practice. Cahalan, *Projects That Matter*, was a practical demonstration of the value of the new practical theology in the daily push-and-pull of church life.

whole or in part; in this sense, they all left their "ghosts" behind. On the other hand, the debate did contribute to a major shift in theological education. Particularly in the practical fields and in systematic theology, an increased emphasis on "doing theology," "theological wisdom," and "reflective practice" became more prominent. In that sense, theological educators largely left behind the old ideas of theory and practice, never very adequate, and made theological thinking an end in itself. Perhaps more important, while the disciplinary model remained strong in church history and in biblical studies, the disciplinary model no longer provided the overall paradigm for seminary education as a whole. Administrators urged teachers to think of themselves as theological educators first and as disciplinary specialists second. Just as the larger trend in theological education was to professionalize various offices, including those of president and dean, so many theological educators saw seminary teaching as a unique profession. As we will see in the next chapter, theological educators increasingly sought the correct pedagogy for theological education as distinct from that appropriate to a university religion department or to other forms of professional education. This supported a deeper change among theological faculties. Historically, seminaries hired ministers who had scholarly specialties to teach. Seminary teaching was, consequently, a special ministry within the church. Now teaching theology was its own profession or calling.[70]

Perhaps more important for the future, the vigorous discussions of the 1980s and early 1990s did contain the heart of a new professional model. The ideal minister or religious leader was a person able to reflect and think theologically about his or her own life and the life of the congregation or agency. If the older professional model had concentrated on the tasks before the minister, the new professional model concentrated on the minister's own formation. The ideal of practice, as defined by such thinkers as Alasdair MacIntyre, or other by adaptations of the ancient ideal of *paideia*, became the overarching goal of theological education. The 1990s and 2000s would elaborate and modify this understanding as theological educators concentrated on new standards, the improvement of teaching, and the use of new technology.

Excursus

It might be useful to compare this discussion with the controversies wracking the Evangelical world. The Mainstream-dominated discussion centered on the question, how can we do theology and theological education after the decline or even the disappearance of biblical authority? The Evangelical argument was over the question, how we continue to affirm biblical authority? In the Catholic Church, the controversies over priesthood occasioned by John Paul II's attempted reforms has a similar division

---

70. This trend may have begun among women teachers in faith traditions that either did not permit ordination or discouraged it.

with one party resolved to maintain the tradition and the other convinced that it could not be salvaged without radical change.

GLOBALIZATION

American higher education and to some extent American secondary education underwent profound changes after 1970. In many ways, American universities became part of an educational order that brought together students and faculty from around the world. As American-based multinational companies increasingly dominated world markets, knowledge of American methods, language, and tools became important economic assets. Another factor increasing the importance of American schools was the rapid urbanization of the world. In the 1960s, Africa was a continent of villages; by the 2000s, it was a continent of cities. Cities in Latin America experienced similar explosive growth. Urban life weakens traditional cultural patterns, and places a high premium on education. The lines between the educated, the less educated, and the uneducated are also lines demarcating the boundaries between social classes. The new urbanization also promoted the growth of mass communications. Beginning with radio and television, the urban areas of the world experienced a communications revolution. News was truly worldwide. Many Third-World countries leapfrogged older technologies such as the land-based telephone and moved directly into cell phones and computers. Since the United States led in communication technology, the communications revolution benefited American companies and American schools. American patterns of education also spread. For example, many Two-Thirds World schools adopted such American degree nomenclature as Bachelor of Arts, Bachelor of Science, and Doctor of Philosophy. The end of the Soviet Union in 1989 increased American power in education. For all their faults, the communist regimes of Eastern Europe and Asia had aggressively promoted education at home and abroad, and their universities had claimed many of the Two-Third World's best minds. The United States won the educational as well as the political cold war.

Another factor promoting an increased American involvement in international education was the fact that American schools had space that they had to fill. The end of the baby boom meant that all schools were involved in an anxious search for students and, not only for numbers, but also for academic talent. In many ways, this search was most intensive in the scientific and mathematical areas where American secondary education was not producing sufficient elite students to support adequately a growing demand for advanced practitioners, but it was common to almost all large institutions. Foreign students became an important part of most student bodies. In short, American universities, both state and private, increasingly became world cities in which people from around the globe and from diverse American backgrounds studied, lived, and worked together. Many of those who came to study stayed to earn and, in turn, claimed important places on the faculties of these schools. Internally, American schools also changed. The heart of the pre-1960s university was the Bachelor of Arts, an educational program designed to produce general knowledge and leadership skills; the new universities stressed science, technology, and professional training. A Master of Business Administration was the key to the new world economy, not a Bachelor of Arts.

The internationalization of American education naturally affected American theological schools. When telling the story of American theological education, we need to note that much of what actually happened in individual schools was the consequence of those schools' participation in the larger American education system. Without any conscious actions by accrediting agencies or their own leadership, these institutions naturally drew an increasing number of students and faculty from around the world. These foreign students and teachers brought with them their own cultures and their own literature. Particularly in the urban areas, where many seminaries were located, the seminaries' nearest neighbors were often new ethnic churches and communities of adherents of different world religions. As the proportion of commuter students increased, theological schools increasingly recruited students and used local churches and religious organizations as part of their educational program. George Braswell, professor of missions at Southeastern Baptist Seminary in Wake Forest, North Carolina, began planning for his seminars on world religions in Washington DC long before the ATS gave him a 1981 grant to complete his preparation.[71] Braswell used the religious diversity of the nation's capital to teach students about the pluralism that they would increasingly encounter in their own ministries. Significantly, Braswell's began his work a decade before Diana Eck investigated the religious pluralism in the Boston area.

Yet seminaries may have lagged behind other American educational institutions in such areas as the enrollment of foreign students and the employment of foreign and ethnic faculty. Like so many issues in theological education, this may have come down to a question of finances and of scale. Larger institutions have the resources to adjust to changing markets more rapidly than smaller ones, and seminaries were often small institutions. In many respects, I suspect, this comparative backwardness may partially account for the intense discussion of the global issue among theological educators. They felt that they had to play catch-up.

Other, less obvious factors may have contributed to the widespread discussion of globalization. The Mainstream churches were in a precipitous and continuing downward spiral, and their seminaries had few resources to help them deal with, not to mention arrest, this trend. They needed students. Further, they needed an expanded sense of mission. Despite the popularity of congregational studies on some campuses, much of the dissatisfaction with the parish and with the denominations remained

---

71. Braswell, "Field-based Learning."

from the 1960s. Faith seemed more vital abroad, and the most socially relevant theologies had roots in the Two-Thirds World. The global was exciting; the local, less so. To be honest, I suspect that for Mainstream seminary leaders, interest in global affairs was a needed diversion. The more seminary leaders fixed their eyes abroad, the easier it was for them to ignore the problems at home.

American Assets for Global Theological Education

In the 1960s, American theological schools seemed well prepared to participate in global education. The American missionary outreach included all the world's continents, and the churches had ministers and other professionals who had mastered many of the world's languages and had begun the study of their cultures. Many Protestant organizations had the word *World* or *International* in their titles. Such organizations included the YMCA, which had hotels in the leading cities of the world, and the World's Fundamentalist Association (a body with members in only the United States and Canada). Such schools as Union Seminary in New York and Yale University had extensive collections of missionary literature and significant numbers of alumni serving around the world. The leading denominational schools, including Princeton and Southwestern Baptist, always had significant numbers of missionaries on furlough studying and teaching at their institutions. Such seminary presidents as John A. Mackay and Henry Pitt Van Dusen were familiar world travelers and eager spokespersons for the newer churches abroad. Many seminaries had professors of missions on their faculties, and most made some provision for the study of non-Christian religions. American theological schools provided many WCC leaders, and many Mainstream seminaries required courses in ecumenical Christianity. Ironically, Mainstream Protestant churches were slowly but surely withdrawing from the missionary movement; as they did, the seminaries gradually dismantled many of their existing programs.

Another American asset was the shared experience of cultural dependency, particularly in theology, with the new churches of Asia and Africa. From early on, American seminaries had used British and German studies as important parts of their curriculum and in individual classes. Much American theological study, particularly in the area of Bible, was directly imported from Europe, and influential chairs in American seminaries were often held by European and British scholars. Only the Chicago School might claim to be American, and, ironically, the process theology that marked its latest incarnation depended on Alfred North Whitehead, an English philosopher. Those engaged in the quest for the Great American Novel, the Great American Epic, and the Great American Theology should have reached out instinctively to those seeking a theology that expressed their own cultural particularities.

At the same time as Mainstream Protestants withdrew from missions, Evangelical Christians became more active abroad. Whereas the more liberal churches saw the decline of imperialism and the rising sense of national identity as a signal to withdraw from world evangelization, conservative missionary theorists saw these same problems as spurs to greater efforts. The churches needed to make gains while they had the opportunity to do so. Moreover, beginning with relatively small numbers, the more entrepreneurial Pentecostal churches rushed into the emerging cities of the Two-Thirds World. Within forty years, they became a major component of the world Christian movement, especially in Africa and Latin America.

Part of Evangelical strength was the tenacity of Evangelical theologians and missionary leaders. Evangelicals refused to give up on their churches in China and in Russia and retained contacts wherever possible with their leaders. Evangelical seminaries, including Fuller, Trinity, Gordon-Conwell, and the Southern Baptist Seminaries, continued to place major emphasis on the theological training of missionaries, and many Evangelical schools expanded their missions programs.[72] Further, evangelical seminaries had a missionary ethos that penetrated all areas of the program, including chapel and the classic theological disciplines.[73] One could not attend an Evangelical or Southern Baptist school without the institution confronting you with the demand that you consider service abroad.

The Association of Theological Schools

The Association of Theological Schools was the major advocate for the globalization of theological schools. In part, this was because the Association provided the one venue where the leaders of theological schools might talk together and make common cause. The Association also had the one big stick in theological education: accreditation. Although accreditation failed to restrain violations of academic freedom, theological leaders, especially in the Mainstream churches, continued to see it as a way of securing or even forcing greater uniformity. The ATS had another asset: it had significant links with important foundations.

When the Association of Theological Schools began to plan the transition in the 1980s, Donald Shriver, president of New York's Union Seminary, moved that the association appoint a Committee on International Theological Education. The motion passed easily, and a decade of discussion and clarification began. Part of the problem was language. *International* gave way to *ecumenical*. By the mid-1980s, the preferred term was *globalization*.[74] Although many reasons for the language existed, one was the need for an equivalent to *ecumenical* without WCC connotations. Some Evangelical and Southern Baptist leaders suspected the WCC and saw it as subservient to liberal

---

72. Missionary Volunteers made up about one fourth of the enrollment of Southwestern Baptist Theological Seminary, which educated about half the extensive SBC contingent of missionaries.

73. This was very true at Southeastern Baptist Theological Seminary when I taught there. Regular missionary chapels were held, missionary history was included in both the required course in Baptist History and Doctrine and in Church History. Southwestern and Southern were even more missions minded.

74. Lesher and Shriver, "Stumbling in the Right Direction," 5.

theological interests.⁷⁵ Ironically, the more the word *globalization* became popular in the ATS, the more it became suspect abroad. By the 1990s, *globalization* had acquired unfortunate economic connotations. Many both at home and abroad used it as shorthand for the influence of multinational corporations. As discussions with theological educators abroad developed, American theological leaders learned that these educators abroad reacted almost viscerally to the term. To African and Asian ministerial educators, *globalization* suggested a theological dominance similar to American economic dominance.⁷⁶ *Globalization* also suggested the attempt to construct a theology that transcended local conditions.⁷⁷ Neither was acceptable, and ATS gradually moved to the language of global perspectives. In retrospect, what was amazing was that the association continued to use the term *globalization* long after the association's dialog partners abroad found the language oppressive.

The term *globalization* also hid some deep divisions among American theological educators. The Roman Catholic Church was a global religious body with much experience in dealing with the massive movement of peoples associated with the new urbanization. As immigration changed the demographics of American life, many Catholic dioceses, including in South Florida and Los Angeles, resembled small world communities. Some Catholic seminaries, including those in Los Angeles and South Florida, experimented with bilingual programs to train priests for the new communities. Further, Vatican II had already carried out a global liturgical revolution. The Mass and other rituals were available in the world's principal languages as well as in many less widely spoken tongues. Translation⁷⁸ is one of the marks of Christianity and represents both a means of the transfer for and the transformation of a message from one culture to another. The Church also encouraged local churches to use a variety of cultural forms, including dance, in worship and evangelization. The key term in much Catholic thinking about the worldwide church was *contextualization*. To contextualize is to adapt something to a new cultural situation. The root theological idea behind contextualization is tradition and its natural development. Tradition expands as each new transmission of faith adds something to the body of received faith. Another, very similar Catholic concept was *enculturation*, the process by which faith becomes part

---

75. SBC Moderate faculty did not share the denomination's antipathy to the councilor movement, and WCC documents were read and assigned during my period at Southeastern Baptist Seminary. *Baptism, Eucharist, and Ministry* was seen as particularly significant. The SBC Conservatives were deeply opposed to the WCC, and the administrations of the Moderate schools downplayed the use of WCC documents in the classroom.

76. The concern about American dominance was not irrational. Many churches abroad sent their most able and ambitious students to the United States or Europe, only to find that they never returned, but took teaching and ministerial positions abroad. American theological educators were often woefully unaware of the damage that this brain drain inflicted on churches abroad.

77. This fear was not completely irrational. One of the hopes of the original ecumenical movement had been that a common theology would be found that transcended differences, and interest in such a world theology has never completely disappeared.

78. Sanneh, *Translating the Message*.

of the everyday assumptions of a people.[79] Catholic liberation theologians used both terms and contributed much to the general Catholic awareness of their importance. In the 1980s when ATS began its own globalization discussion, however, the Catholic Church restricted its liberation theologians, partly because of the Church's nervousness over the influence of Marxism, and removed a handful from their teaching positions. The fact that liberation theology deeply influenced many Mainstream leaders created an atmosphere of suspicion in some more conservative Catholic circles. Was ATS going down a road that Rome did not want to travel?

Evangelicals were also initially uneasy around the new emphasis. Evangelicals suspected, perhaps rightly, that the Mainstream leaders advocating globalization were primarily concerned with the type of global Christianity found in the WCC and in Marxist forms of liberation theology. While many Evangelical members and leaders (particularly in the Lausanne movement) were deeply concerned with the social application of the gospel to human situations, they also recognized a distinction between the gospel and any human application of it. Perhaps because Evangelical seminary leaders had more contact with Christian leaders in other nations, they realized that not all movements of liberation were inherently Christian or favorable to Christian faith. When the Soviet Union fell, Evangelical churches and seminaries helped those congregations and national church bodies that had survived the period of communist persecution. Long-standing ties also enabled them to reach out to Chinese and Cuban churches as the restrictions on religion became less oppressive in the 1990s.

The Mainstream leaders who were most passionate about globalization tended to be committed to some form of liberation theology. The cause of South African liberation from the oppressive system of apartheid energized Mainstream seminary interest in international affairs. Bishop Desmond Tutu, who had headed up the WCC Theological Education Fund, was the exemplar of this style of thinking. Tutu used his worldwide connections to organize fellow Christians against the South African regime, and when independence was achieved, Tutu used his considerable influence in South Africa to help secure a more peaceful settlement. To many, Tutu and Nelson Mandela seemed almost reincarnations of Martin Luther King Jr. and the nonviolent civil rights movement. Yet liberation theology was not only Tutu and Mandela. Many liberation theologians were committed to Marxist analysis and, in particular, to the Marxist idea of *praxis*. While such theologies supposedly had roots in the non-Western world, Marxism was Western in origin and in assumptions. Like earlier forms of academic Marxism, Marxist liberation theology was more or less imperious to the course of events. Thus, while the fall of the Soviet Union had much influence

---

79. See the very insightful speech of Cardinal Arinze to the 1986 ATS meeting (Arinze, "Globalization of Theological Education"): "Inculturation is the incarnation of the Gospel message in a culture. It is the process by which the Gospel message enters the soul of a culture, in such a way that not only are the Christian message and life expressed with elements proper to this culture, but also the culture itself gets evangelized and becomes an enrichment of the Christian life and experience" (19).

in bringing about the apparent death of ideology, Mainstream theologians only rarely believed it worthy of theological notice.

The Three Faces of Globalization: Issue, Cause, and Standard

As globalization developed, these deep divisions gave globalization three different faces. The first, as an issue, was part of the initial proposal by Donald Shriver that the Association of Theological Schools appoint a committee to study internationalization. In many ways, globalization was a classic issue, similar to the other basic issues that occupied so much attention in the 1980s. No one understanding of globalization as an issue ever dominated, and yet a rich debate ensued that involved many of the best theological minds. From 1980 to 2000, the Association of Theological Schools hosted a series of conferences, complete with academic papers, covering different aspects of the topic, and the association's journal, *Theological Education*, published essays that illumined the different dimensions of the question.[80] In 1999, William Lesher and Donald Shriver observed:

> Few activities of the A.T.S. have engaged so many people in virtually all the aspects of the theological enterprise. Hundreds of professors in all the seminary disciplines have attended conferences. Many have written papers; virtually all have participated in discussions about globalization at their individual schools. Administrators have engaged in dialogues at several Biennial Meetings. They have been consulted through surveys regarding resources that would help to introduce themes of globalization on their campuses.[81]

Just as the debate over what was theological about theological education enriched the literature of theological education, so these discussions about globalization made a rich contribution to the understanding and practice of theological schools.[82] However, globalization was not only an issue. Globalization was also a cause and a standard. As I am using the language, a cause is goal-directed behavior often supported by a movement and a sense that the cause is the voice of the future. Movements always want to gain new adherents, to reach new benchmarks and, above all, to maintain their momentum. In contrast, a standard is a mark or measure of how far the members of a group may have attained a goal. In education, *standard* may have a more precise meaning as an agreed-upon mark or level of attainment that is a condition for accreditation. Within these perimeters, the same event may have the character of a movement for some and of a standard for others. Higher representation for women

---

80. For an insightful overview, see *Theological Education*, "Decade of Special Issues."

81. Lesher and Shriver, "Stumbling in the Right Direction"; Evans et al., *The Globalization of Theological Education*; Featherstong, *Global Culture*; Robertson, *Globalization*; Robertson and Garrett, *Religion and Global Order*.

82. Cobb and Hough had included global perspectives as an essential element in theological education.

and minorities was, for instance, a movement for some and a standard for others. The distinction between a movement and a standard is admittedly a historical and analytical device. The distinction allows us to discuss some very complex events and to reach different judgments about those events when we consider them as different aspects of the same story. In the case of globalization, I will argue that globalization, as a basic issue, was one of the great successes of the 1980s and 1990s but that it was less successful as a movement, and that it was even less fruitful as a standard.

The depths revealed by the discussion of globalization as an issue help to explain why it was less successful as a movement or a standard. As they view most issues, scholars viewed globalization from a variety of perspectives. This variety enhanced the discussion and avoided many of the quick and simple solutions that a more superficial examination might have concealed. Yet it was this very depth that limited the globalization movement. Like most movements, globalization was intensely concerned with the reform of existing institutions. The problem was the discussion of globalization as an issue made consensus on what needed to be difficult to attain. Yet, the globalization movement did get many people and institutions motivated. Globalization was always a matter of passionate belief as well as calculated policy. This problem was more acute in the attempt to make globalization a standard. While the ATS leadership has labored to keep its standards from depending solely on quantification, standards require a degree of precision to be enforceable. Agreement with a standard is not sufficient; schools must give evidence that they have attained the mark. The complexities of globalization as an issue meant that globalization remained more a pious hope than a genuine benchmark. As cash-strapped institutions struggled to provide very expensive cross-cultural education, foreign experiences, and international recruitment programs, their leaders found it easy to ask how high they needed to jump to clear the hurdle. Lack of precision meant that schools claimed more and more for less and less.[83]

Globalization as an Issue

As an issue, globalization was concerned with the theological questions involved in providing theological education for a worldwide Christian movement. These issues were not trivial, nor were they of one order or type. Many vexing questions involved the ambiguities of postcolonial national and international politics: How should churches

---

83. For another view, see Roozen, "'If Our Words Could Make It So,'" 34:

> The above cautions notwithstanding, the weight of evidence contained in the 1989 survey strongly suggests that the emphasis given to globalization in our theological institutions has increased over the last six years. Regardless of whether the future judges globalization to have been a passing fancy or a fundamental reconceptualization of preparation for ministry, there is little doubt that at the current time it is an energizing and catalytic concern within theological education.

regard movements of national liberation and national economic development? Should they see these movements as steps toward the attainment of God's rule and reign, or should they see them as part of the secular order? Was violence justified against nonmilitary targets such as economic organizations that followed oppressive policies? Another equally serious set of questions concerned the influence that context has on Christian teaching. Was there a doctrine of the Trinity that incorporated elements of African or Asian philosophy and religion analogous to the way that the ancient creeds incorporated ancient philosophy? Should theologians assume that Asian and African churches and theology will pass through the same struggle with modernity as the American and European churches experienced in the nineteenth century? What is the proper role of culture in theological reflection? Is the religious culture of newly established churches the Old Testament of those churches, so to speak? If so, what was normative in those cultures? Was current Western postmodernism able to provide the rationale or rationales for a theological relativism?

I can only sample the discussion in this narrative. My own discussion will highlight the work of two theologians: Robert Schreiter of Chicago Theological Union and Max L. Stackhouse, then of Andover Newton and later of Princeton. Both thinkers took an active part in the discussions within the Association of Theological Schools, and both published important works about theology and ethics in an international context. Perhaps, equally important, both taught in schools deeply involved in world Christianity. Will later historians agree with my selection? I do not know. However, even if they highlight other thinkers, those thinkers will share much with these two leaders.

Robert Schreiter is a member of the Missionaries of the Most Precious Blood, an Roman Catholic religious order that was part of the Chicago Theological Union, a school established by a variety of different Catholic religious orders. At present, nine orders participating in CTU have extensive missionary work, and they use CTU to prepare their students for service abroad. In addition to their own candidates, these orders also sponsor students from their own mission fields, giving the school an international student body. Although not organized into a school of missions, CTU offered specialized MA and MDiv degrees in missions.

Further, Chicago was a world city with a variety of ethnic groups, religious organizations, and social agencies. CTU was also enriched by its location in the midst of a number of colleges, universities, and theological seminaries. In addition to rich library resources, teachers at the CTU have access to scholars in a number of disciplines relevant to missionary work and theory. These include anthropology, Asian studies, African studies, and comparative religion. Schreiter was a distinguished missiologist, serving at one time as president of the American Society of Missiologists. From the

1970s onward, one of his concerns was how the gospel fit into different localities: that is to say, in contextualization.

Schreiter's contribution to the larger globalization discussion was his sense of the fluidity of the world's cultures and the constantly shifting relationships between them. In two 1993 essays in *Theological Education*, "Contextualization from a World Perspective" and "Christian Theology between the Local and the Global,"[84] he set forth a compelling picture of the shifting context of the Christian missions. The period from 1492 to 1960 was the period of Western imperialism and the spread of Christian faith around the world. A new period began with the end of colonialism and continued until 1989. During this period, the great hope was for a new synthesis:

> In the 1960s and early 1970s, there was considerable optimism about the contextualization of forms of Christianity around the planet. The newly formed democracies in Africa looked forward to being truly Christian, truly African. The Second Vatican Council and the World Council of Churches urged greater sensitivity to cultures.[85]

The fall of the Soviet Union marked the beginning of the third period. This event made global capitalism the primary shaper of the world's cultures. This meant that people increasingly moved from their local cultures into a global culture, often losing their own identity. The churches and their theologians needed to find a way to stand between the emerging world consciousness and the various remaining local cultures:

> A theology that is truly globalized will have to stand at this intersection of the global and the local. It will need to understand the context within which it is global—both the exciting aspects of a new unity among human communities made possible by channels of communication and information, and the need for a non-alienating, participative mode of being together at the local level.[86]

The dialogical or dialectical relationship between the local and the global was crucial to both. Schreiter was conscious that some local theologies, such as the 1930s German Christian movement, were diabolical. For him, the global and Catholic counterbalanced those tendencies and called them to account. When universal and local theologies met in an atmosphere of mutual respect, they informed and enriched each other. The image was somewhat like a mosaic with contrasting tiles of many colors. To understand Schreiter's position, it is essential to recognize that the universal is not the Western or even the ecumenical. The universal is the Catholic that provides the unity between local and national churches. Local churches can dare much because they are part of the Catholic Church.

---

84. Schreiter, "Christian Theology'"; Schreiter, "Contextualization from a World Perspective."
85. Schreiter, "Contextualization from a World Perspective," 70.
86. Schreiter, "Christian Theology," 117.

Like Schreiter, Max Stackhouse began his work on globalization with a deep awareness of worldwide Christianity. He taught at Andover Newton, a school whose two primary leaders in the 1980s, President George Peck and Dean Orlando Costas, had missionary experience and were active in world Christianity. In addition, Stackhouse served for two years as a theological teacher in the Two-Thirds World and had a firsthand knowledge of the situation(s) abroad. He had worked closely with leaders of churches in communist countries, including East Germany. In addition, Stackhouse often represented the United Church of Christ in international church discussions, and he knew church leaders in China, Russia, the former East Germany, and elsewhere.

Stackhouse had other advantages as a theological interpreter of the globalization issue. Stackhouse had studied theology in Holland and was influenced both by the Dutch history-of-religions school and by such Dutch theologians as Abraham Kuyper. These theologians stressed the close relationship between cultures and their religious foundations, even after secularization obscured their religious roots. His work with James Luther Adams, as well as his study of Reinhold Niebuhr and Walter Rauschenbusch, reinforced this basic orientation. Perhaps most important, although Stackhouse identified with liberal Christianity's insistence on justice, he was skeptical of Marxism intellectually and practically.[87]

Stackhouse participated in the globalization of theological education at every level. He was an active participant in the ATS discussions and a contributor to *Theological Education*; he served as coordinating editor of the Center for Theological Inquiry's God and Globalization project, the most significant attempt to discuss the theological issues posed by globalization;[88] and he worked as an evaluator of programs. His work, *Apologia*, edited together with Nanthawan Boonsprasat-Lewis, J. G. F. Collison, Lamin Sanneh, Lee Harding, Ilse von Lowenclau, and Robert W. Pazmiño,[89] reported on extensive conversations on global themes by his own faculty. *Apologia* originated in the Basic Issues Research Program of ATS, funded by the Lilly Endowment. It was also inspired by the excitement generated by the one-hundred-seventy-fifth anniversary of Andover Newton and the election of George Peck as president. In many ways, *Apologia* was several books in one. On the one hand, the book reported on the discussion among Andover Newton faculty of current issues in theological education, including Edward Farley's *Theologia*. This part of the book provides important evidence of the extent of the discussion generated by Farley's work and of unpublished reactions to it. Whatever else, Farley struck a raw nerve among theological educators. The Andover Newton discussion confirmed the diversity within the faculty: "What we found is that the contemporary ecumenical, liberationist, semiotic, and phenomenological

---

87. Stackhouse, "Global Engagement."

88. The results of the God and Globalization project appeared in four volumes published from 2000 to 2007. The last volume, *Globalization and Grace*, was Stackhouse's own statement of the questions.

89. Stackhouse et al., *Apologia*.

perspectives that are so widely influential today contribute rich resources for contemporary reflection and action."[90] In other words, the usual theological reaction to any proposal: we have learned much, but my perspective is still on the table.[91] Yet, *Apologia* is more than the local history of the reception of a broader discussion. Particularly in the Third Part, "A proposal," Stackhouse makes a very important contribution to both the discussion of what makes theological education theological and to the globalization discussion.

Stackhouse began with the fact that religion makes truth claims. People within and without the religion have to take these claims seriously and critically. While admitting the truth of many critiques of religion, Stackhouse wrote:

> it would have to be claimed that not all religion is of that sort, that some of what we call religion is in fact a manifestation of a metaphysical-moral reality that can be, in some sense, known with relative clarity and security, and shown to be inherently true, at least in principle, and just in its effects. A critique of what is invalid requires some acquaintance with what with what is valid. Otherwise, we have only competing opinions.[92]

The object of theology is, thus, God, and in knowing God, theology can analyze and affirm various religious claims about God and ultimate reality.[93] If so, then theology's task is continuous with the ancient idea of *apologia* or apology. An *apologia* requires a willingness to enter into the thought forms of those outside the tradition, to give an account of what is most dear to Christian faith, to hear and evaluate claims not one's own, and to refute unwarranted objections to one's own faith.[94] As an ethicist, Stackhouse was also concerned with the consequences of such beliefs for the larger social and cultural realm. Part of the glory and the agony of world Christianity is that Christianity was unable completely to Christianize its environment, allowing the powers and principalities to use Christian language for non-Christian purposes.

In other words, the current global situation of the church is very similar to the situation faced by the church in the ancient Roman Empire. In Rome, the church confronted a developed culture that had made great advances in philosophy, science, and hermeneutics with a well-developed religious system that was a serious alternative to the church. What the apologists did (and early church theologians did in general) was to so penetrate this culture that they were able to bring their truth to bear on it and able to use it to clarify their own truth.[95] This formed the basis of a religion that

---

90. Ibid., 139.

91. The purpose of the discussion of a basic issue was, we must remind ourselves, not to resolve the issue but to cast light on it.

92. Stackhouse et al., *Apologia*, 147.

93. Ibid., 150–51.

94. Ibid., 7.

95. See Cochrane, *Christianity and Classical Culture*.

"attempted to give inner coherence to one of the most complex, cosmopolitan civilizations that the world has known. And it almost succeeded."[96] Stackhouse believes that we are in a

> new cosmopolitan age, one significantly different in scope and complexity than Christianity has ever met before. Christianity now faces world religions that are deeper, richer, and broader than any that it has previously encountered (or developed). Further, Christianity now confronts cultures and civilizations which have also developed complex systems of philosophy, law, technology, and science that have been—in shaping people's minds, societies, and natural environments—as powerful and pervasive as any in world history.[97]

The image of the "new cosmopolitan age" is subtly, but very importantly, different from other images of globalization. A cosmopolitan age is one in which diverse people met in common sites, have common tasks, and share a common good. Just as Paul could not avoid the Gentiles once he stepped out of Damascus, so modern Christians confront the world's cultures throughout their experience: at work, in school, in politics, and even in charities. This cosmopolitan experience may be like that of ancient Rome, somewhat lumpy, with people retaining aspects of their traditional cultures and religions in a variety of settings, but that does not rob it of its reality. Nor does it rob it of its power to draw others into its orb. Just as one day's German barbarian was the next day's compiler of Latin dictionaries, so the new cosmopolitan world draws people into its values, positive and negative.[98]

Stackhouse believed that every human culture, no matter how apparently secularized, has a religious core that shares and occasionally misshapes its inner life. This religious core underlies such fundamental activities as economics, justice, art, and education. Much of the confusion between people in today's world results from the failure of people to realize that these religious foundations have continuing influence. Banking, for example, has very different meanings in Islamic cultures just as human rights have different political and social meanings in the East and West. In an article in *Theological Education*, Stackhouse wrote:

> A complex set of questions must be asked in regard, at least, to the great, civilization-forming religions—Hinduism, Buddhism, Confucianism, Islam, and likely some Tribal traditions—for they have already long engaged the powers, thrones, and authorities, and have come to arrangements with them. Because no enduring civilization has ever developed without a dominant religion at its core, it is unlikely that a global society can develop in creative directions without one. But it makes a great difference which religion becomes dominant, how it does so, and how it treats other traditions. Today, the commonly

---

96. Stackhouse et al., *Apologia*, 155.
97. Ibid., 160.
98. Ibid., 160. See Stackhouse, *Ethics and the Urban Ethos*.

accepted study of religions is "non-theological" and "non-evaluative," yet one of the tasks of theological ethics in our era will surely be to seek to identify the valid and the non-valid forms of religious belief and practice not only within the Christian tradition but in the world religions, specifically as they shape the spheres and institutions of the common life. How to do so is one of the greatest issues of our time.[99]

The new cosmopolitan world will also have religious foundations that sustain its common life. Stackhouse frequently used the image of powers and principalities to describe these influences. As the new global culture forms, the powers and principalities that will shape it have also gradually acquired power. Stackhouse has done more than stand Marx on his head. He knows that ideologies have deep social and economic roots and that these can and do distort human life. Yet, religion is not only ideology. As societies form, their cultural life reflects the struggle within and between the various powers and principalities that determine its common life. If so, then the most serious sin is idolatry, the putting of something less than God in God's place. In his 2007 restatement of this theme, Stackhouse developed the idea of "sphere sovereignty" as an elaboration of his position.

How then can theological education participate in the shaping of this coming global world? This is where Stackhouse's root metaphor of an *apologia* comes to the fore. Although religion has many aspects, including piety, ministry, and mission, the one that is more involved with education is teaching or doctrine. Of course, he realizes that critics can attack this position from a variety of positions, but he feels that without certain fundamental truth claims, the church cannot morally participate in the public arena, much less seek to spread its message to others. The four foundational doctrines, as Stackhouse sees them, are sin and salvation, biblical revelation, the Trinity, and Christology. Theology seeks to make the case that these teachings are warranted and worthy of acceptance. In his discussion of the Bible, Stackhouse gives one picture of how this model relates to the current discussion among the world's religions:

> It could be argued that the ways in which biblical authors drew on, recast, and transformed material that derived from Egyptian, Babylonian, Greek, and other sources provide the normative model of how authentic interaction takes place between truly inspired religious traditions rooted in the knowledge of the true God and the significant wisdoms of the world.[100]

Schools, of course, are the primary place where such cultural exchanges take place and flourish.

To their treatment of globalization as an issue Stackhouse and Schreiter brought considerable theological skill. They demonstrated that the new global order in religion and education offered new and creative ways to conceive the task of theological

---

99. Stackhouse, "Globalization, Faith, and Theological Education," 75.
100. Stackhouse et al., *Apologia,* 176.

education and suggested creative directions that the discussion might take in the future. If much of the basic-issues discussion revolved around the vexing issue of what makes theological education theological, they offered a vision of how theological education might be theological on a global stage. As the strength of global Christianity became more evident after 2000, their suggestions have even more relevance.

The Theology of World Religions:

Another feature of the discussion of globalization as an issue, noted in both Schreiter and Stackhouse, was the relationship between Christianity and other world religions. Although seminaries continued to offer courses in world religions, usually as an elective, the study of the world's religious traditions was part of the bread-and-butter offerings of religion departments. Often modeled on other courses in the liberal arts, the history-of-religion course featured a general historical approach with some attention paid to significant texts. In this sense, it fit the general liberal-arts paradigm, and religion was frequently accepted as part of the humanities requirement. The expanding graduate departments of religion often taught this approach to the study of religion, although anthropologists and ethnographers added significantly to their work. Only a handful of seminaries, including the divinity schools of Harvard and Chicago, insisted that knowledge of another religion was essential to Christian ministry. This approach to world religions was primarily phenomenological. Religions were part of the world that a scholar might describe in much the same way as any other aspect of human culture.

The discussion of globalization, however, was primarily concerned with the theological questions posed by world religions, especially among Mainstream and liberal Christians. By the 1980s, the problem was attracting the attention of many serious theologians, including John Cobb, Mark Heim, Paul Knitter, Max Stackhouse, and others.[101] The question was also of practical import. Congregational members increasingly asked ministers to perform multireligious rites of passage, especially marriages, and to offer solace to members of multireligious families at funerals. The increasing globalization of business also meant that American business representatives abroad had to deal sensitively with the religious customs and practices of their non-American partners.

Ironically, this aspect of globalization received less formal attention from theological educators. Although writers on globalization treated other religions, so to speak, through the back door of enculturation or contextualization, the general approach to globalization, especially among the Mainstream, was through liberation theologies. Yet, time may show that the question of other religions was the most important issue

---

101. For examples, see Cobb, *Beyond Dialogue*; Hick, *God Has Many Names*; Hick and Knitter, *The Myth of Christian Uniqueness*; Knitter, *No Other Name?*; Sanders, *What about Those Who Have Never Heard?*; Smith, *Religious Diversity*.

facing seminaries as they learned to live in a religiously plural world.[102] As often in the discussion of theological education, irony abounded here. In Africa, ministerial students often attended universities that included Islamic studies and traditional African religions in their theology departments. Something similar was true in Asian universities as well. Yet American schools rarely considered combining instruction for other religion's leaders among their goals and purposes. Hartford was, of course, the great exception.[103] A few tentative beginnings in this direction exist in California. The Graduate Theological Union has some affiliates devoted to non-Western religions, and Claremont proposed in 2010 to work toward the building of a theological university. But, by and large, it is unexplored territory.

Globalization as an Accrediting Standard

The rich discussion of globalization as an issue in theological education gave way to different types of discussion and action after 1986, particularly, in the Association of Theological Schools. During the 1980s, the ATS was increasingly becoming a three-pronged agency: a professional association for theological education, especially for presidents and deans; an organization for the serious discussion of theological education; and an accrediting agency. Institutionally, the legal separation of the work of the Accrediting Commission from the other work of the agency marked a formal recognition of the way that the association developed. While these three activities are closely related, success in one area does not necessarily mean success across the board.

Don Browning and the Fourfold Meaning of Globalization

The event that more than any other contributed to globalization as a standard was the 1986 address of Don Browning at the ATS biennial meeting.[104] Browning was a leading

---

102. My own sense was that Mainstream liberal theology was so reified that it could not take much world theology seriously. There was no liberal experiment as daring as the signs-and-wonders theology that developed at Fuller. The Signs and Wonders course took seriously missionary reports of the demonic powers at work among the people with whom missionaries worked, and it sought to develop a Christian demonology in response. Although Fuller's leadership for good reasons ended the Signs and Wonders course and distanced the school from much Third-Wave charismatic thought, one wonders whether charismatic and Pentecostal theology did not represent a theological entry into a global religious experience far different from anything the global theologians envisioned. The question of the ancestors in Korean and Native American culture and religion is another area where the need to speak theologically is part of a global apprehension of Christianity.

103. For Africa, see Oduyoye, "Contextualization." Interestingly, Claremont proposed such a model of a theological university in 2011, hoping to offer training for Jewish and Islamic students. The Graduate Theological Union has three centers providing graduate work for the leadership of non-Christian religions: the Asian Center, the Islamic Center, and the Richard Dinner Center for Jewish Studies.

104. Browning, "Globalization and the Task of Theological Education." I base my claims about the importance of this speech on the large number of people who subsequently cited it and on the article's

participant in the larger discussion of what made theological education theological, as well as a major contributor to the reinterpretation of practical theology.[105] He argued that the practical theologian was a scholar who enabled the church and the public to see the options before them, should they elect to follow a definite path on a specific issue. His 1986 address was an example of just how valuable such practical theology might be.[106] As Browning saw the globalization discussion, there were at least four components of the larger discussion:

> For some, globalization means the church's universal mission to evangelize the world, i.e., to take the message of the gospel to all people, all nations, all cultures, and all religious faiths. Second, there is the idea of globalization as ecumenical cooperation between the various manifestations of the Christian church throughout the world. This includes a growing mutuality and equality between churches in First and Third World countries. It involves a new openness to and respect for the great variety of local theologies that are springing up within the church in its various concrete situations. Third, globalization sometimes refers to the dialogue between Christianity and other religions. Finally, globalization refers to the mission of the church to the world, not only to convert and to evangelize, but to improve and develop the lives of the millions of poor, starving, and politically disadvantaged people.[107]

These distinctions named the disagreements between members of ATS.[108] The Evangelicals clearly supported the first two of the above. Many Evangelical schools had separate schools of foreign missions, including Fuller's School of World Missions, Asbury's E. Stanley Jones School of World Missions and Evangelism, and Southwest-

clarity. While people responded to the speech when it was delivered, especially in the extension of the mandate on globalization, it did unleash a wave of enthusiastic assent among those present. ATS meetings can never be confused with revivals.

105. See below.

106. Determining the importance of addresses at ATS meetings is difficult. My own sense (as well as the memory of others who were there) is that the address was not greeted with extraordinary enthusiasm. However, it was cited by almost everyone who did subsequent work on globalization.

107. Browning, "Globalization and the Task," 15.

108. Heim, "Mapping Globalization" suggested that each of Browning's types could be further subdivided as much as it was something in its own right.

> To get some idea of the full range of approaches to globalization we need to cross-cut Browning's definitions with another set of variables relating to social analysis. All views of globalization express or imply some kind of social analysis. There are clearly many varieties of such analysis, including ones primarily oriented toward a culture's symbols and images (*symbolic* varieties); other types of analysis directed at intellectual systems and convictions (*philosophical* varieties); still others focused on a culture's functional structures for maintaining identity and meaning or legitimating authority (*functional* varieties); yet others attending to the economic conditions for the culture's organization (*economic* varieties); and those which take up the organization of power (*psychic* varieties). These five sets of approaches may be applied within any of the four categories we have reviewed (14).

ern's Roy Fish School of Evangelism and Missions. Although such schools were the most visible sign of Evangelical global interest, all evangelical schools invested heavily in the education of people for service abroad. While the ecumenical dimensions of evangelicalism are easily overlooked, Evangelical missions, at home and abroad, were often interdenominational, and the various groups involved in the Lausanne movement even more markedly so. In contrast, such Mainstream leaders as Lesher and Shriver, who headed up the Taskforce on Globalization, leaned heavily towards the second and fourth meanings of globalization. In contrast to the Evangelical view, their interpretation of *ecumenical* tended to support the federative model of the National and, particularly, the World Council of Churches. If Evangelical ecumenism stressed practical cooperation on the field, Mainstream ecumenism responded to the social and political activism found in liberation theologies.

Browning's analysis suggested that ATS could go forward with globalization despite the ambiguities in the basic understanding of the term. The association selected a new Task Force on Globalization and charged it with the task of designing a globalization standard that would be part of the accreditation standards. ATS adopted the standard in 1990, and when the association redeveloped the standards later in that decade, the new document mandated globalization as part of each separate standard. Currently, the amended form of the standards uses the language of global perspective. An additional action, originally moved by Orlando Costas of Andover Newton, clearly reflected a movement among theological educators toward the global future: the ATS was to mandate globalization as its principal emphasis during the decade of the 1990s. In addition to other events and publications, ATS held two important consultations: the Consultation on Globalization and the Classical Theological Disciplines in March 1992, and the Consultation on Globalization and the Practical Theological Disciplines in March 1993.

One consequence of the action was a concern on the part of schools to develop ways to provide their students with an experience in another culture. The educational consultant firm Plowshares, headed by Robert and Alice Evans, was an important partner in this endeavor. Aided by a two-million-dollar grant from the Pew Charitable Trust, Plowshares established the Pilot Immersion Project to work with a limited number of seminaries.[109] The Evanses had extensive contacts both in theological education, where they had served as leaders in the case-study movement, and in worldwide Christianity. The immersions that they arranged brought together representatives of different schools on a common site, allowing the diverse interests of the participants to inform each other. Other schools arranged immersion-type experiences, often using the contacts provided by their sponsoring denominations. Immersion education was not new. The East Harlem Protestant Parish, headed by George W. (Bill) Webber

---

109. King and Pacala, "Patterns of Globalization."

was an important precedent, as was the more recent Appalachian Ministries Educational Resource Center, founded in 1985.[110]

This type of education was not new. American theologians, especially in the biblical disciplines, had earlier made an almost mandatory pilgrimage to Germany or England, and study in a European university was a popular faculty sabbatical project. What made the new emphasis significant was the focus on firsthand experience of the Two-Thirds World or its equivalents in the United States.

Many critics saw this type of short-term exchange as theological tourism or even as convincing people that they understood other cultures more accurately than they did. In some cases, these criticisms may have been warranted. Authors have used the well-intentioned but bumbling American abroad as a stock character at least since Mark Twain's *Innocents Abroad*. The popular tours of the Holy Land, promising a new understanding of the Bible, if one "walks where Jesus walked" often more enrich their leaders than their participants. Yet granting all the limitations, the immersion's combination of observation, personal relationships, and—especially in those immersions that took place within the United States—active service were often transformative. If neither individuals nor institutions changed as much one might have hoped, they did change, and that change potentially improved instruction.[111]

Globalization's impact on the curricula of theological schools is harder to measure. Throughout the 1990s and 2000s, administrations pressured faculty to include resources from a variety of underrepresented constituencies as well as from the worldwide church. In the best of times, no single faculty member had the training or leisure to incorporate all those demands into their classes. These were not, however, the best of times. Even many prominent schools had to adjust to an increasingly part-time student body that had less time to devote to study and whose ability to travel was often limited by commitments to full-time jobs. Immersion-style education might have fit more easily into earlier patterns of seminary study where students attended classes full time and had only minor part-time work commitments. The schools also faced increasing competition from alternative forms of theological education that required even less class time and that used and provided fewer library resources. In a world where every enrollment is precious, administrations found it harder to build support for expensive, time-intensive programs.

Globalization also exerted considerable pressure on seminary libraries.[112] In part, the problem was the sheer mass of material and the variety of languages in which it appeared. Even with English functioning as a new *lingua franca* for some theological work, the number of non-European publications increased geometrically. Many of

---

110. Thistlethwaite and Cairns, *Beyond Theological Tourism*.

111 At Bangor we were able to send three faculty members on an extended immersion to Indonesia using contacts provided by the UCC. It was a crucial experience for all who were able to participate in it, and it did increase awareness of the Two-Thirds World on our campus.

112. Smalley, "Librarians and Archivists"; Reid, "Acquiring Materials."

these sources, furthermore, appeared primarily in fragile formats: on cheaper papers and with less-permanent inks. Important theological sources might also appear in media that were not long lasting, such as photocopying. Only large libraries with links to other large libraries, especially thorough interlibrary loan, could hope to have even a token collection, not to mention the extensive resources needed for serious research.

Perhaps the judgment that we ought to pass on globalization as a standard was that it was too expensive for more than a handful of schools to implement. Most schools, faced with internal financial problems, even in the comparatively prosperous 1990s, could not implement the standard, and many found that they had to resort to evasions and halfway measures. The silver lining in this cloud was that schools faced with the vast expenses of operating internationally discovered the global in their own neighborhoods. A growing awareness of the diversity of American communities was an important by-product of the globalization movement. The neighborhood was a less expensive alternative to study abroad, and readily available for placements. Further, ethnic students required less aid than students from abroad did.

The World Conference of Associations of Theological Institutions

Perhaps the most important consequence of the globalization movement was the establishment of the World Conference of Associations of Theological Institutions. The 1986 meeting of the Association of Theological Schools adopted a resolution that called on ATS to establish closer relationships with other theological institutions in the world. As Leon Pacala noted, ATS had not been significantly involved with the WCC, in part because the denominations and parachurch bodies that sponsored many ATS seminaries were not part of the WCC and in some cases hostile to it.[113] The new initiative permitted ATS to enter into a closer, although still informal, relationship with the WCC and its Program for Theological Education. In 1987, representatives of fifteen different theological associations met at Singapore and passed a resolution, introduced by Leon Pacala, to investigate the feasibility of a new world body. Two years later (in 1989), the World Conference was established at a meeting at Yogyakarta, with sixteen charter members. Significantly, representatives of the WCC, the Vatican, and various Orthodox bodies participated in the meeting. ATS, using its contacts with American foundations, provided much of the financing for the new organization. The new organization, called the World Conference of Theological Institutions, met in conjunction with the ATS biennial meeting in 1992. Two of the principal early officers, Leon Pacata, vice president, and Barbara Brown Zikmund, secretary-treasurer, were important ATS leaders. Barbara Brown Zikmund later served as president of the organization. Like Pacala, Zikmund, the president of Hartford Seminary Foundation, was an enthusiastic supporter of international theological education. Significantly,

---

113. Pacala, *The Role of ATS*, 61.

she was the president of the one of the few seminaries that was genuinely religiously pluralistic, having one of the finest Islamic programs in the country.[114]

Leon Pacala wrote the constitution of the new body using the ATS constitution as his model:

> Much of the organizational structure and purpose of WOCATI are patterned after ATS, the effectiveness and benefits of which have been confirmed by the lengthening history of the Association. As the author of the draft constitution for WOCATI, I was convinced that no small part of the organizational nature and experience of ATS was applicable at the world level and modeled much of the World Conference according to ATS structures and relations with such inclusive organizations as the Council on Postsecondary Accreditation.[115]

Pacala went on to say:

> In many respects, WOCATI is an invention of ATS. It provided the initiatives, unrelenting advocacy, the leadership, all but ten per cent of the financial resources, and much of the supporting staff required to inaugurate and sustain the Conference from the time of its inception.[116]

Yet, the new organization was not ATS on a global scale. Perhaps the most significant difference is that WOCATI is neither an accrediting organization nor an organization that somehow accredits theological-accreditation agencies. Although WOCATI has been an valuable help to theological educators in the United States and Europe trying to understand the various degrees granted by non-American and European schools, WOCATI does not define the standards for those degrees. In this sense, WOCATI has primarily followed the ATS model as a location for serious discussion and as an equipper of leadership. This gives the organization a freedom that it might not have, were it more closely connected to the governance processes of the schools or the various national educational agencies. Interestingly, ATS was itself encouraged to separate legally its advocacy and accreditation funds and did so. WOCATI is ATS without the Commission on Accrediting.

WOCATI's greatest service to American theological education may lie in the future. American religion, especially American Mainstream Protestantism, is changing

---

114. The Hartford program developed out of the old Kennedy School of Missions which had the most important center for the study of Islam in the United States and published an influential journal. However, more by evolution than by design, the program began to train people for leadership in various American Islamic communities. Some of those who enrolled wanted to learn the Arabic needed to lead worship, others wanted to run Islamic centers at universities. One must be careful not to equate Imams with Protestant or Catholic clergy, although some Islamic communities seem to be moving in that direction. Islam is a much more "lay" movement with different people, including political leaders, having different roles in the community. I tried to capture both the comprehensiveness and the continued scholarly relevance in the phrase "Islamic studies."

115. Ibid., 62.

116. Ibid.

rapidly, and these changes may require substantial changes in how the United States educates its ministers. While the US will continue, at least in all probability, to require many fully credentialed pastors, finances may force many congregations to hire people with very different qualifications. Just as America provided much of the world with the model of the graduate theological seminary, so the rest of the world may provide American Christians with fresh understandings and strategies of how to train their ministry.

7 Under the Hood
A New Professional Model

THERE ARE NO EASY chronological lines in the history of theological education. Earlier chapters noted that the struggles over race, feminism, and ethnicity continued into the 1990s and 2000s. Likewise, the great debate over the theological nature of theological education continued in the early 1990s, especially in the discussion of David Kelsey's work, although much less so after the turn of the century. Yet, we can see the two decades after 1990 as bringing some long-range changes into greater prominence and starting some new and important trends. The revolution in theological management, begun in the late 1970s, came to its fruition with larger and more complex management teams. Shared governance matured and established patterns of accountability. Accreditation standards increasingly shifted focus from an emphasis on resources to assessment and evaluation. The technological revolution revamped first seminary libraries and their procedures, then entered into the classroom, and in some instances, replaced the classroom. Theological educators developed an interest in teaching and its improvement. Residential study, at least in the classic sense, gave way in many schools to part-time commuter study. An emphasis on multiculturalism replaced the older emphasis on minorities (underrepresented constituencies); and the debate over the ordination of homosexual persons moved to center stage. In short, seminaries were very different institutions in 2010 than they were in 1990.

The ecclesiastical context of theological education was also in flux. The decline of the Mainstream accelerated, and their membership aged significantly. The evangelical revival of the late twentieth century weakened and in some Evangelical churches, including the Southern Baptists, may have ended or reversed. Although Catholics generally did better than Mainstream Protestants in retaining membership, apart from newer immigrants, American Catholicism also experienced declining membership, attendance, and vocations. The most growing religious demographic was those who had no religious preference, the so-called nones. These changes affected theological schools singularly and as a group. New theological schools were often Evangelical or moderate.[1] By 2010, Evangelical seminaries enrolled twice as many students as Mainstream schools, and the largest seminaries were firmly in the Evangelical camp. Significantly, many of these schools rejected the older, free-standing model of the seminary and embedded themselves in Christian colleges and other educational institutions.[2]

FOLLOW THE MONEY

Almost from the beginning, American seminaries were—with few exceptions—small institutions with limited resources. This means that they are unusually responsive to changes in the larger national economy. In the 1960s through the early 1980s, they suffered from the stagflation that accompanied and followed the Vietnam War. A period of relative prosperity followed, especially during the Clinton years, only to be shaken by the dot-com crisis and then by 9/11. After a slow and painful recovery, the recession of 2007 shook them again. At the same time, denominational financial support for the schools declined steadily, even among denominations like the Lutherans, who have a long history of strong support for theological education.

Among the few schools that partially avoided this cycle of boom and bust was Princeton Seminary, the flagship of the Presbyterian Church. In 1960, few might have chosen Princeton as a financial leader among American seminaries, although its endowment was respectable. Under the leadership of President James I. McCord (1959–1983) and Trustee John M. Templeton, the school flourished. Beginning with only eighteen million dollars, the endowment stood at three hundred fifty million dollars when Templeton left the Board in 1988. At its peak, Princeton's endowment reached a billion dollars.[3]

---

1. The Divinity School of Wake Forest University was a major exception. Despite its ecclesiastical location, the school was clearly in the Mainstream, even liberal, camp.

2. ATS's willingness to accept this model was perhaps the most evident result of the SBC controversy. The Association had earlier worked to end some influential Conservative seminaries' links with colleges, including the links between Eastern and Eastern College, Northern and Judson, and Gordon College and Gordon Seminary. This was one of the quiet revolutions that followed the 1980s explosions.

3. Gillespie, "The Seminary President." In addition to skillful fundraising, Princeton developed an artful administration that included very able financial people. The heart of the school's success, however, was the combination of fundraising and investment done by McCord and Templeton.

Organizing for Funding

By 1975, Robert W. Lynn, vice president of Lilly Endowment, recognized that seminary finance needed a fundamental overhaul. Lynn's strategy involved three central components of seminary life: development officers, seminary presidents, and trustees. These were the three foundations of a new order of seminary finance. Changes in how these three types of leader function had profound effects on the structure of the schools overall.

The establishment and encouragement of development offices was a key part of this strategy. Even with the addition of a director or a vice president in charge of development, the development office was a complicated affair. Erskine Clarke gave this description in his account of the seminary presidency:

> The increased demands for fundraising . . . meant enlarged development offices: secretaries were needed to handle expanding mailing lists, directors of seminary publications began to be employed, and more development officers were needed to write funding proposals, meet with prospective donors, and maintain cordial relationships with alumni/alumnae.[4]

The relatively small size of theological schools and their limited budgets meant that most seminaries could not hire people with established records in fundraising, and, hence, that seminary development officers needed both continued training and continued colleague support. In addition to grants to individual schools for development work, Lynn and Fred Hofheinz[5] worked with ATS to establish a professional network of seminary development officers, who met face-to-face once a year, and kept in touch with each other by newsletter and later by e-mail. The Development and Institutional Advancement Program (DIAP), the oldest ATS program for administrators, was a direct result of their work. The structure of the DIAP was to become a familiar pattern in training new seminary administrators: meetings, conversations, and exchange between members.

Presidents, Chief Financial Officers, and Deans

The history of the seminary presidency is a complicated one. In the period before 1970, the office had almost as many definitions as there were seminaries. In some schools, strong presidents, such as Henry Pitney Van Dusen of Union, John MacKay of Princeton, or Duke McCall of Southern, almost personified their institutions and imposed their own stamp on almost every aspect of their school's life. In others, the president was little more than a figurehead. The corporate memory of many

---

4. Clarke, "The President as Administrator," 35.
5. Hofheinz also worked with the Lilly Endowment. One of his areas of special knowledge was seminary finances and development.

seminaries had a golden age, when the faculty directed the school according to more pristine academic principles.[6] This memory was inaccurate; earlier seminary faculties rarely had the free range that their successors supposed. In fact, faculty gained power in the 1960s, especially over faculty appointments and the academic program. Yet the unrest of that decade exposed both the weakness and the necessity for a further development of the presidential office. Cries for shared governance, a constant feature of the last fifty years, weakened the president's role, particularly in schools that had had strong presidents, while the increasing need for money, students, and financial support made the president's office even more central.[7]

Perhaps because of the influence of Warren Deem, the first major attempt to reform the seminary presidency took the shape of management training. One constant in seminary history is that presidents tend to come to their office with little preparation for their new employment.[8] The Association of Theological Schools, working with funding and advice from Robert W. Lynn and the Lilly Endowment, enlisted the Riverside Group, a continuing education of the Columbia University Graduate School of Management, to establish a summer program, the Warren Deem Institute for Theological Education Management. In some ways, the program was similar to a program in the Harvard University Graduate School of Education that worked with newly appointed deans and presidents of colleges. What distinguished the Warren Deem Institute approach from other such programs were two emphases. First, the Warren Deem Institute adjusted management theory and educational best practices to the realities of small institutions with limited staff. Second, the Institute stressed the importance of theological reflection on the seminaries' unique mission as part of the work of seminary leaders. Despite these modifications, the program centered on such classical approaches to management as cost accounting, financial and particularly strategic planning, marketing, and computer skills. By 1990, over one-fourth of ATS seminary presidents had completed the program. Yet the number of seminary presidents attending the program declined steadily; other seminary officers, particularly financial officers, became more numerous.

The gradual decline in the percentage of presidents attending the Institute was the major reason for the discontinuation of the program. At the time, people offered a variety of reasons for this drop. The Lilly grant that financed the program required that it become self-supporting, and the cost gradually rose to six thousand dollars a session. For schools that had to watch every penny, this was a major burden. Further—or so Leon Pacala reasoned—many presidents felt that they could not afford the

---

6. Interestingly, this myth was often shared by faculties and administrators. The supposed power of the faculty was, of course, a ready-made excuse for most problems that schools encountered.

7. See chapter 1, above.

8. Wheeler et al., "Leadership That Works," contains some of the best thinking about the office in the early 1990s. See also Pacala, *The Role of ATS*, 114–15.

time away from their busy offices or from needed vacations.[9] Not as noted at the time was the fact that seminary management grew to include highly trained chief financial officers, most of whom had an MBA from a major business school. It was less necessary for the chief executive officers to have similar skills.

While the hiring of a chief financial officer did not take place in all institutions simultaneously, the days were largely over when theological schools as a whole were "Mom-and-Pop" institutions in which a competent but not necessarily sophisticated bookkeeper handled a seminary's finances. Many factors hurried this evolution along. The growing importance of the federal government and the seminaries' expanding dependence on guaranteed student loans was one factor. Another was the increasing role of accrediting associations, especially the regional agencies. Accrediting standards, both ATS and regional, required more sophisticated financial analysis, long-range planning, and improved accounting procedures.

A similar development also occurred in the academic management of the school, particularly in faculty and program development.[10] Although the title of dean goes back to the 1920s, modern academic deans originated gradually in the larger theological schools, such as Princeton, Southern Baptist, Southwestern Baptist, and Hartford, as those schools became larger and more academically complex. Beginning in the 1980s, the academic work of other seminaries became likewise more complicated. The number of degrees increased and included the Master of Divinity, one or more Master of Arts programs, additional specialized master's programs, a Doctor of Ministry, and some research-oriented degrees. The faculty was also more self-consciously professional and deeply aware of the importance of its own academic standards and their maintenance.[11] Even scheduling, long a simple matter of matching hours to professors, became more complicated as one-hour classes gave way in many schools to three-hour blocks, weekend courses, extension classes, and summer work. Since many schools had multiple deans, the traditional academic dean became the chief academic officer—and in some schools, the vice president for academic affairs. Although the presidents retained considerable structural authority over the academic programs of their institutions, including the formal right of nomination and the right of recommendation for promotion, the day-by-day work passed *de facto* to the academic dean, who directed the increasingly complex processes on which hiring and promotion rested.

---

9. Pacala, *The Role of ATS*, 115.

10. Lynn, "Living on Two Levels"; Ferris, "The Work of a Dean."

11. The phrase *academic guilds* is a loose one that occurs frequently in the literature of theological education. At its best, the phrase describes the advancing professionalization of American scholarship. Common standards and modes of thought do characterize various fields of study, and scholars naturally try to have their work measured by those standards. Yet, the phrase is very misleading when applied to theological disciplines. Few professional organizations elect their members, and almost none expel them. They have no recognized input into decisions about tenure, rank, promotion, or salary.

The development of the chief financial officer and the chief academic officer was fundamental to the further development of the presidency. Freed from many routine administrative tasks, the president was able to concentrate on the two most difficult parts of a very complicated position: fundraising and institutional vision and direction. These two were intimately connected. The president's capacity to create a vision for the school often determined the president's ability to raise funds; and conversely, the capacity of a president to articulate a viable vision often rested on that person's ability to raise funds. Writing in 2010, Barbara Wheeler and her coauthors noted:

> Auburn's research also shows that fundraising for theological schools is president-dependent. Development officers raise millions on their own for colleges and universities. This is not the case in theological education: few big gifts are made to seminaries unless the president is personally involved in seeking them.[12]

Visioning and fundraising were two sides of the same coin: defining the school and its supporting publics. David Allan Hubbard's work on Fuller's 1983 programmatic statement, "The Mission Beyond the Mission," combined theological acuity, simple and direct language, and institutional direction. While providing direction for the school as a whole, the "Mission Beyond the Mission" invited those who caught the vision to join the school as it journeyed to its future.

The president's tasks included working with major givers. But the president's work in fundraising and vision directly related to the various endowments and foundations that supported theological education. Although other officers did much of the work of grant writing and information gathering (the grunt work necessary for a sound grant proposal), the success of the proposal rested on the vision of the chief executive officer, on that person's success in marshaling resources to accomplish institutional goals. Some of the more able presidents of the 1990s and 2000s made foundation work almost an art. Gordon-Conwell's Robert Cooley, Washington Theological Union's Vincent Cushing, Bangor's Malcolm Warford, and Fuller's David Allan Hubbard were masters of the craft.[13]

There were other changes in the presidency that moved it beyond the office envisioned by the Warren Deem Institute. It is helpful to distinguish two aspects of the seminary presidency after the 1980s: the president's job and the president's role in governance. The president's job—what a president does day by day—increasingly shifted toward fundraising and envisioning. The president was the one who had the daily task of taking care of the institution's heritage and future. The president did much of this work, almost necessarily, off campus and on the road. At the same time,

---

12. Wheeler et al., "Leadership That Works."

13. The purpose of the Mission within the Mission was not only or even primarily grant writing, of course. My own claim at this point is only that this document had considerable value with those who made grants

presidents had an important place in their seminary's governance. For want of a better description, governance is the way people exert authority in the seminary structure, especially over matters of policy. It may include the formal (more than the administrative) aspects of faculty employment, especially tenure-track appointments and the conveying of tenure,[14] the budget, and the capacity to expend funds.

Crises test patterns and habits of governance. The unrest of the 1960s, for example, resulted in demands for shared governance. In many ways, the schools spent the next fifty years working out what this meant in practice. The schools were too diverse for any one pattern to fit all. To give only the most obvious variation, the bishop or ordinary under canon law owned and operated the diocesan seminary, and various religious superiors had roles, including formal ownership, in the governance of other Catholic schools. Even a school like St. Meinrad's, a Benedictine monastery, had to define formal and informal roles for the bishops, who provided the bulk of its student body. University- and college-related Protestant and Catholic seminaries provide yet another basic variation in governance. In these schools, the chief executive officer of the theological school is part of a larger bureaucracy under the university president. The chief executive officer is one of many deans who participates in a council of similar officers under the direction of a vice president or provost. While some divinity-school deans, such as Thomas Langford of Duke, had considerable influence in the overall direction of their universities, most did not.

In considering the evolving role of the president in governance, the Reformed concept of an office might be useful. An office exists somewhat independent of its occupant and somewhat independent of the work of the occupant. What is essential to the functioning of the church is that someone holds the office and fulfills its constitutionally mandated functions. The elder of a congregation might do many things—counseling, visiting, administration, education, and so forth—but the office of the elder is to provide the specific ministry of Word and Sacrament. The elder wears the sign of office, the stole, only when performing these specifically mandated tasks. Of course, particular people hold different offices, and their individual talents and personalities affect their performance. Some people are good at what they do, others not so much.

The president is the keystone in the various systems of shared governance. On the one hand, the president directly relates to the board that elects him or her. The president serves at the board's pleasure. Since most seminaries are public, nonprofit corporations, the Board holds title to the school and its property "in trust" for its various publics and particularly for those who have financially supported the school. As part of its responsibility for the institution, the board evaluates the president. The president reports to the board on the institution's performance, and, at least ideally,

---

14. Generally speaking, non-tenure-track appointments and part-time appointments are *de facto* made by the Chief Academic Officer. In schools without tenure but with long-term contracts, the long-term contracts are customarily approved by the school's governance structures.

helps them in their evaluation of that performance. Whether *de facto* or *ex officio*, the president has the power of the agenda and sets the tone and the direction of the board. The president ordinarily presents the budget, or another officer presents it in the president's name. Although the law often confines the right to name its successors to the board of trustees, the president makes important input into this process, and new board members are often de facto presidential appointments.[15] The president also is usually present at meetings of the board's executive committee and often is an *ex officio* member of that committee. The president and board thus share with each other the authority for the ordering of the school. The president is, then, responsible for supporting the board and its decisions with the other components of seminary governance. In other words, the president mediates the will of the trustees, legally ultimate, with faculty and other publics.

In a similar way, the president shares authority with the faculty. Shared governance assumes that the faculty will have proximate authority to set or recommend academic policies, including requirements for degrees, to determine the curriculum, and to nominate its successors. The faculty customarily has authority to recommend tenure to the president and through the president to the board. In many schools, the faculty recommends students for graduation. Faculty and board share the authority for policies governing the faculty. Faculty members are usually understood to have a stake in the overall management of the school, and their representative often sits with the board or its academic committee. In some cases, a faculty member is actually a member of the board. Again, the president's role is ideally and often actually to mediate between the two principal sources of academic policy: the board and the faculty.

The president's role as the mediator includes far more than faculty and board. Although some schools have student representatives on the board and at faculty meetings, the president is usually the one who mediates student concerns to the faculty, administration, and, if necessary, to the board. In most schools, students have some representation on search committees and in tenure or retention committees. In addition to the mediator to students, the president also serves as the mediator between the school and its ecclesiastical sponsor or publics. Just as the president represents the faculty to the board and the board to the faculty, so the president represents the school to its ecclesiastical sponsors or publics, and those sponsors and publics to the school. In some cases, various presidents have come to embody the ecclesiastical persona of their institutions.

The president's relationship to other administrators is somewhat different. Most schools assume that the president is the chief executive officer and that the administrators of the school report to the president. Like any good senior administrator, the president often carries out a twofold assignment: to find effective people to accomplish

---

15. Consequently, over a relatively short period of time, many board members are friends of the president. This is a problem that most programs of trustee education have sought to correct, but without the effects that those programs hoped to achieve.

the needed task and to see that they have what they need to perform that task. So far, this discussion of the president's role with administration has more to do with the president's job than with the presidential role in shared governance, but the administration also functions as a unit in most schools, with its own identity and its own vision of what the school ought to be. While the president cannot relinquish his role as chief administrator, he is also the voice of the administration with the faculty and with the board. The president's role is to see that the process of the formation of academic and financial policy includes the voice of the school's administrators.

A useful metaphor for the president's role in governance is conversation. The president is the one who talks with everyone about the matters most important to them and sees that other conversations reflect those diverse points of view. Thomas Gillespie's image of a person playing six simultaneous chess games against different opponents is apt. Although there is much discussion of shared governance in larger institutions, its implementation in seminaries and divinity schools differs from its implementation elsewhere. For one thing, most seminaries are small enough for conversation and exchange to play a major role in setting policy. Perhaps more important, most seminary presidents have either served congregations as pastors or have been active in church work on a variety of levels. Successful seminary shared governance depends on pastoral leadership skills, including the prime skill of patience, and on the art of consensus building.[16] At least as long as they are relatively small institutions, the intensely personal role of the president in shared governance will be a reflection of the seminary's character as a Christian community as much as of bureaucratic structures.

The patterns of education and training provided presidents after the close of the Warren Deem Institute reflected these complex, changing realties. At the heart of the various studies and evaluations of seminary presidents, certain themes emerged. Perhaps the most important was that one learned the job only by confronting its problems. Thus, Robert Cooley of Gordon-Conwell, widely acknowledged as a successful president, reported that his presidency passed through at least three stages, and other presidents reported a similar shift in their understanding of their positions.[17] In his summary of the experience of presidents, Malcolm Warford also noted their sense of a continually changing landscape that formed and reformed their understanding of the work before them.[18] The response was to try to create and use informal networks where presidents could exchange information and insights. New-president seminars were part of this approach, as were mentoring programs and the publication of studies.

Although the focus of the work of In Trust was on work with boards, this necessitated work with presidents as well. An important way of working with presidents was the development of consultants who could provide public or private advice to presidents. The ATS, In Trust, and the Auburn Center for the Study of Theological

16. Oldenburg, "Reflections of a Pastor/President."
17. Cooley, "Toward Understanding the Seminary Presidency."
18. Warford, "Work and Calling."

Education had important lists of those ready and able to serve. Both Robert Cooley of Gordon-Conwell and Vincent Cushing of the Washington Theological Union had strong reputations as behind-the-scenes advisors and trainers. The ATS and In Trust established programs and networks designed to enable the presidents to become reflective practitioners.

In 2006, the Association of Theological Schools published A *Handbook for Seminary Presidents*.[19] The Lilly Endowment, under the leadership of Craig Dykstra and John Wimmer, financed the project and helped with its conception. The work included articles coauthored by many of the most successful presidents of the last two decades, including Robert Cooley, Louis Weeks, David L. Tiede, Susan Thistlewait, Vincent Cushing, and Richard Mouw—with an advisory committee that included Daniel Aleshire, Cornelius Plantinga, and Barbara Wheeler. The *Handbook* is comprehensive in its scope, covering every aspect of what had become a very complex office, embedded in more or less defined bureaucracies. One of the key phrases used throughout the discussions was "the president's role in," as in "The President's Role in Financial Management." The phrase indicated that the task was assigned primarily to another officers, such as the chief academic officer or the chief financial officer, but that the president brought his or her vision of the whole as an important part of decision making in that area. The president's vision, not his or her expertise, is the basis of the president's super-vision.[20] Clearly, the *Handbook* came after many schools had developed elaborate administrative structures. In addition, the *Handbook* dealt with the unique problems faced by women and representatives of racial and ethnic minorities. One of the most interesting features of the *Handbook* was the special attention that it devoted to the problems of being a chief executive office in a university-related divinity school or a Canadian theological school.[21] Yet, when all the diversity and particular areas of concern are considered, the *Handbook* featured the president as the only individual who had an organic relationship to the various components of the seminary:

> The president is often the only individual who relates to all the constituencies of a school. While this means that the president has the difficult tasks of interpreting the constituencies to one another, and sometimes mediating among them, it also means that the president is the one person in the institution who can share a common story with all constituencies. While this sometimes puts

---

19. Lewis and Weems, *A Handbook for Seminary Presidents*.

20. Thus, "The President's Role in Administration and Personnel Management, the President's Role in Governance, the President's Role in Defining Mission, etc. *Super-vision* is written with a hyphen to emphasize its root meaning as "over-vision" or "view from above."

21. Although Canadian theological education has many features in common with theological education in the United States, the Canadian context is very different. Part of this difference can be seen in the various titles given to chief executive officers (with Dean and Principal often being preferred) and in the Canadian tradition of associating theological schools with universities.

the president in the difficult position of being the person in the middle, it also provides the arena in which leadership is exercised.[22]

While it might be an overstatement to say so, the presidency in less than fifty years moved from an office in which hands-on management was possible to one in which individuals had to lead from the center. One has only to compare a president in the new century with a Henry Van Dusen or a Duke McCall to sense the depth and significance of the change.

Finances drove the development of the new presidency and administration. While these new structures made raising funds and managing resources more efficient and effective, institutions did pay a price for these improvements. By 2010, seminaries were spending between 45 and 55 percent of their income on facilities and administration.[23] Whether this is sustainable over the long run will be determined by the next fifty years of seminary development.

Trustee Development

The third pillar of Lynn's vision of improved funding for seminaries was the trustees, who, like the president, were an essential part of shared government. In many ways, three men, J. Irwin Miller, J. L. Zwingle, and Robert K. Greenleaf, shaped Lynn's understanding of trusteeship. J. Irwin Miller was one of the great post-Rockefeller Christian philanthropists and an active participant in the creation of Christian Theological Seminary in Indianapolis. Miller, sometime vice president and then president of the Cummins Corporation, was an active Disciples of Christ layperson. He was the first lay president of the NCC and one of the architects of that organization's response to the race issue. He also served as an active trustee of the Ford Foundation and of the Yale Corporation. Robert K. Greenleaf had retired from AT&T to found the Center for Applied Ethics, today the Robert K. Greenleaf Center for Applied Ethics, and he wrote a book, *Servant Leadership*, that spelled out his belief that the servant was the incarnation of effective leadership. The relevance of "servant leadership" to the larger issue of trusteeship was almost self-evident. The trustee, a person who stands 'in trust" for another, serves without compensation and without administrative power. Yet the ultimate fate of the institution that the trustee serves is in the hands of just such people. J. L. Zwingle was the former executive director of the Association of Governing Boards of Universities and Colleges. He had resuscitated that organization in the 1960s and understood the social and financial capital that well-positioned trustees could invest to give theological schools the cultural prominence they did not have.

Lynn held a series of seminars on trusteeship and on the future of theological education conducted by himself, occasionally accompanied by Robert K. Greenleaf,

---

22. Aleshire et al., "The President's Vocation and Leadership," 16.
23. E-mail with Aleshire, October 2012.

or John C. Fletcher. Using the bully pulpit provided by his position at Lilly, Lynn urged seminary presidents to take seriously the need for trustee education. These seminars did not take the same form. Some were addresses and discussions conducted during a trustee meeting; others lasted several days and were conducted as a retreat. Despite this diversity of format, some common elements characterized the meetings: the contemporary situation of theological education, the need for the board to use its knowledge of a school's mission and work as the basis for its fiduciary decisions, and the need for the board to act from an awareness of its own leadership potential.

Lilly also worked with the Association of Governing Boards of Colleges and Universities to prepare resources specifically for seminaries. With a grant from Lilly, the AGB provided considerable expertise, including a set of performance standards for board self-evaluation and a sample set of board bylaws. Barbara Taylor of the AGB staff organized a series of meetings for board chairs and seminary presidents led by David Nygren, a Roman Catholic priest and institutional consultant and Malcolm Warford, then president of Bangor Seminary. In addition to the trustee workshops, the AGB published a collection of essays by seminary leaders on governance and trusteeship in 1983, *The Good Steward: A Guide to Theological School Trusteeship*, edited by Joseph C. Gies of the AGB Staff.[24] In subsequent years, the AGB published a monograph on recruiting seminary trustees and another book on trusteeship: *Good Stewardship: A Handbook for Seminary Trustees*.[25] In the early 1990s, Lilly financed a series of weeklong seminars for board chairs and seminary presidents created by Malcolm Warford that included Robert W. Lynn and Christa Klein in the leadership of the seminars.

Although it was less public, the Lilly Endowment made a major contribution to trusteeship among Catholics through the patient work of Fred Hofheinz. Hofheinz recognized that canon law and Catholic custom and tradition required Catholic institutions to adjust the trusteeship system of governance to their canonical status. At times, this meant that particular boards might be formally only advisory, although they had much greater actual power than such language might imply, or that they might have to make specific adjustments to the way that religious orders worked, both singularly and corporately. One of the hopes for Catholic trustees was that they might be able to help the Church adjust its governance to the changing landscape of theological education and find ways for the schools to complement each other's work and not simply duplicate it.[26]

In some ways, the work with Catholic schools evolved in tandem with the work with Protestant institutions. Vincent Cushing decided, after participating in the first of the trustee seminars in Maine led by Lynn, Klein, and Warford, to launch a similar project for Catholic seminary leaders. With the assistance of Lilly and a Catholic

24. The Association of Governing Boards, *The Good Steward*.
25. Taylor and Warford, *Good Stewardship*; Warford, *Recruiting Seminary Trustees*.
26. See Lynn, "Coming over the Horizon," 62–63.

foundation, the Bonfils-Stanton Trust controlled by the Holy Name Province of the Order of Franciscans Minor, these seminars, known as the Keystone Seminars because of their location in Keystone, Colorado, continued for a number of years and provided a significant context for engaging distinctive issues for trustees in Catholic seminaries. Fred Hofheinz, a Lilly officer, provided much of the behind-the-scenes guidance that made these seminars successful. Eventually, these trustee seminars developed into seminars on theological teaching and learning for Catholic theological schools, directed by Kevin J. O'Neil, a Redemptorist priest and faculty member at the Washington Theological Union.

Publications and seminars did not end trustee education. After all, most boards added new members yearly, and schools had to educate these members for their task. New trustee workshops and trustee handbooks became part of the standard operating procedures of most seminaries, as did formal rituals to induct those new trustees. The ideal was for trustee education to become part of a board's standard agenda. Malcolm Warford wrote:

> To continue developing as a community of leadership, it is vital that the board provide for teaching moments in its life. At the least, fulfilling this objective involves an annual retreat when trustees can be together for an extended time to think about the seminary, the nature of trusteeship, and issues in the life of the church and the world that calls them to responsibility. It also helpful for the board to engage in such reflection on a regular, ongoing basis.[27]

Boards were to engage thoughtfully in the evaluation of their own work and become more self-conscious of their role in the ongoing life of the seminary.

The Association of Governing Boards was a key partner during the development of trustee education in the 1980s, but its focus was naturally on the role of boards in larger colleges and universities. In 1989, Vincent Cushing and Christa Klein founded *In Trust* with initial funding and planning help from the Lilly Endowment. At first, *In Trust* was a journal devoted to seminary trustees and the problems of governance. William R. MacKaye served as the first editor of the journal. *In Trust* had a distinctive style, combining short articles, illustrations, charts, and nontechnical language. As time passed, the journal's coverage included general articles on seminaries. Later, the need for more concrete advice to particular institutions led *In Trust* to provide seminary boards, presidents, and administrative teams with a variety of services, including consultations, educational sessions at board meetings, board-assessment instruments, and seminars.

Once the journal had developed into the corporation, In Trust Inc., more organization was required to carry out the expanded mission. In part, this organizational growth was a response to the need to become financially secure. The Lilly Endowment, originally the sole funder, urged the journal and its other activities to become

---

27. Ibid., 80.

self-supporting. Although In Trust charged for its services, the charges rarely covered all the expenses, not to mention the overhead. This meant that the editor had to become an executive director supported by a board of Trustees. William MacKaye led a creative development program that his successor, President Christa Klein, continued. The response demonstrated the importance of In Trust for the seminary community. Perhaps one of the best illustrations of the vitality of In Trust was the care that it took to develop its own board. The board attracted many of the most capable leaders in theological education.

Did the emphasis on trustees and trustee education make a major impact on theological education? Trustees make their major contributions to seminary life by advising the president and by providing leadership in time of crisis, particularly financial crisis. The first of these leaves only a small evidential trail. The president, after all, speaks for the institution and its policies. The second is harder to determine. At least since 1960, seminaries have faced numerous financial crises, any one of which might have weakened or destroyed some theological institutions. That so few schools have closed or had to made major adjustments indicates that the boards are functioning well. However, seminary board members on the average have not become major givers or important partners in fundraising.[28] In that sense, the backgrounds of those appointed to trustee boards is relatively consistent. Boards comprised and continue to comprise an overrepresentation of clergy and of laypeople involved in denominational life. Few were wealthy. Notable exceptions to this generalization exist. C. Davis Weyerhaeuser was one of the key supporters of Fuller Seminary in its formative years, and Gordon-Conwell's board was instrumental in enabling the seminary to survive after the death of J. Howard Pew ended his substantial annual contributions to the school's operating budget. Seminary boards of trustees more resembled the governing boards of church judicatories than they do the boards of other major nonprofits or of colleges and universities.[29] While the quality and training of boards improved, most boards did not become the keystones of their seminary's development efforts. In turn, this increased the pressure on the chief executive officer to take the lead in financial development.

New Seminary Standards

By 1990, the ATS was under pressure to rewrite its accrediting standards. Much of the pressure came from other accrediting bodies. In the 1990s, these agencies redeveloped their own standards and expected the ATS to act in a similar manner. Since the 1960s, theological schools increasingly sought dual accreditation from the regional accrediting bodies in addition to ATS. In some cases, regional bodies granted some

---

28. Wheeler, "In Whose Hands"; and Miller et al., "Great Expectations."

29. Wheeler notes that seminaries are not getting the younger, wealthier trustees that might have make a financial difference.

schools accreditation before they became members of the ATS. Regional accreditation became more important as seminaries expanded the number of their degrees and as students used seminaries for more than ordained ministry. Cooperation between the agencies was vital. For most seminaries, the ten-year reaccreditation visits were joint undertakings for which schools prepared one report. Both ATS and the regional association appointed the visiting teams. The cost of these visits in time and treasure put a heavy drain on faculty and staff during the three years before the visit and immediately thereafter. Few institutions were rich enough to prepare for two separate accreditations. Further, although they could not receive direct federal grants, seminaries were financially dependent on the Federal Student Loan Program. Federal student loans enabled the school to charge higher tuition to students, who then deferred payment until later. The ATS had to maintain good relationships with both the federal government and the other accrediting agencies in order to do the job of certifying schools to participate in the student-loan program.

Why was there so much pressure in the 1990s? Nothing is harder to manage than success. In 1990, American higher education had reaped the benefits of fifty years of accelerated growth and development. Although the traditional demographic of young white males had declined, the schools had replaced them with women, minorities, and foreign students. Further, the percentage of adult Americans with some college education greatly increased. Part of the reason for the popularity of college education was the widespread belief, encouraged by college educators, that a college degree almost guaranteed a good job. The parents who labored to put their children through college were, thus, making the most important single investment in their children's future imaginable. Many people believed that the same argument applied to professional education. Medical schools had far more applicants than they could admit, and law and business schools became increasingly selective.

Yet all was not well in the academic Zion. The rapid expansion of higher education and its economic role as the provider of employment credentials inspired widespread questions about academic quality. There were reports that some colleges had graduated people who were barely literate, and employer complaints about the preparation of graduates were widespread. Many critics and others believed that grade inflation was rampant and that academic standards had sagged. Some observers believed that political correctness weakened the curriculum when ethnic and racial studies entered the program of studies. In 1991 James Davison Hunter, a sociologist at the University of Virginia, published *Culture Wars: The Struggle to Define America*.[30] Like many sociological studies, Hunter's book detailed conditions and situations that lay readily at hand for anyone who had eyes to see them, but the title of his book highlighted the educational center of many of these debates. Whatever else educational institutions do or do not do, part of their function is to transmit culture from generation to generation. The rising influence of postmodernism among many educators further stirred

---

30. Hunter, *Culture Wars*.

the waters. Postmodernism's questioning of absolutes, although hardly new, seemed to imply an intellectual world in which there was no standard beyond the individual's own will to power.

In short, higher education faced some fundamental questions. Was higher education worth it? Were its graduates in fact prepared to work in their chosen fields? Did students learn in proportion to the cost of their education? What were students studying?

Congress responded to this public dissatisfaction in its debates over the periodic reauthorization of the Higher Education Act that governed the student-loan program. Many people, especially in accrediting circles, wondered whether the country might not be on the verge of adopting federal standards for higher education that would, *de facto* if not *de jure*, bypass the accrediting agencies. Many within and without the Department of Education questioned whether voluntary agencies, controlled by those whom they were regulating, had the necessary independence to enforce standards adequately. The Department of Education through its periodical recertification of accrediting bodies exerted pressure for increased clarity about academic achievements, and many expected the government to take further regulatory steps.

In effect, the government hoped for an educational consumer's Bill of Rights. In part, this demand was for public access to important information, including such data as graduation rates and posteducational employment, the names of members of the governing board, and basic financial information. On a more basic level, the demand was for the evaluation of teaching and learning. What assurance did parents and students have that what a school claimed to teach was actually what that schools taught or that students learned what the school taught? How valid were educational institutions promises of quality? With the difference in price between top schools and the others so pronounced, people wanted to know what actual differences between institutions might justify or not justify those increased costs.

The controversy highlighted the uniqueness of American education. American higher education is the least regulated in any advanced country. Although the states charter schools and the Department of Education establishes rules for receiving federal aid, the main check on educational quality is accreditation, standards maintained by independent associations of schools. Each institution voluntarily accepts the standards and each institution evaluates its own compliance with them. The system promotes institutional freedom and creativity. This self-governing regulation allows schools to experiment with different programs and to seek diverse goals. The pressing question was whether accreditation could also promote educational quality.

The ATS approach to accreditation had traditionally centered on two emphases: institutional purpose or mission and resources. The ATS designed its pre-1996 standards around one question: did a school have the resources to accomplish its stated mission? As time had passed, the way that specific standards posed that basic question and the details required to answer it varied, but the core question about adequacy of resources remained front and center. ATS did not want to abandon this approach completely. Some theological schools were still comparatively thin in resources, particularly in finances and in library resources, and the redeveped standards needed to set requirements in these areas clear enough to secure minimum institutional viability. The other historic characteristic of ATS accreditation was that the standards specified characteristics and nomenclature for each of a seminary's degrees. Originally, the ATS did this to protect the integrity of the BD/MDiv program, but it had proved valuable as theological schools developed new degree programs in the 1980s and 1990s. Hence, the Association wanted to retain this practice. However, the redeveped standards focused on two related questions: what is the character of a good theological school, and how does a school demonstrate that it merited that designation? While this presupposed the Basic Issues discussions, including the debate over what made theological education theological, ATS wanted to expand those discussions by placing them in an institutional context. ATS hoped to reorient the accreditation process around the basic question of academic quality and its measurement.

The ATS demonstrated the seriousness of the new undertaking by devising a four-year process that began in academic year 1992–1993 and climaxed at the biennial meeting in 1996.[31] The focus on quality was clear. The name of the program was The Good Theological School. As Daniel Aleshire, who headed up the project, explained: ATS designed the first stage of the process to "the perceptions about good theological education that exist both among ATS member institutions and more broadly in North America." In the second stage, the Association was to redeveop the standards with a view to adopting them in 1996. At the heart of the first stage were four questions:

> What is the character of curriculum, formation, and cultivation of ministerial leadership in the good theological school? (2) What is the character of teaching, learning, and the scholarly task in the good theological school? (3) What is the character of the institutional resources needed for the good theological school? and (4) What is the character of administration and governance in the good theological school?[32]

The questions were open ended, designed to provoke basic thought about what schools were doing to define and achieve quality. The focus was what it meant to be a *good* school.

To begin, ATS convened a group of fifty (50) theological educators in Chicago and divided them into four groups to consider the questions. Writers summarized these discussions and published them in *Theological Education* in 1994. The published essays indicate the seriousness with which the participants took the questions. Each essay approached the major trends in theological education, including part-time students, degree proliferation, financial struggles, faculty training, student formation,

---

31. Aleshire, "The ATS Quality."
32. Ibid., 10.

and governance, from its own perspective. At times, the essays state conclusions with unusual honesty. In discussing the increasingly part-time character of theological schools, James Evans and Jane I. Smith summarized the reality in a single sentence: "Most schools face an enrollment with a lower full-time equivalent and a higher head count, that translates into a demand for more services."[33] Donald Senior and Timothy P. Weber admitted that the reason for the proliferation of degree programs was "to starve off financial ruin."[34] If one theme dominated all four essays, however, that theme was the increasing diversity of the various schools, both within each school and among the various schools. The only way forward was for ATS to find ways to embrace this diversity and use it as part of its definition of quality theological education. The standards had to reach from dispensationalist Dallas through almost every shade of Protestant theological opinion, and cover Catholic and Eastern Orthodox schools as well. Perhaps we can grasp the full dimensions of the problem by mentioning a few of the theologically laden images that educators might use to describe their graduates: learned ministers, mirrors of Christ, ministers of Word and Sacrament, or community leaders.

These early discussions revealed the loss of traditional benchmarks for theological education. During the period from 1933 to 1990, for example, the general academic standards of the university provided the implicit benchmark for seminaries, especially for those schools in the Reformation traditions. Using these criteria, the best practices of the university schools provided benchmarks for other institutions. For example, if the university-related schools taught classes that featured the latest and best biblical scholarship, other schools could judge their own courses by comparing them to university divinity practices. Yale's academic programs and policies served many schools as benchmarks.[35] Yet, theological educators increasingly questioned the role of the various academic disciplines in setting seminary standards. The widespread use of the word *guild* as a pejorative term indicated the extent of the change.

After the discussion in the 1995 biennial, the ATS developed "framework statements" that it believed it might develop into standards. Sister Katarina Schuth described the next step:

> As the 1994–95 academic year began, the Framework Statement was published and distributed to all member institutions for their response and comment. Together, these efforts succeeded in identifying the range of characteristics that are seen by the Association's constituents as important in the "good theological school."[36]

---

33. Evans, and Smith, "What Is the Character," 49.

34. Senior and Weber, "What Is the Character" 21.

35. Most Southern theological schools openly or secretly hoped to be the "Yale of the South." The rigor of individual courses, particularly in history and Bible, was often judged by a comparison of the course's requirements to those expected of Yale students.

36. Steering Committee, "The Quality and Accreditation Project," 2.

After the Association received these responses, the four task forces begin to translate the language of these fundamental discussions into concrete standards. This process involved a careful consideration of the standards of the six regional accrediting bodies and the circulation and criticism of two drafts before Association sent the final draft to the 1996 meeting. The member schools, then, further refined the draft through amendments. The ATS was not alone in its revision of its standards; each regional and professional accrediting association was also reevaluating its own standards, but it was unique in the extent of the participatory and consultative character of the process by which it arrived at its new benchmarks.

Although the new standards did have a few specific requirements,[37] ATS hoped that these new standards would set in motion a process of continued evaluation and assessment followed by review. The ideal was for institutions to create evaluative loops in which what the school learned from one study might function as the basis for institutional changes. In turn, the school evaluated the new situation and made further improvements. The process had no stated termination point. The goal was a series of evaluative loops that moved the process forward. At the same time, ATS hoped that its standards might create a reflective mood in its members. While many regional accrediting bodies defined their new standards in language that invited statistical analysis, the ATS leadership took care to avoid reducing the complex variables of theological education to a system of numbers. In reflecting on the Character and Assessment of learning for Religious Vocation project, Daniel Aleshire, whose doctoral work was in psychology, noted:

> I have, on the one hand, been intrigued my entire career about how things can be measured and the kind of understanding and insight that can accrue from appropriate analyses of statistical data. On the other hand, I do not think that all that is worth knowing can be known statistically. John Harris, a thoughtful assessment theorist, cites a quote that reportedly hung on the wall in Albert Einstein's Princeton office: "Not everything that counts can be counted, and not everything that can be counted counts."[38]

The combination of evaluation and reflection envisioned in the standards was perhaps easiest applied to administrative tasks where various management techniques, including management by objectives, could provide a baseline for effective performance. Library evaluation also seemed to fit most easily into this new mode, especially, with the emphasis on cooperative ventures with other libraries and with access, rather than possession, used as a measurement for the adequacy of holdings.

ATS divided its redeveloped standards into two sections. The first, General Educational Standards, included such matters as planning, purpose, and evaluation; institutional integrity; learning, teaching, and research: theological scholarship (after 2010

---

37. These largely involved financial matters and matters of federal mandate.
38. Aleshire, "The Character," 2.

Theological Curriculum: Learning, Teaching, and Research); library; faculty; student services; authority and governance; and institutional resources.[39] The second section included standards for the individual degrees. The definition of a theological school was particularly important:

> A theological school is a community of faith and learning that cultivates habits of theological reflection, nurtures wise and skilled ministerial practice, and contributes to the formation of spiritual awareness and moral sensitivity.[40]

In some ways, we might call this a new professional model. In the older professional model, the ministry was characterized by emphasis on the various functions of ministry; in the new professional model, the ideal is the civic professional who is actively engaged in the larger interactive world of religious life.[41] Like the earlier professional model, this understanding permitted individual institutions to fill in the blanks and tailor the standards to their own needs. Thus, where the standards call for the "intellectual grasp of the tradition of a faith community,"[42] the individual school might insert, "the Reformed Tradition" or the "activist tradition" depending on the school's own statements of purpose and mission. This general approach allowed the standards to speak in general of such matters as scholarship without too much specificity. The General Standards, thus, rested on the ability of schools to be specific and clear about their own work and mission.

The Association followed the same general format in its definition of the various theological degrees. With the exception of some terms that were in general use, such as theological disciplines, the standards sought to allow schools to supply specifics that they could fit into the standards' generalities. This made the standard broad enough, at least theoretically, to embrace the diverse understandings of the degrees that institutions offered. Again, the new standards rested on a school's capacity to be clear about what it believed its programs accomplished, and to demonstrate that the program actually produced those outcomes.

PLURALISM AND STANDARDS

From the initial adoption of the redeveloped standards through the revisions of 2010 and 2012, the area that occupied the most time, both of the ATS and of the schools it accredited, was educational effectiveness and learning incomes. While documenting the account of time and effort devoted to the task is relatively easy, understanding where the problem lay is not. Thus, the general approach of the standards to allow individual schools to define how they understand the basic terms might have seemed

---

39. *ATS Bulletin* #50 (2012) G-2. The list compares the original categories and the 2012 revision.
40. Ibid., G-5.
41. The term *civic professional* comes from Charles R. Foster et al., *Educating Clergy*, 10–11.
42. ATS, Bulletin, #50, G-5.

to permit an easy solution. In theory, a school could define its education outcomes according to its own institutional purpose and determine whether its courses and programs delivered those goals. Yet in practice, learning outcomes has proven difficult to formulate and to document. Why, given the successful nature of the general approach, has this area remained so difficult for ATS and its member schools?

When a historian comes close to the present, especially in a disputed area, the line between analysis and opinion becomes blurred. If only to avoid silence, I need to attempt some analysis. My contention is that the external and the internal pluralism of the schools made the determination of the benchmarks for teaching and learning difficult to determine. A contrast with the relatively homogeneous case of schools of aviation, law, and physical therapy may illustrate this observation. Education for these occupations has relatively clear outcomes. State examinations, hopefully periodically reviewed and updated, measure many of these expectations. A student who became a licensed pilot and was hired was a successful outcome for the school of aviation; the percentage of students taking and passing the bar examination was a convenient measure for law schools. Likewise the capacity to be licensed and employed is a significant measure of the success of a physical-therapy program. In this sense, one has a clear line establishing basic competence. If a school does not reach that line, the school can focus its programs more on the basics. If the school attains the line, it can work on more advanced skills that might give its graduates an advantage in the marketplace.

In contrast, theological schools are more like prisms. Seminaries are multiuse institutions who admit a variety of students, and who graduate people destined for a variety of possible employments. The Association adopted its new standards in the midst of a period of rapid and fundamental change in theological education, all of which added to the complexity of the schools.

During the 1980s, the seminaries had adopted a plethora of new degrees that pointed to a number of possible outcomes, ranging from the traditional specialized ministries, such as education and chaplaincy, to Master of Arts programs that prepared students for further graduate work, to advanced programs for missionaries. Almost all schools became theological universities. Yet, with the partial exception of the largest schools, they did not develop specialized faculties or departments to handle the new programs. Many seminaries relied on core courses, common to all the various master's degrees, to lay the foundations for the different programs. Further, within each degree program, the ultimate professional certification came from religious communities that had their own standards and expectations. Although many seminaries retained some denominational affiliation, the schools admitted students from different denominational and religious backgrounds. A Catholic school might have Baptists and others enrolled in its Master of Divinity program, and most Protestant schools have students from across the denominational spectrum. While more unusual, students from non-Christian religions also enrolled, as did students with no formal religious affiliation. The seminaries also attracted students who accepted very diverse understandings of their own traditions. An American Baptist Evangelical student, for example, differed more from an American Baptist liberal student than he or she did from an Evangelical Methodist.

At the same time, many schools served large numbers of commuting students, and many had multiple campuses. The new student body was older, more often than not part time and burdened with full-time employment. In addition to the so-called traditional students,[43] the seminaries had a wide range of second- and third-career students whose ages ranged from thirty to sixty, and a handful of students in their sixties seeking part-time work in their retirement years. Residence, even in the somewhat attenuated form of full-time attendance, was in rapid decline. Without changing a course or modifying a curriculum, this changed the character of theological education. Since the founding of Andover, residential theological education mixed students of diverse backgrounds together in a community that combined instruction and life together. Whatever took the place of residence in a student's formation, the decline of the resident student population radically changed theological schools and the nature of seminary communities. The system of dormitories, dining halls, and student apartments was less needed, and no longer provided some unity for seminary experience. Only the classrooms remained to provide common experiences. Students were often on campus only the proverbial ten minutes before and after class. Interestingly, Catholic seminaries resisted the end of residence for those entering the priesthood, while lay students and women were commuters. This further divided the student bodies of Catholic seminaries. One part was composed of candidates remarkably like those in mainstream Protestant schools; the other was composed of residents participating in a program of formation.

Distance education further complicated the picture. In 1996, when the ATS adopted the redeveloped standards, distance education was in its infancy, with few schools offering more than a few technologically rooted courses, often using tapes or phones. By 2012, distance learning was a major component of American higher education. Ironically, since many distance programs required some time physically present on campus—the so-called mixed programs—these students may have experienced more community than nonresident commuters.

A further complication was that students no longer shared a common educational background. Few had a traditional liberal-arts background, and even those with that background often had done their liberal-arts study many years earlier.[44] In part,

---

43. The tradition was, like many traditions, present more in the minds of commentators than in the historical record. Only for a brief span of time—the period between 1955 and 1970—were most seminary students just out of undergraduate school. In earlier times, most took a few years between completing their undergraduate studies and enrolling in seminary. In many cases, they served as pastors during this period.

44. At Bangor, where I taught, we had the Bangor Plan for those who had not graduated from college. Part of this plan was a two-year intense program in liberal arts that included courses in philosophy, history, literature, and basic scientific reasoning. We found that our candidates who had gone

these new students lacked knowledge that was a useful precedent for theological study, but prerequisites were not the principal defect. The new students often lacked critical thinking skills, an outcome that many liberal-arts educators worked hard to impart. They also lacked the leadership capacities that liberal-arts education had encouraged. The Association had recognized these changes by gradually dropping from its documents any reference to recommended educational requirements before seminary, but this left the requirement for admission simply graduation from an accredited school.

This internal pluralism made it difficult to determine outcomes. Seminary students were like runners who began and ended their race at different places on the track. While the new professional model, enshrined in the standards, offered some possible places for measurement, most of these places were subjective or self-reported. The hard question remained: What did seminary add to a student's preparation for ministry that was not already present? Even more difficult to answer was the question of how that might be measured.

At the same time as internal pluralism made educational outcomes difficult to predict, external pluralism made it difficult to define outcomes. Despite the tendency to combine very different groups under broader categories, American religion, especially, American Protestantism, remains very diverse organizationally and theologically. Further, each denomination contains ethnic and other divisions. The more diverse seminaries became in faculty and students, the more denominations and other groups hiring seminary graduates felt that they had to act to ensure the type of graduate they wanted. Most denominations adopted guidelines for those attending seminaries. These ranged from specific courses in denominational history and polity to courses in evangelism and missions. The monitoring of seminary students while they were studying also was intensified. Students had to meet with church committees or judicatory representatives frequently, and many of these meetings resulted in the judicatory urging the student to take certain courses or have certain experiences. Many denominations required Clinical Pastoral Education in either a hospital or another organization for ordination. In short, the seminaries had to share responsibility with the denominations for the outcomes of their programs, and this meant responding to changes in denominational expectations as the denominations changed those expectations.

The United Methodists went a step further than most denominations in the 1980s, directing their University Senate to examine the work of all seminaries with United Methodist students in the light of various criteria or standards. Although the United Methodists insisted that this was not a form of accreditation, it was—and one with serious consequences. The University Senate review was a way for the United Methodists to exert control over schools that they did not support financially. Since many seminaries, especially smaller schools, needed the revenue from every student

---

through this program were often better prepared for theological study than our students with a variety of undergraduate degrees.

that they could enroll, a negative decision by the United Methodist Senate might mean the difference between a school staying open or closing. The loss of United Methodist certification was, thus, more serious than an ATS notation and equal to any sanction other than loss of accreditation itself. If the United Methodist solution was extreme, other judicatories required students to take no more than one or two years in a non-denominational school before completing their work at a denominational seminary.

Many distinctions prized by the denominations were matters of ethos, historically taught through residence, field education, and spiritual experiences, such as prayer, small groups, and chapel. To attain these values, churches had to require at least the majority of their candidates to have sustained experience of their style of religious life. Yet many candidates came to seminary with little or no recent church experience. With residence no longer expected, the question of where that religious seasoning would take place was as difficult to answer as it was important.

Religious organizations also have a theological character. United Methodists, for all their diversity, thought theologically in ways that differed from Baptists, Presbyterians, and Episcopalians. In turn, these denominations had their own ways of resolving theological issues that differed from one another. Reformed theological educators established the traditional form of American theological education, and their work represented their tradition of a theologically literate ministry. Other denominations adopted that form to their own purposes, in many cases, only with considerable difficulty.

In the 1990s and 2000s, American religion, including American Protestantism, became even more diverse. Different forms of church competed for members and leaders. American independent churches, a category that includes the so-called megachurches, tended to stress evangelistic efficiency as the mark of good ministry. Some of these churches undertook the education of their own ministers, partly through on-the-job training. For many potential ministers considering a career in the church, these in-church or in-service programs were an option. They also presented a clear set of outcomes that were different from those advocated by seminaries.

The Mainstream and smaller Protestant churches also turned increasingly to alternative programs of ministerial preparation. The old split between rural and small-town Protestantism and urban and suburban Protestantism reemerged and forced denominations to consider other ways to prepare leaders. To understand this dynamic, one must note the ways that changes in seminary demographics disrupted the traditional clergy career pattern. Historically, young graduates, usually male, spent the first years of ministry in a small, poorly paying congregation, hoping that subsequent appointments would bring substantial financial improvement. In effect, the first churches were an internship. As candidates became older and more diverse, fewer were willing or able to follow this traditional route. If nothing else, the increasing burden of student loans made it difficult to serve poorer churches, as did the fact that spouses often had good jobs that they were unwilling or unable to leave. In response, most denominations either continued and strengthened their traditional lay ministry programs or developed new ones.[45] Multiple paths to ordination became the rule rather than the exception.

In short, the difficulties with learning outcomes among ATS schools reflected the increasing internal and external pluralism of American religious life. Aleshire was right when he stated his own preference for numbers. The problem with numbers is not with statistical analysis; the problem is determining what to measure. In that sense, seminaries represented the worse of all possible worlds. In the main, they were small institutions that sought to meet a wide variety of educational needs, some of which were complementary, and others, less so. The benchmark that defines quality in one degree may not define quality in another, although both degrees may share the same courses. The same observation can be made about the fit of individual degrees and programs with denominational styles.

Accreditation and Reform

Historically, accreditation is a slow path to reform. Changes in accreditation standards take decades before they become part of the practice of member institutions. Not all accreditation initiatives are effective. Institutional inertia may slow the pace of change, and an institution's course is often more immediately determined by such variables as the need for more students or revenue than it is by external agencies. The long struggle over the nature of preseminary preparation is a case in point. Yet, accreditation does produce lasting and abiding changes. Some examples may illustrate the transformative effect of standards. Without the common understanding of theological education provided by the ATS and its standards, seminaries might well have remained locked in rigid denominational patterns. The life of most modern ATS-related schools thus rests on the ability of many different groups to see their own position reflected in the common expectations of all schools. Significantly, the ATS is the broadest ecumenical agency in America, uniting Roman Catholics, Eastern Orthodox, and Mainstream and Evangelical Protestants. For all the problems of contemporary seminaries, the schools have improved in their capacity to deliver high-level education. Perhaps the most dramatic example of this success was the ATS work with the rapidly expanding world of seminary degrees. By examining each new degree program and working with schools to achieve some common understanding of these programs, they prevented an expansion that well might have lowered the general level of theological study. The redeveloped standards have not had their full effect, but they seem to have set theological education on a slow, steady path to manifesting the good theological school.

45. Barker and Martin, "Judicatory-Based Theological Education"; Barker and Martin, *Multiple Paths to Ministry*. Much of this paragraph repeats material presented in Miller, "Why the Seminary?," in Barker and Martin, *Multiple Paths to Ministry*.

Perhaps the most important outcome of these new standards was the impetus that they gave to the new professional model of seminary education. Taking seriously the belief that theological education seeks to provide its students with the capacity to think theologically or pastorally, the new professional model pointed to a high level of religious and personal integration as the goal of theological study. The model is professional in that it assumes, consciously and unconsciously, that the leadership of religious organizations rests on the capacity of that leadership to articulate and apply the organization's basic theological stance. In the place of the multitude of separate ministerial tasks prized in the older professional model, the new model sought to see every aspect of the minister's day as supported by religious and theological thought. As experience accumulated, the theological reflection became (or should have become) richer and more rooted in the substance of the faith tradition.

TEACHING AND LEARNING

The redeveloped standards marked a period of renewed interest in teaching and learning in theological schools. For some time, administrators had worried about whether graduate schools adequately prepared faculty to teach in seminaries. Theological faculties change very slowly. Most are small, and many teachers spend their careers in one or two institutions. Worries and difficulties, hence, tend to surface slowly. By the 1990s, these worries occupied those who thought most seriously about theological schools. Circumstances drove this concern, at least in part. Many believed that the 1990s would see a significant turnover in theological faculties. Many schools had rapidly expanded in the 1950s and early 1960s, and the schools expected those professors to retire during the 1990s. The generally optimistic financial picture in the 1990s also pointed in the same direction. In 1991, the Association of Theological School devoted its autumn issue of *Theological Education* to the subject, and Auburn published four studies related to the topic from 1996 to 2010.[46]

The discussion in the 1980s had often pointed to the scholarly guilds as a central problem for theological education. As many saw it, the scholarly guilds set the effectual standards for seminary teaching and for the hiring and retention of faculty. Supposedly, guild standards, particularly those related to theological research, had the most weight in determining how faculty lived out their vocations. To put this point succinctly, many faculty members may have seen themselves as disciplinary scholars first and as seminary teachers second. As Barbara Wheeler demonstrated, this worry had some sociological basis. A handful of doctoral programs trained the majority of

---

46. Kelsey and Wheeler, "Thinking about Theological Education"; Kelsey, "Conjuring Future Faculties"; Evans, "The Graduate Education of Future Faculties"; McBrien, *The Graduate Education of Future Theological Faculties.*" This issue of *Theological Education* was devoted to concerns about faculty. See King, "Building Theological Faculties"; Hough, "Seminary Faculties." The Auburn Studies were Wheeler, "True and False"; Wheeler and Wilhelm, "Tending Talents"; Wheeler et al., "Signs of the Times"; and Wheeler and Blier, "A Report on a Study of Doctoral Programs."

faculties, and the schools on this list were remarkably constant over time.[47] The schools on the list were not surprising. With the exception of such institutions as Union (New York), they were the same schools that educated faculty members in other academic fields. Religious and theological studies were usually part of the Graduate School of Arts and Sciences. As a result, seminary faculties shared similar understandings of scholarship with their peers in other fields. This situation was not particularly new. During the last century, seminaries had drawn their academic standards from the same German and British universities as other American graduate schools.

These same schools were also leaders in the education of faculty members for the increasingly secular departments of religion in colleges and universities. Although religion departments had begun by teaching a collegiate version of the Protestant theological encyclopedia and courses in comparative religion, they had matured in their methods and self-understanding. In addition to a greatly expanded interest in history-of-religion courses, many new synthetic approaches were developed. These new directions often saw religious life as integral to the various cultures in which a particular religion was located. Not surprisingly, these new directions influenced the study of the classic Western theological disciplines as well. Hebrew Scripture studies were increasingly rooted in the religious history of the Ancient Near East, and New Testament studies in the religious culture of late antiquity. Church history, historically closely tied to its secular counterpart, moved naturally in this direction. Significantly, the American Society of Church History changed the title of its journal to *Church History: Studies in Christianity and Culture*. Many graduate departments, even where they were rooted in divinity schools, such as Yale and Duke, placed their PhD programs in independent graduate departments of religion.[48]

The leading graduate departments of religion had to serve two publics. Like the seminaries, they had to use a relatively small faculty to accomplish diverse goals. In many cases, religionists and theologians shared the some classes, seminars, and dissertation advisors. The academic job market, tight throughout the last fifty years, also dictated breadth of instruction. Wherever a potential PhD might hope to teach, they rarely could choose their first or second assignment in advance.[49]

Many people were uneasy about whether graduate departments could and should continue to train people for both religion departments and theological schools. The Lilly Endowment, led by Craig Dykstra, helped to finance some experimental

47. This point is made in all the Auburn Studies of faculty.

48. In some ways, the situation was similar to the past. Throughout much of western history, philosophy provided the background for theology and other academic disciplines. Hegelians, for example, taught every discipline, including history, literature, and arts. In the modern school of arts and sciences, culture has replaced philosophy as a lingua franca. Postmodernism accentuates this change.

49. Interestingly, seminary-based PhD programs also had a similar dual and even threefold market. Some of the graduates went to large churches, especially to congregations that prized academic ability; some went to seminary teaching; and some to church-related colleges. The programs had to serve multiple publics.

alternatives. Vanderbilt established a special program, the Program in Theology and Practice, for prospective seminary teachers. In addition to completing the requirements in one of Vanderbilt's eight special areas of study, the program supplemented that study with electives, two core seminars, an externship in theological education, and travel grants.[50] The Vanderbilt program looked in two directions. First, the emphasis on research in ministry and the requirement of electives chosen from the program in Theology and Practice pointed to the education of a new generation of practical theologians. This was a response to a widespread need for more academically qualified candidates in that area. But, second, the program also allowed people in such areas as theology and biblical studies to focus their work towards future teaching in theological schools. The new Duke Doctor of Theology program was not as integrated into the PhD program as its Vanderbilt counterpart. That program concentrated on such practical disciplines as worship, preaching, evangelism, and the arts.

The Wabash Center for Teaching in Theology and Religion represented another approach to the problem of the transition between disciplinarily defined doctoral study and teaching. The Wabash Center originated in a 1995 meeting hosted by Craig Dykstra, the Lilly staff, and fifty scholars in religion and theology.[51] The first two directors of the center were Raymond Williams and Lucinda Huffaker, who joined the center in 1997 and became director in 2002. The purpose of the center and its work was to improve the quality of the teaching of new faculty in theology and religion. The methods involved bringing together new faculty with experienced teachers and providing them with the opportunity to ask questions about their new profession in a safe space. The center also provided its fellows with the chance to work intensively on one of their courses. The center subsequently published the best of this work in its journal, *Teaching Theology and Religion*. Wabash played an important role in popularizing the use of technology in teaching, including the Internet, and published a Guide to Internet Resources on its website. The center was an important partner with the Louisville Institute, a Lilly-funded agency for the study of American religion, in the evaluation and distribution of the 1997 Lilly grants for the use of educational technology.

Educating Clergy

Did seminary teaching have its own distinctive pedagogy? This question was at the heart of the major study, *Educating Clergy*, which the Carnegie Foundation for the Advancement of Teaching undertook as part of its inquiries into the varieties of professional education in the United States.[52] The Lilly Endowment and Atlantic Philanthropies provided the funding for the work. Charles Foster, who earlier served on

---

50. Vanderbilt University, "The Program in Theology and Practice."
51. For an introduction to the work of the center, see Foster, "The Wabash Center in the Scholarship of Teaching"; Foster, "The Scholarship of Teaching in Theology and Religion."
52. Foster et al., *Educating Clergy*, 384.

the board of the Wabash Center and was an emeritus professor at Emory University, directed the project. Foster and his team drew on the expert knowledge of a number of consultants in preparing for the project, including Craig Dykstra, Barbara Wheeler, Daniel Aleshire, David Kelsey, and Jeremiah McCarthy. The advisory committee that worked with the researchers was equally distinguished. The method that the team adopted was "appreciative inquiry." Appreciative inquiry begins with the belief that the practices used by a group or a school actually achieve their goals, at least partially, and the purpose of the study is to assert how those goals are achieved.

The key idea in this influential study was Craig Dykstra's understanding of pastoral imagination.[53] The purpose of the study was as follows:

> How do seminary educators foster among their students a pastoral, priestly, or rabbinic imagination that integrates knowledge and skill, moral integrity, and religious commitment in their roles, relationships, and responsibilities that they will be assuming in clergy practice.[54]

Basically, pastoral imagination was the capacity to see the world from the perspective of a pastor; that is, the ability to understand the world from the perspective of faith. The idea was an application of Alasdair MacIntyre's concept of a practice. Like other practices, pastoral imagination develops over a long period and deepens through use. The development of pastoral imagination, thus, begins before formal theological schooling and continues long afterward. Dykstra's sense of the long-term process required to produce a pastor informed the Lilly grants that the Lilly Endowment made for high school theological programs and for programs for a pastor's first years in ministry. The seminary thus stands as a keystone in this development, enabling the student to establish patterns of thought and action that will carry over into the myriad tasks of concrete religious leadership. In this sense, theological education is transformative education. The word *transformative* was important to the study. When we transform something, we change its basic shape, often radically, while we retain its substance. In that sense, transformation differs from creativity or from purification. Foster writes:

> Clerical practice is itself a transformative art, reinvesting inherited traditions with new meanings and strategies in response to changing circumstances and shifting contexts. From this perspective, the pastoral, priestly, or rabbinic imagination requires not only capacities for engaging, integrating, and adapting learning, but also what might be called new forms of religious production. Both Protestant evangelical clergy who interpret a Scripture passage to authorize a new outreach program and Catholic priests who present the Gospel in

---

53. Ibid.
54. Ibid.

the language and cultural forms of a new immigrant population are participating in transformative practices that produce new forms of ministry.[55]

The pedagogy that produces such transformative practice must itself be transformative.

While noting the distinctive role of the study of texts, particularly Scripture, in the training of clergy, Foster's team noted that seminary pedagogies studied texts with four types of goals in mind:

> Developing in students the facility for *interpreting* texts, situations, and relationships
>
> Nurturing dispositions and habits integral to the spiritual and *vocational* formation of clergy.
>
> Heightening student consciousness of the content and agency of historical and contemporary *contexts.*
>
> Cultivating student *performance* in clergy roles and ways of thinking.[56]

These general goals enabled the team studying clergy education to realize that while no single "signature pedagogy" existed in seminaries—indeed successful teachers often used a variety of pedagogic approaches—there were four families of pedagogic techniques that enabled individual classroom teachers to attain their goals: pedagogies of interpretation, pedagogies of formation, pedagogies of contextualization, and pedagogies of performance. Yet perhaps more interesting than these distinctions was the studies' acknowledgement that for theological seminaries, "the implicit curriculum" was as important as what was formally advocated in the classroom:

> In making these distinctions, we are again building on Elliot Eisner's insight into the influence of implicit curriculum of schools on student learning. By that term, Eisner means what a school teaches unintentionally "because of the type of place it is." . . . His attention was drawn to the influence of teacher methods, school organization, building, and arrangement of classroom furniture on student learning. We have also been intrigued by how the seminary community that is the school shares student learning.[57]

Foster noted two particular areas where this implicit curriculum took center stage: field education and programs of spiritual formation. These areas, significantly, were the ones that most varied among schools and the areas of seminary life that transmitted significant ecclesiastical traditions, including African American traditions of liberation and Catholic practices of contextualization. Interestingly enough, these are also the areas where the seminaries most clearly mirrored the congregations

---

55. Ibid., 23
56. Ibid., 33.
57. Ibid., 188.

that their graduates would be called to serve.[58] Yet the study did note a problem that was common to an increasing number of schools. In Roman Catholic, Episcopalian, and Eastern Catholic seminaries, where liturgical practice was part of the life of a residential community, these worship activities enrolled and apparently influenced a high percentage of the community. In many other seminaries, research indicated that many, if not most, students were not on campus when the services were offered.[59]

Like the discussions of what makes theological education theological, Foster's book worked a very high level of abstraction, despite his use of certain teachers as exemplars of good seminary practice. Foster's team presupposed a new professional model (akin to the way the ATS redeveloped its standards), enriched by a deeper sense of the religious work of the ministry. The clergy exist to make God known and to enable people to worship. In many ways, the strength of the book was similar to the strength of the Lilly grants for high school theological study and for new pastors. The book clearly identified seminary as a moment, perhaps even a transformative moment, in the development of a religious leader. Yet, the question of who and when the substance that the seminary transformed was imparted was unanswered. Transformation implies a before and an afterward, a comparison between the beginning point and the conclusion. Without clear pictures of where students begin and where they end, the belief that seminary teachers play a transformative role in the development of ministers is more an assertion than a conclusion.

The Lexington Seminars

Malcolm Warford conducted a series of influential seminars, the Lexington Seminars, from 1998 to 2008. The Lexington Seminar: Theological Teaching for the Church's Ministries brought together teams of administrators and faculty members from diverse seminaries to work on problems of teaching and learning. Although the seminars focused on collaborative faculty projects, proposed and conducted by the schools, the purpose of the seminars was to forge habits of cooperation between faculties, deans, and presidents that might make further progress possible. In effect, the seminars aimed to create a common language for the discussion of concrete problems encountered in the work of preparing men and women for Christian work. The design of the seminars was to gather five schools every year at the Asticou Inn in Northeast Harbor, Maine. The setting promoted conversation and fellowship that was often more important than the material exchanged in their more formal meetings.[60]

---

58. Ibid., 275–76.
59. Ibid., 280.
60. Warford, *Practical Wisdom*.

Faculty as Scholars

If *Educating Clergy,* the Wabash Center, and the Lexington Seminars pointed to the crucial role of seminary faculty as teachers and advisors, what about the faculty as scholars. One strong constant in seminary history is the belief that seminary faculty, especially those in the classical fields, will conduct a rigorous academic examination of the faith. To be sure, the definition of scholarship evolved over this complex history. In the early nineteenth century, such scholars as Moses Stuart and Charles Hodge spent long hours reading and absorbing the best literature on a subject, and later the various doctoral programs became the primary form of scholarly preparation. Further, throughout American seminary history, theological scholarship is a public discipline. Scholars expect other scholars to publish their work and receive criticism for it. The book review existed before the graduate seminar.

Throughout the last fifty years, the Association of Theological Schools has maintained programs that help finance seminary research. Beginning with the Sealantic grants of the 1950s, the Association has administered grants designed to improve faculty scholarship. These grants have included substantial amounts from the Lilly Endowment, the Arthur Vining Davis Foundation, and the Henry Luce Foundation. Those receiving grants as young scholars often became leading scholars later in their careers.

Another important innovation directed towards theological schools was the establishment of the Center for Theological Inquiry at Princeton. James I. McCord envisioned the center while president of Princeton Seminary and served as its first president. McCord's models for the Center included the National Humanities Center in Triangle Park, North Carolina. Like Humanities Center, the Center for Theological Inquiry was to provide a space and resources for skilled researchers to do their work. Libraries, office space, computers, and assistants were at hand to facilitate advanced study. Most important, scholars had access to each other. Formally and informally, the Center provided an opportunity for sharing work in progress and sharpening arguments. Part of the genius of the Center's design was that the Center was to sponsor fundamental theological thought on the cutting edge of current study.

What has changed about theological scholarship over the last fifty years? Perhaps the most important shift has been the rise of religious studies. Before the 1960s, seminary teachers, particularly those in the university-related schools, had a monopoly on high-level theological and religious study. Before 1960, one could write the history of religious studies, including history of religions, by tracing the work of scholars in the university divinity schools in the card catalog and the Religion Index. This situation changed rapidly in the 1960s and 1970s. New religion departments, many of which were located in universities, appeared on the scene, and these institutions required publication as a condition of employment. The book display at the American Academy of Religion grew as its membership increased. In many ways, the AAR and

SBL defined the scholarly task. Seminary teachers had to conduct their research in a context that included scholars whose context was different from their own.

At the same time, religious publishing was undergoing a major shift. The traditional presses that had published important Protestant books, such as Harper's, shortened their lists considerably. At the same time, the principal Protestant denominations lowered their production of serious scholarly texts. In the past, they had supported the scholarly products of their presses by publishing a number of highly profitable items for churches, including Sunday school materials, hymnals, devotionals, and popular study books. In part, this decline in sales reflected the decline in the membership of these denominations. Moreover, the passionate theological cultural warfare in many denominations encouraged churches to purchase their materials from a variety of sources. In particular, more conservative Mainstream congregations often purchased their church materials from Evangelical sources, further reducing the sales of the church presses most profitable items. As a result, the denominational presses had less money to use to cover the losses associated with scholarly publishing.[61] The university presses, particularly Oxford and Yale, continued to publish impressive lists of scholarly books in religion, although the faculty of the new religion departments used these presses as well.

A major change in scholarly publication came from the rise of the Evangelical presses, including Eerdmans, Baker, and Zondervan. In addition to publications aimed at the Evangelical market, these publishers also published many books by Mainstream seminary faculty. Despite this openness, the increased market share of the Evangelical publishers pointed to a new competitiveness in the religious marketplace. One can get a sense of this shift by noting that the New Revised Standard Version of the Bible, which many believed would inherit the dominant position previously enjoyed by the Revised Standard Version, faced stiff competition from the New International Version and other more Evangelical Bible translations. In order to have broader appeal, *The New Interpreter's Bible* commentary printed both the NRSV and the NIV in parallel columns.

Another factor complicating seminary research was the complexity of seminary life. Although most schools had sabbatical programs and encouraged faculty members to seek grants, the daily life of faculty members was becoming more difficult. Few schools concentrated on one degree, and this meant that faculty had to teach diverse student populations. Most of the new degrees carried demands for more individualized courses (directed and independent studies) and more effort on such time-consuming tasks as DMin projects and MA theses. Little time existed for writing. Still, faculty members remained proud of their status as scholars, took active roles in professional societies, and kept up with their disciplines. Aside from in the university-related schools, little evidence exists that the publish-or-perish mentality of the

---

61. Wheeler, "Theological Publishing."

research schools influenced faculty at other seminaries. Few published, but many were tenured.

Changes in the larger culture of American higher education enabled American theological schools to appreciate their own scholarly work, apart from articles and monographs. In 1990, Ernest L. Boyer of the Carnegie Foundation for Teaching published his very influential study, "Scholarship Reconsidered." His basic point was that present-day considerations of scholarship should include four different types of inquiry: the scholarship of discovery, the scholarship of integration, the scholarship of application, and the scholarship of teaching.[62] Boyer's essay was a key element in helping faculties and administrators throughout higher education reassess the meaning of scholarship for tenure and promotion. Seminaries also adopted this broader understanding of scholarship, whether explicitly or implicitly, in their faculty handbooks. Many seminary faculty members who had not published extensively clearly had done outstanding work in one or more of Boyer's types of inquiry.

Boyer's typology also fits the actual diversity of theological schools. Faculty in university divinity schools conduct the basic research and publication in theology for two reasons. First, the university generally holds divinity faculty members to standards similar to those in the humanities. Research is the price of admission to a research university. Second, university divinity schools have doctoral programs, extensive libraries, and multidisciplinary conversations that equip them for the research task.[63] They also have a degree of academic freedom not yet established in all seminaries. Many Evangelical seminaries have strict confessional standards that inhibit research or at least publication, and the power of the *magisterium,* particularly in the training of diocesan priests, may inhibit research in some Catholic seminaries.[64] However, many theological teachers do fit neatly into one or another of Boyer's categories; in particular, faculty often practice the scholarship of application and the scholarship of integration at high levels. In many ways, theological schools, especially the smaller ones, are more analogous in size and achievement to liberal-arts colleges than to the universities that loom so large in seminary mythology.

THEOLOGICAL LIBRARIES, TECHNOLOGY, AND THE EMERGENCE OF A NEW FORM OF THEOLOGICAL EDUCATION

In 1984, Stephen L. Peterson, librarian of Trinity College, published "Theological Libraries for the Twenty-First Century: Project 2000 Final Report." The report was the result of a study of seminary libraries, financed by the Lilly Endowment and done under the auspices of both the Association of Theological Schools and the American Theological Library Association. In many ways, it was a conservative document.

62. Boyer, *Scholarship Reconsidered*, 16.
63. Kitagawa, *Religious Studies*; Cherry, *Hurrying toward Zion*, chapter 3.
64. *Theological Education*, "ATS Luce Consultation."

Peterson believed that the essential tasks of seminary libraries would remain constant: a good library would represent the historical breath of theological thought and religious practice; it would preserve the intellectual diversity of both past and present theology; it would support the school's current curriculum; and it would nurture research and fresh understandings of faith. In other words, libraries were essentially collections of materials. The remainder of the report focused on the resources needed to fulfill these purposes. In particular, it highlighted the need for funding to enable seminaries to expand their collections of materials about world Christianity and to care for their special collections, many of which might not be replaceable. Like almost all material on libraries, the report noted that the combination of heat, acid, and age had damaged many items, and called on seminaries to support efforts such as microfilming to save that material.

The most significant major change that Peterson noted[65] was a shift in how seminaries cataloged their collections. A collection has value only when users can access the materials that they need for particular tasks. The catalogs were guides to the collection. Libraries were increasingly abandoning traditional systems of classification, such as the Union System, in favor of the Library of Congress classification. Peterson traced this change to the use of computer technology:

> The decided movement towards computer assisted cataloguing that has been taking place in the theological libraries no less than in other academic libraries. Ninety-two seminary libraries are now members of a bibliographic utility; 15 anticipate joining a utility or network within five years, and another 10 schools anticipate joining within a decade. OCLC (Online Computer Library Center, formerly the Ohio College Library Center) is and will remain the utility servicing the majority of theological libraries. UTLAS (University of Toronto Library Automated Services) may have eight members, and RLIN (Research Library Information Network), three or four. Thus, even more than is the case with library classification, the theological libraries have cast their lot with large and complex bibliographic utilities. Our libraries will have to accept the products and services of these utilities or find effective ways to modify them.[66]

Although these changes substantially decreased the time between purchasing and shelving, they were back-office changes, rarely noted by the average library user. Yet most users saw one important consequence of these changes. As digital cataloging advanced, computer terminals or networked personal computers gradually became part of the furniture of libraries, often placed conveniently near the traditional card catalogs. Libraries had traditionally housed their card catalogs in massive cases that dominated the library's public space. Shortly after digital cataloging was complete, the

---

65. Peterson, "Theological Libraries."
66. Ibid., 77.

card catalogs themselves disappeared, leaving behind a number of workstations, often placed at different locations in the reading room. The library may not have changed, but the feel of the space was very different.

In the early 1980s, Petersen did not think that the new microcomputers (PCs) had made a substantial difference:

> Microcomputers also are making their presence felt in the theological libraries although not to the extent one might expect... One might have expected that schools that are not members of bibliographic utilities might rely more heavily on micro-computers, but this is not the case. Apparently, schools that have committed themselves to the electronic technologies are using these technologies in several ways and through several machines. The anticipated growth in the use of micro-computers is substantial and may be about 255 percent over the next five years.[67]

Peterson's five-year span was prescient. In 1990, Peterson returned to the themes of his earlier study.[68] By this date, the new technology had become commonplace:

> The personal computer, better referred to as a scholar's workstation, is not a glorified typewriter or even a desktop library catalog. It is a tool of such multiple capabilities that most humanists have yet to begin to understand the effective range of services the microcomputer can render. The chief virtues of the workstation are (1) the power of linkages it provides, both internally and externally, to other scholars and resources, and (2) its powers of integration, i.e., its ability to bring multiple sources and resources to bear on a single problem.[69]

At this time, he estimated that "perhaps now half of all persons directly involved in theological study are computer literate," and he expected that number to grow.[70]

The 1990s were to confirm this prediction. During that decade, the Internet, originally designed for government and research-university use, expanded, and easily used search engines made its rich file sharing capacities available to people with fewer advanced computer skills.

Peterson recognized that these developments would change the character of theological library work. Whether the librarian actually managed the new technology or whether a seminary assigned that task to a new office, later called IT, or information technology, the librarian and the library staff were the people who had the expertise to educate faculty and staff in the use of the new systems.[71] Whenever a teacher or

---

67. Ibid., 79.
68. Peterson, "The More Things Change."
69. Ibid., 139.
70. Ibid., 139–40.
71. The new technology required two levels of skill and expertise. One level was the physical management of the computers, networks, wi-fi systems, etc. Someone had to understand where the servers

student needed help in gathering information or using the new information technology, the library was the natural place to begin.

Libraries responded to the new opportunities in different ways. A 1997 Lilly grant permitted schools to explore the use of computers and information technology in the classroom. Computers opened up various new means of teaching to faculty, including such tools as PowerPoint.[72] These new classroom techniques were information intensive and often faculty found themselves needing new material to supplement their own study and research. To use the new technology effectively, many faculty needed advice and even guidance from the library. Internet-based platforms such as Blackboard, first marketed in 1997, also required considerable library input.

The new technology, particularly the Internet, had a hidden problem. The Internet was an open source, which anyone, at least anyone with technical skills, could use to disseminate information. In contrast, the traditional library was a collection, a consciously assembled set of resources chosen from among many options. A library was only as good as its collection policy. While electronic cataloging and the new interlibrary resources such as OCLC expanded the collections that a student or a scholar might search, they did not fundamentally change the selective character of collections.[73] However, the Web was not only a place where one could examine a collection of collections. The Internet also contained materials of varying quality, ranging from scholarly writing, carefully juried, to rants. Religion, of course, attracted both the most and the least reliable Web authors. The ATLA made a major contribution to the usefulness of the Internet when it resolved to publish full-text editions of significant journals, and the Wabash Center published an online list of websites. Various databases also made useful selections, but the number of such databases available depended on a particular seminary's library budget. Trained librarians who understood the nature and use of the various means of electronic access were as valuable, if not more so, than trained research librarians were to more traditional libraries.

An immediate challenge for librarians was to find ways to provide the new distance- and extension-education programs with library services. In some ways, the extension programs were the easiest. Librarians typically continued the established pattern of negotiating with local libraries for use, either as part of an exchange, or upon payment of a fee. As electronic cataloging advanced, extension centers received

---

were located and how they were connected. While some schools assigned these tasks to the library or put them under the supervision of the librarian, some schools created a separate information-technology (IT) department. The second level of skill was the application of the new technology to education. This was the area where the librarian and its staff became central to the schools. Few faculty, for example, care about the details of the network that puts their computer into contact with the seminary system; they are vitally concerned with what materials they can access for teaching and learning.

72. Microsoft PowerPoint was probably overused. PowerPoint had the advantage of being easy to learn. An instructor could use the program to integrate visual materials, such as art or photographs, music, and text into a single presentation.

73. Crawford et al., "Is There Anything Worthwhile on the Web?"

their own terminals that, in turn, made it easier for students to order specific works from the central libraries. The home libraries could, in turn, mail the student the requested works; or where the extension center was in frequent contact with the home campus, send them by carrier or even, as in the Boston Theological Institute—a Boston-area consortium—distribute books and other resources by van. In effect, electronic cataloging gave every extension its own copy of the catalog and made it possible to search and use the library at a distance. When the Internet became more available, of course, electronic catalogs became accessible from any computer, along with such interlibrary-loan sources as WorldCat.

It can be useful to distinguish extension from distance education.[74] Seminaries conducted extension education in centers where the school maintained a variety of programs and resources. The larger extensions might provide some or all of the academic degree programs available at the main campus, while smaller extensions might only offer a handful of the courses needed for a degree. Some extensions had television connections to the main campus, enabling students to participate in their regular classes. Reformed Seminary's extension program in Orlando was larger than its home campus in Jackson, Mississippi. In contrast, distance education was education that was not classroom dependent. The earliest forms of distance education used such technology as audio and video tapes, although the future was with the Internet. Directed and independent studies were also part of distance education, although they usually counted as residential courses.

After 2000, distance education blossomed as the seminaries, together with many colleges and universities, made an increasing percentage of their program available online. The new delivery system developed in pace with new computer technology. As the use of broadband and other speedy forms of Internet access increased, seminaries increasingly taught more complex courses. Some of these mimicked classroom courses, requiring students to be present at their computers at a set time. Others, perhaps the most common, allowed students to access the course at any time day or night. In the case of synchronic courses, the instructor involved students directly with one another; in the case of the diachronic courses, teachers employed other computer-enabled forms of interaction, such as chat rooms and e-mail exchanges. The use of other electronic technologies in the classroom, such as Blackboard, facilitated the introduction of distance learning. Both technologically aided teaching in the classroom and distance education required the use of information technologies and the integration of a variety of media, including video.

---

74. ATS took this approach in its revision of the standards in 2012. Here distance education is defined as "a mode of education in which a course is offered without students and instructors being in the same location. Instruction may be synchronous or asynchronous and employs the use of technology. Distance education courses may consist of exclusively online or other technologically assisted instruction or a blend of intensive classroom and online instruction" (ES.4.1). At the risk of anachronism, I read this distinction back into the analysis of the material.

Distance education was less expensive than extension centers, and much less bound to the specific location of the student. The student might be located in New York City, surrounded by ample resources, or in rural North Dakota, many miles from a traditional library. Although "blended" programs that required some time on campus, usually in the form of intensives, were one approach to this problem, they did not solve it. Almost by definition, intensive classes required a student's attendance through much of a working day, leaving little time or energy to use the library or other resources. More important for seminaries was that the distance program itself had to provide resources for each course. Although some courses might use textbooks, institutions needed to provide additional resources electronically. In effect, librarians faced the problem of creating virtual libraries for each course.

Libraries were and are capital-intensive enterprises. The same observation is true of technology. For many schools neither the will of their administrators nor the technical abilities of faculty and staff set the limits of the new technological methods. The real constraint was financial. The younger Evangelical schools had some substantial advantages here. Whether or not Evangelicalism was more open to new media than Mainstream Protestantism,[75] Evangelical institutions had two advantages in adopting new techniques. The first is that Evangelical seminaries were comparatively young institutions with a small capital base. Since they had fewer expensive investments in buildings and land, they could invest their resources as the current seminary market dictated. Second, Evangelicalism is a popular movement that depends on the religious excitement of its members, particularly the young. The same youthful openness to cultural innovation that movements create in music and speaking styles encourages Evangelical institutions' openness to technological innovation. Just as it is culturally natural for members of a movement to play Christian music on a portable device, so it is culturally natural for the same group to use other new technologies as they become popular. When a seminary like Asbury used the new technology to redesign its library around information technology and its use,[76] the school's faculty supported the innovation, and its students accepted and applauded the change

The close relationship between libraries and the new technology has an almost Niebuhrian irony. Librarians have often felt that they were an unappreciated component in theological education. Most administrators and faculty have not understood or appreciated the technical and education skills needed to administer a modern library, as the almost endless debates over whether librarians should have faculty status attest. Yet the marriage of technical skills and new technologies has made the library

---

75. Wesley and Whitefield had almost invented the religious use of the new popular press, and Wesley used the press to finance his movement. Whitefield's skills as an actor are well known. Nineteenth-century evangelicals used tracts, often printed with four-color technology, and their publications kept up with the popular taste for illustration. The willingness of evangelicals in the twentieth century to use radio, television, and other technology is well known.

76. The Asbury story is told in American Theological Library Association, "The Information Commons Model"; Boyd, "The Library's Role."

and librarians central to the most visible changes in current theological education. At a time when institutions are increasingly using part-time and adjunctive faculty, the need for librarians with the ability to help students and teachers use the new technology is growing. To exaggerate somewhat, the person able to teach people to use information technology is as central to the new style of education as faculty members were in a less technological age. While I doubt whether the time will come when the new technological librarians will demand faculty status as information technologists, it is not unthinkable.

FINDING A VOICE

In the course of discussing different topics, we have mentioned some of the significant changes that affected theological education during the last twenty years: the decline of residence and the increase in part-time and older students; continuing financial crises; new understandings of teaching and learning; technological innovations; and the increasing presence of women and of racial and ethnic minorities in student bodies, faculty, and administrations. To these we should add the gradual evolution of seminary administrations, new ideas of teaching and learning, new accreditation procedures, and the continuing financial problems of small, often independent, institutions. Historians like dates and symbolic events that have clear locations in time. Alas, few such historical markers exist in the history of theological education. The most significant changes in theological education over the last fifty years have been incremental. Only when the historian looks back can he or she realize how much has changed.

If historians looking back have this much difficulty understanding the rate and direction of change, how do leaders in theological education get the information to enable them to make intelligent decisions about their institutions? Conversations are, of course, part of this process. In a high-level discussion, leaders exchange information, but that is not all they exchange. A good dialog has room for discussion, interpretation, rebuttal, and transformation. There are many structured places for such fruitful exchanges. Most denominational seminary presidents and deans met together once or twice a year. In addition, the yearly meetings of the Fellowship of Evangelical Seminary Presidents, the Mid-Atlantic Association of Theological Schools (Catholic), and newer meetings of Catholic seminary presidents and rectors under the aegis of the Seminary Department of the National Catholic Education Association, as well as the biennial meetings of the ATS, were important places for the exchange of information. We have already mentioned *In Trust,* a lively well-written journal that presented needed information to trustees and others, which enabled them to put their institutions into a meaningful context. The Lilly Endowment, often jokingly called "the church's one foundation," was another important source of dialog and exchange. The Lilly technology grants, for example, were the bellwether of the technological revolution, and Lilly's substantial investments in the recruitment of younger students indicated the need for seminaries to broaden their appeal to youth. In competing for grants, institutions get a clear picture of important trends.

Two institutions were particularly important sources of information: The Association of Theological Schools and the Auburn Center for the Study of Theological Education. The Association had long been a very complex organization. In addition to its work in accreditation, ATS served as the advocate for theological education; the source of information about schools and about training for presidents, deans, and other officers; and the professional society for seminary leaders. In 2004, the Association became two separate legal corporations, dividing its accrediting from its other functions.[77] Although ATS decisions about standards had impact on schools, the impact of conversations at or sponsored by the Association may have had equal impact.

Daniel Aleshire as an Interpreter of Theological Education

Daniel Aleshire was the new century's most influential interpreter of theological education. Aleshire became executive director of ATS in 2002. Aleshire was well prepared for his new position. He had headed up the work in accreditation and supervised the reformulation of the Association's accrediting standards in the 1990s. Aleshire had contributed to the Readiness for Ministry project in the 1970s. He had also served as a professor of religious education. As a former member of the Southern Baptist Theological Seminary faculty, Aleshire experienced the nasty Southern Baptist battles of the 1980s, but he had avoided the angry anti-Evangelicalism that characterized many SBC survivors. While at ATS, Aleshire transferred his ordination to the United Methodist Church. He was a naturally irenic figure who was able to work effectively across the wide spectrum of ATS schools.

Over his time in theological education, Aleshire became a skilled interpreter of theological schools. One of the most important studies that prepared him to interpret the work of ATS and its schools was his partnership with Jackson Carroll, Barbara Wheeler, and Penny Long Marler in the writing of *Being There: Culture and Formation in Two Theological Schools*.[78] The team presented both wings of American Protestantism. Jackson Carroll, a prominent sociologist of religion, had long conducted social research for the Association of Theological Schools. In many ways, he was the go-to person for information about seminaries and their social context. He would later head the influential Pew and Pulpit Research project, sponsored by the Pew Charitable Trusts. Barbara Wheeler was the president of Auburn Seminary in New York and had participated actively in the Basic Issues research, both as commentator and as a Lilly evaluator. Her work on this project helped prepare her for her work at the Auburn Center for Theological Education. Penny Long Marler, also a Southern Baptist Theological Seminary graduate, taught religion at Samford University, a Baptist

---

77. Miller, *A Community of Conversation*, 35–36.
78. Carroll et al., *Being There*.

institution in Birmingham, Alabama. The team project was an ethnographic study of two schools. The decision to employ ethnographic methods was an attempt to avoid the hackneyed type of comparative-educational study that stressed differences in curriculum and other formal items. Instead, the researchers wanted to examine how the two schools shaped their students—intellectually, socially, and religiously.[79]

The research for *Being There* began in 1989, just as Robert Wuthnow's *The Restructuring of American Religion*[80] was at the height of its popularity. Wuthnow's book was on most religious leaders' required-reading list for a variety of reasons, including its lucid and clear style; but the book was important because it linked two important events: the decline of the Mainstream churches and the rise of the Evangelicals. While others had noted both of these separately, Wuthnow's book highlighted their interrelation. At much the same time, James Davison Hunter was popularizing the idea of "culture wars," an almost epic struggle for the soul of a nation. *Being There* was not a treatise about the culture wars, but the researchers worked in its shadow. The fact that the authors called one school a Mainstream seminary and the other an Evangelical seminary indicates the influence of the larger context on their work.

Being There, like all significant studies, functioned on a variety of levels. Its primary focus was on the question of how seminaries socialized their students into the profession of ministry.

> For these reasons our two schools have come to share a number of similar formal characteristics in spite of the sharp differences in the content of their normative cultures . . . Each has some somewhat similar governance structures, each has faculty with similar faculty rank structures; the faculty and students operate with relatively similar rules governing behavior and interaction; each school follows a curriculum structure that has some formal similarities ; each organizes its degree programs according to a common set of standards; and each, with the constraints of its normative culture, emphasizes the norm of the freedom of inquiry.[81]

Significantly, both schools, Evangelical and Mainstream, were reformist institutions. Their cultures hoped to transform the students into their own image, and both reserved much of their scorn for those in their own party who did not accept their program.

In many ways, reform formed the bedrock of much that happened in both schools. *Being There*'s picture of the seminaries is one that features intense internal conflict. Students come to each school with their own theologies and confront the

---

79. Speculation on exactly which schools were involved was commonplace among theological educators when the book appeared. My own guess, based on no research whatever, is either Wesley Seminary in Washington or Drew for the Mainstream Seminary, and Gordon-Conwell in Massachusetts for the Evangelical Seminary.
80. Wuthnow, *The Restructuring*.
81. Carroll et al., *Being There*, 261.

school's dominant understanding of the faith and of ministry. Over the course of the program, the combination of classes, special events, conversations (especially meals together), chapel services, and so forth results in a compromise in which the old is retained and changed by the new.[82] Interestingly enough, the tools that both faculties used to effect this expected change are often rhetorical. This may hide a deeper, less pleasant truth. Although the authors did not draw this conclusion, the reader feels that persuasion has replaced scholarship as the foundation of the each school's pedagogy. The goal is "to get things straight."[83] The Mainstream seminary wants a church that reflects the need for gender and racial equality; the Evangelical seminary wants a scholarly conservatism, rooted in a more Calvinist, less revivalist, understanding of faith. In many ways, this picture of seminary pedagogy is similar to the one presented in *Educating Clergy*. As Foster and his fellow researchers noted, the goal of the diverse pedagogies employed by theological education is the transformation of the student's deposit of faith. Both Mainstream and Evangelical seminaries respond to the growing popularity of postmodernism. For the postmodernist, education had a primarily volitional character that makes the shaping of the student's will, particularly the student's political will, the paramount educational goal.

Being There did note some differences between the two schools. One significant difference was that Evangelical seminary students "do not move through its program in cohorts," while Mainstream seminary's students did. Equally significant, fewer students at the Mainstream school were commuters or part time. In that sense, the Evangelical seminary was much more like the future than its Mainstream counterpart was. By 2010, most Protestant schools had a majority of part-time students following their own way through the seminary. Reading between the lines, this may have guaranteed Evangelical students a greater freedom in their use of the seminary. At the end of the program, the reformist emphasis of their school had influenced them less than the reformist program of Mainstream seminary influenced its students. Yet, as the authors noted, the Evangelical seminary's general culture did not necessarily imply a greater freedom than the Mainstream's. For instance, Evangelical culture had less room for certain questions, especially questions about such politically hot issues as abortion. By 1990, to be an Evangelical was to oppose abortion, no matter how liberal or even radical one might be on such issues as war and peace or poverty.

The careful description in *Being There* provides some important insight into two of theological education's most explicit and angry critics: John H. Leith[84] and Thomas C. Oden.[85] Both worked in Mainstream seminaries where the contested nature of social and theological issues was most evident, and the sharp edge of both authors' books suggests that the enemy under attack was much closer to home than their cri-

---

82. Ibid., 223–24.
83. Ibid., 240
84. Leith, *Crisis in the Church*.
85. Oden, *Requiem*.

tiques stated or let on. Unlike more abstract understandings of learning, reformist and other transformative understandings of education leave little room for disagreement. Although Leith was neo-orthodox and Oden was moving toward Evangelical, both shared a passion for the truth of theology and for theology as faithful inquiry. In that model, participation in the larger historical discussion was more important than the actual resolution of special issues. That two such establishment figures should become bitter jeremiahs confirms much about the world pictured in *Being There*. Whatever the leaders and writers about seminaries might project about their work and mission, what actually occurred on the field might be quite different. Ethos, mentioned in almost all discussions of theological education, may have trumped theology and scholarship in many schools.

Aleshire's work in accreditation educated him further about theological education. During this period directing accreditation, he visited many ATS schools and read the paperwork submitted by others. If the type of study in *Being There* concerned an overarching view or macroview of theological education, the work in accreditation provided him with a close look or microview of individual schools. As executive director, he added to this knowledge. Aleshire's talks to different constituencies, including at the biennial meetings of the Association, provided snapshots of where theological education was at that moment, and made suggestions about possible futures. These periodic reports interpreted contemporary theological education and placed the schools in their religious and cultural milieus. These addresses confirmed ATS standing as the primary interpreter of American theological education and were widely referred to by seminary presidents and board chairs.

Aleshire demonstrated his command of American theological education as a highly valued speaker who received annual invitations to address all of the major constituent groups of the ATS in their meetings. The scope of his interpretation is especially clear in his 2010 volume *Earthen Vessels: Hopeful Reflections on the Work and Future of Theological Schools*.[86] The title was significant. Aleshire recognized that many different types of institutions prepared people for ministry. What he wanted to explore was the case for theological seminaries "like the more than 250 members of the Association of Theological Schools." Theological schools maintain faculties, have libraries, and grant professional and research degrees.[87] Although they are not eternal, theological schools are institutions designed to last over time; their mission links the churches' and their own past to a shared future. Schools provide, consequently, one of the best places for the critical examination and transmission of the tradition. Aleshire argued that

> theological Schools provide more than the sum of three activities. When learning for religious vocation, teaching leaders, and theological research are

---

86. Aleshire, *Earthen Vessels*.
87. Ibid., 21.

undertaken in close connection with each other, over time, in communities of common interest, the result is fundamentally different than if these activities are done separately. Each of them is improved when performed in the presence of the others, and a school provides the single context that brings them together in both expectation and practice.[88]

In other words, the schools promote three types of learning: professional learning, academic learning, and personal learning. As Aleshire and other commentators note, theological schools are expensive, and often their graduates face an increasing burden of debt. The question is, in simple terms, is it worth it? Reading and rereading Aleshire's argument at this point, I wish that he had continued the earlier threefold analysis of theological education (as including professional learning, academic learning, and personal learning). It might be, for example, that theological schools are not particularly well equipped as places for advanced graduate study (academic learning). Universities with their capacity to absorb the high costs of research programs might well be better suited to this specific task. We might make a similar observation about personal learning. Granted that laypeople and seekers need something more than the usual adult church education, is the seminary the proper place to provide it, or do seminaries do this by default? Lay institutes on the European model have not been particularly successful in America,[89] and seminaries seem to be the only current means to meet this need. However, setting aside such criticisms, Aleshire made his point directly and with little fanfare:

> Is the work these schools do worth the price tag? If theological education is a commodity to be produced at the least expense for the most recipients, then the question is legitimate. If the goal, however, is the preparation of religious leaders who are deeply formed in an understanding of faith, who can guide congregations in a culture that is less than convinced that religion is a cultural asset, who can lead in the context of significant change in congregational practice, and who know the tradition and can teach it to the increasing percentage of people who do not know the tradition or understand it, then theological education is not a commodity. Seminaries are founded when religious expressions are growing, and their greatest need might be when those expressions are struggling.[90]

In other words, the value of theological education is proportional to the values of those for whom their graduates ultimately work. With this assertion, we are back to the great question of the 1980s, perhaps somewhat restated: What is the theological value of theological education?

---

88. Ibid., 24.

89. Andover Newton made a major commitment to lay education during the presidency of George Peck, which the school was ultimately unable to sustain.

90. Aleshire, *Earthen Vessels*, 145

The Auburn Center for the Study of Theological Education

The other great interpreter of theological education was the Center for the Study of Theological Education, headed by Barbara Wheeler, president of Auburn Seminary. The Center received its initial funding from the Lilly Endowment. The first volume of Auburn Studies, *Reaching Out*, published in 1993, made the Center's relationship to the 1980s research plain:

> The last decade has seen an unprecedented amount of research and reflection on theological education, efforts with which Auburn's staff and board leaders were well-acquainted. In 1990, Auburn completed an evaluation of ten years of research that had been funded by Lilly Endowment Inc., the largest sponsor of such studies. Led by Auburn's President, Barbara Wheeler, and David Kelsey, professor of theology at the Yale Divinity School and an Auburn consultant, a team of evaluators assessed the quality and impact of 50 research projects supported by nearly $5 million in grants and producing more than 75 published products. They found the amount and quality of work to be impressive and learned that several studies had already exerted significant influence.[91]

The Auburn Center contributed high-quality research on theological schools in its periodic reports. The most able of these studies were on seminary finance. Anthony G. Ruger, who had served earlier at McCormick and at ATS, was third in a secession of nationally known experts on seminary finances, following in the footsteps of Badgett Dillard and Warren Deem. Ruger continued the every-ten-year examination of seminary finances, pointing to much continuity in seminary economies, including the continued decline of denominational support and the continual need for more individual donors. Like Deem and Dillard, Ruger had a breadth of knowledge of seminaries and their business practices that enabled him to advise schools on such varied practices as strategic planning, fundraising, and educational debt. Ruger's work both as researcher for Auburn and as a consultant to individual schools, like Dillard's and Deem's, was sober. Like his predecessors, Ruger continued to note that theological schools were underfinanced and often irresponsibly hopeful about their own initiatives. One can see the Ruger studies as part of a long-ranged emphasis on "best practices" in seminary finance and financial planning.

The Auburn Center's research program also included periodic studies of seminary presidents, faculties, and boards. The primary value of these studies was their use of quantification and careful measurement. In a sense, the various studies proceeded by comparing common or received perceptions with what the researcher learned from statistical and survey data. This method meant that the results of the studies were rarely surprising. One exception to this rule was the Center's report on the public knowledge of seminaries in their midst: *Missing Connections: Public Perceptions*

---

91. Wheeler and Delloff, "Reaching Out."

of *Theological Education and Religious Leadership*.[92] This study indicated how poorly known seminaries were in their own locations. Many seminary leaders recognized in the study a program that they had not anticipated.

The work of the Auburn Center researchers as consultants for various schools was perhaps as important as the Center's publications. Particularly in such areas as finance, Auburn's researchers had access to considerable data and expertise. Private conversations with seminary leaders often did not point to popular results. Many seminaries were in financial trouble before they met with the Auburn consultants, and those called in to examine dark clouds rarely find silver linings. Their recommendations, in whole or more often in part, affected the way that many schools conducted their business and may have been instrumental in helping some schools to determine whether they should struggle on, reorganize, or close.

BRINGING TO A CLOSE

Like all contemporary histories, this narrative ends arbitrarily as we approach the present. The story began with the seminaries increasingly aware of their own financial fragility and, in many ways, it ends on the same note, with the various reports of the Auburn Center. The goal of achieving some type of financial stability pushed the seminaries to professionalize their administrations, to steadily develop the offices of the president, the dean, the chief financial officer, and, above all, the director (now often called the vice president) of development. The Auburn Studies provide graphic evidence of how far the schools have come in developing an increasingly skilled and well-supported staff.

The financial crisis has, of course, not ended, as the recession of 2008 demonstrated. Few seminaries have the money or other resources to realize their potential fully, and this perpetual crisis shows no sign of alleviating itself in the near future. More schools will face exigency, and many more will find that their opinions are limited by their bottom lines. The decline of American Christian institutions will only make this situation worse, not better, as schools compete for a handful of students and other resources.

Yet the poverty of American theological schools has not been wholly a bad situation. The fact that the schools desperately needed students and money helped them adjust to the rights revolution. Without women students, for example, many seminaries would have closed or faced a substantial lowering of their academic standards. The same was true to a more limited extent of African Americans and Latina/Latino students. If these new constituencies did not completely transform the seminaries, as their more vocal supporters hoped, they did change them substantially.

---

92. Lynn and Wheeler, "Missing Connections."

8 Visions
A Concluding Reflective Postscript

OUR STORY BEGAN WITH the general sense of financial crisis that overtook American theological schools in the late 1960s. Much of the thought about the administration and direction of theological schools that subsequently took place was fired by the sense that these financial woes could be overcome by a combination of strong and able presidents (or in schools related to universities, deans), sound financial planning, and above all, ably led development programs. The more adventuresome thinkers among theological educators, including many denominational executives, believed that only the consolidation of schools into larger, more financially viable institutions offered any future for theological education. These prophets could point to the success of the Southern Baptist schools, to the rising importance of Evangelical institutions (especially such powerful schools as Fuller Theological Seminary, Gordon-Conwell Theological Seminary, Trinity Evangelical Divinity School, and Dallas Theological Seminary), as well as the classic university schools. Yet this prescription was by and large not followed. The Mainstream seminaries found it difficult to consolidate their schools, with only a handful of mergers succeeding, and ironically, the Southern Baptists and the Evangelicals, inspired in part by theological controversy, went on a binge of new school foundings. Had the half century been one of revival and religious prosperity, this activity might have sustainable. It was not. Reversing almost one hundred years of growth, American religious organizations shrank steadily during the period, as an increasing secularization of society and declining birthrates took a progressively larger toll on church membership. Pundits might argue that the Roman Catholic Church was the largest religious body and ex–Roman Catholics the next largest, but the decline was real. As a result, the story arrives at the present in the midst of yet another financial crisis for American theological schools.

The financial condition of theological schools is influenced by many factors, but the most important is that theological education is a dependent market. Ultimately, the health of theological schools depends on the ability of many small and very fragile churches to generate students, contributions, and placements. The equation is simple: when the congregations are strong, the schools flourish; when they are weak, they do not. Although theological schools bear some resemblance to other nonprofits, they differ in one important aspect. Both other nonprofits and seminaries depend on alliances for their support, but the public for theological schools is considerably more restricted than the market for other charities.

In other words, the phrase "follow the money" is as important for the history of theological schools as it is for many mysteries and thrillers. Part of what makes the problem so difficult for seminaries is that they live in two worlds: the world of the academy and the world of the church. Perhaps in a less structured time, seminaries could have lived in sectarian isolation from the larger world of higher education, although there is no evidence that they ever did, but that was not a possibility for schools in our period. For good or ill, the larger world of higher education established many of the institutional and academic standards that the theological schools believed they had to attain. Further, the virtual monopoly of advanced religious thought that the seminaries had enjoyed before 1960 was shattered by the rise of the academic study of religion in colleges and universities. Not only did the new departments compete for teachers, often successfully, but they also had many perks, including more generous salaries, that the seminaries had to match. And on the research level, the universities had the resources—including libraries—that the seminaries could not match. Competition often results in winners and losers, and the seminaries were in many ways the losers in this competition.

Like most of American life, American higher education was a tangle of regulations, formal and informal, legal and customary. Seminaries had, of course, always struggled with the many local regulations around buildings, but the last fifty years saw these regulations multiply as schools sought to become accessible to people with disabilities and to use less energy. But the real gateway to regulation was through the new federal student-loan programs that mandated, at least if one wanted one's students to have access to the money, meeting federal standards, including accreditation. Many of these regulations were good, some very good, but they did require increased sophistication, and sophistication comes at a price.

Federal loans were a gentle trap for the school. On the one hand, these loans permitted seminaries to pass more and more of their expenses on to their students, who could defer payment (hopefully) until a more convenient season. What this meant was that seminary tuition was, for the first time, somewhat elastic. Moreover, the federal program permitted theological students to borrow amounts in line with other students in professional schools. Yet a world of difference existed between the future earnings of a lawyer or surgeon and the future earnings of a pastor. In addition, the relative elasticity of seminary tuition resulted in a labyrinth of financial-aid programs that made it difficult to figure out what the amount paid to schools by the average student might be.

The administrator's vision of theological education was largely expressed through the Association of Theological Schools and its standards. Basically, their vision was what the Association of Theological Schools called the Good Theological School. The Good Theological School was a well-financed institution that served its public well and met contemporary expectations for sound financial planning and management. In many ways, this vision, especially as it was shared by the majority of ATS administrators, was open ended. They believed, or at least the documents that they formulated and publicly shared affirmed, that each institution was capable and obligated to form its own picture of its mission in the world. The pressure of the federal government for more accountability also influenced this picture of the ideal seminary. Theological schools carefully worked through the requirements for public disclosure and labored to find ways to establish that they identified and measured the learning outcomes of their programs. In simple terms, seminaries shared a common form but not necessarily a common substance.

This understanding of the nature of theological schools did not so much change as it deepened and became more sophisticated. Information gathering and analysis became more sophisticated as both outside agency and internal administrative decisions required more detailed information about the schools, individually and as a system of similar institutions.

Perhaps the biggest system-wide shock was the long rights revolution that was slowly but surely winning ground in America. Basically, the American political, educational, and economic system moved from being largely a world dominated by White, male heads of households to being a complex world that included racial, ethnic, and gender diversity. Although some social tensions resulted from these changes, basically the society and with it the churches and seminaries made these changes with relative ease. Even the incorporation of women into ordained ministry, a striking departure from tradition, was accomplished with relative dispatch. From one perspective, it was a peaceful revolution with little difficulty. The seminaries basically moved in tandem with the larger society and culture.

Yet, and this is one of the decisive differences between theological education and other forms of professional training, the existential dimension of theology, the fact that theology always addresses head and heart, meant that the study of theology—not just its application—had to be affected by social change. The closest analogies to these might be the many programs in Hispanic American studies, women's studies, or African American studies in undergraduate schools and universities. In general, those programs used various disciplines—history, social science, philosophy,and so forth—to examine a particular subject matter. Some important analogs to these programs existed in theological schools as courses in women's history and in African American and Hispanic culture multiplied. However, what was different was the assertion by many minority theologians that their experiences ought to modify the structure of faith and its articulation. In some ways, this was a variation on the theme of culture and theology that had concerned theologians since Schleiermacher. No serious theologian doubted that cultural context influenced religious and theological affirmation. What was different was the assertion that cultural norms could and should be used as critical principles in theological inquiry. The result was a natural fragmenting of theological studies, as courses were offered in black theology, feminist and womanist theology, Latin American theology, and so forth. A similar fragmenting occurred in biblical studies, where the historical-critical method, although not replaced or ignored, was supplemented by a variety of hermeneutics that sought to provide a perspective on the text and its interpretation.

Judging the significance of these theologies will take more perspective than we currently have. Clearly, some work of lasting and abiding significance was done and some conclusions reached that have become part of the commonplaces of current seminary life. Taken as a whole, these theological directions did sustain a fairly consistent picture of the seminary and its mission. Basically, this vision was that theological reflection must primarily serve the needs of various social groups for liberation and support, and the churches' larger goals and purposes must include such social transformation as one (if not the overarching) purpose of Christian faith. Although represented on most faculties, particularly those related to Mainstream Protestantism, it rarely dominated those schools. It was, however, an important vision of what the schools ought to become.

In many ways, the rights revolution may have been the seminaries' fiscal savior. Beginning in the 1960s, the number of white males interested in the ministry progressively declined. As in Europe, secularization appears to have advanced much more radically among established males than among females or immigrants. Church attendance and membership also show a rapid decline in white male participation. Had the seminaries continued to rely on the white male demographic for their budgets, most could not have met their expenses. Even with significant enrollments by underrepresented groups, they have struggled to maintain enrollments, a significant statistic for schools that are largely tuition driven.

The pace of change in theological schools was increased by the progressive integration of minority people into American economic and political culture. As the people attending minority churches became better educated and more prosperous, they wanted pastors with professional and educational standing in the community. They also wanted leaders whose sophistication equaled their own. In modern professionalized America, the seminaries as graduate professional schools have the prestige to help minority pastors grow with their congregations. Of course, this is not only or merely a matter of social prestige. Seminary graduates have knowledge and skills that enable them to work effectively in a middle-classed environment; that is, the degree certifies substantial ability to serve as a minister to a particular clientele.

Many factors combined to slow the rate of change in theological schools. As often was the case, finances played a role. No school could add the faculty that it desired to meet the needs of its new student bodies, and underrepresented constituencies have continued to lag behind in the number of faculty and administrative positions that their members have attained. In part, this is because administrative positions require substantial professional experience before appointment, but it is more complicated than that. Small institutions tend to add new personnel at a very slow rate, and they tend to retain personnel over long periods of service. If this is less true for the twentieth century than for the nineteenth, when whole faculties might change over a few short years, the slow rate of retirements and the lack of substantial institutional growth necessarily slow the rate of theological and institutional change.

The bitter battle among American religious conservatives in the 1980s came, ironically, at the point when religious conservatism had made remarkable gains in theological education. These controversies involved some of America's largest and most successful seminaries. These included the Southern Baptist schools, Concordia (the largest Lutheran theological faculty in the world), and the flagship of western-US conservatism, Fuller Theological Seminary. In the case of both Concordia and the Southern Baptist schools, these controversies resulted in the largest sudden shift in theological direction in the history of American theological education, and other conservative institutions have had to work more carefully and cautiously thereafter.[1]

The debate over the aims and purposes of theological education in these controversies needs to be seen in the larger context of American theological education. By and large, all sides in the debate shared a common belief in theological education as professional education, and religious education—ironically one of the great new approaches to theological education pioneered by liberal Christians—was particularly prized by Southern Baptists. The same was true of pastoral psychology, another liberal innovation that also found strong support among Southern Baptists, and, interestingly enough, at Fuller, which established a full school of psychology. These remnants of the old professional model would not be challenged by the inerrancy debate, and all these emphases would continue after the transformation of the various institutions. To be sure, Concordia, which followed more continental theological models than most American schools, did not embrace these directions with the passion or consistency of other conservative schools, but these newer emphases were there as well.

So much of the ill will from those disputes is still present that one hesitates to try to summarize the issues with fairness to both sides. Nonetheless, one can say that at the heart of the conservative movement was the strong conviction that any compromise of the doctrine of biblical inerrancy led schools sooner or later to embrace an understanding of theological education that encouraged or advocated intellectual

---

1. In contrast, the change from confessional to liberal among denominational seminaries took almost thirty years of trial and error. The changes at Concordia took place almost in a year, and the process of change in SBC seminaries took less than a decade.

and social accommodations with current intellectual fashion. To use an analogy from earlier church history, these conservatives saw biblical inerrancy much as classical Christians saw the Nicene formulation: as a bulwark against serious departures from the faith. In this sense, inerrancy was a core doctrine that defined the conservative world of discourse. Thus, one might not believe that the story of the conquest of Canaan had much contemporary theological relevance, but the denial of the historicity of the biblical account of that conquest had far-reaching theological implications. The better conservative theologians were aware that many very different theologies might be constructed on this foundation—after all, both the Council of Trent and the Book of Concord interpreted inerrancy as a mark of biblical authority. Yet this did not necessarily mean that the doctrine was not relevant. In most sports, the rule book defines the field of play and its dimensions. Likewise, inerrancy defined the language game of conservative theology and church life. Both believers in the real presence and deniers of the doctrine could argue, because they shared a similar point of view of the field of play.

Were all conservatives that sophisticated in their understanding of the issues? I doubt it. Many subscribed to a very simple doctrine of biblical supremacy: "God said it; I believe it." Others held to other simple biblicisms.[2] This should not obscure the fact that serious people, often with very good theological educations, held the conservative point of view. Conservatives were not the "bozarks of the Ozarks" as many liberals and moderates charged.

The moderate position was less sharply defined. At their best, the Moderates believed that they offered a conservative, even confessional, understanding of contemporary theological discussion. This meant openness to modern biblical criticism and its conclusions, a willingness to consider existential and process perspectives on theological education, and a general acceptance of the broader social ministry of the churches. In that sense, the field of theological discourse was defined by the contemporary theological discussion among diverse participants. In other words, they shared the field with schools that ranged from the most progressive to conservative. The desire to be part of this larger language game meant conformity to the rules by which it was played: the priority of research and reasoned discourse, the importance of academic freedom, and engagement in the broader discussion through publication (including oral presentation). On that field, they were confident that they represented an intelligent and articulate understanding of their traditions. Yet, the belief in reasoned discourse and dialog demanded that the field represented by a particular school have a variety of positions. Most moderate schools had faculty and students who ranged from positions almost indistinguishable from their conservative opponents to scholars who were much closer to the Mainstream Protestant or even to progressive Protestant positions.

2. The plural is deliberate.

The different understandings of the task of theology made dialog across the divide between the two positions almost impossible. In a real sense, they were playing different games with different rules and different players. What constituted a winning argument in one language game did not score in the other. Perhaps that was the reason for the constantly rising tensions between the advocates of the different positions. It also may help to explain why the carefully nuanced Chicago Statement on Biblical Inerrancy did not satisfy most of the combatants. It may also explain why many very conservative schools continued to leave such questions as the historicity of Adam and Eve open to discussion in the classroom, if the inerrancy of Genesis was nonetheless maintained.

Both sides were deeply affected by the passion for relevance and political activism that was part of the heritage of the 1960s. Both moderates and conservatives hoped to address society, but what they believed that society needed was substantially different. Most conservatives, following a deep Protestant tradition of support for the traditional family, lined up around family-related issues, including private schooling and an anti-abortion viewpoint, while most moderates tended to support the newer social emphases of their time and to be open to attempts to state those emphases in theological terms. In time, these differences reflected different sides in the widespread culture wars of the 1990s and 2000s, but one must be careful not to move too quickly to identify the politics with the theological convictions. Conservatives knew many played on their field with much more progressive political commitments, and the moderates were well aware that deep differences were present among their supporters. Nonetheless, the movement towards political conservatism, especially around the issue of abortion, greatly aided the conservative side of the debate. Many moderates, particularly those in Southern Baptist circles, recognized the truth of both positions, but they tended to see the issue as one for individuals to decide. Perhaps to everyone's surprise the abortion issue, especially in the 1980s, gave the conservatives a real advantage in the conflict. Yet one must be careful. The theological debate had profound political and social implications, as all theological discussion has, but that does not mean that the discussion can be reduced to politics. A moderate might believe that his theological position inclined him to support Democratic social politics without believing that the two issues are one and the same.

There was another issue in the debate—a profound issue of vision even if it was not seen as one by many at that time or this—and that was whether seminaries were ecclesiastical or public bodies. Those seminaries that had independent boards, including Fuller, managed to find ways to contain the institutional consequences of the controversy. Those schools whose governance was integrated into the governance of their denominations were unable to do so. In many ways, this paralleled the final result of the earlier fundamentalist-modernist controversy. The more independent a school's board, the more the members of the board have an investment in the administration and faculty and trust them to carry out the school's basic mission. Interestingly enough, the case of Ramsey Michaels at Gordon-Conwell indirectly confirms this point. The charges against Michaels were brought by the faculty, not by the board or by outsiders, and the board sustained the faculty.

Was there a common vision of theological education that united either party in the conservative debates of the 1980s? Although one is tempted to say that the conservatives advocated a confessional understanding of theological education in which the churches' public positions formed the starting point for theological inquiry, this vision was only shared by a handful of the conservative champions. Instead, the vision that the conservatives shared was that of a Bible under attack, consciously or unconsciously, by those who ought to have defended it as the Word of God. The proper response to this vision was to circle the wagons. The Chicago Statement was one way to erect a defensive wall around the Bible; strict control by a board of trustees was another. Yet, when all is said and done, the demand was not an attempt to end theological diversity. Biblical inerrancy only set the perimeter of the field of theology; it was not the field itself.

Did the conservative-moderate debates on the Right influence theological education as a whole? In one sense, the question is misplaced. Theological education as a whole had a substantial Evangelical contingent—between 40 and 60 percent of Protestant enrollments—and included many of the largest and financially strongest institutions. If they were not the whole, they were a very large part of the theological-education community. At a minimum, these intense battles reinforced the conviction of non-Evangelical schools that "we were not like those people." Yet, it is no accident that the inerrancy debate raged at the same time as the broad discussion of the theological nature of theological education.

The connection between the two debates is the Bible. The Mainsteam discussion was rich in nuance and in intellectual precision, so all generalizations are suspect. Yet I would suggest that these discussions assumed that the world of theological education had to operate in an environment where classical theological authority was no longer recognized. There was a deep and abiding fissure between the critical study of the Bible and of Christian history, and attempts to formulate a larger understanding of Christian faith or to understand contemporary Christian practice. In simple terms, no obvious bridge existed between the scholarly study of religion and its normative intellectual or social/institutional application. Such categories as theory and practice, although long used, did not seem to be applicable. The rise of a plethora of biblical hermeneutics served to highlight the gap between what was done in the classroom and what was needed by the churches. There was also a sense that directing theological education towards the preparation of ministers—Farley's clerical paradigm—was not legitimate or, perhaps more accurately, was not adequate. Theological education should be rooted somehow in the nature of theology itself, an expression of the inner logic of theological inquiry. The hope was that a line of thinking about theological schools that had been common among those involved in the enterprise might be either refined or even surpassed. Despite an emphasis on congregational studies, one has a sense that many in the debate wanted to escape the messy world of Christianity as it is actually lived and experienced in favor of a church that somehow more conformed to the ideal, no matter how that the ideal was substantiated. Charles M. Wood was the clearest about this critical standpoint. For him, the focus had to be on the adequacy of theological reflection to the church's proclamation, but the others shared an uneasiness with lived religious experience, especially among the middle classes.

To draw one vision from this rich debate is neither easy nor possible. Nonetheless, I would suggest that taken together, this discussion hoped to refocus theological education around the category of wisdom and around the formation of its students. The advantage of wisdom as a mode of thought for theological education was that while the wise person might be aware of the results of scholarly inquiry, wisdom was not the same as scientific inquiry. Equally important, although the wise person needed skills, wisdom was not a technology that sought inherently to transmit a certain skill or skill set. A wise person was the one who was able to see what needed to be done, thought, or advocated in a situation, and who was able to communicate that to others. At its best, wisdom was both social and participatory. The wise person was attuned and responsive to the world around and able to see the direction in which things were moving.

A useful term for this type of intellectual endeavor is *reflection*. Reflection brings together past and present experience, the reading of a situation as well as all the resources available to a person. The reflective person is not necessarily seeking new knowledge or new or refined skills, although those might be needed, but an insight, a vision, or a comprehensive point of view. As David Kelsey, among others, emphasized the study of the Christian thing—marked as it was by pluralism and diversity among students, teachers, and institutions—almost necessarily leads to such a goal for theological education. And if this is true of the apprehension of Christianity as a religion, the observation is even more accurate when the purpose of theological education is to know God truly. Every apprehension of the divine is necessarily limited, even if that apprehension is true.

How does theological schooling fit into the development of theological wisdom or discernment? Almost by definition, wisdom is always a work in progress in which past learning and experience are continually mined for new insights. Wisdom is also continually open to vision and reexamination. What schools can do is to help students form the habits of mind that will enable them to view life from within their Christian perspective. If the school does its job well, the student will leave in possession of a practice that will deepen as years pass. Ancient ideas of education, especially the Greek understanding of *paideia* and the educational practices of Christian monasteries, suggest what that education was like in the past. The student has to be formed, not in the Catholic sense of preparation for sacramental life, but as a responsible thinker and leader. To be sure, such training has great value for those who might take up ordained leadership in the churches, but its value is not confined to them.

This vision has many similarities to the earlier one that Schleiermacher proposed. In both cases, we hear many of the notes characteristic of the romantic mode of life: a grudging but real reverence for the achievements of science, a trust in the cultured individual whose *Bildung* (*paideia*, formation) provides guidance both internally and socially, the appeal to the whole and its apprehension, not to any particular part. In many ways, the vision was similar to one common in the liberal-arts tradition where cultural knowledge and sensitivity is seen as ideal preparation for leadership.

Those romantic overtones also point to the weakness of the model. Romantic understandings of truth depend on apprehension or appreciation. One discerns the truth in the midst of the various options presented by the situation. In many ways, the physician in general practice, who draws on his or her breadth of education and experience, or the wily attorney make good analogies for this understanding of ministry and theological education. Yet every wisdom is limited in its scope. When a new disease appears, the experienced physician must rely on the work of the researcher to begin the process of understanding the new condition, and the complex problems posed by the tax codes of advanced nations require something more than discernment. Although all the advocates of this understanding saw theology as having a role in evaluating the truth or adequacy of theological statements, the place of science (*Wissenschaft*) received less consideration; yet, even in a postmodern age, scientific methods and validation have some import. After all, if Jesus said no such thing, it is difficult to use his teachings as warrants for a particular action.

The discussion of the globalization of theological education in the 1980s did not produce nearly as clear a vision of theological education as the formal discussion of what makes theological education theological. In part this was because the globalization movement attempted too much and tried to cover too great a territory. Part of the discussion was the theological counterpart of what was becoming an obvious fact: American educational institutions were increasingly setting the norms of much of education around the world. In this, American schools were occupying much the same position in the world educational system as British and German universities held in the previous century. At the same time, immigrants from much of the world were entering the United States. Their children, often raised in both cultures, were likewise entering American colleges and universities. The result was that America's schools were international in their student bodies and increasingly in their faculties as well. This presented both opportunities and problems for the educational system. On the one hand, declining American birthrates opened spaces in classrooms and dormitories. These needed to be filled. On the other hand, the United States, although long known for its innovative industrial techniques and inventions, was ill prepared for the new technological world. The nation lacked qualified students in the vitally important scientific and mathematical fields.

To a lesser extent, the same thing was happening in theological education. The American missionary movement had made a significant contribution to worldwide Christianity, and the newer churches found themselves with a deficit in highly educated leadership. Moreover, although American and European theology continued to have considerable prestige, the leaders of these churches were increasingly aware that their own cultural traditions had a contribution to make to the larger theological tradition. The Latin American theology of liberation had already become part of the standard theological curriculum, and liberation theology had exerted significant influence on the various minority theologies in the United States. For at least some of its advocates, theological globalization was the American equivalent of the style of ecumenism associated with the WCC, which had been moving in an increasingly radical direction.

Was globalization a variation on the pluralistic model favored by many minority theologians? This was definitely the case with some passionate advocates of globalization, such as Donald Shriver of Union Seminary in New York, and some global theological leaders shared this perspective. Yet almost by definition, the global included different voices as well. Liberalist models for theology, while continuing to have some impact on Catholic theology, had passed their peak in that communion, and other Catholic voices had influence on the worldwide church. Furthermore, Evangelicals were by far the most important presence abroad, and the combination of the Lausanne movement and the withdrawal of the Mainstream churches from traditional missions served to increase their presence. Consequently, no one compelling vision of globalization emerged. Catholics, Evangelicals, and Mainstreamers had different understandings of the term *globalization* and of the discussion itself.

What is often most significant is what did not happen. In this case, the very complexity of globalization worked against theological education concentrating on the most difficult question: how does Christianity, and with it theological education, relate to the various religions of the world? This was not only a question for Christians outside of the United States but increasingly for Christians within the United States. America's largest cities often had various temples, Buddhist dharma centers, mosques, and synagogues. Many of these religions were in neighborhoods nearby existing seminaries. Moreover, the Second Vatican Council had raised the issue as one of the central questions before the Catholic Church as it worked for peace in the world. The question of the relationship between the religions, also, potentially might have required a radical thinking of the goals and purposes of theological education. Yet, perhaps in part because of the more immediate issue of the global diversity of Christianity, this issue never generated the fresh thinking that might have moved it to center stage.

Did Catholicism produce a new vision of theological education? Both Catholic and non-Catholic observers of the Second Vatican Council believed that the new directions affirmed the Council would produce a new vision of ministry and education.

On the one level, these visionaries were right. American Catholic education changed rapidly in its teaching methods, its philosophy, and its basic curriculum. In many ways, these changes were on the magnitude of those that accompanied the Reformation and the Council of Trent. The most dramatic of these changes was that the Catholic schools found a place in their program of studies for those interested in the study of religion and for those interested in nonordained ministry. Many Catholic administrators and scholars became leaders in the larger world of American theological education, and some were exemplary leaders who served as consultants to other presidents and institutions. Vatican II had directed national churches to shape their programs around the demands of their own national needs, and the American Church did that. When the seminaries and the Church looked at the American environment, they found models for theological education ready at hand.

In the main, Catholic schools grafted their inherited formational mission onto the trunk of the standard American seminary program. The resultant institutions often looked very similar to the standard American schools, with courses in church history and biblical studies taught on historical and critical principles, courses in pastoral practice, and classes in doctrine. In many ways, the changes in the doctrine courses were particularly striking: many courses sought to allow for a dialog with the full range of discussion among past Catholic theologians. At the same time, the exclusively clerical character of Catholic theological schools was altered. Laymen and laywomen joined the faculties, as did some Protestants, and the schools accepted substantial numbers of laypeople who, like their counterparts in other schools, were preparing for a variety of religious occupations. Interestingly, these programs for non-priestly candidates tended to be commuter programs that lacked formal formation programs. Organizationally, while still following canon law about ultimate authority, the leadership of many schools went *de facto* to the rector or chief executive officer and a board of trustees. Like their Protestant counterparts, Catholic institutions, with new programs to train laypeople, were expensive to run, and the whole plethora of administrative and other offices followed in the wake of these changes. The closest analog to these new seminaries in Catholic experience were the state Catholic universities of Europe that likewise separated intellectual and sacramental formation.

Vatican II had said little about religious orders; yet, the education of priests for religious orders had its own demands. Each order had its own distinctive charisma and its own set of ideals. Traditionally the orders had educated their own members for ministry in their communities, and this education had been heavily formational. In many ways, the traditional order seminary resembled a monastery. Such schools tended to be rural, to be largely staffed by members of the order, and to have included much indoctrination. The Jesuits, of course, had their own pattern. Although generations are always dangerous, the tendency of religious orders was to form union seminaries that educated members for many orders. Each order retained its own formation program, while sharing libraries, classrooms, and administrative services. This created institutions with a notable freedom from authority and ability to innovate, especially around mission.

What remained of the older Catholic foundations? One important continuity was that, despite the disappearance of high school and college seminaries, the Church continued to insist that philosophy was a necessary part of preparation for theology. The program was pointedly divided into two years of philosophy followed by four years of theology. This existed in some tension with formal requirements for degrees that often required a college degree and three years of study for a Master of Divinity. Consequently, the attainment of the MDiv was not sufficient for ordination. This enabled Catholic seminaries to prepare significant numbers of women for religious leadership without preparing them for ordained leadership. This approach also allowed schools to see theology as a liberal art in which students might earn a Master of Arts degree.

The most distinctive and traditional element in this understanding of theological education was the determination to maintain the formation program. Formation was a rich idea in Catholic tradition, and it would be too easy to identify any one element as its foundational meaning. The best meaning is sacramental: the candidate for priesthood is to be shaped to receive the sacrament of ordination and to be, consequently, a bearer of grace to the world. In more Protestant terms, the prospective priest is to prepare to receive a new identity, a new self-understanding that will manifest itself in all areas of their priestly work. Naturally, both mind and heart, both intellect and will, must form this new man. Ultimately, formation is a matter of the conversion of the person. The process naturally places a heavy emphasis on preparation for a life of celibacy. Perhaps the most striking, nontraditional element in the current understanding of formation is the emphasis on the use of psychology and psychological tests.

The conservative turn during the papacies of John Paul II and Benedict XVI seemed to many contemporaries to threaten the end of innovation in Catholic theological education, and many traditional elements, particularly in piety, were reintroduced. Yet what is remarkable is how much of the basic structure of post-Vatican II Catholic theological education remained intact, despite debate, controversy, and theological changes.

Was this the transformation that many expected in the 1960s? The answer must be given carefully. Vatican II raised expectations, especially among liberal Catholics, that the Church might not have been able to fulfill. The Roman Catholic Church, after all, is both an ancient and an international body that touches the lives of many people in varied cultures. Ironically, both John Paul and Benedict may have raised conservative expectations higher than the Church might fulfill for much the same reasons. In that sense, despite theoretical doctrine of papal supremacy and the role of Councils, the actual exercise of authority in the Church is very complex. In other words, neither popes nor councils can do everything that they might desire.

The last fifteen years has seen much reflection around pedagogy in theological schools. In part, this is because of the federal government's emphasis on educational outcomes. The interest in pedagogy also reflected a deep sense among many seminary leaders that the scholarly preparation that teachers received in graduate schools did not equip them adequately for the classroom. Although much of this discussion included teachers in both undergraduate religion departments and seminaries, the sense of a disconnect between theological studies and graduate education pointed to a deep confusion about what and how a theological school ought to be conducting its educational mission. The fact that there was no signature pedagogy commonly accepted among seminary teachers highlighted this confusion. Instead, seminaries had a variety of very effective teachers with very different methods, and divergent goals and objectives. The earlier discussions of the theological nature of theological education, the discussions of the nature of practical theology, and Alasdair MacIntyre's concept of practices as intellectual traditions of mind and action combined to suggest a new professional model in which theological education contributed to a sensitivity to the theological (religious) work of the pastor. Of course, like the idea of practice on which much of this model was based, the new professional model was progressive. Pastoral imagination and sensitivity began in the person's experience before seminary, the seminary deepened and equipped this awareness, and this practice had its fullest development only after seminary was completed. As in MacIntyre's well-known example of playing chess, every game contributed, but no game was determinative. What was important was the formation of the virtue of a chess player. One is reminded of Schleiermacher's belief in the virtuoso of religion who is able to awaken the depths of faith in another.

The advantage of this model is its comprehensiveness. It provides some insight almost regardless of which religious or theological position an individual or, more importantly, a community might hold. A rabbi would develop a Jewish religious sensitivity, a Protestant Christian a Protestant sensitivity, and so on. Professional and spiritual skill would necessarily develop together so that the minister's own spiritual growth would reinforce professional growth, and vice versa. Further, each pastoral practice—whether preaching, counseling, social witness, or what have you—could be seen as an expression of a whole ministry.

Part of the difficulty in implementing this new professional model is that it is largely an attempt to describe theological education from outside the circle of particularities that define concrete experience. From without, the young Southern Baptist pastor who is on fire with a passion for souls can be seen as developing a practice highly valued by his or her community; but from within, this Evangelical passion is seen and experienced as a divine mandate, a response to the divine commissioning of the ministry. A similar point could be made about other aspects of ministerial practice in different communions. To designate something as the Word of God is to put that something above everything else. The irony of this is that the new professional model was developed, in part, to deal with the irreducible plurality of American religious practice. Yet to do so it must work at a level of generality potentially too separated from concrete religious practice to deal adequately with it from within.

The still relatively new application of computer technology to theological education has not yet yielded its own vision of the goals and purposes of theological education. This is understandable. No one quite knows what this new direction in theological education will yield, and much discussion has necessarily concerned such items as balances between residence and distance education, the difference between online communities and face-to-face communities (if any), and the use of multimedia techniques. If there is one mantra that runs through this discussion, it is accessibility. Schools should make theological education readily available to anyone desiring it. At times, the advocates of this method of theological training have tended to repeat the old saw: "anything you can do, I can do better." Fortunately, this stage in the discussion appears to be drawing to a close. Yet one wonders whether there are concealed problems in the midst of this passionate exchange. One of the most obvious is that the Internet is essentially a consumer tool that people use to make choices among various options: consider the usual search result of several thousand items. Thus, one purchases something from among these options depending on one's own goals and purposes. Students potentially can choose a course in New Testament from among many different courses offered online, subject only to the question of where and how those courses can be combined into a degree. This might be a great gain for some students: imagine someone in my generation who could have had theology courses with both Niebuhrs, with Tillich, and with Carl F. Henry, as well as access to courses of special interest, including, say, an introduction to Coptic. The downside is equally imaginable: a student who, for whatever reason, elected to take courses wherever the workload was lightest or in which their own point of view was vigorous affirmed. My own sense is that a new style of institution will ultimately be needed to correlate the diversity available to students and to provide some larger coherence for the distance degrees. But this is a matter for another study.

We began this volume with a confession: the last fifty years of theological education did not seem to yield a common theme. If the result of my study and reflection is not piety and confusion, the conclusion remains that the last fifty years have seen a substantial plurality in the goals and purposes of theological schools. Ultimately, this conclusion rests on an awareness that over the last fifty years the United States has become a much more complex, much more diverse society and that its culture in general has likewise become more complex and much more diverse. After all, neither society nor culture are independent variables. Changes in one contributes to changes in the other. On a less cosmic level, however, it is also a judgment on the course of theological thought. The seminary ideal described in *Piety and Intellect* ultimately rested on the grand intellectual vision of Orthodox Christianity. In the midst of revival and nation building, the church had to show that its deposit of faith was intellectually as well as emotionally satisfying. Only then could the church fulfill its grand mission both in the United States and around the world. The seminary ideal in *Piety and Profession* emerged out of the deterioration of this ideal. Biblical criticism and modern science weakened the sense of intellectual certainty that had supported the earlier sense of seminary identity. Perhaps, ironically, the faculty members who introduced the new understandings represented the fruit of the older understanding of the seminary's work. Yet from this work of intellectual deconstruction and reconstruction, a new understanding of the seminary emerged that saw the school more as a graduate professional school. As part of this newer understanding of the study of theology, new practical disciplines sought to apply the best insights of modern social science to the tasks of ministerial work. Part of the genius of these disciplines was that they stressed ministerial functions, such as directing Christian education, over particular tasks imposed by church tradition. The new practical disciplines had other origins as well. American Protestantism was intensely activist, especially in its more evangelistic forms, and the Bible schools and other mission-centered institutions experimented with teaching students "how-to" courses in ministry and in missions. Yet the predominant influence, at least on seminaries, was the new theology.

The new model was perhaps most fully implemented in the university divinity schools, which were almost by definition interdenominational, but it influenced all theological schools, including almost all that retained conservative theology. Conservative Gordon, Eastern, and Northern all had excellent programs in religious education, as did Southern Baptist Theological Seminary. In many ways, the professional ideal served as a bridge for the graduates of these schools as they used their degrees, especially after they were accredited, as bridges into Mainstream denominations and church leadership positions. Later, other minority persons, particularly women, would find professionalism a useful way into participation.

Beginning in the 1960s, the professional model began to fray around the edges and to lose its persuasive power. While it did not completely disappear—indeed some of its most interesting experiments, including Readiness for Ministry, continue—the professional model lost the power to inspire. The various visions that we discussed earlier in this chapter were an attempt, in part, to replace it with another vision or, in some cases, to supplement it. Although each had some effect on theological education, none became dominant. The vision of the goals and purposes of theological education remained plural and diverse. In that sense, theological education was and has remained contested territory.

I am not sure that theological schools, even those affiliated with the Mainstream churches, are any weaker than they were in 1960. In fact, I would say that the administrations of these schools are much stronger, and that they have increasingly sophisticated tools to use in accomplishing their tasks. Such aspects of institutional life as fundraising are much improved. Despite their poverty, real and imagined, the schools are better off today than they were in the 1960s and their faculties more adequately compensated. Information about theological education is also much more readily available. Indeed, the plurality that I have attempted to describe may be possible only because of these changes and their very positive effects.

What then is my last word on the complex world of theological schools that I have studied? The future is open. Perhaps the future will bring new unity; perhaps new diversity. The one thing that history suggests is that it will be different from the past.

Bibliography

Academe. "Report." July–August 1996.

Achtemeier, Elizabeth. "Evaluating the Feminist Approach to Bible and Theology." *Interpretation* 42 (1998) 45–57.

Adams, James E. *Preus of Missouri and the Great Lutheran Civil War.* New York: Harper & Row, 1977.

Albanese, Catherine. *A Republic of Mind and Spirit: A Cultural History of American Metaphysical Religion.* New Haven: Yale University Press, 2006.

Aleshire, Daniel O. "The ATS Quality and Accreditation Project." *ThEd* 30/2 (1994) 5–16.

———. "The Character and Assessment of Learning for Religious Vocation: M.Div. Education and Numbering the Levites." *ThEd* 39/1 (2003) 1–15.

———. *Earthen Vessels: Hopeful Reflections on the Work and Future of Theological Schools.* Grand Rapids: Eerdmans, 2008.

———. "Gifts Differing: The Educational Value of Race and Ethnicity." *ThEd* 45/1(2009) 1–18.

Aleshire, Daniel O. et al. "The President's Vocation and Leadership." In *A Handbook for Seminary Presidents*, edited by G. Douglass Lewis and Lovett H. Weems, 1–17. Grand Rapids: Eerdmans, 2006.

Allen, William Lloyd. "The Review & Expositor: A Century of Engagement and Encouragement." *Review & Expositor* 101 (2004) 21–34.

Ammerman, Nancy Tatom et al. *Congregation & Community.* New Brunswick, NJ: Rutgers University Press, 1997.

Ammerman, Nancy T. et al., eds. *Studying Congregations: A New Handbook.* Nashville: Abingdon, 1998.

Appleby, R. Scott. *"Church and Age Unite!": The Modernist Movement in American Catholicism.* Notre Dame Studies in American Catholicism. Notre Dame: University of Notre Dame Press, 1992.

American Theological Library Association. "The Information Commons Model in Theological Education." Panel discussion. *American Theological Library Association Summary of Proceedings* 61 (2007) 113–21.

Arinze, Francis. "Globalization of Theological Education." *ThEd* 23/1 (1986) 7–42.

The Association of Governing Boards of Universities and Colleges, *The Good Steward: A Guide to Theological School Trusteeship.* Washington, DC: the Association of Governing Boards, 1983.

Barker, Lance R., and Edmon B. Martin. "Judicatory-Based Theological Education." *ThEd* 39/1 (2003) 155–73.

———, eds. *Multiple Paths to Ministry: New Models for Theological Education.* Cleveland: Pilgrim, 2004.

Bass, Dorothy C., and Craig Dykstra, eds. *For Life Abundant: Practical Theology, Theological Education, and Christian Ministry.* Grand Rapids: Eerdmans, 2008.

Batsel, John David. "Faculty Status of Academic Librarians." *American Theological Library Association Summary of Proceedings* 26 (1972) 151–56.

Baumgaertner, William L. "A Retrospective Study of the Institute for Theological Education Management." *ThEd* 29/1 (1992) 39–54.

Bechtold, Paul I. *Catholic Theological Union at Chicago: The Founding Years.* Chicago: Catholic Theological Union, 1993.

Becker, Russell J. "In Parish Pastoral Studies 1960–1966." *ThEd* 3/3 (1967) 403–18.

———. "The Place of the Parish in Theological Education." *Journal of Pastoral Care* 21 (1967) 163–70.

Board of Control. "Exodus from Concordia: A Report on the 1974 Walkout." St. Louis: The Board, 1977.

Boyd, Ken. "The Library's Role in Media and Instructional Design—A Summary." *American Theological Library Association Summary of Proceedings* 42 (1988) 169–75.

Boyer, Ernest L. *Scholarship Reconsidered: Priorities of the Professoriate.* Princeton: Carnegie Foundation for the Advancement of Teaching. 1990.

Braaten, Carl E. "What Price Unity? The Presbyterians and the Re-Imaginging Conference." *Pro Ecclesia* 3 (1994) 407–10.

Braswell, George W. "Field-based Learning in World Religions." *Missiology* 13 (1985) 461–72.

Bridston, Keith R., and Dwight W. Culver. *Pre-Seminary Education.* Minneapolis: Augsburg, 1965.

Bright, John. "The Academic Teacher and the Practical Needs of the Clergy." *ThEd* 1/1 (1964) 35–52.

Brokaw, Tom. *The Greatest Generation.* New York: Random House, 1998.

Browning, Don S. *A Fundamental Practical Theology: Descriptive and Strategic Proposals.* Minneapolis: Fortress, 1991.

———. "Globalization and the Task of Theological Education in North America: A Plenary Address at the 1986 ATS Biennial Meeting." Supplement 1, *ThEd* 30 (1993) 15–28.

———, ed. *Practical Theology: The Emerging Field in Theology, Church, and World.* Harper Forum Books. San Francisco: Harper & Row, 1983.

Browning, Don S. et al., eds. *The Education of the Practical Theologian: Responses to Joseph Hough and John Cobb's "Christian Identity and Theological Education."* Studies in Theological Education. Atlanta: Scholars, 1989.

Bulman, Raymond F., and Frederick T. Parella. *From Trent to Vatican II: Historical and Theological Investigations.* New York: Oxford University Press, 2006.

Burkee, James C. *Power, Politics, and the Missouri Synod: A Conflict That Changed American Christianity.* Minneapolis: Fortress, 2011.

Cahalan, Kathleen A. *Projects That Matter: Successive Planning and Evaluation for Religious Organizations.* Bethesda, MD: Alban Institute, 2003.

Cahalan, Kathleen A., and James R. Nieman. "Mapping the Field of Practical Theology." In *For Life Abundant: Practical Theology, Theological Education, and Christian Ministry,* edited by Dorothy C. Bass and Craig Dykstra, 62–85. Grand Rapids: Eerdmans, 2008.

Campbell, Thomas C. et al. "Theological Curriculum for the 1970's." *ThEd* 4/3 (1968) 671–727.

Cannon, Katie, and the Mudflower Collective. *God's Fierce Whimsy: Christian Feminism and Theological Education.* New York: Pilgrim, 1985.

Cardwell, Sue Webb. "The Theological School Inventory: Is It Still Valid?" *ThEd* 10/2 (1974) 94–103.

Carey, Patrick W. *Catholics in America: A History.* Lanham, MD: Rowman & Littlefield, 2008.

Carey, Patrick W., and. Earl C. Muller, SJ, eds. *Theological Education in the Catholic Tradition: Contemporary Challenges.* New York: Crossroad, 1997.

Carpenter, Joel A. *Revive Us Again: The Reawakening of American Fundamentalism.* New York: Oxford University Press, 1997.

Carr, Aute L. "The Federated Theological Faculty of the University of Chicago: An Analysis of the Agreements, Structures, and Relationships, 1943-60." Supplement 1 *ThEd* 4/4 (1968) 61-80.

Carroll, Jackson W. "Project Transition: An Assessment of ATS Programs and Services." *ThEd* 18 (1981) 45-165.

———. "Why Is the DMin So Popular?" *Christian Century* 105 (1988) 106.

Carroll, Jackson W., and Penny Long Marler. "Culture Wars? Insights from Ethnographies of Two Protestant Seminaries." *Sociology of Religion* 56 (1995) 1-20.

Carroll, Jackson W., and Barbara G. Wheeler. "Doctor of Ministry Program: History, Summary of Findings and Recommendations." *ThEd* 23/2 (1987) 7-52.

Carroll, Jackson W. et al. *Being There: Culture and Formation in Two Theological Schools.* Religion in America Series. New York: Oxford University Press, 1997.

Carroll, Jackson W. et al., eds. *Handbook for Congregational Studies.* Nashville: Abingdon. 1986.

Cartwright, John H. "The Cultural Context: A Historical/Social Analysis." *ThEd* 20/1 (1983) 20-36.

Chaves, Mark. *Ordaining Women: Culture and Conflict in Religious Organizations.* Cambridge: Harvard University Press, 1997.

Cherry, Conrad. *Hurrying toward Zion: Universities, Divinity Schools, and American Protestantism.* Bloomington: Indiana University Press, 1995.

Chinnici, Joseph P. "The Reception of Vatican II in the United States." *Theological Studies* 64 (2003) 461-94.

Chopp, Rebecca S. *Saving Work: Feminist Practices of Theological Education.* Louisville: Westminster John Knox, 1995.

Christ, Carol P. "Heretics and Outsiders: The Struggle over Female Power in Western Religion." *Soundings* 61 (1978) 60-80.

———. *Laughter of Aphrodite: Reflections on a Journey to the Goddess.* San Francisco: Harper & Row, 1987.

———. "New Feminist Theology: A Review of the Literature." *Religious Studies Review* 3 (1977) 203-12.

———. "Reflections on the Initiation of a Woman Scholar into the Symbols and Rituals of the Ancient Goddesses." *Journal of Feminist Studies in Religion* 3/1 (1987) 57-66.

Christian Century. "Bennett Elected Union President." 81 (1964) 7.

———. "Breaking Ranks: A Seminary Librarian Is Fired." 115 (1998) 100-101.

———. "Princeton Declaration Opposes Ordaining Gays." 110 (1993) 592-93.

———. "Princetonians against 'Princeton Declaration.'" 110 (1993) 737.

———. "SBC Seminary President Fired." 111 (1994) 308.

———. "Tenured SBC Woman Forced to Resign." 111 (1994) 847-48.

Ciuba, Edward J. "The Impact of Changing Ecclesiological and Christological Models on Roman Catholic Seminary Education." *ThEd* 24/1 (1987) 57-72.

Clark, Ryan. "Twilight Breaking: The State of Baptist Theological Education in a Global Christian Era and Implications for the Future." *Baptist History and Heritage* 44/2 (2009) 47–63.

Clarke, Erskine. "The President as Administrator." Supplement 2, *ThEd* 32 (1995) 33–45.

Cobb, John C., Jr. *Beyond Dialogue: Toward a Mutual Transformation of Christianity and Buddhism.* Philadelphia: Fortress, 1982.

Cochrane, Charles N. *Christianity and Classical Culture: A Study of Thought and Action from Augustus to Augustine.* Oxford: Clarendon, 1940.

Colwell, Ernest Cadman. "A Tertium Quid: The Church's Seminary and the University." *ThEd* 1/2 (1965) 96–103.

Colson, Charles W. "Evangelicals & Catholics Together: The Christian Mission in the Third Millennium." *First Things* 43 (May 1994) 15–22.

Conde-Frazier, Elizabeth. *Hispanic Bible Institutes: A Community of Theological Construction.* Scranton, PA: University of Scranton Press.

Cone, James H. "Black Power, Black Theology, and the Study of Theology and Ethics." *ThEd* 6/3 (1970) 202–15.

———. *Black Theology and Black Power.* Original Seabury Paperback. New York: Seabury, 1969.

———. *The Cross and the Lynching Tree.* Maryknoll, NY: Orbis, 2011.

———. *Martin & Malcolm & America: A Dream or a Nightmare?.* Maryknoll, NY: Orbis, 1991.

Cone, James H., and Gayraud Wilmore, eds. *Black Theology: A Documentary History.* Maryknoll, NY: Orbis, 1979.

Cook, Donald E. "'Our Message Be the Gospel Plain': The Teaching of the Bible and Biblical Languages at Southeastern Baptist Theological Seminary, 1950–1988." In *Servant Songs: Reflections on the History and Mission of Southeastern Baptist Theological Seminary, 1950–1988*, by W. Randall Lolley, et al., edited by Thomas A. Bland Jr., 114–16. Macon, GA: Smyth & Helwys, 1994.

Cooley, Robert E. "Toward Understanding the Seminary Presidency: Reflections of One President." *ThEd* 32 (1996) 19–58.

Costen, James H. "Black Theological Education: Its Context, Content and Conduct." *Journal of the Interdenominational Theological Center* 12 (1985) 1–8.

Cox, Harvey. *The Secular City.* New York: Macmillan, 1965.

Crawford, Eileen et al. "Is There Anything Worthwhile on the Web? A Cooperative Project to Identify Scholarly Web Resources in Theology and Religion." *ThEd* 40/1 (2004) 49–57.

Culpepper, R. Alan. "Reflections on Baptist Theological Education in the Twentieth Century." *Baptist History and Heritage* 35/3 (2000) 24–52.

Curran, Charles E. "Academic Freedom and Catholic Institutions of Higher Learning." *Journal of the American Academy of Religion* 55 (1987) 108–21.

Cushing, Vincent. "Some Reflections on Institutional and Cultural Issues Facing Theological Education." *ThEd* 36/2 (2000) 1–10.

Daly, Mary. *Beyond God the Father.* Boston: Beacon, 1973.

———. *Beyond God the Father.* Boston: Beacon, 1985.

———. *The Church and the Second Sex.* New York: Harper & Row, 1968.

Dart, John. "Iliff Seminary Warned on Diversity Issues." *Christian Century* 121 (2004) 24.

Day, Heather F. *Protestant Theological Education in America: A Bibliography.* ATLA. Bibliography Series 15. Chicago: American Theological Library Association, 1985.

Deem Warren H. "Evaluative Criteria for Seminary Governing Boards." *ThEd* 10/2 (1974) 73–78.

———. "Observations of an Organizational Birdwatcher." *ThEd* 12/1 (1975) 63–67.

Deem, Warren H., and George Van de Mark. "1970s: Alternatives for Change." Supplement 2, *ThEd* 4/4 (1968) 42–78.

Deering, Ronald F. "Library Service in the Theological Seminary: Today and Tomorrow." *Review & Expositor* 65 (1968) 209–20.

Dolan, Jay P. *The American Catholic Experience: A History from Colonial Times to the Present.* Garden City, NY: Doubleday, 1985.

Dolan, Jay P. et al., eds. *Transforming Parish Ministry: The Changing Roles of Catholic Clergy, Laity, and Women Religious.* New York: Crossroad, 1990.

Dorrien, Gary. *The Making of American Liberal Theology.* Vol. 3, *Crisis, Irony & Post-modernity, 1950–2005.* 3 vols. Louisville: Westminster John Knox, 2006.

Douglas, Ann. *The Feminization of American Culture.* New York: Knopf, 1977.

Dulles, Avery. *Vatican II and the Extraordinary Synod: An Overview.* Collegeville, MN: Liturgical, 1986.

Edwards, Tilden. "Integrating Contemplation and Action." *ThEd* 15/1 (1978) 73–79.

Edwards-Armstrong, Janice. "CORE: An Evolving Initiative." *ThEd* 45/1 (2009) 71–76.

Elliott, Ralph H. *The "Genesis Controversy" and Continuity in Southern Baptist Chaos: A Eulogy for a Great Tradition.* Macon, GA: Mercer University Press, 1992.

Ellis, John Tracy. "American Catholics and the Intellectual Life." *Thought* 30 (1955) 351–88.

Erskine, Noel Leo. *King among the Theologians.* Cleveland: Pilgrim, 1994.

Evans, Alice Frazer et al., eds. *The Globalization of Theological Education.* Maryknoll, NY: Orbis, 1993.

Evans, James H. "The Graduate Education of Future Faculties." *ThEd* 28/1 (1991) 85–89.

Evans, James H., and Jane I. Smith. "What Is the Character of the Institutional Resources Needed for the Good Theological School?" *ThEd* 30/2 (1994) 45–59.

Farley, Edward. *Requiem for a Lost Piety: The Contemporary Search for the Christian Life.* Philadelphia: Westminster, 1968.

———. *Theologia: The Fragmentation and Unity of Theological Education.* Philadelphia: Fortress, 1983.

Featherstone, Mike, ed. *Global Culture: Nationalism, Globalization and Modernity.* London: Sage, 1990.

Feilding, Charles R. et al., eds. "Education for Ministry." *ThEd* 3/1 (1966) 1–252.

Ferré, Frederick. "Toward Transformational Theology: A Dialogue with My Father." *Religion in Life* 67 (1978) 6–22.

Ferris, Robert W. "The Work of a Dean." *Evangelical Review of Theology* 32 (2008) 65–73.

Fey, Harold Edward. "Editorial: The Ideas of a Seminary." *Christian Century* (1963) 518.

Fletcher, John C. "Theological Seminaries in the Future." *ThEd* 21/1 (1984) 71–86.

Fogarty, Gerald P. "American Catholic Biblical Scholarship: A Review." *Theological Studies* 50 (1989) 219–43.

———. *American Catholic Biblical Scholarship: A History from the Early Republic to Vatican II.* Confessional Perspective Series. San Francisco: Harper & Row, 1989.

Foster, Charles R. "The Scholarship of Teaching in Theology and Religion: A Wabash Center Advisory Committee Conversation." *Teaching Theology & Religion* 5 (2002) 192–200.

———. "The Wabash Center in the Scholarship of Teaching." *Teaching Theology & Religion* 10/3 (2007) 156–58.

Foster, Charles R. et al. *Educating Clergy: Teaching Practices and Pastoral Imagination*. San Francisco: Jossey-Bass, 2006.
Fowler. James W. "Practical Theology and Theological Education: Some Models and Questions." *Theology Today* 42 (1985) 43–58.
Fraser, James W. et al. *Cooperative Ventures in Theological Education*. Lanham, MD: University Press of America 1989.
Gagnon, Robert A. J. *The Bible and Homosexual Practice: Texts and Hermeneutics*. Nashville: Abingdon, 2001.
Gay, George A. "Hispanic Ministries Education at Fuller Theological Seminary." *ThEd* 13/2 (1977) 85–89.
Geyer, Alan F., ed. "Black Theological Education: Successes and Failures." *Christian Century* 88 (1971) 91–93, 97–104, 106–108, 122–31.
Gezork, Herbert. "An End and a Beginning: Commencement Address." *Andover-Newton Quarterly* 6 (1965) 8–14.
Gillespie, Thomas W. "The Seminary President as Chess Player." *Theology Today* 61 (2004) 149–54.
Gilpin, W. Clark. "Basic Issues in Theological Education: A Selected Bibliography." *ThEd* 25/2 (1989) 115–21.
González, Justo L. *The Changing Shape of Church History*. St. Louis: Chalice, 2002.
———. *The Theological Education of Hispanics: A Study Commissioned by the Fund for Theological Education*. New York: Fund For Theological Education, 1988.
Graves, Thomas H. "The Influence of Morris Ashcraft on the Future of Baptist Theological Education." *Perspectives in Religious Studies* 25 (1998) 185–92.
Grenz, Stanley J. *Welcoming but Not Affirming: An Evangelical Response to Homosexuality*. Louisville: Westminster John Knox, 1998.
Grigsby, Marshall C. "The Black Religious Experience and Theological Education—1970-1976." *ThEd* 13 (1977) 73–84
Hamilton, Michael S., and Johanna G. Yngvason. "Patrons of the Evangelical Mind: Why Has Evangelical Scholarship Soared in the Last Few Decades? Native Intellectual Talent is One Reason, to Be Sure. But an Infusion of Cash Didn't Hurt." *Christianity Today* 46/8 (2002) 42–47.
Handy, Robert T. "The Problem of Purpose in the Theological University." *ThEd* 2/2 (1966) 102–6.
Hankins, Barry. *Uneasy in Babylon: Southern Baptist Conservatives and American Culture*. Religion and American Culture. Tusculoosa: University of Alabama Press, 2002.
Hannah, John D. *An Uncommon Union: Dallas Theological Seminary and American Evangelicalism*. Grand Rapids: Zondervan, 2009.
Harding, Vincent. *Martin Luther King, the Inconvenient Hero*. Nashville: Abingdon, 1996.
Harper, George W. "Regensburg Redux: Have Colson and Neuhaus Succeeded Where Bucer and Contarini Failed?" *Evangelical Review of Theology* 30 (2006) 309–21.
Harrelson, Walter J. "Introduction." *ThEd* 3/4 (1967) 437–40.
Harvard University Libraries. *Afro-American Studies: A Guide to Resources of the Harvard University Library*. Cambridge: Harvard University Press, 1969.
Hazelton, Roger. "Ministry as Servanthood." *Christian Century* 80 (1963) 521–24.
Heim, S. Mark. "Mapping Globalization for Theological Education." Supplement 1, *ThEd* 26 (1990) 7–34.

Henry, Carl F. H. "American Evangelicals in a Turning Time: A Theology Perpetually on the Make Will Not Do." How My Mind Has Changed." *Christian Century* 97 (1980) 1058–62.

Hernández, Edwin I., and Kevin Davies III. *Reconstructing the Sacred Tower: Challenge and Promise of Latina/o Theological Education*. Scranton: University of Scranton Press, 2003.

Hernández, Edwin I. et al. "The Theological Education of U.S. Hispanics." *ThEd* 38/2 (2002) 71–85.

Hester, Richard L. "AAUP Censures Southeastern Seminary." *Christian Century* 106 (1989) 742–44.

Hick, John, and Paul F. Knitter, eds. *The Myth of Christian Uniqueness: Toward a Pluralistic Theology of Religions*. Faith Meets Faith Series. Maryknoll, NY: Orbis, 1989.

Hick, John. *God Has Many Names*. Philadelphia: Westminster, 1982.

Hill, Johnny Bernard. *The Theology of Martin Luther King Jr. and Desmond Mpilo Tutu*. Black Religion, Womanist Thought, Social Justice. New York: Palgrave Macmillan, 2008.

Honeycutt, Roy. "To Your Tents O Israel!: A Biblical Call to Duty, Unity and Honor." In *Going for the Jugular: A Documentary History of the SBC Holy War*, edited by Walter B. Shurden and Randy Shepley, 124–34. Macon, GA: Mercer University Press, 1996.

Hopewell, James F. *Congregation: Stories and Structures*. Philadelphia: Fortress, 1987.

———. "A Congregational Paradigm for Theological Education." In *Beyond Clericalism: The Congregation as a Focus for Theological Education*, edited by Joseph C. Hough and Barbara G. Wheeler, 1–9. Scholars Press Studies in Religious and Theological Scholarship. Atlanta: Scholars, 1988.

Horn, Henry E. "The University Environment and Future Seminary Life." *Lutheran Quarterly* 18 (1966) 305–50.

Hough, Joseph C., Jr. "Seminary Faculties, Changing the Guard." *Christianity and Crisis* 52 (1992) 127–30.

Hough, Joseph C., Jr., and John B. Cobb, Jr. *Christian Identity and Theological Education*. Scholars Studies in Religious and Theological Scholarship. Chico, CA: Scholars, 1985.

Howe, Claude L., Jr. "From Houston to Dallas: Recent Controversy in the Southern Baptist Convention." Special issue, *Theological Educator* (1985) 31–43. Reprinted *Theological Educator* 41 (1990).

Howe, Leroy T. "A Future for Pastoral Theology." *Perkins School of Theology Journal* 42 (1989) 7–13.

Hunter, James Davidson. *Culture Wars: The Struggle to Define America*. New York: Basic Books, 1991.

Hutson, Christopher Roy. "Case Study: Hood Theological Seminary." *ThEd* 45/1 (2009) 35–40.

Jensen, Kenneth A. "Protestant Theological Education in 1968." *ThEd* 4/4 (1968) 5–41.

John Jay College Research Team. "The Causes and Context of Sexual Abuse of Minors by Catholic Priests in the United States, 1950–2010: A Report Presented to the United States Conference of Catholic Bishops." Online: http://www.usccb.org/issues-and-action/child-and-youth-protection/upload/The-Causes-and-Context-of-Sexual-Abuse-of-Minors-by-Catholic-Priests-in-the-United-States-1950-2010.pdf/.

John Paul II, Pope. *Apostolic Constitution: On Catholic Universities*. Online: http://www.vatican.va/holy_father/john_paul_ii/apost_constitutions/documents/hf_jp-ii_apc_15081990_ex-corde-ecclesiae_en.html/.

———. *Apostolic Letter Ordinatio Sacerdotallis of John Paul II to the Bishops of the Catholic Church on Reserving Priestly Ordination to Men Alone*. Online: http://www.vatican.va/

holy_father/john_paul_ii/apost_letters/documents/hf_jp-ii_apl_22051994_ordinatio-sacerdotalis_en.html/.

———. *Post-Synodal Apostolic Exhortation Pastores Dabo Vobis*. Online: http://www.vatican.va/holy_father/john_paul_ii/apost_exhortations/documents/hf_jp-ii_exh_25031992_pastores-dabo-vobis_en.html/.

Jones, Lawrence. "To Seize the Times." *ThEd* 9 (1973) 333–39.

Kauffman, Christopher J. *Tradition and Transformation in Catholic Culture: The Priests of Saint Sulpice in the United States from 1791 to the Present.* New York: Macmillan, 1988.

Kelsey, David H. *Between Athens and Berlin: The Theological Education Debate.* Grand Rapids: Eerdmans, 1993.

———. "Conjuring Future Faculties." *ThEd* 28 (1991) 27–35.

———. *The Fabric of Paul Tillich's Theology.* Yale Publications in Religion 13. New Haven: Yale University Press, 1967.

———. "Reflections on Convocation '84: Issues in Theological Education." *ThEd* 21 (1985) 116–38.

———. *To Understand God Truly: What's Theological about a Theological School.* Louisville: Westminster John Knox, 1992.

Kelsey, David H., and Barbara G. Wheeler. "Thinking about Theological Education: The Implications of 'Issues Research' for Criteria of Faculty Excellence." In "Building Theological Faculties for the Future." Edited by Gail Buchwalter King. Special issue, *ThEd* 28/1 (1991) 11–26.

Kimmel, Michael. *Manhood in America: A Cultural History.* 2nd ed. New York: Oxford University Press, 2006.

King, Gail Buchwalter, ed. "Building Theological Faculties for the Future." Special issue, *ThEd* 28/1 (1991).

King, Gail Buchwalter, and Leon Pacala, eds. "Patterns of Globalization: Six Studies." Special issue, *ThEd* 27/2 (1991).

Kinghorn, Kenneth Cain. *The Story of Asbury Seminary.* Wilmore KY: Asbury Seminary, 2010.

Kitagawa, Joseph Mitsuo. ed. *Religious Studies, Theological Studies, and the University-Divinity School.* Scholars Studies in Theological Education. Atlanta: Scholars, 1992.

Klimoski, Victor J. et al. *Educating Leaders for Ministry: Issues and Responses.* Collegeville, MN: Liturgical, 2005.

Knitter, Paul F. *No Other Name? A Critical Survey of Christian Attitudes toward the World Religions.* American Society of Missiology Series 7. Maryknoll, NY: Orbis, 1986.

Laney, James T. "The Identity Crisis in the Seminaries." *Christian Century* 94 (1977) 95.

Lehman, Edward C., Jr. *Women's Path into Ministry: Six Major Studies.* Pulpit & Pew Research Report 1. Durham, NC: Duke Divinity School, 2002.

Leith, John H. *Crisis in the Church: The Plight of Theological Education.* Louisville: Westminster John Knox, 1997.

Leonard, Bill J. *God's Last and Only Hope: The Fragmentation of the Southern Baptist Convention* Grand Rapids: Eerdmans, 1990.

———. "Roy Lee Honeycutt as President of Southern Seminary: Right Man—Wrong Season." *Review & Expositor* 102 (2005) 615–45.

Lesher, William E., and Donald W. Shriver Jr. "Stumbling in the Right Direction." *ThEd* 35/2 (1999) 3–16.

Lewis, G. Douglass, and Lovett H. Weems, eds. *A Handbook for Seminary Presidents*. Grand Rapids: Eerdmans, 2006.

Lincoln, C. Eric, and Lawrence H. Mamiya. *The Black Church in the African American Experience*. Durham, NC: Duke University Press, 1990.

Lindbeck, George. *University Divinity Schools: A Report on Ecclesiastically Independent Theological Education*. Working Papers—The Rockefeller Foundation. New York: The Rockefeller Foundation, 1976.

Lindsell, Harold. *The Battle for the Bible*. Grand Rapids: Zondervan, 1976.

———. *The Bible in the Balance*. Grand Rapids: Zondervan, 1979.

Lolley, W. Randall et al. *Servant Songs: Reflections on the History and Mission of Southeastern Baptist Theological Seminary, 1950-1988*. Edited by Thomas A Bland Jr. Macon, GA: Smyth & Helwys, 1994.

Lynn, Elizabeth, and Barbara G. Wheeler. "Missing Connections: Public Perceptions of Theological Education and Religious Leadership." *Auburn Studies* 6 (1999) 1-16. Online: http://www.auburnseminary.org/sites/default/files/Missing%20Connections.pdf/.

Lynn, Robert W. "Coming over the Horizon." In *Good Stewardship: A Handbook for Seminary Trustees*, edited by Barbara Taylor and Malcolm Warford, 51-66. Washington DC: Association of Governing Boards of Universities and Colleges, 1991.

———. "Living on Two Levels: The Work of the Academic Dean in North American Theological Education." *ThEd* 24/1 (1987) 75-87.

Machado, Daisy L. "Ethnic Diversity and the Issue of Education: Latina/o Perspectives." *Lexington Theological Quarterly* 41/3-4 (2006) 263-80.

MacIntyre, Alasdair. *After Virtue: A Study in Moral Theory*. 2nd ed. Notre Dame: University of Notre Dame Press, 1984.

Maldonado, David. "Latino/a Theological Education: Defining the Table." *ThEd* 45/1 (2009) 27-33.

Manschreck Clyde, and Barbara Brown Zikmund, eds. *The American Religious Experiment*. Chicago: Exploration Press, 1976.

Marquart, Kurt. *Anatomy of an Explosion: A Theological Analysis of the Missouri Synod Conflict*. Grand Rapids: Baker Book House, 1978.

Marsden, George. *Reforming Fundamentalism: Fuller Seminary and the New Evangelicalism*. Grand Rapids: Eerdmans, 1987.

Marty, Martin E. "Showdown in the Missouri Synod." *Christian Century* 89 (1972), 943-46.

May, Lynn E. "Southern Baptist Perspectives on Education." *Baptist History and Heritage* 29/2 (1994) 4-32.

McBrien, Richard P. "The Graduate Education of Future Theological Faculties: A Catholic Perspective." *ThEd* 28/1 (1991) 90-94.

McCall, Emmanuel L. "Theological Education and the Black Community." *Review & Expositor* 75 (1978) 417-21.

McCord, James I. "Financing Theological Education." *Christian Century* 88 (1971) 106-7.

———. "The Understanding of Purpose in a Seminary Closely Related to the Church." *ThEd* 14/2 (1978) 59-66.

McDougall, Joy Ann. "Keeping Feminist Faith with Christian Traditions: A Look at Christian Feminist Theology Today." *Modern Theology* 24 (2008) 103-24.

McFague, Sallie. *Life Abundant: Rethinking Theology and Economy for a Planet in Peril*. Minneapolis: Fortress, 2001.

———. *Metaphorical Theology: Models of God in Religious Language.* Philadelphia: Fortress, 1982.

———. *Models of God: Theology for an Ecological, Nuclear Age.* Philadelphia: Fortress, 1987.

McKay, Arthur Raymond. "Resources Planning in Theological Education." *ThEd* 4/4 (1968) 751–845.

McSwain, Larry L. "Roy Lee Honeycutt as Theological Educator." *Review & Expositor* 102 (2005) 591–614.

Michaels, J. Ramsey. *Servant and Son: Jesus in Parable and Gospel.* Atlanta: John Knox, 1981.

Miller, Donald G. "Contemporary Threats to Theological Education." *American Theological Library Association Summary of Proceedings* 23 (1969) 139–44.

Miller, Glenn T. *A Community of Conversation: A Retrospective of the Association of Theological Schools and Ninety Years of North American Theological Education.* Pittsburgh: The Association of Theological Schools, 2008.

———. *Piety and Profession: American Protestant Theological Education, 1870–1970.* Grand Rapids: Eerdmans, 2007.

Miller, Keith D. *Voice of Deliverance: The Language of Martin Luther King, Jr., and Its Sources.* New York: Free Press, 1992.

Miller, Sharon et al. "Great Expectations: Fund-Raising Prospects for Theological Schools." *Auburn Studies* 14 (2000).

Mollenkott, Virginia Ramey. *Sensuous Spirituality: Out from Fundamentalism.* New York: Crossroad, 1992.

Montgomery, John Warwick. *Crisis in Lutheran Theology: The Validity and Relevance of Historic Lutheranism vs. Its Contemporary Rivals.* Grand Rapids: Baker Book House 1967.

Mouw, Richard J. "Evangelicalism and Philosophy." *Theology Today* 44 (1987) 329–37.

———. "Evangelicals in Search of Maturity." *Theology Today* 35 (1978) 42–51.

Mudge, Lewis S., and James N. Poling, eds. *Formation and Reflection: The Promise of Practical Theology.* Philadelphia: Fortress, 1987.

Nelson, Robert E. "Trusteeship: The Tradition of Voluntary Action." *ThEd* 12/1 (1975) 57–63.

Neuhaus, Richard John. "Theological Education and Moral Education." In *Theological Education and Moral Formation*, edited by Richard John Neuhaus, vii–x. Encounter Series. Grand Rapids: Eerdmans, 1992.

Niebuhr, H. Richard et al. *The Advancement of Theological Education.* New York: Harper & Row, 1957.

Noll, Mark A. "Evangelicals and the Study of the Bible." *Reformed Journal* 34/4 (1984) 11–19.

———. "What Has Wheaton to Do with Jerusalem? Lessons from Evangelicals for the Reformed." *Reformed Journal* 32 (1982) 8–15.

———. *The Scandal of the Evangelical Mind.* Grand Rapids: Eerdmans, 1994.

Novak, Michael. *The Rise of the Unmeltable Ethnics: Politics and Culture in the Seventies.* New York: Macmillan 1972.

O'Brien, Elmer J. "Challenges and Difficulties for the Independent Seminary Library." *American Theological Library Association Summary of Proceedings* 29 (1975) 71–75.

Oden, Thomas C. *Requiem: A Lament in Three Movements.* Nashville: Abingdon, 1995.

Oduyoye, Mary Mercy. "Contextualization as a Dynamic in Theological Education." Supplement, *ThEd* 30/1 (1993) 107–20.

Ogden, Schubert. "What Is Theology?" *The Journal of Religion* 53 (1972) 22–40.

Oldenburg, Douglas W. "Reflections of a Pastor/President." Supplement, *ThEd* 32/3 (1996) 101–14.
O'Malley, John W. *What Happened at Vatican II*. Cambridge, MA: Belknap, 2008.
Orsy, Ladislas M. "The Mandate to Teach Theological Disciplines: Glosses on Canon 812 of the New Code." *Theological Studies* 44 (1983) 476–88.
Pacala, Leon. "ATS and the Corporate Imperatives of Theological Education." *ThEd* 19/1 (1982) 62–72.
———. *The Role of ATS in Theological Education, 1980–1990*. ATS Publications. Atlanta: Scholars, 1998.
Paris, Peter J. "Overcoming Alienation in Theological Education." In *Shifting Boundaries: Contextual Approaches to the Structure of Theological Education*, by Barbara Wheeler and Edward Farley, 181–200. Louisville: Westminster John Knox, 1991.
———. *The Spirituality of African People: The Search for a Common Moral Discourse*. Minneapolis: Fortress, 1995.
Patterson, James. *Shining Lights: A History of the Council for Christian Colleges & Universities*. Grand Rapids: Baker Academic, 2001.
Payne, J. Barton. "Ethical Issues in the Responses to the Battle for the Bible." *Presbyterian* 3 (1977) 95–105.
Peacock, Heber. "Seminary Loses Another Teacher." *Christian Century* 80 (1963) 326.
Peterson, Stephen L. "The More Things Change—The More Things Change: Theological Libraries in the 1990s." *ThEd* 26/2 (1990) 137–51.
———, ed. "Theological Libraries for the Twenty-First Century: Project 2000 Final Report." Supplement, *ThEd* 20/3 (1984).
Piepkorn, Arthur C. "What Does Inerrancy Mean?" *Concordia Theological Monthly* 36 (1965) 577–93.
Pierard, Richard V. "Evangelicals Seek Their Roots." *Christian Century* 100 (1983) 517–18.
Poling, James N., and Donald E. Miller. *Foundations for a Practical Theology of Ministry*. Nashville: Abingdon, 1985.
Poole, Stafford. "Preparation of the Roman Catholic Priest as Person in the Community." *ThEd* 2/1 (1965) 9–15.
Porterfield, Amanda. *The Transformation of American Religion: The Story of a Late-Twentieth-Century Awakening*. Oxford: Oxford University Press, 2001.
Pulliam, Sarah. "Westminster Theological Suspension: Professor's View of Biblical Inspiration Draws Reaction from the Seminary Board." *Christianity Today* 52 (2008) 17–18. Online: http://www.christianitytoday.com/ct/2008/aprilweb-only/114-24.0.html/.
Pressler, Paul. An Interview with Paul Pressler, *Theological Educator*, (1985) 15–24.
Preus, Daniel. "The Lutheran Church–Missouri Synod: Holiday from History; The 25th Anniversary of the *Walkout*." Online: http://www.confessionallutherans.org/papers/dantalk.htm/.
Ratzinger, Joseph (now Pope Emeritus Benedict XVI). *Theological Highlights of Vatican II*. New York: Paulist, 2009.
Reid, Thomas G, Jr. "Acquiring Materials on World Christianity in a Small Theological Seminary Library." *American Theological Library Association Summary of Proceedings* 54 (2000) 103–6.
Roberts, J. Deotis. "And We Are Not Saved: A Black Theologian Looks At Theological Education." *Religious Education* 87/3 (1992) 353–69.

Robertson, Roland. *Globalization: Social Theory and Global Culture*. Theology, Culture & Society. London: Sage, 1992.

Robertson, Roland, and W. R. Garrett, eds. *Religion and Global Order*. Religion and the Political Order 4. New York: Paragon, 1991.

Robinson, David A., ed. "Toward the Renewal of Perkins: Self-Study." Special issue, *Perkins School of Theology Journal* 22/1 (1969) 5–37.

Rodríguez, Daniel A. "Hispanic Ministry Where Language Is No Barrier: Church Growth among U.S.-Born, English-Dominant Latinos." *Missiology* 38 (2010) 432–42.

Rooks, Charles Shelby. "The First Dozen Years Are the Hardest." *Journal of the Interdenominational Theological Center* 1 (1973) 95–102.

———. *Revolution in Zion: Reshaping African American Ministry, 1960–1974: A Biography in the First Person*. New York: Pilgrim, 1990.

———. "Vision, Reality and Challenge: Black Americans and North American Theological Education, 1959–83." *ThEd* 20/1 (1983) 37–52.

Roozen, David A. "'If Our Words Could Make It So': Comparative Perspectives from the 1983 and 1989 Surveys on Globalization in Theological Education." Supplement, *ThEd* 30/1 (1993) 29–42.

Ruether, Rosemary Radford. "Rosemary Radford Ruether: Retrospective." *Religious Studies Review* 15 (1989) 1–11.

Rust, Eric C. "Theological Emphases of the Past Three Decades." *Review & Expositor* 78 (1981) 259–70.

Salazar, Pamela Reed. "Theological Education of Women for Ordination." *Religious Education* 82 (1987) 67–79.

Sanders, John, ed. *What about Those Who Have Never Heard? Three Views on the Destiny of the Unevangelized*. Downers Grove, IL: InterVarsity, 1995.

Sandoval, Moises. *On the Move: A History of the Hispanic Church in the United States*. Maryknoll, NY: Orbis, 1988.

Sanneh, Lamin. *Translating the Message: The Missionary Impact on Culture*. American Society of Missiology Series 42. Maryknoll, NY: Orbis, 2009.

Schaeffer, Francis A., and C. Everett Koop. *Whatever Happened to the Human Race?* DVD. Worcester, PA.: Vision Video, 2010.

Schreiter, Robert J. "Christian Theology between the Global and the Local." *ThEd* 29/2 (1993) 112–26.

———. "Contextualization from a World Perspective." Supplement, *ThEd* 30 (1993) 63–86.

Schuller, David S. "Graduate Theological Union: A Descriptive-Evaluative Study, supplement, *ThEd* 4/4 (1968) 3–21.

Schuller, David S. et al. *Readiness for Ministry*. 2 vols. Vandalia, OH: Association of Theological Schools in the United States and Canada, 1975.

Schüssler Fiorenza, Elisabeth, ed. *Aspects of Religious Propaganda in Judaism and Early Christianity*. Studies in Judaism and Christianity in Antiquity 2. Notre Dame: University of Notre Dame Press, 1978.

———. *The Book of Revelation—Justice and Judgment*. Philadelphia: Fortress, 1984.

———. *Bread Not Stone: The Challenge of Feminist Biblical Interpretation*. Boston: Beacon, 1984.

———. *But She Said: Feminist Principles of Biblical Interpretation*. Boston: Beacon, 1992.

———. *In Memory of Her: A Feminist Theological Reconstruction of Christian Origins*. New York: Crossroad, 1983, 1995.

Schuth, Katarina. *Educating Leaders for Ministry: Issues and Responses.* Collegeville, MN: Liturgical, 2005.

———. *Reasons for the Hope: The Futures of Roman Catholic Theologates.* Wilmington, DE: Glazier, 1989.

———. *Seminaries, Theologates, and the Future of Church Ministry: An Analysis of Trends and Transitions.* Collegeville, MN: Liturgical, 1999.

Senior, Donald, and Timothy P. Weber. "What Is the Character of Curriculum, Formation, and Cultivation of Ministerial Leadership in the Good Theological School?" *ThEd* 30/2 (1994) 17–33.

Shaw, Susan M., and Tisa Lewis. "'Once There Was a Camelot': Women Doctoral Graduates of the Southern Baptist Theological Seminary, 1982–1992: Talk about the Seminary, the Fundamentalist Takeover, and Their Lives Since SBTS." *Review & Expositor* 95 (1998) 397–423.

Shea, William M. *The Lion and the Lamb: Evangelicals and Catholics in America.* Oxford: Oxford University Press, 2004.

Shurden, Walter B., and Randy Shepley, compilers. *Going for the Jugular: A Documentary History of the SBC Holy War.* Macon, GA: Mercer University Press, 1996.

Skillrud, Harold C. "The Fruits of Merger." *ThEd* 3/3 (1967) 424–26.

Smalley, Martha Lund. "Librarians and Archivists as Partners with Faculty in the Globalization of Theological Education." *American Theological Library Association Summary of Proceedings* 54 (2000) 263–65.

Smith, Wilfred Cantwell. *Religious Diversity: Essays.* Edited by Willard B. Oxtoby. New York: Harper & Row, 1976.

Stackhouse, Max L. "Global Engagement." How My Mind Has Changed. *Christian Century* 128 (2011) 30–34.

———. "Globalization, Faith, and Theological Education." *ThEd* 35/2 (1999) 67–77.

———. *Ethics and the Urban Ethos: An Essay in Social Theory and Theological Reconstruction.* Boston: Beacon, 1972.

Stackhouse, Max L. et al. *Apologia: Contextualization, Globalization, and Mission in Theological Education.* Grand Rapids: Eerdmans, 1988.

Stackhouse, Max et al., eds. *God and Globalization.* Vol. 4, *Globalization and Grace.* Theology for the Twenty-First Century. London: Contiuum, 2007.

Stallsworth, Paul T. "The Story of an Encounter" in *Theological Education and Moral Formation*, edited by Richard John Neuhaus, 132–233. Encounter Series. Grand Rapids: Eerdmans, 1992.

Steering Committee for the Quality and Accreditation Project, and Katarina Schuth (chair). "The Quality and Accreditation Project." *ThEd* 32/2 (1996).

Strege, Merle D. "Chasing Schleiermacher's Ghost: The Reform of Theological Education in the 1980s." *This World* 26 (1989) 102–15.

Suchocki, Marjorie. "The Challenge of Mary Daly." *Encounter* 41 (1980) 307–17.

Taylor, Barbara and Malcolm Warford. *Good Stewardship: A Handbook for Seminary Trustees.* Washington DC: Association of Governing Boards of Universities and Colleges, 1991.

Taylor, Charles L. "Do Churches Support the Seminaries?" *Christian Century* 79 (1962) 548–49.

Tentler, Leslie Woodcock. "'God's Representative in Our Midst': Toward a History of the Catholic Diocesan Clergy in the United States." *Church History* 67 (1998) 326–49.

Theological Education. "ATS Luce Consultation on Theological Scholarship, May 2003." 40 (2005) 93–114.

———. "Cooperative Structures for Theological Education." Supplement 1. *ThEd* 4/4 (1968).

———. "Decade of Special Issues on Globalization in Theological Education." *ThEd* 35/2 (1999) 79–84.

Thistlethwaite, Susan B., and George F. Cairns, eds. *Beyond Theological Tourism: Mentoring as a Grassroots Approach to Theological Education*. Maryknoll, NY: Orbis, 1994.

Tietjen, John H. *Fact Finding or Fault Finding?: An Analysis of President J. A. O. Preus' Investigation of Concordia Seminary*. St. Louis: Concordia Seminary, 1972.

———. *Memoirs in Exile: Confessional Hope and Institutional Conflict*. Minneapolis: Fortress, 1990.

Todd, Mary. *Authority Vested: A Story of Identity and Change in the Lutheran Church–Missouri Synod*. Grand Rapids: Eerdmans, 2000.

Traynham, Warner R. "Black Studies in Theological Education: The Camel Comes of Age." *Harvard Theological Review* 66 (1973) 257–71.

Trible, Phyllis. *God and the Rhetoric of Sexuality*. Overtures to Biblical Theology 2. Philadelphia: Fortress, 1978.

———. *Rhetorical Criticism: Context, Method, and the Book of Jonah*. Guides to Biblical Theology. Old Testament Series. Minneapolis: Fortress, 1994.

———. *Texts of Terror: Literary Feminist Readings of Biblical Narratives*. Overtures to Biblical Theology 13. Philadelphia: Fortress, 1984.

Trotti, John B. "Dealing with Pain: Preservation, Automation, Interpretation and Negotiation." *ThEd* 17/1 (1980) 78–84.

United States Conference of Catholic Bishops. *Encuentro and Mission: A Renewed Pastoral Framework for Hispanic Ministry*. Washington DC: United States Conference of Catholic Bishops, 2002.

———. *Program of Priestly Formation*. 5th ed. Washington DC: United States Conference of Catholic Bishops, 2006. Online: http://www.usccb.org/upload/program-priestly-formation-fifth-edition.pdf/.

Vanderbilt University. Website. "Program in Theology & Practice." Online: http://www.vanderbilt.edu/theology-and-practice/.

Vatican II Documents. Online: http://www.vatican.va/archive/hist_councils/ii_vatican_council/.

Voyage, Vision, Venture: Report of the Task Force on Spiritual Development." *ThEd* 8/3 (1972) 153–97.

Wacker, Grant. *Heaven Below: Early Pentecostals and American Culture*. Cambridge: Harvard University Press, 2001.

Wagoner, Walter. "A Model for Theological Education." *ThEd* 1/2 (1965) 90–95.

Waits, James, ed. "Globalization in the Practical Theological Disciplines." *ThEd* 29/1 (1993).

———, ed. "The Study of Chief Academic Officers in Theological Schools: Reflections on Academic Leadership." Supplement, *ThEd* 33 (1996).

Warford, Malcolm L. *Practical Wisdom: On Theological Teaching and Learning*. New York: Lang, 2004.

———. "Work and Calling: An Interpretation of Presidents' Reflections on the Nature of Their Office." Supplement 3, *ThEd* 32 (1996) 1–18.

Warford, Malcolm L. *Recruiting Seminary Trustees*. Washington DC: Association of Governing Boards of Universities and Colleges, 1985.

Weaver, C. Douglas, and Nathan A. Finn. "Youth for Calvin: Reformed Theology and Baptist Collegians." *Baptist History and Heritage*. 39/2 (2004) 40–55.
Webber, George W. "The Christian Minister and the Social Problems of the Day." *ThEd* 1/1 (1964) 15–34.
Welch, Claude. "Between Athens and Berlin: The Theological Education Debate." *Journal of Religion* 75 (1995) 144–45.
———. *Graduate Education in Religion: A Critical Appraisal*. Missoula: University of Montana Press, 1971.
West, Cornel. *Prophetic Fragments*. Grand Rapids: Eerdmans, 1988.
Westmoreland-White, Michael. "Reading Scripture in the Baptist Vision: James Wm. Mc-Clendon, Jr., and the Hermeneutics of Participation." *Perspectives In Religious Studies* 27/1 (2000) 63–70.
Wheeler, Barbara G. "In Whose Hands: A Study of Theological School Trustees." *Auburn Studies* 9 (2002).
———. "Theological Publishing: In Need of a Mandate." *Christian Century* 105 (1988) 1066–70.
———. "True and False: Reports from a Study of Theological School Faculty." *Auburn Studies* 4 (1996) 2–21. Online: http://www.auburnseminary.org/sites/default/files/True%20 and%20False%20Final.pdf
Wheeler Barbara G., and Helen M. Blier. "Report on a Study of Doctoral Programs that Prepare Faculty for teaching in Theological Schools." New York: Auburn Center for the Study of Theological Education, 2010. Online: http://www.auburnseminary.org/sites/ default/files/Report%20on%20a%20Study%20of%20Doctoral%20Programs_0.pdf/.
Wheeler, Barbara G., and Linda-Marie Delloff. "Reaching Out: Auburn Seminary Launches the Center for the Study of Theological Education." *Auburn Studies* 1 (1993).
Wheeler, Barbara G., and Mark N. Wilhelm. "Tending Talents: Reports from a Study of Theological School Faculty." *Auburn Studies* 5 (1997).
Wheeler, Barbara G. et al. "Signs of the Times: Present and Future Theological Faculty." *Auburn Studies* 10 (2005).
———. "Leadership That Works: A Study of Theological School Presidents." *Auburn Studies* 15 (2010).
White, Joseph M. *The Diocesan Seminary in the United States: A History from the 1780s to the Present*. Notre Dame Studies in American Catholicism. Notre Dame, IN: University of Notre Dame Press, 1989.
Wills, Gregory. *Southern Baptist Theological Seminary, 1859–2009*. Oxford: Oxford University Press, 2009.
Wilkie, Owen. "Tremendous Growth in Latin American Churches." Assemblies of God, World Missions. Online: http://worldmissions.ag.org/regions/latinamcab/__.cfm ?targetBay=ac6d31db-8d8e-42ff-9454-08eb791d73e7&Process=DisplayArticle&RSS _RSSContentID=9208&RSS_OriginatingChannelID=1164&RSS_Originating RSSFeedID=3692&RSS_Source/.
Wilmore, Gayraud S. *Black Religion and Black Radicalism: An Examination of the Religion of the Religious History of African Americans*. Maryknoll, NY: Orbis, 1998.
Wilmore, Gayraud S. et al. "Black Pastors/White Professors: Dialogic Education." Supplement, *ThEd* 16/1 (1980) 83–169.
Wind, James P., and James Welborn Lewis, eds. *American Congregations*. 2 vols. Chicago: University of Chicago Press, 1994.

Wister, Robert J. "The Effects of Institutional Change on the Office of Rector and President in the Roman Catholic Theological Seminaries: 1965–1994." Supplement, *ThEd* 32 (1995) 47–160.

Wittman, Derek E. "Freedom and Irresponsibility: Fundamentalism's Effect on Academic Freedom in Southern Baptist Life" *Baptist History and Heritage*, 39/1 (2004) 80–96.

Wood, Charles Monroe. *Vision and Discernment: An Orientation in Theological Study*. Scholars Press Studies in Religion and Theological Scholarship. Decatur, GA: Scholars, 1985.

Wuthnow, Robert. *The Restructuring of American Religion: Society and Faith since World War II*. Studies in Church and State. Princeton: Princeton University Press, 1988.

Yates, Wilson. *The Arts in Theological Education: New Possibilities for Integration*. Scholars Press Studies in Religion and Theological Scholarship. Atlanta: Scholars, 1987.

Young, Andrew. "Recent Directions in Black Theological Education." *Journal of the Interdenominational Theological Center* 8 (1981) 105–10.

Ziegler, Jesse H. "The AATS and Theological Education." *ThEd* 2 (1966) 67–83.

———. *ATS through Two Decades: Reflections on Theological Education, 1960–1980* Vandalia, OH: J. H. Ziegler, 1984.

———. "Conservation and Change in Theological Education." *St. Vladimir's Theolog-ical Quarterly* 13 (1969) 103–10.

Zikmund, Barbara Brown, ed. *Hidden Histories in the United Church of Christ*. New York: United Church Press, 1984.

———, ed. *The Living Theological Heritage of the United Church of Christ*. 3 vols. Cleveland: Pilgrim, 1995–1998.

———. "The Protestant Women's Ordination Movement." In *Encyclopedia of Women and Religion in North America*, edited by Rosemary Skinner Keller and Rosemary Radford Ruether, 2:940–50. 3 vols. Bloomington: Indiana University Press, 2006.

———. "Three Coins in the Fountain: Female Leadership in Theological Education." *ThEd* 45/2 (2010) 1–60.

———. "Walking the Narrow Path: Female Administrators in ATS Schools." *ThEd* 29/2 (1992) 55–68.

Zikmund, Barbara Brown et al. *Clergy Women: An Uphill Calling*. Louisville: Westminster John Knox, 1998.

Zimmerman, Paul A. *A Seminary in Crisis: The Inside Story of the Preus Fact-Finding Committee*. St. Louis: Concordia, 2007.

Index

abortion, 96, 136, 195, 204–5, 223, 232, 233, 234, 243, 248, 342, 343, 353
academic freedom, 6, 8, 83, 148, 159, 167, 206, 217, 221, 227, 228, 237, 239, 240, 248, 249, 256, 281, 333, 352
accreditation, x, 15–18, 47, 58, 59, 97, 125, 126, 148, 159, 161, 167, 174, 206, 217, 281, 284, 295, 298, 300, 313–24, 339, 349, 343, 348
Achtemeier, Elizabeth, 106
Adams, Robert, 202
Advancement of Theological Education, ix, 4, 32, 251
Affirm, 212
African American, xii, 12, 13, 29, 63, 64, 65, 66, 67–88, 94, 98, 101, 111, 112, 115, 116, 128, 130, 131, 132, 134, 135, 137, 139, 191, 195, 208, 231, 252, 261, 329, 346, 349, 351
Aleshire, Daniel O., xiv, 58, 63, 102–3, 194, 309, 316, 318, 325, 328, 340–44
Alston, William, 202
alternative theological education, 323
Apuntes, 113
Asbury Theological Seminary, 48, 186, 196, 229, 294, 338
Ashcraft, Morris, 238, 240
Asociación para la Educación Teológica Hispana, 113
Assemblies of God Seminary, 186
Association of Governing Boards, 310, 311, 312
Association of Theological Schools, American Association of Theological Schools (ATS), x, 4, 5, 11, 15, 32, 38, 49, 50, 54, 60, 63, 64, 73, 77, 79, 85, 92, 97, 98, 112, 125, 138, 158, 159, 161, 163, 181, 206, 217, 246, 249, 253, 281, 284, 286, 297, 303, 309, 331, 333, 339, 340, 343, 349
Auburn Center for the Study of Theological Education, 308, 340, 344–46
Auburn Studies, xv, 325, 326, 345, 346

Baker, Robert, 222
Baptist Faith and Message, 94, 206, 207, 223, 227, 229, 238, 243
Baptist Seminary at Richmond, 240–41, 246
Baptist Seminary of the Americas, 126

Basic Issues, 249–55, 316, 340
Bass, Dorothy C., 277
Baum, William Cardinal, 174–75
Becker, Russell J., 23–24
Beckwith, Francis, 203
Being There, 102, 194, 340–43
Benedict XV (Ratzinger), 93, 121, 152, 158, 169, 173, 174, 176, 177, 359
Bible Colleges, 2, 17, 44, 47, 87, 113, 127, 134, 182, 185, 196, 230
Bible institutions (Hispanic), 127–28
Bible, xiii, 1–2, 5, 7, 8, 9, 46, 53, 58, 87, 94, 103–6, 136, 154, 155, 164, 177, 185, 186, 188, 189, 190, 191, 192, 197–202, 207–8, 213, 216–17, 222, 226, 228–29, 232, 237–38, 281, 291, 296, 317, 332, 354, 362
Billy Graham Center for the Study of American Evangelicals, 195, 199
BIOLA (Bible Institute of Los Angeles), 47, 117, 182, 202
birth control, 20, 90, 136, 152, 156, 165
black theology, 80, 81, 82–85, 350
Blue Book, 212–14, 218
Blumhofer, Edith, 198
Boff, Leonardo, 118
Boyer, Ernest L., 332–33
Braswell, George W., 279
Browning, Don S., 274, 275, 293, 294, 295

Carpenter, Joel A., 45, 198, 199, 203
Castro, Fidel, 114, 125
Catholic theologians, xiv, 93, 121, 134, 152, 156, 167–71, 358
Catholics (Roman Catholic), x, xi, xii, xiii, 2, 3, 8, 10, 14, 16, 17, 22, 23, 26, 28, 30, 46, 59, 60, 61, 63, 66, 74, 77, 90, 92, 95, 94, 95, 96, 97, 98, 115, 116, 117–25, 128, 129, 131, 133, 134, 137, 139, 140–81, 201, 203–6, 207, 210, 217, 232, 243, 245, 249, 255, 276, 277, 282, 284, 286, 287, 298, 300, 301, 306, 311, 312, 317, 324, 328, 329, 330, 333, 339, 347, 356, 357–59
Celibacy, 137, 141, 142, 156, 171, 172, 359
Center for Theological Inquiry, 288, 331
Chávez, César, 112, 116

381

Chicago Statement, 190–91, 238, 240, 353, 354
Chicago Theological Union, 121, 163, 286
Chief Financial Officer, 55, 161, 302–5, 309, 346
Chopp, Rebecca S., 273
Christ, Carol P., 108, 109
Clemmons, William, 60
Clinical Pastoral Education, 22–24, 322
Cobb, John B., Jr., 253, 255, 262–64, 267, 275, 284, 292
Colwell, Ernst Cadman, 11, 13
computers, see technology
Concordia Seminary, ix, 18, 189–220, 351
Cone, James H., 80–81, 82, 83
Confessing Church, 214–16, 233, 248
Congregation, Congregational Studies, 250, 270, 271, 272, 279, 355
Constitution on the Sacred Liturgy, 153
Cooley, Robert E., 187, 188, 305, 308, 309
Costen, James H., 74
counter-seminaries, 219, 220, 229–30, 240, 245–46
Criswell, W. A., 223, 228, 229, 230, 231, 236–37
Cuba, Cubans, 67, 113–14, 117, 125, 128, 129, 130, 132, 133, 283
Curran, Charles E., 152, 167, 168
Curriculum for the 1970s, 34–35, 49
Cushing, Vincent, 163, 178, 305, 309, 311, 312

Dallas Theological Seminary, 197, 347
Daly, Mary, 93, 107–8
Davies, G. Henton, 228–29
Dayton, Donald, 198, 200
Deem, Warren H., 33, 34, 36, 37, 38, 54–57, 303, 345
Dignitatis humanae, 154
Dilday, Russell, 222, 236, 244–45
Dillenberger, John, 33
Diocesan seminaries, 117, 141, 145, 161, 163, 164, 170, 175, 180, 207, 306, 333
Distance Education, x, 48, 61, 92, 321, 337–38, 361
DMin (Doctor of Ministry), 28, 42, 49–53, 98, 100, 111, 128, 251, 271, 276, 304, 332, 337
Dorcas, Gordon, 98
Dorrien, Gary, 80, 250, 274
Drummond, Lewis A., 239–40
Dykstra, Craig, xv, 98, 264, 276, 309, 326, 327

Earthen Vessels, 343–44
Eck, Diana, 279
Eden Theological Seminary, 219
Edge, Findlay, 60
Educating Clergy, 319, 327–30, 342
Ehlen, Arlis, 218

Elert, Werner, 214
Elliott, Ralph H., 221, 226–27, 228, 229
encuentro, 123–24
Enns, Peter, 192
Evangelical, Evangelicalism, x, xiii, 2, 4, 24, 26, 33, 41–49, 60, 65, 67, 71, 76, 85, 87, 88, 95, 96, 97, 98, 102, 103, 104, 117, 125, 126, 127, 128, 136, 137, 162, 164, 169, 182–206, 220, 221, 222, 233, 242, 243, 246, 249, 250, 251, 255, 277, 281, 283, 294, 295, 300, 301, 324, 328, 332, 333, 338, 339, 340, 341, 342, 343, 347, 354, 357, 360
Evangelicals & Catholics Together, 205–6
Evangelical Seminary of Puerto Rico, 125
Evangelical Theological Society, 193
Evans, Alice, 295
Evans, Robert, 295
Ex corde ecclesiae, 169

Farley, Edward, 53, 60, 83, 189, 253, 255, 256, 258–62, 264, 267, 272, 278, 288, 354
Farley, Margaret A., 168
Federated Faculty, 12, 14
feminist, feminism, 82, 84, 90, 100, 101–11, 133, 134, 194, 208, 231, 242, 248, 273, 350
Fitchue, Leah Gaskin, 73
formation, priestly, ix, xiii, 28, 59, 96, 121, 122, 124, 131, 141, 144, 145, 146, 147, 155, 157, 158, 159, 160, 161, 162, 163, 164, 166, 170, 171, 174, 175–80, 181, 206
Foster, Charles R., 319, 327–30, 342
Fowler, James W., 275
Francisco, Clyde, 229
French Revolution, 142
French, France, 114, 119, 122, 141, 142, 143, 149, 151, 268
Friedan, Betty, 89
Fuller Theological Seminary, 2, 45, 47, 48, 76, 86, 88, 102, 117, 126, 130, 183, 186–90, 194, 195, 196, 197, 213, 281, 293, 313, 347, 351, 353
fundraising, 6, 44, 54, 161, 197, 301, 302, 305, 313, 345, 362

Gagnon, Robert A. J., 136
Gardner Taylor Lectures (Duke), 85
Garland, Diana, 242–43
Gaudium et spes, 153–54, 162
German, Germany, ix, x, 8, 10, 20, 22, 67, 87, 115, 122, 124, 129, 133, 141, 143, 159, 160, 195, 207, 209, 214, 215, 216, 219, 233, 248, 256, 257, 258, 268, 280, 287, 288, 290, 296, 327, 356
Gezork, Herbert, 3
globalization, xiii, xiv, 278–97, 299, 356, 357

Index

Glorieta Statement, 237–38, 241
Goldstein, Valerie Sawing, 106
González, Justo L., 113, 120, 122, 128, 134
Good Stewardship, 311
Good Theological School, 57, 316–18, 324, 349
Gordon-Conwell Theological Seminary, 48, 87, 187, 188–89, 191, 195, 196, 246, 281, 305, 308, 309, 313, 341, 347, 354
graduate professional education, 5, 17, 18, 32, 54, 62, 159
Graduate Theological Union, 11, 13–14, 33, 37, 54, 162, 249, 293
Graham, William (Billy), 2, 3, 43, 45, 48, 88, 184, 187, 188, 189, 195, 196, 199, 200, 208, 239
Graves, Thomas H., 240
Green, Molly Marshal, 94, 242–44
Greenleaf, Robert K., 311
Grenz, Stanley, 137, 143
Gundry, Robert H., 189
Gutiérrez, Gustavo, 118

Handbook for Congregational Studies, 270
Handbook for Seminary Presidents, 309
Harms, Oliver Raymond, 210–12
Harrison, Paul M., 33
Hatch, Nathan, 198, 199, 203
Hazelton, Roger, 21
Heim, S. Mark, 292, 294
Henry, Carl F. H., 43, 184, 189, 195, 196, 200, 242, 361
Higher Ground Sermon, 236
Hinson, E. Glenn, 60
Hobbs, Hershel, 227, 229
Hofheinz, Fred, 161, 163, 181, 303, 311, 312
Holy War Sermon, 235–36, 241
Honeycutt, Roy, 94, 99, 222, 228, 233, 235–36, 237, 238, 241–42, 243, 244
Horne, Martha, 98
Hough, Joseph, 253, 255, 262–64, 267, 268, 274, 284, 325
Howard University School of Religion, 13, 69, 73, 79, 83
Howe, Claude L., 226, 228, 230
Howe, Leroy, 275
Hubbard, David Allen, 43, 47, 102, 130, 187, 305
Huffaker, Lucinda, 327

Immersions, xiv, 28, 295–96
In Trust, 308, 312–13, 339
inclusive language, 101, 104
inerrancy, 46, 183, 187, 188, 189, 190, 191, 192, 200, 205, 210, 213, 232, 237, 238, 240, 244, 351, 352, 353, 354

Institute for Biblical Research, 191–92
Interdenominational Theological Center, 11, 12, 72, 76, 78, 81, 83
Internet, 40, 41, 327, 335, 336, 337, 361
Irish, Ireland, 79, 120, 124, 142, 143

James, Allix B., 73, 74
Jesus People, 4, 46, 185
John Paul II, 93, 121, 169, 173, 175–76, 177, 270, 360
Johnson, Elizabeth A., 168
Jones, Lawrence, 73, 88–89
Journal of Hispanic/Latino Theology, 134

Kantzer, Kenneth, 43, 47, 188
Kelsey, David H., 98, 253, 254, 255, 256, 257, 267–73, 276, 325, 328, 345, 355
King, Martin Luther, Jr., 4, 68, 70–72, 80, 82, 84, 150, 248, 251, 283
Kinney, John W., 74
Klein, Christa, x, 311, 312–13
Knitter, Paul F., 292

Latina/Latino, xii, 63, 64, 68, 74, 77, 84, 112–35, 191, 208, 248, 252, 346
Lawrence Neale Jones Library, 73
Leavenworth, Lynn, 33
Leith, John H., 342–43
lesbian, lesbianism, xii, 63, 65, 102, 110, 111, 135–38
Lesher, William E., 284, 295
Lewis, Tisa, 99
Lexington Seminars, 330–31
LGBT, xii, 63, 135–38
Library of Congress, 39, 334
library, librarians, 6, 13, 14, 15, 35, 36, 37, 38–41, 51, 73, 81, 148, 152, 162, 164, 165, 179, 199, 243, 286, 296, 297, 316, 318, 319, 332, 333–38, 344, 349, 359
Lilly Endowment, xv, 7, 9, 17, 21, 54, 55, 56, 87, 98, 161, 163, 181, 199, 252, 253, 264, 288, 302, 303, 304, 310, 311, 312, 326, 327, 328, 333, 336, 339, 340, 344, 345
Lilly Technology Grants, 340
Lindsell, Harold, 188–90, 194, 197
Lolley, W. Randall, 43, 94, 102, 222, 237, 238, 239, 242
Lumen gentium, 153
Lutherans, 14, 17, 18, 22, 36, 67, 68, 92, 94, 95, 110, 138, 140, 182, 184, 185, 203, 206–20, 221, 228, 301, 351
Lynn, Robert W., xv, 54, 55, 56, 98. 199, 253, 255, 260, 264, 271, 302, 303, 310, 311

Mackay, John A. 30, 45, 280, 302

MacKaye, William, 312-313
Maddox, Mickey, 203
Mainstream, x, xiii, xiv, 1, 3, 4, 20-21, 26, 31, 32, 35, 42, 43, 45, 46, 47, 60, 65, 66, 67, 74, 75, 83, 88, 91, 92, 94, 99, 101, 102, 104, 109, 110, 126, 127, 128, 132, 137, 139, 158, 171, 182, 183, 185, 186, 187, 190, 194, 195, 196, 197, 199, 203, 231, 232, 242, 249, 250, 251, 273, 277, 279, 280, 281, 283, 284, 292, 295, 298, 300, 301, 321, 323, 324, 332, 338, 341, 343, 351, 352, 357, 362
Maldonado, David, 132
Malone, Edward, 33
mandatum, 168-69
Marsden, George, 169, 188, 198, 199, 201, 203
Marshall, John, 174
McBeth, Leon, 222
McCall, Duke, 30, 43, 241, 302, 310
McCall, Emmanuel, 70
McClendon, James W., 226
McCord, James I., 30, 42, 59, 301, 331
McEnroy, M. Carmel, 93
McIntire, Carl, 195
Mexico, Mexican, 67, 113, 115-17, 119, 122, 126, 129, 130, 132
Michaels, J. Ramsey, 191
microfilm, 15, 41, 334
Midwestern Baptist Theological Seminary, 222, 226-28, 244
Missouri Synod, ix, 18, 94, 95, 113, 182, 183, 184, 185, 192, 206-20, 221, 222
Mohler, Albert, 94, 242-44
Moody, Dale, 222, 235, 244
Moss, Robert, Jr., 33
Mouw, Richard, 187, 202, 309
Mudflower Collective, 110, 273
Mullins, E. Y., 223, 224, 247-48

National Association of Bible Instructors (NABI), 9
National Association of Evangelicals, 2, 184, 195, 196
National Commission on Accrediting, 16-17
National Pastoral Plan for Hispanic Ministry, 123
Naylor, Robert, 43
Nazarene Theological Seminary, 186
Nelson, C. Ellis, 160, 274
Neo-Orthodoxy, x, 19, 45, 57, 190, 207-8, 214, 215, 222, 226, 229, 250
Neuhaus, Richard, 203, 205, 206, 218, 239
Newman, John Henry, 169, 267
Newport, John, 222
Niebuhr, H. Richard, ix, 4, 7, 13, 19, 32, 44, 209, 219, 250, 251, 361

Niebuhr, Reinhold, 103, 251, 288, 338, 361
Noll, Mark, 169, 191, 198, 199, 200-201, 203
Notre Dame, 143, 148, 169, 203, 245

O'Neil, Kevin J., 312
oath against modernism, 144
Ockenga, Harold, 43, 45, 184, 188, 189, 195, 196, 200
OCLC, 40, 41, 334, 336
Oden, Thomas, 342-43
Optatam totius, 155-56
ordination, 8, 22, 24, 58, 59, 66, 69, 73, 83, 91-92, 93, 94, 95, 96, 97, 104, 135, 136, 138, 140, 141, 142, 145, 158, 159, 160, 161, 163, 166, 167, 172, 175, 177, 179, 210, 219, 243, 244, 250, 261, 300, 322, 324, 340, 349, 359
Osborne, Grant, 189
Otten, Herman, 210-11

Pacala, Leon, 252, 253, 254, 255, 295, 297-99, 303
PADRES, 122
Paris, Peter J., 83
Pastores dabo vobis, 158, 174, 175-79, 179
Patterson, Dorothy, 243
Patterson, Paige, 223, 230, 231, 232, 237, 240
Paul VI, 93, 121, 151, 171
Peace Committee, 237-38
Peacock, Heber, 227
Pentecostal Theological Seminary, 186
Pentecostals, Pentecostalism, 46, 63, 64, 67, 69, 74, 76, 78, 87, 94, 95, 112, 119, 126-28, 132, 134, 185, 186, 197, 199, 200, 281, 293
Peterson, Stephen L., 39, 333-35
Pew Charitable Trust, 48, 131, 188, 295, 340
Piepkorn, Arthur C., 210
Pinnock, Clark, 187, 192, 193, 230
Plantinga, Alvin, 202, 203
Plaskow, Judith, 108
practical theology, 49, 250, 258, 274-76, 294, 360
Pre-Seminary Education, 9
presidents, 29, 38, 48, 55, 56, 73, 75, 89, 98, 132, 163, 183, 186, 187, 188, 262, 277, 301-10, 311, 312, 313, 330, 339, 340, 343, 345, 346, 346, 347, 358
Pressler, Paul, 230-31, 232, 236
Preus, Jacob O. A., 210-19
Princeton, ix, 28, 30, 42, 45, 54, 59, 110, 136, 185, 190, 198, 201, 208, 228, 236, 280, 287, 301, 302, 304, 318, 331
profession, professionalism, ix-xiv, 1-30, 32, 33, 34, 35, 37, 38, 44, 47, 48, 49-54, 55, 57, 58, 60, 61, 62, 65, 69, 78, 89, 90, 91, 92, 96, 99, 100-101, 114, 119, 128, 139, 145,

148, 158, 159–60, 161, 162, 165, 166, 167, 170, 172, 173, 174, 176, 177, 181, 188, 191, 193, 198, 230, 231, 250, 251, 252, 253, 254, 255, 256, 257, 259, 262, 263, 267, 269, 273, 274, 275, 276, 277, 278, 279, 294, 302, 304, 314, 318, 319, 320, 322, 325, 327, 340, 340, 341, 343, 344, 346, 348, 349, 350, 351, 352, 360, 362
Program in Theology and Practice, 327
Program of Priestly Formation, xiii, 121, 144, 147, 155, 157–58, 160, 161, 171, 174, 175, 176, 179, 180
Puerto Rico, 67, 113–15, 117, 125, 129, 130, 131, 132

Readiness for Ministry, 5, 57–59, 60, 73
Re-Imagining Conference, 109–10
Reno, R. R., 203
Resources Commission, 11, 32–38, 51, 54, 162, 252
Rice, John R., 195, 211
Rockefeller, Rockefeller Brothers Fund, 4, 7, 10, 12, 60, 73, 77–79
Rooks, Charles Shelby, 77–80, 81
Ruether, Rosemary Radford, 93, 107, 108
Ruger, Tony, 54, 345

Scarborough, Lee, 223
Schaeffer, Francis, 189, 204, 231, 233
scholarship, faculty, 330–33
Schreiter, Robert, 285–87
Schüssler Florenza, Elisabeth, 104–6
Second Vatican Council (Vatican II), xiv, 3, 10, 17, 61, 92, 121, 123, 133, 142, 145, 148, 149–57, 158, 159, 160, 162, 164, 165, 166, 170, 171, 172, 174, 175, 178, 179, 180–81, 203, 282, 287, 357, 359
Seminex (Christ's Seminary) 219–20
sexual abuse scandals, 137, 178
shared governance, 181, 238, 300, 303, 306–7, 308
Shaw, Susan, 99
Sherwood, David, 242
Shriver, Donald, 281, 284, 295, 357
Sloan, Robert, 203
Smith, Jane I., 317
Smith, Timothy, 199, 200
Southeastern Baptist Theological Seminary, 8, 43, 60, 94, 102, 206, 207, 221, 222, 228, 231, 233, 237, 238–40, 241, 242, 246, 279
Southern Baptist Theological Seminary, 30, 43, 60, 70, 71, 94, 189, 190, 206, 207, 224, 227, 228, 231, 234–38, 241–48, 340, 363
Southern Baptist Convention, x, xi, xiii, 11, 19, 30, 33, 43, 44, 49, 46, 60, 66, 67, 70, 74, 86, 87, 94, 95, 99, 125, 126, 220–49, 282, 300, 302, 304, 340, 347, 351, 354, 360, 362
Southwestern Baptist Theological Seminary, 43, 44, 48, 222, 223, 224, 228, 229, 236, 240, 244, 245, 280, 296, 304
specialized ministry, 25–26
spirituality, 59–61
Saint Louis University, 219
St. Mary's Seminary and University, x, 148, 164
Stackhouse, Max L., 287, 288–92
student unrest, 28–31
Suchocki, Marjorie Hewitt, 103, 108

Taylor, Charles L., 4–5, 9
Teaching Theology and Religion, 327
technology, x, 6, 38–41, 61, 116, 154, 164, 176, 184, 263, 278, 279, 290, 327, 333–39, 355, 356, 357, 361
Templeton, John, 42, 301
The Good Steward, 311
Theological Education by Extension (TEE), 47, 125
theological reflection, 354–56
theology of world religions, 292–93
Tietjen, John, 209, 212–18, 219, 220
Tillich, Paul, 7, 19, 20, 44, 71, 103, 107, 222, 235, 250, 268, 269, 361
Trent, Council of, x, 119, 141, 142, 149, 152, 352, 358
Trible, Phyllis, 104–6
Trinity Evangelical Divinity School, 43, 47, 186, 243, 347
trustees, 42, 56, 69, 100, 174, 181, 183, 192, 194, 195, 224, 225, 227, 233, 238, 239, 241, 245, 246, 253, 301, 302, 307, 308, 310–13, 354, 358
Tull, James, 222
Tutu, Desmond, 71, 283

Union Theological Seminary (New York), ix, xi, 6, 7, 8, 9, 13, 14, 18, 27, 29, 31, 39, 41, 42, 44, 48, 65, 74, 76, 77, 83, 98, 104, 111, 116, 156, 163, 208, 221, 228, 250, 253, 280, 281, 302, 326, 335, 357
United Methodist University Senate, 132, 322–23
United Planning Council, 212
university divinity schools, 6–8, 13, 17, 48, 57, 66, 73, 156, 168, 170, 174, 186, 198, 249, 256, 268, 273, 331, 333, 362
Urban Training Programs, 26–28

Vanderbilt University Divinity School, 10, 49, 189, 327

Van Dusen, Henry Pitt, xi, 13, 30, 33, 48, 280, 302, 310
Vatican II, see Second Vatican Council
Verbum dei, 154–55
Vietnam, 3, 4, 18, 19, 29, 66, 91, 151, 301
vocations crisis, 66, 124–25, 144, 149, 154, 158, 164, 166, 169, 172, 173, 175 178, 301

Wacker, Grant, 198, 199
Wagoner, Walter, 10, 78
Waltke, Bruce, 192
Warford, Malcolm L., 305, 308, 311, 312, 330
Warren Deem Institute, 55, 303–5, 308
Washington Theological Union, 60, 164, 178, 305, 309, 312
Waits, James, 245
Webber, George (Bill), 18–19, 27, 28, 128, 295
Webber, Robert, 204
Weeks, Louis, 309

Wheeler, Barbara G., 50, 52, 55, 86, 98, 102, 194, 255, 271, 305, 309, 314, 326, 328, 333, 340, 345, 346
Wilkens, Robert L., 203
Williams, Delores, 111
Williams, Raymond, 327
Wimmer, John, 309
Wolterstorff, Nicholas, 202
Womanist theologians 95, 111, 112, 350
Wood, Charles, 254, 255, 257, 258, 264–67, 272, 276, 355
Woodstock, 146, 163
World Cat, 40
World Conference of Associations of Theological Institutions 297–99

Ziegler, Jesse, 4, 5, 15, 28, 29, 33, 54, 55, 58, 79, 92, 97, 138, 159, 181, 252
Zikmund, Barbara Brown, 95, 97–98, 297–98.

www.ingramcontent.com/pod-product-compliance
Lightning Source LLC
Chambersburg PA
CBHW081533300426
44116CB00015B/2619